ON THE OCEAN

For Sean McGrail

ON THE
OCEAN

*The Mediterranean and the Atlantic
from Prehistory to* AD 1500

BARRY CUNLIFFE

OXFORD

UNIVERSITY PRESS

OXFORD

UNIVERSITY PRESS

Great Clarendon Street, Oxford, OX2 6DP
United Kingdom

Oxford University Press is a department of the University of Oxford.
It furthers the University's objective of excellence in research, scholarship,
and education by publishing worldwide. Oxford is a registered trade mark of
Oxford University Press in the UK and in certain other countries

© Barry Cunliffe 2017

The moral rights of the author have been asserted

First Edition published in 2017

Impression: 1

Published in the United States of America by Oxford University Press
198 Madison Avenue, New York, NY 10016, United States of America

British Library Cataloguing in Publication Data
Data available

Library of Congress Control Number: 2016960648

ISBN 978–0–19–875789–4

Typeset by Sparks—www.sparkspublishing.com

Printed in Great Britain by
Bell & Bain Ltd., Glasgow

PREFACE

People who live on the interface of the land and the sea are usually fortunate. Not only do they have the resources of the two contrasting worlds to support them, but the sea is present in another guise, challenging and demanding engagement. Its stimulus has driven technological invention, allowing humans to harness the power of the winds and the currents, it has stimulated abstract thought about the nature of the world and of the universe, and it has given full rein to that innate human inquisitiveness that craves unfettered mobility. The sea, then, is an inspiration to humans: it cajoles and lures them into its presence and it drives them on to great feats of achievement. Yet the relationship between humans and the sea has always been ambiguous. The sea may have much to offer, but it has an animate quality, a wilfulness and an unpredictability which means that at any time it may turn against the intruder. The sea is known to be alien and dangerous, yet few can resist its challenge.

This book is about that contest between humans and the sea played out against the narrative of early European history, including, of course, prehistory. It contrasts the contained Mediterranean with the endless Atlantic, exploring the relationship between them and the different world-views that they have engendered. Archaeology is fast extending our understanding of these matters. It is enabling us to begin to glimpse the beginnings of seafaring as Palaeolithic hunters tentatively set out to explore the larger islands of the eastern Mediterranean, it is demonstrating the astonishing exploits of the Phoenicians, and it is allowing us to trace the Atlantic journeys of Byzantine traders probing new horizons as their Mediterranean world was crumbling. Meanwhile, nautical archaeology is developing apace, with major new ship discoveries like those at the port towns of Thonis-Heraklion in the Nile delta, in the Theodosian harbour of Constantinople, and in and around the early medieval town of Roskilde in Denmark. The discoveries of the last two decades have totally refocused our perceptions on the central importance of the sea in human development.

We cover a long period, from the exploits of those sea-going Palaeolithic hunters to the first decade of the sixteenth century AD, when the limits of the Atlantic were first charted. It has to be. The story of seafaring is a continuum and is best treated as such, unconstrained by conventional period divisions. It is the only way to appreciate the grandeur of the human achievement.

Finally, a word on the maps. Although it is a modern convention to present maps with north at the top, our cognitive geographies change depending on where we are. To understand the past better, therefore, we should try to visualize space as people might then have done. Concepts of space no doubt varied with time and place, but the phenomenon that would have impacted upon everyone throughout time would have been the rising and the setting of the sun. For this reason, and also to jolt us out of our comfortable geographical complacency, I have chosen to orient our maps with west at the top, giving prime place to the setting of the sun. I find this offers a more stimulating way of trying to empathize with the people of the Mediterranean, while for people living along the Atlantic façade it conforms to the natural orientation of their world. I hope it may help the reader to see things differently—to be able to take a sea-wise view of the world.

B.C.
Oxford
February 2017

CONTENTS

1

Those in Peril on the Sea

This is the story of two seas and of the humans who challenged them. The enclosed Mediterranean—the familiar Mare Nostrum of classical times—and the fearsome, unending Ocean—the Sea of Perpetual Gloom as it was known by the Arabs. Humans evolved as land-based animals and yet by the sixteenth century AD many thousands, every year, were facing the dangers of the sea: pilgrims crossing the Bay of Biscay from Bristol to Galicia to converge on the shrine of St James at Compostela, traders sailing south round Africa to the Indian Ocean and the rich markets of the east, and shiploads of excited young men crossing the Atlantic, drawn by the gold of the Aztecs and Incas to seek a new life as conquistadors, comforted by the belief that they were doing God's work. Nor should we forget the flotillas of fishing ships leaving the ports of Iberia, Brittany, and Britain every year for the North Atlantic to reap the seas and return with their salted catch to feed the burgeoning population of Europe. For all of them the sea offered passage, and for the lucky ones it provided reward.

But the human engagement with the sea was a complex matter. By no means all felt its draw. The Breton writer P.-J. Hélias, in his widely read book *Le Cheval d'orgueil*, describes how, early in the twentieth century, communities living only a few kilometres from the coast shunned the sea. Much earlier, in the eighth century BC, the bucolic poet Hesiod, content in his remote farming village on the flanks of Mount Helicon in Boeotia, felt compelled to give some advice on sailing in his *Works and Days*, but he prefaced his remarks with 'If now the desire to go to sea, disagreeable as it is, has got hold of you …'. The sea, then, drew men to itself, but that attraction came from proximity. What is it about the sea that so fascinates and entices humans into acts of irrationality?

The Sea Is Different

For land-dwelling animals like humans, the sea is other: an alien world different in every way from the land. While the land is scarred with human activity—with settlements, field boundaries, burial mounds—reflecting the deep heritage of human interaction, the sea has no history: it is timeless. On land one is constantly reminded of how the landscape we see today fossilizes past human activity. The sea is a place for forgetting. Land appears static, stable; the sea is ever in motion, varying in colour from deep greys to blues and greens, changing voice from a gentle mumble to a roar, tranquil one moment and raging the next. For those ever fascinated by the sea there is never a dull moment.

The enigma of the sea is brilliantly captured by Victor Hugo in his *Toilers of the Sea*:

> Wind is full of this mystery. So, too, is the sea. Like wind, it is composite in nature; under the waves of water, which we can see, are waves of force, which we cannot see. Its constituents are—everything. Of all the jumbles of matter in the world the sea is the most indivisible and the most profound.

It is a place of danger. The sea gives, but the sea takes. In the words of a Breton song, 'At sea all is anguish, all is prayer.' Early classical literature is full of stories of the dangers of the sea, often in the guise of monsters and beasts. Odysseus was beset by fearsome forces while at sea, not least the Sirens, whose island was strewn with the bleached bones of the sailors unable to resist the lure of their song. The Phoenician explorer Himilco, venturing into the Atlantic, encountered 'monsters of the deep and beasts [that] swim around the slow and sluggish crawling ships'. Such horrors, vividly imagined by medieval cartographers, enliven the oceans on early maps. The beasts of the deep feature large in Christian belief systems. The sea was the home of the Leviathan so vividly described in the Old Testament: 'its snorting throws out flashes of light; its eyes are like the rays of dawn—flames stream from its mouth … Nothing on earth is its equal—a creature without fear' (Job 41: 18–33); and it was from the Ocean that the Beast of the Apocalypse would come to destroy the world, fearsome with its seven heads and ten horns (Revelation 11: 7, 12: 3). Brought up to believe in such images, it is hardly surprising that the Victorian congregation would sing lustily, begging God's protection for 'those in peril on the sea'. There is, however, an interesting ambivalence here. All the creatures of the sea, including the Leviathan, were created by God; yet they threatened the earth, and if St John's vision was to be believed, they would be its destruction. Perhaps, embedded here in Christian belief are deep echoes of an earlier vision of the world in which the sea is a wild, uncontrolled force, congenial at times but always poised to destroy.

1.1 Monsters living in the ocean deep are a recurring theme in literature and art and find a place in many religious beliefs, including Christianity. Here, in the engraving taken from Gustave Doré's famous painting *The Destruction of Leviathan* (1865), the monster is confronted by the powers of righteousness

3

1.2 The Sirens in Homer's great epic of Odysseus lured sailors to their destruction by the beguiling beauty of their song. In this scene Odysseus has himself tied to the mast so that he can hear the Sirens' song while being powerless to do their bidding. The sailors have their ears blocked and so are oblivious of the Sirens' temptations. Greek red-figure vase of the late sixth to early fifth century

The concept of the demanding sea, ready to claim its dues, pervades the myth and folklore of the Atlantic shores. The Breton legend of the lost town of Ker-Is, the Welsh story of the submergence of Cantre'r Gwaelod in the bay of Cardigan, and the Cornish belief in the flooding of the land of Lyonesse between Cornwall and the Scilly Isles, offer a consistent theme of catastrophic inundation by the Atlantic. While these stories may be rooted in Christian allegory, reflecting the fate of the sinful, it is significant that the agent of death and destruction is always the sea. The reality that inspired the stories may have included the striking remnants of fossil forests exposed around the Atlantic shores at very low tides and folk memories of violent storm surges or even tsunamis.

4

1.3 Fearsome sea creatures were often used to enliven maps and charts. This hungry monster is depicted on a map of 1598 by Olaus Magnus

Belief in the demanding nature of the sea is also evident in stories told around the Atlantic coasts of Europe. In many communities there is a strong belief that a drowning man belongs to the sea and should not be saved lest the sea claims the rescuer as one of his family in recompense. One story, recorded in the twentieth century on Galway Bay, tells of a drowning man who, clinging to the side of a boat, had his fingers hammered so that he would not be able to hold on.

The presence of a powerful female spirit is a pervading theme of many myths told about the sea. Often she is in the form of a mermaid who entices a man into her realm and keeps him there. The personification of the sea as a predatory female is given full rein in Pierre Loti's famous novel *Pêcheur d'Islande*. In it the fisherman hero, Yann, after a life of engagement with the ocean, is finally drowned off Iceland, embraced by the jealous, sexually demanding sea, while his wife is left waiting on the cliffs for his return, mocked by the rising and falling of the tide. It is a powerful piece of writing embodying the beliefs and superstitions pervading the world of Breton seafarers in the nineteenth century. They would all have understood that, while the sea gave them a livelihood, she inevitably demanded something in return.

The close relationship between death and the sea is a motif running through Celtic belief systems. In Irish mythology Donn, 'the dark one', god of the dead, lives on the rocky island called Tech Duinn (the House of Donn) off the south-west coast of Ireland. The rock has a sea-cave eroded from one side to the other and, looking

5

towards it from the nearby land, the setting sun can be seen shining through the cave. Such a spectacular place can hardly have failed to impress. The belief was that the god, from whom all the Irish were descended, invited the dead to sail through his house to the Other World in the west. This association of the west, where the sun set, with the place where the worthy dead go to spend eternity is a theme prevalent in early Greek mythology, as we shall see (p. 14).

In early Irish law texts, the sea is used as a mediator in cases of serious crimes, committed usually by women. The guilty person is put in a boat with a single paddle and a pot of gruel and set adrift on an offshore wind. If she (or he) survives, it is assumed that God has made a judgement and they are allowed to live. Similarly, a child born of incest is put into a small leather boat and taken out to sea 'as far as a white shield is visible'. It was left to God to decide the child's fate. We know of these laws through their codification in Christian times, but in all probability the practice dates back to

1.4 The rocky island of Tech Duinn off the south-west coast of Ireland was the place where, in Celtic belief, the great god Donn resided and to which the spirits of the departed made their way. The sea-cave runs right through the island, and at certain times the setting sun shines strongly through it, indicating the way for souls to travel

the pre-Christian era, when it was the sea itself, guided by the gods residing therein, that was the arbiter.

The sea, then, is another world, a dangerous world, an uncertain place to venture. It is fickle, treacherous, demanding, with rules entirely of its own, only half-understood. It is other.

To enter the world of the sea requires a deliberate act—a passage from the Known, across a liminal zone, to the Unknown. That liminal zone, the narrow shoreline in the almost tideless Mediterranean and the much wider intertidal littoral of the Atlantic, was conceived of as a place of unusual power. It was a sacred space allowing contact with the gods. It was also a place of danger, where things happened of themselves or could be made to happen. The point is nicely made in the tenth-century Irish text *The Colloquy of the Two Sages*, which tells of the visit of a young man to the shore, to the 'brink of the sea', deemed by poets to be 'a place of revelation'. Concerned to understand 'the chant of the wailing sadness' coming from the waves, he casts a spell on the sea so that she will reveal her meaning.

The intertidal zone featured large in the lives of many Atlantic-facing communities. In a fascinating series of personal stories collected from among the seaweed-gathering communities of Connemara and the Aran islands in the 1930s and 1940s (published as *Seaweed Memories: In the Jaws of the Sea*) the magic of the shore zone is palpable. Mermen and mermaids are encountered; fairies and storm witches intervene in the work of the gatherers. One young girl, caught by a freak wave and thrown up unconscious on the storm beach, describes how 'the sea took me with her in her mouth'. For the seaweed gatherers the dangerous liminality of the shore was ever present.

Fear of the sea may well have been behind an ill-reported incident in AD 40, when the Roman emperor Gaius (Caligula, as we know him) drew up his legions facing the Channel in preparation for the invasion of Britain:

> suddenly he gave the order: 'Gather sea-shells!' He referred to the shells as 'plunder from the sea due to the Capitol and to the Palace', and he made the troops fill their helmets and tunic-tops with them, commemorating this victory by the erection of a tall lighthouse … in which fires were to be kept going all night to guide ships.
>
> (Suetonius, *The Twelve Caesars* 46)

While this incident is often presented as simply a sign of the emperor's madness, it may relate to the army's refusal to cross the sea. The gathering of shells from the sea-shore and the building of the lighthouse may have been the emperor's attempt to negotiate with the gods in anticipation of another attempt. The fact that three years later the emperor Claudius faced near-rebellion when he led his troops to the Channel coast is clear indication of the emotional power which the Ocean had on the minds of the army.

Another curious tale is the famous story of King Cnut, who is said to have stood on the sea-shore in an attempt to command the sea. Cnut, in choosing to commune with the sea from the shore, was behaving much as the young man in *The Colloquy of the Two Sages*.

Sometimes promontories of land jutting far out into the sea were endowed with the same supernatural powers as shorelines. They, too, were interfaces between land and sea. Such places are usually referred to in the classical literature as 'sacred promontories'. One of the best known is the headland of Sounion at the extreme tip of Attica, Greece, dominated still by the temple of Poseidon built in the fifth century BC. That Homer describes it as the 'sacred cape of Sounion' shows that its sanctity goes back much earlier. It was the first sight of land that an Athenian sailor would have had when returning from the Aegean. Sea-marks of this kind would have been of special importance to the navigator, allowing him to position himself on his cognitive map of the world. The Massaliot Periplus, sailing instructions possibly written in the fifth century BC giving a description of sea-marks between Massalia (Marseille) and the Atlantic coast of Portugal, has several mentions of sacred capes. Their identification when sailing in foreign waters would have given reassurance for ships' masters as their journeys progressed. There was a sense of wonder, too, when approaching such places from the land. With the sea pounding all around, it would have been difficult to resist the feeling that the fragile projecting land was entirely at the mercy of the sea. This same kind of wonder attached to the Victorian seaside pier: its fascination for the holidaymaker is that it is neither of the land nor of the sea: it is another world—a world apart.

The Lure of Distant Places

In a world in which accurate maps, air photographs, and satellite images are available at the click of a mouse, it is not easy to imagine how early societies may have envisaged the world, how they comprehended the spaces they inhabited, their concept of distance and of what lay outside their immediate environment. But comparative ethnographic and ethnohistorical studies offer some useful insights. Humans generally conceive of space with themselves at the centre. Space then resolves itself into the horizontal and the vertical. Horizontal space is the place on which we live—the surface of the land (and the sea). That which is closest to us—our house, settlement, territory—we consider as 'place', to which we ascribe names, ownership, history: it is

1.5 Since it was essential for sailors to recognize where they were when approaching land, memorizing distinctive land forms was a necessary part of the navigator's art. Sometimes significant promontories were visually signed by constructions, more recently by lighthouses. Some promontories were sacred and, as in this case at Cape Sounion on the southern tip of Attica, were graced with temples. Here at Sounion the temple is appropriately dedicated to the sea-god Poseidon

familiar. Beyond lies largely undifferentiated space, becoming rapidly less comprehensible and increasingly supernatural with distance from the centre. However, distance is not absolute. Distances within our place can be measured in terms of hours or days of travel, but, once outside, we are in the realm of supernatural distance, where things are unnervingly flexible. Vertical distance can be thought of in the same way. Above is air, or ether, until we reach the sky, which is often conceived of as a solid with some kind of heaven close by. Below the surface on which we live are depths which may be watery or include some kind of spirit underworld. Thus, above and below us lie the confines of the supernatural. It is at the horizon that these two realms meet, at the most distant boundary of the cognitive world. Such a boundary is especially powerful. When humans die, they leave the known world for the supernatural realms, for heaven, for the underworld, or they travel across the sea to the distant horizon.

Translated into real-life situations, a person who moves away from his home into distant lands, which become increasingly mysterious and powerful the further he ventures, gains experiences of the unknown. When he returns, he brings with him esoteric knowledge: stories of people and places never before seen, understandings of new technologies and cosmologies, and exotic materials to be used as gifts. All this enhances his status. The further he travels, the more heroic he becomes. In early Greek mythology men like Jason and the Argonauts, Herakles, and Odysseus fulfil the role of the farfaring hero. Knowledge is also an important attribute of leadership. The successful leader should travel himself or encourage travellers to his court so that he can embrace their knowledge. When the travel-worn Telemachos and his companions arrived at the palace of Nestor, Homer reports how they were treated as honoured guests. Only after being bathed and fed, as the rules of hospitality required, could Nestor turn to them and say, 'Now that our visitors have regaled themselves, it will be no breach of manners to put some question to them and inquire who they may be.' The old man was about to gather in their travellers' tales and thus enhance his own knowledge and status. In the more complex societies kings would positively encourage wise strangers to settle in their households. The greater the number, the greater the king's standing. The welcome given to Marco Polo by Qubilai Khan, and the fact that he was encouraged to stay for years in the Mongol court, reflected his perceived value as a 'wise stranger' from afar. Kings might also gain status by embarking on lengthy journeys themselves. One of the most extreme cases is that of Alexander III of Macedon, whose exploits gained him the sobriquet 'the Great'.

Later history is full of examples of farfaring. Heroic overseas expeditions became an essential part of Nordic life in the eighth century. Population pressures at home limited the ambition of young men, whose only outlet was to take to the sea as Vikings. Some sought new lands to settle, but others used the opportunity to acquire plunder and to enhance their reputations. The leaders of the vast Viking fleet, starting out as 150 vessels, which sailed into the Guadalquivir to raid Seville in the 840s were attracted as much by adventure, and the prestige that adventure brought, as by the prospect of loot. The fact that the Moors beheaded two hundred of them and hanged many more from the city's palm trees made the stories of the survivors all the more impressive. When, later, another band of Vikings, intent on pillaging Rome, raided Luna, far to the north-west, in error, the great distances travelled and the exotic aura of Italy would still have endowed the adventurers with huge prestige in spite of their missing their target.

The lure of distant places of wonder played well to the code of chivalry, which so inspired the elites of medieval Europe. Young men were drawn in their tens of thousands to join the various Crusades to the Near East and North Africa, their reckless adventures sanctified by the prospect of defeating the infidel. In the fifteenth century other opportunities were offered, under the patronage of Infante Dom Henrique of Portugal (Prince Henry the Navigator, as he became popularly known to Victorian audiences), for the exploration of the Atlantic coast of Africa and thus to blaze a trail to the riches and mysteries of the Indian Ocean. A little later the Spanish royal house sponsored the opening up of the Americas, initiated by Christopher Columbus, offering untold opportunities for eager young men to pillage their way across the new continent. The conquistadors, as they became known, were able to indulge their desire for adventure and self-aggrandizement with the justification that they were bringing Christianity to the ignorant natives.

Vikings, Crusaders, navigators, and conquistadors were all alike. They were human animals conditioned by their genetics to be mobile, compelled to travel into the distance to see what lay beyond, and in doing so to acquire esoteric knowledge and exotic goods. The innate desire for travel and acquisition has made humans the most successful of the animal species in colonizing almost every ecological niche in the world. By assigning value to this knowledge of the beyond, and status to those who have acquired it, societies have given added impetus and reward to those who wish to travel. Add to this the periodic pressures created by the uncontrolled growth of populations in areas of restricted resource, and the restless drive of people to move away from home to face danger and discomfort in anticipation of discovering the unknown can begin

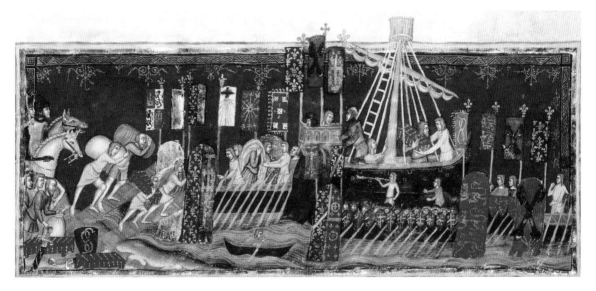

1.6 The innate human desire to travel in part accounts for the popularity of the Crusades, which gave ordinary people the opportunity to leave their villages and see the world. This fourteenth-century French manuscript shows men embarking from Europe on their way to the Holy Land under the flags of the French and English kings

to be understood. It is this restless mobility that distinguishes the human race from all other animals.

One further example needs to be considered since it gets close to the core of the relationship of men and the sea: that of the travelling Irish monks, the *peregrini*, of the early Middle Ages. Many monks travelled extensively by sea. For some the motive was to find a remote place, often a small island, wherein to isolate themselves from the broader community, the better to contemplate God. For others it was to take their distinctive Celtic Christianity to foreign lands, many establishing monasteries in north-western France while the more adventurous reached central Europe and Italy. Some of the *peregrini* were more extreme; for them it was sufficient simply to take to the sea and be guided by God. Tales of these voyages, the *immrama*, telling of the magic places encountered in the ocean, were popular from the eighth century

1.7 The discovery of islands way out in the Ocean by monks in search of solitude has been a popular theme for literature and art. These Icelandic postage stamps issued in 1994, designed by Colin Harrison, show St Brendan landing on the Faroes—the islands of sheep—and on Iceland, characterized by its volcanoes

and propounded a specific Christian view of the world. It is a matter to which we shall return (pp. 25–8), but what is significant for the present discussion is that, for the monk, it was the journey itself that was important rather than the acquisition of riches or status-enhancing knowledge. The act of travelling empowered the person. Perhaps it is this very deep-rooted feeling that really drives the confusion of mobility that characterizes history.

The Nature of the Universe

Through time people have felt the need to understand the complexities of the world around them. Nowadays modern science has provided us with models to help us to contain our insecurities—models for the coming into existence of the universe, the origin of the solar system, the evolution of life. Previously societies had to construct creation myths from little more than their own imaginings. One of the most familiar to modern readers is likely to be the account given in Genesis:

> and darkness was upon the face of the deep. And the Spirit of God moved upon the face of the waters … And God made the firmament, and divided the waters which were under the firmament from the waters which were above the firma-ment … And God said … '… let the dry land appear' …
>
> (Genesis 1: 2–9)

The Old Testament creation story is a reshaping of myths which probably go back to Babylonian times. The same sonorous tones and the same succession of separate events of creation are evident in the *Theogony* of Hesiod, probably written towards the end of the eighth century BC:

> First came Chaos and then broad-breasted Earth … Out of Chaos came Erebos [Hades] and Dark Night: and from Night in turn came Aether and Day … and Earth first bore starry Heaven … and she bore the long mountains and the undraining Sea and its fearsome swell but afterwards she lay with Heaven and the deep swirling Ocean.
>
> (lines 135–55)

Hesiod goes on to relate stories of the coming into being of successions of gods, many hundreds in all. All this is unlikely to be the result of his vivid imaginings, dreamed up as he looked after his sheep on a Greek mountainside. What he brought together in his remarkable work was disparate oral traditions going back deep into time which he had heard in storytellings over his lifetime and had woven together in a single poetic narrative.

For Hesiod the 'undraining Sea' (the Mediterranean), divided from earth, was a separate act of creation from that of the 'deep swirling Ocean', which was later born of the union of Earth and Heaven. The vision here is of the land and the inner sea surrounded by the Ocean Stream. The same idea is evident in Homer's description of the great shield made for Achilles by the god Hephaestos: 'He decorated the face of it with a number of designs ... representing first of all, Earth, Sky and Sea, the indefatigable Sun, the Moon at the full and all the constellations ... Finally, round the very rim of the wonderful shield he put the mighty Ocean Stream' (*Iliad* 18.483–608). For Homer, the 'Ocean Stream' encircling the world was a distant place of extreme power. All the stars, except the circumpolar star, 'bathe in Oceanus' (that is, rise and set in it): so, too, does the sun. At one point Homer implies that the sun, once it has passed below the horizon, travels beneath the earth to rise again in the east, though later poets believed that the sun floated along the Ocean Stream around the earth, from west to east. Homer also says that it was from Ocean that all the immortals were born.

Beyond the Ocean Stream to the west lies a zone of great potency, where the canopy of the sky meets the distant horizon. It is here, Hesiod tells us, that the Gorgon lives 'beyond famed Oceanus at the edge of the world hard by Night where the shrill-voiced Hesperides are'. Here at the edge of the world 'by deep eddying Ocean' are the 'isles of the blest', where 'untroubled in spirit ... [dwell] happy heroes for whom the grain-giving fields bear rich honey-sweet fruit three times a year'. Here, too, standing at the limits of the earth, is Atlas, who 'on his head and tireless arms carries the broad heavens', keeping the canopy of the sky apart from the earth. The Hesperides, the daughters of Atlas, were charged with guarding the Golden Apples given to the goddess Hera on her marriage. The eleventh labour of Herakles was to steal the apples, a task he managed by a customary mixture of violence and subterfuge. Clearly this far distant space at the limit of the world between heaven and earth was perceived by the Greeks to be a place of particular power, where heroes and gods could be in competition and where the worthy dead could exist in luxury for eternity.

The recurring mention of the Ocean Stream raises the interesting question of whether the Greeks of the eighth century were aware of the Atlantic Ocean beyond the Mediterranean, stretching west to the far-distant horizon, or whether the Ocean Stream was simply a theoretical concept, a neat edging to the world rather like the rim binding of Achilles' shield. Although no Greek is likely at this stage to have seen the Atlantic, it is quite possible that knowledge of the outer Ocean had been acquired from Phoenicians who were setting up trading entrepôts along the Atlantic coast of

Iberia in the ninth century or earlier. The Greek geographer Strabo, writing in the early first century AD, was of the opinion that Homer knew of the Atlantic, and even speculated that the Ocean was the setting for the wanderings of Odysseus. This has also become a popular theme pursued by several recent authors, but, like Strabo's, their arguments are speculative and unconvincing.

With the foundation of the Greek colony of Massalia (Marseille) about 600 BC, the Greek presence at the western end of the Mediterranean became established, and knowledge of the western edge of Europe and of the great ocean that bounded it would have become widespread, eventually extending the length of the Mediterranean to ports like Miletos on the Aegean coast of Asia Minor. By 600 BC Miletos had become the foremost maritime centre of the Ionian Greeks, a place well known for its ability to organize successful colonizing expeditions, especially to the Black Sea. Because of its central position in an intricate maritime network, Miletos was a focus for the accumulation of knowledge flowing in from the ever-expanding world, not only from the Mediterranean and the Black Sea but also from Egypt and the Near East. It was a time of great intellectual excitement, and it was here in the sixth and fifth centuries that a succession of original thinkers began to discard the old mythologies and to develop a more objective and questioning view of the world.

The first of the Ionian philosophers was Thales (*c.*636–546 BC). Later Greek writers looking back on these times believed that he was a merchant who had travelled widely, visiting Egypt, where he studied mathematics and learned something of Babylonian astronomy. Many stories are told of his scientific beliefs and achievements. How much his thinking was conditioned by deep-rooted traditional myths it is difficult to say, but it is unlikely that he was able to cut loose entirely from them. When considering the central question of the origin of the world, he decided that everything came from water. Perhaps in this he was still influenced by the beliefs that informed Homer's remarks in the *Iliad*, 'Okeanos, from where the seed of all the Immortals comes', encapsulating the myth that everything arose from the mingling of the freshwater stream Tethys and the salt-water sea Okeanos. What Thales was doing, however, was formulating the central questions and distilling from the tangle of stories answers that could be used as a basis for building more complex models. Thus began the tradition of rational thought.

It was Anaximander, quite possibly a pupil of Thales and twenty-five years his junior, who made the next significant advance. He, too, was concerned with the primeval substance from which the world was created. Breaking away now entirely from the mythological traditions, he theorized that the primary matter was not water but an 'undefined something' or an 'unlimited' that had no specific physical properties but was composed of oppositions in perpetual motion. From the 'unlimited' all known substances were derived, existing for a brief time before decaying back into it. This was a daring leap into pure theory with intriguing resonances in modern theoretical physics.

Anaximander also speculated about the nature of the world, rejecting Thales' idea that the world rested on water in favour of a revolutionary concept. He considered the world to be a three-dimensional entity, possibly a cylinder hanging free in space, in a vortex of perpetual motion, kept there by a balance of forces. The inhabited world existed on the circular concave upper surface of this form. Though the basic concept was entirely new, he still retained the traditional idea of the earth as a disc.

By the mid-sixth century, when Anaximander was developing his theories, knowledge of the real world was accumulating fast and it was said that he was the first to draw a map of the inhabited world. About 500 BC this was improved by the much-travelled historian Hecataeus, also a citizen of Miletos. The prevailing Ionian view of the world was of an inner sea, the Mediterranean, and its adjunct, the Black Sea, opening through the Pillars of Herakles to the Atlantic Ocean, which was part of the Ocean Stream surrounding the inhabited land. Through the Mediterranean, from Rhodes to the Pillars, ran an equator dividing the world into halves with a high degree of bilateral symmetry. To the north lay the Celts and the Scythians, to the south the Ethiopians and the Indians. South of the Ethiopians the land was too hot to inhabit, while to the north of the Scythians it was too cold to support human life, though in the extreme north, beyond the Rhipaean Mountains, were the Hyperboreans, a mythical people who lived 'beyond the North Wind' in a land where the sun never set. The pleasing symmetry of this perceived world commended itself to the orderly Greek mind.

As knowledge of the real world accumulated, so the map was modified and a more questioning attitude developed to critique the simplistic vision of neat symmetricality. The historian Herodotus (c.484–c.424 BC) was instrumental in introducing a more evidence-based approach. Born at the port city of Halicarnassus at the south-western corner of Asia Minor, he was part of the intellectual renaissance gripping the Greek cities of the

1.8 A conjectural map of the world as envisaged by the Greek geographer Hecataeus of Miletos in the late sixth century BC

eastern Aegean. He travelled widely throughout Greece and around the Black Sea, where he came into contact with the Scythians. He visited Syria and went overland to Babylon and Susa, and, like others before him, he was drawn to Egypt, travelling south along the Nile as far as Elephantine. The information he gathered provided the basis for his *Histories*, which survives to this day as one of the great classics of historical writing. Like all good historians, he rooted his historical narrative deep in geography and anthropology, augmenting his own knowledge with information gleaned from other travellers, all carefully assessed for its reliability. Writing of people and places distant from the familiar civilized world, he was particularly critical of his sources. Of the far west he mentions a river, the Eridanus, said to flow into the outer Ocean, whence came amber, and also the tin-producing islands out in the ocean, warning us that he has no first-hand knowledge of them. He continues:

> Though I have taken great trouble, I have never been able to get any assurance from an eyewitness that there is a sea on the far side of Europe. Yet tin and amber do come to us from the ends of the earth. The northern parts of Europe are much richer in gold than any other region, but I do not know for certain how it is processed. There is a story that the one-eyed Arimaspi steal it from the griffins, but I can hardly believe this.
>
> (Herodotus, *Histories* 3.115–16)

Here, then, is the careful scholar determined to be objective but unable to resist introducing stories of marvels just in case there may be a grain of truth in them. For Herodotus the world was flat, but whether or not it was contained within a continuous Ocean Stream he leaves as an open question. Yet for all his critical scholarship, he still could not quite give up the Ionian concept of symmetry. The Danube, he knew, began in mountains somewhere in the west of Europe and flowed eastwards into the Black Sea. To balance it, on the other side of the Mediterranean the Nile must also rise in western mountains in Africa and flow east before turning north to reach the inner sea. Even the most enquiring mind finds it difficult to abandon some entrenched ideas.

Herodotus spent the last twenty or so years of his life in the newly founded Greek city of Thurii in southern Italy and would almost certainly have been aware of the theories of Pythagoras, who had lived in the southern Italian town of Croton about a century earlier, about 530 BC. The cities were only about ninety kilometres apart. What credence, if any, he gave to the theories we shall never know. The Pythagoreans were enamoured by number, believing that 'the whole heaven is harmony and number'. Since the most perfect shape is the sphere, the heavenly bodies, including the earth, the sun, and the moon, must be spheres and must revolve in a circle. In the middle, they theorized, was a great central fire. That the fire was not visible to us was explained by the belief that the occupied part of the earth faced away from it. It was, of course, a theory, based on abstract reasoning, but the idea of the earth as a sphere was seen to have some explanatory value. It would explain why, as you travelled north, the polar stars rose higher and the days grew longer. Similarly, it would account for the appearance of new stars as you travelled south.

Further observation refined the basic theory. Parmenides (c.512–c.450 BC), from the southern Italian Greek city of Elea, concluded that the moon encircled the earth and shone with light reflected from the sun. A little later Anaxagoras (c.500–c.428 BC) was instrumental in introducing these new western ideas to Athens, where they began to replace the old Ionian concepts. Socrates and Plato accepted that the earth was a sphere, while, about 370 BC, Eudoxus of Knidos carried out observations to enable the circumference of the earth to be estimated. Although his estimate was almost twice the actual circumference, it was a significant effort, marking the beginnings of a new experimental approach.

Theories were all very well, but without scientific observation there could be no real advance. This new mood was simply expressed by Aristotle (384–322 BC), with his assertion 'we must collect facts'. In his numerous writings he surveyed many areas of knowledge, bringing together the thoughts and observations of others and adding original contributions of his own. He, like others before him, believed that the world was a globe, giving us as proof that the earth's shadow on the face of the moon at the time of an eclipse is circular. He accepted the idea of a celestial sphere but believed that it was the earth, and not an unseen fire, that lay at its centre. The earth, he argued, must be quite small since the arrangement of the stars changed markedly over short distances. Because of this, the distance from Iberia to India across the Ocean could not be particularly great.

The concept of the world had changed dramatically in the four centuries since Hesiod composed his poem in his pastoral tranquillity. Although new discoveries would be made, it was not until the time of Galileo that the Greek vision of the universe would be seriously challenged.

Beyond Mare Nostrum

That the Mediterranean was an enclosed sea opening through a narrow strait into an endless Ocean was known to the Phoenicians, who were already sailing the length of the Mediterranean and through the strait to explore the Ocean shores as early as the tenth century. Two centuries later they had established a major port of call, Gadir

(Latin: Gades) on a pair of Atlantic islands, now Cádiz. Knowledge of the distant Ocean will have spread quickly among Mediterranean seafarers. But it may well be, as we shall see (pp. 213–17), that even earlier maritime networks linking the Atlantic to the western Mediterranean provided the vector by which stories of the outer Ocean reached the Mediterranean at least as early as the twelfth century BC. It may, indeed, have been these stories that inspired or contributed to the belief in the encircling Ocean.

Already in the seventh century Greek seafarers like Kolaios (pp. 250–3) were passing through the Strait of Gibraltar to trade with the Tartessians of south-western Iberia, bringing back first-hand accounts of the Ocean. With the foundation of the Greek colony of Massalia about 600 BC, Greek knowledge of the western extremity of the Mediterranean will have increased still further through trading expeditions and exchanges of information with other seafarers. But by this time the Phoenicians had begun to establish a monopoly in the region.

In Greek mythology the Mediterranean ended at the Pillars of Herakles, beyond which lay the Ocean. This was the scene of Herakles' tenth labour, which required the hero to fetch the red cattle of Geryon from the island of Erythia. Here Herakles erected two columns, one on either side of the strait, to mark the western limit of his adventures. It was generally assumed that the northern pillar is to be equated with the Rock of Gibraltar while the southern pillar is Jebel Musa in Morocco, but Strabo, quoting a lost passage of the poet Pindar, says that the writer referred to the pillars as the 'gates of Gades'. This raises the possibility that the pillars may have been those of the temple of Melqart at Gades. The Phoenician god Melqart can be identified with the Greek Herakles. Another, rather more colourful myth favoured by Roman writers was that Herakles, while travelling west on his way to the garden of the Hesperides, was confronted with a mountain range, which he proceeded to smash through, creating the strait and thereby joining the Atlantic to the Mediterranean. It is hardly surprising that such a spectacular phenomenon should have acquired a rich mythology. The narrow seaway was itself a liminal space: it was a place of danger and of wonder, particularly for seafarers travelling from the familiar Mediterranean to the unknown outer Ocean.

Although some Greek ships did make the journey through the strait in the seventh and sixth centuries, Pindar, writing in the early fifth century, was in no doubt that the Atlantic was a place to be avoided. Describing the Pillars of Herakles, situated at the western extremity of the known world far from home, he advises: 'What lies beyond cannot be trodden by the wise or the unwise … One cannot cross from Gadir towards the dark west. Turn again the sails towards the dry land of Europe' (*Nemean Odes* 3.5.19–20).

The Phoenicians were far more adventurous. About 600 BC an expedition spon-sored by the pharaoh Necho II had assembled on the Red Sea and had sailed around Africa, arriving home three years later having passed through the Pillars of Herakles. Two centuries or so after the circumnavigation, other Phoenician sailors were explor-ing the Atlantic coastal waters. Two are named: Hanno, who sailed down the west coast of Africa, and Himilco, who seems to have ventured further out into the Ocean. We shall return to the geography of their adventures (pp. 301–7), but here it is their perception of the Ocean that concerns us. The fullest description is given by Himilco, whose report, 'published long ago in the secret annals of the Carthaginians', is selec-tively quoted in a grossly pretentious poem compiled by a Roman administrator, Rufus Festus Avienus, in the fourth century AD. A few lines of his *Ora Maritima* will suffice to give the flavour:

> To the west of these Pillars, Himilco reports that the swell is boundless, the sea extends widely, the salt water streaks forth. No one has approached these waters, no one has brought his keel into that sea because there are no propelling breezes at sea and no breath of heaven's air aids the ship. Hence because the mist cloaks the air with a kind of garment, a cloud always holds the swell and persists throughout the humid day.
>
> (lines 375–84)

Elsewhere he talks of 'monsters of the deep and beasts who swim amid the slow and sluggish crawling ships'. And again, 'great fear of monsters stalks the deep'. When the wind falls, 'the sluggish liquid of the lazy sea is … at a standstill', while 'thick seaweed often tops the sea and the tide is hindered by the marshy wrack'. Himilco was evi-dently not enamoured of his encounter with the Ocean. Perhaps his vessel was drawn south into the doldrums and reached the Sargasso Sea, as some commentators have suggested, or perhaps he reported in this dispiriting way simply to aggrandize his own achievement and to deter others. Another possibility is that his original report was embroidered by Avienus. Yet one point of particular interest stands out: he asserted that the Atlantic 'can scarcely be crossed in four months'. Is this perhaps a clue that he sailed west hoping to reach the Isles of the Blest and was forced to return? Later writers, like Pytheas the Massaliot, who sailed on the Atlantic from the Gironde to circumnavigate Britain at the end of the fourth century (pp. 310–17), give a more realistic impression of the ocean, stressing its fearsome waves and massive tidal reach, characteristics that were bound to intrigue sailors used only to the Mediterranean.

How extensive was the interaction between Mediterranean seafarers and the Atlantic is a question to be explored in some detail in the chapters to follow. Archaeological evidence leaves little doubt that Phoenician trading colonies were established all along the Atlantic façade from the river Mondego, in Portugal, to the island of Mogador, off the Moroccan coast, and there must have been a lively cabotage between them. A scatter of references in the classical texts suggest that ships' masters, including some Greeks, were also making exploratory journeys, but the implication is that they were interested more in seeking trading opportunities with coastal communities than in venturing far out to sea.

By the time that Aristotle was compiling his treatises in the mid-fourth century BC, the widely accepted view that the world was a sphere would have encouraged a new curiosity. By sailing out across the ocean one would reach not the dangerous space of the end of the world, where sky and earth met, but India. To the adventurous here was an opportunity to gain knowledge and reputation. Nor would the more commercially minded have overlooked the opportunity for trade. If the calculations which Aristotle favoured were correct, the distance to the Far East was less by ocean, sailing westwards, than by land travelling eastwards. This new understanding is neatly encapsulated in a brief statement by the Greek geographer Eratosthenes of Kyrene (c.285–c.205 BC) that it would be possible, by starting out from the Iberian coast and sailing along a latitude parallel, to reach India. Assessing all this information, Strabo concludes: 'Those who have tried to circumnavigate the Ocean and then turned back say that the voyage beyond the limit reached was prevented not through opposition or any constraint but through destitution and loneliness, the sea nevertheless permitting further passage' (*Geography* 1.1.8). The implication of this remarkable text is that some people did, indeed, try to cross the ocean. How many set out and how many managed to get back we shall never know.

The seafarers from the Mediterranean who had penetrated the outer Ocean would have come into contact with sailors from the indigenous communities living along the ocean fringe, people who from the Mesolithic period had mastered the arts of sailing and navigation in Atlantic coastal waters and had developed vessels able to contend with the rigours of Atlantic storms. These indigenous populations would have had a special relationship with the sea—more intensive perhaps than did Mediterranean sailors with their own sea. They would daily have experienced the marvel of the sun sinking into the sea, the after-light still colouring the clouds even after it had disappeared from sight. The wonder of the setting sun never fails to impress. Observing the position of the sunset gradually moving along the horizon as the season advances would have introduced an awareness of the periodicity of time. On a different scale the passing of time is also evident in the tides, both in their varying amplitude and in the changing times of high and low water: it was not an insuperable step to collate these observations with the cycles of the moon. All this would have become embedded in mythology and belief systems, but of this, without writing, there is little evidence. One hint, however, is provided by the recurring images found in Scandinavian Bronze Age iconography of a sun borne on a boat. Perhaps behind this lies a belief in the daily journey of the sun carried across the water beneath the earth from sunset to sunrise.

That a distinctive solar-based cosmology was widespread in Atlantic regions from the fifth millennium BC is evident from the careful siting exhibited by many megalithic monuments. Best known is Stonehenge, which, by 2000 BC, was arranged so that its axis aligned with sunrise on the midsummer solstice and sunset on the midwinter solstice. But this refinement comes at the end of millennia of development. A thousand

1.9 In Scandinavian rock art and in contemporary decoration on bronze implements, the image of the ship carrying one or more sun discs is sometimes found, suggesting a belief in the sun being transported by sea under the world from its place of setting in the west to its place of rising at dawn. (*a*) This example, from Egely in Bornholm, Denmark, showing two sun discs, dates to the Late Bronze Age. (*b*) The second ship image, from Tanum, Sweden, is carrying a giant figure, possibly a god

1.10 Many megalithic monuments in Atlantic Europe were constructed to relate to celestial phenomena. Stonehenge, on Salisbury Plain, is a prime example. Its axis is aligned with sunrise on the midsummer solstice and sunset on the midwinter solstice. The more spectacular of the two is the midwinter event as the sun's descent is glimpsed in the gap between the two uprights of the great central trilithon

years earlier megalithic passage graves found at Newgrange in Ireland, Maes Howe on Orkney, and elsewhere were carefully aligned to capture the sun's rays at the solstices. The ability to do this must have been based on a detailed understanding of solar activity and a long period of observation and experiment, all quite independent of developments in the Mediterranean. Indeed, it is quite possible that the cosmology of the Atlantic-facing Neolithic communities was in advance of that of the Mediterranean. But evidence is lacking, though later Hesiod, at least, had a good knowledge of the basic issues, including the existence of the solstices. Why it was that solar phenomena featured large in belief systems along the Atlantic façade is difficult to say, except that those living on the ocean's margin would have been daily reminded of the sun sinking into the sea.

In Ireland the central importance of the setting sun continued to be reflected in the wedge tombs clustering in the west of the island and dating to the second half of the second millennium BC. Those that have been studied in detail face west towards the setting sun so that the last of the sun's rays will shine into them. The belief system that lay behind these sitings may well be the same as that which we later find in the Irish vernacular literature recalling the great god Donn, whose home was the rock off the south-west coast where the spirits of the dead were encouraged to come, drawn by the light of the setting sun.

1.11 The setting of the sun on the western Ocean is a dramatic event. In the south-west of Ireland many of the wedge-shaped galley graves of the second millennium which occupy promontories seem to have been aligned in the direction of the setting sun, as does this example at Altar, County Cork

The Sea as an Allegory of Life

The deep emotional significance of the western ocean to the pagan Irish, when combined with the beliefs of the Celtic Church, has given rise to a highly distinctive literary form: *immrama* (tales of voyages). Early Celtic Christianity was deeply influenced by the teachings of the desert fathers, for whom the aesthetic life, far away from the comforting reassurance of the community, was the only sure way to achieve closer communion with God. Driven by these beliefs, monks chose to isolate themselves in remote locations, often islands. Thus, while the desert fathers sought deliverance in the sandy wastes of the Near East, for the Irish monks the western sea was their desert.

The sea, like the desert, was also perceived to be a place to wander seeking self-knowledge and salvation. The *immrama* deal with the dual themes of the Journey and the Other World. Men take to a boat and, while travelling randomly across the sea, they encounter strange and miraculous places. These are imaginary tales rooted in pagan Celtic concepts of the Other World and enlivened with fragments gleaned from the voyages of the many seafarers who had stories to tell: hermits, missionaries, and fishermen. The monks who compiled the tales may also have drawn from their knowledge of Vergil's *Aeneid* and Ovid's *Metamorphoses*. The results are vivid: highly imaginative, adventurous, gripping, often humorous and full of surprises. The travellers, hopelessly caught up in it all, are forced to make choices and to consider values. Those who come through it are better men for the experience. As allegories of life's journey the *immrama* are incomparable.

Of the seven *immrama* noted in the lists of sagas only three now survive, of which the oldest is *The Voyage of Máel Dúin*. The extant manuscript is of the tenth century, but the original was probably composed in the eighth century and was the direct inspiration for *The Voyage of St Brendan* (*Navigatio Brendani*), which became so influential in the Middle Ages.

The voyage of Máel Dúin begins with the hero setting out with his companions to find his father's murderer, but because the specific instructions of a druid he had consulted were not followed, the mission failed and a storm took their boat out to sea. Being unsure what course to follow, the men left their boat to sail wherever God decided to guide it. And so their wild adventure began, the boat being taken from one island to another, thirty-one in all, introducing them to a gallimaufry of weird beasts and bizarre happenings, every encounter bristling with the magic of the Other World. One example will suffice:

1.12 To find a 'desert' where they could be free of the comforting domesticity of family life, the better to contemplate God, Irish Christian monks took to the sea to seek out remote islands. The most spectacular of these is the gaunt pyramidal rock of Skellig Michael off the south-west coast of Ireland, where a small community of monks established themselves high above the waves, often shrouded in mist and clouds

> They found another island surrounded by a stone wall. When they came near, a great beast arose and ran round the island … It went to the summit of the island and stretched itself on the ground with its feet in the air. It would turn in its skin, the flesh and bones revolving and the skin unmoved; or at another time the skin turning as well, the bones and flesh quite still.
>
> *Immram Curaig Maíle Dúin*

Reading the entire story, one cannot help but admire the sheer inventiveness and sense of fun of the author. The enthralled listeners would have been led to reflect on the

ſt belua in mari que grece aſpido delone dicꝰ Aſpido ꭟ
Latine ū aſpido teſtuudo. Cete etam dicta. ob ſete.
mmmnantate corporıſ. eſt enī ſicut ille q̃ excepꞇ

1.13 St Brendan and his followers land on an island only to find that it is a giant sea creature

deeper meaning of the adventures that God had put before the travellers and upon the
unexpected situations that life can suddenly spring. The skill of the storyteller was to
link the moral teaching of the Church to deeply held beliefs in the power of the sea,
the excitement of travel, and the natural expectation that, in the vastness of the Ocean,
there were islands to be discovered.

The Voyage of St Brendan, composed in the late ninth or early tenth century, was closely based on earlier *immrama*, but its purpose was to present, implicitly, the picture of the ideal monastic life and to show Brendan as one who upheld monastic values and observances. In this example the *Voyage* is the vehicle for displaying a man of piety. The narrative encompasses three separate voyages: the first, the voyage of the old monk Barinthus to visit Mernoc on the Island of Delights; secondly, the voyage of both men to the Land of Promise of the Saints; and, finally, the voyage of St Brendan and his followers to discover the Land of Promise for themselves. The Land of Promise in this context is clearly the 'promised land' in the biblical sense, a land of abundance and peace reached by the righteous after the trials and tribulations of life. *The Voyage of St Brendan* gained great popularity during the Middle Ages. It was widely translated and served as an inspiration to many who later set out into the Atlantic believing the *Voyage* to be an accurate account of the real world when, in reality, it was an allegory of the good Christian life.

Islands in the Ocean

The persistence of the belief in Isles of the Blest far out in the ocean is one of the most remarkable features of Atlantic mythology. It was first committed to writing, as we have seen, by Hesiod in the eighth century BC and still finds echoes as late as the late nineteenth century AD. The basic myth is a simple construct: the Ocean Stream bordered the world, so beyond the stream, in the supernatural zone where sky and sea met, was the place where the souls of the worthy, guided to their destination by the path of the setting sun, would find eternal peace and plenty. This paradise was usually conceptualized as miraculous islands variously called the garden of the Hesperides, Insulae Fortunatae, and the Land of Promise of the Saints.

The concept was further developed by Plato, who created a vision of a huge island, which he called Atlantis, lying in the ocean beyond the Pillars of Herakles. It was the preserve of the god Poseidon and was larger than Asia and Africa together. Atlantis features in two of his dialogues, *Timaeus* and *Critias*, written in the mid-fourth century BC. At the beginning the inhabitants were wealthy and prosperous, but they became corrupt, seeking to conquer the world: only Athens stood up against them. Eventually Zeus lost patience with the Atlantians and

> there occurred portentous earthquakes and floods, and on one grievous day and
> night all the warriors were swallowed up by the earth, and the Island of Atlantis
> in like manner was swallowed up by the sea and vanished. The Ocean at this spot

has now become impossible and unsearchable, being blocked up with shoals of
mud created as the island settled down.

(Plato, Timaeus 25c–d)

These events, said Plato, had taken place nine thousand years before and were recorded
by the Egyptians, the story later to be brought to Greece about 600 BC by Solon.

That such a vivid and powerful story has featured large in debate and discussions
since Plato's time is hardly surprising. Perhaps there were some Egyptian myths that
inspired Plato, but the entire story is best regarded as an allegory, a neat piece of struc-
turalism created by Plato to facilitate discussion about the ideal state, a major theme of
The Republic. The story is constructed around oppositions: Atlantis outside the Pillars,
mythical and corrupt; Athens inside the Pillars, real and worthy. In the end the ideal
state triumphs while the imperfect polity sinks into oblivion. The effort and ingenuity
spent by so many writers over the years in trying to locate Atlantis would no doubt
have surprised and amused Plato.

Knowledge of the myths and allegories about Atlantic islands encouraged seafarers
to explore the ocean. While many, like the Phoenician explorer Hanno, preferred to
keep to coastal waters, others, like Himilco, seem to have ventured further out to sea.
Himilco claims to have found nothing but shoals and seaweed, but other Phoenicians
reached the Canary islands and some may have made landfall on Madeira. The Greek
historian Plutarch, writing in the early second century AD, knew of the Canaries and
considered them to be the Elysian Fields mentioned by Homer. A little later in the
century the geographer Ptolemy confidently names them Insulae Fortunatae, making
them his westernmost prime meridian of longitude—a practice still followed by the
French into the nineteenth century.

Classical concepts of the world were transmitted to early medieval scholarship in
a variety of ways, through the monastic libraries in which early texts were preserved,
through the writing of Arab scientists and geographers, and through encyclopedic
compilations like *Etymologiae*, written by Isidore of Seville (c.560–636). It was
through the monastic tradition that the idea of Isles of the Blest entered the consciousness of the Irish monks, there to be conflated with the Christian notion of the earthly
paradise. Isidore also believed in Atlantic islands, naming specifically the Insulae
Fortunatae, the Gorgades, and the Hesperides. His other contribution was to transmit
a concept of the world not at all unlike that of the early Ionian geographers, with the
land, surrounded by an encircling ocean, divided into three: Asia, Europe, and Africa.
In its simplest form this was expressed symbolically as a T and O map—an image that
became widespread in the Middle Ages.

Along the Atlantic façade, belief in miraculous islands was not restricted to the Irish Christian communities. One Breton legend tells the story of a hundred monks sailing out into the ocean 'to contemplate [its] innumerable wonders'. Under divine guidance they were led to an island with a golden mountain and a town built of gold, eventually returning safely home after a journey lasting three years. A more pervasive story was that of the Seven Bishops. During the Muslim conquest of Iberia in the early eighth century, we are told that the bishop of Oporto together with six other bishops took ship to flee from the Arab army, taking with them their Christian followers, their livestock, and other supplies. They sailed westwards into the Atlantic and after a while they discovered a large island and decided to settle there, founding seven cities, one for each bishop. The island was known as Antillia, or the Isle of the Seven Cities. The name Antillia has been variously interpreted but probably came from the Portuguese 'Ante-Ilha', 'Opposite Island', referring to the belief that it lay opposite Portugal. Although the circumstantial detail of the story carries a certain conviction, no such island exists and so the story must be relegated to the status of myth.

The advance of the Arab armies along the north coast of Africa was spectacularly rapid. Fustat (Old Cairo) was taken in AD 642, and forty years later Uqba ibn Nafi, in a furious dash westwards from Carthage, rode his horse into the Atlantic shouting that only the ocean prevented him from advancing still further. In 711 the Muslim forces crossed the Strait of Gibraltar to begin the conquest of Iberia, and so by the mid-eighth century the Arabs confronted the Atlantic from the north of Iberia to the south of Morocco.

The tenth-century Arab geographer and historian al-Mas'udi was unexcited by what lay before him. Describing lighthouses 'where the Mediterranean and the Ocean meet', he says they are surmounted by statues which point as if to say, 'There is no way beyond me; beyond me there is no passage for thou who enter the Ocean from the Mediterranean. No ship can enter the Ocean. It contains no inhabited land and no rational animals dwell there. Where it begins and where it ends are both unknown.' In this al-Mas'udi was echoing the views of Pindar fifteen hundred years before. For the Arabs the ocean had various names: the Green Sea, the Sea of the Atlas Mountains, the Circumambient Ocean, this last echoing the old Ionian idea of the Ocean Stream. But for many who knew it well, it was the Sea of Perpetual Gloom.

The Canary islands were known to al-Mas'udi from his reading of Ptolemy. For him they were Jaza'ir al-Khalidat (the Eternal Isles). A later geographer, al-Idrisi, writing in the twelfth century, claims, 'There are twenty-seven thousand islands in this sea, some are inhabited, others not. We have mentioned those closest to the mainland which are inhabited. As for the others, there is no need to mention them here.' He, too, seems to have been relying on Ptolemy for this estimate. He goes on to tell of an expedition to the Eternal Isles which came to nothing because of the death of the admiral in command, but he is able to name two of the islands: Masfahan (perhaps Tenerife) and Laghus (perhaps Gran Canaria).

How extensive were the Arab explorations of the Atlantic it is difficult to say. In the early tenth century an inhabitant of Córdoba, Khashkhash, led a contingent of young men from the city on a maritime adventure. What course they took is unrecorded, but since they returned safely with rich booty it is more likely that they were engaged in coastal raiding than Atlantic exploration. A more famous expedition took place in the late eleventh or early twelfth century and involved eighty *mugharrirun* (intrepid explorers) from Lisbon who 'set out to sail the Sea of Perpetual Gloom in order to discover what there was and where it ended'. Al-Idrisi gives an account of the adventure that is detailed enough to suggest that this was a real event which may have involved landings on Madeira and the Canaries. The details of the story are kept for a later chapter (pp. 396–7). Suffice it to say that the *mugharrirun* ended up on the Moroccan coast and returned home to Lisbon, where they were honoured by having a street named after them. Al-Idrisi names a number of other islands in the Atlantic, identifying their special characteristics, all gleaned, no doubt, from sailors' tales, some based on sightings of the Canaries, Madeira, or even the Azores, others imaginative inventions, but all adding to the rich lore of the ocean.

As more men took to the Atlantic and began to venture further and further out from coastal waters, more islands were discovered and their positions established so that they could be fixed on the maps that were beginning to be drawn in increasing numbers from the early fourteenth century. But what of the mythical islands? Some could be collated with newly discovered islands, as Ptolemy was content to do when he identified the Canaries with the Fortunate islands, a Romanized version of the much earlier Hesperides of Hesiod and Homer. Others preferred to think of these elusive paradises as still to be discovered, and so, as knowledge increased, map-makers were forced to move them further and further out into the unknown ocean.

One of the more persistent of the phantom islands, as we have seen, was Antillia, the Isle of the Seven Cities. The island first appears on a chart of 1424 sited due west of Iberia far out into the ocean. A later map of 1492 also shows the island labelled with a caption telling of its settlement and adding enigmatically, 'In 1414 a ship from Spain approached very close to the island.' Other sightings were mentioned. About 1430 a Portuguese ship blown off course claimed to have landed there, its crew praying in one of its churches. So real did the island seem that in the later fifteenth century many attempts were made to rediscover it. Contemporary maps show it as a massive rectangular island lying in the open ocean beyond the Azores, difficult for any competent navigator to miss. Yet it remained puzzlingly elusive. For many the problem was finally resolved when Columbus discovered the Caribbean islands and the adjacent coast of America. Various identifications were suggested for Antillia: Cuba, Hispaniola, Florida. On the map of Cantino from 1502, the cartographer could confidently label the West Indies as 'Antillias de Reg de Castella'. The mystery of Antillia, which had intrigued seafarers for nearly eight hundred years, had finally gone away, but no one ever explained why the seven Christian cities founded by the bishop were never found.

An even more persistent mythical island was Hy-Brasil, which was believed to lie somewhere off the west coast of Ireland. In Celtic mythology it is the enchanted Other World of peace and plenty sought by the many who were prepared to face the ocean. It first appears in the seventh-century adventures of Bran son of Febal, who was lured to make the journey to the Land of Women by a fairy who described its wonders:

> The island was supported on four pillars of gold. The chariots are of gold, silver and bronze and there is no sadness, anger or sorrow, and no sickness or death. There the sun god presides who comes at sunrise to light up the level lands. He rides over the white plain against which the ocean murmurs. He stirs the sea into blood.

In Christian mythology this became the Tir Tairngiri (Land of Promise) sought by many heroes and is given substance on maps from the early fourteenth century as a circular island labelled Hy-Brasil, Brazir, or one of its other variants. Its longevity is remarkable. It first appears on a map of 1325 by the Genoese map-maker Angelino de Dalorto and remained on sea-charts as Brazil Rock until it was finally removed in 1865. Hy-Brasil has fascinated the Irish for centuries. In an academic assessment of the many stories told about it, published in 1912 in the *Proceedings of the Royal Irish Academy*, the antiquarian T. J. Westropp recorded that he had seen the island himself no fewer than three times. The last occasion was late on a summer's day in 1872. It was 'a clear evening, with a fine golden sunset, when just as the sun went down, a dark island suddenly appeared far out to sea, but not on the horizon. It had two hills, one wooded; between these, from a low plain, rose towers and curls of smoke.' Those with him, including his mother, all saw it at the same time, 'with such realistic appearances'. No one can doubt the veracity of the vision published in the august pages of the *Proceedings*, but what was it they were seeing? In these rational times we might fall back with relief on the suggestion that it was a mirage probably caused by thermal inversion.

The western ocean, where the sun sets, has always had a supernatural aura. It was the place where paradise lay and about which the imagination could run wild. Little wonder,

1.14 (*Opposite*) Map by Bartolomeo Pareto dating to 1455 showing Atlantic islands, some real, others imaginary

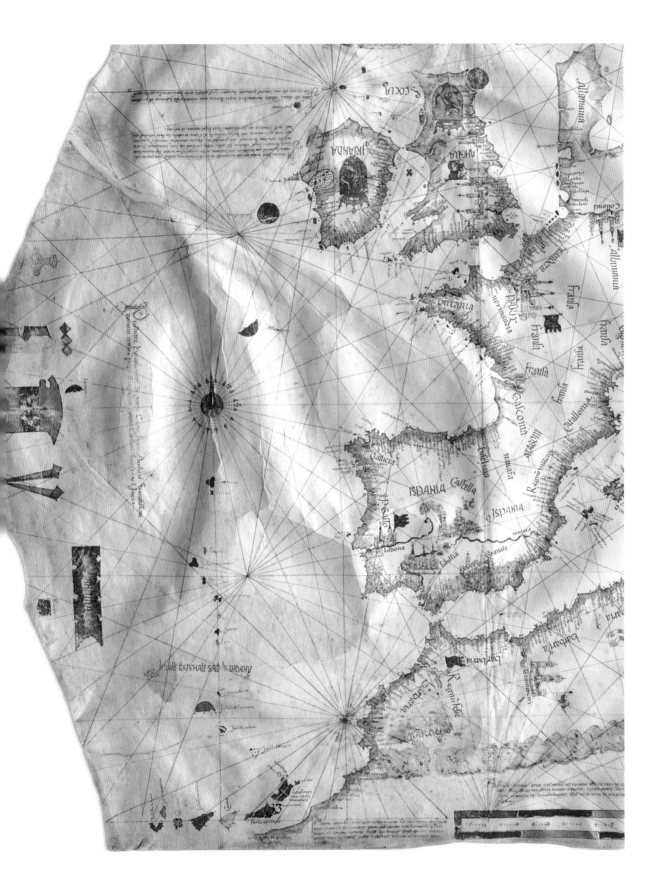

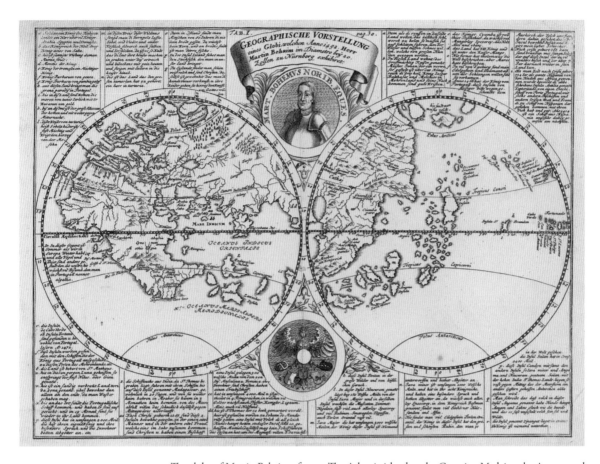

1.15 The globe of Martin Behaim of 1492. The Atlantic islands—the Canaries, Madeira, the Azores, and the Cape Verde islands—are reasonably accurate, but beyond, to the west, the map is pure speculation. The illustration comes from an engraving by Johann Gabriel Doppelmayr

then, that it has drawn the inquisitive over the ages. To begin with it was a beyond, a place to be conceptualized. Then, as men became more adventurous and technically competent, it was a region to be tentatively probed, an esoteric world to be experienced. But after the discoveries of Columbus all this changed. By the early sixteenth century people realized that there was a New World to be colonized beyond the ocean. And so the westward flow of population began. First the Spanish and the Portuguese adventurers, then the French and the British settlers, and later the Irish and other Europeans fleeing economic deprivation and tyranny. Before AD 1500 it was the journey that was important: the experience of being on the ocean at the ocean's mercy and returning to tell the tale. After that, when the imperative became the destination, the ocean was reduced to little more than an inconvenience to be crossed as quickly as possible.

34

2

The Combat That Is Called Navigation

With rare exceptions, like the seafaring monks of Ireland who found reassurance in leaving their fate to God, most people who took to the sea had two concerns in the forefront of their minds: to stay alive, and to be able to return home if they wished. To accomplish these essentials the successful mariner had to have a wide range of knowledge, and the skills to apply it. For navigation on the open sea he needed to have an understanding of the movement of the stars and sun, of the sea currents and of winds. For pilotage—the art of bringing a vessel safely to shore—he must in addition have understood tides and been familiar with coastal land forms. Over the long prehistoric period this knowledge was learned from experience and transmitted orally. Later it was committed to writing in the form of periploi (manuals of navigation) in the Greek and Roman periods and portolans (pilot books) in the Middle Ages. Sea-charts began to be produced in significant numbers only from the fourteenth century. Whatever the mariner might have believed or feared about the sea, it was upon accurate factual information and the wisdom to use it effectively that his life, and the lives of those under his command, depended.

In the Beginning

By observing fossil sea-shells high above contemporary sea-level the Greeks were aware that the relationship between the land and the sea was not constant, but it was not until 1858, after fifty years of scholarly speculation, that a French scientist, Antonio Snider-Pellegrini, set out a clear formulation of how the present-day continents had been part of a single mega-continent and had subsequently split apart. The mega-continent, known as Pangaea, was surrounded by the ocean, Panthalassa, with one wide inlet, the Tethys Sea, thrusting deep inland. In the Triassic period, about 180 million years ago, Pangaea began to split into two land-masses, Laurasia and Gondwana, along the Tethys Sea axis. Other splits then began to open up and the individual plates thus formed moved separately in relation to each other. Two of these movements are of direct relevance to our seas. About 65 million years ago, at the end of the Cretaceous period, the African and Eurasian plates moved more closely together, capturing the western part of the Tethys Sea to become the proto-Mediterranean, while together they moved away from the American plate, creating the Atlantic Ocean. These two movements are still in operation today. While the Atlantic is widening, the Mediterranean is narrowing, with each year the coast of North Africa moving closer to Europe. Our two seas, then, were created in two different ways: the Mediterranean by constriction, isolating part of the old Tethys Sea, and the Atlantic by expansion as the plates are torn further apart.

These very *longue durée* geological processes have contributed to the character of the seas. As the African plate pushes against the Eurasian plate, its northern edge dips down beneath the southern rim of Eurasia. The effect is that the North African coast is, for the most part, low and comparatively featureless, while the southern edge of Europe is rucked up, creating mountain ranges and a deeply denticulate coastline. These differences have had a constraining effect on the way in which humans have dealt with the land–sea interface. Plate tectonics have also imposed character on the Atlantic since the tearing apart of the two land-masses has weakened the earth's crust, creating a sinuous zone of volcanic activity, the Mid-Atlantic Ridge, along which a number of volcanic islands have appeared—Tristan da Cunha, Ascension, and the Azores—and the volcanoes of Iceland. Nearer the east coast, volcanic activity has created the Cape Verde islands, the Canaries, and Madeira—islands which have played a significant part in the later exploration of the ocean.

2.1 (*a*) The world about 200 million years ago, when there was a single land-mass, which is known as Pangaea. As a result of continental drift, the plates of the earth's crust began to move in relation to each other (and are still moving today). (*b*) The situation 65 million years ago with the Atlantic beginning to form as the plates pulled apart while the Tethys Sea was squeezed to create the proto-Mediterranean

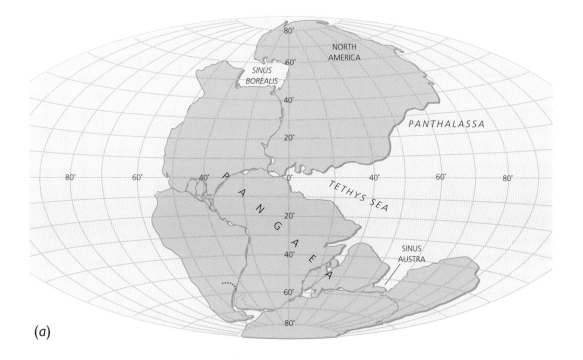

(a)

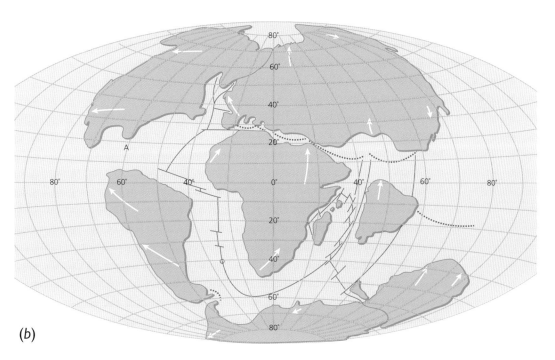

(b)

The ever-expanding Atlantic has changed comparatively little over the last 10 million years, apart from growing wider, but the Mediterranean has had a more tortured geological history. The closing of the African and Eurasian plates at what is now the Near East cut off the western end of the Tethys Sea but opened a gap at the east end between Iberia and North Africa so that the remnant Tethys became joined to the Atlantic, roughly along the line of what was to become the Strait of Gibraltar. About 5.96 million years ago this gap closed, initiating what is known as the Messinian Salinity Crisis, which lasted for more than half a million years before the Atlantic was reunited once more with the Mediterranean. The Messinian Salinity Crisis is so named because the closing of the strait to inflow from the Atlantic caused the Mediterranean to evaporate at a faster rate than the inflowing rivers could match. At times the sea had all but dried out, leaving only a few hypersaline pockets some 3–5 kilometres below contemporary ocean-level. Changes in world climate affected the severity of the desiccation, but eventually, about 5.33 million years ago, conditions were such that the Atlantic began to flood into the Mediterranean basin in a phenomenon known as the Zanclean flood. Some writers have suggested that it was a sudden spectacular event, with a massive waterfall or waterfalls dropping more than a kilometre from the Atlantic, allowing huge volumes of water to gush in at such a rate that the level of the Mediterranean rose 10 metres per day, filling the basin in not more than two years. Others favour a more leisurely event spread over a longer period. Whichever is true, the result was the same. The Mediterranean and the Atlantic became conjoined and thenceforth continuous inflows from the Atlantic replenished the constantly evaporating Mediterranean.

The final sealing of the east end of the Mediterranean about 10 million years ago, and the mountain-building associated with the plates coming together, separated the westward remnant of the Tethys into two separate seas, one open to the Atlantic, the other, called the Paratethys, becoming a massive brackish inland sea stretching from the Carpathian basin to the Pamir mountains, fed by a number of rivers bringing Arctic meltwater from the northern plains. Eventually, over the millennia, the Paratethys shrank to become the three inland seas: the Black Sea, the Caspian Sea, and the Aral Sea, the last now fast disappearing. The Black Sea remained a contained lake, the Neoeuxine Lake, until about 5200 BC, when the rising level of the Mediterranean overtopped the ridge separating the two and salt water began to pour into the lake, cutting a deep channel, now the Bosporus. Original estimates suggesting that the water-level in the Neoeuxine Lake was at this time 100 metres below the Mediterranean level have since been revised to 18 metres, rather diminishing the dramatic effect of the event, but it would still have greatly extended the sea's boundaries by flooding the surrounding lands.

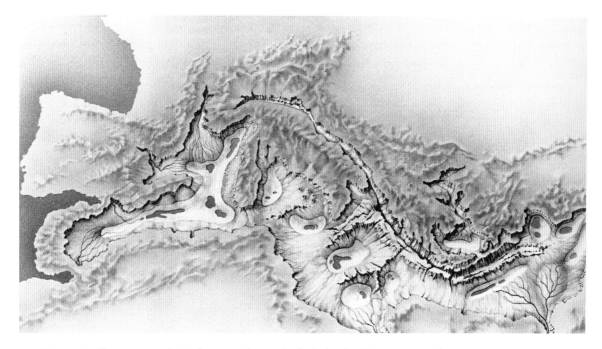

2.2 About 5.96 million years ago the Mediterranean became landlocked and, without constant inflow from the Atlantic, began to evaporate—an event known as the Messinian Salinity Crisis—reducing the water to a few excessively salty lakes occupying the deepest troughs

By 5000 BC a certain equilibrium had been reached. The Mediterranean was still prone to massive evaporation, but its level was maintained by inflows of fresh water from its own rivers, especially the Ebro, Rhône, Po, and Nile, and, via the Black Sea, from the rivers of the Pontic steppe. But this inflow amounts to only a fraction of its needs. By far the greatest volume of the water required to top it up pours in continuously from the Atlantic, the rate of flow dominating the rhythm of their coexistence.

Mare Nostrum

'Our Sea'—the familiar world of the Mediterranean—is really many seas, each with their individual characters. A glance at the map immediately makes apparent the divide between the eastern and western Mediterranean basins, the two separated by the elongated peninsula of Italy and offshore Sicily. This leaves two points of communication between the two seas: the narrow Strait of Messina, 3.5 kilometres wide at its narrowest point, and the broader seaway, the Sicilian Channel, 147 kilometres wide, between Marsala at the westernmost tip of Sicily and the Cap Bon peninsula of Tunisia. The island of Pantelleria lies roughly between, providing a convenient point of reference for navigators. Between these connecting narrows and the Strait of Gibraltar lies the expanse of the western Mediterranean divided into smaller maritime regions by the island barriers: Corsica–Sardinia and the Balearics. A seafarer who roamed these waters would have developed a cognitive geography of the different seas which comprise the whole. The most distinctive is the Tyrrhenian Sea, protected to the west by the island masses of Corsica and Sardinia and to the east by the Italian peninsula. Another distant enclosed sea lies between the east coast of Iberia and the extended network of the Balearics. Other discrete expanses are the two wide gulfs of the north coast, the Gulf of Genoa and the Golfe du Lion, and the Alboran Sea, between the southern Iberian coast and the coast of North Africa, at the end of which lies the way through to the ocean. Each one of these stretches of water had its own personality and mood that had to be learned. The proximity of land conditioned the currents, while the prevailing wind patterns added another variable. And then there was the nearby land itself, variously offering hazards and tempting havens and resources. There was much for the seafarer to observe and commit to memory.

The eastern Mediterranean differs from the western Mediterranean in many ways, but perhaps the most significant is that much of it lies much further to the south. Whereas the southern shore of the western sea averages 36° north, that of the eastern end is at about 33° north. There is also a difference in the altitude of the coastal region. The Atlas Mountains run close to the southern shore of the western Mediterranean, beginning massively on the Atlantic and running out at the Cap Bon peninsula, but most of the southern shore of the eastern Mediterranean, except for the hills of Cyrenaica (the eastern coastal region of modern Libya), is low-lying. The result is that the southern shore of the western Mediterranean offers a congenial coastline, with an indented coast providing recognizable headlands and easy landings. Moreover, its higher latitude brings it within a productive ecological zone, well watered by the moist winds blowing in off the Atlantic. In contrast, the south coast of the eastern Mediterranean is unfriendly low-lying desert or semi-desert, with few natural havens or sea-marks, difficult for navigation and dangerous to approach because of offshore reefs and sand-bars.

The northern shores of the eastern Mediterranean were far friendlier both ecologically and from a navigator's point of view. Contorted by plate tectonics, the northern waters divide into four very different seas. The Adriatic is a long, narrow waterway, its southern approach between Italy and Albania, guarded by the island of Corfu, being only 74 kilometres wide. To the south lies the Ionian Sea, bounded to the west, north, and east by an arc of land and islands—Malta, Sicily, Italy, Greece, and

Crete—providing ample sea-marks and safe havens. Further east lay the almost land-locked Aegean, partially closed on its southern side by a string of islands: Kythera, Crete, Kasos, Karpathos, and Rhodes. Surrounded by deeply indented coasts and liberally scattered with islands, the Aegean was a highly attractive place for seafarers and it is hardly surprising that much of the earliest evidence for ships and sailing is to be found there. Finally, there is the easternmost end of the Mediterranean, which we might call the Levantine Sea, enclosed on three sides by the coast of Egypt, the Levant, and Turkey and given focus by the large and productive island of Cyprus. It was a populated region with a connecting sea easy to navigate because of favourable currents and gentle winds. What is left after defining these specific maritime zones is the southern part of the eastern Mediterranean, a largely empty sea which could be traversed from the Levant to Tunisia out of sight of land for almost the entire journey. Phoenicians made good use of its 'emptiness' in travelling its length on their outward journeys to the west, safe from the dangers of coastal waters. Separate local coastal networks also grew up, linking the ports of Cyrenaica and those of Tripolitania. Even so, the empty sea lay apart from its lively, interconnected northern neighbours.

The Mediterranean, as we have seen, is an evaporating sea which, left unreplenished, would soon dry up; so, too, is its adjunct the Black Sea. Both receive influxes of fresh water from the rivers that flow into them. The Black Sea is more than topped up by the Danube and the rivers of the Pontic steppe, its surplus spilling through the Bosporus and Dardanelles into the Mediterranean, providing about 4 per cent of the water the Mediterranean needs to maintain itself. Another few per cent is made up by the Ebro, Rhône, Po, and Nile. But by far the greatest quantity of top-up water comes from the Atlantic funnelled through the Strait of Gibraltar, creating a constant east-flowing surface current which, with a following wind, can reach six knots. Once into the Mediterranean, the flow slows to about one to two knots and is maintained along the entire North African coast. At the east end it swings round anti-clockwise to flow back westwards along the northern shore, where the peninsulas and islands deflect it into a series of gyratory systems serving each of the separate seas and making it comparatively easy to find a current to travel in any direction. That said, the power of the currents is often overshadowed by winds, which can reach thirty knots.

The Mediterranean winds are created by depressions, about a third of which form in the Atlantic and move eastwards into the Mediterranean basin, some from the Bay of Biscay, others across the Moroccan coast and Western Sahara or along the Strait of Gibraltar. The remaining two-thirds are generated in the Mediterranean itself, usually in the Gulf of Genoa. The eastward passage of depressions along the length of the sea draws in winds blowing off the land, which were so important to the livelihood of seafarers that each was identified by its characteristics and given a name. From the

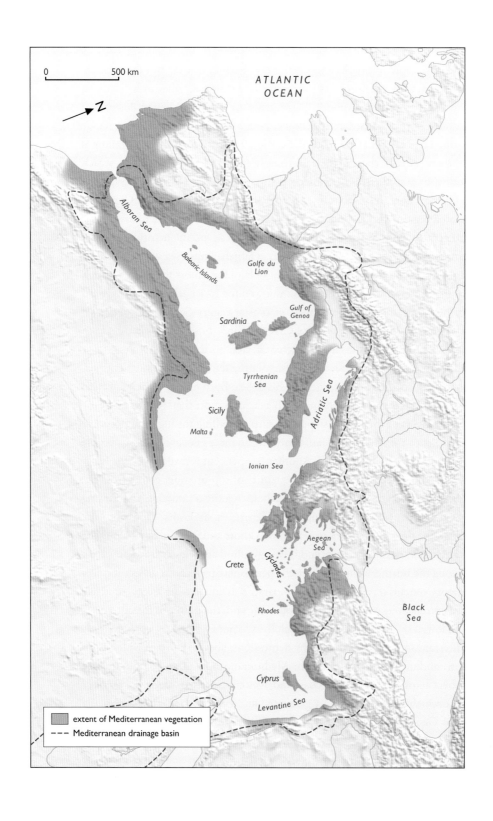

ATLANTIC
OCEAN

0   500 km

N

Alboran Sea

Balearic Islands

Golfe du
Lion

Gulf of
Genoa

Sardinia

Tyrrhenian
Sea

Adriatic Sea

Sicily

Malta

Ionian Sea

Aegean
Sea

Crete

Cyclades

Rhodes

Black
Sea

Cyprus

Levantine Sea

extent of Mediterranean vegetation

--- Mediterranean drainage basin

north comes the mistral, blowing with great strength into the Golfe du Lion, creating a continuous roar that gave the gulf its name. Another powerful wind, the bora, blows from the European plains into the head of the Adriatic, while from the Pontic steppe comes the fierce summer wind the meltemi, funnelling along the Bosporus and the Dardanelles and over the mountains of Bulgaria into the Aegean. These three great winds are at their strongest where they leave the northern coasts, their velocity decreasing as they move south. The northerly winds are complemented by winds blowing from the Sahara: warm, dry winds carrying fine red dust. For the most part these are together called the sirocco, but there are also local names like the ghibli from Tripolitania and the khamsin from Egypt. Over the sea the north and south systems compete. It is the fierce northerlies that usually dominate, but when they falter the sirocco can drive up the Adriatic, forcing the sea-level to rise along the Ligurian coast and spreading its Saharan dust across the land.

The natural currents, the varying intensity of the prevailing winds, and the distortion created by peninsulas and islands together create the marine microcosms that the Mediterranean seafarer has to learn. A ship's captain sailing eastwards along the North African coast could rely on the current to take him with it, enhanced when the gale blew by northerlies deflected east along the coast. His journey would have carried him through the calmest waters of the Mediterranean. Should he, however, have wished to sail north, following the current along the west coast of Sardinia and Corsica towards Marseille, he could have found himself battling against fierce offshore gales with a higher frequency in the Golfe du Lion than anywhere else in the Mediterranean. But knowing the sea and its predominant winds and tides was no assurance: winds could vary and storms appear out of nowhere. The unpredictability of it all was a fact of life at sea.

There is another way to characterize the Mediterranean and one which would have been of importance to early seafarers. It can be divided into two separate zones: those parts which, in good conditions, are in sight of land and those where no land can ever be seen. Since ease of sighting is dependent on the height of the land, it follows that the mountainous coasts and islands around the northern shores would come into view from further out to sea than would the low-lying shores of much of the North African coast. Keeping land in sight had numerous advantages, not least of which was being able to position the vessel in relation to known landmarks. A mountainous coast allowed this to be done with the vessel still well out from the shore, clear of all coastal hazards. The low-lying North African coast, with its many offshore shoals and reefs and the added danger of being caught on a lee shore if land was approached, was best

2.3 (*Opposite*) The seas comprising the Mediterranean. The map shows the extent of the river systems flowing into the sea, defining the catchment and the vegetational zone which characterize the Mediterranean

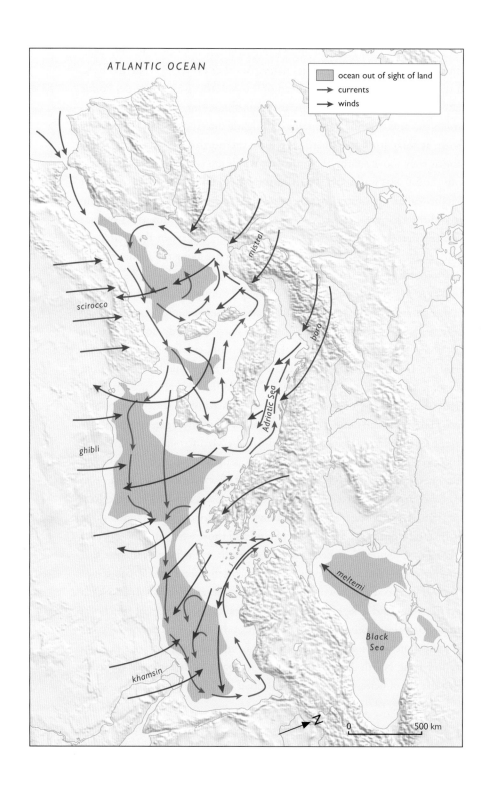

ATLANTIC OCEAN

ocean out of sight of land
currents
winds

mistral

boro

scirocco

Adriatic Sea

ghibli

meltemi

Black
Sea

khamsin

N

0   500 km

avoided. In many ways the empty seas offered greater safety. If a storm blew up, it could be more safely weathered in the open, there being no risk of being driven onto the shore. Once seafarers had mastered the rudiments of navigating by the stars, sailing out of sight of land would have begun to be an attractive option for those making long sea journeys.

The Mediterranean offers a generally hospitable environment for humans. Its semi-arid climate with hot, dry summers and mild, wet winters is a factor of its southerly latitude moderated by the inflow of moist air from the Atlantic. This results in a distinctive ecology characterized by dense, scrubby aromatic vegetation, generally known as garrigue or maquis, interspersed with broad-leafed evergreen shrubs and small trees like olive and holm oak, with pine becoming denser at higher altitudes and stands of deciduous trees thriving where the land is sufficiently well watered. The Mediterranean ecological zone is restricted to the coastal regions bordered by the deserts to the south and east and the mountain chains, rising to over a thousand metres, forming a limit to the north. In many regions, like the south coast of Asia Minor and the western coasts of the Adriatic, there is little more than a narrow coastal strip between the mountain and the sea. Elsewhere, along the coast of the Maghrib, both sides of the Italian peninsula, and around the Aegean, land suitable for cultivation is more extensive. Wherever suitable land exists, the three Mediterranean staples—olives, grain, and vines—can flourish, with flocks of sheep and goats kept on the hills above. The sea, too, has food to offer, but the fish stocks are never large. The high salinity of the sea means that fish can only thrive in the fresher surface levels, but the water here is poor in nutrients and there are few rivers to replenish the minerals needed to support the plankton upon which the fish feed. That said, in the Neolithic period a variety of fish was readily available for those with time to gather them. Other products of the sea included the red corals off the west coast of Italy, used for jewellery, and the murex shells found along the North African coast, which could produce a much-sought-after purple dye.

The Mediterranean was also well endowed with desirable mineral deposits. Gold was to be had at various places around the northern and eastern Aegean, silver in workable quantities came from south-eastern Iberia, Sardinia, Etruria, Attica, and north-western Asia Minor, while copper was found in quantity on Cyprus, Sardinia, Etruria, and south-eastern Iberia. Another vital commodity in this period was the volcanic glass obsidian, which flakes easily and could be made into a variety of sharp cutting

2.4 (*Opposite*) For much of the time sailors in the Mediterranean would have been able to stay in sight of land, but there were large expanses of sea from which no land was visible. The currents that determined shipping routes are essentially a series of gyratory systems created by the constant inflow of water from the Atlantic. The winds from the north and south created another variable with which the navigator had to contend

tools. The island of Melos was a major supplier in the Aegean, while in the central Mediterranean obsidian came from a number of island sources: Lipari (the largest of the Aeolian islands), Sardinia, Palmarola, and Pantelleria.

Those living around the Mediterranean enjoyed a productive environment where, so long as population growth was kept under control, a comfortable livelihood could be won from the soil. But for many occupying the narrower coastal strips, geography conspired to force them to look outwards towards the sea, and rumours of rare raw materials—obsidian, metals, and other luxuries—drew the more adventurous onto the water. The rarity of these materials and the unevenness of their distribution led to the formation of networks of connectivity. These became increasingly active and complex as time progressed and generated the rhythm that gave life around the sea its very being.

Between Sea and Ocean

The Strait of Gibraltar is a waterway of some complexity. In length 58 kilometres, it varies in width from 43 kilometres at its western extremity between Cape Trafalgar and Cape Spartel to 23 kilometres at its eastern end, between the two pillars of Gibraltar and Jebel Musa. At its narrowest it reduces to 13 kilometres. It is through this channel that water from the Atlantic surges into the Mediterranean to maintain its level. But the water flows are complex. As the less salty Atlantic floods eastwards, below it, at a depth of about 120 metres, colder, salty, and denser water from the Mediterranean flows westwards into the Atlantic. The surface (eastward) flow runs at two to three knots, but Atlantic tides can increase this to as much as six to seven knots. Winds, too, can have an effect. The levanter, an easterly blowing from the Mediterranean, visible in the curious cloud that curls and tumbles over the Rock of Gibraltar, will constrain the east-flowing surface current, while the vendaval, blowing from the Atlantic, will enhance it. The winds are, within limits, predictable. The levanter blows in March, from July to September, and in December, while the vendaval dominates the intervening months.

For the mariner wishing to make the journey through the strait, it was the interplay of wind and current that controlled his actions. Few would attempt to challenge a contrary wind: better to find a convenient port and wait until the winds became favourable. The current presents a more complex picture. The main current, occupying most of the width of the channel, flowed eastwards, making return to the Mediterranean comparatively straightforward, but there was also a much narrower counter-current to the north of it, closer to the Iberian coast, which favoured a westward course to the Atlantic when the wind conditions allowed. For seafarers prepared to take the risk of sailing even closer to the coast, there were two very narrow coastal currents, one against the African coast flowing westwards and one against the Iberian coast flowing eastwards. A ship's master wishing to run the strait had to understand this complex interplay of winds, currents, and tides. Nothing could be easier than sailing into the Mediterranean on a rising tide with the vendaval blowing, but the return to the Atlantic had to be planned more carefully and, if the winds remained unfavourable, could have involved much tacking and zigzagging. And then the winds might suddenly change, throwing the best-laid plans into confusion and danger. When the vendaval was blowing strongly, a ship wishing to sail west through the strait had little option but to find a safe port on the Iberian coast and wait. Over thousands of years the port of choice has been Malaka (Málaga). If the contrary winds persisted, the decision might be made to go by land. According to classical sources, the journey from Malaka westwards to Tartessos could be made in four or five days. For a ship-owner wishing to complete a trade deal, an overland trek would be preferable to waiting for months for the wind to change.

Complex though the conditions in the strait were, seamen familiar with the waters would have had little difficulty in using their knowledge and experience to plan their journeys, making the most of whatever opportunities presented themselves. And for those less familiar there would have been plenty of advice to be had in the ports on either side of the narrows.

The Ocean

The Mediterranean and the Atlantic could not have been more different, the one small with defined and well-comprehended boundaries, the other vast and seemingly without end. But an even greater difference is that, while the Mediterranean is contained within only one ecological zone (named after it), the west-facing Atlantic façade straddles many. At its northern extremity Iceland touches the Arctic Circle. Then comes Britain, Ireland, France, and northern Iberia, all within a temperate zone. Southern Iberia and Morocco share a Mediterranean climate down to the edge of the Sahara, roughly in the latitude of the Canary islands. Beyond that the desert confronts the ocean for about 1,200 kilometres, extending south down to the river Senegal, which marks the northern edge of the broad zone of savannah and equatorial forest straddling the equator. Further south the desert picks up again in Angola and extends for 2,100 kilometres, mainly along the Atlantic coast of Namibia, to the Mediterranean ecozone of Cape Province at the foot of Africa. For the purposes of the present book the emphasis will be on the northern part of the Atlantic coast from the edge of the

2.5 The Strait of Gibraltar, with Europe to the north (*left*) and Africa to the south (*right*). The westernmost part of the Mediterranean, just before the strait is reached, is known as the Alboran Sea

2.6 The currents and the winds through the Strait of Gibraltar determined the timing of sea passages between the Atlantic and the Mediterranean. There were times when the combination of winds and currents prevented ships from leaving the Mediterranean for days or even weeks

Sahara at about 27° north to the Arctic Circle at 66° north, though the rest of the African coast does, from time to time, enter the narrative. For the Greek geographers the Arctic and the Sahara defined the boundaries of the inhabited world.

The ragged edge of Europe and North Africa varies dramatically from place to place. At one moment it is towering cliffs of hard rock thrusting out into the sea, at another, endless dreary sand-bars built up by longshore drift and backed by marshes. Both are uncongenial to seafarers, though the distinctive headlands do provide useful points of reference. But many parts of the coast are more inviting. North-western Iberia, Brittany, south-western Britain, south Wales, and the south-west of Ireland all share the characteristics of a ria coastline (so named after the rias of north-western Iberia). The rias are river valleys that have been drowned by rising sea-levels, allowing the sea to penetrate deep inland, creating sheltered anchorages for ships. Modern ports like Vigo and El Ferrol in Galicia, Brest in Brittany, Plymouth and Milford Haven in Britain, and Cork in Ireland all owe their prosperity to the deep and well-protected anchorages provided by the rias on which they were established.

Another aspect of the Atlantic coast bringing great benefit to those who lived along it are the many substantial rivers that flow into the Ocean, rivers like the Sous, Lixos, Guadalquivir, Guadiana, Tagus, Douro, Miño, Garonne, Loire, Seine, Somme, Rhine,

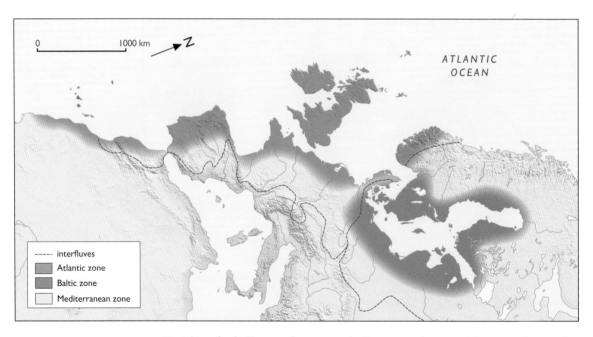

2.7 The Atlantic façade. The rivers draining into the Ocean create the greater Atlantic zone, but in reality only a narrow coastal strip is really oceanic in its cultural systems

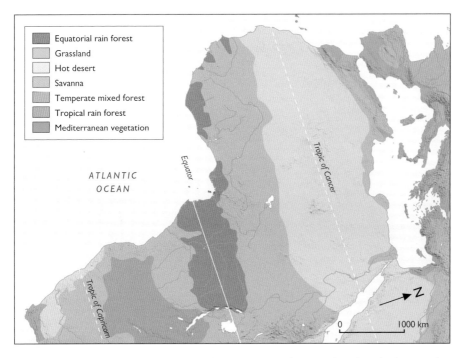

2.8 The Atlantic coast of Africa crosses many climatic zones. The long stretches where the desert reaches the sea would have been daunting to early explorers

Severn. All allowed sea-going vessels to sail far up their sheltered estuaries to offload cargoes at riverside market towns, there to be transferred to riverboats for the onward journey deep into the hinterland. An added advantage of these major rivers was that they carried heavy loads of silt and other nutrients, spewing them into coastal waters for the benefit of phytoplankton and, further up the food chain, fish and their human predators. Silt deposited offshore also created fertile lowlands and marshes, ecologically beneficial to human communities. It would be no exaggeration to say that the Atlantic-flowing rivers of Europe were the prime reason why the Atlantic zone became a focus of energy and innovation in both prehistoric and more recent times.

Much of the zone was also rich in minerals and other desirable commodities. The most sought-after metal was tin, which is rarely found elsewhere in Europe and never in useful quantity in the Mediterranean region. Copious amounts were to be had in Galicia in north-western Iberia, in Brittany, and in south-western Britain—remote and mysterious places fascinating to the ancient Mediterranean world. The same regions produced gold. Gold also came from Ireland and south Wales and equatorial Africa, from where it was traded across the Sahara to ports on the Moroccan coast.

2.9 The ria coastline—a coast of drowned river valleys stretching far inland and named after the coastal topography of Galicia—is characteristic of Brittany, south-western England and Wales, and southern Ireland. The deep, sheltered inlets provided welcome havens for sailors. Some of the deep rias, like Plymouth in this photograph, developed into major naval bases in more recent times. The promontory in the centre of the picture is Mount Batten. It was a major trading post in the first millennium BC

South-western Iberia yielded huge supplies of silver, and copper was found extensively across western Iberia, Brittany, south-western Britain, Wales, and southern Ireland. In short, Atlantic Europe was a metal-rich zone—a fact that encouraged maritime connectivity and attracted the attention of Mediterranean entrepreneurs from an early date. Beside metals, the trading ports of the African coast were able to offer ivory and ostrich shells from the African interior, while from Jutland and the Baltic came the much-desired amber. Those engaged in trade along the Atlantic coasts were never short of raw materials to exploit. Herodotus may have regretted that he had little to say of the distant Atlantic region when he wrote in the fifth century BC, but he was well aware that it was the source of tin, amber, and gold.

The communities of the Atlantic façade have benefited from the ocean in many ways, but crucial for their very existence is the Gulf Stream. The Gulf Stream is a warm ocean current originating in the Gulf of Mexico and flowing north between Florida and Cuba into the North Atlantic along the coast of North America. Past Newfoundland (and now called the North Atlantic Drift Current) it is deflected by the south-flowing cold Labrador current towards Europe, where it divides into three, one branch flowing northwards towards Iceland and Greenland, the second, the Norwegian Current, flowing north-eastwards around the north of Britain and along the coast of Norway, and the third, the Canary Current, flowing southwards along the coast of Atlantic Europe and North Africa. Within the Gulf of Mexico the current is narrow—only about 80 kilometres wide—and flows at a rate of 2.7 knots, but in the North Atlantic it widens to several hundred kilometres and slows to about one knot. The temperature, which begins at 24 °C, cools considerably as the current proceeds, but it is still a few degrees warmer than the surrounding sea temperature when it reaches Europe. The ameliorating effect on the climate of Europe is significant. The average low December temperature for London is 5 °C. At St John's in Newfoundland, which lies a few degrees of latitude south of London, it is −3 °C. Recent work has suggested that the milder climate of western Europe is also, in part, due to the westerly winds originating in the Rocky Mountains which blow across the warm Atlantic, helping to transfer the heat of the current to the European coasts.

The current has another significant impact on Atlantic Europe. The turbulence caused by the flow churns up the sea bed, especially where it passes over the shallow European continental shelf, bringing nutrients up into the warm surface levels and creating ideal conditions for the growth of phytoplankton and the zooplankton that feed on them. It is this abundance of zooplankton that accounts for the vast shoals of fish found in the waters around Newfoundland. In the more southerly latitudes the biomass carried by the sea is further increased by the warm Mediterranean climate. It was to these waters that the Phoenicians from Gadir (Cádiz) sailed in their hippoi (small boats rowed by three to five rowers), taking four days to reach the prolific fishing grounds off the Atlantic coast of Mauretania, where shoals of tuna abounded. The fishermen returning with their loaded boats to the home port may have understood little of warm currents and nutrients, but they would have been well aware that the gods favoured the Atlantic, making the fish of the lush ocean waters far more prolific than those of the sluggish inland sea.

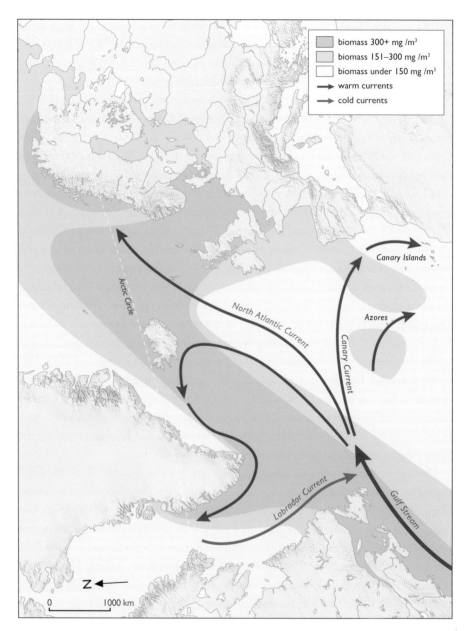

2.10 The warm Gulf Stream, originating in the Caribbean and sweeping around to Europe, ensures that the Atlantic face of Europe remains warmer than equivalent latitudes on the east coast of America. The warmth and nutrients carried in the stream encourage the growth of the plankton biomass, which in turn supports prolific shoals of fish

The configuration of the Atlantic coast, conditioned by its geology and climate, offered many opportunities to those who wished to travel by sea. We have already seen that on a micro-scale there were congenial and uncongenial coasts, but on a macro-scale the deep bights and promontories and the channels between the islands encouraged humans to react to what the coastline had to offer in particular ways. Standing back from the infinite variety of it all, we can define two core areas where the Atlantic funnelled to narrow channels giving way to different seas. The Southern Core comprises the wide gulf between south-western Iberia and the Moroccan coast, leading to the Strait of Gibraltar and the Mediterranean beyond. The Northern Core is more complex, incorporating the promontories of old, hard rock extending from south-western Ireland to Brittany separating two sea passages, the English Channel, leading to the North Sea, and St George's Channel, offering a passage via the Celtic Sea and North Channel to the north-western Atlantic. These two core zones have been focuses for mercantile and naval activity throughout time, transcending the individual histories of their constituent territories. Between them lies Galicia (north-western Iberia), jutting out into the sea and offering its friendly ria coastline to seafarers travelling between the cores. The experienced navigator would have preferred to use it as a safe stepping stone, thus avoiding the long sand-bars and treacherous, sheer cliffs of the coasts between.

The North Sea, with its adjunct the Baltic, was a closed environment with its own distinctive characteristics. It was not an easy sea to navigate and, until the rise of the Vikings in the late eighth century AD, most of the shipping seems to have chosen to hug the coasts, preferring to make the journey between the Continent and Britain across the narrower southern reaches of the sea.

Beyond the two cores lay the ocean borders, offering passages leading to the unknown. Northward from Britain the Northern Isles of Orkney and Shetland were settled by the Neolithic period, but beyond, the Faroe islands and Iceland had to wait for the Christian *peregrini* from Ireland, who sailed north in search of remote places to establish their monastic cells. What drew them to venture this way into the open sea is never stated, but observing the annual flights of migrating birds they would have been able to make the reasonable guess that there was land to be found somewhere in that direction. It was left to the Norwegians to establish permanent settlements in these remote North Atlantic islands: the Faroes, about AD 800, Iceland in the late ninth century, and Greenland about a century later.

South from the Southern Core adventurers would have followed the coast, some, like the Phoenician Hanno, reaching the equatorial region of Africa in the fifth century BC. But the onset of the desert beyond Cape Juby would have deterred all but the most persistent. Offshore, in latitudes 25–27° north, lie the seven Canary islands. The

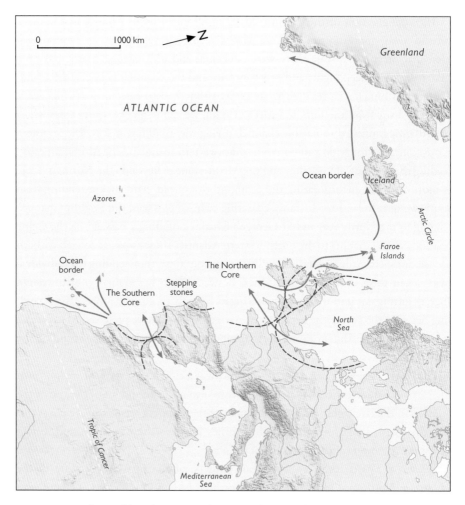

2.11 A conceptual map of the Atlantic coast of Europe and North Africa

nearest to the African coast, Fuerteventura, is only 100 kilometres from Cape Juby and would have been known to sailors plying the coastal routes. The proximity of the islands to each other (none was further than 100 kilometres from a neighbour) and the height of the main islands of Tenerife (3,718 metres) and Gran Canaria (1,949 metres) created a high degree of intervisibility. It is hardly surprising, therefore, that they had been settled in the prehistoric period from the adjacent African mainland and were known to classical writers. By the fourteenth century AD the Canaries were well integrated into the maritime networks, and from the late fifteenth century the archipelago served as a starting point for explorers bound for America.

2.12 The Canary archipelago was much fought over, both Spain and Portugal attempting to subdue the indigenous people. The islands formed a convenient setting-off point for journeys south along the African coast and west across the Ocean

Three other groups of islands lie in the eastern part of the Atlantic. The ten Cape Verde islands, 480 kilometres off the African coast, were first occupied by the Portuguese in the fifteenth century. The same is true of Madeira and Porto Santo, which lie much further out to sea, some 700 kilometres from the coast of Morocco. There are some hints that these islands may have been sighted as early as the fourth century BC. But only in the first century BC were credible sightings made. The final group, the Azores, lies in the centre of the Atlantic west of Cabo da Roca in Portugal,

1,330 kilometres from the European mainland. The ten islands are spread out over a distance of some 640 kilometres. They were settled by the Portuguese in the fifteenth century, but it may well be that the Genoese already knew of them and there are tantalizing hints of much earlier landfall, as we shall see (p. 513). The Azores took on a key role in the sixteenth century as the port of call for ships homeward bound from the Americas and from the Indies making for Iberia.

That the Canaries and the Azores became integrated into the Atlantic trading network is entirely due to the winds and currents prevailing in the ocean. On each side of the equator these create gyratory systems. In the North Atlantic the system is dominated by two sets of winds. The north-easterly trades blow southwards down the coast of Europe and North Africa, veering westwards across the ocean as they near the equator to hit the Caribbean. The contrary winds, the prevailing westerlies, blow off North America in a north-easterly direction across the Atlantic to northern Europe. Between the two systems lie the horse latitudes (or subtropical highs), characterized by variable winds alternating with calms caused by a ridge of high pressure. In the southern hemisphere the system is similar, with south-easterly trades blowing northwards along the coast of Africa, then veering westwards towards the northern part of South America, while the prevailing westerlies blow from South America around the southern tip of Africa. Between the two systems lie the doldrums, or equatorial trough, which in January is located on either side of the equator. In July, as the prevailing westerlies in the northern hemisphere decrease in force, the other zones move north by about 5° of latitude.

The ocean currents follow much the same gyratory patterns as the winds, with the Canary Current and the North Equatorial Current equating to north-easterly trades, and the Gulf Stream and North Atlantic Drift following the prevailing westerlies. The combination of wind and current means that it is comparatively easy to sail with the current and a following wind southwards down the coast of Iberia and North Africa as far as the Cape Verde islands, where it is possible to pick up an inshore current, the Guinea Current, to get to the Bight of Bonny (fringed by modern Cameroon). Journeying further south by sail is more difficult. When the winds allowed, it would have involved much tacking and patience. The return journey from Cameroon along the coast would have had to be made against prevailing winds and currents, which, while possible, would have been tedious. This is why ships returning from the Indian Ocean in the sixteenth century preferred to use the south-easterly trades to make a loop far out into the ocean, then to cut across the north-easterly trades to try to pick up the prevailing westerlies back to Europe. The run to America and back, opened up by Columbus, was comparatively straightforward. The north-easterly trades and the Canary and North Equatorial currents led directly to the Caribbean, while the prevailing westerlies and North Atlantic Drift, once reached, would bring a ship safely back to Iberia via the Azores.

These ocean-wide patterns dominated the sailing routes taken by the European trading vessels from the fifteenth century, but in earlier periods they were of much less significance to seafarers, whose prime concern was to move safely between coastal ports or to reach offshore fishing grounds. For them it was the intricacies of the local wind patterns and currents, affected by the proximity of land and the massive tidal reaches, that controlled their sailing routines. Only in those rare cases when ships were blown out to sea, or ventured to explore beyond sight of land, did the rhythms of the open ocean come into play.

The Mediterranean seafarers who ventured into Atlantic waters encountered significant tides for the first time. The average tidal range along the coast of Iberia was 3 metres, and further north around Brittany it could rise to 5 metres. On exceptional occasions, when the lunar high tide coincided with the alignment of the sun and moon, in areas where the seas suddenly narrow, much higher tides could be experienced. Every eighteen years, in the Bay of Mont St Michel between Brittany and Normandy, the tide reaches a height of 14 metres and may be a metre higher in the estuary of the river Severn. If this conjunction is accompanied by low atmospheric pressure and onshore winds, even higher tidal surges can be experienced.

The rhythm of the tides is controlled by a number of phenomena, the most significant being the gravitational pull on the earth's seas by the moon and the mitigating effects of sea-floor topography and coastline. For much of the European coast the most common tidal type is semi-diurnal, that is, there are two high tides in each tidal day (24 hours 50 minutes). But the phase of the moon and its alignment with the sun can variously influence the tidal range. Thus, when the sun and moon are aligned at the new and full phases of the moon, high spring tides are experienced. When the moon is at right angles to the sun–earth alignment (that is, is in its first quarter or last quarter), the coefficient is reduced, creating lower high waters and higher low waters: these are called neap tides. While all this may seem rather abstract, to a ship's master planning to sail in shallow coastal waters threaded with reefs and sand-bars, overlooking or misjudging such details could mean disaster.

For those communities that lived along the Atlantic coast, the tides, as well as the pattern of currents and the winds, were part of their cognitive geography: for the Phoenicians, the Greeks, and later the Romans who sailed the Atlantic, these were new realities that had to be learned fast. The Phoenicians were the first of the Mediterranean states to enter the Atlantic in the tenth century BC, and their main home port of Gadir was on the Atlantic. It was from the sailors of Gadir that the Greek ethnographer Poseidonios gained his knowledge of the ocean tides at the end of the second century BC and wrote about them in his book *On the Ocean*. Although the book is lost, the geographer Strabo quotes extensively from it (*Geography* 3.5.9),

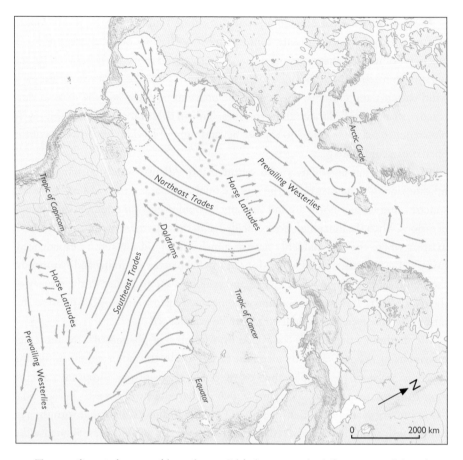

2.13 The prevailing wind patterns (shown here in July) characterize the different zones of the Atlantic and determined sailing routes. The horse latitudes, or subtropical highs, are ridges of high pressure where the winds are variable and are interspersed with calms

leaving little doubt that Poseidonios' informers understood that the tides were affected by the moon, though they did not fully grasp the subtleties of the relationship.

News of the Atlantic tides was also brought back to the Mediterranean by the Massaliot explorer Pytheas, who travelled the seas around Brittany and Britain at the end of the fourth century BC and is quoted as saying the tides in this region are related to 'the fullness and faintness of the moon'. Pytheas also said that tides at the north of Britain could reach 80 cubits, which equates to 36.5 metres. This is something of an exaggeration, but tidal surges at lunar high tide driven by high winds at times of low pressure could give the appearance of reaching such amplitude.

Yet not all sailors from the Mediterranean fully understood Atlantic tides. Even Julius Caesar, who had experienced the Atlantic off the north-west of Iberia and

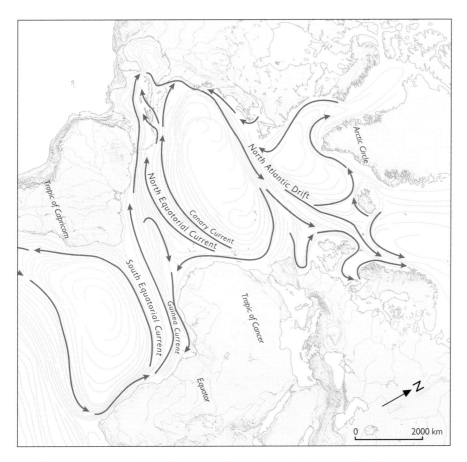

2.14 The gyratory currents of the Atlantic, together with the wind patterns, offered both constraints and opportunities to those taking to the Ocean and relying on sail. To make headway the mariner had to develop a deep understanding of the moods of the Ocean

around Brittany during his campaigns in the middle of the first century BC, made serious misjudgements. In describing his landing in Britain in 55 BC he records:

> That night there happened to be a full moon. This time of the month, though we did not realize it, regularly brings the highest tides in the Atlantic. So the warships ... which had been hauled up on the beach were engulfed by the tide and at the same time the transports that were riding at anchor were battered by the storm.
>
> (*Gallic Wars* 4.29)

There was much for a Mediterranean to learn about the Atlantic.

On the Sea

The cautious Hesiod is very specific in his advice on when to take to the sea:

> For fifty days after the solstice [21 June], when the summer has entered its last stage … then is the time for mortals to sail. You are not likely to smash your ship, nor the sea to destroy the crew, unless it be the will of Poseidon … At that time the breezes are well defined and the sea harmless.
>
> (*Works and Days*, lines 663–7)

But, he advises, come back before the autumn rains set in and the south winds stir up the sea. Then it is time to

> pull the ship onto the land and pack it with stones all around to withstand the fury of the wet-blowing winds, taking out the plug so that the heaven's rains do not cause rot. Lay away the tackle under lock in your house, tidily stowing the sails and oars … hang the well-crafted steering oar up in the smoke.
>
> (*Works and Days*, lines 618–30)

One can almost sense the relief in his voice that the disagreeable business of sailing was over for another year. There was also a brief period in spring when sailing was possible, but 'I do not recommend it … A snatched sailing: you would have difficulty in avoiding trouble.'

Hesiod's distaste for the sea may have caused him to be over-cautious with his advice. More than a thousand years later the fourth-century Roman author Vegetius took a more relaxed view. Sailing could be undertaken from mid-March to mid-November, but only from June to mid-September was it reasonably safe. From mid-November to mid-March sailing was ill-advised.

Once at sea the ship's master had to bring his skills in navigation and pilotage to bear. Navigation involved taking the vessel from home port to its destination and being able to determine the vessel's position. Pilotage, more specifically, was the art of navigating the vessel safely in coastal waters, where reefs, shoals, currents, and winds had to be contended with.

Many a ship's master would have chosen to keep his ship in sight of land using his knowledge of the landmarks to guide his course. Homer, in the *Odyssey*, makes several references to this. Approaching Ithaca, Odysseus gets his bearings from 'the wooded peak of windswept Neriton'. Prominent natural features viewed against the sky would have been fixed on the mental map carried by all successful mariners. Artificial constructions gave distinction to less obvious headlands. The temple of Poseidon on Cape Sounion is a well-known example, but there were many others. Homer mentions the burial mound of Achilles, 'a great and glorious mound … on a foreland jetty over the broad waters of the Hellespont so that it might be seen far out to sea by the sailors of today and future ages' (*Odyssey* 24.80–5).

In another case one of Odysseus' crew was buried in a similar mound, identified by an oar set upright to guide sailors. And along Atlantic coasts in the first millennium BC promontories were often defined by banks and ditches creating 'cliff castles', each with their own distinctive profile when viewed from the sea. Later, in the Roman period, lighthouses were built, like the Pharos guiding sailors to the harbour of Alexandria and the Tower of Hercules at La Coruña to aid those rounding the treacherous north-western corner of Iberia. An experienced sailor would have been able to read the profile of the land like a map to fix his position.

But not all journeys were made in sight of land. On their return home from Troy some of the heroes gathered at the island of Lesbos in the northern Aegean to debate which route to take back to their home ports in Greece:

> We were hesitating whether to choose the long passage outside the rugged coast of Khios by way of Psyria, keeping that island on our left, or to sail inside Khios past the windy heights of Minas. In this dilemma we prayed for a sign, and heaven made it clear that we should cut straight across the open sea to Euboea. A westerly wind blew up and our ships made a splendid running down the highways of the fish.
>
> (Homer, *Odyssey* 3.165–75)

By choosing the open sea-route they would have been out of sight of land for long periods of time. The other route via Khios would have enabled them to use the Cyclades as landmarks. Elsewhere Odysseus tells of a journey on a Phoenician ship sailing from a port on the Levant bound for North Africa. Rather than following the coastal route south to Egypt and then west, keeping the coast in sight, the ship's master chose the 'central route', sailing to within sight of Crete and then due west, following the southern shore of the island, before turning south across the open sea to Africa. Nor should we forget the Irish monks who, in the ninth century AD, were prepared to submit themselves to a six-day journey out of sight of land to reach ultimate seclusion in Iceland, or, a little later, the Norwegians who sailed west from their home fjords braving the fogs and storms of the open sea to set up new homes in Iceland.

For those sailing out of sight of land hoping to make a specific landfall, knowing the precise direction was essential. This requires an accurate knowledge of the movements of the sun and the stars. Such awareness was not restricted to those travelling on the sea.

It most probably developed in Palaeolithic or Mesolithic times, when bands of hunters travelled far from the home base in pursuit of game. Homer gives an intriguing account of Odysseus' departure from Calypso's island. Once at sea, 'he never closed his eyes', keeping them on the constellations: the Pleiades, Boötes, the Great Bear, and Orion. It was the Great Bear 'that the wise goddess Calypso had told him to keep on his left hand as he made across the sea'. Since the Great Bear (Ursa Major), which contains the Plough, 'never bathes in Ocean's Stream'—that is, it never sinks below the horizon in the northern hemisphere—it is particularly useful in identifying the Celestial Pole, the null point around which it, and all the other stars, appear to rotate. By using its pointer stars it is possible to identify the direction of the North Pole, a direction marked today by the North Star (Polaris) but in the first millennium BC more closely by Kochab. The even greater usefulness of the constellation of the Little Bear (Ursa Minor) for sailing at night was discovered by the Phoenicians, for which reason it was known as Phoinike to sailors in the classical period.

The concept of latitude was well understood in the ancient world and would probably have featured large in navigation. To sail on the latitude gave assurance of position and this could be achieved by keeping the zenith (highest point) reached by the sun above the horizon, the same each day. At night the zenith of a chosen star could be taken. The measurement could be made in terms of finger widths or fists at arm's length, by holding a measuring stick or by reference to a fixed point on the vessel, for example, against a mast. Over short distances these simple methods would have been accurate enough. By sailing from a port, keeping to a fixed latitude, and reaching a foreign shore, a ship's master would then sail north or south along the coast to his port of destination. Repeating the same journey in reverse, he would have a reasonable chance of arriving home. It is quite probable that the Phoenicians adopted latitude sailing in their journeys westwards along the length of the Mediterranean. Leaving the coast of the Levant at about 34° north, they could have kept Cyprus and Crete in sight on the starboard side, repositioning themselves at the western end of Crete by a degree or two to follow the latitude to Malta. Another leg of the journey, from southern Sardinia to Ibiza, also involved latitude sailing.

In the late fourth century BC the Massaliot explorer Pytheas set out to explore the coasts of north-western Europe (pp. 310–17). In order to be able to establish his relative position he took a measurement of the sun's zenith at Massalia and recorded a number of similar measurements at successive points on his journey north. By adjusting them to an estimate of zenith on the midsummer solstice his recalculated measurements could be directly compared to show how far north he had travelled. This data was later used by the astronomer Hipparchos to calculate actual degrees of latitude. Eratosthenes clearly understood latitude sailing when he said that by leaving Iberia and sailing on the same latitude it would be possible to reach India. The Norwegians also used latitude extensively in their sailing directions. In the thirteenth century it was known that the promontory of Hvarf in Greenland was on more or less the same latitude as Bergen, so to reach it all that was necessary was to sail due west. This did not stop one compiler of the *Landnámabók* (Book of Settlements, a medieval account of the settlement of Iceland) from offering additional reassuring detail:

> From Hernar in Norway sail due west for Hvarf in Greenland; and then you will
> sail north of Shetland so that you can just sight it in clear weather; but south of the
> Faroe islands, so that the sea appears halfway up the mountain slopes; but steer
> south of Iceland so that you may have birds and whales therefrom.

A navigator would use as many sources of evidence as possible to establish his position and direction. The sun at its zenith indicates the south, while sunrise and sunset can be taken as an approximation of east and west. Understanding the winds can also help. The north wind is cold, the south is hot and dry, while the west wind tends to be wet. These generalizations were well known to Homer, and the division of the winds continued to serve sailors well. The eight elements of the wind rose (a device for showing wind direction) are depicted on the Horologion of Andronicos—better known as the Tower of the Winds—erected in Athens in the second century AD. Even when the wind ceased to blow, the motion of the swell reflected its direction, often for days to come, so long as it was not distorted by a nearby land-mass.

Establishing direction of sail was paramount, but it was also necessary to be able to gauge speed in order to calculate distance travelled to fix position. In the ancient world distance at sea was usually measured in terms of a day's sail for a well-found vessel in a fair wind. Thus, from the mouth of the main branch of the Nile to the island of Pharos was a day's sail, while from the Nile to Crete was four days' sail. Records from the Mediterranean in the classical period suggest that speeds averaged four to five knots, whereas in the North Sea in the early Middle Ages they were nearer six to seven knots. An experienced sailor would have known the number of days normally taken to sail between ports and so, to establish his position at sea, he needed to compare his own speed with the average. This could be done in various ways, by measuring the time needed to pass between two landmarks, by observing the distance of the second bow-wave from the bow or the magnitude of the spray, or by throwing a buoyant object overboard at the bow and measuring the time taken for it to reach the stern (this was later a log). Armed with these observations, he could then estimate time of arrival and thus his present position.

The impending approach of land was always a tense time at sea because of the uncertainties of landfall and the increased dangers of shoals and reefs. Early signs that land was near might be the orographic cloud which often formed above land rising from the sea, the flight of birds, the appearance of driftwood, changes in the swell pattern, or even smells blowing in the wind. The lead and line would also have come into its own to indicate the changing depth and character of the seabed. Herodotus gives a specific instance when writing of the sea approach to Egypt: 'when you are still a day's sail from the land, if you let down a sounding line you will bring up mud, and find yourself in eleven fathoms' water, which shows that soil washed down by the river extends to that distance' (*Histories* 2.5.2).

The sounding lead used in this instance would have had a hollow base, possibly lined with beeswax to catch the bottom sediment. Such indications of approaching land would have been invaluable, particularly in the case of Egypt with its low coastline difficult to see except near in, and its dangerous offshore reefs. However skilled the navigator, the weather could close in, causing all sense of direction to be lost. This was a constant risk faced by seafarers in the North Atlantic, and compilers of the Icelandic sagas had a specific word for it: *hafvilla*. *Hafvilla* is usually preceded by the failure of the wind. Then the fog (*myrkr*) would come in, cutting out all sight of the sun and stars. These frightening conditions of total isolation could last for days or even weeks while the vessel drifted aimlessly. When the skies eventually cleared and the winds picked up again, the navigator would have to use all his skills to re-establish his vessel's reckoning.

Transmitting the Knowledge

For any sea or stretch of coast the accumulated sea lore would have been vast. It was essential to the well-being of maritime communities that it was kept up to date and passed on from one generation to the next. In preliterate times this would have been done by word of mouth, possibly in the form of chants or songs, or at least in rhythms that allowed the instructions to be easily committed to memory. Later they could have been written down. Such sailing directions, known as periploi, though probably quite common in the ancient world, seldom survive. The best known, and most comprehensive, is the *Periplus Maris Erythraei*, compiled in Greek in the first century AD, detailing the ports and sea-routes of the Red Sea and Indian Ocean. Another, rather earlier periplus, dated to between the sixth and fourth centuries BC, survives embedded in Avienus' grandiose *Ora Maritima*, written in the fourth century AD (pp. 282–4). It is rather difficult to extract the original text from the complex of information that Avienus interwove, but it appears to have given sailing instructions for a journey from somewhere north of the Tagus estuary to Massalia. Assuming Massalia to have been the home port of the compiler, it is usually referred to as the Massaliot Periplus. Periploi of this kind are likely to have existed for much of the Mediterranean and, as explorers began to brave the Atlantic, for stretches of the ocean coast as well. But, even so, information gained from observation, committed to memory, and passed on from one generation to the next by word of mouth will still have featured large. A sensible ship's master intending to sail in unfamiliar waters will have taken the advice of locals before venturing out of port, much as Odysseus did in seeking instructions from Calypso. In this way networks of knowledge were constructed.

By the early medieval period sailing instructions were regularly written down in mariners' handbooks known in English as rutters (from the French *routier*). The widespread adoption of the magnetic compass in the thirteenth century brought a new formality to sailing instructions. The compass was first used for maritime navigation in Song dynasty China at the beginning of the twelfth century, and by the middle of the thirteenth century it was widespread throughout the Mediterranean. It was in the Mediterranean at this time, in the Italian trading ports of Venice, Genoa, Pisa, and Amalfi, that maritime handbooks—portolans—began to be produced, embodying a wide range of information, not only about the physical character of the coastline but about the use of navigational instruments, astronomical tables, customs regulations in the different ports, and much else besides to aid the mariner. Instructions were given on coastal cabotage (*per starea*) and open-sea sailing (*per peleggio*), with directions now expressed in terms of distances and compass rose points. Since portolans were valuable compilations incorporating much commercially sensitive information, they were jealously guarded and were not allowed to fall into the hands of rivals.

By the late thirteenth century charts—portolan charts—were being produced to accompany the handbooks. The oldest extant chart is the Carta Pisana, dating to 1275–1300. It was found in Pisa but could have been made in one of the other Italian maritime cities. It covers the whole of the Mediterranean and Black Sea and the Atlantic coast from Morocco to the Netherlands. Like all portolan charts it has a wind compass, in this case divided into sixteen points; later charts favour thirty-two points. Lines drawn radiating from the centres of these wind roses, known as rhumb lines, were used to lay courses from one harbour to the next. Although the portolan charts themselves contained a great deal of accurate information, they were designed to be used with the written portolans. Unlike the medieval T and O maps, which focused on Jerusalem with the world, the *orbis terrarum*, encircled by the ocean—conventions redolent of Christianity but embedded in a more ancient classical tradition—the portolan charts were rigorously accurate in their desire to express the real world for the benefit of navigators. One map, produced in Genoa in 1403, boasted that the cartographer had included information provided by seamen and had checked his details against 'efficacious experience'. To be of use the charts not only had to be accurate but they had to be kept up to date, particularly at a time when knowledge of the world was fast expanding.

In the fourteenth and fifteenth centuries map-making became a fine art in many of the Italian ports, but few could rival the Majorcan cartographic school, which became the best known in Europe. Information was gathered from every port, largely through the Jewish community, whose contacts spread wide, and the cartographers busied themselves producing not only functional portolan charts for their merchant patrons but splendid maps adorned with all manner of decoration for princes and kings who wished to display their erudition. One of the most magnificent of those to survive is the famous Catalan Atlas, produced in 1375 by the Jewish book illuminator Cresques Abraham.

2.15 Charts of the seas, produced in number from the fourteenth century, were a valuable commercial asset and were carefully guarded. The Carta Pisana, illustrated here, was made at the end of the thirteenth century and was found in Pisa, though was not necessarily created there. It is the oldest serving portolan chart giving a detailed survey of the Mediterranean coast. The better-preserved western part is illustrated here

2.16 (*Opposite*) The Catalan Atlas, created at the end of the fourteenth century by the map-makers of Majorca, originally consisted of six vellum leaves. It is elaborately painted in bright colours, including gold and silver, and was evidently designed for the aristocratic market. Since the time of Charles V it has been in the Royal Library of France

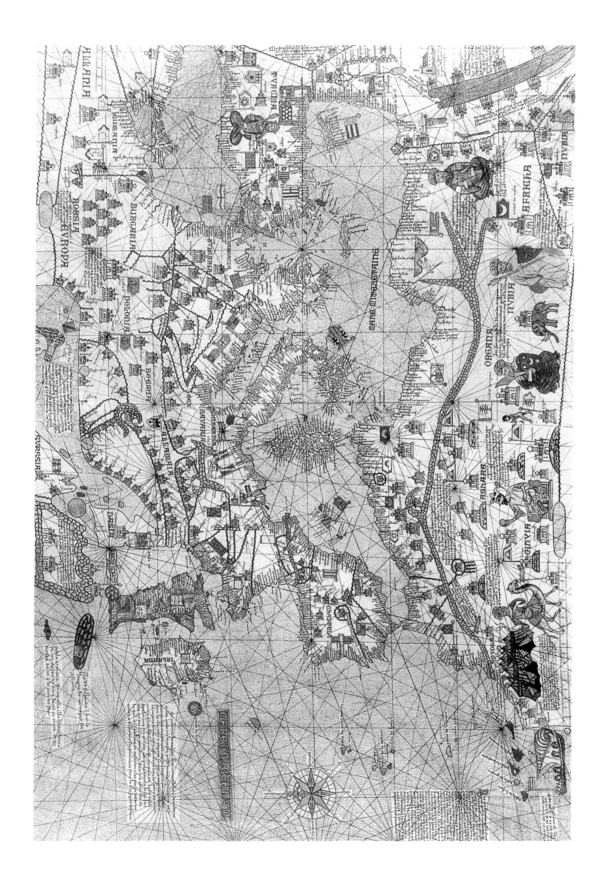

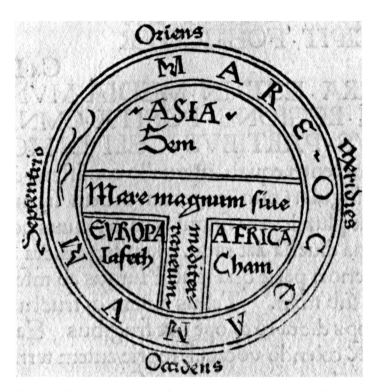

2.17 (*a*) (*Above*) The T and O map from the earliest printed version of Isidore of Seville's *Etymologia*, originally compiled in the seventh century. Isidore believed that the world was spherical and that dry land occupied half the sphere. T and O maps embodied a popular conception of the world. (*b*) (*Opposite*) Much the same idea is apparent in Muhammad al-Idrisi's world map of 1154. Shown here is a fifteenth-century copy. North is at the bottom

It was composed of six vellum leaves elaborately painted, two of text, in Catalan, on astronomy and cosmography and other subjects, and four of maps. The atlas was for a while in the collection of the emperor Charles V (1500–58) and thereafter in the Royal Library of France. Grand productions of this kind, reflecting the intense interest of the west European elite in the fast-expanding world, grew from the incremental discoveries of seamen who were now exploring the ocean. Even at this early date the Catalan Atlas shows the Canary islands, Madeira, and the Azores in more or less their current positions. What now remained was to see what lay beyond.

For all the navigational aids that developed—astronomical tables, charts, portolans, compasses—successful navigation can be reduced to the contest fought by the seaman

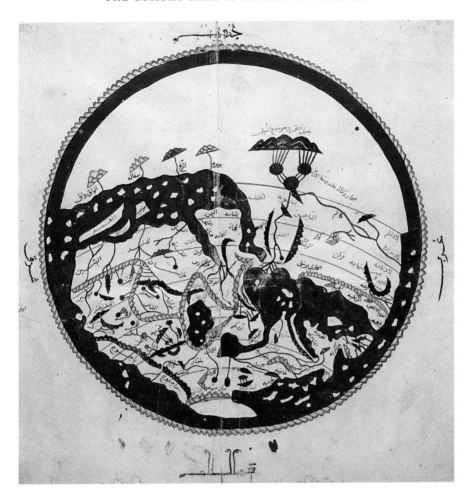

and his vessel against the sea and the winds. This is nowhere better summed up than in the words of Victor Hugo: 'The sea, in conjunction with the wind, is a composite of mechanisms. The sea's forces are mechanisms of infinite power: the ship's mechanisms are forces of limited power. Between the two organisms, the one inexhaustible, the other intelligent, takes place the combat that is called navigation' (*The Toilers of the Sea*, 1866).

3

Taking to the Sea

The further back in time one goes, the more difficult it becomes to discover evidence of the human past. This is particularly true when trying to assess the seagoing activities of our ancestors in the Palaeolithic period. Until comparatively recently most archaeologists dealing with Europe have assumed that until about 10,800 BC, at the onset of the last cold spell known as the Younger Dryas, the sea played little part in human history and that it was only the rapid climatic change at this time that drove people to explore the maritime world as an alternative subsistence resource. There is, as we shall see, some truth in this assumption, but there are now hints that the reality was far more complex, and more interesting.

The reason why so little is known of early maritime prehistory is that tangible evidence is difficult to find. The earliest remains of a boat so far known date to about 5500 BC, and changes in sea-level of more than a hundred metres have eroded or submerged old coastlines where people may have lived. But, as every archaeologist knows, absence of evidence is not necessarily evidence of absence, and there are ways of using surrogate evidence to fill in some of the gaps. Thus, while the boats may be lacking, the fact that human groups established themselves on oceanic islands, as shown by artefact scatters, implies that there were ways of crossing the sea. Similarly, the mainland use of exotic material like obsidian found only on certain islands demands that some kind of maritime transport was available. But, even so, positive evidence of these occurrences is sparse in the extreme, and a single discovery may completely overturn cherished beliefs. To give just one example, it was long believed

75

that the island of Crete was not settled by humans until the Early Neolithic period about 7000 BC, but in 2008 and 2009 programmes of field-walking focusing in the region of Plakias on the south coast discovered stone tools embedded in geological deposits dating to 130,000–100,000 years ago. A few weeks of fieldwork can require prehistory to be written.

There are also lessons for European archaeologists to learn from other parts of the world. About 50,000 years ago human groups made multiple sea-crossings of some 70–90 kilometres from South East Asia to Sahul (the single land-mass that, at the time, included Australia, Tasmania, and New Guinea); we know they were multiple because they moved in sufficient numbers to establish a successful breeding population. A little later, between 38,000 and 17,000 years ago, other human groups were making the deep-water crossing of 75–150 kilometres between Taiwan and the Japanese Ryukyu islands and settling in Okinawa. Some archaeologists have suggested that these movements should be seen in a much broader perspective, arguing that the early modern humans who moved out of Africa followed the rim of the Indian Ocean as a convenient passage eastwards. In this scenario the groups would have moved between favourable ecological niches, particularly estuaries and other wetlands, using simple watercraft to transport people and fresh water. Such coastal journeys would pre-adapt them for the longer crossings. A similar argument has been made that maritime migration around the North Pacific Rim may have contributed to the colonization of America from 16,000 years ago.

For maritime migrations of this kind to be possible a number of factors favourable to movement had to be met. The presence of offshore islands and indented coastlines with periodic estuaries and good pelagic resources was of prime importance, while unprotected coastlines battered by heavy winds and high seas had to be at a minimum. There had also to be suitable raw materials for building sea-craft. These conditions are met around the Indian Ocean and North Pacific Rim. They are also met in the Mediterranean and along the Atlantic coast of Europe and North Africa. There is no reason, therefore, why the Palaeolithic inhabitants of these regions should not have been successful as sailors, as were their contemporaries in the Indian Ocean and North Pacific.

But why did these migrations take place? What encouraged people to move? The usual reasons given are a combination of factors, principally resource depletion caused by over-exploitation, often exacerbated by climatic change and population growth. There can be no doubt that these were sometimes significant drivers, but we should not overlook human curiosity—the desire to see what lay round the next headland or what that distant island had to offer.

In the Beginning

By as early as 1.2 million years ago early hominids known as *Homo heidelbergensis* were moving out of eastern Africa into North Africa and into Europe, reaching as far west as Britain by about 750,000 years ago. The population roaming the European peninsula began to evolve to become Neanderthals (*Homo neanderthalensis*), a process under way by about 230,000 and completed by 150,000 years ago, while those in Africa evolved in a divergent way to become *Homo sapiens*, with anatomically modern humans developing about 200,000 years ago. For a long period of time, until the anatomically modern humans began to move into Europe about 50,000 years ago—a movement which contributed to the demise of the Neanderthals within 20,000 years—the two very different human races seem to have been separated by the Mediterranean.

Surprisingly there is yet no evidence of any movement between Africa and Europe across the Strait of Gibraltar, which at times of low sea-level was only ten kilometres across with a convenient island at about the halfway point. Nor is there at present any convincing evidence for human presence on the larger islands of Sicily, Corsica, Sardinia, and Cyprus. However, the recent discovery of Middle Palaeolithic tools dating to 130,000–100,000 years ago on Crete is a stark reminder of the fragility of negative evidence. It shows, beyond reasonable doubt, that humans, presumably from the European mainland, were able and willing to island-hop across the open sea in sufficient numbers to establish themselves on the island. Nor is this the only example. Middle Palaeolithic tools have now been found on Kefalonia, the Sporades, and Melos, all islands at the time but requiring shorter crossings than the journey to Crete.

It is usually assumed that the humans who were making these adventurous sea-crossings to the islands came from the European mainland and were therefore Neanderthals, but this runs contrary to the beliefs of some archaeologists who argue that Neanderthals would not have had the mental agility to mount such expeditions. An alternative explanation would be to suppose that the hunters were *Homo sapiens* sailing from the North African coast, but this would require them to have travelled across three hundred kilometres of open sea, which might be thought unlikely. The only evidence that could be used to give some slight support to the hypothesis is that it was the south coast of Crete where the traces of human activity were found, and there have been recent claims that Middle Palaeolithic tools have been found on the island of Gavdos, thirty-two kilometres south of Crete. The debate is likely to continue for some time as new evidence accumulates.

These discoveries raise the question of what manner of transport was used. Commentators unimpressed by the achievement suggest enhanced flotation or assisted drifting using perhaps bundles of driftwood or even inflated skins or a few logs lashed together. This may, indeed, have been the case for some of the shorter crossings, but to reach Crete implies a more robust vessel and an ability to guide it. Even if it were little more than a log raft manipulated with paddles and driven by winds and currents, it represents the beginning of seafaring.

Evidence that the European Neanderthals were exploiting maritime resources comes from recent excavations at Gorham's Cave and Vanguard Cave in Gibraltar. Here midden deposits dating to 49,000–45,000 years ago produced bones of dolphin and monk seal together with quantities of marine molluscs, including mussels and limpets, which could have been gathered within four kilometres of the caves. A study of the mussels showed that they were collected in mid-spring at the end of the growing season when at their prime as a food source. This careful utilization of the maritime environment would have offered an assured protein source at a time when other forms of food were scarce. Whether the monk seal and dolphins were the result of deliberate hunting or casual collection of stranded beasts, they will have provided a valuable source of oils as a supplement to the diet. The Gibraltar caves are not alone. More than a dozen sites are known around the Mediterranean Rim where Middle Palaeolithic communities exploited shellfish. While this does not, in itself, imply the use of boats, it demonstrates foraging strategies geared to the exploitation of maritime resources. Taking this evidence together with that for human presence on islands, it is becoming difficult to resist the conclusion that premodern humans were already familiar with the sea and with its huge potential.

The Arrival of Modern Humans

Anatomically modern humans began to penetrate Europe about 50,000 years ago, moving northwards out of Africa, most probably around the east end of the Mediterranean. Within about 20,000 years they had replaced the resident Neanderthals, though, as recent research has shown, there was some interbreeding, resulting in there being between 1 and 4 per cent of Neanderthal genetic material in modern human populations. The replacement of the European population was played out against great changes in climate which can be charted in some detail by reference to micropalaeontological and isotopic data derived from cores drilled through deposits of deep-sea sediments and polar ice caps. The most significant climatic downturn during this period was the Last Glacial Maximum, lasting from 21,000 to 18,000 BC, when temperatures fell to at least 10 °C below present-day levels. During this time extremely cold water currents flowed from the polar regions down the Atlantic coast of Europe, and this, combined with changes in wind patterns, introduced a continental pattern of climate

0   500 km

Z

Last Glacial Maximum ice caps
inland lakes
sea level drop of 110m
modern coastline

3.1 During the Last Glacial Maximum (*c.*24,500–*c.*10,000 BC) huge volumes of the earth's water were captured in the ice sheets that covered much of northern Europe. This reduced sea-level by as much as 110 metres. At the time the Mediterranean was more restricted and was separated from the Black Sea. The Caspian Sea was larger and received meltwater from the ice cap

to much of Europe, with the result that a massive ice sheet developed over Scandinavia, the Baltic, and much of the North Sea, Britain, and Ireland. More limited ice sheets extended over the Alps and the Pyrenees. South of the main ice sheet was a vast swath of tundra extending from the Atlantic eastwards into Russia. Further south this gave way to park tundra and steppe, with forests restricted to the north coastal regions of the Mediterranean, much of Iberia, and the coastal zone of north-west Africa.

With so much of the world's water now locked up in ice sheets, the sea-level fell by probably as much as 110–120 metres. This meant that those parts of the North Sea not beneath the ice were now land, with the Atlantic shore being up to 100 kilometres

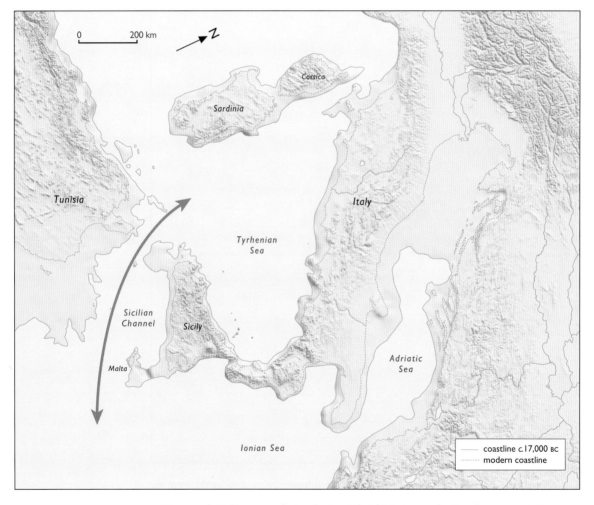

3.2 The central Mediterranean during the Last Glacial Maximum, showing the comparatively narrow channel joining the eastern and western basins

west of Ireland and 150 kilometres west of the present coast of western France. In the Mediterranean, coastlines extended out by, on average, 30–50 kilometres. Much of the Adriatic was now land, Corsica and Sardinia were a single island, and Sicily extended south to include Malta. The Black Sea became a freshwater lake once again, joined to a much-extended Caspian Sea. For people living around the Mediterranean and along the Atlantic coast of Iberia the forested coasts and the littoral zone together offered a favourable environment with a plentiful supply of animal protein. This is nowhere more dramatically expressed than in the paintings found on the walls of the Cosquer Cave, near Marseille. At the time of its use by hunting groups, between 21,500 and 20,000 BC, the cave mouth was about ninety metres above sea-level and was some distance from the contemporary coast, but subsequent sea-level rise after the Last Glacial Maximum has inundated the lower levels and its entrance, and it was discovered by divers only in 1985. Having penetrated the long, narrow approach tunnel, they found themselves in a partially flooded chamber, the walls of which were covered with paintings and engravings of the animals familiar to the early occupants as prey. The majority of the animals illustrated are woodland beasts that would have been the principal source of protein—ibex, aurochs, horse, and red deer—but 11 per cent of the illustrations were of sea or shoreline creatures including nine seals, one fish, and three auks—large flightless birds. Some of the seals were shown speared by projectile points, while the three auks made up a single scene with two males fighting over a female. The seals and auks, rich in fat, would have made a valuable addition to a diet composed predominantly of lean meat.

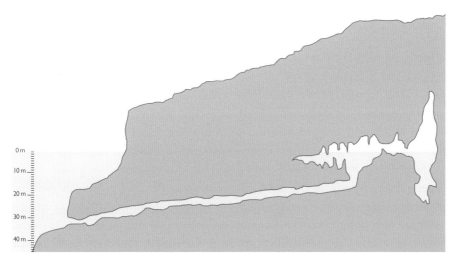

3.3 The Cosquer Cave on the Mediterranean coast of France, not far from Cap Morgiou, was discovered by divers in 1985. The only entrance is now thirty-six metres below sea-level, but when the cave was first used *c*.25,000 BC the entrance was well above the contemporary sea-level and the cave was easily accessible

81

3.4 Among the many animal paintings on the walls of the Cosquer Cave, featuring mainly bison, ibex, and horses, are marine creatures including auks (pictured here), seals, and possibly a jellyfish

Another cave site, Nerja, on the Bay of Málaga, now some four kilometres from the sea, was occupied between 21,000 and 10,800 BC. Excavation recovered the physical remains of food brought to the shelter. The animals represented were mainly small game, including goats and rabbits, augmented with pine nuts, snails, and fish. Among the thirty or so species of fish represented were Atlantic fish—cod, haddock, and pollock—which moved into the western end of the Mediterranean at certain times of year in pursuit of their food sources. While many of the fish species could have been caught in inshore waters, the presence of deep-sea species suggests that sea-going vessels may have been in use.

There is clear evidence in this period that sea-crossings were being made to the larger offshore islands. In western Crete an anatomically modern human skull was found with extant deer at Simonelli Cave. On Sardinia, at Corbeddu Cave, a fragment of human bone was recovered in a context suggesting a deposition in the Late Glacial Maximum, while Upper Palaeolithic tools of the same period were found on the Campidano. That the large island at the time comprising Corsica and Sardinia should have been occupied is no surprise since the narrowest crossing from the mainland was barely fifteen kilometres wide. The crossing from Italy to Sicily across the Strait of

Messina was much narrower. Given the length of the sea passages to Crete and from Crete to Gavdos already accomplished in the Middle Palaeolithic period, Palaeolithic foragers living around the Mediterranean could, and probably did, make long sea journeys over extended periods of time. The rapidly growing archaeological evidence no longer allows this very considerable achievement to be dismissed or played down.

The Warming Climate

At the end of the Last Glacial Maximum the climate began to warm up, reaching the Bølling–Allerød interstadial in the period 12,700–10,700 BC. Forest replaced the vast swaths of the open tundra and steppe of central and northern Europe, and, as temperatures approached those of the present day, sea-levels began to rise at certain periods, reaching a rate of as much as two centimetres per year. The climatic amelioration brought with it a much greater range of plant and animal species beneficial for those living in inland areas, but communities utilizing the coastal plains found their traditional resource zone shrank with the rapidly rising sea-level. Their response was to diversify the range of food resources procured and to intensify gathering from the littoral and the sea. This is reflected in the great increase in the number and size of shell middens found around the Tyrrhenian Sea. Molluscs were now being gathered before they had reached prime size, indicating that the resource was under pressure from over-collecting. In southern Iberia food remains found at settlement sites show that a greater reliance was now being placed on Atlantic open-water fish caught in the Alboran Sea, while the presence of increasing quantities of sardine is an indication that trawling nets were now being used. Meanwhile, in the Gulf of Argos communities

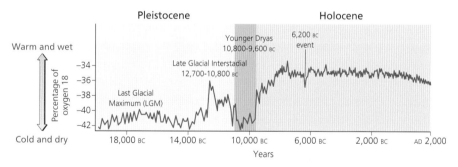

3.5 One way of charting climate change during the distant past is to measure the changing ratios of oxygen isotopes along the length of cores bored through the Greenland ice cap. The diagram derived from these calculations shows the sudden rise in temperature c.12,700 BC at the end of the Last Glacial Maximum and the short cold period of the Younger Dryas (10,800–9600 BC) before the temperature levels out to roughly what it is today

using the Franchthi Cave for shelter were beginning to augment their diet by collecting marine molluscs and fishing in inshore waters. Their successors, as we shall see, were to demonstrate their growing competence at open-sea sailing.

Standing back from all the detail, there is sufficient evidence to show that by the eleventh millennium BC foragers around the Mediterranean were making extensive use of the sea both for fishing and for travelling, building on experience gained by their predecessors over the previous hundred thousand years. They must have been able to build serviceable vessels and to navigate effectively, albeit usually within sight of land. We can fairly claim that seafaring was now well under way.

The Return of the Cold

About 10,800 BC the temperature plunged suddenly and dramatically. It was the beginning of the last period of intensive cold known as the Younger Dryas, a period that was to last twelve hundred years before, equally rapidly, the temperature began to rise again. This rise marked the end of the Pleistocene period and the beginning of the Holocene, the climatic era in which we currently live. There has been much debate about the cause of the Younger Dryas cold snap, but it is generally agreed that the rapid melting of the North American ice sheet during the Bølling–Allerød unleashed torrents of icy meltwater into the North Atlantic, deflecting the warm Gulf Stream away from Atlantic Europe. Partly as a consequence of this, wind patterns changed and Europe experienced cold airstreams blowing off the American continent across the icy Atlantic. The multiplier effect of these factors sent the temperature of Europe tumbling. The effects varied with geography. In Britain the mean annual temperature dropped to −5 °C, whereas in the Fertile Crescent, stretching along the east coast of the Mediterranean and across Syria to Iraq, the woodland and forest died back, leaving only pockets of trees isolated in vast swaths of grass and legumes. The varied ecozones of the Mediterranean were all affected, but in different ways, changing the balance of the resources upon which the human communities depended. The speed of change, coming at a time when the population was steadily rising, forced foraging groups to experiment with new food-gathering strategies. Some, like those living in the Fertile Crescent, intensified their gathering and adopted strategies leading to the domestication of animals, especially sheep and goats, and the selection of certain cereals and legumes for cultivation. This created a more sedentary lifestyle, setting the communities on a trajectory that soon led to settled farming. In other areas, particularly those near the sea, the new survival strategies involved a more extensive exploitation of the coastal and maritime resources.

3.6 The Franchthi Cave (*left*) in the Argolid, Greece, was occupied from the Upper Palaeolithic period to the Neolithic. Today the sea comes close to the entrance, but in times of lower sea-level it looked out over a wide plain abounding in plants and animals

The changes brought about by the Younger Dryas cold spell are evident in the stratified occupation levels found in the Franchthi Cave in the Peloponnese overlooking the Gulf of Argos. The cave was used on many occasions from about 38,000 to 3000 BC, spanning the Upper Palaeolithic to the Neolithic periods, during a time of fast-changing sea-levels. The improvement of climate from the Last Glacial Maximum to the warmer Bølling–Allerød saw a modification in the foraging strategies of those communities who used the cave. Earlier hunting patterns, targeting ibex, chamois, steppe ass, and aurochs, became much more diversified, with the hunting of wild pig and deer, the collection of land-snails, wild legumes, cereals, and marine molluscs, and the beginning of inshore fishing. This focus on the resources of the sea is also reflected in the appearance, about 13,000 BC, of obsidian, a black volcanic glass originating from the island of Melos about 120 kilometres away and brought in for making tools. The onset of the Younger Dryas saw the cave abandoned, but with the climatic

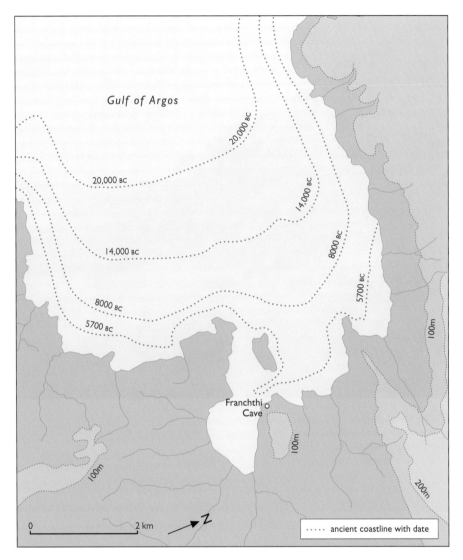

Gulf of Argos

20,000 BC

20,000 BC

14,000 BC

14,000 BC

8000 BC

8000 BC

5700 BC

5700 BC

100m

Franchthi Cave

100m

100m

200m

0   2 km   N

····· ancient coastline with date

3.7 The location of the Franchthi Cave in relation to changing sea-levels

improvement about 7900 BC it was reoccupied by communities who had access to increased quantities of obsidian and were now catching tuna.

What can be made of this evidence? Certainly we are seeing diversification in food-procuring strategies over time, with increasing emphasis on resources from the sea, but, while the appearance of tuna hints that more open-sea sailing was being practised, it is not in itself conclusive proof since tuna can be found inshore. The presence of obsidian from Melos, even in the small quantities in which it is found before the Younger Dryas, does, however, show that long sea trips were now being undertaken, but probably by other mainland communities from whom the inhabitants of the Franchthi Cave acquired their limited supply. But by the eighth millennium the quantities available had increased significantly, hinting that the cave users may now have been making the journey for themselves. The direct route would have involved sea trips of up to thirty-five kilometres crossing difficult seas. A safer route would have been from the tip of Attica, island-hopping through the western Cyclades with sea-crossings of no more than twenty kilometres on each step. Knowledge of the obsidian source on Melos implies that mainland foragers must have been making extensive sea-voyages, already well under way by 13,000 BC, motivated originally either by curiosity or by the desire to follow shoals of fish. The discovery of the obsidian was probably a by-product of this activity. At any event, it was the shock of the Younger Dryas downturn that encouraged a greater involvement with the sea.

One question, unanswerable at the moment, is, what kind of sea-going vessels were in use at this time? Given the technology available, the boats they used were probably made either of a light wooden framework covered in skins or of bundles of reeds sewn together. Without direct archaeological evidence the issue cannot be resolved, but an experiment using a reed-bundle boat island-hopping from Attica with six paddles showed that such craft were viable. It took two weeks to reach Melos, but this included time lost for bad weather. More experienced sailors in better weather might have been able to halve the time.

Further evidence for seafaring comes from Cyprus, where several early sites have been identified on the south coast. The most significant to date is Akrotiri Aetokremnos, a rock shelter some forty metres above present sea-level on a near-precipitous cliff. The excavation identified four distinct stratified layers. Below a mixed-surface deposit were two levels (2 and 4) separated by a layer of wind-blown sand. The earliest layer (4) contained over two hundred thousand bones of pigmy hippopotamus (a species that had evolved on the island), representing some 505 individual beasts, mixed with a few bones of dwarf elephants (another island native). A high proportion of the bone had been burned and was mixed with a few stone artefacts, which, assuming they had not been intruded later, would indicate human activity. After the sterile sand had blown in, layer 2 accumulated, incorporating ample signs of human activity including hearths, stone tools, and a few shell and stone ornaments. Associated animal bones included dwarf hippopotamus, many sea-birds, a few foot bones of wild boar, and large quantities of marine molluscs, crabs, and sea urchins. Radiocarbon dates suggest that layer 2 should be dated to between c.10,900 and c.10,100, that is, towards the beginning of the Younger Dryas.

There has been much debate about the interpretation of this evidence (and, indeed, the integrity of the deposits), some commentators finding it difficult to accept the excavators' conclusions that it was human intervention that led to the rapid extinction

3.8 The obsidian found in the occupation layers in the Franchthi Cave came from the island of Melos by sea. The route taken to the island would probably have started from Attica and would have involved a series of short sea trips hopping between the islands of Kea, Kythnos, and Seriphos. Nothing is known of the types of boat used at the time. A successful experimental crossing, using a boat made of reed bundles, showed that such a vessel was at least a viable mode of transport

of the native megafauna. However these issues are resolved, if they ever are, the inescapable conclusion is that the rock shelter was used by humans during the eleventh millennium BC and that they adopted a wide-ranging foraging strategy involving a thorough exploration of the maritime resource.

Evidence of broadly contemporary human activity comes from three other sites in the coastal region of Cyprus: Nissi Beach on the south-east coast, Aspros on the west coast, and Alimman close to Aspros. All three sites are located on fossil sand-dunes and are represented by scatters of stone implements comparable to those found at Akrotiri Aetokremnos. At the time, when the sea-level was seventy metres lower than it is at present, these locations were elevated, looking out over a wide coastal plain with minor rivers running across it, fringed by sandy beaches. They would have provided comfortable places to camp for foragers intent on exploiting the littoral zone and the sea. An added attraction may have been the nearby natural rock basins where sea-water evaporated, leaving crusts of salt.

The evidence for epipalaeolithic activity on Cyprus, albeit at present limited, is sufficient to show that hunters and fisher-foragers were now regularly sailing to the island from the mainland, from the Levant or southern Asia Minor, to exploit the varied coastal resources and to hunt the local megafauna of dwarf hippopotamus and

88

elephant to extinction. To begin with these foragers probably came on annual expeditions, returning home with whatever they were able to preserve by smoking, drying, or salting, but over the years some bands may have decided to stay.

There has been much discussion about what drove these people to the open sea. One favoured possibility is that it was the effects of the climatic deterioration following the onset of the Younger Dryas, when cold and extremely arid conditions began to take their toll, depleting the resources of the homeland. Under such pressures coastal communities, already used to the sea, may have set out to find new territories

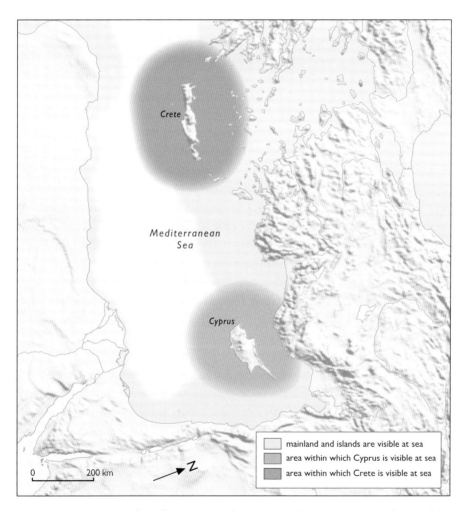

3.9 Intervisibility was a significant factor in early seafaring. The map shows various aspects of intervisibility in the eastern Mediterranean. A large area of the sea is out of sight of any land, but Crete is visible from mainland Greece, and Cyprus from mainland Asia Minor

to exploit. The situation may also have been exacerbated by steady population growth. These factors, taken together with the innate curiosity of humans, encouraged the more adventurous spirits to make longer and longer journeys at sea. But to argue that the Younger Dryas kick-started seafaring (as opposed to sea-going) is to overstate the case. The evidence for the Middle Palaeolithic settlement of Crete and the exchange of obsidian from Melos sometime later in the thirteenth millennium BC shows that the practice of open-sea sailing was already well established in the Aegean before the onset of the Younger Dryas. When the need to open up new ecological niches became pressing, the sea-going expertise was there to harness.

Other Worlds: Similar Responses

On the Atlantic front the end of the Last Glacial Maximum set in motion a series of changes that reshaped the landscape in a far more dramatic manner than in the Mediterranean. When the ice sheet was at its maximum, it blanketed much of northern Europe, including large parts of Britain and Ireland, locking up so much of the world's water that the sea-level fell to 110–20 metres below present levels. The enormous weight of the ice sheet also depressed the land. Thus, when the ice sheet began to recede, two processes were set in motion: eustatic rise in sea-level and, for the depressed regions, an isostatic uplift of the land. While the sea-level rise affected the entire world, isostatic uplift was limited to the areas that had been directly affected by the weight of the ice. In the north-west the two processes continued together, on occasions one outstripping the other, causing shorelines to fluctuate, but the overall effect was that sea-level rise dominated. Even so, isostatic uplift is still active in some areas: Scotland is still rising by three millimetres per year, while in the northern Baltic the rise is as much as nine millimetres.

One of the most dramatic effects of these processes was that the large expanse of what had been lowlands between Britain and Scandinavia gradually sank beneath a marine transgression as the North Atlantic expanded southwards to become the North Sea. The process continued until about 6000 BC, when Britain became an island.

As the ice retreated northwards from Denmark and southern Sweden, the expanding ocean quickly invaded the deep channel known as the Norwegian Trench, which flanks southern Norway, creating a wide inlet between Denmark and southern Sweden, the precursor of the present-day Kattegat and Skagerrak. Into this gulf flowed the warm Jutland Current, bringing sediments and dissolved nutrients from the fast-eroding North Sea Plain. At the same time meltwater from the receding ice sheet built up in the area later to become the Baltic Sea. Sometimes this inland sea opened directly onto

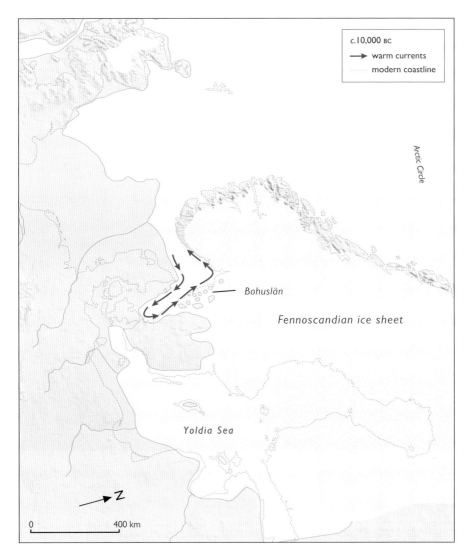

3.10 North-western Europe *c*.10,000 BC, with the remnant of the ice sheet still present. The islands of Bohuslän, off the north-west coast of Sweden, benefited from warm currents flowing in from the North Sea as the Gulf Stream began to be established. The favoured islands, offering a range of food resources, could be reached overland or by river from the forested North European Plain to the south

the Skagerrak, at others it was dammed, becoming a freshwater lake which drained to the Kattegat by two narrow waterways, the Øresund Strait and the Storebælt Strait, the situation depending on the dynamic relationship between eustatic and isostatic forces. In both cases nutrient-rich meltwater entered the Skagerrak to mix with that of the Jutland Current.

3.11 The archipelago of islands close to the ice margin *c.*10,000 BC provided a favoured hunting ground, particularly for seals. The gradual rise in land-level, which is still going on, has now incorporated many of the islands into the mainland coastal region of Bohuslän, western Sweden

This preamble has been necessary to explain why the west coast of Sweden north of Göteborg, the area known as Bohuslän, developed a remarkably rich and distinctive ecosystem benefiting from the nutrient-bearing currents and the warming conditions. During the Younger Dryas it comprised a belt of islands, small at first but getting larger as isostatic readjustment took effect, which supported a varied maritime ecosystem rich in fish, marine molluscs, sea mammals and their predators, and polar bears. The warmer conditions also allowed a woodland flora to develop at an early stage. It was a welcoming ecological niche in an otherwise rather hostile part of the world.

Recent archaeological surveys in Bohuslän have shown there to be a remarkable number of hunter-gatherer campsites dating to the Younger Dryas, beginning about 10,800 BC. In some areas the density is as much as fifteen sites per square kilometre, and, since the islands cover an area of about five hundred square kilometres, there may be as many as 750 separate locations where hunter-gatherer groups stopped for a while and left a scatter of stone debris. There can be little doubt that the attraction of the region was the rich maritime fauna. The artefacts and debitage have been classified as the Henbacka culture, which represents the summer foraging activities of the Ahrensburgian reindeer hunters whose usual zone of activity was the tundra of the North European Plain. In other words, during the Younger Dryas some members of these hunting bands set out on a trek of some three to five hundred kilometres north to the Bohuslän islands to gather food for the winter. They would have brought back dried or smoked fish and, more importantly, seal oil. Ethnographic studies have shown that hunters who live mainly on lean meat suffer from dizzy spells, feelings of extreme weakness, and diarrhoea, which can be counteracted by eating 'bone grease' derived from processed animal bones. Seal oil would have been a far more effective supplement, and its ready availability in a region abounding with sea food would have made the long expedition to the north a diversion to be encouraged. Over the centuries it is likely that some of the maritime foraging groups stayed in Bohuslän rather than make the annual return journey. That this was so is shown by the gradual divergence of artefact types between the two areas over time. Thus it was that seasonal visitors eventually became settlers.

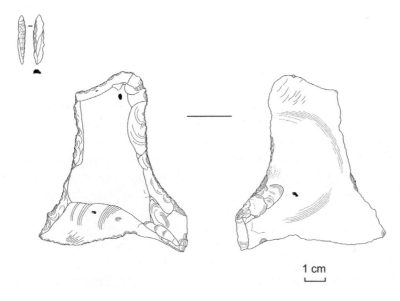

1 cm

3.12 Axes made from flakes of stone were used by Upper Palaeolithic hunters to butcher seals caught on the Bohuslän islands. This example is from Nösund. The small boring tool would have been useful for perforating skins to facilitate stitching

The distinctive toolkit of the Henbacka foragers included awls for boring holes in skins and flake axes with a wide cutting edge useful for slicing up seal blubber and for preparing sealskins for clothing and other uses. The blubber would probably have been packed in sealskin 'pokes' (containers) and either hung in the sun or buried in beach gravel for about two weeks to render it into oil, a process used by the Inuits in the recent past. In addition to being an essential dietary supplement, the oil would have had a variety of other uses. One of great importance to the foragers would have been to waterproof the sealskin boats which must have been in regular use for moving between the islands and for fishing. Indeed, much of the journey northwards from the reindeer-hunting camps is likely to have been by river and sea. We know nothing of the boats themselves, but it is a reasonable assumption that the sea-going vessels would have been made of sealskin stretched over a light wooden framework much in the style of the umiaks used by the Inuits. Umiaks are highly efficient craft which can carry ten to twenty people, but to function safely they have to be hauled out of the water, dried, and re-oiled every four days or so. This implies that on long foraging journeys among the islands and skerries either supplies of oil were carried or caches had been left on earlier occasions at points along the anticipated routes.

The closing phases of the Younger Dryas, then, saw groups travelling from the North European Plain to exploit the rich resources of the Bohuslän islands. In doing so, they developed expertise as sea-goers and eventually began to establish pioneer groups in the region. From here, during the tenth millennium, seafarers began to explore and later to set up permanent bases all along the Atlantic coast of Norway, reaching as far north as Finnmark by about 9500 BC. This process, extending along two thousand kilometres of coast, may have taken as little as two hundred years. To accomplish this, the pioneers must have been skilled navigators using sea-craft well adapted to the fjords and islands of this deeply indented coast.

The maritime colonization of, first, the Bohuslän region of Sweden and then the entire Atlantic coast of Norway, beginning in the Younger Dryas and continuing into the following centuries, by reindeer hunters of the North European Plain is one of the most spectacular examples of maritime endeavour in the whole of European prehistory. True, those engaged in the adventure would not have needed to spend long periods at sea or to sail out of sight of land, but the sturdy quality of the skin vessels and their skills in navigation show that they were seafarers of some competence. Why they should have embarked on the colonization of so extensive a coastal expanse is a matter of debate. No doubt the changing climatic conditions were a significant factor. The retreat of the ice sheets, creating nutrient-rich environments for maritime faunas to flourish, offered new opportunities for foraging. Population pressure will also have played its part. But we return to the question of human curiosity: was the driving force the desire to know what lay beyond the next headland?

That we can trace this story in some detail is due largely to the fact that the Scandinavian region has been rising in relation to sea-level as a result of isostatic readjustment, and therefore the campsites of the maritime foragers have survived. Further south, along the coasts of southern Britain, France, and Iberia, sea-level rise has been the dominant factor, resulting in the erosion or inundation of the coastal archaeology of this crucial period. Although evidence is sparse or lacking, we can be sure that along the whole of the Atlantic coast Upper Palaeolithic communities would have exploited the marine and littoral resources offered by the prolific ocean. In doing so, they too would have become skilled seamen.

The Sea Gives: Littoral Strategies

The dry, cold period of the Younger Dryas ended quite suddenly about 9600 BC and temperatures rose rapidly, at first as much as 7 °C in a generation or two. By about 7000 BC it had peaked and then settled down to fluctuate more or less around present-day temperatures with one brief cold event occurring about 6200 BC. The climatic amelioration beginning in 9600 BC marks the start of the Holocene era. In terms of archaeological cultures this is the beginning of the Mesolithic (or Epipalaeolithic in the Levant) when hunter-gatherers were fast readjusting to the improving climate and the more extensive opportunities for food-getting that this provided.

Over much of Europe the steppe and tundra of the Younger Dryas was colonized by trees, the early pioneers of birch, pine, and hazel gradually being replaced by elm, oak, lime, and alder. In the more southerly region of Europe change came more slowly, held back by the continued lack of moisture rather than the cold. Pine colonized the higher regions, while elsewhere deciduous oak began to spread, but the other broad-leafed trees that came to dominate the European forests were much sparser. With the change of vegetation came a change in fauna. Large mammals like the woolly rhinoceros and the mammoth died out, and the vast herds of migrating reindeer of the north European tundra moved north to be replaced by more sedentary beasts: elk, aurochs, red deer, roe deer, and wild pig. The increase in sea temperature also encouraged the growth of plankton, which, in turn, supported a richer and more varied marine fauna. The gradual rise in sea-levels during this period brought changes to the coastlines, sometimes reducing the extent of the coastal plains but also generating sand-bars, behind which marshes, rich in varied resources, could develop. The larger rivers, often carrying increased loads of silt, created wide flood-plains and extensive deltas.

After a period of abandonment during the Younger Dryas, the Franchthi Cave, overlooking the Gulf of Argos, was brought back into active use by early Mesolithic hunter-gatherers, but the environment had changed. A rise in sea-level by about thirty metres had greatly reduced the coastal plain, bringing the shoreline to within a kilometre or so. The cave now overlooked coastal wetlands and was backed by hills blanketed with deciduous oak and pine, providing habitats for wild pigs and red deer and offering many wild plant resources including barley, lentils, pears, acorns, almonds, pistachios, and medicinal herbs. A study of the plant remains from the cave suggests that the site was occupied from early spring to at least late autumn and may have continued to be used throughout the winter. In other words, it had become the main residential base for the community—a fact further emphasized by the creation of a burial-ground just outside the cave mouth. Reliance on the sea is shown by the arrival of supplies of obsidian from Melos, while the diet was augmented by fishing and the collection of marine molluscs.

In the early eighth millennium the economic strategy of the community changed in a way that probably involved the use of other sites as bases for longer periods of time. As a result, the cave was less intensively used and burial declined. Then, for a brief period, there was a significant change. Much greater quantities of obsidian were introduced and fishing became far more evident. Not only were specialized tools for fish-processing found in some quantity, but large numbers of tuna were caught, some of them weighing up to two hundred kilograms. Though tuna do swim in coastal waters, where they can be netted or perhaps speared, they are habitually a deep-water fish. Taken together the evidence suggests that the occupants were now going on tuna-fishing expeditions, possibly combining these with visits to Melos to collect obsidian. This does not imply the sudden development of a maritime capability since, as we have seen, this already existed five thousand years earlier, but it does show that the maritime resource was now being more intensively used.

Contemporary discoveries from elsewhere in the Aegean point to the seasonal use of small islands as temporary bases for specialist fishing expeditions. At Gioura in the Sporades, an archaeological deposit excavated at the Cyclops Cave produced obsidian tools associated with bone hooks suitable for catching large fish. The faunal remains included tuna, bonito, and mackerel which had already been decapitated before being taken to the cave for drying or smoking. On another island, Kythnos, one of the strings of islands on the route between Melos and Attica, an open-air hunter-gatherer site was found producing large quantities of obsidian. Thus, although the evidence is not yet extensive, it is already sufficient to show that by the eighth millennium a maritime network had grown up in the Aegean involving long-haul sailing expeditions using the smaller islands as convenient bases at least for part of the year.

It is too early to assess the position of Crete in these networks. As we have seen (p. 77), recent fieldwork has shown that the island was populated during the Middle Palaeolithic period. The same programme has also discovered twenty sites near Plakias, on the southern side of the island, producing quartz and chert artefacts of Mesolithic type, dating to the ninth and eighth millennia BC, scattered along a coastal zone nearly two kilometres wide and ten kilometres long. Although the survey focused on an area of the coastal wetlands, an ecozone favourable for coastal foragers where there were convenient rock shelters, the number of sites found was surprisingly large. Clearly there are many more Mesolithic sites to be found on the island. The broad similarities between the tool type found in the Plakias survey and those from the Franchthi Cave suggest that the Cretan foragers may have been part of the maritime network that embraced Kythnos, Gioura, and the Argolid, but whether they were seasonal visitors or residents it is impossible to say. The most likely explanation is that from the time when hunger-gatherer communities reached Crete in the Middle Palaeolithic the island continued to be part of the broader Aegean maritime system, but, unlike the smaller Aegean islands of Kythnos and Gioura, Crete was large enough to sustain a resident population.

We have seen that on Cyprus there was a flourishing maritime-forager community using the Aetokremnos rock shelter and neighbouring beaches in the eleventh millennium BC, and we shall consider below the beginnings of permanent Neolithic settlement in the early ninth millennium. What happened in the thousand years in between is at present unclear, but in all probability the island continued to be part of an eastern Mediterranean network during this period, bound to the coastal communities of Asia Minor and the Levant. The Neolithic settlers who began to arrive on the island in the ninth millennium were using seafaring skills and technology long established in the region.

The rise in sea-levels in the Mediterranean is unlikely to have significantly affected the accessibility of Sicily from the mainland of Italy, but the channel between the island and North Africa widened and Malta became separated. The importance of the sea to late foragers is vividly demonstrated by the sequence of occupation deposits found in the Grotta dell'Uzzo, a cave site on the north-east coast of Sicily, with occupation spanning the transition from Mesolithic foraging to Neolithic cultivation and domestication over the period 9000–5500 BC. In the earlier Mesolithic layers, bones of large game, small mammals, and birds occur in about equal quantities, but it was the large game—red deer, wild cattle, and wild boar—that would have supplied the bulk of the food. Thereafter fish became increasingly important, making up 25–40 per cent of the bone detritus. Most common were grouper, with wrasse, white bream, and moray eel providing significant percentages of the catch. Other

3.13 The well-watered narrow coastal plain of the south coast of Crete in the vicinity of Plakias provided an ideal environment for Mesolithic hunter-gatherers

maritime resources gathered included very large quantities of marine molluscs, dolphins, pilot whales, large whales, seals, and a turtle. While the whales, represented largely by their vertebrae, were probably found stranded on the shore rather than being harpooned at sea, there can be little doubt that fishing out at sea featured large in the food-gathering activities of the foragers. The discovery at a contemporary inland settlement of blades of obsidian from the island of Lipari off the north coast of Sicily is sufficient to show that journeys of at least thirty kilometres were being made across the open sea.

A study of the faunal remains from the Grotta dell'Uzzo suggests that the cave was probably the home base occupied throughout the year from which hunting and gathering parties would have gone to procure food, some in pursuit of large game herds in the uplands, others to the shore and the sea. The growing scarcity of the game herds, resulting from climatic change and over-hunting, meant that the community was forced to rely increasingly on the sea for its livelihood. If this was the situation elsewhere in the central Mediterranean, it would have led to the scope of the fishing becoming more adventurous, causing local networks to join up, the sea now becoming the connective tissue linking distant and disparate coastal peoples together.

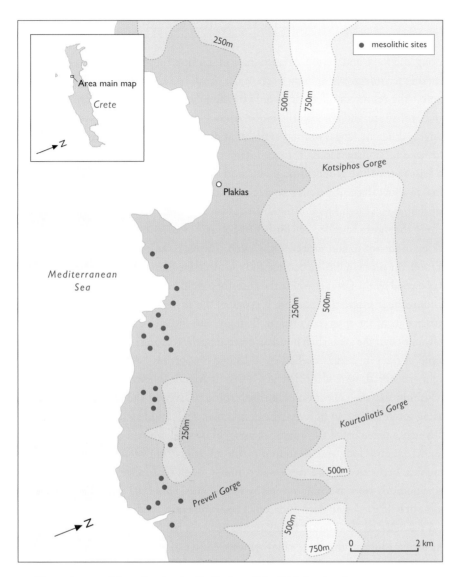

3.14 The south coast of Crete showing the distribution of Mesolithic hunting sites

Standing back from the evidence for the two millennia following the end of the Younger Dryas, sparse though it still is in the Mediterranean basin, it is clear that the sea played a rapidly increasing role in daily life. We are still completely ignorant of the shipbuilding skills of the people, but after many thousands of years of experience the vessels used were likely to have been skilfully designed to suit local conditions and sailed by people raised in the traditions of the sea.

99

Reaping the Outer Ocean

Along the long and varied Atlantic face of Europe those Mesolithic communities working territories within easy reach of the ocean had the advantage of being able to exploit the resources offered not only by the inland forests but also by coastal wetlands, the shore, and the sea. The four ecozones, often found in close proximity, could provide different ranges of food available at different times of the year, thus reducing the need for constant long-distance foraging, allowing base camps to be occupied by at least part of the group throughout most of the year. From these bases, optimally sited to allow all the different resource zones to be reached, experienced hunters could concentrate on catching game in the forests while the very old and very young could be sent to the shores to collect shellfish. Others might fish in the rivers and lagoons, some taking to the sea to add variety to the catch. The more varied were the assured sources of food, the more stable life became and the more the home base camp became a property owned by the families where the ancestors could be laid to rest, creating memories binding the living to the location. It is one of the characteristics of Mesolithic coastal settlements as far apart as Portugal, Brittany, and Denmark that the dead were carefully buried in the great shell middens created by the feasting of successive generations. Some of the cemeteries reached considerable proportions. At Skateholm in Sweden eighty-six burials were identified; at Cabeço da Arruda in Portugal there were 175.

Fishing and the collection of shellfish featured large in the life of many Atlantic-facing communities. In Portugal the best-known shell middens are found in the valley of Muge, a tributary of the Tagus where an individual midden could be as much as a hundred metres long and up to four metres in height. They tended to be sited at the interface between salt and fresh water in easy reach of a range of fish and shellfish. Aquatic birds were available in nearby marshlands, while the scrub beyond was the home of wild cattle and deer. Such a rich environment with all the food sources within easy reach led to the mounds being used as places of habitation throughout the year.

Further south in the Sado valley another cluster of shell middens has been examined. These tend to be slighter, and analysis of the faunal remains suggests that the individual sites were occupied for more limited periods of time by specialist foraging groups. Most of the molluscs of which the mounds were composed were common cockle-shell or peppery furrow shell, found in a ratio of roughly 2:1. Cockles live in clean, sandy deposits in the intertidal region of estuaries, while the peppery furrow shells prefer the more stagnant, muddy parts of inner estuaries. Of the fish found in the middens, meagre (similar to sea-bass) were the most common. They could be caught offshore but also favoured shallow estuaries with sandy bottoms. Other food sources included red deer, wild pig, and aurochs, as well as hare and rabbit. The huge quantity

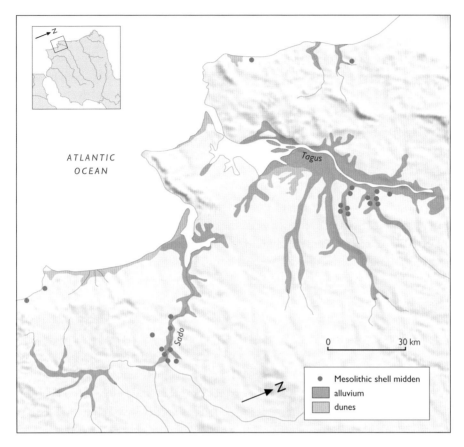

3.15 The valleys of the Tagus and Sado in southern Portugal offer a rich range of aquatic resources—rivers, marshes, and estuaries—for Mesolithic hunter-gatherers

of marine molluscs that accumulated is impressive, but it is worth remembering that their contribution to the calorific intake of the community was comparatively small. It has been calculated that a single red deer provides the food equivalent of 157,000 cockles, 52,000 oysters, or 31,000 limpets. Even a 1.5-metre meagre would compensate for a considerable weight of cockles.

The Mesolithic midden sites in the Muge, Sado, and Mira valleys of Portugal reflect well-established communities with a specialized, balanced food-gathering system based on upper estuaries. But while there can be little doubt that boats were regularly used, there would have been no need for the foragers to venture far beyond the estuaries: all they required for a comfortable life was close to hand.

Much further to the north, in Denmark, it is possible to trace the emergence of coastal adaptations in many ways very similar to those found in the Portuguese estuaries.

In the early stages of Holocene development, named after the type site of Maglemose (9000–6400 BC), communities were still largely hunters of game animals. Such boats that there were were probably still made of skin stretched around a light-wood framework or of birch bark since there were few suitable trees for building anything more substantial, but with the spread of forests during the late Maglemose and the subsequent Kongemose period (6400–5400 BC) it is likely that log boats began to be developed. The only traces of water-going vessels in these early periods are a few isolated paddles. It is only from the last phase of the Mesolithic, the Ertebølle period (5400–3900 BC), that actual log boats have been recovered—currently some twenty-one individual examples.

By the Kongemose period hunting and foraging were being organized to utilize both inland and coastal environments. Inland camps, by rivers or lakes, were used by groups hunting large game animals, while the coastal camps set up on sheltered bays or on islands close to the mainland allowed for the gathering of marine molluscs, fishing, and the hunting of marsh birds. Already, in this period, coastal camps seem to have become the main bases to which the hunters would return from inland with their prey. By the fifth millennium the emphasis on the coastal camps had grown still more and they now supported a sedentary population for much of the year with small hunting bands leaving for the inland areas in the summer months.

The coastal camps of the Ertebølle period are characterized by vast shell middens up to two metres deep and twenty metres wide, sometimes stretching for up to 150 metres along the contemporary shorelines: they represent the accumulation of food detritus over many generations, in some cases for periods of up to seven hundred years, and provide an invaluable resource for the study of the Mesolithic economy. Game hunted

3.16 The bone of an aurochs decorated with human figures inscribed by Mesolithic hunter-gatherers. From Ryemarksgård, Denmark

in the inland regions and brought to the base camp included roe deer, red deer, and wild pig, with lesser numbers of elk and aurochs as well as fur-bearing animals like lynx, wild cat, otter, and pine marten. At the nearby marshland swans and ducks were shot or netted, while the shoreline offered grey seals and unlimited quantities of oysters, mussels, cockles, and periwinkles.

A detailed study of the fish-bones recovered from the middens identified more than forty species, including salt- and freshwater fish and fish migrating between the sea and estuaries. The percentages of the species caught vary from site to site. At Ertebølle, which produced twenty-one different species, the commonest by far were cyprinids, mainly roach, with smaller quantities of eel, cod, saithe, and perch. Nearby, at the broadly contemporary site of Bjørnholm, more than half the catch was eel, while at Norsminde on the east coast of Jutland flat-fish, mostly flounder, were found. These differences probably reflect availability rather than deliberate choice. Looking at the fish remains overall, it is clear that they represent the gathering of whatever fish were available in local coastal waters during the summer months. The majority were

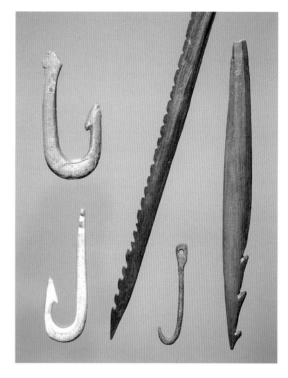

3.17 Mesolithic fish-hooks and harpoons found from Danish Mesolithic sites are evidence that large fish were being sought, indicating the possibility of deep-water fishing

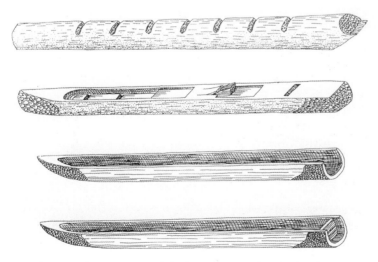

3.18 Suggested stages in the construction of a log boat using a simple technology based on stone axes and wooden wedges

small species like stickleback and roach as well as young individuals of larger species. In other words, the fishing seems to have been non-selective. This, and the type of fish caught, would suggest that the catch was made by placing stationary fish-traps close to the coast. That said, finds of fish-hooks and leister prongs from a fishing spear indicate that there were also expeditions out to sea to catch bigger fish.

The twenty or so log boats of Mesolithic date found around the coasts of Denmark give an unprecedented insight into sea-craft of the fifth millennium used for coastal fishing and possibly for making longer journeys at sea. They were made from hollowed-out trunks of lime wood, typically 6–7 metres long and about 1 metre broad. The hollowing left the walls of the vessel 3–4 centimetres thick at the bottom, thinning to 1–2 centimetres at the sides. The bow was thicker and was pointed, while the stern was cut square and fitted with a bulkhead. The hollowing was done by chopping slots across the trunk and wedging out the timber in between. A number of the vessels were provided with clay hearths set aft, but some also had forward hearths, the implication being that they were at sea for extended periods. Experiments with replicas showed them to be seaworthy and capable of carrying up to five people. Such vessels would have been ideal for travelling and fishing in coastal waters, but trials showed that they would also have been able to cross the Great Belt—the seaway between Sjælland and Funen, a distance of some twenty kilometres—with little difficulty in five hours. In the Ertebølle period sea journeys of twice that length were being made. The only disadvantage of log boats of this kind was their tendency to crack and to need regular repair.

By the Ertebølle period the Mesolithic foragers of Denmark were well adapted to their coastal environment and, while they were clearly well able to work the fishing grounds and make journeys between the islands, there is nothing to show conclusively that they undertook longer sea-voyages. Like the foragers of the Portuguese estuaries, they had little need to stray far from these familiar coastal waters.

On the west coast of Scotland and on many of the islands of the Inner and Outer Hebrides there is ample evidence of mobile hunter-gatherer groups living well off the rich coastal resources. The foragers who camped on the island of Risga in the mouth of Loch Sunart collected many different types of marine molluscs as well as catching crab and fish including conger eel, skate, grey mullet, haddock, and sea bream. They also hunted a range of marsh birds and seals and had access to supplies of red deer and wild pig. With the seaweeds and other plants they could gather, the diet could hardly have been more varied. How mobile the community was it is difficult to say, but on the tiny island of Oronsay, some seventy kilometres away, temporary fishing camps were set up where, amid the abundant shellfish, sea-fish, notably saithe, were processed. By studying the growth of the ear bones of the saithe, specialists were able to suggest that the camps were occupied at different times during the year, early summer, midsummer, autumn, and winter, the implication being that the fishing parties used the island for short periods, returning to other bases in between.

This impression of inter-island mobility is given greater visibility when the distribution of different types of stone used to make implements is considered. Bloodstone from Rhum, pitchstone from Arran, and mudstone from Katis Bay on Skye were all distributed well beyond the island of origin. Not all finds are closely dated to the Mesolithic period, and indeed most of the pitchstone finds that have been dated belong to the fourth millennium, but the complex maritime networks represented in these distributions must have their roots in the time when the first hunter-gatherers were moving into the archipelago. To sustain a life in such an environment mobility was essential: the sea provided the only practical means of travel. Unlike their contemporaries enjoying the comparatively placid waters around Denmark, the Mesolithic inhabitants of western Scotland had to face the fast-changing tempers of the Atlantic. We know nothing of their boats, but it is a fair assumption that they must have been robust and able to run before the wind without shipping too much water. Log boats would have been serviceable in sheltered inland waters, but for longer journeys on the more open sea, skin boats like the Inuit umiaks would have been a much safer option since they ride the waves more easily.

Enter the First Farmers

The emergence of societies whose livelihoods were based on food production—the cultivation of crops and the domestication of animals—took place in South West Asia in an arc stretching from the Levantine coastal region, across what is now northern Syria and southern Turkey, to the Zagros Mountains of Iran. It was a complex and long-drawn-out process that started with the move to larger and more sedentary settlements in the early Epipalaeolithic (18,000–12,000 BC). People began to rely increasingly on collecting selected wild cereals and pulses and exploiting wild sheep—strategies that were sharpened by the climatic downturn of the Younger Dryas. The crucial period, when the careful selection of wild crops like einkorn wheat, barley, and chickpea led imperceptibly to cultivation and the husbanding of wild sheep, goats, cattle, and pigs created domesticated flocks and herds, took place between 9600 and 6900 BC. The period is generally known as the Aceramic Neolithic and is divided about 8000 BC into an early and a late phase. An alternative terminology, widely used in the Levant, is to refer to the period as the Pre-Pottery Neolithic, the division being into Pre-Pottery Neolithic A (PPNA) and Pre-Pottery Neolithic B (PPNB). The amelioration of the climate following the end of the Younger Dryas set in motion a number of interacting processes.

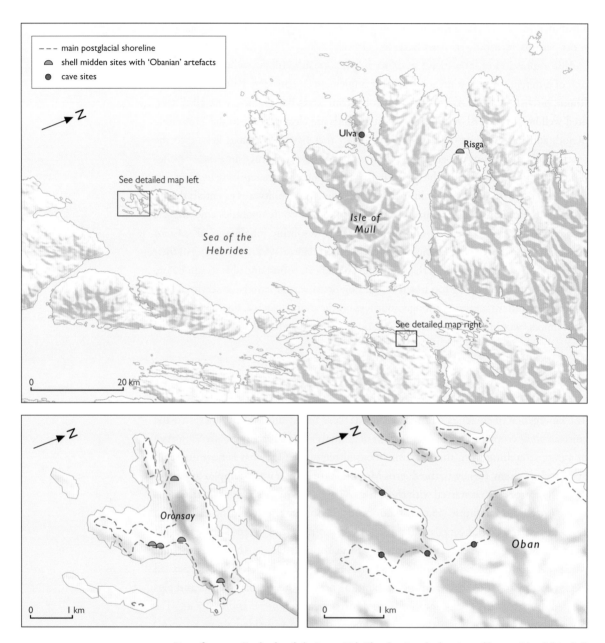

3.19 Part of western Scotland and the Inner Hebrides showing the location of known Mesolithic shell middens. Many more sites in similar locations no doubt remain to be found

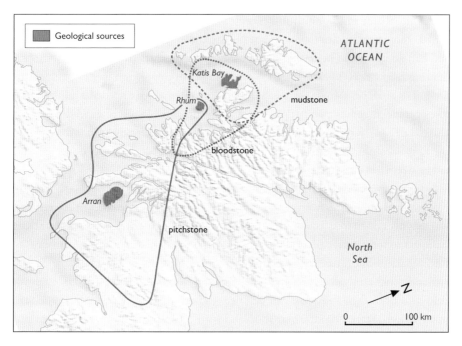

3.20 Nothing demonstrates maritime mobility more clearly than the transport of distinctive types of stone favoured for tool-making from island sources off the west coast of Scotland in the Mesolithic and Early Neolithic periods. The sea must have been the principal mode of transportation

The warmer, damper weather made the land more prolific, removing constraints on population growth, but the ensuing exponential rise in population set up new stresses as expansive exploitation began to damage and deplete the environment. A steady rise in sea-level also meant that large expanses of the highly productive coastal plain around the eastern end of the Mediterranean were inundated. The momentum of a rising population soon outstripped society's ability to deal with the loss of production. In other words, in many regions where the Neolithic economy was taking root, the holding capacity of the land could no longer accommodate the increasing numbers of people. The inevitable results were twofold: new economic strategies had to be developed, and people moved away to find and settle new ecological niches. In the east of the region this led eventually to the colonization of the alluvial valley of the Tigris and Euphrates. In the west Neolithic communities spread to Cyprus in the late tenth millennium BC, into southern Turkey in the early ninth millennium, to Crete about 7000 BC, and to the plains of eastern Greece between 7500 and 6500 BC.

The earliest known Neolithic settlement in Cyprus is Asprokremnos, in the centre of the island, dating to the period 9100–8500 BC. Here a small settled community used a tool assemblage similar to that of the PPNA of the Levant and fed off domesticated

pig. A little later in the ninth millennium, in PPNB, more settlements were established. Those living at Shillourokambos close to the south coast were cultivating pulses
and had domesticated herds and flocks of sheep, goats, cattle, and pigs and were also
hunting fallow deer. How extensive was the influx of population it is difficult yet to
say, but to establish a single sustainable community would have needed a minimum of
forty people. Breeding populations of the farmyard animals as well as seed-grain had
also to be brought to the island by boat. The wild pigs had already been introduced in
the Epipalaeolithic period, but the domesticated sheep, goats, and cattle and the wild
fallow deer to boost the stock of wild game were all shipped in by the early farmers.
This must have involved multiple sea journeys, either making the open sea-crossing
of a hundred kilometres from the Levant, or setting off from the coast of Asia Minor
some eighty kilometres distant. Transporting wild boar across the open sea in sufficient
numbers to form a breeding population was an impressive achievement managed by
the Epipalaeolithic foragers. When the first farmers arrived about 9000 BC, the earliest
settlers brought only dogs to help in the hunt and the seed-grains needed to establish
cultivation, but their ships also carried mice—a pest which demanded the immediate
importation of cats. Over the next thousand years cattle, goats, sheep, fallow deer, and
domesticated pigs were introduced, the sheep being the latest arrivals about 8000 BC.
Nothing is known of the vessels used, whether dug-out log boats, reed-bundle boats,
hide boats, or rafts, but certain speculations are possible.

While young pigs could travel the distance trussed up in the bottom of a dug-out
without significant harm, the transport of ruminants was a different matter since they
needed to stand and had to be moved quickly. The most appropriate way to do this
would have been to join two or more dug-outs together in the manner of a catamaran
with a platform built across them for the animals, suitably tethered, to stand on. Since
speed was of the essence if the animals were to survive, it is possible that some kind
of sail was rigged. A study of the mice adds a further interesting detail. Mice breed
fast, and natural mutations will lead to evolutionary drift if the population is isolated
for long. That this was not the case with the Cyprus mice shows that there must have
been a constant inflow of new blood from the mainland, estimated to have been at a
rate of at least two inputs of fresh mice each year. In other words, once established, the
farmers of Cyprus maintained regular contact with the mainland.

3.21 (*Opposite*) The spread of Neolithic farming practices from the Near East to Europe was a complex
process taking some two thousand years to complete its first stage. One of the main routes of advance was
through the heart of Europe making use of the great rivers; the other was by way of the Mediterranean
by a process of coastal enclave colonization, which allowed rapid progress to be made, beginning in the
Balkans *c*.6000 BC and ending on the Atlantic coast of Portugal five hundred years later

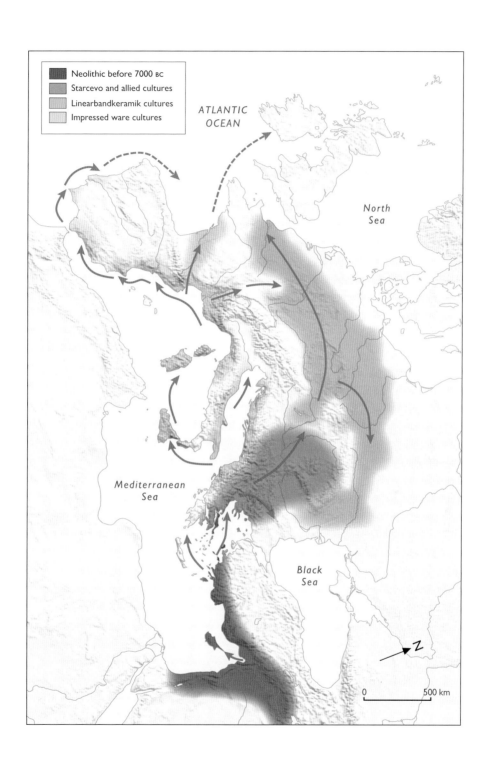

ATLANTIC
OCEAN

Neolithic before 7000 BC
Starcevo and allied cultures
Linearbandkeramik cultures
Impressed ware cultures

North
Sea

Mediterranean
Sea

Black
Sea

N

0   500 km

In the seventh millennium farmers and their stock were leaving the south and west coasts of Asia Minor for Crete and the plains of eastern Greece in considerable numbers, sufficient to establish a fast-expanding farming population. To reach Crete it would have been possible to island-hop via Rhodes, Karpathos, and Kasos in order to break up the 190-kilometre sea journey, while to reach the Greek mainland there was a variety of possible routes via the Cyclades. But whichever routes were favoured, the scale of the operation implies the existence of well-built boats and experienced navigators used to the local waters. As we have seen, such facilities existed at least as early as the twelfth millennium BC among the coastal foragers of the regions, who were rooted in a maritime tradition going back many millennia earlier. When the land-based farmers of South West Asia decided to set out on their colonizing journeys to the west, they will have found foragers well used to the vagaries of the sea ready to help them.

The Race to the West

Early Neolithic communities expanded across the plains of eastern Greece during the millennium from 7500 to 6500 BC, creating a dense network of farming villages. From these pioneering settlements the farming package spread westwards across Europe by land and by sea until, by about 5000 BC, farming was being practised as far west as the Atlantic coast of Europe in such remote regions as western Portugal and the Channel Islands. There were two principal routes of advance. From eastern Greece groups practising food production moved northwards along the valleys of the rivers Vardar and Morava into the lower and middle Danube basin by 6000 BC, and from there farming spread rapidly along the river valley systems and through the deciduous forests of middle Europe, reaching Normandy and Brittany about 5300 BC, covering a distance of fifteen hundred kilometres in about seven hundred years. There has been much debate about the processes involved in this astonishing advance, but the archaeological evidence, combined with a rapidly growing body of ancient DNA data, shows that, while acculturation of the early Mesolithic hunter-gatherers was a factor, new people with South West Asian genes were involved in the forward push. To create the momentum there must have been a strong social imperative for pioneering groups to split off from established settlements and move into the unknown to colonize new territories. The simplest way to understand this is to suppose that society believed it to be socially desirable for the young to move away from home. To embrace mobility was a way of gaining status.

The spread of the Neolithic package westwards the length of the Mediterranean and out through the Strait of Gibraltar to the Atlantic coast of Portugal was even more rapid than the continental, riverine expansion. From Greece to Portugal, a distance of 2,500 kilometres as the crow flies (and considerably more by following the coast), it took less than five hundred years, a speed made possible by the use of the sea. In this maritime environment pioneer settlers and their livestock could sail along coasts or by way of islands until they found a suitable place to establish their new farming settlements. They could select areas that were not intensively used by indigenous Mesolithic hunter-gatherers or they could choose to develop symbiotic relations with the locals. The needs of the farmers for light, dry soil and those of the foragers for coastal and riverine wetlands complemented each other. Both groups in their different niches could procure resources desirable to the other, facilitating reciprocal exchange and coexistence. That said, the stories of the pioneer enclaves are likely to have differed considerably one from another.

The spread of the first farmers around the Mediterranean can be traced by the sudden appearance of the Neolithic package: cultivated wheat and barley, domesticated sheep, goats, cattle, and pigs, ground-stone artefacts, and pottery. Characteristically the pottery was extensively covered with decorations impressed into the clay before firing—a highly distinctive style known to archaeologists, unsurprisingly, as Impressed Ware. After about 5400 BC the favoured way to impress the patterns was by using the cockle-shell (*Cardium edule*), creating Cardial Ware, which remained the common style until about 5000 BC, after which a variety of local types emerged using a range of tools. These are known as Epicardial Wares. The distribution of these impressed wares around the Mediterranean and into the Atlantic shows the extent of the early phase of colonization. Radiocarbon dates allow the progress of the colonization to be charted.

The starting-off point seems to have been western Greece just before 6000 BC. From here settlers sailed up the Dalmatian coast, some crossing the Adriatic to the east coast of Italy. Both zones were settled, and within a century or two Neolithic enclaves were being established at the head of the Adriatic in Istria and the Po valley. Meanwhile, other groups were crossing to Calabria and to Sicily and Malta, where the earliest Neolithic presence is attested soon after 6000 BC. The introduction of the new way of life is vividly shown at the Grotta dell'Uzzo, where occupation continued, but after about 5700 BC domestic sheep and cattle make their appearance in the

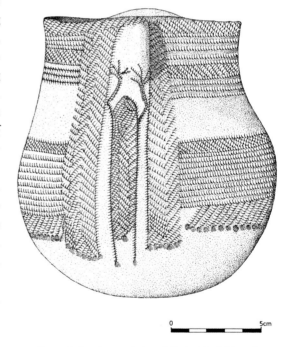

0   5cm

3.22 One of the characteristics of Early Neolithic cultures was the use of pottery heavily decorated before firing with impressions made by a *Cardium* shell. This example comes from Cova de l'Or, Valencia, Spain

cave deposits, increasing rapidly in quantity as the component of wild fauna decreases. In parallel, fishing declines and marine molluscs all but disappear. Exactly what this sequence means in terms of human interactions it is difficult to say. Did the farmers stay aloof from the foragers at first, supplying them with mutton and beef through reciprocal exchange, or was there a rapid fusion of the population? The archaeological evidence is unable to distinguish.

From Calabria and Sicily pioneers moved north through the Tyrrhenian Sea. The earliest known settlement on the eastern Italian coast dates to 5500 BC, but they had already reached the Gulf of Genoa, where an Impressed Ware horizon identified in the cave of Arene Candide is dated to 5700 BC. It was during this period that enclaves were established on Corsica and Sardinia. To Corsica they brought sheep and pigs at first, with cattle arriving after 5000 BC. The full range of domesticated animals was introduced to Sardinia from the beginning, in addition to red deer brought to provide a new game stock to augment the only other wild source of meat, the indigenous hare-like *Prolagus sardus*.

From the Gulf of Genoa and possibly from Corsica the colonization of the north coast of the Mediterranean began. The present evidence suggests that between here and the Strait of Gibraltar four main coastal settlements were established, in Languedoc, Catalonia, Valencia, and Andalucía. The earliest radiocarbon dates for Neolithic settlements in this zone all lie within the century 5550–5450 BC, and it was during this period that farmers sailed through the strait to colonize the coast of Portugal. Over a mere hundred years boatloads of farmers carrying their livestock with them had hopped along the coast, setting up viable enclaves over a distance of two thousand kilometres. The detailed study of sheep bones from some of these sites, focusing on the morphological differences, suggests that it was not a linear progression, but rather that the different settler communities were sending off pioneer groups leapfrogging over each other. Even so, it was a remarkable rate of advance. The motivation can hardly have been lack of resources or pressure of population. It must have been conditioned by an innate restlessness, driven, perhaps, by a desire to reach for the sunset. Though the sea was the principal vector of movement, some groups, once established on the coast, sent off bands of adventurers by land along the Ebro valley and the Aude–Garonne: by these routes Neolithic settlers eventually reached the Atlantic coast.

The agricultural communities who had settled on the islands and coasts of the central Mediterranean soon developed a maritime network incorporating, no doubt, the knowledge and expertise of the indigenous foragers they encountered. Once more it is the distribution of obsidian that illuminates the individual spheres of interaction. There were four favoured sources of obsidian in the region: Monte Arci on the eastern side of Sardinia, and three small islands, Lipari north-east of Sicily, Pantelleria between

Sicily and Tunisia, and Palmarola off the Italian coast between Rome and Naples. Each produced a distinctive type of obsidian. The patterns of distribution from these different sources changed over time. In the late sixth millennium Lipari obsidian reached Sicily, Malta, and Calabria; that from Sardinia was used throughout the island and northwards in Corsica, Elba, and northern Italy; Palmarola served central Italy; while the obsidian from Pantelleria was distributed from western Sicily to eastern Tunisia. Each of these patterns is a reflection of the extent of the maritime networks at an early stage of their development. Later, by the end of the fifth millennium, the patterns had changed, with Lipari now supplying the entire central Mediterranean and Sardinia extending its influence to southern France and northern Italy. The change clearly reflects the growing use of the sea and the interconnectedness this allowed.

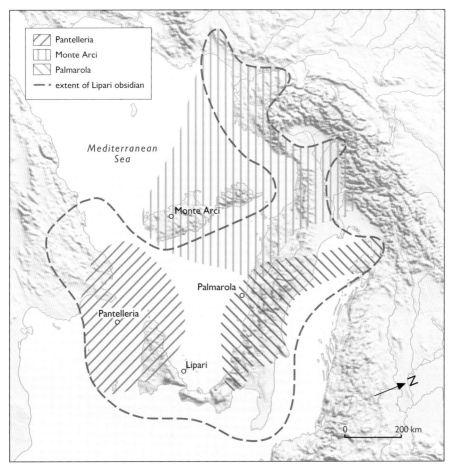

3.23 Throughout the Neolithic period obsidian from four main sources in the central Mediterranean circulated widely, carried mainly by sea. Eventually the source from Lipari dominated

The boats, so essential to the original westward expansions and the subsequent development of the maritime network, are unknown. The only hint of what may have been available is provided by a log boat found at the lakeside settlement of La Marmotta on Lake Bracciano near Rome and dated to the mid-sixth millennium. It was 10 metres long and a metre wide, carved from a single trunk of oak with four strengthening ridges left in place crossing the bottom of the vessel. It is very similar to the slightly later log boats of the Ertebølle foragers in Denmark. Whether boats of this kind were used on long sea journeys and, if so, how well they functioned must remain unknown. Sea trials of a replica paddled by a crew of eleven showed that the vessel performed well, averaging 1.6–2.2 knots. A ship's master choosing the right conditions would have been able to make the journey from Pantelleria to Sicily or Tunisia in three days. If vessels of this kind were used to transport heavy loads, such as pioneer settlers and their livestock, two boats could have been joined together in the style of a catamaran to provide greater stability and storage capacity. It is not impossible that they towed rafts piled with goods or animals.

The central and western Mediterranean networks demanded few long sea journeys other than the crossings between Corsica and the Italian mainland and between Sicily and Tunisia and Sicily and Malta. For the rest of it sailors could have hugged the coast, keeping land in sight and making such landfalls as were necessary. That the exploration of the open sea was not an imperative at the time is suggested by the fact that the Balearic islands, at their closest only eighty-five kilometres from the Iberian coast, appear not yet to have been settled. The Neolithic pioneers setting out to explore the west were content to allow the current to carry them along in sight of the mainland.

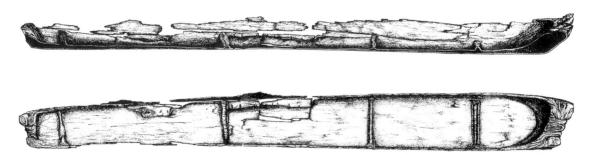

3.24 The log boat found at La Marmotta on Lake Bracciano, north of Rome, dates to the middle of the sixth millennium BC at the time when the western Mediterranean was being colonized by farmers. Such vessels, perhaps with outriggers, could have been used at sea. A replica with a crew of eleven made speeds averaging about two knots in sea trials

Into the Atlantic

About 5500 BC pioneers setting out in these boats from the enclaves along the coasts of Valencia or Andalucía made the epic passage through the Strait of Gibraltar into the Atlantic, some settling on the Algarve, others continuing their journey northwards along the coast to set up new farming communities on the limestone uplands between the Tagus and the Mondego. They found themselves in an environment that was at once familiar and alien. The familiarity came from the fact that southern Portugal was part of the Mediterranean ecozone, with climate and geology similar to those they were used to. The alien character was provided by the sea, no longer the predictable Mediterranean but a fierce sea stirred up by onshore winds with a mysterious tidal rhythm that had to be understood and respected.

The fine detail of the archaeological record of Portugal shows how, at first, the new settlers coexisted with the Mesolithic foragers dependent on the wetlands of the Tagus, Sado, and Mira estuaries for their sustenance, but by the opening centuries of the fifth millennium farming had spread throughout much of southern Portugal, leaving only a few communities of hunter-gatherers still hanging onto their traditional lifestyle in the Sado valley. In this Atlantic example the farmers and foragers seem to have had little cultural interaction, a result of the very different environments demanded by their divergent economic strategies.

The Neolithic colonists of Portugal are the earliest seafarers known to have sailed from the Mediterranean to the Atlantic: they had reached the far west and could daily watch the sun set in the ocean. Once settled in their new land, there is little evidence to suggest that they engaged with the sea with any enthusiasm, yet it was from this population that there emerged successive cultures that were to be instrumental in the development of the maritime networks which, by the end of the Bronze Age, bound the whole Atlantic face of Europe together in a single system. Perhaps there was something in the genetic make-up of these pioneers that made them and their successors respond to the challenge and opportunities of the ocean.

So When Did Seafaring Begin?

Archaeologists in the past tended to underestimate the ability of our prehistoric ancestors to engage with the sea. This is understandable because there is an absence of direct evidence: all that survives is surrogates—scatters of tools and the detritus of meals. But the picture is fast changing as new, and sometimes startling, evidence is

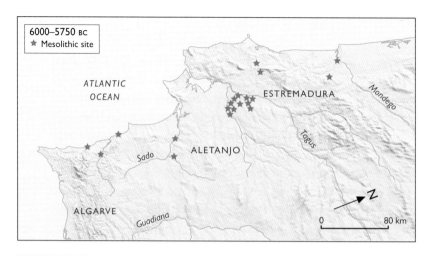

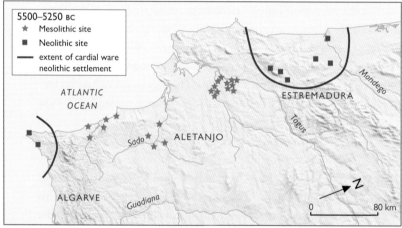

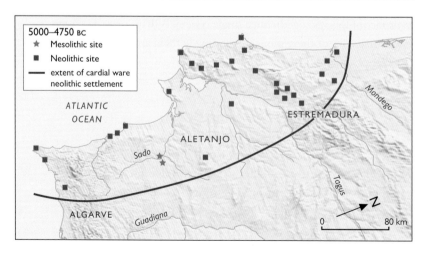

discovered. The recent discovery of Palaeolithic tools dating to more than a hundred thousand years ago on Crete and other Aegean islands has demanded our preconceptions be rethought. It used to be argued that seafaring only really got under way when the Younger Dryas cold spell, combined with population growth, kick-started maritime exploration. While these factors certainly exacerbated the exploration of new maritime environments, it is now clear that sea-going had a much longer ancestry. The hunters who reached Crete in the Middle Palaeolithic period must have made long sea-crossings in sufficient numbers to allow a sustainable population to survive, at least for some generations. By the twelfth millennium BC, before the onset of the Younger Dryas, sea journeys were being made from the Greek mainland to Melos and from the Levant to Cyprus. These cases are probably only the tip of the iceberg—rare examples, dimly visible in the all-too-sparse archaeological record. That seafaring was a fact of life for coastal dwellers in the Palaeolithic period must be accepted. Not just sea-going but seafaring, used here in the sense of repeatable journeys at sea requiring skills of navigation, a robust craft, and an intention to return.

The discovery of a Middle Palaeolithic presence on Crete has raised many fascinating questions. If the settlers came from Europe, then we must allow that premodern humans had already developed a surprising range of cognitive skills. The other possibility, that they were *Homo sapiens* coming from the North African coast, would open up the whole question of the routes by which anatomically modern humans reached the European peninsula. These are intriguing questions and we can only await further evidence.

However far back the origins of the seafaring may lie, it is clear that the period 12,000–7000 BC saw the emergence of seafaring communities where livelihood was predicated on maritime resources all around the Mediterranean and along the Atlantic coasts of Europe. These maritime foragers seem largely to have developed patterns of restricted mobility within stable localized systems. But there were exceptions: for example, the spread of foragers from the North European Plain first to Sweden and later along the entire Atlantic coast of Norway. These were maritime adventurers. So, too, were the farmers from the South West Asian mainland who settled Cyprus, Crete, and Greece and, after about 6500 BC, set in motion series of pioneer expeditions that saw farmers and their livestock reaching the Atlantic coast of Iberia within a thousand years. The sea facilitated these extraordinary ventures, but it was human inquisitiveness that drove them.

3.25 (*Opposite*) The earliest Neolithic enclaves were established on the Atlantic coast of Portugal between 5500 and 5250 BC, living alongside indigenous hunter-gatherer groups. In the period 5000–4750 BC farming spread to almost the entire region

117

4

Two Seas, Many Responses, 5300–1200 BC

One helpful way to conceptualize western Europe is as a peninsula washed by two seas: the Atlantic and the Mediterranean. The two faces of the peninsula are very different. The Atlantic face is dominated by nine major rivers extending from the Guadalquivir to the Elbe, creating extensive lowland plains with wide estuarine reaches allowing sea-going ships to sail deep inland, while the western Mediterranean face is characterized by mountains nudging close to the sea, with only a few major rivers—the Rhône, Ebro, and Segura—managing to cut their way through. Another difference is that, while the western Mediterranean face is comparatively uniform, though a little sinuous, the Atlantic face is far more complex and is best viewed as three quite distinct maritime regions: a northern region comprising the seas around Britain, a central region focused on the Bay of Biscay, and a southern region incorporating southern Iberia and north-west Africa. These separate worlds nurtured discrete cultural systems connected to each other by the ocean, and it was the sea, flowing through the Strait of Gibraltar, that brought the communities of the Atlantic and western Mediterranean into contact.

The two faces of peninsular western Europe and its encompassing seas provide the context for us to explore the next four thousand years of maritime history.

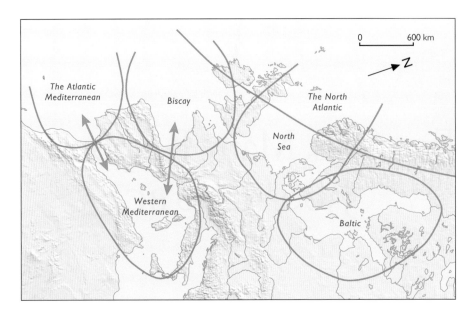

4.1 The Atlantic face of Europe can be divided into a number of separate seas, all interlinked. The western Mediterranean can be regarded as one of these seas

The Farmers Take Over

We saw in the last chapter that farming communities using pottery in the Impressed–Cardial Ware tradition were setting up successful enclaves around the Mediterranean coast of Iberia in Catalonia, Valencia, and Andalucía in the period 5700–5550 BC, and that they had begun to colonize the Atlantic coast of central and southern Portugal between 5500 and 5400 BC. At about the same time another group reached Morocco just to the south of the Strait of Gibraltar. From these early beginnings the Neolithic way of life spread inland, probably by a combination of processes from new colonial enclaves budding off established settlements to the acculturation of indigenous hunter-gatherers. The advance was far from even, and it took a long time for the practice of farming to reach the centre of Iberia, but the upper Ebro valley was settled by farmers by 5200 BC at the latest. The sixth millennium also saw farming systems moving north-wards from the Cardial Ware communities of Languedoc and Provence. One line of advance was along the Rhône, the other along the Aude–Garonne axis leading to the Atlantic, where a number of Impressed Ware settlements are found along the coast of the Vendée. The dating of this process is still imprecise, but distinctive arrowheads and other lithics of Mediterranean type were being used in the west by the middle of

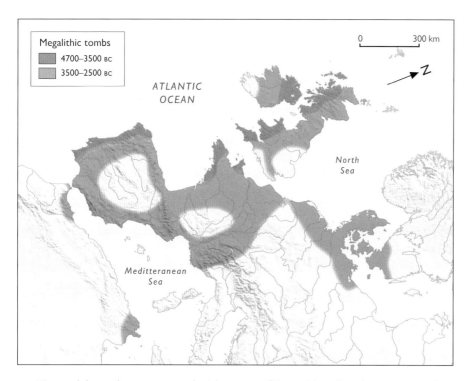

4.2 The megalithic tombs concentrate in the Atlantic zone of Europe. The earliest, the passage graves, have a distinctly maritime distribution and share similarities suggesting that belief systems and cosmological knowledge were communicated along the Atlantic façade

the sixth millennium, and by the end of the millennium farming was well under way. While there can be little doubt that Impressed Ware and farming spread to western France from Languedoc, it remains possible that some of the coastal farming communities may have been set up by pioneers from the Portuguese enclaves drawn on by the restless desire to explore the ocean coasts of the north. If this is so, then considerable navigational skills would have been required to contend with the Bay of Biscay.

One scrap of evidence which reflects on the sailing abilities of the early farmers comes from a late Mesolithic hunter-gatherer site at Ferriter's Cove on the coast of County Kerry in the south-west of Ireland. Here, among the remains of wild fauna hunted for food, were found several bones of domesticated cattle. One was dated to 4790–4550 BC, another to 4500–4180 BC—well before the introduction of farming to Britain and Ireland. These exotic beasts, if carried alive, must have been brought to south-western Ireland along the Atlantic seaways from western France by pioneer farmers who may have intended to set up a viable community in remote Ireland but failed. Whether they came from the Vendée or from Brittany, to have transported cattle across so great an expanse of sea speaks to their sailing skills, their experience, and their audacity.

Farming was also being introduced to western Europe by Danubian (Bandkeramik) farmers moving with some rapidity through middle Europe along the major rivers threading the deciduous forest zone. They had reached the eastern and southern parts of the Paris basin by about 5300 BC, and a successor group, named after the site of Villeneuve-Saint-Germain, continued the western thrust through Normandy, getting as far as central Brittany by 5000 BC. Although this was largely a land-based advance, the sea clearly played a part in bringing Neolithic settlers to Guernsey in the Channel Islands, fifty kilometres off the French coast, where Early Neolithic sites are known with dates between 5400 and 5000 BC. These dates seem to be very early but might suggest that the potential of the offshore islands was being explored before the settlers had penetrated far into the Breton massif. More radiocarbon dates will be needed before the final stages of the westward spread of farming can be properly understood. One matter is not, however, in doubt: the sea must have played a significant part in the life of the Early Neolithic community—a point vividly made by the predominantly coastal distribution of the stelae (standing stones) and passage graves of Brittany erected during the fifth millennium.

By 5000 BC farming had spread across the face of Europe to the Atlantic and to the continental coast of the English Channel. As we have seen, at least one abortive attempt seems to have been made to establish a farming settlement in the south-west of Ireland, and other sea-going expeditions may have set out to explore the potential of Britain and Ireland, though positive evidence is at present lacking. It was to be seven or eight centuries before farmers made a concerted, and successful, attempt to tame these wild offshore islands.

Ancestors and Megaliths in Iberia and Brittany: The First Steps

One of the most striking features of the Atlantic façade in the fifth and fourth millennia was the way in which the disparate communities honoured their ancestors by depositing their remains in collective tombs often built of large stones (megaliths). The earliest manifestations of this phenomenon are found in Portugal, Galicia, and Brittany in the period 4700–4500 BC, but the rite of collective burial in graves sometimes lined with stone slabs begins in the Mesolithic period and is evident in shell midden sites found in the Muge and Sado valleys in Portugal and on the islands of Hoëdic and Téviec off the south coast of Brittany. At Moita do Sebastião in the Muge valley twenty-six graves containing fifty-nine adults were found, and not far

4.3 One of the Mesolithic burials found on the island of Hoëdic off the south coast of Brittany was adorned with sea-shells and red deer antlers. It dates to c.4600 BC. A similar range of burial rites is apparent in Mesolithic coastal communities from Portugal to Sweden

away eight children were buried in individual pits arranged in a semicircle. At Téviec there were ten graves with twenty-three individuals, while at Hoëdic nine graves contained a total of thirteen individuals. At both these sites there are strong hints that the shell midden formed after the cemetery had been established. So what can be made of these observations? One obvious conclusion is that, by the late stage of the Mesolithic in these two regions, foragers were stating their group identities and their claims to place and territory by creating cemeteries, and they were returning to those places for long periods each year, over many generations, to congregate and to feast—activities which led to the accumulation of vast mounds of debris, mainly composed of marine molluscs. It may be that the mounds were deliberately built up to be symbolic of group stability.

We have already seen that in Portugal groups of farmers were moving in soon after 5500 BC, gradually taking over the land until about 4750 BC, when the lifestyle of the last foragers, in the Sado valley, came to an end. In Brittany the Neolithic penetration seems to have begun about 5300 BC, with the shell middens ceasing to be used by 4800

BC. In both regions the long period when farmers and hunter-gatherers coexisted was a time for them to learn from each other. In central southern Portugal the farmers who had originally buried their dead in ones or twos in rock shelters began to adopt a more collective style of burial. First, small closed cists were used, but later more monumental structures were erected comprising megalithic chambers reached by a short passage allowing access to the burials. The earliest of these early passage graves probably date to the mid-fifth millennium or a little earlier. In Galicia in the north-western corner of Iberia a similar sequence can be recognized. Here the earliest passage graves so far dated belong to the early fourth millennium.

In Brittany monumentalization took a different route. Among the earliest monuments are shaped and decorated stelae, or menhirs, of which the most impressive is the Grand Menhir Brisé at Locmariaquer, once standing to a height of sixteen metres at the end of an alignment of twenty menhirs of decreasing size. There are three principal concentrations of menhirs, all coastal, in the southern Morbihan, Bas-Léon, and Saint-Malo regions. Such dating evidence as there is suggests that the main period of erection probably lay in the middle of the fifth millennium, about 4700–4300 BC. Of broadly similar date are a series of *tertres* (long mounds) which cluster in southern Morbihan. Typically these mounds are quite low, often with a stone kerb or wall defining them. They cover a variety of structures including stone-built cists, small menhirs, hearths, and settings of posts. The larger cists were probably intended for human burial, though in the local acid conditions bone seldom survives.

4.4 The Grand Menhir Brisé (broken) was once a single stone standing to a height of seventeen metres (with a further three metres below ground). It marked the termination of a row of menhirs at Locmariaquer in Morbihan on the south coast of Brittany. The stone was brought from a source more than ten kilometres away. Its transport and erection were a triumph of the coercive power at work within the Early Neolithic community

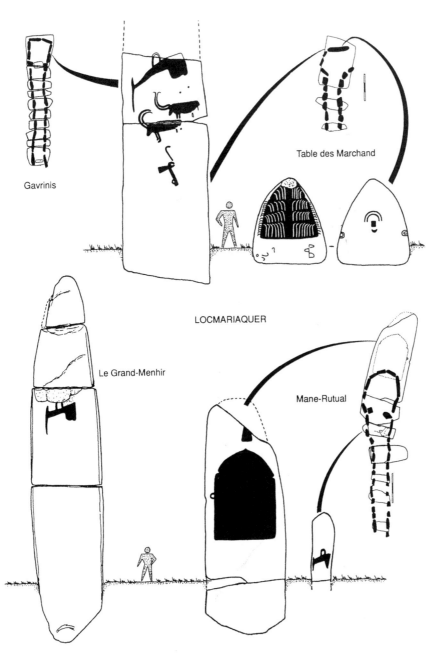

Gavrinis

Table des Marchand

LOCMARIAQUER

Le Grand-Menhir

Mane-Rutual

4.5 A number of the early menhirs in southern Brittany, sometimes broken up, were used in the construction of passage tombs. It is possible that the Grand Menhir was pulled down at the time. Many of the menhirs were decorated with carved motifs. It has been suggested that the single motif on the Grand Menhir, and a similar one on the piece of stone used in the tomb on the island of Gavrinis in the Gulf of Morbihan, may have been intended to represent a sperm whale

There has been much debate about the origin of the menhirs and *tertres*. One possibility is that both originate in the local Mesolithic tradition. There is an alignment of small stelae at Douet on the island of Hoëdic, associated with Neolithic pottery with radiocarbon dates of 4708–4536 BC, which might relate to the late use of the shell midden. Similarly, the stone cists containing burials beneath the shell midden at Téviec could be the prototypes for the cists beneath the *tertres*. It has even been argued that the *tertres* themselves were intended to copy elongated shell middens, though another possibility is that they were modelled on the domestic longhouses introduced by the farmers of Villeneuve-Saint-Germain. Whatever the solution to these intriguing matters, the menhirs and *tertres* represent an indigenous development lying at the beginning of what was to become a rich tradition of monumental building in Brittany.

At the beginning of the fourth millennium a sudden change can be recognized in the mortuary architecture of Morbihan when the *tertres*, with their enclosed burial cists, were replaced by large mounds containing one or more passage graves, each comprising a megalithic chamber, roofed with a capstone or corbelling, linked by a passage to the outside of the mound. Some of these new passage graves incorporated decorated menhirs, broken or entire, in the walls or roofs. Two possible explanations have been offered for this change. Either it was the result of internal development or it was the forced replacement of one belief system by another. In favour of the first it could be argued that a natural catastrophe like an earthquake may have brought the menhirs tumbling to the ground, their fragments being used to give legitimacy to the post-earthquake generations who adopted a new tomb type. Alternatively it could be that the menhirs were destroyed in an act of iconoclasm driven by an alien ideology and the pieces desecrated by use in the tombs of a new elite. Such is the imaginative latitude allowed by limited archaeological evidence.

Whatever the favoured explanation, the question of the origins of the passage grave idea remains. While it could have evolved locally in the Morbihan region, there is some evidence to suggest that the passage grave tradition evident on the north-west coast of Brittany has an earlier origin than its appearance in Morbihan. The famous passage grave monument at Barnenez on the Bay of Térénéz, close to the town of Morlaix, has produced a series of radiocarbon dates which suggest that the first phase of the monument was built before the middle of the fifth millennium and was modified in the third quarter of the millennium. If so, a vibrant passage grave tradition existed on the north Breton coast for centuries before it appeared in Morbihan. Stepping back from the confusion of the regional detail, and always mindful of the uncertainties created by having too little reliable radiocarbon data, a plausible scenario can be sketched out predicated on the idea that, while collective burial practices developed at many points along the interface between indigenous Mesolithic foragers and incoming farmers, the highly specific passage grave tradition emerged first in central southern Portugal in the early sixth millennium BC and quickly spread to Galicia and to north-western Brittany. From these initial focuses the tradition spread still further, by the beginning of the fifth millennium or soon after reaching all the coastal regions of western Iberia and north-western France from the Garonne to the Seine. It was this expansion that saw the decorated menhir–*tertre* mound tradition of Morbihan replaced by passage graves about 4000 BC. Behind such a hypothesis lies the implication that a network of Atlantic sea-routes was in operation throughout, facilitating a degree of human mobility sufficient to allow belief systems and technological know-how to be transmitted between central southern Portugal, Galicia, and Brittany. How such a system might have functioned is beyond recovery, nor can we guess with what periodicity people made the long sea journeys involved. But, once established in the fifth millennium, the maritime links remained in existence and can be amply attested in the archaeological record until the ninth century BC, when external factors finally led to a breakdown into more restricted regional systems.

That the maritime network may, at times, have extended further north than Brittany is hinted at by the discovery, in western Wales, western Scotland, and the north of Ireland, of a distinctive range of small megalithic grave monuments characterized by closed chambers and simple passage tombs. The coastal distribution of these monuments and their similarity to tombs found in Morbihan has led to the suggestion that they represent a movement of people from Brittany to the Irish Sea region about 4200–4000 BC. One tomb, excavated at Achnacreebeag in Argyll and Bute, produced a pottery vessel very similar to Breton pottery of this date. A possible context for such a migration from Morbihan could be the social disruptions that there must have been at the time when the menhirs and *tertre* mounds were being replaced by passage graves. Once introduced into Britain, these simple megalithic monuments fared differently in different regions. In western Scotland and northern Ireland they initiated local developments, but in Wales they seem to have died out. If this interpretation of the evidence is correct, it would further support the suggestion that the sea played a significant part in the life of the early farming communities along the Atlantic façade.

Britain and Ireland Incorporated

The spread of the Neolithic way of life across mainland Europe was rapid. By about 5000 BC it had reached the Atlantic and the Channel coast as far north as the Rhine.

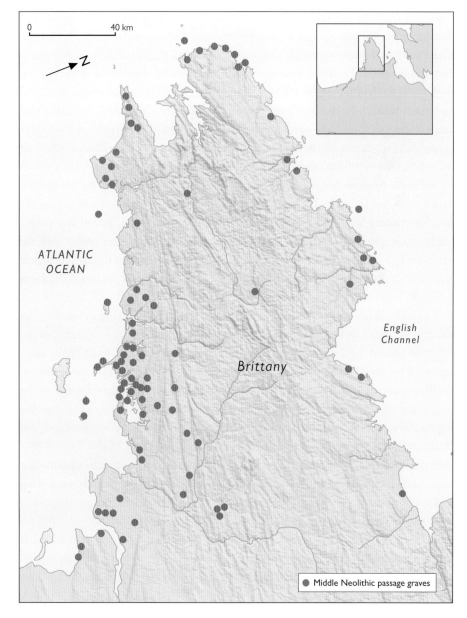

4.6 The passage graves of Brittany belonging to the Early and Middle Neolithic have a distinctly coastal distribution, which might suggest, but by no means proves, that the earliest Neolithic communities favoured coastal locations for their settlements, attracted by the range of available resources

4.7 The Neolithic passage grave of Barnenez on the north coast of Brittany occupies a prominent hill and is visible from the sea. It was built in two parts. The eastern part (*right*), containing five passage graves, was constructed first. The western part, with six passage graves, was added later

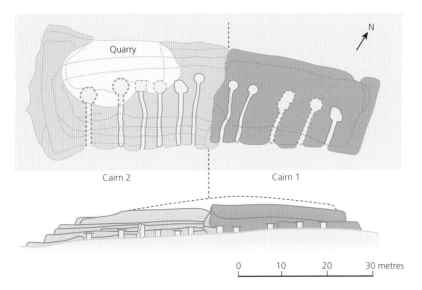

4.8 The plan and elevation of Barnenez shows the way in which the grave monument was extended. The large scoop on the north-western side is the quarry, dug by a farmer in search of building stone, which first brought the monument to light

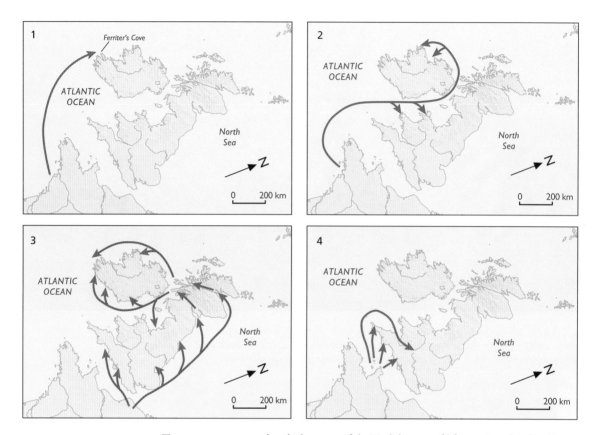

4.9 There were many routes by which aspects of the Neolithic way of life were introduced to Britain and Ireland. The earliest (map 1) is represented by the appearance of domesticated cattle in south-western Ireland c.4500 BC. Later (map 2), burials in closed chambers, similar to examples found in southern Brittany, appear in the Irish Sea region c.4200 BC. A more massive influx of populations from northern France and the Low Countries (map 3) took place c.4000 BC, and a century or two later (map 4) there seems to have been an incursion into south-western Britain from Normandy. In all of these the sea played an essential part

Here it paused until about 4300 BC, when there were small-scale movements, first in south-western Ireland and later in the Irish Sea region. It was not until 4000 BC that Britain and Ireland began to experience a wave of new settlers, this time coming from the Nord and Pas-de-Calais regions of France and settling in the south-east of the country before spreading rapidly to colonize much of Britain and Ireland over the next two centuries. It was an astonishing phenomenon, brought into focus only recently by an intensive campaign of radiocarbon dating. The details of the spread—its geography and the processes by which the farming packages were taken up—have still to be worked out, but there can be little doubt that the sea was a prime factor in the speed of advance, with networks quickly established along the North Sea coast of Britain to the north of Scotland and along the Channel coast, and others developing in the Irish Sea and around the Atlantic coast of Ireland. A little later, about 3800 BC, there is some evidence to suggest contact between Lower Normandy and south-western Britain, introducing, in addition to farming practices, simple forms of passage graves.

Why, then, did it take continental farmers seven centuries or more to take to their boats, starting in a small way about 4300 BC, reaching a climax about 4000 BC, and continuing until about 3800 BC? Demography probably plays a part. The initial pioneering movements across Europe introduced farming into a sparsely populated landscape. After a thousand years the population had grown and in many areas the land will have reached its holding capacity, creating a new impetus for some communities to move away to find new ecological niches to settle. There was also a climatic factor that may have influenced mobility. The period 4100–3800 BC saw an increase in the annual temperature range, giving rise to colder winters and warmer summers, while at the same time there was a reduction in winter rainfall. The combined effect of these changes was to improve significantly conditions for cereal growing across north-western Europe, encouraging expansion. But while demography and climate will have played their part, the insatiable curiosity inherent in the human psyche must have been a significant factor enticing people to cross the sea to explore new lands.

Cosmologies

The spread of farming communities to Britain and Ireland brought these offshore islands firmly into the European ambit, but there is little evidence that active communications were maintained across the Channel or the southern North Sea in the millennium and a half following the initial pioneering movements. The Atlantic network, however, seems to have thrived during the fourth millennium, allowing the belief systems and cosmologies associated with the passage graves to spread and develop in parallel along the entire Atlantic façade from Portugal to the Orkney islands. While many regional variants appeared, they shared much in common: the complex beliefs that required selected ancestors to be laid out together in chambers set beneath large mounds, methods of building involving megalithic construction and corbelling, and a style of art expressed in a broad repertoire of carving and painting. But even more significant was a shared cosmology which acknowledged the setting or rising of the

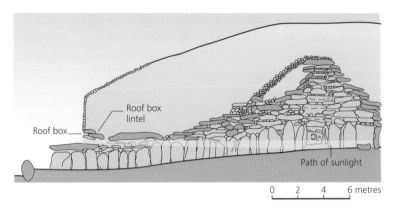

4.10 The great passage grave of Newgrange in Ireland was built c.3000 BC. Its passage was carefully aligned so that the rising sun on the midwinter solstice would shine through a specially constructed 'roof box' along the full length of the passage

4.11 The entrance to the passage grave of Newgrange is now heavily restored. The 'roof box' is visible above the door. In front is a kerb of intricately decorated stones

132

sun on the solstices and sought to incorporate these perennial phenomena into the alignments of some of their tombs and other monuments. There are few things more awe-inspiring than standing in the great passage grave of Maes Howe on Orkney on the solstice eve, watching the rays of the setting midwinter sun move to light up the passage and the end chamber. Here, encapsulated in the tombs of the ancestors, was a universal wisdom discovered by keen observation and passed down the generations. For this knowledge to be shared across such distances implies an intellectual connectivity of an intense kind. It is difficult to resist the thought that the many rhythms of the sea and the daily drama of the sun setting beyond the ocean created, among those living along the ocean fringe, a shared awareness of the power of the heavens—a power manifested in a predictability that had to be revered.

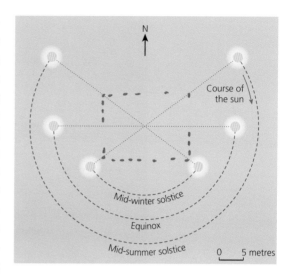

4.12 The rectangular stone setting at Crucuno, Plouharnel, Brittany, laid out in relation to the sun's position at the solstices and the equinox, demonstrates an intimate understanding of cosmology

Some Practicalities

That people took to the sea and transported themselves, their animals, and their seed-grain over considerable distances is implicit in the archaeological evidence, but little is known of their boats. It can be assumed that log boats were in universal use at this time. Two, dating to the period 3700–3400 BC, were found in Lough Larne, County Antrim, and many others are known from inland locations in Ireland dating from the second to the first millennium. Vessels of this kind would have been serviceable on the lakes and rivers and in sheltered coastal waters, but without suitable modification they would not have functioned well in the swells and gales of the Atlantic. However, with outriggers to provide greater stability, or with added strakes to increase the freeboard, they could have managed moderate seas under a ship's master able to judge the right weather conditions.

Far more appropriate to Atlantic waters would have been hide boats made by sewing cows' hides onto a light wooden framework in much the same way as the currachs of western Ireland were made in the Middle Ages and later. Skin boats plying the Atlantic coast of Europe are mentioned in texts of the late first millennium BC (pp. 332–6) and in all probability such craft had a long ancestry, but as yet no physical traces have been found. The only hint we have of what Atlantic vessels of the Neolithic period may

4.13 Lough Corrib in County Galway, Ireland, has provided a surprising array of boat remains, among them the Annaghkeen log boat dating to *c.*2500 BC. Its central spine and cross-ribs left to strengthen the vessel can be clearly seen

have looked like is provided by engravings on the orthostats (upright stones) of the megalithic passage grave of Mané Lud in Morbihan. The depictions are simple but can be interpreted as vessels with high prows and sterns powered by four or five paddlers. A distinction seems to have been made between the prow and the stern. Other engravings from the same tomb, which look like the handlebars of a bicycle, may, with some imagination, be considered boat-like, but they are usually referred to as 'yokes' or 'horns' by the more cautious. Simple motifs of this kind carved on a rock at Borna in the Bay of Vigo in north-western Spain are considered by some to be boats, but in themselves they are barely convincing.

Iberia: Displays of Strength and Power

The Pyrite Belt sweeps in a great arc across Iberia from Galicia in the north-west to Almería in the south-east. It is a complex of geological structures, heavily mineral-ized, providing an incomparable source of metal ores. Over much of the western arm of the arc gold and tin prevail, while the southern arm divides into zones that are rich in silver and others that abound in copper. It was this copper that was the first to be extracted and utilized and was to change dramatically the trajectory of social development.

When copper extraction began in Iberia is a matter of debate. Evidence of cop-per smelting has been claimed at the Neolithic settlement of Cerro Virtud in Almería from a context dating to 5000–4500 BC. This would be by far the earliest occurrence and some commentators are not prepared to accept it. After this, the earliest dates centre around 3200 BC for well-attested smelting sites in Almería and the Tagus region. Thereafter copper smelting becomes more common and more widespread across southern Iberia. The possibility that the technology of copper extraction was introduced into Iberia from northern Italy or the Alpine region has to be considered. Metalworking is known at Cabrières in Hérault in southern France about 3000 BC, where the extraction technologies used are comparable to those of northern Italy, but they differ from those practised in Iberia. It remains a possibility, therefore, that the art of copper smelting was independently developed in Iberia and could date back to the early fourth millennium or earlier.

From the beginning copper and the items fashioned from it had a high social value. It was comparatively rare, and its extraction and working required the consolidated labour of a large number of specialists. Thus, those who controlled its supply had power and could use that power to build or to reinforce social hierarchies. This is well illustrated by the settlement of Cabezo Juré, which overlooks the valley of the river Odiel in south-western Iberia. The settlement was arranged in three distinct zones. On the summit of the hill lay the elite area strongly fortified with its own water cisterns. Below, on the northern slope, was a residential area for the metalworkers, while on the southern slope the ore-smelting furnaces were concentrated. Luxury goods—gold sheet, marble cups, linen cloth, and horses—were restricted to the fortified residence. The settlement began about 2900 BC and lasted for some seven hundred years. While it would be tempting to suggest that it was the control of copper production that led to the emergence of the social hierarchy, there are ample signs to show that Neolithic societies were already developing social inequalities: copper production simply offered an easy way for those already with power to consolidate their hold. Since access to the new metal was restricted and uneven, it immediately became an item of desire,

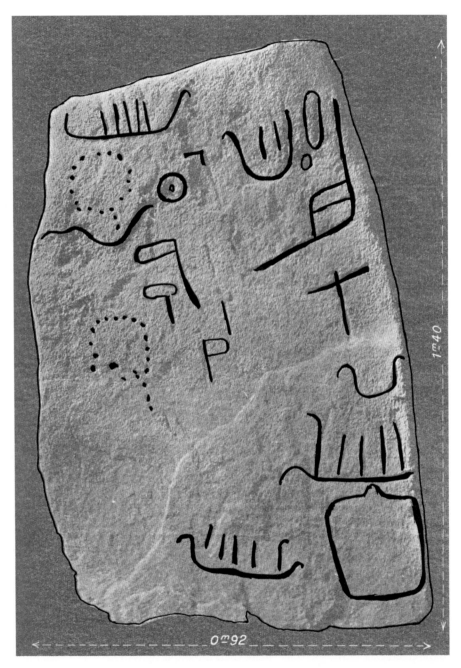

4.14 One of the upright stones comprising the megalithic tomb of Mané Lud in southern Brittany is engraved with a number of motifs, including what might be representations of boats carrying four or five people

4.15 Petroglyphs, possibly of ships, were carved on a rock at Borna, Pontevedra, north-western Spain. They are undated but may be Neolithic

encouraging the development of exchange networks, which led to an increase in the mobility of other raw materials such as gold, cloth, ivory, and ostrich shell. The result of all this was twofold. While enhanced exchange created greater connectivity, loosely binding hitherto isolated communities together, the growth of hierarchies led to increased competition between polities and a desire to proclaim their identities through defensive architecture.

Thus it was that, throughout the third millennium BC, strongly fortified settlements were built across southern Iberia from the Atlantic to the Mediterranean coast. Some were quite small, like Leceia, Zambujal, and Vila Nova de São Pedro in Portugal, where the central fortified areas were barely fifty metres across, while others, like Los Millares in Almería, were massive. Here, on a promontory between the river Andarax and a tributary, Rambla de Huéchar, lay a settlement covering more than two hectares protected by concentric lines of defensive walls. The outermost, more than two hundred metres long, was strengthened with nineteen towers, while the approach to the site was guarded by a line of four small stone forts. Outside the main entrance lay a cemetery of circular corbelled collective tombs, of which eighty-three survive, representing the last resting places of the elite dynasties. The grave goods with which the dead were supplied—gold, copper, marble, ivory, ostrich shell, jet, amber, and variscite

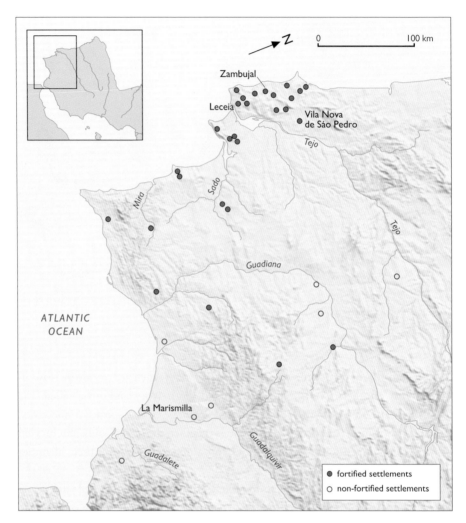

4.16 In the third millennium BC powerful communities arose in southern Iberia, their prestige often demonstrated by the erection of massive walls to enclose the settlement. The map of the principal Chalcolithic settlements shows a particular concentration of elite settlements around the estuary of the Tagus

(an attractive green stone)—are a vivid reflection of the trading networks now serving the population.

The third-millennium settlements range in size and complexity and no doubt functioned in different ways depending upon the extent and social structure of the community they served, but they are all likely to have been focal points within discrete territories. One site, Valencina de la Concepción, stands out as an exception to the rule. Valencina, near Seville, is now far inland, but originally it would have lain at the

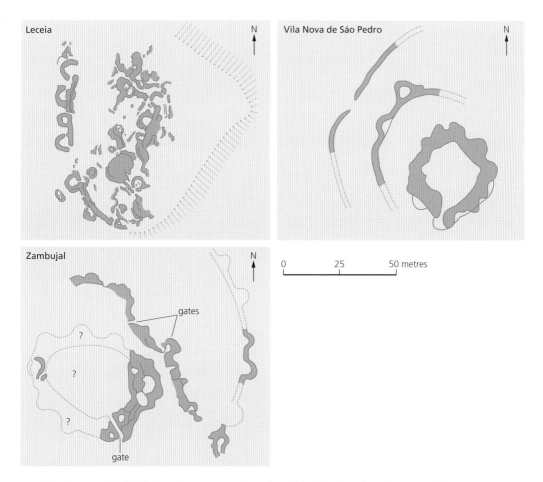

4.17 A selection of the fortified settlements dating from the third millennium from the region of the Tagus estuary

head of a large lagoon (now silted and comprising the Coto Doñana nature reserve) into which the river Guadalquivir flowed. Contemporary activity covered a huge area, some three to four hundred hectares, and included a zone devoted to metalworking, areas of habitation, and a cemetery. Among the finds were exotic materials from afar. It is difficult to resist the conclusion that Valencina was super-regional in its function, providing facilities for exchange for the many polities of the lower Guadalquivir valley. It was an interface with the wider world reached by the sea and would have been a convenient port of entry for the elephant ivory and the ostrich shell so much in demand. It may have been from Valencina that the first copper was exported to Morocco in exchange for these exotics and perhaps also for gold.

4.18 The most extensively examined of the third-millennium defended settlements from south-eastern Iberia is Los Millares in Almería. Its multiple lines of defences, developing over time, protected a cluster of houses. Outside the walls a large cemetery extended along the approach road. The reconstruction gives an impression of how the settlement might have looked

The Beaker Phenomenon

The pioneer farmers who had sailed from the Mediterranean in the mid-sixth millennium to settle on the limestone uplands between the Tagus and the Atlantic coast chose their new homeland with care. The soil was light but rich in minerals, the region enjoyed a Mediterranean climate, and the ocean, with its high level of nutrients, offered a rich harvest of sea food. They and their successors flourished, and by the middle of the fourth millennium the communities were investing their surpluses in strong walled settlements like Zambujal and Vila Nova de São Pedro and in megalithic funerary monuments to honour their ancestors. Before the end of the millennium they had learned to smelt copper and were using it to make flat axes, saws, knives, daggers, awls, chisels, and arrowheads.

About 2800 BC the local potters began to develop a distinctive assemblage of wares characterized by having the outer surfaces decorated with zones of impressions or shallow incisions making up a series of standard motifs. One of the recurring forms was a beaker, with a capacity of about two litres, of a kind suitable for holding an alcoholic beverage. The beaker forms were variously decorated, but one frequently recurring style was for the decoration to be restricted to thin horizontal bands infilled with comb impressions set diagonally, the direction of slope alternating between bands. This type is known as a Maritime Bell Beaker of herring-bone variety. They were well made and were carefully fired in an oxidizing atmosphere to a rich red-brown or red colour. What is remarkable about this specific type is that it is widely distributed throughout western Europe, reaching as far east as the Rhine valley and the Po valley with particular concentrations in the Tagus region (where the type originated), Almería, Languedoc and Provence, and the south coast of Brittany. Along the Atlantic coast, where detailed studies of the fabrics have been made, it is clear that, although of exotic type, the Maritime Bell Beakers were made of locally sourced clay. In other words, it was not the beakers that travelled but the concept of the beaker together with the skill to make it.

The situation is greatly complicated by developments in the North European Plain, where a cultural complex known as the Corded Ware–Single Grave complex had developed with beaker types of its own. The cultural phenomenon overlapped with the Bell Beaker phenomenon in the broad zone along the Rhine valley, where the two pottery styles interacted to give rise to a number of varieties. It was from here that new styles of Beaker pottery spread, southwards along the Rhine–Rhône corridor, westwards across northern France to the Loire valley and the ocean, and from northern France and the Low Countries across the English Channel and the southern North Sea to Britain. This, in its broadest outline, seems to be the scenario for the third millennium, but it is couched, as archaeologists so often tend to do, in terms of animated ceramics. What the pottery styles reflect, of course, is the highly complex movement of people, skills, beliefs, and values. The Beaker phenomenon has received a formidable amount of detailed investigation, most recently using isotope studies of human teeth and ancient DNA to identify population mobility. The resulting picture is one of some intricacy with many issues still to be resolved, but what is abundantly clear is that the third millennium saw a continent-wide mobility on a scale never before experienced. The river valleys and the sea provided the corridors of connectivity.

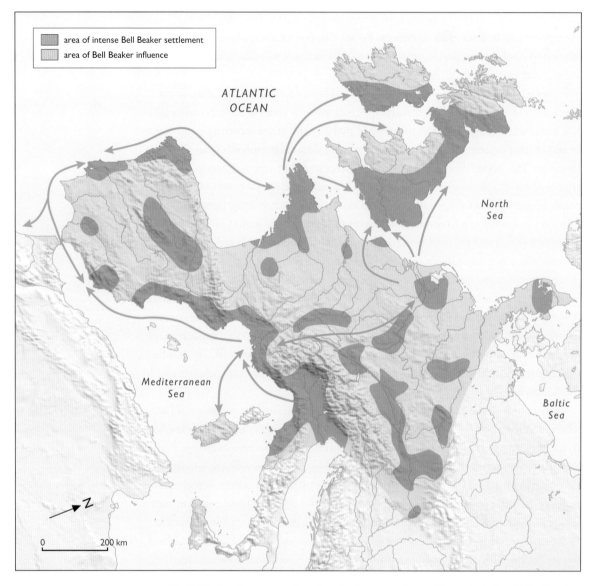

4.19 The Bell Beaker phenomena embraced much of western and central Europe in the late third millennium and reflect an enhanced mobility both of material and of people. The denser areas of settlement occur around the coasts and along the major rivers, which would have provided the main communication routes

But to return to the herringbone-decorated Maritime Bell Beakers which originated in the Tagus region: their distribution leaves little doubt that the sea was the vector of their original dispersal. One route led northwards, via Galicia and across the Bay of Biscay to southern Brittany, utilizing networks already two millennia old. The other

142

led south to the Strait of Gibraltar, one branch continuing down the coast of Morocco and the other into the Mediterranean and along the coast of Iberia to the Languedoc–Provence region. Although this route is not well attested earlier in the archaeological record, it may already, before the dispersal of the beakers, have been in use linking the copper-producing regions. Further back in time it was along this coast that the Neolithic pioneers set up their enclaves as they moved west. The Beaker distribution may, then, have been utilizing networks first established in the mid-sixth millennium.

The Maritime Bell Beakers have usually been found in funerary contexts, almost invariably associated with existing megalithic tombs, thus continuing ancestral traditions. But subtle changes can be seen. In most of the passage graves of the Tagus region and in the dolmens of Alentejo and Extremadura the dead were laid either in separate niches or around the monument and most were accompanied by grave goods, often specific to gender. The same separation is found in the reused megalith tombs of Brittany and the Channel Islands. For example, at Ville ès Nouaux on Jersey a number of separate burial cists were constructed within the early monument. Taken together the evidence suggests a change in value systems. While the ancestral burial places continued to be hallowed, there was now a much greater emphasis on the individual identified with specific grave goods—beakers, arrowheads, wrist guards, knives, awls, and ornaments—signifying gender, status, and skills.

Archaeology can at best provide an incomplete and shadowy picture of human reality. What did the sudden spread of the Maritime Bell Beakers really mean? Clearly people made journeys carrying with them skills and a strong belief in the symbols that gave them their individuality and status, and they persuaded the people they encountered that these values were worth accepting. The initial journeys from the Tagus, made by sea in the period about 2800–2500 BC, followed long-established routes along which people had interacted over very many generations. It is not difficult to imagine how, at a time of increased mobility motivated by an interest in metals and other rare raw materials, those who made these heroic journeys were honoured and emulated.

Beakers in Ireland and Britain

The new mobility evident around the Atlantic and western Mediterranean shores had also gripped much of the rest of western Europe, where the main river valleys became the axes of connectivity. After about 2500 BC interaction between Iberia and France and the rest of Europe intensified, as a result of which elements of the single-grave belief systems developing in the Rhine corridor spread south and west and many regional groups emerged, combining elements of the disparate ideologies.

The spread of beakers to Ireland seems on present evidence to have been coincident with the development of copper extraction. Copper mining and smelting is first attested on Ross Island in Lough Leane in County Kerry about 2400 BC and is associated with Beaker pottery. The mining continued for about five hundred years, producing most of the copper in use in Britain and Ireland at that time, but was eventually replaced by other sources in Ireland and Wales. The implication is that the new technology was introduced by Beaker specialists coming perhaps from Brittany, where there were also ample copper sources to be had. Within a century gold from Ireland or south-western Britain was being exploited, and by 2100 BC the first bronze, an alloy of copper and tin, was being produced, implying that there was now a regular supply of tin in circulation coming from south-western Britain or Brittany. This remarkable efflorescence of metalworking skills, binding together the metal-rich Atlantic peninsulas of southern Ireland, south-western Britain, and Brittany, is strongly suggestive of a highly active maritime network facilitating the movement of metalworking specialists and their products. The distribution of gold lunulae (sheets of gold designed to be worn around the neck and to cover the upper chest) illustrates the geographical range of the network, with examples being found in Ireland, Wales, Cornwall, Normandy, Brittany, and western France. Most were probably made in Ireland, but a few came from a more provincial school, perhaps in Cornwall.

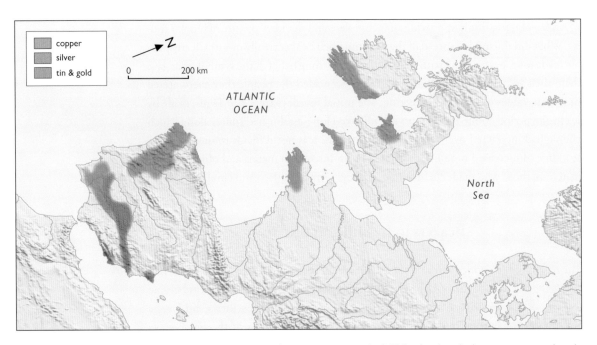

4.20 The western extremities of Europe are composed of old, hard rocks, which in some areas are heavily mineralized. The map shows the major occurrences of tin, gold, silver, and copper

The intensification of Beaker activity evident on the Continent from 2500 BC coincides with the beginning of the spread of the Beaker package to Britain. A careful analysis of the form of the beakers and the associated grave finds suggests they arrived as the result of a series of movements from the continental coast between the Seine and the Rhine over the period 2500–2250 BC and that the east coastal route played a part in their appearance in northern Britain. Thereafter, until about 1950 BC, active contacts were maintained across the Channel and southern North Sea. That exactly the same routes had been used by the pioneer farmers who had settled Britain fifteen hundred years earlier may be due to little more than the constraints and opportunities imposed by geography, but it is a reminder that the maritime network serving the English Channel and southern North Sea, once established about 4000 BC, continued to function, but with different intensities as conditions changed over time.

4.21 A gold lunula from Blessington, County Wicklow, Ireland. Sheet-gold ornaments of this kind were worn around the neck. They have been found mainly in Ireland, with a few from Cornwall and Armorica. Traditionally they were thought to have been made in southern Ireland, but recent analysis has hinted that the gold may have come from Cornwall

The first three centuries of the second millennium saw the elites of Wessex and Brittany involved in reciprocal exchange, while in the second half of the millennium the intensity of communication was such that the communities facing each other on either side of the Channel developed close cultural similarities of a kind that implies regular movements of people. Trade and exchange will have played its part. So, too, would the exchange of skilled men and of brides, but there may also have been some limited movements of small communities. Thus, once the sea-crossings got under way about 4000 BC, the sea connected Britain and the Continent rather than dividing them.

The Integration of North Africa

The proximity of southern Iberia to the Maghrib and the Atlantic coast of Morocco would suggest that the two regions developed maritime contacts from an early date. While this can indeed be demonstrated from the archaeological record, the evidence from north-west Africa is sparse and the narrative is, accordingly, rather ill-focused. Elements of the Neolithic lifestyle spread down the Atlantic coast of Morocco in the early fifth millennium, reaching as far south as Tarfaya in the south of the country, but for the most part, it seems, the foraging subsistence economies persisted.

The first clear evidence of revived maritime contact comes in the late fourth and early third millennia—the Pre-Beaker Chalcolithic—with the importation, to the Tagus region and the estuary of the Guadalquivir, of ivory from the African savannah elephant (*Loxodonta africana*), which at this time would have been found roaming the grasslands of the Maghrib on the foothills of the Atlas Mountains. Since no Iberian goods of this period have yet been found in Africa, it is impossible to say who initiated the exchange, or indeed how intensive it was, but the strong probability is that it was the demand for luxury goods among the Iberian elite that encouraged the exploration of the Atlantic coast south of the Strait of Gibraltar. Once the contact had been set up, it was maintained and developed throughout the third millennium. This is clearly shown by the appearance in some quantity of Maritime Bell Beakers of the herringbone variety along the North African coast in caves such as Caf Taht el Gar, near Tétouan, and Gar Cahal, near Ceuta. The importance of these assemblages is that they also included the other ceramic types in use at this time in the Tagus region, suggesting that there was close and lasting contact between these two regions. Other Maritime Bell Beakers are found on the Algerian steppe and on the Atlantic coast near Rabat. The Atlantic network continued in use into the later Beaker period, characterized by what is known as the Palmela complex in Portugal. Pottery of this type from the Tagus region or the mouth of the Guadalquivir is found at coastal sites all along the Moroccan coast as far south as Casablanca. All this time elephant ivory and ostrich shells were being transported to Atlantic Iberia. Taken together, the evidence shows that an Atlantic coastal network established towards the end of the fourth millennium continued in operation well into the second half of the third millennium.

Scientific analysis of the ivory found along the south coast of Iberia showed that it was not until the Early Bronze Age (late third and early second millennia) that ivory of the African savannah elephant began to be used in the south-east of Iberia. Before that the Iberians made use of supplies of Asian ivory (*Elephas maximus*), presumably from the eastern Mediterranean. In other words, the settlements of Almería and the Levant were not part of the original Atlantic system but were only brought into it about 2000 BC or later. It was the now extended system embracing the Alboran Sea as well as the Atlantic that saw bronze implements of the type characteristic of the Argaric culture of south-eastern Spain—flat axes, daggers, and halberds—being introduced to north-west Africa. Although few actual specimens have been found, the types are well represented in rock engravings found high in the Atlas Mountains, suggesting that they once had a wide distribution.

The distribution of ivory, ostrich shells, pottery, and bronze implements exchanged between southern Iberia and north-west Africa reflects maritime communication spread over more than a thousand years. For the most part it would have involved Iberian boats setting out for the Tagus estuary, perhaps to be joined by other vessels from the mouth of the Guadalquivir, stopping off at the natural harbour of Tangier and then making their way down the coast of Morocco with its dangerous offshore reefs and westerly winds ready to drive the vessels onto the lee shore. It was hardly an easy journey, but there were sheltered estuaries to be found like those of the rivers Loukkos and Bou Regreg, where safe landfall could be made. Of the boats plying these coasts we are entirely ignorant.

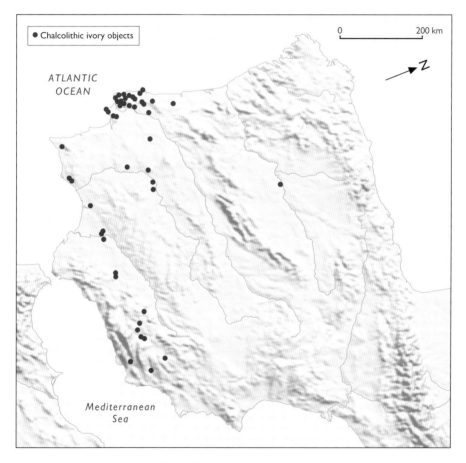

4.22 Ivory, mostly coming from North Africa, was used to make a variety of ornaments for the elite communities of southern Iberia in the third millennium. The quantity in use suggests a lively maritime trade with Africa

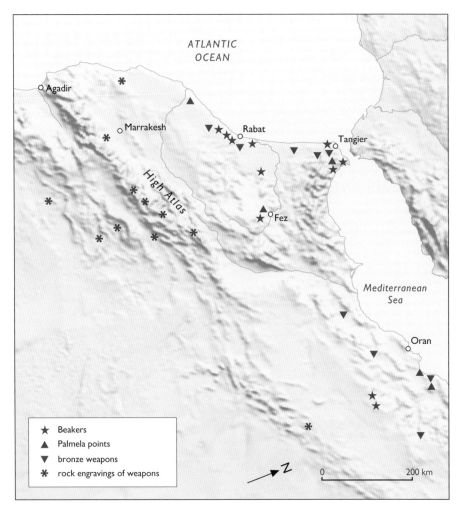

4.23 In return for North African commodities such as gold, ivory, and ostrich eggs, Chalcolithic metalwork and Bell Beaker pottery made in Iberia found their way to the coastal regions of Morocco. European bronzes were probably once widely used in the region and are depicted on rock engravings found in the Atlas Mountains

Into the Mediterranean

The maritime networks functioning in the western Mediterranean can be pieced together from the distribution of characteristic artefacts. The most obvious is that revealed by the distribution of obsidian obtained from various volcanic sources around the Tyrrhenian Sea. The four centres being worked in the mid-fifth millennium continued, but by the beginning of the fourth millennium Lipari, off the north

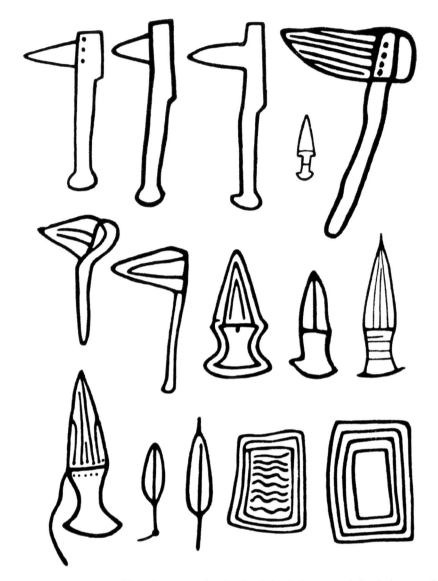

4.24 The weapons represented by rock engravings found in the High Atlas Mountains, halberds, daggers, and spears, were probably imported from southern Iberia, where they are found in Chalcolithic and Early Bronze Age contexts

coast of Sicily, had begun to dominate, its output reaching North Africa, most of Italy, and along the Ligurian coast as far west as Languedoc. Lipari obsidian was evidently much prized, but by what methods it was distributed we can only guess. Most likely it was by down-the-line methods with cargoes being traded at intermediate ports from one ship to another, each serving its own discrete territory: the journey from Lipari to the French coast is likely to have involved many transhipments. A network of a similar kind served the long coastal stretch from Andalucía to the Gulf of Genoa, the short-haul shipping helping to maintain contact between the coastal farming communities.

These localized cabotage systems were the successors of those set up by the initial Neolithic pioneers, but there is little to suggest actual long-distance maritime endeavour in the western Mediterranean until the appearance of the Maritime Bell Beakers in the mid-second millennium. The distinctive herringbone variety, originating in the Tagus area, spread along the entire Iberian coast to the Golfe du Lion. The rapidity of the spread, the highly distinctive nature of the Beaker, and the way in which local communities interpreted it within their own ceramic assemblages, suggest that the Beaker was symbolic of a new and widely accepted value system. The manner of its introduction is a matter of speculation, but it implies the movement of people, per-haps high-status specialists. It is tempting to believe that the search for metals and other commodities may have been involved. Some support for this is provided by the copper-working settlement at Cabrières in southern France. The technology used to extract copper was probably introduced from the Alpine or northern Italian region about 3000 BC, but about 2550 BC new influences can be identified, including the use of the smelting crucible, a characteristic of Iberian copper extraction. It may have been specialists from the Tagus region, drawn to the region by knowledge of its metal resources, who introduced the new technology along with the Maritime Bell Beakers.

That the Beaker period explorations in the western Mediterranean may have included some who were more adventurous is suggested by the discovery of the her-ringbone variety of Bell Beaker on the west coast of Sardinia and western Sicily. In both cases, however, the alien types were rapidly assimilated into local ceramic traditions. At best these finds reflect only a brief exploration of the possibilities of the wider sea by people coming either directly from the Tagus region or more likely from Languedoc. The initial contacts do not seem to have been followed up. It was about this time, in the middle of the third millennium, that the Balearic islands were discovered and settled. It may have been the exploration initiated by the Atlantic Beaker-using com-munities that provided the stimulus for this, if only indirectly.

The maritime network in operation along the south-east coast of Iberia continued to develop during the Argaric Early Bronze Age, eventually combining with the Atlantic networks, thus linking the entire southern Iberian shore to North Africa, making ostrich shell and the ivory of African savannah elephants available to all the Iberian elites. The maritime systems of the western Mediterranean are not well known in this early period and much of the North African coast remains a blank. While this may, in some part, be due to the unfocused nature of the archaeological evidence, it may also be that the sea had not yet begun to feature significantly in the lives of those who lived around it.

Copper: Improved Technology and Boatbuilding

In the west copper first began to be produced in significant quantity in Iberia towards the end of the fourth millennium, and from there the technology spread along the metal-rich Atlantic façade, reaching the south-west of Ireland about 2400 BC and western Britain at the end of the third millennium. The earliest copper, extracted from the Ross Island mines in Ireland, had a high arsenic content, which gave the metal a hardness that pure copper lacked. About 2100 BC, as the arsenical ores were beginning to run out and other types of ore came on stream, someone, somewhere in the south-western arc of Ireland, Cornwall, and Brittany, discovered that by adding about 11 per cent tin to the copper an alloy resulted that combined hardness with an attractive golden colour. How that observation was made and how the knowledge was put into general practice we shall never know, but it was a significant advance. It was not, however, until about 1700 BC that regular bronze replaced copper over most of the rest of western and central Europe.

To begin with, in the Atlantic zone, copper and its alloys were used to make a limited range of items: flat axes, daggers, arrowheads (Palmela points), and a few tools like awls, chisels, and gouges. Later the range increased to include halberds, palstaves (a type of axe), and various ornaments. The different items were used in different ways, among which displaying status featured large. To own copper artefacts was itself a mark of status. Some items, like arrows and daggers, denoted prowess as an archer or a warrior; others symbolized different skills: the awl for the leather-worker, the axes, gouges, and chisels for the woodworker. There can be little doubt that the development of these sharp and precise carpentry tools created a revolution in woodworking, and this will have impacted directly on boatbuilding.

Before the advent of copper, polished stone axes and various small bladed tools and awls made from chipped flint were the only cutting implements available. Such a toolkit was perfectly adequate to shape and hollow out log boats and to make hide boats, but it was not suited to cutting planks with precision or boring holes of the kind needed if planks were to be sewn together. The appearance of a copper toolkit changed all this, enabling new styles of boatbuilding to evolve alongside the more traditional methods, which continued little changed.

Boats of the British and Irish Seas

Until the end of the third millennium the only boats to be found around the islands are log boats. For the most part they were simple structures, but the vessel found at Annaghkeen, on the shores of Lough Corrib, County Galway, showed unusual features.

It was 12 metres long, suitable for ten to twelve paddlers. In hollowing out the boat, the carpenters had left ridges of wood 2–3 centimetres high to give additional strength. One ridge ran laterally along the vessel, creating a spine, while four others at right angles formed cross-ribs. It may be that the carpenters, impressed by the way in which a wooden frame gave rigidity to a skin boat, transferred the concept to this solid wooden vessel. It is dated by radiocarbon to about 2500 BC, before the development of the local copper industries, and is likely, therefore, to have been crafted with polished stone axes.

From the beginning of the second millennium a new and far more sophisticated type of boat appears in the archaeological record built of planks sewn together with yew withies. Seven have so far been identified around the coast and estuaries of Britain dating to the second millennium, three in the Humber estuary at Ferriby, one at Kilnsey on the Holderness coast, one at Dover, one at Southampton, and two at Caldicot in the Severn estuary. They were built of planks carefully trimmed so that they butted together. The joints between the planks were packed with moss held in place by a lath and bound together with individual lashings of yew withies made pliable by twisting to separate the fibres. To give rigidity to the structure cleats had been left proud on the upper surface of the planks with holes cut through them, so arranged that the cleats on adjacent planks lined up, allowing transverse timbers to be wedged between them. The vessels were constructed with flat bottoms, to which wide strakes were sewn, the lowest strake being hollowed to make the transition between the side and the bottom. The two best-preserved examples, Ferriby 1 and Dover, show significant differences in their design. The bottom of the Dover boat is composed of two planks placed side by side. Each had an upturned cleat rail left along their adjacent edges through which wedges were driven, holding in place a lath set between the rails covering the joint. At intervals there were transverse timbers passing through individual cleats left in the centre of the planks. One end of the vessel survives. Here the bottom planks and side strakes were joined to allow for a transom board held in place by a combination of wedges and withy lashings. The treatment of the other end is unknown, but it may well have been finished in the same style. The Ferriby 1 boat was also flat-bottomed, though it may have been slightly curved, or 'rocked', about its length. The bottom was composed of a thick central keel plank made of two lengths scarfed together, to which the side planks were sewn. The treatment of the ends is not certain, but it is possible that transom boards were added.

Since the Dover vessel dated to 1550 BC and Ferriby 1 is two or three centuries younger, their differences in structure may reflect changes in boatbuilding technology over time. It has been suggested that the Dover boat may have developed out of the practice of jointing two log boats together along their length. Be that as it may, the single thickened keel plank of the Ferriby boat has the appearance of being an advance

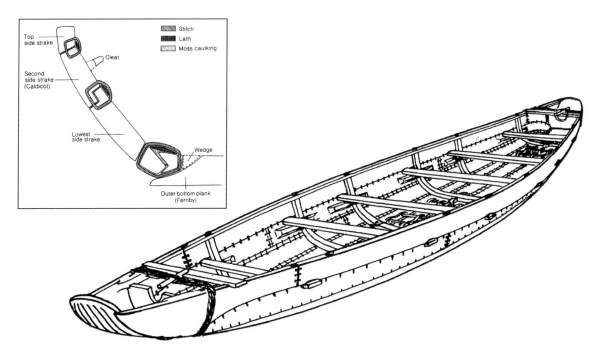

4.25 Reconstruction by Edward Wright of the Ferriby 1 boat, dating to the late second millennium BC, found in the Humber estuary. The inset shows the method by which the timbers were sewn together

on the more over-engineered basal structure of the Dover vessel. More examples are needed before these issues of sequential development can be resolved.

No sewn-plank boats have yet been recovered in Ireland, but a log boat found off Lea's Island in Lough Corrib, dating to 1400 BC, appears to show that some elements of the new technology were being adopted in log boat construction. Cleats were found in the floor, anchoring slender rods holding two parts of the hull together, and a split in the stern was rebound using moss caulking and yew withy stitching. While it could be argued that the stitching of cracks might have been developed anywhere at any time, the cleats are part of the new technology developed in British waters facilitated by copper alloy tools.

Once in use, the sewn-plank tradition continued in Britain into the first millennium BC. It was evident in the Brigg raft from northern Lincolnshire, a flat-bottomed vessel with five base planks sewn together which dates to about 800 BC, and in an oak fragment with a cleat found at Ferriby dating to about 400 BC. Much has been written about the sea-going capabilities of these sewn-plank boats. One view, influenced perhaps by the fact that most have been found in sheltered estuaries, is that they were designed not for the open sea but for use on rivers and estuaries, or, at best, for

153

4.26 The Dover boat, dating to *c.*1550 BC, seen here *in situ* during excavations

making short coastal journeys. But this underestimates the capacity of the craft and the spirit of those who sailed them. Paddled by an experienced crew in fair weather, they would certainly have been able to make longer sea-crossings. Speeds are difficult to judge, but with crews of ten paddlers, who would have fitted comfortably into an 11–13-metre vessel of the Ferriby 1–Dover type, reasonable headway could have been made. Sea trials in the Channel with a half-scale replica of the Dover boat and a crew not used to handling such a vessel reached average speeds of 2.9 knots over 8 nautical miles with top speeds approaching 7 knots. Thus, average speeds of 3–4 knots may have been the norm for experienced seamen, meaning that a crossing from Dover to France in fair conditions could probably have been accomplished in five to six hours given effective use of the tidal flow. The possibility of boats being fitted with a temporary sail must also be considered. While there is no convincing evidence of sails, it would have been feasible for a simple

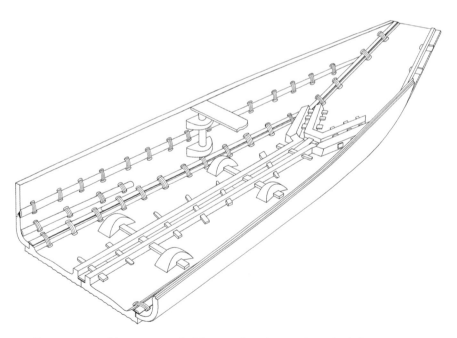

4.27 Reconstruction of the surviving end of the Dover boat showing the method of construction

bipod mast and yard to have been erected. If set well forward of midships, a small sail would have been quite effective in a following wind, though with such a narrow beam and low freeboard the vessel would have needed skilled handling.

The sewn-plank boats sailed by men of experience had the potential to make sea journeys around the British coasts and between Britain and the Continent. Nor should we forget the amount of skilled labour invested in their construction. These were artefacts of high value, the ownership and successful sailing of which would have carried much prestige. It is not too fanciful to see them as symbols of high status used by the elite to make the long journeys so necessary to keeping alive cross-Channel social networks to ensure that rare commodities like copper, tin, gold, amber, and jet were kept in circulation and to bring back news of other worlds.

Nordic Traditions

The two wide channels the Skagerrak and the Kattegat, which divide Denmark from the coasts of western Sweden and southern Norway, were, throughout prehistory and in the early historic period, a forcing ground for seafaring. It was here, after the end of the Last Glacial Maximum, where foragers from the North European Plain came to feast off the rich resources of Bohuslän, Sweden, and to send expeditions on to settle the Atlantic coast of Norway (pp. 90–5); and later, in the later sixth and fifth millennia, where the Ertebølle hunter-gatherers established their base camps, creating the huge shell middens from the debris of their marine foraging (pp. 102–4). Their successors eventually began to adopt aspects of the Neolithic lifestyle, gradually at first and then, after 3900 BC, embracing the new ways with enthusiasm. Although the introduction of farming dramatically changed the subsistence patterns and led to fertile land being cleared and settled, the coastal resources remained important for those living within reach of the sea.

Among the material resources that Denmark had to offer, two commodities were of particular value in long-distance exchange systems because of their scarcity: amber and flint. Amber was found in concentrations along the west coast of Jutland and the south coast of the Baltic and was exchanged, at first within the North Sea and Baltic region and then, after the beginning of the second millennium, more widely across Europe, eventually reaching the Mediterranean. In all probability the extension of the trade in amber after 2000 BC was driven by the desire of the Scandinavian communities to acquire bronze and gold, which were becoming increasingly desirable but in which the region was entirely deficient. High-quality flint occurred in the chalk and limestone deposits of northern Jutland and the island of Fyn, and by the Late Neolithic was being worked into finely finished thin-butted polished axes used in exchange. Later, in the Early Bronze Age, the flint masters turned their attention to making exquisite, finely flaked daggers imitating the form of bronze daggers now coming into circulation. These flat daggers were an important commodity in the exchange systems linking northern Jutland with the west coast of Norway. Flint daggers predominated, but the north-bound cargoes also contained bronze weapons and, more rarely, gold. The principal point of entry along the west coast of Norway was in the Jæren region, two hundred kilometres by sea across the Skagerrak from northern Jutland, though some ships sailed much further along the coast to Sunnmøre, adding another four hundred kilometres to the journey. What commodities the Norwegian coastal dwellers could give in exchange we can only guess, but seal oil, dried fish, and furs would probably have featured large in their offer.

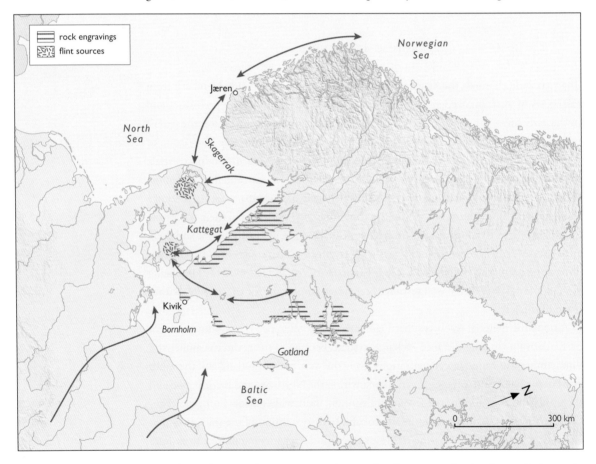

4.28 The southern Scandinavian region in the second millennium BC showing the principal routes by which resources such as flint were being distributed. Copper reached the area from central Europe along the river routes

The sailors making these northern journeys in the early second millennium were following the routes first pioneered by the foragers who settled these coasts in the tenth millennium. How much maritime traffic had passed in the intervening eight millennia it is impossible to say, but once the route had been opened and people were settled along the Norwegian coasts, it is likely that contacts by sea continued, even if long-distance trading expeditions happened only sporadically. That boats were in active use by local people along the remote Atlantic coast of Norway is illustrated in rock engravings from Alta in northern Norway, dating to 3300–2200 BC, showing a series of boats chasing a swimming deer. There is a similar scene, undated, from Repparfjord, Finnmark. The vessels illustrated are small, with high freeboard and prows accentuated to look like animal heads. These are surely skin boats, the precursors of the Greenland umiak.

The waters between Denmark and southern Scandinavia, and the Baltic Sea to which they gave access, would have been alive with sailing craft in the second millennium, transporting the rare commodities demanded by the elites to display their status. Such expeditions provided opportunities for aspiring young men to prove their daring and powers of leadership. That

4.29 Flint daggers of the Late Neolithic period were made in Denmark, where flint naturally occurs, and were exported to communities in Sweden and along the Norwegian coast using the now well-established sea-routes

the boat now played a vital part in social, economic, and religious life is amply demonstrated by the astonishing number of boat images carved on exposed rock faces in the coastal region of eastern Norway and southern Sweden and that haunt the bronze-work of the period. The rock carvings are the most prolific source. Spread across some five thousand sites, there are estimated to be depictions of seventy-five thousand boats. In Bohuslän alone, on the west coast of Sweden, there are more than ten thousand images of individual boats, by far the most common motif to be displayed. Of the eight hundred or so bronzes recorded, ship images are found on, or influence the form of, 420. They occur on swords, razors, knives, and neck rings. In Bronze Age Scandinavia boats were everywhere to be seen.

The earliest closely datable boat image from the Nordic region is found on the side of a single-edged sword, one of a pair found in a bog at Rørby in western Sjælland, Denmark. A careful examination shows that it had been engraved on the wax model,

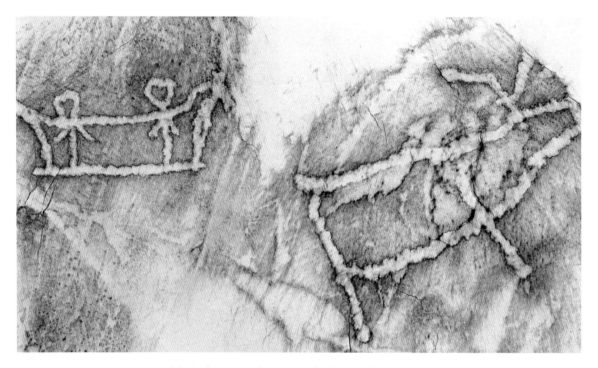

4.30 This rock engraving from Repparfjord, Finnmark, in Norway clearly shows two people in a boat. One interpretation is that they are hunting a swimming reindeer depicted nearby

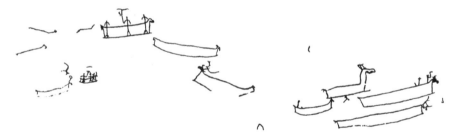

4.31 Rock carvings of boats found at Alta in northern Norway, dating to 3300–2200 BC

from which the mould for the sword was made. This is an important observation because it means that the image is of the date of manufacture of the sword and was not engraved at some later time: since the sword dates to the sixteenth century BC, so too must the image. The essence of the boat is conveyed with great simplicity. The hull is delineated by two parallel lines, one representing the gunwale, the other the keel-line. The keel-line continues fore and aft. At the bow it forms a pointed keel-extension, while at the stern it is expanded to become some kind of stabilizer. The

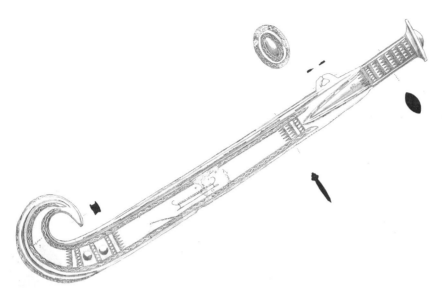

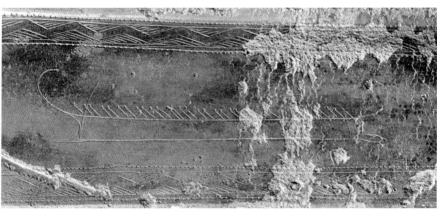

4.32 A sword found at Rørby, western Sjælland, Denmark, dating to *c.*1600 BC, is decorated with a representation of a boat. Vessels similar to this are represented on rock engravings

gunwale-line also continues fore and aft, turning up at both ends in a sweeping curve. The crew, some thirty-four or thirty-five of them, are indicated by simple strokes ending in dots for the heads. They incline in the direction in which the boat is moving, suggesting bodies tensed forward with paddling. The strokes indicating people are paired to indicate paddlers sitting side by side, with single strokes at the fore and aft perhaps to represent the leader and the steersman. For such a simple line drawing the Rørby engraving is full of detail. All the characteristics it shows can be matched on rock engravings.

The importance of the boats shown on, or influencing the shape of, metal objects is that the objects can be dated by typology and context and ascribed to one of the seven periods into which the Nordic Bronze Age is divided. The rock engravings, for which there is no direct means of dating, can then be matched with the bronze images, thereby acquiring a broad date. Just how close the similarities are can be appreciated by comparing the Rørby boat with rock carvings from Bergel, Østfold, Norway. Over time the images chart a change in boatbuilding styles. In the period from 1500 to 1300 BC horses' heads were introduced to adorn the stem- and stern-posts and continue to remain popular until the end of the Bronze Age, about 500 BC. About 1100 BC aquatic birds make their appearance as adornments to stem and stern. At the same time the fore keel-extension becomes a major feature, curving up high out of the water. Some of these changes may have resulted from technical improvements, but more likely they were fashions responding to the evolving belief system.

The boats depicted are clearly long canoes powered by many pairs of paddlers. The Rørby boat with its thirty-four or thirty-five paddlers, if a real vessel, would have been somewhere in the order of 15 metres long, which is not unreasonable, but other boats are shown with impossibly large numbers of paddlers. The boat carved at Torsbo, Bohuslän, with about 120 figures on board, is more a boastful exaggeration than a practical possibility. The actual structure of the boats has been much discussed. Some

4.33 Rock engraving from Halden, Østfold, Norway, showing a procession of boats. The rock is clearly visible on the edge of a valley close to the sea

writers, noting vertical lines sometimes shown on the sides of the vessels, have favoured the conclusion that they were skin boats with ribs showing in the sunlight. Others, noting horizontal lines on the engravings, have argued for sewn-plank construction. The latter method seems more likely for long, narrow vessels of this kind. Sewn-plank technology was already being used on the other side of the North Sea, and the Iron Age successors of the Bronze Age boats, known from an actual example found at Hjortspring on the Danish island of Als, dating to the third century BC, was a sewn-plank craft (p. 369 below). Sleek vessels of this kind, powered by a team of experienced paddlers, would have been impressive to watch as they streaked across the sea, the fore keel-extension making it possible to run far up a beach without damaging the vessel.

The proliferation of images leaves little doubt that boats featured large in the lives of the people. They symbolized many things: power and wealth, connectivity, and the ability to acquire rare commodities and esoteric knowledge. They also allowed those who commanded them to show enterprise and daring. The boat crews who crossed the treacherous Skagerrak to trade along the western Norwegian coast in the Late Neolithic and Early Bronze Age would have gained glory from these ventures, as well as bringing back cargoes of furs to distribute. How far they ventured out of their home waters is largely a matter of guesswork. That they sailed far up the Norwegian coast is well attested in the archaeological record; they might also have journeyed south along the coast, perhaps crossing the southern North Sea to Britain with cargoes of amber. They would, of course, have commanded the Baltic and been able to paddle up north European rivers like the Oder and the Vistula to make contact with the elites of central and eastern Europe. That they actually did so is suggested by the distribution of east European bronzes extending northwards from Hungary to Denmark, reflecting the routes

Amøy, Jæren

Tanum, Bohuslän

Amøy, Jæren

Amøy, Jæren

Tanum, Bohuslän

Hegre, Trøndelag

4.34 A selection of rock engravings from south-west Norway and Sweden. It has been suggested that the horizontal lines on some of the representations might indicate that the vessels were built of planks

4.35 Rock engraving found at Södra Ödsmål, Bohuslän, Sweden. The vessels appear to be anchored while their occupants are engaged in fishing

along which bronze (so necessary to the Nordic world) flowed, together with knowledge of new technologies like the two-wheeled chariot and stories of distant alien lands.

In the great tapestries of images carved into the ice-smoothed granite of Bohuslän and Østfold the action-packed world of the Bronze Age springs to life. It is all there: the boats, the ploughs, the carts, the animals, and the warriors, often armed and threatening. To a contemporary observer the meaning of it all would have been obvious; we, at our distance, can only make guesses. Perhaps the boat engravings tell narratives of individual vessels, their departures and arrivals, and of grand expeditions setting sail. But boats also had other parts to play. Some seem to have been stages for performances, with jumping acrobats or warriors engaged in combat. At the other end of the scale is a tranquil scene of two men fishing from a tiny craft. And then there are the enigmatic depictions showing a single person (a god perhaps) defiantly holding a boat aloft. Was this to remind us of powers beyond human control? At the very least, the rock carvings provide ample scope for the imagination.

The Nordic boats so vividly brought to life in the rock art images are part of a maritime tradition which began in the tenth millennium BC with pioneering foragers and continued without interruption up to the Viking outpourings beginning in the eighth century AD. It is a tradition fostered, indeed demanded, by the close intertwining of land and sea so characteristic of the Nordic region.

Emerging Traditions

What becomes clear from all the detail considered here is that there are three distinct maritime networks. Two of them, the Nordic and the British networks, were regional in that they were responses by local communities to the environment in which they found themselves. The third, the Maritime Bell Beaker network, was super-regional, extending its tentacles south to the coast of Morocco, north to Brittany, and beyond and east into the Mediterranean. The British network is given its coherence by its characteristic sewn-plank boats found along the east, south, and west coast of the island— vessels that were robust enough in fair-weather conditions to cross the southern North Sea, the English Channel, and the Irish Sea. These boats facilitated contacts between Britain and Ireland and the adjacent continent, allowing many communities to share in a broadly similar cultural development. The Nordic network has the appearance of being more dynamic. The Nordic boats, like the British, encouraged social connectivity, but by venturing along the west coast of Norway and along the European rivers the Nordic boat-masters were being more adventurous than the British—or so it might appear. We should remember, however, that the differences may be more apparent than real: lively rock engravings are able to inspire the imagination more than sodden planks.

The Maritime Bell Beaker enterprise was quite different. Though we know virtually nothing of the boats, the extent of the networks was spectacular. Whatever were the driving forces, it is evident that the quest for metal featured large. It was in this period that the Pyrite Belt of Iberia began to be fully exploited, and that the production of copper, tin, and gold first got under way in the metal-rich arc from Brittany to southern Ireland; and it is not impossible that voyaging along the Moroccan coast was in part motivated by the availability of West African gold. Some of the more enterprising travellers also began to explore the metal-rich regions of Mediterranean Iberia and southern France.

The boats that we know of from their remains preserved in British waters, from the rock carvings in the Nordic region, and from the few enigmatic engravings in western Iberia and Brittany, all seem to be long, narrow craft, 12 or more metres in length, powered by many pairs of paddlers. Such craft would have been ideal for ceremonial visits or for raids, but would have been less suited for carrying bulk cargo. Alongside them were other craft: log boats well suited for travel in rivers, lakes, and estuaries, and, very probably, skin boats, buoyant on the open seas and broad in the beam to provide stability. Such vessels would have had a greater carrying capacity than the longboats. In the period covered by this chapter little evidence for skin boats has yet come to light, but they will take greater prominence later in the narrative. We can, however, assume their presence, carrying on traditions which probably went back to the Upper Palaeolithic period, adding to the variety of sea-craft now plying the ocean fringes.

5

The Eastern Mediterranean Cauldron, 5300–1200 BC

The narrative history of the eastern Mediterranean over the four thousand years or so covered by this chapter is the story of competing states and polities and of the kings and pharaohs who ruled them. Dynasties came and went, and states acquired huge territorial power only to be overwhelmed and to fragment. It was a time of intense competition, when status was measured by the ability to acquire rare raw materials and to consume them in ever-increasing volumes. This is nowhere better demonstrated than in burial monuments, be they in Saqqara, Ur, or Mycenae. Real power lay in the facility to command the flow of goods and commodities and, since the sea provided many of the vital transport routes, its mastery became an imperative.

In very broad terms the period considered here can be divided into two: before and after two centuries or so of confusion and upset caused by system collapse between about 2100 and 1900 BC. In the first period the two seas which made up the eastern Mediterranean—the Aegean and the unnamed eastern cul-de-sac which we can refer to as the Levantine Sea—developed as separate entities. The Aegean, closed on its southern side by Crete, was largely inward-looking, serving its many islands, while the Levantine Sea formed the principal link between Egypt and the fast-developing states of Mesopotamia and Asia Minor. Egypt seems to have taken the lead in maritime technology, building on its long experience with the Nile, its ships now opening up the sea-routes to the ports along the Levant coast.

After the phase of widespread social dislocation about 2000 BC Crete rapidly emerged as a new maritime force dominating the southern Aegean and Greece, extending its operations to the coasts of Asia Minor and to Egypt. By the middle of the second millennium power had begun to pass to the Mycenaeans on the Greek mainland. Thereafter ties with the east were further strengthened and new trading opportunities were opened up with the Tyrrhenian Sea to the west. By the thirteenth century BC Mycenaean pottery—a useful archaeological surrogate for the trading networks—is found from Sardinia to the Levant and deep into Egypt. The sea had brought the Near Eastern states into direct engagement with the developing polities of barbaric Europe for the first time.

The Two Seas

The eastern Mediterranean divides into two well-peopled seas, the Aegean and the Levantine Sea, joined by a coastal route along the southern shores of Asia Minor. Between them and the long and largely desert coast of North Africa west of the Nile lies an empty sea requiring considerable navigational skill, and no little faith, to cross. The Aegean and the Levantine Sea, while nurturing maritime systems of their own, provided interfaces between the fast-evolving states of the Near East and the intricate complexity of the European peninsula.

The hinterland of the Levantine Sea well demonstrates the importance of geography to human agency. To the south lies the Nile delta, isolated by great tracts of desert extending to the shore, the Western Desert between the delta and Cyrenaica, and the Sinai desert, creating a hostile zone from the delta to the vicinity of Gaza, beyond which the coast takes on a more benign aspect. Along the northern shore the Taurus Mountains nudge close to the water, except for the more friendly plain around the Gulf of Iskenderun. From the gulf to Gaza lie five hundred kilometres of sinuous coastline currently divided between the modern states of Turkey, Syria, Lebanon, Israel, and Palestine. The immediate hinterland of this Levant coast was formed by immense tectonic pressures which have created a wide faulted valley—the northwards continuation of the African Rift Valley—flanked by mountain ranges to east and to west. This mountain spine, cleft by its valley, separates a narrow coastal plain, in some places barely fifteen kilometres wide, from the vast Syrian and Jordanian deserts stretching interminably to the east. The only approaches to this coastal plain from the Nile delta are by way of an overland desert route along the coast, or by sea. At the northern end of

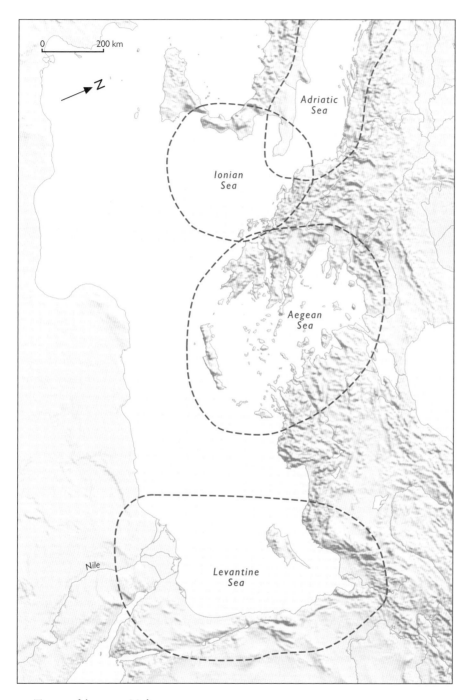

5.1 The seas of the eastern Mediterranean

the plain, where the upper valley of the Euphrates comes within 120 kilometres of the Mediterranean shore, lies the most convenient route to Mesopotamia, long dominated by the ancient city of Aleppo. Geography, then, demands that, if the rapidly developing states of Mesopotamia and Egypt were to interact, they would do so in the coastal lowlands of the Levant. This, as we shall see, is exactly what happened.

The coast of the Levant can be divided into three regions. The southern part as far north as Haifa, sited where the promontory of Mount Carmel provides protected waters, is an uncongenial coast, much of it rather arid with few natural locations suitable for ports. Further north lies the coast of Lebanon, its more varied geography of headlands with a scattering of small offshore islands making it a far more friendly place for seamen. It was along this stretch that the famous ports of Tyre, Sidon, Beirut, and Byblos were to develop. Although the coastal zone was narrow, it was exceedingly fertile, benefiting from the moist westerly airstream coming from the Atlantic along the length of the Mediterranean. Behind the plain the mountains of Lebanon rise to heights of over three thousand metres, forcing the clouds to rise, releasing the rains and creating swiftly flowing torrents to water and to fertilize the plains. The warm, moist climate of the mountains saw the growth of extensive forests of cypress, pine, and cedar so much in demand for shipbuilding. If this second zone—the Lebanese Levant—was closed in upon itself by the mountains and had little option but to look out to the sea, the third zone to the north (north of Tripoli) was more open, with overland routes threading to the east. One, beginning on the coast at Tell Kazel, led to Homs in the valley of the Orontes, then due east across the desert to the oasis of Palmyra and eventually to the Euphrates. Further up the coast from the port of Al Mina at the mouth of the Orontes it was possible to reach the Euphrates by the much shorter route by way of Aleppo. Between the two ports of Tell Kazel and Al Mina there were many others, but none more important than Ugarit, in modern Ras Shamra, which grew to be an independent city of some power. Sailing due west, Cyprus could be reached. It lay outside the major maritime networks for much of the Neolithic period, but with the discovery of its rich copper resource it was rapidly integrated and its southern ports began to flourish.

This has been a long excursion into geography, but only by understanding the constraints and opportunities offered by the landscape will we be able to appreciate how it was that the Levantine Sea came to play so crucial a part in European prehistory.

The second sea, the Aegean, is simpler to understand and needs less of an introduction. Landlocked on three sides, its fourth partially closed by Crete, the Aegean provided a fine mesh of sea-routes linking the west coast of Asia Minor and the Balkan peninsula. It can be divided into three parts. The north is a comparatively open sea, with a few large islands like Lemnos and Lesbos and a scattering of smaller ones, surrounded

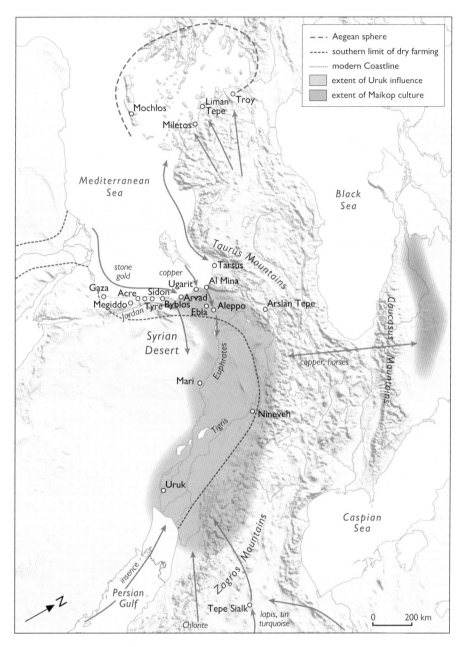

Aegean sphere
southern limit of dry farming
modern Coastline
extent of Uruk influence
extent of Maikop culture

Troy

Liman
Tepe

Mochlos

Miletos

*Mediterranean
Sea*

*Black
Sea*

Taurus Mountains

Tarsus

copper

stone
gold

Ugarit
Al Mina

Gaza
Acre
Sidon
Arvad
Aleppo
Arslan Tepe

Megiddo
Tyre
Byblos

Jordan
Ebla

*Syrian
Desert*

Euphrates

Caucasus Mountains

copper, horses

Mari

Tigris

Nineveh

Uruk

*Caspian
Sea*

Zagros Mountains

insence

*Persian
Gulf*

Tepe Sialk

lapis, tin
turquoise

Chlorite

N

0   200 km

5.2 The Levantine coast of the Mediterranean provided an interface between the consuming states of the Near East and the productive world of the Mediterranean and Europe

5.3 Ras Shamra in Syria, close to the Mediterranean coast, is the location of the ancient city of Ugarit, the entrance to which was through a well-defended gate

by a ragged coastline, mountainous in part but with plenty of sheltered places for harbours. At the north-eastern corner the narrow sea channel, the Dardanelles, gives access through the Sea of Marmara and the Bosporus to the Black Sea, while on the southern side the islands of Euboea and Khios flank the hundred-kilometre-wide sea passage to the central Aegean.

The central Aegean is quite different from the north, littered with a confetti of small islands, the Cyclades in the centre and the Dodecanese towards the coast of Asia Minor. So many and so close are these islands that they provided the natural stepping stones between Asia and Attica, a journey that could be made by many different routes seldom requiring sailings of more than thirty kilometres in one haul. It was probably this way that the pioneer farming groups made their way to the Greek mainland in

5.4 (*Opposite*) Ugarit lies close to the coast and was served by the port of Minet el-Beida. The town is well sited to command the route from the coast through the mountains to the upper Euphrates

170

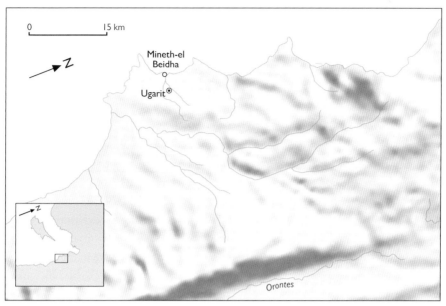

courtyards

fortifications

the seventh millennium. Many of the islands were large enough to support farming populations and some had the added attraction of mineral wealth, between them producing copper, silver, obsidian, marble, and emery. Altogether the Cyclades offered a welcoming environment, with their communities able to maintain an island identity and yet be part of a more extensive network.

The southern Aegean was different again, an open sea, the Sea of Candia, fringed along its southern side by a string of islands, Kythera, Antikythera, Crete, Kasos, Karpathos, and Rhodes. Crete, with its long mountain spine, was by far the largest and, blessed with a warm climate and fertile soil, was productive enough to support a sizeable population. There were other factors in its favour. From its position on the southern rim of the Aegean it could engage with the Cyclades and also with the mainlands of Asia Minor and Greece. But it was part of a wider world, a natural goal for the sea-routes along the southern shore of Asia Minor from the Levantine Sea and a starting point for those brave enough to make the open-sea journey south to the North African coast en route to the Nile delta. Crete would grow to become a major player in this global world of the second millennium.

The Urban States of Mesopotamia, 5400–2000 BC

For a long while after the development of regular farming economies in the Near East, the farming villages were restricted to the hilly region stretching as a wide zone from the Levant coast of the Mediterranean across southern Turkey and northern Syria, northern Iraq, and western Iran, the southern boundary of the zone corresponding to the southern limit beyond which farming without irrigation was not possible. In the early sixth millennium this boundary was successfully crossed when communities moved down to the rich alluvial plain of the Tigris and Euphrates and set up villages, compensating for lack of rain by irrigating their fields by systems of ditches fed from the great rivers. This initiated the Early Ubaid culture (5900–5400 BC), named after Tell el-Ubaid on the river Euphrates. Tied to the land by the need to maintain the irrigation system, the settlements took on a more permanent aspect and began to grow, and with this came the need for inter-village cooperation and the emergence of more complex political systems. Soon aspects of the Ubaid culture were to spread throughout the farming communities of the hilly flanks zone (known as the Late Ubaid culture, 5400–4200 BC), creating a wide corridor of farming villages extending from the Persian Gulf, which became known in contemporary texts as the Lower Sea, to the north-eastern corner of the Mediterranean, the Upper Sea.

The succeeding period, the Uruk period (4200–3100 BC), was one of rapid and dramatic change which saw the emergence of the first towns. More permanent settlements and greater productivity, relieving the constraint of the holding capacity of the land, allowed populations to increase, a process which, once under way, took on a momentum of its own. Another factor was the pulling power of the burgeoning settlements in attracting semi-nomadic people from the surrounding country. It was not long before some of them had increased both in size and in social complexity to become small towns of thirty to fifty hectares. By the end of the period the city of Uruk, which had the additional benefit of lying at the head of the Persian Gulf, had grown to a hundred hectares and was surrounded by a number of satellite settlements.

Growth in the size of the towns drove other changes. While a high percentage of the resident population would have engaged directly in agricultural production, others developed specialist skills to service the community, to provide them with pottery, metalwork, and clothing. Alongside these productive specialists there were others who became administrators to run the increasingly complex state systems headed by a priest-king supported by a theocracy. The state also required scribes and bookkeepers for overseeing taxes, seal-cutters to manufacture the symbols of authority used to control the movement of goods, and architects, stone carvers, and brickmakers to build the increasingly impressive temples that grew to dominate the towns. Such an escalation in complex social and economic interactions inevitably led to the creation of a script, which soon evolved into cuneiform. The emergence of complex urban society created demands for materials that could not be sourced locally. Elite display craved such luxuries as copper, silver, gold, lapis lazuli, turquoise, and carnelian, while the desire to build monumental structures required the importation of timber and stone, in both of which the alluvial valleys were deficient. So it was that the trading networks strengthened and expanded and specialists began to oversee the inflow of goods from the Persian Gulf, from the Iranian plateau and Afghanistan beyond, from Asia Minor and the more distant Caucasus, and from Egypt coming via the Mediterranean. To ensure the flow of goods Uruk trading communities were established in border towns and beyond, and it may be that garrisons were sent to protect them. The Uruk expansion, as it is called, got under way about 3700 BC, reaching its peak after 3400 BC, but it came to an abrupt end about 3100 BC amid signs of growing internal tensions in society.

During the third millennium waves of warfare washed through Mesopotamia. The causes of the unrest were various. Continued population rise put increasing pressure on the land, a problem made much worse by widening social inequality leading to slavery, mentioned in various written sources for the first time, and the rise of secular rulers alongside the other elites and the traditional priesthoods. All needed to express their power through rich palaces and extravagant burials, and in doing so used up even more of the agrarian surpluses generated by the land-workers. The two factors working together put intolerable stress on society and the underlying economy. To add to the woes nomads from the Zagros Mountains and the Syrian desert began to raid the urban centres.

In the atmosphere of warlike competition which developed between the many rival city states, some rose to dominance, others became subservient, and fortunes changed rapidly. By the end of this long period of inter-state rivalry (known as the Early Dynastic period) two powerful polities remained: Sumer and Akkad. But Akkad was gaining ascendancy. Under its charismatic leader Sargon (reigned c.2334–2279 BC), Sumer was beaten, and Sargon went on, by conquest and diplomacy, to bring many city states and neighbouring territories under his control, creating the first Mesopotamian empire. The empire was to outlive him, but not for long, and in 2193 BC it collapsed under pressure from nomads who had begun raiding from the Zagros Mountains and the desert. The king of Ur now assumed leadership, but in 2004 BC Ur fell to the Elamites, and Mesopotamia dissolved into another period of confusion as city states dissipated their energies, vying with each other and beating off attacks by external enemies. Yet, in spite of the state of endemic warfare and waves of disruption sweeping across the plains, individual city states, now strongly fortified, held out and many of them flourished, their leaders going to even greater efforts to draw to themselves the rare commodities from distant sources so necessary if they were to continue to display their power and manage their patronage.

One of the interfaces between the Mesopotamian core and the outside world was the three-hundred-kilometre or so coastline of the eastern Mediterranean extending from the Gulf of Iskenderun southwards to the port of Byblos. Centrally placed along the stretch was the city of Ugarit, situated on a low hill a few kilometres from its well-protected port of Minet el-Beida (fifteen kilometres north of the modern port of Latakia). Ugarit was ideally sited. It looked out across the sea to copper-rich Cyprus and had easy access by sea to the copper- and silver-producing regions of the Taurus Mountains. In its immediate hinterland the climate and soil favoured the production of olive oil while the sea offered murex shells, from which a deep-red dye was extracted—two products much in demand in the Mesopotamian cities. From Ugarit an overland caravan route led to the flourishing city of Ebla, which commanded the road to the Euphrates. As Mesopotamia's gateway to the Upper Sea, Ugarit could hardly have been better placed. It flourished through the fourth and third millennia but suffered depopulation and destruction in the troubled time about 2000 BC.

The other Mediterranean port town of importance was Byblos, lying at the southern extremity of the Mesopotamian sphere of influence, on a narrow coastal strip backed by the mountains of Lebanon, blessed by the forests of cedar. Though it remained only a small town of some five hectares, Byblos became a favoured port of call for Egyptian merchants avid for regular supplies of high-quality timber. The gifts they brought, well

5.5 The city of Byblos in Lebanon occupied a promontory overlooking the sea. The ruins of the ancient city are now dominated by a Crusader castle. The modern town covers much of the archaeological site

represented in the archaeological record, enabled the local rulers to maintain a comfortable residence and to aggrandize the temple of the Lady of Byblos (Ba'alat Gebel). Byblos, then, could command two markets: Egypt and Mesopotamia.

Meanwhile in Egypt

There is no better example of the impact of geography on social and political development than Egypt—a sinuous, narrow strip of fertile land hemmed in by unending desert, which protects and isolates, forcing the valley communities to develop their own peculiar brand of hothouse culture unleavened by the experiences of others and deeply inward-looking. It is geography, again, that divides the fertile part of Egypt into its two very different zones, the tightly constrained Nile corridor and the splaying

175

delta. There are several oases in the Western Desert, but they played only a marginal role in the state's development.

Already by the beginning of the seventh millennium foragers on the fringes of the Sahara in southern Egypt were harvesting wild fruits and grasses and managing herds of wild cattle, but the full Neolithic package of domesticated species—sheep, goats, cattle, and pigs, and the cultivates emmer wheat, barley, and flax—was not introduced from the Levant until about 5000 BC. Farming practices were taken up in the delta region and the Fayum oasis within the next five hundred years and spread along the Nile valley between 4500 and 3000 BC. The delta and valley offered a benign environment for farmers, whose lives were strictly controlled by the reassuring regularity of the annual Nile flood. The flood rose in the late summer, falling in the autumn and leaving the valley floor blanketed with a layer of fresh silt. The crops could now be sown so that they would grow during the warm winter and be ready for harvesting in spring. It was a system outside human control, needing minimum effort to produce good harvests. The only significant factor influencing yield was the volume of the annual flood, which affected the silt load carried by the river.

Along the valley and in the delta region communities were able to create permanent settlements and to produce surpluses. Already by 3300 BC towns were beginning to appear at intervals along the valley, but growing populations and the severe restriction on space led to competition and conflict, and the emergence of strong leaders. By the end of the fourth millennium a unified kingdom had emerged in Upper Egypt led by the king of Hierakonpolis. The kingdom rapidly extended its influence along the Nile valley, and about 3000 BC the valley and the delta were united under a single authority with a new capital city founded at Memphis at the northern end of the valley before it fanned out into the delta. It was on the desert-edge plateau west of the city that the early pharaohs built their mastabas (small tombs) and pyramids. The powerful rulers of the Early Dynastic period (c.3000–2686 BC) and the Old Kingdom (2686–2125 BC), by directing a highly efficient administration, were able to hold Egypt together as a unified state for nearly a millennium. But by about 2400 BC the rulers began to make land grants to the lesser elite, including the provincial governors, thus weakening the hold of the state. Matters came to a head about 2150 BC, when a succession of low Nile floods drastically reduced crop yield to levels unable to sustain the growing population and to meet the high consumption expectations of the elite. Famine and disruption followed, and unified government fell apart.

Throughout the late fourth and third millennia Egypt was a consumer state requiring an inflow of raw materials to sustain its social systems. A variety of goods came from the south, from Nubia and from the region of East Africa known as the kingdom of Punt, to which trading missions were being sent after the middle of the third millennium.

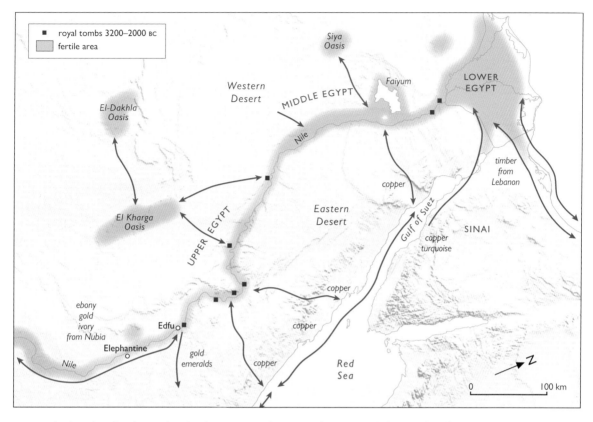

5.6 The fertile Nile valley, hemmed in by the Eastern and Western deserts, provided a corridor of communication as well as a rich and congenial environment for human settlement. A wide range of commodities were drawn to it by elite demand. The delta region created an interface with the Mediterranean

Gold was the principal import together with aromatic resins, ebony and other African hardwoods, ivory, slaves, and wild animals. Gold, copper, and amethyst were also available in the Eastern Desert of Nubia not far from the first cataract. Below this point lay Aswan, the most southerly of the Egyptian cities. Significantly its name comes from the word *swenet*, meaning trade. The Eastern Desert also provided copper and a range of building stone including granite, so much in demand for monumental buildings and statues. Sinai could also supply copper and turquoise. Taken together Egypt was well supplied from its African hinterland, but its Mediterranean interface allowed another range of materials to be accessed: silver from Asia Minor, lapis lazuli from Afghanistan, cedar-wood from Lebanon, and oils, food, and wine from the Levant coast. One tomb found at Abydos dating to about 3200 BC contained four hundred Palestinian storage containers which had probably been used for transporting and storing wine.

Resources from the Levant could be acquired either by land or by sea. The land route along the Mediterranean edge of Sinai, known as the Ways of Horus, became a protected passage under Egyptian control, making it possible for caravans to reach southern Palestine in a ten-day trek. Fortified bases led as far north as the vicinity of modern Tel Aviv. But by the beginning of the Old Kingdom (c.2700 BC) the land route had lost is popularity. With ships now able to face the ocean, it was more convenient to allow the sea-route to take over.

The Boats of the Nile: The Third Millennium

The very existence of the Nile demanded skilled boatbuilders. The river was the artery of Egypt, providing easy connectivity between those living on opposing banks and between the many settlements strung along its length. It was a forcing ground for the skills of the boatbuilder. Those wishing to travel downstream could simply go with the flow, paddling when necessary to adjust the course. Those needing to travel upstream would find it hard to make headway under their own efforts unless they stuck to the shallow river margins, but with a wind constantly blowing from the north it took little imagination to realize that to harness it with a sail would make the boatmen's lives much easier. Given this simple geographical reality, it is hardly surprising that the first sails to be attested in the Mediterranean zone are Egyptian.

The boatbuilding skills learned in the river valley and the delta were soon being employed on the two seas that the Egyptian state came to master, the eastern end of the Mediterranean and the Red Sea, the first easily accessible from the delta, the second reached only after a long trek across the Eastern Desert. The Mediterranean gave access to the resources of the Levant, while the Red Sea allowed the more adventurous to harvest exotic products from East Africa: the Land of Punt. Both networks were essential to satisfy the massive demands of the consumer state.

The overland route from the delta to the productive lands of the Levant—the Ways of Horus—began to be eclipsed by the coast-hugging sea-route from about 2700 BC. A text of the reign of Sneferu dating to about 2600 BC refers to the arrival of forty ships loaded with cedar-wood, presumably from Lebanon, while the famous Palermo Stone, an inscribed slab of basalt of the fifth dynasty (2494–2345 BC) recording royal annals stretching back to the prehistoric period, refers to the Egyptians building ships of meru wood (a kind of oak) and of cedar. More expressive are the reliefs on the mortuary temple of the pharaoh Sahure (reigned 2487–2475 BC) at Abusir, which show a fleet of ships leaving Egypt for the Levant and returning with Asian prisoners, bears, and a cargo of jugs. These scraps leave little doubt that coastal trade was now

5.7 The Egyptian ship depicted on a relief in the fifth-dynasty burial temple of Sahure at Abusir dates to *c.*2475 BC. The hogging hawser running from stem to stern, supported on crutches, kept the vessel taut and prevented it from buckling in the middle. The bipole mast is shown here lowered

well under way. Much of it will have been beneficial to all parties directly involved. Even if the ships depicted at Sahure's temple do show prisoners, they are more likely to have been captives acquired by the local Levantine rulers and passed down the line to the Egyptian trading partners as yet another marketable commodity than the result of Egyptian raiding.

The building of watercraft in the Nile valley and delta was under way by the early Neolithic period. The earliest craft would probably have been rafts made of bundles

5.8 Egyptian relief showing the construction of a reed-bundle boat. From the fifth-dynasty tomb of Ptahhotep at Saqqara

5.9 The Cheops boat, built c.2600 BC, was dismantled into its 1,224 component parts and buried in a pit at the base of the pyramid. Perfectly preserved in the desert conditions, it has been reconstructed and is now displayed in its former glory

of reeds tightly bound and lashed together. The materials were ready to hand and the technology was simple. Reed-bundle rafts, so well adapted to the riverine environment, remained popular on the Nile even until recent times, and are frequently depicted. Propelled by pole and paddle, they would have served most of the needs of the local riverside farmers.

There may also have been log dug-outs, but given the lack of available local timber this type of craft can never have been common. The construction of more elaborate plank-built vessels is not likely to have begun before the appearance of copper tools at the end of the fourth millennium, but once under way the skills of the boatbuilder developed apace, and it may have been this technological surge, exacerbated by the need for good wood, that drove the demand for Lebanon cedar. The results were spectacular, as the famous Cheops boat—the oldest plank-built vessel in the world—bears witness. The boat was buried about 2560 BC in a specially constructed chamber at the foot of the pyramid of a fourth-dynasty pharaoh. The Cheops boat is massive, 43 metres long, nearly 6 metres broad, and 1.8 metres high, with the stem- and stern-posts rising to more than 7 metres. It was built, shell first, of thick planks of cedar-wood, with the frames added later. The planks were positioned in relation to each other with joggles, tenons, and dowels, and then lashed together with ropes of halfa grass, which held in place battens covering the joins between the planks. The holes for the lashings were cut within the thickness of the planks so that the lashings were not visible from the outside, removing the danger that they could be snagged or torn by rocks scouring the outside of the hull. The vessel was propelled by five oars on each side and was steadied by a rudder on each quarter attached to a transverse beam. Although the Cheops boat was, presumably, built to attend the pharaoh in life and afterlife, and was therefore ceremonial in its intent, it was a functional structure reflecting the very best of contemporary boatbuilding technology.

There are no convincing representations of plank-built vessels pre-dating the Cheops boat, though such craft must have existed, but from the fifth dynasty onwards paintings and reliefs provide much detail. One recurring feature is the hogging hawser, a multi-strand rope attached to bow and stern and taken over a vertical support in the centre of the vessel. By tightening the hawser the boat's planking could be pre-stressed to prevent the centre from buckling and rising up when the vessel was afloat. Another frequently occurring fitting was an aft deck for the helmsmen working the steering oars. The sail first appears in depictions about 3200 BC as a small rectangular construction raised on a single pole set well forward. In the fifth dynasty, about 2450 BC, the bipod mast begins to come into regular use. When sufficient detail is shown, the sails are square or rectangular, square-rigged to the yard at the head with a boom attached to the foot. An intriguing relief of 2500 BC found in the tomb of Ipi at Saqqara shows the method by which the sails were managed. The helmsman squatting on his raised deck held the

5.10 The hull of the Cheops boat was built of cedar, probably brought in from Lebanon. The planks were originally sewn together with halfa grass

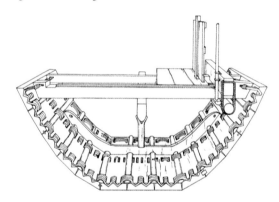

5.11 Diagrammatic section of the Cheops boat showing the way in which the planks were positioned in relation to each other with tenons and sewn together so that the cords did not protrude through the planks to the outside of the vessel, where they would have been in danger of being snagged and broken

ropes coming from the yard while another man standing below him controlled the ropes from the boom. In this particular case the boom appears to be held aft of the mast. Rigged in this way with the sail set well forward of centre, the boats could sail with a strong wind up to four points (about 45 degrees) on either side of dead astern. A wind outside that range would have made the vessel difficult to control.

Most of the vessels represented in the Egyptian reliefs and paintings were built for use on the river, but many of the techniques involved in their construction were adopted for the design of larger, sea-going ships. This is nowhere better shown than in the reliefs of the mortuary temple of Sahure. The ships are large, elegant vessels, some tensed with hogging hawsers and with horizontal rope girdles binding the hull just below the gunwale, attached to vertical girdles, under-girthing the ends. On one vessel the bipod mast is lowered, with the top steadied on a frame. Aft, three steersmen stand on their platform, their steering oars drawn out of the water while the oars of the seven pairs of oarsmen are at rest. A squadron of these great vessels manoeuvring themselves into the harbours of the Levant must have been an awe-inspiring sight. There would have been much for the local boatbuilders to learn and to incorporate into their own repertoires.

The Old Kingdom ships making their way along the coastal waters of the Levant in the middle of the third millennium were a remarkable achievement. Nurtured in a long tradition of riverboat building and given a new lease of life with the introduction about 3000 BC of sharp copper cutting tools, the Nile craftsmen were able to rise to the challenges of the rapidly growing and demanding state system. It was the elite

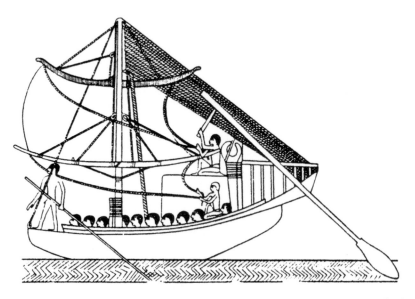

5.12 Egyptian sailing ships from the tomb of Ipi at Saqqara, dating to the fifth dynasty (mid-third millennium BC)

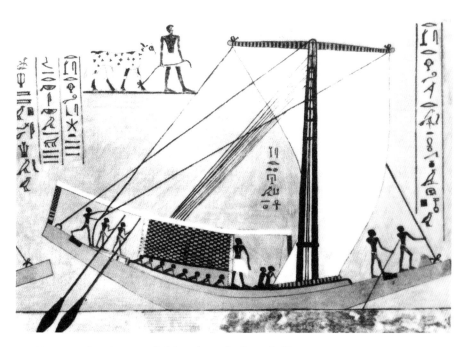

5.13 Egyptian sailing ship on a relief from the tomb of Kaem'onkh at Giza, *c*.2400–2300 BC

passion for exotic materials that drove entrepreneurs to foreign lands. Here they also found the cedar and other woods needed for shipbuilding and brought them back in increasing quantities to the Egyptian shipyards. So it was that in a brief four hundred years a new revolutionary type of sailing ship emerged in the Mediterranean.

The Inward-Looking Aegean, 4000–2000 BC

The Neolithic colonization of the Aegean islands began with Crete about 7000 BC and gradually spread to the rest of the islands. Settlers coming from Asia Minor and from the Greek mainland had taken over the larger islands by the end of the fourth millennium, and had embraced most of the minor islands capable of sustaining a resident population by the middle of the third millennium. The Aegean was a comfortable place to live. The sea was a major resource, while climate and soils combined to make most of the islands able to support farming communities, though in differing degrees. There were also mineral resources to be had: the much-desired obsidian from Melos, silver from Sifnos, copper from Kythnos, and marble from Naxos and Paros. The uneven distribution of resources encouraged mobility between the islands

183

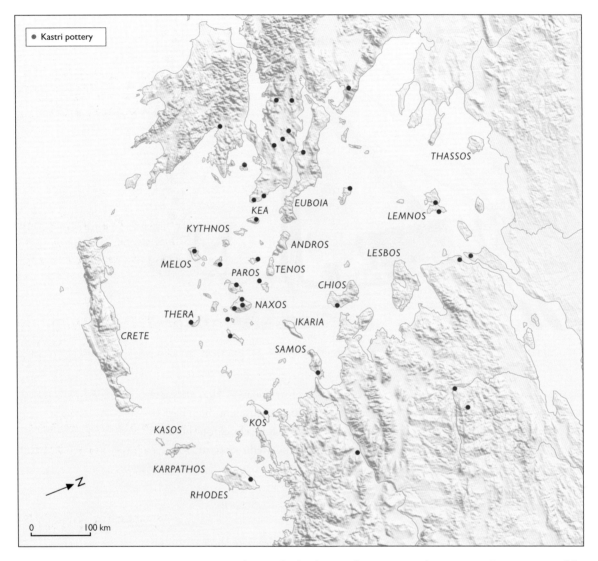

5.14 The Aegean Sea showing the distribution of Kastri pottery, demonstrating the connectivity of the Cyclades and Attica

and it is easy to see how a distinctive maritime culture could soon emerge, each island developing flotillas of boats used in cycles of trading embedded, no doubt, in a complex web of ceremonial. The same vessels would have been effective in the raids which took place when competition between island elites could no longer be constrained by social convention. Such was the situation that developed in the Cyclades in the period 3100–2700 BC: it was essentially an inward-looking island-bound system.

8.18 The Aegean Sea, almost enclosed by Greece, Turkey, and Crete, with its scattered islands forming stepping stones for sailors

In the twenty-seventh century a new internationalism began to take hold, driven by the expansionist interests of the Near Eastern states whose influence was beginning to spread into Anatolia. While the sea-routes along the south coast of Asia Minor continued to be active, new overland trade routes emerged linking the Near East to ports along the Aegean coast—places like Troy, Liman Tepe, and Miletos—from which direct contacts could be established with the Aegean maritime networks. This was a time of increased mobility both of goods and of people involving a widening world. At Lerna, on the Argolid, clay seals were found reflecting the registering and securing of goods in transit, an activity located at a grand megaron house belonging to a member of the local elite, while at the port of Agia Photia in north-western Crete some of the graves in the cemetery were furnished with Cycladic grave goods buried in a manner which suggests that the deceased may have been members of a Cycladic trading colony. Taken together the evidence is strongly suggestive of an expanding trading network drawing Greece and the Aegean islands closer to the Near Eastern world.

The period 2500–2200 BC saw a further intensification of these trends accompanied by the appearance of an assemblage of pottery known as the Kastri group (from Kastri, on the island of Kythera), inspired by Anatolian prototypes. The vessels included drinking cups and pouring jugs made in a monochrome black or brown colour with a lightly burnished surface intended to imitate metallic drinking sets. At the same time there were changes to the settlement system with the abandonment of some sites and the fortification of others. How to interpret all this is a matter of debate. While it is possible that it reflects a hostile intrusion of people from Asia Minor, a more likely explanation is that we are witnessing social dislocations caused by internal factors such as inter-island competition or social unrest. The widespread distribution of the new ceramic drinking set need mean little more than the adoption of a drinking ritual learned from contact with Anatolians.

One further factor should be mentioned: the relationship between Crete and the Cyclades altered. Whereas at first there appears to have been comparatively free inter-change between the two realms, after the middle of the second millennium the only Cycladic goods found on Crete are obsidian and copper. The implication is that Crete had now taken charge of the surrounding seas, relying on its own seafarers to bring in the commodities it required to the exclusion of all other carriers. By the end of the third millennium Crete had emerged as a major maritime power with trading routes extending to the Peloponnese and to the Asian mainland, and there is evidence to sug-gest that at Kastri and Miletos colonies of Cretan traders were now settled through whom engagement with the mainland was manipulated.

The vessels used in these various maritime transactions are known from clay models, lead models, rock engravings, and schematic images inscribed on ritual pots. A clay model at Mochlos on Crete represents a relatively short boat with a protrusion at water-level at both ends and with rising ends of equal proportion, making no distinc-tion between bow and stern. The model found at Palaikastro in eastern Crete has the two ends treated differently. At one end, assumed to be the stern, the width of the vessel tapers into a high-rising structure while the bow is more bulbous and terminates with a short projection at about the waterline, possibly designed to facilitate beaching. The same kind of vessel, with a high stern and a short bow projection, is depicted on a rock engraving discovered on Naxos, which shows a man loading an animal, probably a goat. It is difficult to estimate size from the models and engraving but the boats were probably quite short, certainly no more than 8 metres in length, and were most likely designed for local journeys involving three or four paddlers.

Quite different are the longboats represented by four lead models from Naxos and from incised decorations on flat ceramic plates of frying-pan shape. The most com-plete of the Naxos models is of a long vessel with a raised tapering bow and a transom stem also rising but at a lesser angle. If, in reality, the boat had been 1 metre wide, its length would have been about 12 metres. This would have allowed about fourteen paddlers, double-banked, together with two steersmen with long paddles at the stern and one man in the bow. The boats depicted on the ceramic plates appear to be longboats of comparable proportion to the Naxos models but with the characteristic high stern and raised bow with a bow projection shown on the Palaikastro clay model. In all cases the stern is surmounted by a fish facing aft, below which hangs a tassel pendant. That all these images were found embedded in motifs representing the sea, on a very distinctive type of pottery designed for ritual use, raises the question of their interpretation. While it is tempting to see them as the boats used in ceremonial visits, trading expeditions, and raids between the islands—a vision inspired by the recent anthropological past of the Pacific islanders—it may be that the image is of a single, particular vessel replicated many times, and it remains a possibility that the vessel was mythical. But even if this extreme interpretation is accepted, the form of the vessel is likely to have had some basis in reality.

The boat forms shown in the models and engravings are clearly not simple log boats, but they could have been logboat-based with sides extended by planking. Alternatively they could have been of sewn-plank construction. How far back the tradition goes is uncertain. The representations discussed above are all from the third millennium, but a simplified rock engraving found at Strophylas on Andros, dating to the fourth millennium, appears to show a vessel with a high stern carrying a number of paddlers. As in other parts of Europe, the ready availability of bronze tools would have greatly empowered boatbuilders, enabling them to create larger, lighter craft that could take to the sea, in fair weather making journeys of up to fifty kilometres a day. In such a vessel, in good weather conditions, the open-sea crossing between the Cyclades and Crete could have been made with only two nights spent on the water.

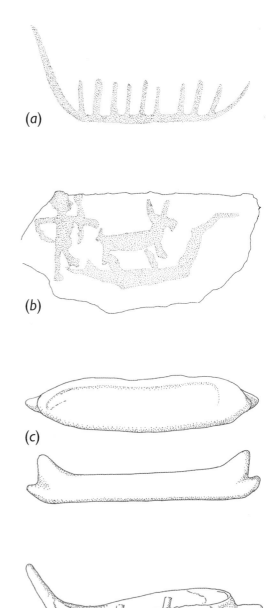

5.16 Various representations of boats from the Aegean: (*a*) rock carving from Strophylas on Andros; (*b*) rock carving from Korphi t'Aroniou on Naxos; (*c*) clay model from Mochlos on Crete; (*d*) clay model from Palaikastro on Crete. All third millennium BC

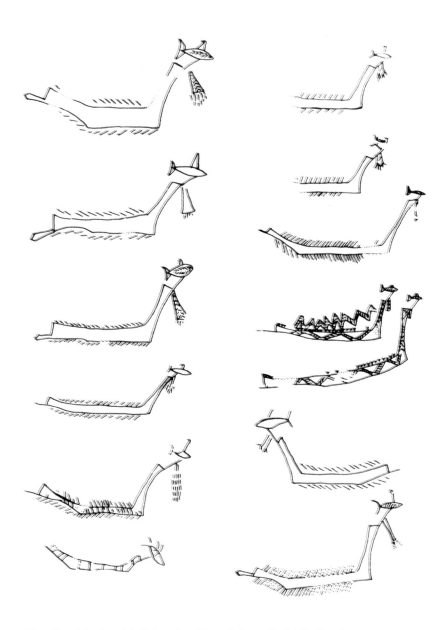

5.17 (*Opposite top*) Lead model of a boat from Naxos dating to the third millennium

5.18 (*Opposite bottom*) Pottery vessels commonly referred to (incorrectly) as frying pans are often decorated with boats depicted against a swirling sea. This example is from the island of Syros

5.19 (*Above*) Drawings of a selection of vessels depicted on 'frying pans'. The striking similarities raise the question of whether it is a particular vessel that is being depicted or an idealized version of a ship

Events in the Near East, 2000–1300 BC

The end of the third millennium saw widespread unrest across the Near East. The causes were many, but the trigger seems to have been a period of climatic oscillation culminating about 2200 BC in a succession of short, very arid phases characterized by low rainfall, leading to depleted rivers and the desertification of some regions which had hitherto been marginally productive. Although more congenial conditions returned soon after 2000 BC, the sudden climatic upsets set in motion a greater mobility in less favoured regions, which impacted on the hitherto more stable states.

In the Nile valley a succession of lower Nile floods undermined what social stability still remained, and in 2125 BC the Old Kingdom collapsed into a chaos of regional rivalries driven by recurrent famines. In Mesopotamia the Akkadian empire fell apart by 2150 BC. A century later the ruler of Ur rose to a brief period of dominance, but this was brought to an end in 2004 BC by an influx of Elamites and Amorites from the borderlands, and once more the region reverted to a patchwork of rival city states in constant conflict with each other. The more distant port cities of Ugarit, Tyre, and Sidon came to a temporary end, the abandonment caused as much by a breakdown of the maritime systems as by regional unrest. Of the Levantine ports only Byblos maintained a tenuous existence. With the return of a more balanced, moister climate after 2000 BC, state systems were once more established. In Egypt the Middle Kingdom came into being in 2055 BC, unified under the eleventh-dynasty pharaohs based at Thebes, and soon began to expand into Lower Nubia. The Middle Kingdom lasted until 1650 BC, when an incursion of the Hyksos, a Semitic people from the Levant, conquered Lower Egypt, but unity was established once more under the New Kingdom in 1550 BC and Egyptian dominance was extended to include the whole of the Levant as far as the Gulf of Iskenderun and the upper Euphrates.

Meanwhile, in Mesopotamia new kingdoms appeared based on Babylon and Ashur in the nineteenth century BC. Later two other powerful states emerged further to the west, the Mitanni, stretching from the Levantine coast to the upper Tigris valley, and the Hittites in central Anatolia. In the mid- and late second millennium these four powerful states together with Egypt acted as competing equals, exchanging correspondence, gifts, and threats. It was an unstable equilibrium that often exploded into open conflict, but what is significant from our point of view is that these mega-states were centres of consumption on a grand scale, avid for ever-increasing supplies of rare raw materials. As their power and their demands grew, so the surrounding territories were drawn ever more closely into the vast trading network which supplied them. So it was that the eastern Mediterranean sea-routes, linking the eastern states to each other and to the Aegean system, developed apace.

The upsurge in trade at the beginning of the second millennium saw the port cities of the Levantine coast, some previously abandoned, re-establish themselves and grow to a new peak of prosperity. They served not only as ports-of-trade between Egypt and the states of Mesopotamia and Anatolia, in the traditional manner, but now showed a more entrepreneurial spirit in opening up networks to the west, drawing the Aegean world into ever-closer trading relations with the east.

Something of the scale of this activity is brought to life by a description of two trading adventurers detailed in the annals of the pharaoh Amenemhat II (reigned 1911–1877 BC) recorded on the Mit Rahina inscription found at Memphis. One expedition returned from the north with 1,554 slaves alongside a cargo of consumer durables. The other, in addition to a small number of captives, brought in a large consignment of Lebanese cedar, seventy-three fig trees, a quantity of silver, bronze, copper, and tin, emery and other grinding sand, decorative stones, oils, resins, and spices. Among the manufactured goods were bronze daggers decorated with gold, silver, and ivory. This expedition, comprising only two ships, was evidently targeted on the Levantine coast.

The imperial venture sponsored by Amenemhat II involved Egyptian ships being sent in the service of the pharaoh, but trade was enacted on various levels, often under the authority of entrepreneurs working out of the port cities. A good illustration of this is provided by a painting in the tomb of the royal official Kenamun, in Thebes, dating to the fourteenth century BC. Here we see a flotilla of Levantine ships docked somewhere along the Nile offloading their goods to their eagerly waiting Egyptian trading partners. The ships differ from vessels of the Old Kingdom in that the masts are now placed nearer midships, which would have enabled them to sail closer to the wind, and the boom was set forward of the mast, making it easier to set the broad sail to give optimum performance. Boatbuilding technology, developed on the Nile, had now been refined to provide ships that could carry large volumes of cargo but had a speed and manoeuvrability that enabled them to outsail predators prowling the sea-lanes.

Minoans and the Wine-Dark Sea

The large island of Crete, closing the southern side of the Aegean Sea, played no significant part in the maritime history of the region until about 2000 BC, when a series of precocious developments in social organization and the appearance of the deep-hulled sailing ship heralded the beginning of the island's dominance of the region through its control of long-distance trading routes. The period from 1950 to 1700 BC, generally referred to as the Protopalatial period, saw the emergence of large nucleated

5.20 Depictions of ships docking and unloading their cargoes from the tomb of Kenamun, Thebes, Egypt, fourteenth century BC. The picture represents the arrival of Levantine merchants

settlements focused on palace complexes which served as administrative, production, and storage centres, as well as providing space for the ceremonies that bound society together. Whether or not they were ruled by kings is a moot point, but at the very least they were places where authority resided and from which the regional population could be coerced into communal behaviour. Some of these centres, like Knossos and Malia on the north coast and Phaistos on the south coast, grew to become major settlements. Knossos at its peak was a hundred hectares in extent, its palace, of 1.3 hectares, being provided with a central court which could accommodate the dispersed population living in villages and farmsteads, who exploited the fertility of the land and returned a tithe on their produce to support the palace economy.

About 1700 BC the island was gripped by a devastating earthquake, which caused extensive damage, but the palaces were quickly rebuilt, heralding the Neopalatial period, which was to last until 1450 BC. During this time several new palatial centres were established, including Khania in the west of the island and Zakros in the east.

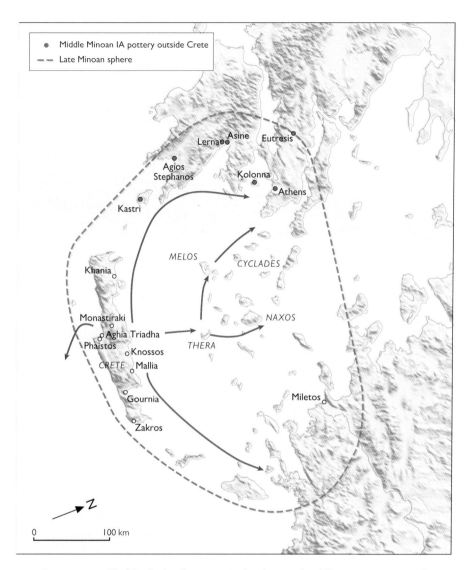

5.21 The Minoan world of the third millennium. The distribution of Middle Minoan IA pottery shows a limited connectivity in the Late Pre-Palatial period (*c.*2100–*c.*1950 BC), but in the early second millennium the Minoans had begun to establish wider networks embracing the southern Aegean

About 1450 there was an episode of widespread destruction when the palaces were extensively damaged by fire. In the Final Palatial period which followed, only Knossos survived, continuing to dominate the island until about 1375 BC.

The complex society responsible for building and maintaining the palatial complexes developed from indigenous origins, but there can be little doubt that the growth

5.22 The Minoan 'palace' of Malia on Crete lies close to the sea. Its rooms were arranged around a large central court

of maritime trade after 2000 BC, which drew Crete into the eastern Mediterranean networks, was a contributing factor in its spectacular success. In the scrabble for rare raw materials among the Near Eastern states, Crete was ideally sited, providing a convenient island base on the interface between the Levant and Egypt on the one hand and the Aegean and Europe on the other. The most dramatic sign of the expanding networks was the appearance of the deep-hulled sailing ship in Cretan waters. No trace of actual vessels has yet been found, but depictions on Minoan seal-stones show that they were now a feature of Cretan culture. Ships of this type were vastly superior to the Cycladic canoe. Sail power meant that fewer rowers were required, thus increasing carrying capacity, which was further enhanced by the deep plank-built hull. Moreover, a lightly manned sailing ship carrying its own supplies could remain at sea for much longer periods, allowing more ambitious voyages to be undertaken. The introduction of the deep-hulled sailing ship to Crete, probably from the Levant and Egypt, was avidly seized on by the Cretan elites. It enabled them to take control of the seas and to become a significant trading partner with their Near Eastern peers.

The growth of Minoan sea-power can be charted through the distribution of Minoan pottery and other artefacts found throughout the eastern Mediterranean.

In the Protopalatial period a Minoan enclave was established at Kastri on Kythera, the settlers not only using their own pottery but burning their dead in their own distinctive way and worshipping at a peak sanctuary as they had been used to in Crete. Kythera formed an important node on the western sea-route linking Crete to the Peloponnese and Attica beyond. Minoan finds at Agios Stefanos in Lakonia and at Lerna in the Argolid indicate the mainland ports frequented by the Cretan traders, while Minoan pottery found on the islands of Thera, Melos, and Kea reflects something of the texture of the maritime networks developing at this time. Among the many resources being sought by these entrepreneurs silver from the mines of Lavrion in Attica would have been a prime attraction. An eastern route via the islands of Kasos and Karpathos led naturally to the Dodecanese and the mainland of Asia Minor. Both islands have produced Protopalatial pottery. On Rhodes there seem to have been Minoan enclaves at the settlements of Ialyssos and Trianda, while on the mainland Minoan traders had already discovered the attraction of Miletos. Although these networks had begun to form in the Prepalatial times, it was in the Protopalatial period, following the revival of eastern Mediterranean trade after 2000 BC, that they developed apace.

The eastern and western routes linking Crete to the Greek mainland and to Asia Minor created what we can regard as the inner core of Minoan maritime activity, but there is ample evidence to show that the Minoans were now beginning to take part in the larger networks serving Egypt, the Levant, and the southern Turkish coast—the gyratory system of anti-clockwise movement conditioned by the sea currents and the winds. The principal indicator of this trade is the distribution of Minoan pottery, particularly the brightly painted Kamares Ware, which was admired and copied in Egypt and the Levant. Protopalatial pottery has been found in reasonable quantity in many far-flung places, at Lahun on the edge of the Fayum Depression in Egypt, at the Levantine ports of Ugarit, Byblos, and Beirut, and on Cyprus. Some of the more elaborate forms will have been transported for their own sake as high-value, low-bulk goods alongside more bulky cargoes of less archaeologically visible commodities such as woollen fabrics, olive oil, wine, scented oils, ointments, medicinal herbs, and timber—all known to have been in high demand in Egypt, a demand that Crete could supply in plenty.

In the Neopalatial period Minoan overseas trade intensified. On the Greek mainland the Mycenaean elite consumed quantities of Minoan luxury goods in their elaborate burial rituals, most notably in the shaft graves at Mycenae dating from between 1650 and 1500 BC. On the Asia Minor mainland the colony of Miletos flourished, while Minoan influence on the Aegean islands increased, particularly in the thriving towns that were now developing on Melos, Kea, and Thera.

3.23 Kamares ware jug from the palace of Phaistos in Crete, eighteenth century BC

Trade with Egypt and the Levant continued to grow, and there are frequent references to people from 'Keftiu', thought to be Crete, in the Egyptian sources. The annals of Tuthmosis III (reigned 1479–1425 BC) mentions ships from Keftiu in Levantine ports loaded with poles, great trees, and masts en route to Egypt. While it is possible that the ships' masters were engaging in cabotage, picking up Levantine timber and carrying it to Egypt, it is equally possible that their cargo originated in Crete, where excellent wood, especially cypress, was available in quantity. Tomb paintings of the same period depicted men from Keftiu, along with Canaanites, Mesopotamians, and Nubians, carrying vases of gold and silver, elephants' tusks, bolts of cloth and oxhide, and ingots of copper as tribute to the pharaoh. This was the time when the rulers of the Near Eastern states demonstrated their power by expecting and receiving tribute from their peers and supplicants. That the Minoans were now a part of the system shows that the palatial elites of Crete had become significant players in the world of high politics.

We have little indication of how the maritime expeditions were organized. The probability is that they were controlled by the Minoan aristocracy, who supplied the goods to be dispatched and expected a return on their investment. They may even have owned the ships. But over the course of time a class of ship-owning middlemen may have emerged—the merchant venturers of the Minoan era—able to mount expeditions of their own and to engage in coastal cabotage. Nor should we forget that Levantine and Egyptian vessels may have sailed to Crete. The archaeological evidence provides the broad patterns of engagement but seldom lets us into the life of the merchants and their ships' masters to share their anxieties, their fears, and their commercial triumphs.

It has long been evident, from engraved Minoan gemstones, that by 2000 BC the Minoan seafarers, like their contemporaries throughout the eastern Mediterranean, were using deep-hulled sailing ships. In 1972, during the excavation of the town of Akrotiri on Thera, another remarkable source of maritime imagery was found painted on the walls of a building called the West House. Akrotiri was buried in ash following the eruption of the volcano that had given form to the island. There has been much debate about the date of the eruption. The traditional approach, based largely upon a

5.24 Painting on the wall of the tomb of the vizier Rekhmire at Thebes, showing Aegeans, probably Minoans, bringing a range of exotic offerings for the pharaoh. The tomb is of the eighteenth dynasty, late second millennium BC

typological consideration of the pottery, suggests a date in the late sixteenth century, but radiocarbon dating, backed by dendrochronology and ice core studies, points to the second half of the seventeenth century. Although the matter is by no means resolved, the older date seems the more likely. In either case the destruction of Akrotiri came during the Neopalatial period in Crete.

The maritime wall paintings in the West House were found on the north and south walls of room 5. The south frieze depicts eighteen vessels, both ships and boats, sailing between two towns. The north frieze has nine vessels sailing offshore, either engaged in a sea-battle or supporting sponge divers, such is the fragmentary nature of the scene. Needless to say, there has been a great deal of speculation about the interpretation of the two compositions, but what is important for us is the detail they give of shipping in the Neopalatial period and of the variety of the vessels in use. The basic ship depicted had a plank-built hull estimated to be between 18 and 35 metres long, with a high prow and a cabin at the stern for the captain, in front of which one or two steersmen plied their oars. The central part of the ship was occupied by a raised structure, which gave shelter to passengers but probably also served as a storage area for the boom, yard, and sail when the central mast was unstepped. Some of the ships are shown with the mast stepped in position and one

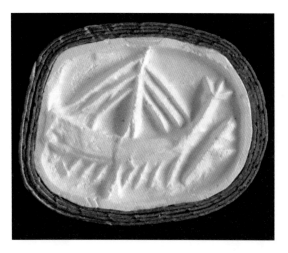

5.25 Cast of a seal-stone of Minoan date from Crete showing a vessel with a mast to take a sail, dating to *c.*2000 BC. This would seem to represent the appearance of deeper-hulled sailing vessels in the Aegean for the first time

has the sail rigged. When the sail was stowed, propulsion would have been by paddling or rowing.

The ships of Akrotiri appear to have been designed to serve multiple purposes. For trading journeys, with the mast stepped and sail rigged, they would have needed only small crews, leaving ample space for cargo. For shorter journeys requiring speed and manoeuvrability the mast would have been unstepped and stored together with the sail and yards, leaving space for rowers or paddlers. In such a mode they would have been ready for inter-island journeys and raiding. There were also occasions when, decked out with garlands, they could have carried dignitaries in regattas, as would appear to be the case with some of the ships appearing in the Akrotiri murals. Enigmatic though these maritime scenes are (and will probably remain), they provide a remarkable insight into the highly flexible vessels available to Aegean sailors in the second millennium.

The Periphery Takes Over

By the middle of the second millennium the Minoans were in command of the southern Aegean seaways. The geographical position of Crete and the skills of the Minoans as shipbuilders and seamen meant that they could serve as middlemen between the consuming states of the Near East and the productive periphery of the Balkans and the rest of the European peninsula beyond. By manipulating these interchanges the Minoans could benefit by acquiring what they most needed: gold, silver, copper, and tin as well as other small luxuries like decorative stones for making vessels and adornments. But systems of this kind are inherently unstable, and so it was for the Minoans.

One of the Minoans' main trading partners on the European interface was a group of Bronze Age polities on the Greek mainland whose centres of power were focused at Pylos, Tiryns, Mycenae, Athens, Thebes, Gla, Orchomenos, and Iolkos. These communities shared a broadly similar culture and are called by archaeologists Mycenaeans. In the Hittite texts the Mycenaeans are called the Akhijawa, though the Egyptians seem to refer to some of the people as coming from the country known as Tanaja. Mycenaean society was competitive and warlike, though if the Homeric epics are a fair reflection of this period, the leaders could form alliances and work together for a common cause, with Mycenae in command.

198

5.26 One of the scenes from a remarkable set of wall paintings preserved in the West House of Akrotiri, on Thera, by volcanic eruption in the mid-second millennium BC. The scene appears to depict a procession of ships approaching the harbour of a town, where the expectant inhabitants are waiting

Sometime about 1450 BC all the Cretan palace centres were destroyed except Knossos, and even there, there were traces of burning in the surrounding town. In the aftermath of this island-wide event, Knossos continued as the sole centre of authority but with a distinct change of culture. Most significant was the introduction of a new script from the Mycenaean world, Linear B, using the Greek language and replacing the Minoan Linear A script, which had transcribed the original local non-Greek language. At the same time, other aspects of Mycenaean material culture and lifestyle become evident. The simplest explanation for these observations is that the Mycenaean elite overcame the Minoan leaders and unified the island. There are, however, alternatives. It could be argued that natural disasters or internal conflict (or both) brought the old, fragmented system to an end, after which commercial contacts with Mycenae intensified. The change of script and of the language of administration, however, suggest that the Mycenaean presence was soon dominant.

From the middle of the second millennium the Mycenaeans assumed control of the maritime networks in the Aegean and further developed trading links with states surrounding the eastern Mediterranean. The Minoan trading colony at Miletos was taken over and there was now a Mycenaean presence at Ephesos, while settlements developed on Rhodes and Kos, strengthening connections with Aegean Turkey and the Hittite state. Further afield large quantities of Mycenaean pottery are found on Cyprus, which had become an important supplier of copper, and a Mycenaean presence is evident at the major Levantine ports. Trade with the area is also demonstrated by the quantities of Canaanite transport amphorae used to carry wine and oil from sea ports such as Ugarit to the Aegean and mainland Greece. Other commodities brought back to the Mycenaean courts from the east include glass beads and, more rarely,

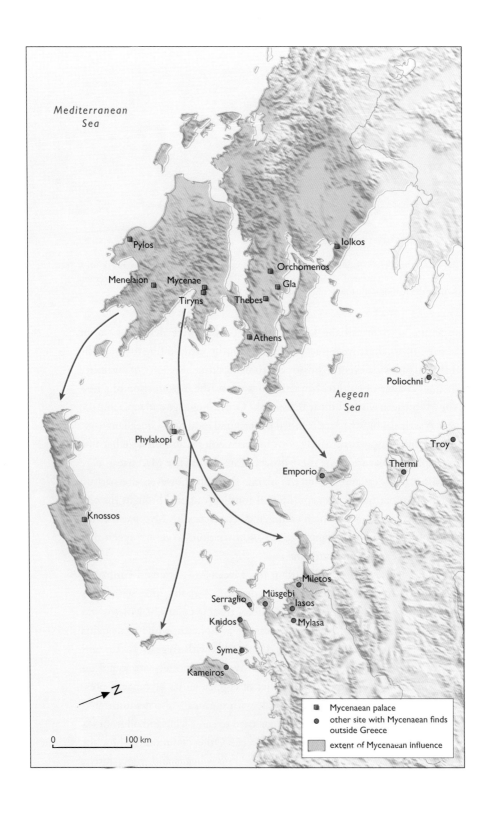

Mediterranean
Sea

Pylos

Menelaion   Mycenae
              Tiryns   Thebes

                                    Orchomenos
                                         Gla

Iolkos

Athens

Aegean
Sea

Poliochni

Phylakopi

Emporio

Troy

Thermi

Knossos

Miletos

Müsgebi

Serraglio   Iasos

Knidos   Mylasa

Syme

Kameiros

N

0   100 km

■ Mycenaean palace
● other site with Mycenaean finds
   outside Greece
   extent of Mycenaean influence

Mesopotamian cylinder seals like the collection of mainly lapis lazuli seals found in the palace of Thebes.

Direct trade with Egypt also flourished. Mycenaean pottery has been found at some fifty sites in Egypt. Memphis on the Nile probably continued to be a main port of entry, but ports like Marsa Matruh and its offshore Bates's Island were used, as was the nearby fortified port of Zawiyet, both lying on the North African coast three hundred kilometres west of the delta, conveniently placed to be the first ports of call for ships sailing south from Crete. There are some hints that Egyptians were also making journeys to Crete and to mainland Greece. One of the Linear B tablets from Knossos mentions 'Aiguptios' ('the Egyptian'), and it would seem that Amenhotep III (reigned 1390–1352 BC) sent a diplomatic or trade mission to visit the powerful Mycenaean centres. The evidence for this comes from an inscription in the pharaoh's mortuary temple at Kom el-Hetan, which lists the places visited by the mission, among them Knossos, Mycenae, and Troy. Could it be that the nine faience plaques with the cartouche of Amenhotep III found at Mycenae were a diplomatic gift made by the Egyptian ambassadors?

In the second half of the second millennium the Aegean and the eastern Mediterranean were alive with ships setting out from the Mycenaean world, Egypt, the Levant, and Cyprus, the sailors meeting up in the many cosmopolitan ports there to tell stories about distant journeys and the riches to be gained. In this way sea lore—the best routes to navigate, how to approach a difficult harbour, and sea-marks to look out for—would have been shared. And in the various harbours cargoes could be assembled to carry to the next port in a cycle of cabotage.

A rare insight into the complexity of trade at this time is provided by the remarkable shipwreck found at Uluburun close to Kaş on the southern Turkish coast. The bulk of the cargo was made up of ten tonnes of copper ingots in the shape of oxhides and one tonne of tin ingots, 175 blocks of cobalt blue and turquoise glass, and 145 Canaanite jars once containing, among other things, oil, wine, and terebinth resin. There was also a large quantity of Cypriot pottery. Among this high-bulk, high-weight cargo were smaller packages of raw materials: elephant and hippopotamus ivory, logs of African blockwood, ostrich eggs, textiles, items of gold, silver, and tin for recycling, and food including figs, olives, grapes, almonds, and pomegranates augmented by fresh fish, evidenced by fishing tackle. Other smaller items included cylinder seals, scarabs, amber, musical instruments, two Mycenaean daggers, and several sets of balance weights conforming to different metric standards, presumably to facilitate trade

5.27 (*Opposite*) The Mycenaean world of mainland Greece and the expansion of Mycenaean influence to the southern Aegean by the fourteenth century BC

in different ports. It is an astonishing haul giving an incomparable insight into trade about 1300 BC, when the ship was driven onto a lee shore and perished. Inevitably it has occasioned much debate. Was the cargo a diplomatic gift en route to a king or was it an eclectic cargo assembled by a wealthy merchant to offload wherever he found a likely market? And where did the ship originate? The bulk of the cargo might suggest that it came from the Levantine coast or from Cyprus, but it could have been built elsewhere and have offloaded its cargo in a Cypriot or Levantine port before taking on local goods. Similarly, its crew could have been recruited or augmented anywhere around the eastern Mediterranean. Maritime trade had now become internationalized.

The vessel itself was quite small, about 15–16 metres long and 5 metres broad. Comparatively little of the hull has been exposed but enough to show that there was a keel plank roughly square in section and several side planks of cedar-wood fastened with oak mortise and tenon joints set within the thickness of the planks and locked in position with pegs. Mortise and tenon joints are known in Egyptian vessels but

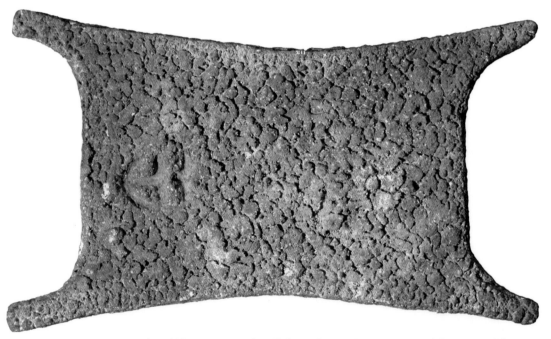

5.28 An oxhide copper ingot from Enkomi, Cyprus. Cyprus was one of the most prolific sources of copper in the late second millennium BC. The shape of the ingot may have been designed for ease of handling

5.29 (*Opposite*) Oxhide copper ingots from Cyprus were exported widely throughout the eastern and central Mediterranean in the late second millennium. Two shipwrecks carrying ingots have been found off the coast of southern Turkey, at Cape Gelidonya and Uluburun. From the cargo found with the Uluburun wreck it is possible to suggest the route that such vessels may have taken

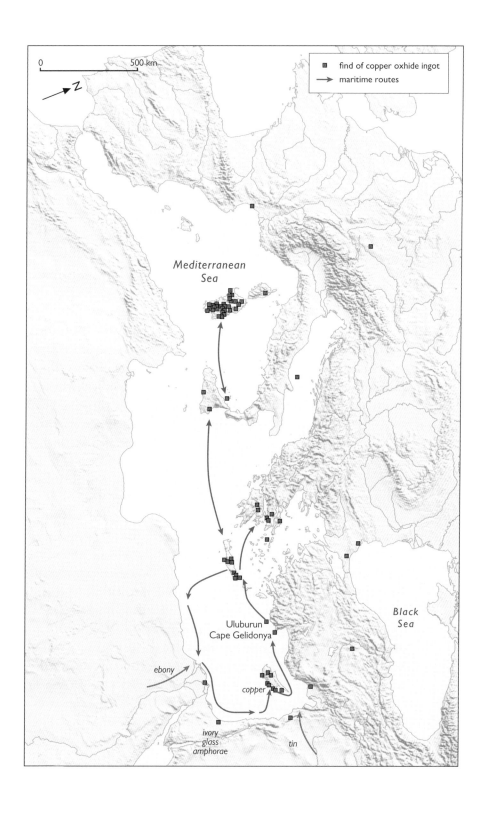

find of copper oxhide ingot

maritime routes

Mediterranean
Sea

Black
Sea

Uluburun
Cape Gelidonya

ebony

copper

ivory
glass
amphorae

tin

0   500 km

N

without the locking device. The ship was provided with oars, of which fragments survive. It would also have had a sail, but no trace of the mast or mast-step has been uncovered. Two other shipwrecks of the late second millennium are known, both dating to about 1200 BC. One, sunk off Cape Gelidonya on the south coast of Turkey, like the Uluburun vessel, has planks joined with locked mortice and tenon joints. It carried a mixed cargo, including thirty-nine copper oxhide ingots. The second wreck sank in the Gulf of Argos off Point Iria. The bulk of its cargo was made up of pottery transport vessels from Cyprus, Crete, and the Mycenaean world. While hardly comparable to the Uluburun vessel, the two later wrecks reflect the variety of goods in transit and the very cosmopolitan nature of the cargoes.

New Centres, New Peripheries

The internationalism of the eastern Mediterranean and the Aegean and the intense connectivity of the different states and polities contrast dramatically with the situation in the central Mediterranean, where a far more insular mood prevailed, the disparate polities tending to look in on themselves and away from the sea. It was almost as though they were relishing their remoteness, enhancing it by developing highly distinctive architectural forms: the temples of Malta, the nuraghi (stone-built megalithic towers) of Sardinia, the statue menhirs of Corsica, and the talayots (stone towers) of Majorca, each proclaiming an identity to differentiate themselves from the 'other'. This is not to say that sea travel was excluded but simply that there is little archaeological evidence to suggest that maritime connectivity, overseas trade, and the interactions that ensued were much of a social imperative. As a result communities remained small and devoted their energies to self-defence.

Soon after 1600 BC this began to change as entrepreneurs from the Mycenaean world started to explore the Tyrrhenian Sea and the Adriatic. One of the earliest of their landfalls was Lipari in the Aeolian islands. The attraction here might have been a ready supply of alum, much in demand in cloth manufacture for fixing dye and for curing leather, and it may be no coincidence that alum is mentioned in the Linear B tablets found in the Mycenaean palaces of Pylos and Tyrins. From Lipari seafarers could access much of the Tyrrhenian Sea, using the island as a convenient base from which to explore and also a place to regroup before returning home to the east. It was not long before landings were being made on the little island of Vivara in the Bay of Naples, situated between Ischia and the mainland. From Vivara it was an easy voyage along the Italian coast to reach Etruria with its rich metal resources. Etruria was also connected overland to the Po valley, which received quantities of the much-desired amber, a fossilized resin extracted along the Baltic coasts and traded across Europe and through the Alpine passes. Much of the amber used in the rich graves in the Mycenaean world was probably acquired in this way, either directly from Etruria or from Sicily, to which it may have been carried by local shipping. By the fourteenth century trade had intensified. A port-of-trade was established at Scoglio del Tonno near Taranto in southern Italy. Later, new bases were being developed at Thapsos on the west coast of Sicily, and Antigori not far from Cagliari on the south coast of Sardinia, while an early landfall at Roca Vecchia on the heel of Italy became the favoured first port of call for those preferring to take the coastal route up the coast of Epirus and across the Strait of Otranto rather than the open-sea route directly to Sicily.

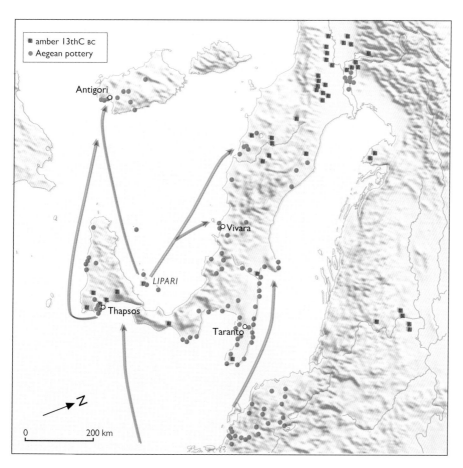

5.30 The central Mediterranean in the late second millennium at the time when the Mycenaeans were extending their trading activity to the west. One of the attractions of the area was that amber from the Baltic traded southwards through the Alpine passes was available to traders in the Tyrrhenian Sea

With the intensification of contact after 1400 BC bringing increasing quantities of Aegean pottery, together with glass, ivory, and figurines, to the central Mediterranean, Cypriot pottery began to make an appearance, suggesting that other entrepreneurs from the eastern Mediterranean may now have been moving in on the market. Judging by the concentration of Cypriot finds, it was to Sardinia that they were most attracted, developing close relations with the island in the twelfth and eleventh centuries. It was Cypriot entrepreneurs who introduced copper oxhide ingots to Sardinia, together with Cypriot toolkits and technologies that contributed to the development of the indigenous copper production. Technology transfer on this scale suggests much more than simple trade: skilled workers from the eastern Mediterranean must now have settled on the island. Similar processes are also implied by the local production of Mycenaean-style pottery and bronzes on Sicily. What began as voyages of exploration in the sixteenth century soon developed into regular cycles of trading, most likely with the eastern ships arriving and departing at about the same times of year on an annual basis. But by the thirteenth century things had changed. Enclaves of traders and tech-nicians had now been set up at the main ports of Italy, Sicily, and Sardinia. It was a prelude to the large-scale colonial movements that were to grip the Mediterranean in the ninth and eighth centuries.

What all this meant for the development and spread of ship technology we can only speculate. Although there is little evidence for extensive maritime activity among the indigenous communities of the central Mediterranean in the third and early second millennia, local boats were certainly in use for fishing and for short-haul journeys. The appearance of eastern Mediterranean deep-hulled sailing ships and the establish-ment of regular trading cycles with the east would have had a significant impact on the local communities. On the one hand it would have introduced them to radically new types of vessel, and on the other it would have led to an intensification of local networks of production and distribution. The overall effect on the Tyrrhenians would have been increased connectivity and the introduction of new technologies, including shipbuilding.

Going West

The Mycenaean and Cypriot presence around the Tyrrhenian Sea in the late second millennium raises the inevitable question of whether a few of the more enterprising sailors might have been drawn to explore the western Mediterranean and beyond, and, if so, whether any archaeological evidence survives. The human spirit of adven-ture being what it is, it would be surprising if no one had ventured beyond Sardinia.

The direct archaeological evidence is, however, sparse, but two shards of undoubtedly Mycenaean pottery of the period 1300–1250 BC were recorded during the excavation of a settlement at Montoro in the valley of the Guadalquivir in Andalucía, together with plain wheel-turned pottery which may also have been imported. How the alien pots reached the heart of Andalucía we shall never know, but perhaps they were offloaded at a port on the southern Iberian coast and traded across the Sierra Nevada.

Another source of potential evidence is provided by the Iberian rock paintings and rock engravings showing ships. One intriguing scene, painted on a cave wall at Laja Alta in the uplands of the province of Cádiz, shows seven ships, some with masts and sails and others with oars. One of the vessels seems to have been docked within a rectangular harbour. The problem with such scenes is that they are without direct dating. Various opinions have been put forward arguing that the scene belongs to the late second or early first millennium, though whether it precedes the arrival of the Phoenicians in the west in the tenth century is uncertain. Several writers have argued for a late second-millennium date, pointing to similarities with eastern Mediterranean vessels, in particular with Egyptian reed-bundle boats with triangular sails.

A more convincing depiction of an eastern Mediterranean ship was found at Oia near Pontevedra on the west coast of Galicia. It is part of a rock carving which also depicts quadrupeds, possibly deer, in a style that belongs to the end of the second millennium. The vessel has a high prow and stern with a central mast braced with rigging. It is highly reminiscent of images of Aegean vessels. This similarity, and the discovery of what is claimed to be a Mycenaean glass bead at an open settlement nearby, have led some writers to argue for a Mycenaean origin.

These ship images are tantalizing. They could well represent the response of local people to the appearance of Mycenaean sailing ships in Atlantic waters. There is nothing unreasonable in supposing that a few spirited adventurers from the Aegean found the lure of the west irresistible and braved the Strait of Gibraltar as early as the thirteenth and twelfth centuries to return with stories of an El Dorado rich in gold, copper, and tin. While the

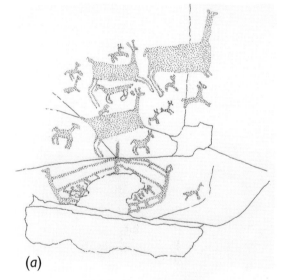

(a)

(b)

5.31 (a) Rock engraving of a sailing ship found at Santa María de Oia, Pontevedra, in Galicia. (b) Rock painting of a sailing vessel from the rock shelter of Laja Alta, Cádiz. Both are undated but are probably from the second millennium

evidence currently available does not prove that such journeys did take place, future discoveries may provide more convincing data.

Travellers' Tales

Those Mycenaean seamen, later joined by Cypriots, who set out to explore the west were making journeys into the unknown. The actual journeys were not particularly adventurous. By sailing up the west coast of Greece to Corfu or just beyond, it required only a short sea-crossing of eighty kilometres to reach the port of Roca Vecchia. From there to the Strait of Messina the journey could be made in sight of land with as many stop-overs as necessary. From Messina journeys to Thapsos in Sicily or to Lipari were comparatively short hauls. Once the new geography was learned, the more direct open-sea route across the Ionian Sea to Sicily became a possibility, and from there the more adventurous could make for Sardinia, crossing more than three hundred kilometres of open water. Over the generations sailing instructions passed on orally will have made the journeys safer and success more assured, but even then these western ventures must have been regarded with awe and respect by those hearing the stories of them at home. The few who sailed even further west into the unknown and returned to tell the tale must have been regarded as heroes.

Stories of all these expeditions to the Tyrrhenian Sea and to the far west, embellished with ever more fanciful detail, would have been told and retold endlessly in the Mycenaean courts, the different tales crystallizing around the names of select heroes to make memorizing and retelling easier. And so it was that the realities of late second-millennium exploration passed into first-millennium myth, formalized in the tales of Jason and the Argonauts, Herakles and his labours, and the long homeward journey of Odysseus. These are, of course, composite sagas with complex geographies, but echoes of the west are there to be heard. The Tyrrhenian Sea features large, with Scylla and Charybdis most likely symbolizing the Strait of Messina; further west there is the Land of Geryon in southern Iberia with the Strait of Gibraltar flanked by the Pillars of Herakles; and beyond, the realms of the Hesperides, guardians of the golden apples. Homer and the other unnamed poets who composed the epics made good use of these early travellers' tales, conjuring up all the fear and wonder which the original pioneers must daily have experienced.

6

Exploring the Ends of the World, 1200–600 BC

The six centuries from 1200 to 600 BC saw the ancient world transformed. In the Aegean and the eastern end of the Mediterranean the stable maritime networks that had been building up for centuries fragmented during the twelfth century into a chaos of piracy, raiding, and mass mobility, with many players—new names and new people—taking to the seas to pursue their individual needs and aspirations, bringing them into direct confrontation with the old order. To the Egyptians these were the 'sea peoples', a ragbag of barbarians who threatened the stability of the state. The Levantine polities suffered too. Here economic stability and the arrival of new people changed everything, while further west the Mycenaean world collapsed, heralding the Greek 'dark age', with some groups of Mycenaeans moving to Cyprus to settle.

Along the Atlantic façade of Europe quite different forces were at work. The maritime connectivity which saw the Beaker phenomenon spread out from Portugal and set in train the exploitation of the rich metal resources of the ocean fringes at the end of the third millennium continued to hold together those living within reach of the sea, neighbours engaging with neighbours in cycles of exchange embedded deeply in social well-being. In this way, even though the discrete groups maintained their individuality, their various beliefs, values, and behaviours, as well as artefacts, spread along the seaways throughout the second millennium until, by the twelfth century, the similarities were such that archaeologists refer to the maritime zone stretching from

Iberia to the Shetlands as belonging to the Atlantic Bronze Age community. Similar phenomena can be observed around the southern North Sea and the Baltic.

Out of the twelfth-century turmoil which so changed the central and eastern Mediterranean the Egyptians, protected by the surrounding deserts, survived largely unshaken. There was also a resurgence among the port cities of the Levant coast, whose inhabitants are from here on referred to by the Greek world as Phoenicians, while in Greece itself and along the Aegean coast of Asia Minor a number of city states began to develop, many of them owing their growing strength to their command of the sea.

The Phoenician port cities of the Levant, with little hinterland to develop, looked outward to the Mediterranean. They continued to provide the link between Egypt and the Mesopotamian states, but increasingly they became the suppliers of raw materials to their powerful eastern neighbours. Their entrepreneurial skills were remarkable. Some founded enclaves on Cyprus, from where they will have learned much about the central maritime network; by the tenth century they were sailing the length of the Mediterranean, venturing out through the Strait of Gibraltar to set up trading colonies along the Atlantic coasts of Morocco and Portugal. Not long after, in the eighth century, some of the more enterprising Greek city states were following in their wake, though they were content at first to restrict themselves to the Tyrrhenian Sea while making the Black Sea their own. During the pioneering days of the eighth and seventh centuries Phoenicians and Greeks seem to have worked the seas in comparative harmony, restricting themselves to their own spheres of interest but able to share harbours when necessary. It is also likely that they were prepared to carry cargoes of any origin, which makes their activities difficult to untangle using only archaeological evidence.

By 600 BC the western Mediterranean had been thoroughly incorporated into the greater Mediterranean system. Settlers from the Greek city of Phokaia in Asia Minor had just founded their colony of Massalia (Marseille) as a prelude to establishing a wider Greek presence around the Golfe du Lion, thereby threatening the overseas enterprises of the Etruscans of northern Italy. Meanwhile, in the Tyrrhenian Sea, Phoenician, Greek, and Etruscan interests were now beginning to compete. The crystallizing of commercial realms and the aspirations of the principal players were soon to lead to conflict.

Meanwhile, along the Atlantic façade the old Bronze Age unity began to fall apart. The Phoenician presence from the tenth century drew North Africa and Iberia into the Mediterranean sphere, weakening traditional contacts across the Bay of Biscay, and, with the gradual demise of bronze as iron became increasingly available, the old long-distance routes sank into abeyance. From about 600 BC Ireland, Brittany, and Britain began to develop in their own distinctive ways.

These six crucial centuries of European history briefly summarized, we can now turn to the detail.

Between the Two Seas

A convenient place to begin is in southern Spain in the estuary of the Odiel and Tinto rivers, dominated today by the modern port city of Huelva. About 1000 BC the topography of the region was very different. Over the past three thousand years since then, huge quantities of silt carried by the rivers have clogged the ancient channels, building land where once there was open water. Originally the two rivers flowed in wide inlets, creating a navigable estuary eight kilometres across, divided by a promontory upon which the prehistoric settlement was located. Apart from having an excellent sheltered harbour the great attraction of the location was that it commanded the two major river routes leading from the metal-rich hinterland to the sea. The Rio Tinto gets its name from its red colour, caused by iron salts washed out of the mineral lodes through which it flows, and in more recent times has given its name to the world-famous metal-producing conglomerate. The historical importance of the location lies in the ancient settlement and its cemetery occupying the promontory beneath the modern city and on a large collection of Late Bronze Age bronzes found when the harbour was being deepened in 1923.

The Huelva hoard, as it is frequently called, was collected over a period of some weeks while the river Odiel was being dredged. More than four hundred items were recovered, including seventy-eight swords, twenty-two short-swords or daggers, eighty-eight spearheads, thirty-five tubular spear butts, fragments of two peaked helmets, and other small objects, including fibulae (small brooches) of eastern Mediterranean origin, belt hooks, and horse-gear. The nature of the deposit has been much debated. Some regard it as deriving from a shipwreck, while others prefer to think of it as a votive hoard thrown on a single occasion into the river. Another possibility is that it was, indeed, a votive deposit but resulted from more than one act of dedication spread over a period of time. Radiocarbon dates from wood still preserved in the sockets of some of the spearheads cluster around 950 BC, suggesting that deposition is best dated to the tenth century.

A number of the swords found in the collection belong to a highly distinctive form known as carp's-tongue swords of the Huelva type, characterized by a heavy slashing blade with a long, narrow, pointed end, combining the style of the typical Atlantic slashing sword with the thrusting rapier more common in the Mediterranean. The distribution of these swords concentrates in southern Spain, suggesting local

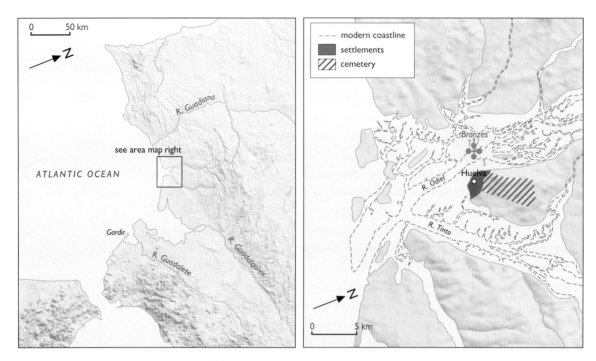

6.1 The port of Huelva is located on a promontory at the confluence of the rivers Odiel and Tinto. In recent times there has been much silting of the estuary. The Tartessian city occupied the southern end of the promontory overlooking the deep-water harbour

manufacture, perhaps in the region around Huelva, but they were also to be found along the Atlantic network to Galicia and to north-western France. Such dating evidence as there is suggests that they developed in the early tenth century. It was in north-western France, probably in the Loire valley, that local swordsmiths made their own version of the Spanish originals, referred to as the Nantes type, which were widely spread across north-western France and south-eastern England in the period 950–875 BC. Some reached as far as the Rhine, a few finding their way south along the sea-route to southern Iberia. The vitality of the Atlantic networks at this time is also shown by the distribution of Irish basal-looped spearheads, which are found widely across Britain and north-western France, while a number reached Galicia; the type is also present in the Huelva collection.

Links with the Mediterranean are also evident in the deposit. The crested helmet fragments are a southern Iberian type, examples of which are found in Sardinia and northern Italy, while the elbow brooches found in some number at Huelva also turn up on sites in Cyprus and the Levant. Huelva, then, is the linchpin that joins the Atlantic system to that of the Mediterranean.

The modern city of Huelva grew up over the prehistoric settlement, which, by the end of the seventh century BC, had reached about twenty hectares in extent. Archaeological traces of it have been found at several locations. At one site, the Plaza de las Monjas, rescue excavation carried out in advance of building work examined layers going back to the first half of the seventh century BC, but the water table prevented careful excavation of the lower levels. These had to be removed mechanically by the contractors, while archaeologists screened the sand and silts dug out in order to recover artefacts. From deposits between five and six metres below the water table they were able to collect a remarkable haul of material which has entirely revolutionized our understanding of the earliest phases of settlement. More than half the pottery recovered was local handmade ware, but nearly 40 per cent of the total was Phoenician, closely comparable to pottery found in the Phoenician city of Tyre at the eastern end of the Mediterranean. Among the rest of the collection there were smaller quantities (seventy-three sherds in all) coming from Attica and Euboea or the Cyclades, and from Cyprus, Sardinia, and northern Italy. Clearly, Phoenician entrepreneurs were prominent among the settlers and, indeed, it was probably they who introduced the other foreign pots, acquiring them from ports visited along the route from the Levant. On typological grounds the pottery dates to the tenth century and the first half of the ninth. Three radiocarbon dates from the deposit lie between 1000 and 820 BC, with the weighted average being in the middle of the tenth century. Thus, the earliest settlement evidence so far recovered from Huelva is broadly contemporary with the date of the bronzes deposited in the estuary. It is important to remember, however, that the early settlement deposits need not represent a short phase of occupation but may have accumulated over a period of time throughout the tenth and early ninth centuries.

The other finds recovered from the settlement deposit are no less remarkable. There is extensive evidence for metalworking in the form of furnaces and tuyères (nozzles for directing the heat from bellows), crucibles for copper smelting, and stone moulds for casting, as well as detritus from processing silver, lead, tin, and iron. Other activities include woodworking, shipbuilding, and the working of ivory, bone, and ostrich eggs, while the presence of murex shells suggests that reddish-purple dye may have been extracted from them. Farming is attested by the usual farmyard animals and cereals as well as wine grapes and figs. A range of sea-fish was also much in evidence. The discovery of an amphora with fish-scales sticking to the interior hints at the salting of fish or the manufacture of fish sauce. Finally, to remind us that this was a commercial emporium, four lead weights were found which conform to the Near Eastern system of shekels. Thus, we have a picture of the thriving cosmopolitan port as it was in the tenth century at the time when traders from the eastern end of the Mediterranean were just beginning to establish commercial relations with the metal-rich west.

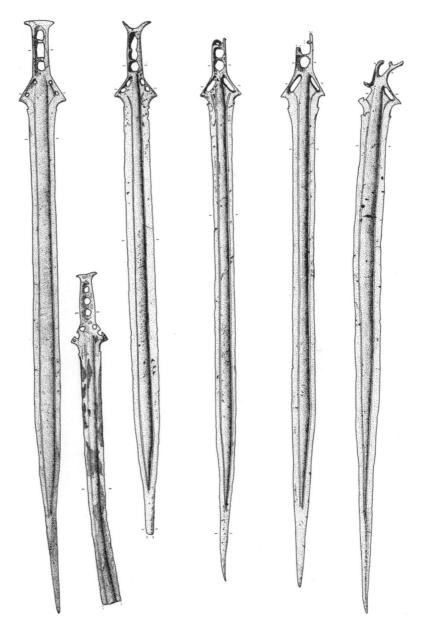

6.2 Carp's-tongue swords from the river Odiel at Huelva formed a major part of the collection of bronze items dredged from the river

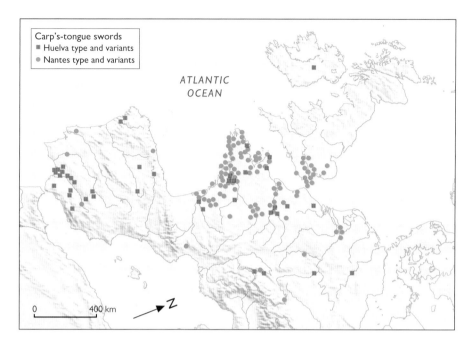

6.3 In the Final Atlantic Bronze Age the distinctive carp's-tongue sword was popular. The earliest examples were made in south-west Iberia, quite possibly in the vicinity of Huelva, and some were exported to north-western France, where local bronze-smiths working near Nantes made copies, which became popular in northern France and south-eastern Britain

It is surely no coincidence that it was at precisely this time, in the mid-tenth century BC, that King Hiram of Tyre and King Solomon of Israel were sponsoring trading trips to distant ports (pp. 227–8 below). 'Ships of Tarshish' are mentioned many times in the Bible in a context implying that they were a Levantine fleet specializing in trade. That Tarshish is to be identified as Tartessos—the name used in late Greek texts for the hinterland of Huelva—has been frequently debated. The recent discoveries at Plaza de las Monjas would add strong support for this view. The Bible mentions that the fleet was away for three years. This would be about right for the round trip from one end of the Mediterranean to the other, allowing for a period on land to trade. A further implication from the text is that at least some of the trading expeditions reaching Huelva were under royal sponsorship. On the jetties and in the markets of Huelva, Phoenician traders and perhaps some Sardinians will have rubbed shoulders with ships' masters arriving from along the Atlantic façade. It was one of those special moments in history when two quite alien cultures confronted each other for the first time.

An End and a Beginning, 1200–1100 BC

The appearance of Phoenician traders in southern Iberia in the tenth century BC heralds the opening of an entirely new phase in the history of the Mediterranean and the Atlantic. But to understand this globalizing phenomenon we must first explore the dramatic changes happening in the central and eastern Mediterranean in the preceding centuries.

We saw in the last chapter how the great states of Egypt, Asia Minor, and Mesopotamia vied with each other, their aggressive tendencies usually being constrained within a system of competitive consumption, though occasionally descending into outright warfare over border disputes. The contemporary texts show the ruling dynasties to have been in tight-lipped correspondence, polite but threatening, over the niceties of mutual respect and the proper observances of status. Their demands for exotic raw materials brought the Aegean palace polities into the eastern Mediterranean trading sphere after about 2000 BC, and by 1600 BC Aegean entrepreneurs had begun to exploit the possibilities of the Tyrrhenian Sea, establishing regular trading missions as far afield as Sicily and Sardinia. While the consuming states of the Near East continued to be served by overland caravans bringing commodities from deep in Central Asia, their dependence on Mediterranean shipping was now, arguably, the greater.

Although we cannot convincingly quantify the volume of maritime trade in the late second millennium, the impression given by the archaeological record is that it was considerable and growing. With technological improvements in sailing ships, all those living within easy reach of the sea became caught up in an enthusiasm to engage in potentially profitable maritime commerce. Cyprus is a case in point. After a long period of comparative isolation, in the fourteenth and thirteenth centuries Cypriot sailors began to take part in trading expeditions to the Tyrrhenian Sea alongside Aegean entrepreneurs. This escalated in the twelfth and eleventh centuries until engagement with Sardinia was such that Cypriot metalworkers were established on the island. Apart from their metal-extracting knowhow and craft skills, the Cypriots offered copper imported to Sardinia in the form of oxhide-shaped ingots. What the particular attraction of Sardinia was is difficult to say. In all probability it lay in metals. Sardinia had good supplies of its own copper and iron and was in easy reach of the metal resources of Etruria, but perhaps more important was that Sardinia had maritime links with the west and the Atlantic, whence came gold, silver, and tin, metals in short supply elsewhere in the Mediterranean. We shall return to these Atlantic links later (pp. 240–3).

By about 1200 BC the volume and variety of shipping criss-crossing the eastern Mediterranean and tramping from port to port in endless cycles of cabotage must have

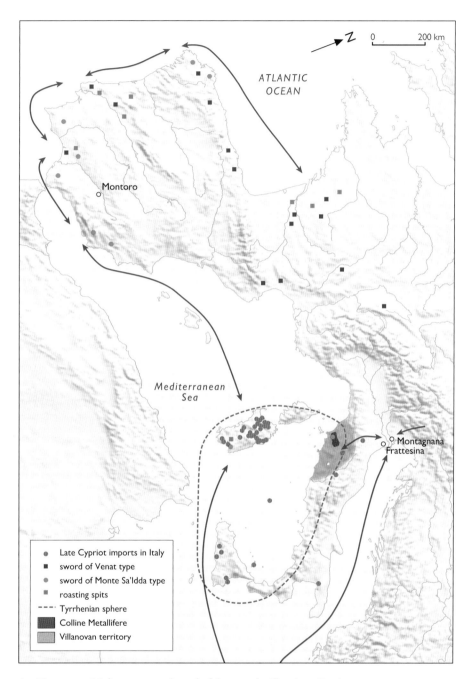

6.4 The western Mediterranean at the end of the second millennium. Cypriot entrepreneurs were now trading with the Tyrrhenian communities and had established a presence on Sardinia, which now also became an important focus for trade with the west

been enormous. Something of the variety of vessels is already evident in the wall paintings of the seventeenth century from the island of Thera (Santorini) (Figure 5.26). Many of the more prestigious trading vessels were probably of the size of the Uluburun ship, dating to about 1300 BC—16 metres in overall length—but two slightly later ships, the Cape Gelidonya vessel and the wreck found off Point Iria in the Gulf of Argos, were considerably smaller at about 10 metres. Vessels of this size are likely to have belonged to ship-owners (possibly the ships' masters) engaging in small-scale private enterprises, the larger vessels perhaps reflecting state enterprises.

With so much commercial shipping now at sea, it would be surprising if piracy and raiding had not become lucrative enterprises in their own right. One justly famous account of the dangers of sea travel in the eleventh century is given by an Egyptian envoy, Wen-Amon, who, in the service of the pharaoh, set out on a sea-voyage from Egypt to Byblos in 1075 BC to acquire logs of cedar-wood. His journey was fraught. Even before leaving the delta his letters of introduction had been confiscated, and not long afterwards one of his escorts ran off with his supply of silver and gold, so when he eventually arrived at the court of Zakar-Baal, prince of Byblos, his bargaining power was severely compromised. However, a deal was finally reached, and in return for seven great cedar logs the Egyptian agreed to send a mixed cargo of gold and silver together with ten linen garments, rolls of linen from Upper Egypt, and '500 rolls of finished papyrus, 500 cows' hides, 500 ropes, 20 bags of lentils and 30 baskets of fish'. Wen-Amon must have breathed a sigh of relief when he finally left Byblos, but his troubles were not entirely over. Contrary winds blew his ship out to the shores of Cyprus, where with his crew he was attacked by an angry mob and only saved by the intervention of a local princess eager not to upset her neighbour, the prince of Byblos. The story goes some way to highlighting the dangers and relative lawlessness of sea travel in the eleventh century. The lot of a sailor was not an easy one.

Something of the uncertainty of the times is recorded in the Egyptian sources. The first reference to trouble comes during the reign of Merenptah (1213–1203 BC), when the delta was attacked by Libyans and peoples coming from the sea named Ekwesh, Lukka, Shekelesh, Sherden, and Teresh. Attempts to identify the intruders are largely speculative, but it has been suggested that the Ekwesh were Achaeans from Greece and the Lukka, Lycians from southern Asia Minor, while similarities in the names link the Sherden to Sardinia and the Shekelesh to Sicily. Merenptah is recorded to have killed six thousand of the invaders and to have dispersed the rest. Later, during the reign of Rameses III (1184–1153 BC), Egypt was attacked by land and by sea: 'The foreign countries made a conspiracy in the islands. All at once the lands were on the move, scattered in war.' These encounters, with Egypt triumphant, are depicted in the relief on the walls of Rameses' mortuary chapel at Medinet Habu. They show shiploads of foreigners, some with horned helmets, others with feathered headdresses, coming under attack from boarding parties as arrows rain down upon them. The varying dress and armour of the foreign attackers and the differences between their ships are meant to indicate that the enemy came from far and wide.

Some of the named peoples attacking Egypt in the late thirteenth and early twelfth centuries had been active in the region earlier. Denen, Lukka, and Sherden are mentioned in the late fourteenth century, and Lukka, Sherden, and Peleset fought on the Egyptian side as mercenaries in the battle of Qadesh (1275 BC). The implication, then, is that at least from the fourteenth century ethnically distinct bands roamed the eastern Mediterranean willing to take up service as mercenaries or to join together in rabble armies whenever the opportunity of a lucrative raid presented itself.

The sea clearly played an important part in the restless mobility that had begun to grip the eastern Mediterranean after the middle of the thirteenth century BC. The Egyptians were not the only ones to suffer. The Levantine coast was now under threat. In a terse exchange of letters between Hammurabi, king of Ugarit, and the king of Cyprus we learn that Ugarit had sent its troops to Hittite territory in central Asia Minor, and its ships were stationed in Lycia, leaving the town unprotected. Hammurabi pleads for help: 'There are seven enemy ships that have come and done much damage.' No record of the response survives, but soon afterwards Ugarit was destroyed.

Unrest was widespread in the eastern Mediterranean. While Egypt, protected by its deserts, survived, other regions fared less well. On the Aegean islands and in Greece the old palace-centred economies collapsed one after another. About 1300 BC some braced themselves with new defences, but fire and destruction swept through the land and by 1150 BC the boasting, self-congratulatory world of the Mycenaeans was no more. The Hittite state, dominating Asia Minor, collapsed and fell apart after the destruction of its capital, Hattusa, in 1180 BC. In the twelfth century, along the Levantine coast, population movement and warfare were a fact of life.

Standing back from the detail of this century of disruption (1250–1150), what impresses is the sheer scale of the mobility, much of it by way of the sea. People were moving over considerable distances, sometimes mercenary bands, sometimes whole populations. There is some evidence to suggest that Mycenaeans settled in Cyprus, bringing the Greek language with them, while the Philistines of the southern Levant may be equated with the Peleset, one of the mercenary bands mentioned by the Egyptian sources. The similarities of their pottery with late Mycenaean types have been taken by some writers to suggest that they may originally have come from the Aegean region. Nor should we forget the similarity in the names of the Shardana and the Sherden of Sardinia and the Shekelesh and the Sikels of Sicily. There are two

6.5 (*Above and opposite*) The images offer a lively depiction of a sea-borne raid on the Nile delta by the 'sea people'. Variously dressed to indicate their different ethnicities and in their distinctive ships, they are shown suffering a devastating attack by the forces of Rameses III. Relief from the Great Temple at Medinet Habu, Egypt

tantalizing possibilities: either that people came from the two Tyrrhenian islands to engage in raiding and mercenary activities in the eastern Mediterranean, or that they were footloose wanderers from the east who chose to settle the two western islands. The evidence, such as it is, could be argued either way.

That mobility on a huge scale was a feature of the time is not in doubt, but why it should have erupted in the twelfth century is a difficult question to address. The favoured prime movers are upheavals caused by social inequality exacerbated by ancillary factors such as exponential population increases and climatic deterioration. Some of these elements may well have been involved in this case. But there may be others. Perhaps the supplies of raw materials, upon which the competitive system, based on conspicuous consumption, was dependent, became unsustainable, causing social order to collapse. Other value systems founded on valour as a warrior and a war leader may,

in some regimes, have taken over. Another contributory factor may have been that a thousand years of intensifying maritime trade may have generated a large floating population of rootless boat people willing to sell their services or to turn a quick profit by brigandage if necessary. At any event, the interaction of some or all of these dynamics created a century or so of intense mobility, erasing much of the old social edifice, destroying long-established centres of power, and setting the scene for an entirely new world order.

The Rise of the Phoenicians

The narrow eastern Mediterranean coastal strip roughly equivalent with modern Lebanon emerged from the chaos of the twelfth century as the home of maritime entrepreneurs whose skill and daring were quite unmatched. This was the land of the Phoenicians—the Phoinikes, as they were known to the Greeks, a word that derives from an Indo-European term meaning 'red', thought to be a reference to the reddish-purple dye which the inhabitants of this coast extracted from the murex shell and for which they were famous. To the Greeks, then, Phoenicia meant 'the land of the purple cloth'. The Phoenicians called themselves Can'ani, Canaanites, which probably derives from the Hebrew word for 'merchant'. The usage goes back to the third millennium BC, but by the second millennium the name Canaan, in addition to being a toponym, had also taken on the connotation of 'purple'. It was this that the Mycenaeans translated into Greek, giving us the familiar 'Phoenician'.

Late usage by classical authors further confuses the picture with the indiscriminate use of 'Phoenician', 'Punic', and 'Carthaginian'. 'Carthaginian' clearly refers to the Phoenician inhabitants of the city of Carthage, founded in the ninth century BC, while 'Punic' tends to be used for Phoenicians who had come under the influence of Carthage after the city had assumed military hegemony from the sixth century BC. For those people of Phoenician origin who had settled in the western Mediterranean between the ninth and sixth centuries BC it is still convenient to retain the word Phoenician or to qualify it as western Phoenician.

In strict archaeological terms the Phoenicians of the Levantine coast who emerged to prominence after the twelfth century were descended from the indigenous population of Canaan, whose roots go back to the third millennium. These were the people whose port cities, like Byblos and Ugarit, grew rich by serving as the middlemen who dealt in trade between Egypt and the state of Mesopotamia, adding to the flow of goods their own cedar, pine, and cypress trees, which grew in profusion on the mountain slopes. Once the political crisis of the twelfth century was over, the favoured coastal interface could again play a central role in the trade networks that were being re-established and extended, but there were now significant differences. As a result of the upheavals, the old land of Canaan had lost three-quarters of its territory. In the south the Philistines had taken over much of the central region of Palestine, while inland the Israelites had conquered the mountain region. At the same time, in the north and north-east (modern Syria), Aramaeans had appropriated large territories. The result was that the land of the Canaanites was reduced to the coastal strip from Mount Carmel near Acre to the island of Arwad near the mouth of the river Nahr al-Kabir, with very little hinterland to support the population. The only option available to the coastal cities to sustain their growing populations was to become the facilitators of trade. With their backs to the mountains they looked out over the sea, and it was the sea that they were to conquer.

The coastal cities of Phoenicia were situated on promontories provided with natural harbours or, in the case of Arwad and Tyre, on offshore islands. Each city had its own territory defined by fast-flowing rivers coming from the mountains, which divide the narrow coastal plain into discrete blocks. Some of the cities had roots going back to the Bronze Age, but not all had survived the twelfth-century crisis. Ugarit and Alalakh had been destroyed and were not rebuilt, but others, like Byblos and Sidon, survived to dominate the region in the immediate aftermath. The legend that Tyre was founded by the Sidonians in 1191 BC suggests that Sidon may have been instrumental in the rebuilding of Tyre: at any event, she claimed Tyre as a daughter city. The seas to the south of Tyre, as far south as Gaza, were at first controlled by the Philistines, but their defeat by the Israelite king David in 975 BC gave Tyre breathing space and contributed to its spectacular growth in power. Under King Hiram I (reigned 969–936 BC), Tyre established hegemony over all the other Phoenician cities and became the foremost port in the entire Mediterranean. Hiram could proudly style himself 'King of Tyre and of Phoenicia'.

Crucial to the success of Tyre was the creation of a close working relationship with the kingdom of Israel to the south. This was achieved by a commercial treaty agreed by Hiram I and Solomon (reigned 960–930 BC) which saw the two polities enter into mutually supportive trade agreements. Hiram supplied building materials, specialist services, and luxury goods to Israel, while Solomon sent silver, farm products, and food for Hiram's royal household. The lists are interesting. Hiram had already shown himself to be an energetic builder at Tyre, where he joined various islets together to create one large island and built several monumental structures, including a grand

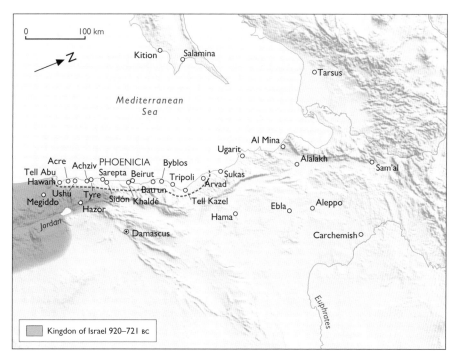

6.6 The Phoenician homeland occupied the coastal strip backed by a mountain range, on the lower slopes of which the famous cedar trees grew. With little hinterland the Phoenicians looked outwards to the sea

6.7 (*a*) The city of Tyre in 1938. At this time the modern city was largely restricted to what had been the island upon which the original Phoenician city was founded. (*b*) Reconstruction of ancient Tyre at its height

6.8 The modern island town of Arwad just off the coast of Syria occupies part of the once-larger island chosen by the Phoenicians as an offshore trading port

temple to Melqart. He also played a role in the construction of Solomon's temple at Jerusalem, no doubt providing cedars for the project. Solomon, for his part, sent food to help support Phoenicia's burgeoning population.

The commercial agreement also allowed the Phoenicians to develop routes into the interior, to the upper Euphrates and thence to Mesopotamia, and to begin to extend their influence along the coasts of northern Syria to Cilicia and the Taurus region. As part of this maritime enterprise Cyprus and Crete were drawn into the Phoenician sphere. Cyprus was already in contact with Phoenicia in the late eleventh century, and inscriptions suggest that under Hiram the eastern part of the island may have become a Phoenician protectorate. In the middle of the ninth century Tyre consolidated its hold over the island by founding a colony at Kition, thus ensuring control over the island's rich sources of copper. These early contacts with Cyprus will have given the Phoenicians access to traditional sea lore about the distant western Mediterranean which Cypriot sailors had gathered over nearly four hundred years of contact.

Another outcome of the commercial treaty between Hiram and Solomon was the development of new overseas trading expeditions. The relevant texts, mainly biblical, have given rise to much debate and disagreement, but there is now a view that two quite separate maritime systems were involved. One concerned the building of a merchant fleet at Ezion-Geber, near Eilat on the Red Sea, to trade with the distant land of Ophir, which probably included Sudan, Somalia, and Arabia, bringing back precious stones, rare wood, gold, and spices. The text (1 Kings 10) mentions what is probably a second and separate trading venture: 'For the King had a fleet of ships of Tarshish at sea with the fleet of Hiram. Once every three years the ships of Tarshish used to come bringing gold, silver, ivory, apes, and [peacocks?].' This reference may plausibly be seen to refer to trade with the far west, in particular with Tartessos in south-western Iberia, where, as we have seen (pp. 215–17 above), there is ample evidence of a Phoenician presence as early as the tenth century.

Standing back from the detail, then, by the end of the eleventh century there was already a significant Phoenician presence on Cyprus, which was further consolidated under Hiram in the tenth century. Since the fourteenth century the Cypriots had been trading with the central Mediterranean, and by the twelfth century there was already a settlement of Cypriot entrepreneurs, including metalworkers, on Sardinia. At about this time or soon after, the archaeological evidence suggests that maritime contacts were being established between Sardinia and south-western Iberia (pp. 206–8 above).

It is not unreasonable, therefore, to suppose that the Phoenician sailors who were engaged in trade with Cyprus would soon have picked up stories of the far west, where all kinds of riches were to be had. By following the long-established route they would have had little difficulty in reaching the ports of Sardinia, where they would have met sailors from the western Mediterranean with first-hand accounts of the thriving markets of Tartessos. That, by the tenth century, they were opening up these markets is amply demonstrated by the archaeological finds from Huelva. To sail the length of the Mediterranean and back within a three-year cycle (if the biblical text is to be believed) would be a considerable feat of seamanship but one founded on long experience.

Something of the world of the Phoenician sailors of this early period is captured in the works of Homer written down in the eighth century but probably reflecting oral accounts of a century or two earlier. Homer followed the disdain of the Greek elite for traders, and consequently had a somewhat jaundiced view of Phoenicians, but even so there is much to learn from his references. Homer makes it clear that Phoenician trade with the Greek world was based on individual enterprises involving buying and selling for profit, slave-trading, and carrying passengers. Phoenician ships were working the ports of Syros, Lemnos, Pylos, Ithaca, and Crete, as well as Egypt and Libya. Nor were they averse to a little kidnapping. In the *Odyssey* Eumaeus, a king's son, tells how, when he was a child, his island was visited 'by a party of those notorious Phoenician sailors, greedy rogues, with a whole cargo of flashy knick-knacks in their black ship … the trader stayed with us for a whole year and took on board a vast store of goods'. Just as they were about to leave, one of his father's servants, a woman of Sidon, led the young boy aboard the ship, where he was kept captive until it sailed, eventually to be sold for a good price on Ithaca. Another story in the same vein is told by Odysseus of how, when in Egypt, he 'fell in with a rascally Phoenician, a thieving knave who had already done a deal of mischief in the world'. He sailed with him to Phoenicia, where the man had an estate, and stayed with him for over a year. He was then lured on board a ship which sailed for Africa, where the Phoenicians intended to sell him as a slave. Fortunately, Zeus intervened and the ship was wrecked, but Odysseus was saved to tell the tale. One particularly interesting detail is that from the Levantine coast the ship sailed due west and 'ran down the lee side of Crete', a route which suggests that the ship's master was sailing on a latitude.

These few anecdotes, biased though they are, give something of a flavour of the freebooting, entrepreneurial nature of Phoenician trade and of the navigational skills of the ships' masters. Yet lying behind the opportunist commercialism there are hints of an earlier system of gift exchange harking back to the elite interactions of the second millennium. In the *Odyssey* we hear of a gold-rimmed krater of chased silver which the king of Sidon gave to Menelaus when he was a house guest, while in the *Iliad* another silver krater, 'a masterpiece of Sidonian craftsmanship', was taken by a Phoenician trader from one Greek port to another until it was presented as a gift to the king of Lemnos. The same krater was later given to Achilles as ransom for one of Priam's daughters and was eventually awarded by him as a prize in the funeral celebrations of Patroclus. The krater had acquired an impressive biography, its value enhanced with every act of giving. Valuable gifts of this kind were very much 'introductory offers' designed to establish relationships between the two parties. Once gifts had been exchanged, more routine trading could follow.

The Thrust West, Tenth–Eighth Centuries BC

We have already stressed that the narrow coastal strip which the Phoenicians occupied forced them to look outwards to the Mediterranean in order to provide the resources to sustain their growing population. Another factor which made them engage with the wider world was their peripheral position in relation to the Assyrians, who by now controlled Mesopotamia and were in expansionist mood. Simply stated, Assyria was a consuming state which needed to be fuelled with a constant input of raw materials and luxury goods. The Phoenician trading cities on their western periphery were able

6.9 The bronze gates of the Neo-Assyrian palace of Balawat, south-east of Mosul, bear this intriguing scene in the upper register of Phoenician boats (hippoi) carrying gifts destined for King Shalmaneser III from the island city of Tyre

6.10 (*Opposite*) In the early first millennium BC a regular traffic developed between Phoenicia and the metal-rich area of Tartessos. From their homeland the Phoenician ships probably took the central route, sailing as far as possible along the latitude past Crete to Malta, then across to southern Sardinia before setting a course for Ibiza and thence to Iberia. The return journey would probably have made use of the favourable east-flowing current along the coast of North Africa

to acquire these exotic materials and to provide the skills to transform them into desirable works of art to satisfy the Assyrian kings.

It was in the interests of Assyria that the Phoenician trading cities should flourish: it was a symbiotic relationship, but not without its tensions. For the Phoenicians the Assyrians provided a degree of protection and a lucrative market for their goods, while in return the Phoenicians were forced to pay tribute to the Assyrian rulers. In the early ninth century the list included gold, silver, tin, linen, monkeys, ebonite, and wooden and ivory chests. The silver krater, the 'masterpiece of Sidonian craftsmanship' given to Menelaus, is an example of the goods on offer. The Phoenicians were also renowned for their ivory carvings used in lavish quantity to adorn the Assyrian palaces. Nor should we forget the monkeys shown on a relief from the ninth-century palace at Nimrud being carried to the king as tribute by Phoenicians. By the end of the ninth century large quantities of iron as well as purple cloth are listed.

The relationship remained at arm's length until the mid-eighth century, when Assyrians, campaigning in the west, captured the island of Arwad and forced the surrender of Tyre. Although Tyre was allowed to continue with its trading operations, the Assyrians demanded a massive tribute in gold and installed their own customs inspectors in the port. Thereafter relations between Assyria and Tyre worsened until 701 BC when the king of Tyre was forced to flee to Kition, the inhabitants were deported, and pro-Assyrian governors installed. The occasion prompted Isaiah to begin his well-known oracle concerning Tyre: 'Howl ye ships of Tarshish, your fortress has been destroyed' (Isaiah 23: 1). Tyre continued to trade throughout the seventh century,

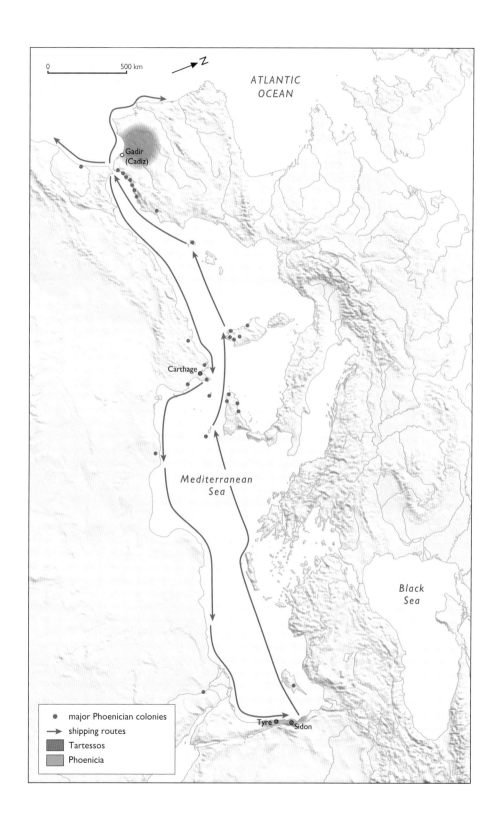

ATLANTIC
OCEAN

Gadir
(Cadiz)

Carthage

Mediterranean
Sea

Black
Sea

Tyre Sidon

0   500 km

N

•   major Phoenician colonies
→   shipping routes
▨   Tartessos
▨   Phoenicia

6.11 Ivory, one of the commodities regularly traded by the Phoenicians, was worked into elaborate decorated items by their craftsmen for their Assyrian patrons. This ivory panel from the palace of Nimrud showing a Nubian boy being mauled by a lioness is Phoenician workmanship at its most accomplished

though under increasingly humbling conditions, but now its overseas colonies like Carthage were beginning to take over its commercial activities in the central and western Mediterranean. The end finally came when the Babylonian king Nebuchadnezzar besieged Tyre for thirteen years (585–572 BC). Although Sidon continued to articulate a level of international trade, the power of Phoenicia had been eclipsed.

From the tenth to the eighth centuries, then, the Phoenicians were actively engaged in developing maritime trading networks throughout the Mediterranean and into the Atlantic. The historical tradition would have us believe that the far-western colonies of Lixus (in Morocco), Gadir (modern Cádiz), and Utica (in Tunisia) were the first to be founded in quick succession about 1100 BC, not many years after the end of the Trojan War. Since no archaeological evidence has been recovered for Phoenician presence in the west for such an early date, the tradition has generally been dismissed, but the recent discovery of incontestable support for a Phoenician trading enclave at the Atlantic port of Huelva as early as the tenth century has focused once more on the question. Late Mycenaean pottery found in Andalucía hints that ships from the eastern or central Mediterranean were making trips to the west as early as the thirteenth century. It is not impossible, then, that early voyages of reconnaissance were beginning to spy out the potential of the west as far as the Atlantic shores of Iberia and North Africa, and it was legends of these pioneering expeditions that the classical writers were reporting. That a Phoenician trading base was flourishing at Huelva by the tenth century or even earlier might suggest that the merchants set out with some foreknowledge of the region's great potential. The fact that no early occupation has yet been found at Lixus or Utica, and that the earliest traces of settlement so far found at Cádiz date to the ninth century, does not mean that there is no earlier material to be found. The earliest levels of these cities are still virtually unknown to archaeologists. On present evidence, then, we may allow the possibility of early exploration before the establishment of a trading colony at Huelva, coinciding with the ambitious overseas ventures sponsored by Hiram I. Whether more trading ports were founded at the time remains to be seen.

The attractions of western Mediterranean ports such as Huelva for the Phoenicians were many. Huelva commanded the supply of copper, silver, and iron from the mineral-rich hinterland; and from further afield, along the western arm of the Pyrite Belt, a zone rich in metal ores which stretches along the south of the Iberian peninsula, gold and tin could be had. The Atlantic maritime network also brought copper, tin, and gold from further north, from Armorica, Britain, and Ireland; and from the south, through the ports along the African coast, gold, ivory, and ostrich shells were readily available. This range of desirable raw materials, together with monkeys and other exotic animals and perhaps furs, would have been shipped the length of the Mediterranean to the Phoenician home ports, there to be worked into high-value products for the Assyrian market and for other consumers around the eastern Mediterranean. During the ninth and eighth centuries, Phoenician colonies began to be founded along the south coast of Iberia from the Strait of Gibraltar to the estuary of the river Segura, along the Atlantic coast of Portugal as far north as the river Mondego, and southwards along the Moroccan coast to the island of Mogador close to modern Essaouira. Although the dating evidence for the foundation of all these colonies has still to be established, those along the Portuguese coast originate in the ninth century. This is also the earliest date so far available for Gadir and for the colonization of the Málaga region. No doubt the colonization of these coasts took place over time, with latecomers seeking out suitable

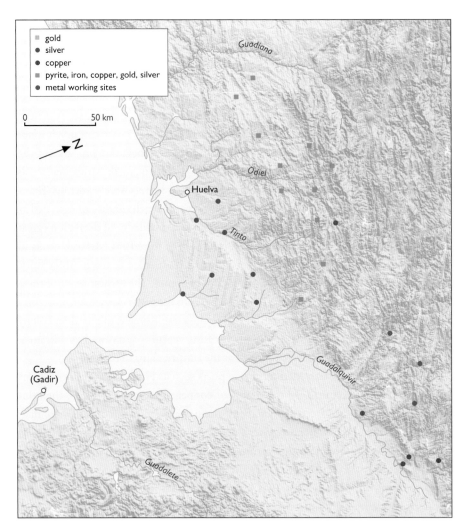

6.12 The Phoenician city of Gadir (modern Cádiz) was established early in the first millennium BC on islands in the estuary of the Guadalete. Its location was a brilliant choice. From here it could engage directly with the native trading community living at Huelva (probably ancient Tartessos), which commanded the rich metal resources of the hinterland, and it could serve as a focus for its trading enclaves established along the Atlantic shores of Portugal and Morocco. Sea level as at *c.*600 BC

locations between existing settlements. The colonists tended to favour estuaries where rivers had created fertile plains and provided easy access to productive hinterlands.

The settlements along the south coast of Iberia differ in that they are much more closely spaced, in some cases barely twenty kilometres apart. Each commanded an area of fruitful, well-watered coastal plain close to a river giving access to the intermontane plateaux of the Sierra Nevada and the fertile plain of the Guadalquivir beyond.

234

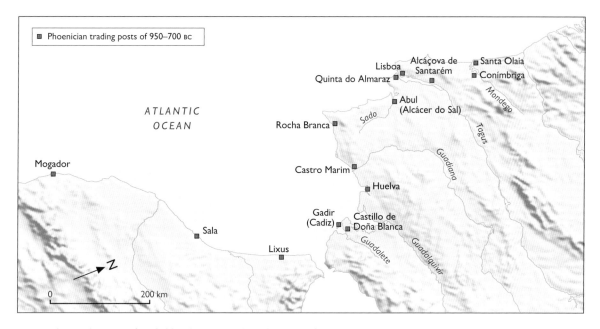

6.13 Trading enclaves were founded by Phoenicians along the coasts of the Atlantic. The density of sites known along the Portuguese coasts is the result of intensive archaeological fieldwork. It is likely that many more trading stations remain to be found along the Moroccan coast

Although the colonists could have acquired silver from the Sierra Morena, flanking the north banks of the Guadalquivir, it is more likely that their prime aim was to collect foodstuffs, including grain, from the lush hinterland to be exported to feed the population of Phoenicia.

The fortunes of the early settlements differed. Most seem to have remained modest, but Gadir, situated on two islands in the estuary of the river Guadalete, grew to become the prime city of the Phoenician enterprise. It was sited on the Atlantic façade nearly ninety kilometres beyond the Strait of Gibraltar, ideally located as a setting-off point for the journey northwards along the European coastline or southwards along the African coast. It was also within easy reach of Huelva and the metal lodes of the Sierra de Aracena.

The Phoenician city of Gadir made use of two islands separated by a narrow channel which provided a safe anchorage. The northern island, Erytheia, was occupied by the settlement, while the narrow, elongated southern island, Kotinoussa, was used as the cemetery. A third island, Antipolis, lay between it and the mainland. The western extremities of both the main islands were dominated by temples, the temple of Astarte on Erytheia and that of Baal Khrones on the opposite side of the channel on

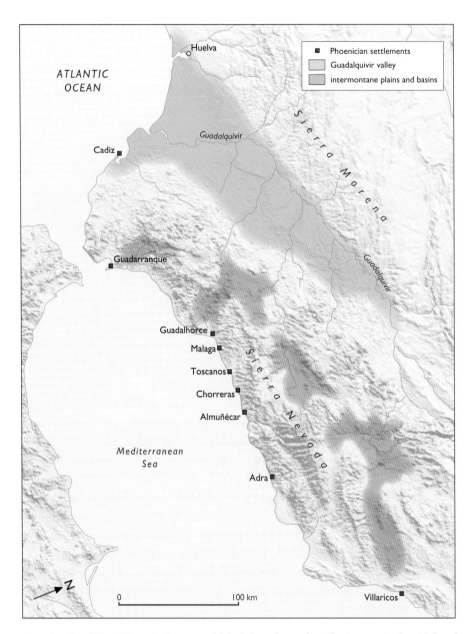

6.14 A series of Phoenician colonies was established along the southern Iberian coast in the eighth and seventh centuries. They occupied the narrow fertile coastal strip, well watered by rivers flowing from the Sierra Nevada. The communities had access to the produce from the intermontane plateaux and the fertile valley of the Guadalquivir as well as to the rich silver deposits of the Sierra Morena

Kotinoussa. At the southern end of Kotinoussa was another temple, to Melqart, providing a welcome sea-mark to greet the traveller arriving from the east. The ancient city and the harbour channel are now buried deep beneath the thriving modern city of Cádiz, but some traces of the early occupation dating back to the ninth century have been found in deep soundings. The topography has changed since Phoenician times. A slight rise in sea-level has inundated the western extremities of both islands, while there has been much silting up of the bays between the islands and the mainland, but the city still maintains its proud maritime character serving as the gateway to the Atlantic.

The Phoenician settlements on the Portuguese coast cluster in four areas, on the leeward Algarve and in the estuaries and valleys of the Sado, Tagus, and Mondego. Since those on the Mondego and Tagus seem to pre-date the others, it suggests that the early settlers were deliberately making for specific locations, which, in turn, hints that they may have been following in the wake of earlier pathfinders whose transit along the coast may be glimpsed in iron knives found in eleventh- and tenth-century contexts on indigenous coastal sites. By the ninth century the enclaves were well established, their inhabitants apparently living in harmony with the indigenous population.

Much less is known about the origins of the Phoenician settlements along the Atlantic coast of Morocco, but Lixus, sited on a promontory in the estuary of the river Loukkos, was believed by classical writers to be the earliest. It is well located to have served as the centre from which the rest of the North African coast could be reached, rather as Gadir served the Portuguese coast. Archaeological examination of the early levels has been minimal, but the earliest pottery so far recorded is of the eighth century. Phoenician enclaves were established down the coast of Morocco at least as far as Mogador, some six hundred kilometres south of Lixus, where occupation has been found to be as early as the seventh century. The earliest settlers established a temple to Astarte identified by a baetyl (a sacred stone pillar) characteristic of Phoenician religious locations. Their presence is also shown by imported pottery, some bearing Phoenician graffiti. From their island base the traders were able to link directly to the Saharan caravan routes carrying gold, resins, and spices, as well as other exotics. Among the debris found on the island were elephant bones—a reminder of the importance of ivory—and the skull of a young lion that had apparently been kept for some time in captivity. Whether it was a live beast for export or simply a lion-skin trophy it is difficult to tell. The archaeological deposits also produced large quantities of fish remains, reflecting trade in salted fish.

For the Phoenician merchants, Mogador would have been the last port of call on the coastal route. Little is yet known of the early phases of this Atlantic African network, but it would not be at all surprising to find that the initial settlement of the African Atlantic coast goes back to at least the ninth century.

Sufficient will have been said to show that the Phoenician discovery of the far west occurred with astonishing speed and represents, by any standards, a major feat of both maritime exploration and colonial enterprise. But it could not have been sustained without a Mediterranean infrastructure to support the year-long voyages between Tyre and Gadir. The outward journey from Tyre would have taken the open-sea route (favoured by Odysseus' abductor), keeping to the latitude and sailing past the southern shore of Crete, perhaps stopping at the port of Kommos to take on supplies. The onward journey would have taken the vessel to Malta, from where, after a change of direction, ports in eastern Sicily and southern Sardinia could have been reached. From here the course would have been set to Ibiza and onward to the Iberian coast. The return journey was probably made along the North African coast using the predominant east-flowing

6.15 Modern Cádiz still occupies the islands first settled by the Phoenicians, but a rise in sea-level has drowned the western extremities of the two islands of Erytheia and Kotinoussa, which can be seen in the photograph just below sea-level, one now supporting the offshore castle of San Sebastián

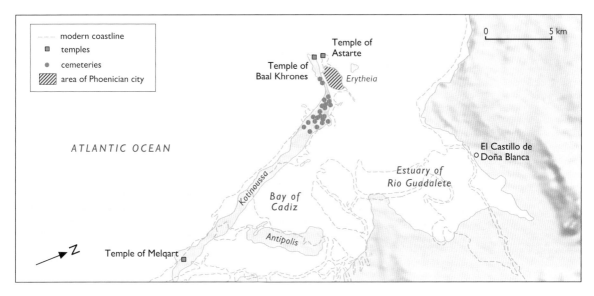

6.16 Gadir was founded on two islands separated by a channel. The main settlement occupied the smaller northern island, Erytheia, while the longer island, Kotinoussa, was used for burials

current, stopping over at Carthage and other North African ports on the way. Along these routes regular ports of call were developed. Some, like Kommos, were already well established. Elsewhere, on Sicily, Sardinia, and the North African coast, new colonies were set up, increasing in number as the maritime trade intensified. At Nora, on Sardinia, an inscription dating to the ninth century was found that referred to a newly built temple indicating an important event in the development of the settlement, which may already have been in existence. Carthage, on the coast of Tunisia, is traditionally said to have been founded in 814 or 813 BC, and this is confirmed by radiocarbon dates of 850–795 BC for the earliest levels so far encountered. But Carthage may have been a new foundation to replace an earlier port at Utica a little to the north, close to the estuary of the river Medjerda, after silt from the river began to clog the harbour. Indeed, for the long-distance trade with the far west to have functioned at all, some of the intermediate ports-of-call must already have been in existence from the tenth century.

Over the years, as the routes became established, Phoenician merchants may have stopped off to settle, making a living through trade with the indigenous populations and by providing services for passing ships. Gradually the enclaves would have grown into colonies complete with temples, tophets (sacred precincts), and systems of government. Thus, the Phoenician settlements in Sicily, Sardinia, and North Africa may well have originated not as pioneer acts of colonization but more as a support infrastructure for the long-distance trade with the west.

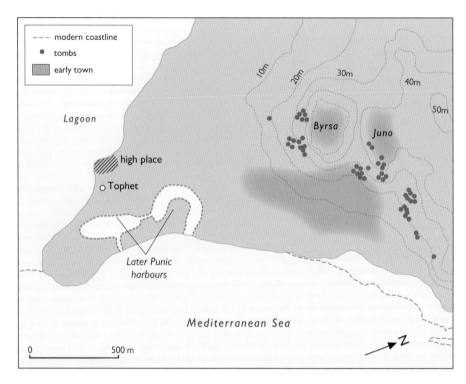

6.17 The location of Carthage as it was in the seventh and sixth centuries before the famous harbours were built. The core of the settlement lay on the flat-topped Byrsa hill with the domestic quarters spreading along the east-facing slope below. To the south was the Tophet. The steep hill immediately adjacent may have been the 'high place' where sacrifices were carried out

When East Meets West

The impact of Phoenician traders on the indigenous communities of south-western Iberia was dramatic, and over the period of intensive contact from the tenth to the seventh century native society was transformed. Before contact the indigenous popu-lations were part of the Atlantic Bronze Age continuum distinguished by certain char-acteristics. The pottery in common use was a distinctive burnished-decorated ware, its typological variation suggesting that two discrete groups were represented, one occu-pying southern Portugal west of the Guadiana, the other lying east of the Guadiana and including much of the Guadalquivir valley. Inland from these two groups, and overlapping with the Guadalquivir region, a large number of carved stone stelae (standing stones) have been found dating to the period 1200–800 BC. They appear to be part of a funerary tradition commemorating individual warriors, but they seldom mark graves. Characteristically they are stelae pecked or incised with a range of motifs arranged in recurring compositions. The oldest depicts a shield flanked by a spear and a sword. On later examples more exotic goods are illustrated, including helmets, two-wheeled chariots, and mirrors, while the latest in the series display human figures and other motifs such as musical instruments, brooches, and combs. The early type, with weapons only, tend to cluster in the Tagus river valley, while the later ones are found in the Guadiana valley, with the latest concentrating in the Guadalquivir valley. The simplest explanation for the change in decorative style is that this long-lasting burial tradition began well before the arrival of the Phoenicians and continued during the early contact period, when eastern Mediterranean novelties such as mirrors and chariots were becoming increasingly available to the native leaders.

A later development of the same funerary tradition, confined largely to the southwestern corner of Iberia west of the Guadiana, sees the appearance of stelae incorporating inscriptions in Phoenician script. These date from the eighth to the fifth century BC. What is notable about them is that the script is used to write the native language, now widely agreed to be Celtic.

The distributions of the different styles of pottery and of inscribed stelae no doubt reflect different socio-economic units within the indigenous population. The kingdom referred to by classical writers as Tartessos is most likely to be the polity occupying the region of the Guadalquivir valley extending westwards to the Guadiana with Huelva as its principal point of entry. The funerary monuments inscribed in Phoenician script form another distinct group which may collate with the Cempsi and Kunetes, tribes referred to by classical sources as occupying the extreme west of the peninsula.

While the finds from the earliest levels of Huelva show the archaeological reality of Phoenician contact in the tenth century, later classical writers looking back on these early days offer a more colourful but surely exaggerated memory. One post-Aristotelian text sums it up thus:

> It is said that those of the Phoenicians who first sailed to Tartessos, after importing to that place oil and other small wares of maritime commerce, obtained for their return cargo so great a quantity of silver, that they were no longer able to keep or receive it, but were forced when sailing away from those parts, to make of silver not only all the other articles which they used but also all the anchors.
>
> (Pseudo-Aristotle, *De Mirabilibus Auscultationibus* 153)

Silver was highly valued in the Phoenician sphere and may well have become the kingdom's principal export. The archaeological evidence shows a marked increase in silver extraction in Tartessos by the eighth century. The import of eastern Mediterranean

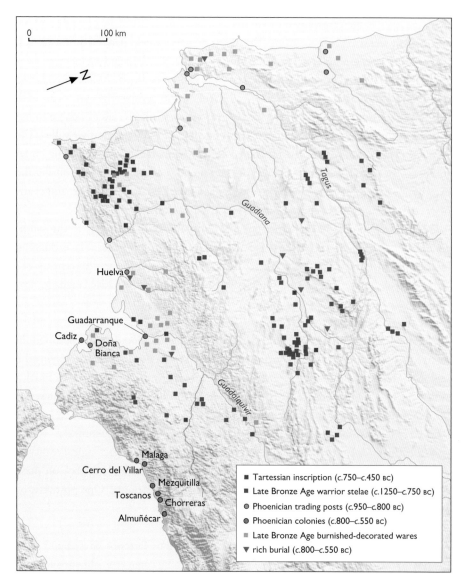

6.18 The culture of the indigenous Late Bronze Age communities living in south-western Iberia changed as contact with Phoenician traders and colonists intensified. One group, living in the extreme south-western corner of the peninsula, started to use Phoenician script to express their Celtic language on memorial stones. Exotic metalwork made in the coastal towns also found its way into the graves of those able to command the routes by which gold and tin were traded to the south

oil is amply demonstrated by the large numbers of Phoenician oil amphorae found in south-western Iberia, but it was probably more than just the commodity that was imported. With it came sets of fine pottery which suggest that new eating and drinking habits were being introduced, accompanied perhaps by exotic herbs and spices. The 'other small wares of maritime commerce' are also interesting. There are likely to have been low-bulk luxury goods like beads, jewellery, and the bronze flagons, dishes, and incense burners found in the rich burials of the local elites. It cannot have been long after the initial contact that Phoenician craftsmen capable of manufacturing these consumer durables settled in Tartessos to develop a market for their skills. Ivory workers are known to have been in residence in Huelva and in Doña Blanca on the mainland opposite Gadir. Some of their products have been found in Carthage.

Of the number of rich burials found in Tartessian territory, none are more remarkable than those found in the cemetery of La Joya close to the settlement at Huelva. Among the many burials found, tomb 17 stands out. The deceased was accompanied by a two-wheeled chariot of walnut wood decorated with silver and bronze fittings and drawn by two horses. Mounted on the chariot was a wooden quiver covered in bronze. Among the other grave goods was an ivory box with silver hinges supported by ivory figures at each corner, a bronze mirror with an ivory handle, iron knives also with ivory handles, and a jug, dish, and incense burner made of bronze and used for libations. Some of the other tombs in the cemetery also contained luxury goods, but others were those of poorer people. Tomb 17 probably dates to the seventh century BC. It reflects the range of Phoenician-inspired goods now available to the indigenous population able to afford them. Some, like the libation set, were probably made locally, but other items like the chariot and the ivory box look like imported eastern Mediterranean products. A close parallel to the chariot was found at Salamis on Cyprus.

6.19 One of the characteristics of indigenous culture in south-western Iberia in the Late Bronze Age (c.1250–c.750 BC) was the setting up of carved stelae (standing stones) to commemorate warriors. Often they depict armour such as circular shields and wheeled vehicles. This example is from Solance de Cabañas, Cáceres, Spain

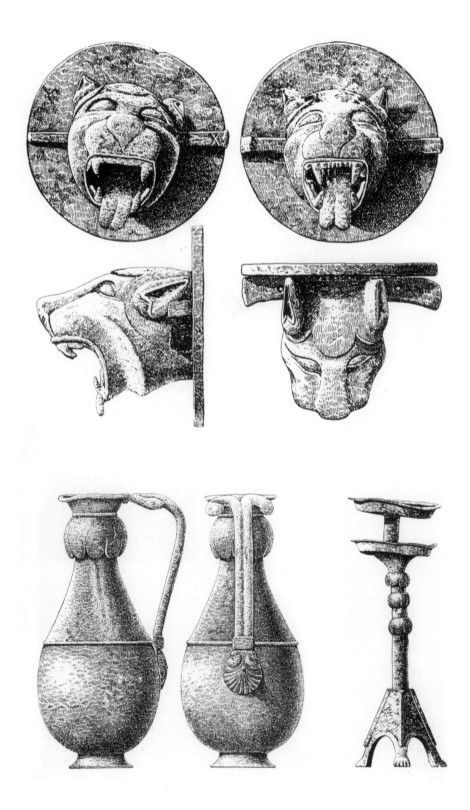

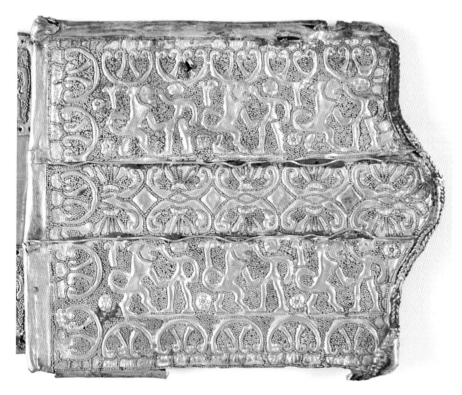

6.20 (*Opposite*) The cemetery at La Joya, just outside the settlement of Huelva, contained a number of tombs, tomb 17 being the richest. Among the grave goods provided for the deceased was a bronze jug and an incense burner and also a four-wheeled vehicle with the hub-caps ornamented with lions' heads. These exotic goods, though probably made locally, were heavily influenced by eastern ideas. Tomb 17 dates to 650–600 BC

6.21 (*Above*) The elite burial at Aliseda, Cáceres, Spain, contained a number of items of gold, among them this belt plate decorated with a recurring scene of a man fighting a rampant lion, typical of Phoenician art

Another rich burial, probably of a woman, dating to the late seventh century, was found at Aliseda in the province of Cáceres in the upper Tagus valley. The burial was accompanied by a spectacular set of gold jewellery including a diadem, a necklace, a belt, bracelets, earrings, and finger rings inset with amethyst, jasper, and carnelian. There was also a green glass bottle decorated with Egyptian hieroglyphs, a gold bowl, a silver dish, and a bronze mirror. While some of the assemblage may have been imported, much of it was probably made by Phoenician craftsmen resident in Tartessos.

Aliseda and La Joya are not alone. Aliseda is one of a series of rich burials found in west central Iberia as far north as the valley of the Douro. It is tempting to see them as the tombs of the local rulers who commanded the routes by which the tin and gold of northern Iberia were traded south to Tartessos and the Phoenician world.

The maritime adventure which saw the Phoenician entrepreneurs make their audacious dash to the far west in the tenth century was unprecedented. In a single move it brought Iberia and the Atlantic façade firmly into the eastern Mediterranean sphere, and incidentally created a series of way-stations strung along the shipping lanes that threaded the southern Mediterranean. The Atlantic was no longer a myth: it was now a tangible new world with high economic potential. News of the resource-rich west spread rapidly in the eastern Mediterranean, eventually reaching the consciousness of the Greek city states that were beginning to emerge around the Aegean.

The Greek Awakening

The disdain with which the early Greek elite regarded traders is nicely summed up by Homer. When the tired and travel-worn Odysseus appears at the Phaeacian games, his refusal to take part brings scorn from a young nobleman: 'I should never take you for an athlete ... but rather some captain of a merchant crew, who spends his life on a hulking tramp worrying about his outward freight or keeping a sharp eye on the cargo when he comes home with the profits he has grabbed' (*Odyssey* 8.161–4). Anyone who indulged in trade (*emporos*) was beyond contempt, yet Homer may be reflecting fast-disappearing values. There is ample archaeological evidence that after about 1000 BC overseas trade began to pick up in the Aegean world.

The most compelling evidence comes from Lefkandi on the south coast of the island of Euboea. Here a small town had developed. In the town's cemeteries, the earliest graves contain only locally accessible grave goods, but after 1000 BC more exotic material begins to appear, including pottery and jewellery from the Levant. A little later in the tenth century a heroon (shrine) was constructed over the grave complex of a member of the local aristocracy. There were two grave shafts: one contained the bodies of four horses, while the other contained the cremated remains of the hero placed in a Cypriot bronze vessel and the body of a woman buried with her jewellery, including an antique gold necklace of Babylonian origin. Other burials in the cemetery in front of the heroon were furnished with grave goods from Attica, the Levant, Cyprus, and Egypt. Clearly the inhabitants of Euboea in the tenth and ninth centuries had access

6.22 (*Opposite*) The Greek island of Euboea was already engaging in extensive trade in the ninth century BC. One of the products of the island was a distinctive painted bowl known as a pendent-semicircle skyphos. The distribution of this pottery type around the eastern Mediterranean gives an indication of the extent of the trading routes with which the Euboeans were engaged

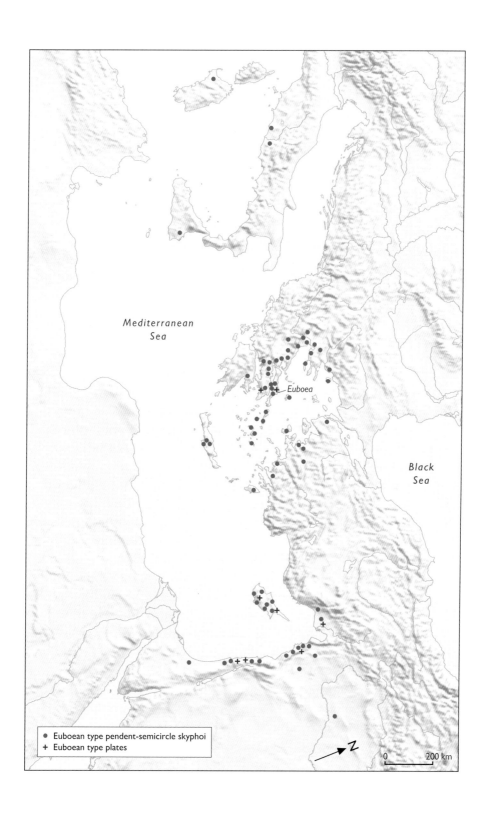

Mediterranean
Sea

Euboea

Black
Sea

● Euboean type pendent-semicircle skyphoi
+ Euboean type plates

N

0   200 km

to luxury goods circulating around the eastern Mediterranean. It could be argued that these trinkets were brought to the Aegean by jobbing Phoenician traders who were the butt of Homer's scorn (pp. 228–9 above). This may be so, but there is convincing evidence to suggest that the Euboeans may themselves have indulged in overseas trade. By the ninth century they were producing a highly distinctive type of fine pottery characterized by skyphoi (drinking vessels) and plates painted with pendent circles. These wares are found throughout the Aegean, on Cyprus, and along the coast of the Levant, with a particular concentration at the port of Al Mina, at the mouth of the Orontes, sufficient to suggest the presence here of a Euboean trading enclave. A few skyphoi found around the Tyrrhenian Sea hint that western journeys were also being made. It is tempting to suggest that some memory of these exploits is reflected in the Hymn to Delian Apollo, which mentions Euboea, 'famous for its ships'.

The tentative exploration of the Tyrrhenian by the Euboeans in the late ninth and early eighth centuries coincided with Phoenician activity in the same sea. At this early stage, before spheres of influence were staked out, there is unlikely to have been much aggressive competition. Euboean pottery is found at Phoenician settlements in Sardinia and at Carthage, while there appears to have been a significant Phoenician presence at the Euboean colony founded at Pithekoussai on the island of Ischia in the Bay of Naples. At the port of Al Mina the Euboeans rubbed shoulders with Cypriots and Phoenicians, but by the seventh century the Euboeans had been eclipsed by traders from Rhodes, Samos, Miletos, and Khios. In Egypt, too, foreign traders were welcomed. Herodotus writes of an enclave of citizens from Tyre who had settled around the temple of Astarte at Memphis to trade, and at the end of the seventh century Greek traders were allowed to settle at Naukratis on the Canopic branch of the Nile some eighty kilometres from the sea. All these examples suggest that in the early centuries of the first millennium trading centres were cosmopolitan, the different ethnic communities working together, sharing each other's knowledge, and trading in each other's commodities.

The Euboean settlement of Pithekoussai, founded about 770 BC, heralds the beginning of Greek interest in establishing overseas colonies. Over the next two centuries or so, many of the Greek polities around the Aegean sponsored groups of pioneers to set up communities on foreign shores. The favoured areas were the Black Sea and the Tyrrhenian Sea, especially Sicily and southern Italy, where the colonies were so numerous that the region became known as Magna Graecia (Greater Greece). Colonies were also founded in Cyrenaica (on the east coast of what is now Libya) and along the east coast of the Adriatic.

The settlement at Pithekoussai shows something of the dynamics of the pioneering phase. The offshore island of Ischia was probably first used as a safe and convenient place for summer markets set up by Euboean and Phoenician traders to do business with the natives of the nearby mainland. From here they could also access Elba with its source of high-quality iron ore. Eventually, about 770 BC, the decision was made to establish a permanent settlement. That the first settlers are likely to have been largely males is suggested by the fact that a significant number of the female burials in the early cemetery were interred with indigenous-style jewellery, as might be expected if the wives had been local women. After a generation or so the trust between the newcomers and the natives was such that a new settlement was set up on the mainland coast at Cumae, an event which coincides with a further influx of new settlers. The new settlement was an immediate success, and by 700 BC it had already begun to eclipse the island colony. The vicissitudes experienced by overseas settlements will have varied, but the overall trajectory was for communities to grow and to set up daughter colonies when the opportunity presented itself.

Greek overseas settlement differed from that of the Phoenicians and was driven by different forces. The prime mover in the Greek world seems to have been population increase at home, where the holding capacity of the territory around the polis was often limited. This led to tensions which drove the more enterprising of the young men to leave home. The freedoms and opportunities of a pioneer settlement on foreign soil would, for many, have been preferable to the restriction of the polis dominated by a conservative hierarchy bound by convention. Thus it was that oracles were consulted and bands of young people eagerly set out for a new life. The scale of this diaspora was considerable. Miletos, for example, is credited with having organized ninety colonies around the Black Sea. Not all would have been successful. Herodotus tells one revealing story of how the inhabitants of Thera were forced by successive bad harvests to choose by lot a sector of the population to be sent away to found a colony. The oracle advised that Cyrenaica in North Africa was a suitable region, but the reluctant colonists opted for an island off the African coast. When the colony failed, the oracle was again consulted and told them that they should have followed her original advice. This time they did what she said and established a successful colony on the African mainland, founding the city of Kyrene, which soon flourished. No doubt the religious hierarchies associated with the principal oracular shrines assembled a fund of knowledge from pilgrims visiting from all over the ancient world. It was this wisdom that they conveyed through the utterances of the oracles to would-be pioneers.

The Greeks distinguished between two kinds of overseas settlement: *apoikia*, a 'home away from home', and *emporion*, an enclave set up to manage trade between the Greek world and the indigenous population. An *apoikia* implies a full citizen colony surrounded by a territory (*khora*) which could support the population, while an *emporion* need have been little more than a community of traders. In reality the difference was probably less stark, and over time the distinction would have become blurred into irrelevance.

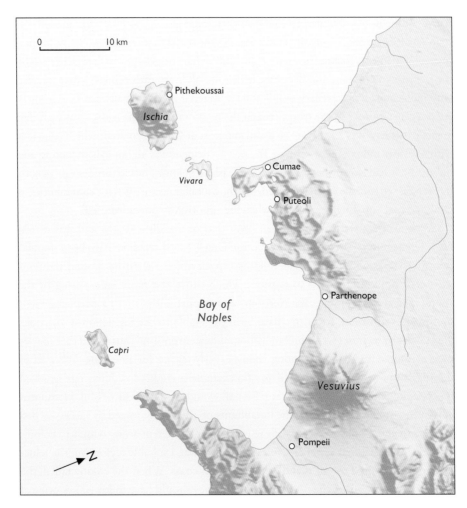

6.23 The region of the Bay of Naples played a significant part in contact between the east and central Mediterranean. The small island of Vivara received Aegean traders in the late second millennium BC, whose presence is known from quantities of pottery which they brought with them. Later, in the eighth century, Euboeans founded a colony at Pithekoussai on the island of Ischia. A century or so later the Greeks moved to the mainland to establish the new colony of Cumae. About 650 BC a later Greek colony, Parthenope, was set up by Rhodians further round the bay, eventually to become Naples (the 'new town', Neapolis). Other Greek enclaves appeared at Puteoli (now Pozzuoli) and Pompeii

Greek interest in the western Mediterranean seems to have come quite late. According to Herodotus it was Phokaians, from the coast of Asia Minor, who opened up the sea-routes to Iberia, establishing a friendly relationship with Arganthonios, king of the Tartessians. The interest of the eastern Greeks in Iberia is further emphasized by the story which Herodotus relates about a remarkable voyage made by a ship's master

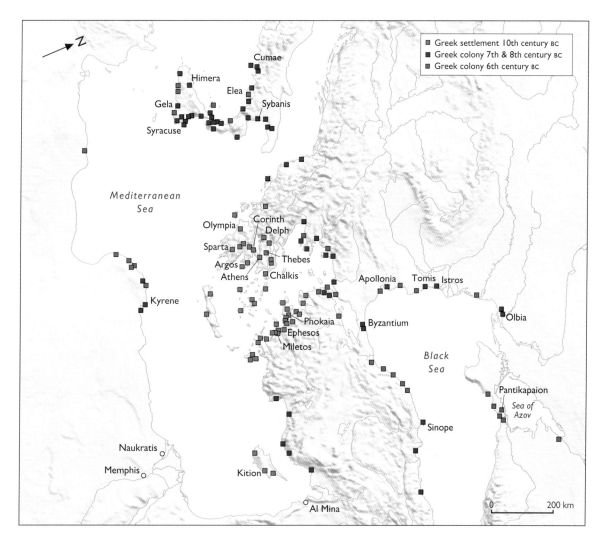

6.24 The waves of colonization emanating from the Greek world in the eighth and seventh centuries engulfed southern Italy and Sicily, which became known as Magna Graecia (Greater Greece). Colonies were also established around the Black Sea and on the North African coast of Cyrenaica. In the sixth century new colonies were set up in these regions and the more adventurous reached the shores of southern France

called Kolaios. Sailing from the island of Samos about 630 BC, bound for Egypt, he was driven off course by fierce winds, ending up, by some miracle, in Tartessos. Here, we are told, he found the town 'unfrequented by merchants', and by skilful trading he came away with an extremely valuable cargo, so valuable that one-tenth of the profit enabled him to commission a sumptuous bronze wine vessel, which he dedicated as a thanks-offering in the temple of Hera on Samos (*Histories* 4.10). The story is not without its problems. It seems extremely unlikely that he could have encountered a storm of sufficient constancy and magnitude to blow his ship the length of the Mediterranean. More probably he had heard stories of the wealth of the west, perhaps from Phoenician sailors, and decided to explore for himself. Tartessos was hardly 'unfrequented by

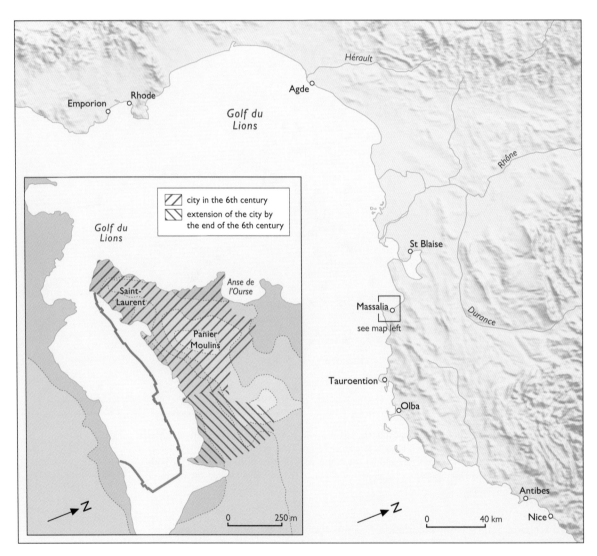

6.25 The colonial city of Massalia (Marseille) was founded by Phokaian Greeks *c.*600 BC, and other colonies soon sprung up around the Golfe du Lion. Massalia lay close to the mouth of the river Rhône, which provided access to the Iron Age chiefdoms of middle Europe. The city occupied a promontory commanding a large, well-protected harbour, now the Calanques

merchants' since the Phoenicians had been established there for at least three hundred years, but it could be that he was the first Greek to get there. Once the contact had been made and the success of the voyage proclaimed, other Greeks would have followed.

Archaeology adds some support to the broad narrative. The first Greek imports found in southern Iberia comprise luxury goods, including Rhodian *oionochoai* (wine jugs), a griffin-headed cauldron, and Rhodian and Corinthian wares found at Huelva and along the south coast. These date to the end of the seventh or early sixth century and could as well have been imported by Phoenicians as by Greeks. But from the end of the seventh century the port city of Huelva received a considerable quantity of Greek pottery, including fine wares from Attica, Corinth, Khios, Lakonia, and Ionia, and transport amphorae from Khios, Corinth, and Samos: a Phokaian coin of the early sixth century was found at Seville. The quantity of imports is sufficient to suggest that Greek ships originating in the eastern Greek world were now making regular voyages to Tartessos, exploiting the contacts that the Phoenicians and Kolaios had pioneered.

It was not long after this, about 600 BC, that the Phokaians established their first colony in the western Mediterranean at Massalia (Marseille) in a territory already

6.26 Marseille is today a thriving international port, but the Calanques (*top left*), no longer large enough to take modern shipping, is given over to pleasure craft. The Greek colony occupied the rising ground immediately to the north (*right*) of the harbour. The excavation in the foreground explored part of the ancient harbour

opened up by Etruscan traders. Other colonies were soon to follow all around the Golfe du Lion, creating a firm base from which the Greeks could exploit the many trading opportunities offered by Iberia.

The Atlantic Contribution

The Atlantic seaways, invigorated in the latter part of the third millennium when the scramble for metals—gold, copper, and tin—created a new mobility, remained a force encouraging connectivity throughout the second millennium. This does not mean that people moved along the whole of the Atlantic façade from one end to the other, but rather that incremental movements between neighbouring communities led to a degree of cultural convergence—a sharing of ideas, values, and, in some cases, artefacts. There were periods when contacts lessened and some regions became isolated, but by the thirteenth century BC—the beginning of what archaeologists call the Final Atlantic Bronze Age—the polities of the Atlantic zone had converged culturally to a remarkable degree. Society was dominated by a heroic male aristocracy; burial seems to have been largely by excarnation; over much of the area, hoards of metalwork were being buried in the ground or deposited in watery places to put them within the realms of the chthonic deities; and, from about 1000 BC, strongly fortified centres were being built in a variety of local styles. All this is clear from the rich archaeological record.

The warrior aristocracy was equipped with a round shield, usually made of leather, and fought with a slashing sword and a spear. Central to maintaining the cohesion of society was the feast, represented by the great communal bronze cauldron, flesh-hooks for dragging out the boiling meat, and rotary spits for roasting joints. At such gatherings the status of the participants would have been reaffirmed or contested, brave deeds remembered, and expeditions planned. The distribution of the artefacts associated with these various activities embraces the whole of Atlantic Europe. A warrior commemorated on one of the engraved stelae from south-western Iberia would not have felt out of place had he visited his contemporaries on the Shetland islands of the far north, or the Aran islands off the west coast of Ireland.

Such a remarkable degree of cultural similarity argues that the people of the Atlantic were able to communicate in a common language. That the language is most likely to have been Celtic gains strong support from the recent demonstration that Celtic was being used in the south-west of Iberia as early as the eighth century. As a lingua franca for Atlantic communication Celtic may have begun to develop as early as the fourth millennium, when contact along the seaways began to get under way.

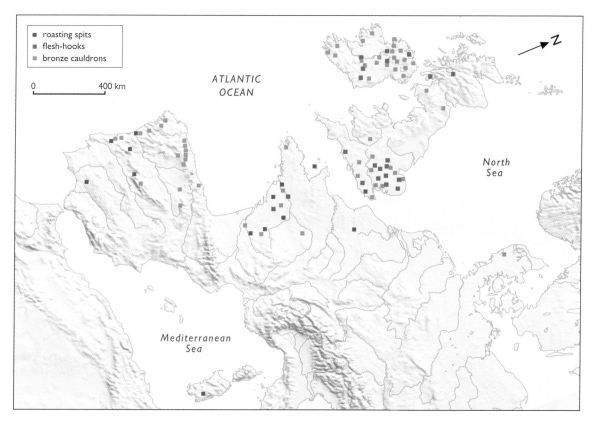

6.27 During the lively Final Atlantic Bronze Age, artefacts were exchanged along the Atlantic coasts of Europe, binding the communities together in networks of exchange. The distribution of items associated with communal feasting, such as cauldrons, flesh-hooks, and roasting spits, shows that similar patterns of social behaviour were shared along the Atlantic façade

The high degree of cultural similarity and the distribution of similar artefacts over so large an area implies that the sea must have been used as a major highway, and yet direct evidence of the boats involved is minimal. Most of the evidence, such as it is, comes from Britain. Three partial wrecks are known, two in the Severn estuary and one on a tributary of the Humber. They are in the tradition of the sewn-plank boats of the second millennium and their dates range between 1200 and 800 BC. To these we can add several probable wreck sites, their presence indicated by large collections of artefacts recovered from the sea bed. One, at Langdon Bay in the shadow of the chalk cliffs of Dover, comprised a cluster of 360 tools, weapons, and other artefacts of French origin dating to 1300–1150 BC. Another, from the Salcombe estuary in Devon, consisted of 259 copper ingots and twenty-seven tin ingots found together with a sword and three gold bracelets dating to about 900 BC. The same estuary has also produced a range of other material that may also have come from wrecks or could have been lost overboard from trading vessels plying between Britain and Brittany. These few scraps from the British waters are a tantalizing reminder of the many Bronze Age wrecks that remain to be recovered.

One of the most notable aspects of the Final Atlantic Bronze Age is that the system was not restricted to the Atlantic but extended into the western Mediterranean, reaching as far as Sardinia, where a comparatively large number of artefacts of Atlantic origin have been found. From Sardinia one or two items, including a rotary spit and distinctive elbow fibulae made in southern Iberia, were carried in the cargoes of other ships to the eastern Mediterranean, while a few artefacts from the Tyrrhenian area, notably shaft-hole axes of Sicilian type, found their way back along the Atlantic seaways to western France and southern Britain. The western Mediterranean system was already under way by the tenth century BC and was probably motivated by a desire for Sardinian copper, which could have been traded for Atlantic tin and gold. The existence of these Atlantic-inspired exchange networks would have facilitated the rapid arrival of the Phoenician traders at Tartessos.

Once the Phoenician presence was established in south-western Iberia, it was not long before Phoenician trading enclaves came into being along the Atlantic coast from Mogador to the Mondego valley—a distance of some fourteen hundred kilometres—served by sailing ships fast enough to outsail the small local boats. By the eighth century this coastal swath had been drawn

6.28 From the eighth century one community living in south-western Iberia began to use Phoenician script on commemorative stelae to write inscriptions in the Celtic language. This example is from Bemsafrim, Lagos, Portugal

firmly into the Mediterranean sphere, undermining the unity of the Final Atlantic Bronze Age. Thereafter north-western France, Britain, and Ireland maintained their connectivity, but increasingly these regions looked across the southern North Sea to continental Europe. The final fragmentation of the old Atlantic system came about 600 BC when the links between Ireland and the rest of north-western Europe withered. Why this should have occurred is not immediately clear, but by now bronze was being replaced by the more ubiquitous iron, and the need to transport large quantities of copper and tin had greatly diminished. The old order was passing.

Epilogue: A Likely Tale

In many ways 600 BC or thereabouts marked a significant watershed. In the Atlantic it signalled the final break-up of the Atlantic Bronze Age continuum, while in the Mediterranean, with the foundation of the Greek colony of Massalia, Greeks, Etruscans, and Carthaginians were beginning to see themselves as commercial rivals. Meanwhile, at the other end of the Mediterranean the curiosity of the pharaoh Necho II led to a momentous discovery—that Africa was surrounded by sea. The story is told by Herodotus. To test his theory, Necho tasked a group of Phoenician sailors to sail from the Red Sea clockwise around Africa and to return, via the Strait of Gibraltar, to Egypt:

> so they sailed into the southern ocean. When autumn came they went ashore wherever they might happen to be, and having sown a tract of land with cereals, waited until the grain was fit to eat. Having reaped it, they again set sail; in this way two whole years went past, and it was not until the third year that they reached the Pillars of Hercules and completed their voyage home.
>
> (*Histories* 4.42)

The story might have been regarded as a fable had not Herodotus offered an additional fact by way of reservation: 'On their return, they said (and I for one do not believe them, but others may) that in sailing around Africa they had the sun on their right hand.' What Herodotus had not realized is that Africa extends to nearly 35° south of the equator, in which case the journey around the southern cape would indeed mean that the sun remained on the right-hand side of the vessel. His expressed doubt goes a long way towards authenticating the voyage. The audacity of the journey should be seen in the context of Phoenician achievements in the Mediterranean and the Atlantic. These were seamen of extraordinary skill, and more adventures were to follow.

7

Of Ships and Sails:
A Technical Interlude

Sufficient will have been said in the last chapter to show that, following the period of disruption in the twelfth century BC, shipbuilding and seamanship played a crucial part in the exploration and exploitation of the Mediterranean and the near Atlantic. The Phoenicians and, later, the Greeks depended for their prosperity, and indeed their livelihoods, on their ability to move huge volumes of food and raw materials over considerable distances. The sea provided corridors of connectivity which, once mastered, could offer quick and comparatively safe passage. The increase in the volume of sea traffic over the course of the first millennium BC provided the incentive for the improvement of shipbuilding technology. It also ensured the rapid evolution of specialist vessels designed not only for carrying cargo, but also for the protection of merchant shipping and the safeguarding of territory.

Evidence for shipping in the thousand years from 1300 to 300 BC is varied. The most direct evidence comes from the shipwrecks themselves, of which over 120 have now been identified in the Mediterranean, but only fourteen of them have yielded details of their hull structures. To this can be added descriptions by classical writers like Homer, Herodotus, and Thucydides, and information gleaned from contemporary depictions on pottery and relief carvings. Taken together it is possible to build up a reasonable understanding of nautical technology and of the various types of ship plying the seas. The principal difficulty comes in attempting to assign specific ships to different ethnic groups, particularly in the earlier part of the period. While it is tempting to try to

259

describe typical Phoenician ships and to distinguish them from Greek ships, there can be little doubt that there was a great deal of borrowing. In international ports like Al Mina on the coast of Syria, ships from all over the eastern Mediterranean docked alongside each other, their crews no doubt taking great interest in each other's vessels. Repairs carried out in such places would have involved people of different ethnicity sharing their technical skills. Similarly, at great ports like Carthage and Huelva, the quantity and variety of imported materials speak of the arrival of vessels from Greece and Phoenicia as well as possibly from Sardinia and Etruria. These were cosmopolitan places and it was not until the fifth century BC that commercial rivalries began to take a hold, leading to conflict and a new isolationism.

An illustration of the issue is provided by the shipwreck found in 1961 in Campese Bay on Giglio, an island off the west coast of Italy. Some structural details of the ship were recovered, including part of the oak keel and some pine planks positioned by treenails (wooden dowels set in the thickness of the planks), which, once fixed, were then sewn together. Its cargo derived from Etruria, Samos, Ionia, and the Phoenician world, so the vessel could have originated from anywhere in the central or eastern Mediterranean. Given the varied nature of the cargoes being carried throughout the Mediterranean, few of the fourteen known wrecks can be assigned with any degree of certainty to a country of origin.

How to Build a Ship

An intriguing do-it-yourself account of how to construct a ship is given in Homer's description of how Odysseus built a sea-going vessel to enable him to leave Calypso's island. Calypso first equips Odysseus with 'a great axe' and an 'adze of polished metal' and takes him to 'where the trees grew tall, alders and poplars and firs … that had long since lost their sap and would make buoyant material for the boat'. There she leaves him to his task:

> He then set to, cutting the planks, and quickly got on with the job. He dragged out twenty felled trees and adzed them with the bronze. He cleverly planed them and made them straight to the line. Then Calypso brought him augers and he cut holes in all the planks and fitted them to each other. He hammered the boat together with *gomphoi* and *harmoniai* and constructed a broad boat (*edaphos*) as wide as a trading vessel built by a skilled carpenter. He next added the decking, which he fixed to the ribs at short intervals, finishing off with long gunwales down the sides. He made a mast to go on the boat with a yard fitted to it and a steering

oar to keep her on course. And from the stem to stern he fenced her sides with plaited osier twigs and a plentiful backing of brushwood as protection against the heavy seas. Meanwhile the goddess brought him cloth with which to make the sail. This he manufactured too; and then lashed the braces, halyards and sheets in their places on board. Finally he dragged her down on rollers into the tranquil sea.

(*Odyssey* 5.243–61)

The description is so immediate and so detailed that it is tempting to believe that Homer was describing an activity he had personally witnessed. Many points of interest emerge, not least the emphasis on the boat being wide-bodied like a merchant ship. Here Homer is making a contrast to the sleek, narrow-bodied warships of the time. What actually is meant by *gomphoi* and *harmoniai* has been much debated but this is probably a reference to the use of treenails to position the planks or perhaps to mortise and tenon joints locked by dowels, a technique observed in the Uluburun ship and in a number of other wrecks. The decking referred to is probably the raised deck at the stern, on which the steersman sits. What Odysseus was doing with the brushwood is less clear but it could be that it was spread between the ribs as dunnage to protect the planking from the cargo. Such an arrangement was found in the Cape Gelidonya wreck.

Some Further Technicalities of Hull Construction

It is clear both from Homer's description and from the recovered wrecks that Mediterranean ships of the late second and early first millennium were built plank first, with strengthening ribs added later. Since the planks were butted edge to edge, the main technical issue was how to hold them in place and how then to keep them together. The problem had been partly solved by the Egyptians. The Cheops ship had made use of mortise and tenon joints as early as the third millennium. Those in the superstructure were locked (that is, held by dowels so the joint could not pull apart), but those in the hull were without locking. The earliest known use of locked mortise and tenon joints in hull construction is found in the Uluburun ship, built about 1300 BC, which was probably of Levantine origin. It is quite possible, therefore, that the technique was developed in Egypt and was adopted in the Levant, along with other Egyptian innovations such as the sail, sometime in the first half of the second millennium. That the Romans referred to this method of jointing as *coagmenta punicana* (Punic joints) supports the idea of transmission via the Levant.

A rather different tradition for securing planks, widely used in the Mediterranean, was by sewing. This involved first positioning the planks relative to each other with

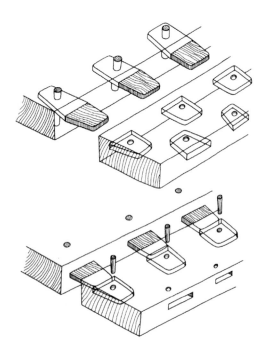

treenails or mortise and tenon fastenings, and then sewing across the seam with a continuous fastening passed through holes bored in the edges of the planks in such a way that the fastenings were not proud of the underside of the planks. The stitches were usually wedged in the hole, and battens, held in place by the stitches, were used to cover the junction between the planks on the inside of the vessel. This method is first recorded in third-millennium Egypt and may be implied in Homer's description of the state of the Greek ship beached for nine years near Troy when he says, 'The timbers ... have rotted and the cords have perished' (*Iliad* 2.135), though 'cords' in this case could refer to rigging.

7.1 One of the key characteristics of early shipbuilding in the Mediterranean was the way in which the hull planks were positioned in relation to each other and fixed with mortise and tenon joinery, a technique first developed in Egypt

7.2 The harbour of Massalia (Marseille) produced ample evidence of shipping. The photograph shows the two wrecks found at place Jules-Verne. To the front is wreck 9, probably a fishing boat. The larger wreck, 7, behind, was probably a cargo ship. Both date to the end of the sixth century BC

Several wrecks with sewn joints are known around the Mediterranean from 600 BC onwards, but, to complicate matters a little further, a few vessels are known with both locked mortise and tenon joints and sewing. Two of the wrecks found during the excavation of place Jules-Verne in Marseille illustrate the point. Both date to the end of the sixth century BC. Wreck 7 was a cargo ship some 14 metres in length. Its planks were mainly secured by locked mortise and tenon joints, but sewing was used for repairs and at the ends of the hull, where shearing stresses would have been at their greatest. Wreck 9, a small fishing boat 5 metres long, used treenails to fix the planks in relation to each other and sewing to attach them tightly together. The Giglio wreck (mentioned above) also had only wedged

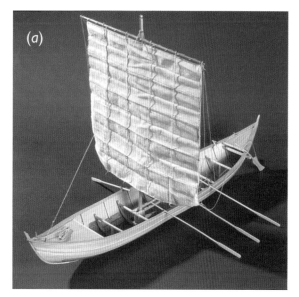

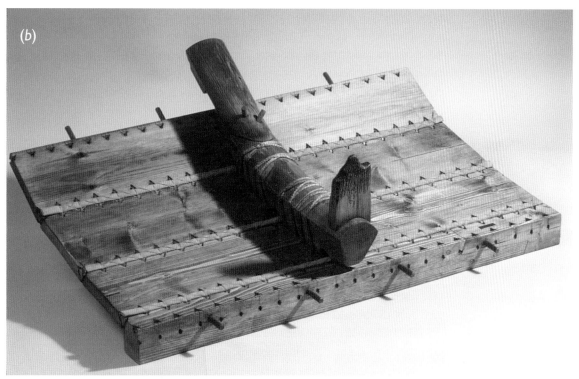

7.3 The model, (a), offers a reconstruction of Jules-Verne 9. (b) shows the way in which the hull planks were positioned with dowels and were sewn together

sewing, while wrecks from Gela, Sicily (*c.*500 BC), and Ma'agan-Michael near Haifa (*c.*400 BC) used a combination of sewing and locked mortise and tenons.

What to make of these variations is not immediately clear, but one interpretation would be to see the locked mortise and tenon technique as developing in the Levant while the sewing technique originated elsewhere in the Mediterranean, perhaps in the Aegean, with hybrids beginning to appear by the sixth century.

Another structural innovation introduced about 500 BC involved the way in which the planks of the hull were attached to the framing ribs. The traditional method, used in the Playa de La Isla wreck dating to the seventh century, were with lashings passed through the planks. This method was still used in the place Jules-Verne fishing boat (wreck 9), built about 500 BC, but the contemporary cargo boat (wreck 7) had iron nails driven through the planks and frames from the outboard and clenched at the ends to secure them. The use of nails is known from other wrecks dating from this period, but usually they are copper. Thereafter nail-fastened framing becomes the norm.

The sample of early first-millennium wrecks so far available is very limited—far too limited for a definitive account of marine technology, with all its regional variants, to be written. The broad picture that is beginning to emerge suggests a highly cosmopolitan world but one in which innovation and conservatism went hand in hand. Whatever the origin of the different construction techniques, by the middle of the millennium they were being widely disseminated throughout the Mediterranean, making it difficult, if not impossible, to assign individual wrecks to their country of origin.

Volume versus Speed

While the evidence from the wrecks provides useful technical detail, it is the depiction of ships carved in relief or painted on pottery that best informs about the styles of the vessels most commonly in use. There were two principal types: the wide-bodied, 'round' merchantmen designed for their large capacity, and the long, narrow warships built to be sleek and fast. While the merchantmen were lightly manned and relied largely on sail, the narrow ships were crammed with rowers to provide manoeuvrability and acceleration when needed. The two types became ubiquitous throughout the Mediterranean, used by both Phoenicians and Greeks and adopted by other nationalities.

In the Phoenician world the two types are frequently, though somewhat schematically, depicted. The best-known representation is a relief from the palace of Sennacherib at Nineveh in Iraq. The scene illustrates the flight of the people of Tyre and Sidon from the advance of the Assyrians in 701 BC. All available vessels were called into use for the evacuation. The cargo ships are shown rounded in longitudinal profile with vertical posts at both ends, while the warships have high curved sterns and sharply pointed rams projecting at the bow. They are square-rigged with the mast stepped at midships, while the cargo ships have no standing mast, though their masts may have been taken down. Both types of ship were propelled by rowers apparently arranged on two levels, and both have pairs of steering oars at the stern. The vessels are shown packed with refugees or soldiers sitting or standing on decks above the rowers. The row of round emblems just below them may be shields. A similar type of warship is shown in a bas-relief from the palace of Sennacherib at Nineveh dating to about the same period. A warship is also incorporated on the obverse of a coin from Byblos dating

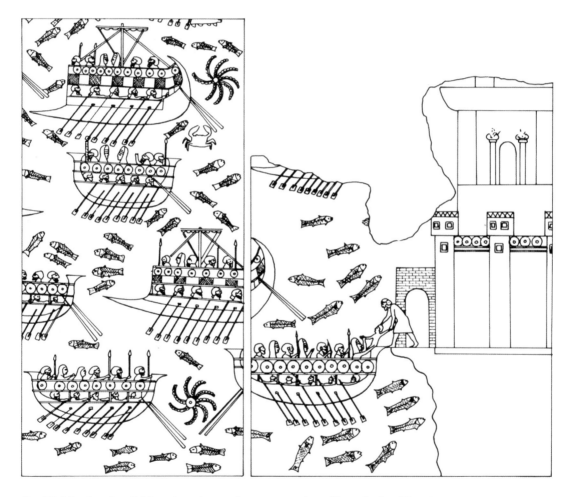

7.4 Simplified drawing of a relief from the early seventh-century BC palace of Sennacherib at Nineveh, northern Iraq, showing King Luli of Tyre fleeing from the city. The building shown to the right is the temple of Melqart

7.5 Detail from a relief from the palace of Sennacherib at Nineveh, northern Iraq, showing a Phoenician warship, seventh century BC

to about 340 BC. The vessel is long with the characteristic high recurved stern and a metal-sheathed battering ram projecting from the bow just above the water-level, but in this case the bow-post is carved with a figurehead representing a lion.

A third type of Phoenician vessel, shown engaged in transporting logs, appears on a relief from the palace of Sargon II at Khorsabad dating to the end of the eighth century BC. The boats are small, with between three and five rowers pulling oars from a standing position, and have high stern- and bow-posts with the top of each bow-post decorated with a horse-head. These are the hippoi mentioned by later writers. The earliest representation of small local craft of this kind is on the bronze frieze from the Gates of Balawat in Nineveh dating to the ninth century. Much later Strabo refers to them being used by fishermen from Gadir exploiting the Atlantic shoals of tuna off Lixus in Morocco. Hippoi were the workhorses of the Phoenician world.

The round cargo ships and the sleek warships with battering rams were probably first developed by the shipbuilders of the Levantine coast. We have already noted the Levantine vessels illustrated in the fourteenth-century tomb of Kenamun in Egypt with their wide, rounded bodies and high vertical stem- and stern-posts (pp. 191–2 above). These are the prototypes for the Phoenician cargo ships shown on the relief from Khorsabad. The first appearance of the battleship powered by two levels of rowers (the bireme, as it became known to the Greeks) is also on the Khorsabad relief. An eastern origin for these warships was accepted by some classical writers, who believed that both the bireme and the trireme were Phoenician developments. But whatever the origin of the different traditions, it is clear that by the eighth century both

7.6 Coin issued by the city of Byblos *c*.340 BC showing a Phoenician warship fitted with a battering ram

7.7 Phoenician ships (hippoi) transporting logs. From a relief in the palace of Sargon II at Khorsabad, Iraq

Phoenicians and Greeks were developing cargo ships and warships to meet their commercial and defensive requirements.

The wide-bellied freighters—the *gauloi* (bath-tubs) to the Greeks, *naves rotundae* to the Romans—were ubiquitous throughout the Mediterranean. Depending on sail and needing only a small crew, they were cheap to run, while their size and shape made them stable at sea and capable of carrying substantial cargoes estimated to be from about ninety to 450 tonnes. They could, however, be slow, though with a favourable wind they could reach speeds of up to five knots, enabling them to cover 160 kilometres in a day's sailing. The basic type had already developed before the end of the second millennium and changed little over the next thousand years.

The evolution of the battleship is, however, a different story. So often in human history the perceived need for defence (which involves the ability to make pre-emptive attacks on potential enemies) has driven technological invention. So it was with the warship. The essential characteristics of speed and manoeuvrability and the facility for carrying a fighting contingent were met by developing long, narrow vessels with provision for a large number of rowers and decking above to house the militia. Such ships may originally have had bow projections at water-level to facilitate beaching. The growing need to engage at sea led to the conversion of this projecting timber into a battering ram by sheathing it with bronze. The art of ramming was to disable the enemy's ship while being able to pull away quickly to reposition for another action. A pointed ram might pierce the enemy at the waterline, but it had the disadvantage of locking the two vessels together, allowing fighting men to swarm between the ships. A much better solution, soon adopted, was to make the ram flat-ended or finned so that a suitably aimed collision would spring the planking of the enemy's ship while allowing the ramming vessel to disengage and reposition. Blunt-ended rams were already in use in the sixth century, but by the time of the Peloponnesian War the finned version had developed, increasing the area of impact and lessening the chance of the ram actually penetrating. The ram sheaths were masterpieces of the bronze caster's art and were immensely costly because of the amount of metal used. One example, the second-century BC ram found in the sea off Atlit, Israel, weighed 465 kilograms and was 2.16 metres long.

Effective use of the ram required skill; it also required a high ratio of oar power to vessel length to create the necessary ramming speed and stability. Thus, once ramming had become an essential tactic in naval warfare, there was an imperative to increase the number of rowers, from twenty in Homer's time, to thirty (triaconters), and eventually to fifty (penteconters). Increasing the number of rowers on a single rowing deck would have meant increasing the length of the vessel, but this would have generated structural weaknesses and instability without improving the ratio of oar power to

7.8 Bronze ram from a Hellenistic or Roman warship found in the sea off the coast of Tobruk, Libya, in 1964. The Belgammel ram, as it is known, weighs twenty kilograms and was cast in a single pouring

vessel length. Other solutions were soon to be found to create more effective fighting vessels, but the standard penteconter remained popular because of its adaptability.

For Greeks engaged in exploration and the establishment of colonies on distant shores the penteconter was the ship of choice. Herodotus writes that the Phokaians were the first Greeks to undertake long voyages of discovery, exploring the Adriatic, the Tyrrhenian Sea, and Iberia. For these journeys they used penteconters rather than round-built merchant ships (*Histories* 4.163). Later, when the inhabitants of Thera decided to send a group of two to three hundred colonists to settle in Cyrenaica, they did so in two penteconters (*Histories* 4.156). Penteconters were also used in exploration and in colonizing missions along the Atlantic coast of Africa (pp. 301–2 below). The accounts imply that ships could be constructed with sufficient capacity to carry passengers and supplies when necessary. Their great advantage lay in their speed and manoeuvrability. Because of their shallow draft they were easy to beach or bring alongside and could slip out of sight quickly behind an island or headland if danger threatened. Such vessels would have been ideal on missions where Greeks or Phoenicians were uncertain of their welcome.

The Rise of the Super-Galley

The race to build more powerful ships with the capacity to carry larger contingents of mariners was driven by the increasing incidence of naval warfare. The obvious solution to the problems of how to increase oar power without greatly increasing vessel length was to introduce a second deck of rowers above the first to create a bireme. This advance had already been adopted by the Phoenicians by the end of the eighth century. The earliest certain image of a Greek bireme appears on an Attic cup of the late sixth century. An earlier image, sometimes claimed as a bireme, on a Late Geometric vase of the eighth century, is best interpreted as an attempt to show two rows of rowers sitting side by side on the same deck. That said, it is quite possible that the Greeks were using biremes as early as the Phoenicians.

Once the idea of multiple rowing decks had been introduced, the next step was the introduction of a third deck to create the trireme, a development that seems to have taken place about 700 BC. Some writers attributed the idea to the Phoenicians. Thucydides' assertion that the earliest Greek triremes were built in Corinth does not necessarily mean that the Greeks were first with the idea. Triremes are mentioned in sixth-century engagements by both Herodotus and Thucydides. By the fifth century they had begun to dominate the Mediterranean.

7.9 Greek vessel depicted on a Late Geometric vase from the Dipylon Gate, Athens, dating to the second half of the eighth century BC, showing a battleship fitted with a battering ram

7.10 Pirates attacking an unsuspecting merchant vessel depicted on a late sixth century Greek cup

Contemporary texts and illustrations on pottery have provided rich material for scholars, enamoured by the technical specifications of these iconic vessels so redolent of Greek naval power, to debate at length. One issue is the meaning of the word. 'Trireme' is an Anglicized version of the Latin *triremis* ('three-oared'). The more precise Greek naval term is *trieres* ('three-fitted'). After centuries of speculation it is now generally agreed that the rowers were placed on three different levels, the highest being accommodated on outriggers extending outwards from each side. So arranged, a vessel of no

7.11 The Krater of Aristonothos, dating to *c*.680–70 BC, showing a sleek warship, perhaps belonging to pirates, attacking a rather more cumbersome merchant vessel

271

7.12 Modern full-sized reconstruction of a trireme under sail. The vessel is named *Olympias*. During sea trials the ship reached a sprint speed of 8.4 knots over a period of a minute or so, with speeds averaging 5.8 knots over a period of one hour

more than 35 metres in length could carry 170 rowers, thereby giving a very favourable ratio of oar power to length. There would also have been an additional crew of thirty, including five officers, about fourteen marines, and various seamen to handle the sails. The equipment carried on the triremes is known in some detail from fourth-century BC inscriptions found at the Athenian naval base at Piraeus. Among the items mentioned are the 'big sail' (mainsail) and the 'boat sail' (foresail) and the various ropes needed to work them: the halyard, the braces, the sheets, and the lifts. There were also two iron anchors and their cables, together with mooring lines.

By the fifth century the trireme had become the prime fighting vessel. At the battle of Salamis, fought in 480 BC, when the Greek fleet of three or four hundred assorted vessels faced a Persian force of about twice the size, both sides relied heavily on triremes. The Greeks had two hundred, requiring thirty-four thousand rowers. Triremes also played a leading part in the Peloponnesian War (431–404 BC), when Athens and her allies confronted Sparta and Corinth. By the fourth century the Athenian navy had grown considerably, the number of triremes reaching four hundred. But by now the trireme was beginning to be dwarfed by much larger warships. It was fast becoming yesterday's technology.

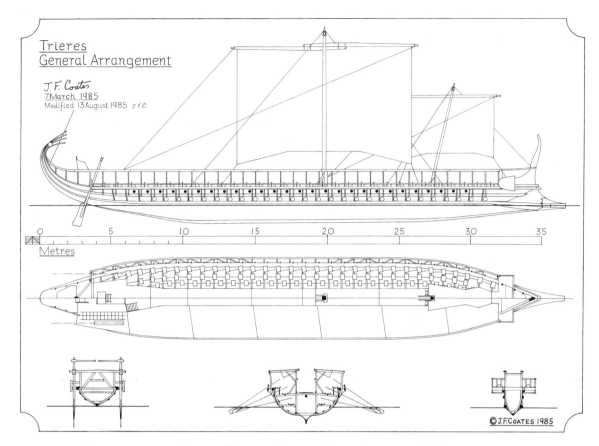

7.13 Drawing of a trireme using a wide range of literary and iconographic evidence upon which the reconstruction of the *Olympias* was based

The new Hellenistic states that began to emerge in the latter part of the fourth century as the power of Athens waned now spearheaded the advances in shipbuilding. Among the formidable navy of Dionysus I of Syracuse (430–367 BC) triremes were overshadowed in size by tetremes ('four-fitted') ships. His son introduced 'six-fitted' vessels. Sizes increased still further under the rulers of the Hellenistic states that emerged after the fragmentation of Alexander's brief empire until Ptolemy IV (reigned 222–204 BC) capped them all by launching a 'forty-fitted' ship. Navies now regularly included squadrons of these mega-ships alongside their triremes and smaller vessels, though Ptolemy's monster was probably built more for show than for practical engagement.

How the rowers were arranged in these super-galleys has been the subject of lively debate. In the trireme and its smaller predecessors each oar was manned by one seated rower. In the larger ships there could be as many as eight men to an oar and, if arranged on more than one deck, the high number of rowers implied in the ships' names could easily be reached. Putting more men to the oar would have increased power. It would also have compensated for lack of skilled rowers. The name *tririka ploia*, sometimes applied to these multi-handed oared vessels, implies that some at least were arranged with three rowing decks, as were the triremes. To have added more would have been to increase the chance of capsizing. And what of the 'forty-fitted' ships? One second-century AD reference discussing a very large vessel described it as 'double-prowed and double-sterned', raising the possibility that it was two vessels joined together in catamaran style, perhaps with a platform between the two to provide space for a large contingent of marines. If each half had three rowing decks with three or four rowers to an oar, the forty rowers could easily be achieved. How manoeuvrable these vast constructions were is a moot point, but their shock-and-awe factor must have been considerable.

7.14 This relief of the late first century BC from Palestrina, Italy, shows a heavy Roman warship with its contingent of marines on the upper deck preparing to disembark

274

The escalation in size of these mega-galleys between the mid-fourth and mid-third centuries was the result of changing naval tactics, away from the ram-and-run style of the earlier period to a grapple, hold, and board approach. Thus, the marines became increasingly important, and many more were now carried. To add to the fighting capacity of the ships removable wooden towers were added to stern and prow to provide platforms for archers and javelin throwers. The larger vessels could also support catapults to hurl a variety of missiles at opponents. Catapults were first used in land warfare about 400 BC. The first recorded sea-battle using catapults took place off Cyprus between Demetrius I of Macedon and Ptolemy I in 307 BC, the catapults both shooting arrows and throwing stones. Another contraption, invented this time by the Romans, was the *corvus* (raven), a boarding device consisting of a long walkway which could be rotated from a fixture in the bows and could be raised and lowered by ropes and pulleys. When its free end was dropped onto the deck of an enemy ship, a sharp iron beak (hence *corvus*) attached to the end penetrated the wood and held fast, allowing marines to board. Naval warfare had changed a lot: ships were now used increasingly to bring armies together.

The destruction of Carthage in 146 BC brought the need for centuries of continuous naval vigilance almost to an end, but it was not until 31 BC, with the triumph of Octavian at Actium, that the last of the old-style sea-battles was fought. Thereafter the navy in the Mediterranean relaxed into peacetime duties, ferrying troops and officials, patrolling the wilder coasts, and occasionally rooting out pirates.

Merchant Fleets

The shipwreck excavated off Kyrenia on the north coast of Cyprus lies at the end of a long tradition of Mediterranean round-ship building which had been evolving throughout the second and first millennia. The vessel, dating to about 300 BC, was built mainly of Aleppo pine. It was comparatively small, some 14 metres in length, with a capacity of about twenty-five tonnes. Its hull planks were fastened solely with locked mortise and tenon joints without any recourse to sewing, while the framing timbers were attached to the planking with long copper nails, driven from outboard through treenails, with their ends hooked and beaten back into the frame. The framing is regular, with floor frames and side timbers alternating with half frames. The mast-step was notched to fit over the frames. A further refinement was that the keel was rockered (it had fore and aft curvature), which facilitated beaching and increased the hull's resistance to stress. Finally, that part of the hull that remained underwater was sheathed in lead primarily to reduce the threat of ship-worms (*Teredo navalis*). The Kyrenian ship was an elegant, carefully crafted vessel incorporating all the boatbuilding skills learned

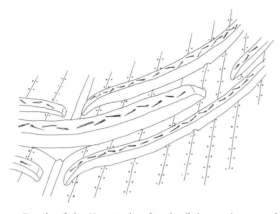

7.15 Details of the Kyrenia ship found off the north coast of Cyprus dating to *c*.300 BC. Its planks were fastened with mortise and tenon joinery and the planks were attached to the frame timbers with long copper nails driven from the outside, their protruding points then being hooked and driven back into the frames

over the centuries, but it was still a small, round ship, little different in capacity from the Uluburun vessel built a thousand years before.

The growing power of Rome, especially after the end of the Second Punic War, and the increasing volume of commercial traffic that ensued, created a demand for larger and larger merchant vessels until, by the first century BC, ships with capacities of four to six hundred tonnes were not at all unusual. The wreck from La Madrague de Giens, off the south coast of Gaul, had a massive hold, 4.5 metres deep, which accommodated three tiers of large amphorae, with boxes of smaller pots stacked above. Vessels of this size called for structural innovations. The strength of the planking shell was increased by broadening the tenons

7.16 The Roman cargo vessel known as the Madrague de Giens wreck, carrying amphorae of wine from northern Italy to Massalia, sank off the French coast in the first half of the first century BC. Here, partially cleared of its cargo, the robust structure of the hull is revealed with its closely spaced framing timbers and the partial boarding of the interior

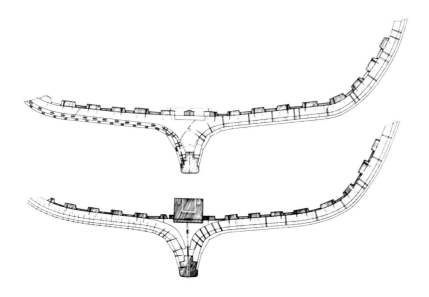

7.17 The sections, here taken through the Madrague de Giens wreck amidships and at the mast-step, show the solidity of the hull structure. It is estimated that the vessel could have carried four hundred tonnes of amphorae stacked in three tiers

used to fasten the planks together; double planking also added to the robustness and integrity of the hull. Keels were now more substantial and their jointing more complex, while the fastening of some frames to the keel added further to the structural strength. The transverse section of the hull also changed to become flatter and deeper to provide greater stowage capacity. With the large merchant ships of the first century BC, Mediterranean shipbuilding had reached a high point.

The Art of the Navigator

Old Testament writers are unanimous in their praise of Phoenician seamanship. For Isaiah the Phoenicians were 'the great ones of the world', while Ezekiel called them 'rulers of the world'. Whatever stereotypes of the wily, cheating trader the Greeks might believe of the Phoenicians, their spectacular seamanship was hard not to acknowledge. Even classical authors reluctantly agree that the maritime feats of the Phoenicians were impressive. To Strabo the Phoenicians were the most skilled of navigators, while Pliny believed that they were the first sailors to apply astronomical knowledge learned from the Chaldaeans to the navigation of the open ocean. It was they who chose to locate the celestial North Pole (at the time not marked by the Pole Star) as the centre point around which the constellation of Ursa Minor rotated—a tighter rotation than that of Ursa Major. The discovery was recognized by the Greeks, who called Ursa Minor 'Phoinike'. Increased contact between Phoenicians and Greeks from the eighth century ensured that knowledge of the navigational arts soon became common among the seamen who frequented the many ports of the Mediterranean. Homer understood the significance of stars for navigating at night, and measurements of star heights above the horizon allowed the ships' masters to steer courses down the latitude, making open-sea crossings a much safer option.

The relationship between the sun's height and latitude was also understood. About 320 BC Pytheas, an explorer to whose travels we shall return (pp. 310–17), set out from Massalia (Marseille) on a journey to north-western Europe using local boats. In order to assess his progress northwards, he calculated the maximum height of the sun above the horizon at midday on the summer solstice, understanding that the height would decrease proportionately as he moved northwards. The first measurement he took was at his home port of Massalia. How this was done we can only guess, but it would have involved calculating the ratio of the height of his measuring staff to the length of the shadow that it cast. To be accurate the measurements had to be taken on land but not necessarily at the midsummer solstice since they could be taken at any time and then corrected, knowing the number of days between the date of the reading and the actual solstice. After leaving Massalia, Pytheas took four sun height readings, enabling him to estimate the distance northwards that his points of reference were from home. He also noted that the number of hours of sunlight at the midsummer solstice increased with distance going north, though he would have had no way to measure this accurately.

It was not until the second century BC that the way of connecting these sun heights to latitude was worked out. This achievement is ascribed to the astronomer Hipparchos of Nicaea, working from an observatory on Rhodes. Having already calculated the obliquity of the sun's observed path and established an accurate estimate for the circumference of the earth, he was able to convert the sun heights, recorded by Pytheas in his book *On the Ocean*, into degrees of latitude assuming the celestial sphere to be 360°. The measurement at Massalia put it at 43° north, while the rest of Pytheas' measurements were taken at 48°, 54°, 58°, and 61° north. The measurement of longitude was far more difficult and, until an accurate chronometer was developed in the eighteenth century AD, the only way to arrive at a rough guide was by estimating speed and direction of travel.

In one of his works, Hipparchos discusses the night sky and the location of the celestial north point. He would have been aware of the Phoenician method of calculating the point in terms of the rotation of Ursa Minor but was interested in arriving

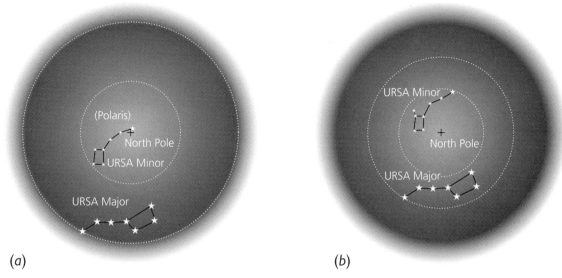

7.18 The diagrams show the position of the North Pole relative to the revolution of Ursa Minor and Ursa Major, (*a*) now, when Polaris is very close to the North Pole; and (*b*) *c.*500 BC, when the position of the pole had to be estimated in relation to the two constellations

at a more accurate method. 'No single star lies at the pole', he writes, 'but an empty space near which lie three stars. The spot marking of the pole, aided by these, encloses a figure resembling a quadrilateral—exactly, in fact, as Pytheas the Massaliot says.' It is an intriguing example of the way knowledge was transmitted. Hipparchos, writing in the mid-second century BC, was quoting from Pytheas' book written 170 years earlier. Where did Pytheas get his information from? His own personal observations, from some other book, or from someone he had met on his travels? An experienced sailor would have had a store of wisdom gleaned over a lifetime. Few would have read books, but the sea lore passed orally from one generation to another would have been immensely rich, far richer than the few scraps recorded in classical sources can begin to suggest. This much is clear from the scale and success of the maritime activity of the first millennium BC.

The Atlantic: Learning from the Inner Sea

The arrival of Phoenician trading ships on the Atlantic coast in the tenth century, and the establishment of trading enclaves along the coasts of Portugal and North Africa during the ninth and eighth centuries, were on a scale that cannot have failed to make an impact on the indigenous maritime people. In the course of a few generations they would have been exposed to revolutionary technologies of shipbuilding—sails, complex rigging, mortise and tenon jointing—and ships' masters whose understanding of celestial phenomena is likely to have been novel and surprising. But the newcomers also had much to learn, not least of Atlantic sea conditions: the frightening phenomenon of the tides and how to cope with persistent onshore winds. Knowledge flows in many directions.

To be able to study this contact period in detail would be fascinating, but sadly the available evidence is sparse in the extreme. We know from Strabo and other classical authors that Phoenician hippoi and penteconters were sailing in Atlantic waters, but no wrecks of Mediterranean or Atlantic vessels of this period are known other than the few sewn-plank boat fragments found in British waters (pp. 151–5 above). There is, however, a small group of tantalizing engravings and paintings which might be relevant. We have already referred to the sailing vessels depicted on rock paintings at Laja Alta, Cádiz, and the rock engraving of a ship with mast and stays from Oia, Pontevedra. While some commentators argue that they record Mediterranean shipping in Iberian waters in the late second millennium, there is nothing to argue that they are not later, reflecting the impact of Phoenician ships on the indigenous imagination. Other images include a creditable impression of a hippos inscribed on a pot from Lisbon and what might be taken for two hippoi engraved on a rock surface at El Cercado on La Palma in the Canary islands. By their very nature, however, the images are without close dating.

The presence of Mediterranean craft must have had an impact on Atlantic shipping. While it is an outside possibility that the sail may already have been in use on the British sewn-plank boats of the second millennium, the appearance of Mediterranean sailing ships would have provided an example of the efficacy of the sail for all to see, and could have led to its widespread adoption along the Atlantic façade. Another lesson to be learned was the value of nailing the planks to the frames, a technique already practised in the Mediterranean by the sixth century. The Venetic vessels against which Julius Caesar battled off the Breton coast in the first century BC were robust, high-sided craft with sails of rawhide, their planking securely fixed with massive iron nails. These indigenous craft were clearly the product of a long-established technology. Perhaps in these Venetic ships we are seeing the culmination of shipbuilding technology carefully honed to suit the fury of the Atlantic, combining traditional local skills with innovations introduced by Phoenicians from the Mediterranean many centuries earlier.

(a)

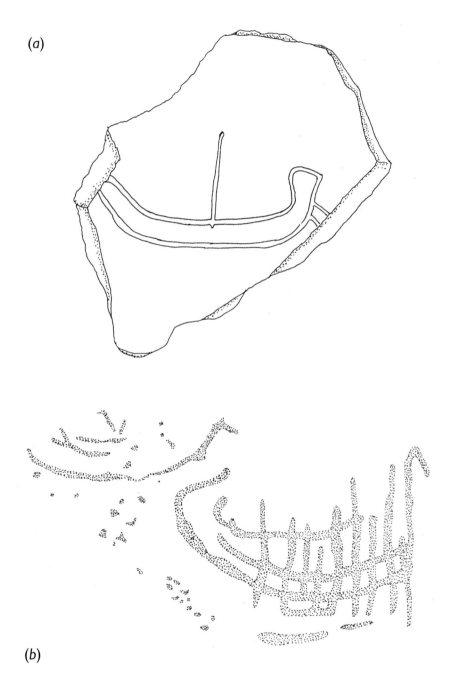

(b)

7.19 Two images of Phoenician ships from the Atlantic seaboard: (*a*) a hippos scratched on a pot sherd found at Lisbon; and (*b*) a hippos depicted on a rock at El Cercado, La Palma, Canary islands

Travelling the Coast: From the Atlantic to the Mediterranean

In the first half of the first millennium BC the volume of maritime traffic passing along the Mediterranean and Atlantic coast of Iberia was considerable, and there can be little doubt that ships' captains acquired a detailed knowledge of the sea-lanes, experiencing the local wind and tide conditions, committing to memory the shape of distinctive headlands, and learning their names and stories about them the better to remember. They would have been aware, too, of convenient anchorages and harbours and of how to approach them safely. Such knowledge was vital. For many it was the stuff of existence to be curated and passed down the generations usually by word of mouth, transmitted perhaps in rhyme. Occasionally these sailing instructions were written down as a periplus. Periploi rarely survive, but one, describing the Iberian coastline, is believed to have formed the basis for the poem *Ora Maritima*, which comes down to us almost in its entirety.

Ora Maritima is a florid, ungainly composition written by the minor Roman official Rufus Festus Avienus, who served in North Africa at the end of the fourth century AD. It was no doubt copied many times, allowing scribal errors to creep in, until the only surviving manuscript surfaced in Venice in published form in 1488. Since then the 714 lines have been pored over by scholars eager to identify the many places mentioned and to distinguish the various sources used. This is no easy task and there are as many different interpretations as there are commentators, but what is broadly agreed is that among the various sources used by Avienus (and he lists a number of them, including Hecataeus, Herodotus, and Thucydides) was a periplus probably composed by a ship's master from Massalia sometime between the sixth and the fourth century BC.

The poem is a cut-and-paste work incorporating snippets of information from various sources stuck onto the periplus, which provides the main storyline—a progression of coastal vignettes beginning on the Atlantic coast of Europe and proceeding down the coast of Portugal, through the Strait of Gibraltar, and along the southern and eastern shores of Spain to Massalia. The main narrative is broken by asides. The fearsome nature of the Atlantic is stressed three times using an unknown source which described a sea journey made by the Carthaginian navigator Himilco (pp. 306–7), while a discursive section on the tribes of the south-western extremity of Iberia may have come from the historian Hecataeus of Miletos or Ephoros of Kyme in Aeolis, Asia Minor. For his description of the strait—which he calls the Pillars of Herakles—Avienus quotes the astronomer Euctemon of Athens and the explorer Scylax of Caryanda. But behind all this lies the relentless progress of the periplus, recording fact after fact about the coastline through the eyes of an experienced sailor:

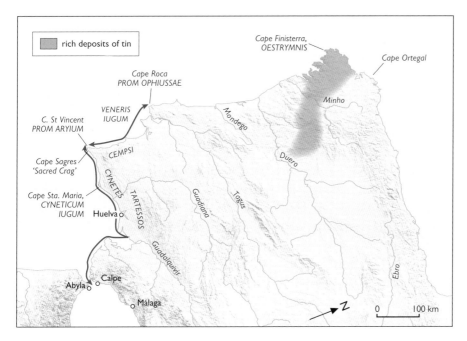

7.20 The periplus embedded in the poem *Ora Maritima* seems to record a journey from Cabo da Roca to Massalia, but the route northwards to Oestrymnis (Cape Finisterre) was also known

The Ana River flows out there through the Cynetes and furrows the land. Again the bay spreads out and hollow land extends to the south. From the aforementioned river, two branches suddenly divide and through the sluggish water of the above mentioned bay—for all this sea is thick with mud—follow their slow courses. Here the tops of two islands raise themselves on high. The smaller one lacks a name, the other tenacious custom has called Agonis. Then there stands ruggedly on the cliffs a crag and it too is sacred to Saturn.

(*Ora Maritima*, lines 205–16)

And so on. Much scholarly effort has been lavished on attempting to identify the places listed, with varying degrees of success. But given the patched-together structure of the poem, its author's partial understanding of his sources, and the scribal errors that are likely to have crept in, no amount of scholarly ingenuity will allow a one-to-one identification. That said, the further the text advances towards the Mediterranean, the more recognizable become the places mentioned.

The most difficult question to answer is, where does the journey begin? The confusion really surrounds the identification of the place called Oestrymnis, described in lines 93–107 as a promontory, a 'lofty mass or rocky height [which] completely faces the warm south wind' and protects a bay in which there are many islands producing tin. The native inhabitants are industrious and much concerned with trade, and they go to sea in boats made of hides sewn together. This fits well with Cape Finisterre in Galicia at the north-western extremity of Iberia, which protects the wide bay of Corcubión to the south, and beyond the islands and promontories of the ria coast of Galicia, an area rich in tin. That Oestrymnis is Cape Finisterre gains some support from a later, rather obscure comment implying that Oestrymnis was an early name for Ophiussa (Spain). The name Ophiussa also seems to be used for a promontory usually identified as Cabo da Roca, the most westerly point of Iberia, close to Lisbon, which, the poem says, is separated from Oestrymnis by 'a great bay of wide sea'—an appropriate description for the inward sweep of the Iberian coast between Cape Finisterre and Cabo da Roca. All this would make sense if the original periplus was describing the journey from the tin-producing coasts of Galicia back to the more familiar part of Iberia around Lisbon before the coastal haul to Massalia could begin.

There is, however, one difficulty. In lines 108–45 Avienus inserts a section saying that from Oestrymnis it is a two-day journey to the Holy Island (Ireland) and Albion (Britain), and then adds some very confused statements about the far north. This could best be accommodated by assuming that this Oestrymnis is the western extremity of the Armorican peninsula. In other words, Oestrymnis was the name used for both Cape Finisterre in Galicia and the westernmost cape of Armorica, and Avienus was confusing the two, overlooking the fact that the Bay of Biscay separated them. If so, then lines 108–45 will be an interpolated text taken from a totally different source, perhaps the work of Pytheas. That the two promontories should be given the same name, Oestrymnis, incorporating the Indo-European word for 'west', need occasion no surprise. Today both promontories are called Finisterre, 'the end of the earth'.

Ora Maritima is a tantalizing text that will continue to fascinate and to tax scholarly ingenuity, but, leaving aside all the academic debates about its constituent parts, what stands out is its core document: the periplus written down by a Massaliot sea-captain, probably in the sixth century BC, to guide those who set out on the long and perilous journey to the ends of the earth in search of tin.

7.21 Cape Finisterre, on the north-western corner of the Iberian peninsula, must have seemed to be the end of the world for those who approached it by land and by sea. To the south (*right in this photograph*) of the great cape lay the more tranquil waters of the ria coast of Galicia, where tin from local sources was widely available

8

Exploring the Outer Ocean, 600–100 BC

The Phoenician pioneers who first ventured into the Atlantic in the tenth and ninth centuries BC found themselves in an alien world—a world dominated by a fearsome unending ocean but one already populated by communities long experienced in using the sea to maintain social contact and to trade in the varied commodities which their hinterlands had to offer. The Phoenician penetration of this new world was explosive, and within a century or so they had set up factories—small enclaves of traders—along a wide front, from Mogador in the south to the Mondego valley in the north. Those enclaves on the European façade used Gadir (Cádiz) as a home base, while the settlers on the African coast looked to Lixus as their anchor. The distances were not great. If the conditions were favourable, a ship could make the passage from the Mondego to Gadir in five days of sailing; from Mogador to Lixus might have taken a day or two longer.

From the factory at Santa Olaia at the mouth of the Mondego, Phoenician traders could make the onward journey to the enticing indented coastline of the Rías Baixas, where tin and probably some gold were to be had from people living in the shadow of the brooding headland of Oestrymnis. A number of the native hill-forts along the coast have produced Phoenician trinkets—iron objects, fibulae, glass beads, and pottery—which speak of Phoenician stop-overs in the estuaries of the Douro, Cávado, and Miño before the ria coastline was reached and where the trade goods concentrate.

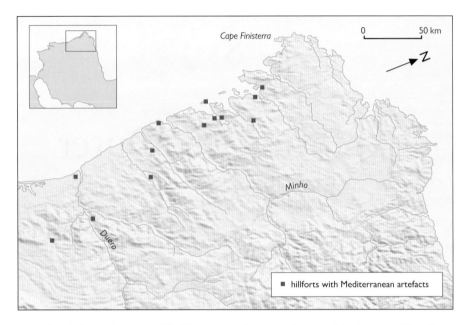

8.1 Although the northernmost of the Phoenician trading ports along the Atlantic coast of Iberia lay in the Mondego estuary, Phoenician ships probably made regular journeys further along the coast to trade for tin and gold. Evidence for this is provided by the distribution of Mediterranean artefacts—pottery, glass beads, armaments, and iron objects—found in the indigenous hill-forts

What is particularly notable is that in this period, from the ninth to the sixth century, Cape Finisterre marked the northernmost limit of Phoenician imports. If all the tin needed could be obtained from Galicia, why venture further north?

Herodotus, writing in the fifth century BC, had heard stories of the tin-rich west, but admits, 'Of the extreme tracts of Europe towards the west I cannot speak with any certainty ... nor do I know of any islands called the Cassiterides where comes the tin which we use' (*Histories* 3.115). Where these tin-rich islands lay has been much debated. Some favour Brittany, others Cornwall, mindful of descriptions of Cornish tin extraction mentioned in much later texts by Diodorus Siculus and Pliny (pp. 312–13 below). But Strabo is in little doubt that the Cassiterides were islands off north-western Iberia. He says that there were ten of them and that they 'lie near each other in the high sea north of the port of the Atabrians'. The Atabrians occupied the northern part of Galicia. He gives a lively picture of the black-cloaked inhabitants and their pastoral lifestyle, adding that they mine tin and lead and 'give these metals and the hides of their cattle to sea-traders in exchange for pottery, salt and copper utensils. In former times it was the Phoenicians alone who carried on this commerce for they kept the voyage secret from everyone else' (*Geography* 3.5.11).

288

At the southern extremity of the Atlantic network lay Mogador, a small island off the African coast opposite the mouth of a minor river, the Ksob. Originally it was one of two islands lying about a kilometre out to sea from the sandy shore of the mainland, but later dune formation and silting joined the other island to the land and it is now occupied by the town of Essaouira. Excavations on the east coast of Mogador have

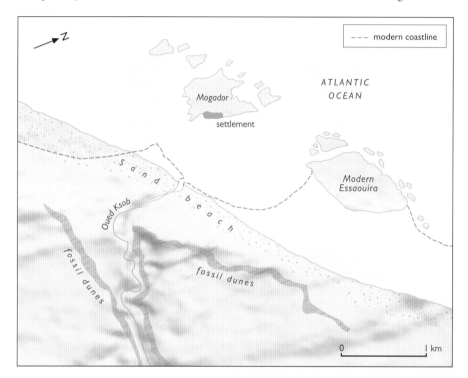

8.2 (*Top*) The island of Mogador, off the coast of Morocco, was chosen by the early Phoenician explorers as a convenient trading base. The topography of much of the coast has changed, but the island still retains its identity

8.3 (*Bottom*) Mogador seen from the mainland. The Phoenician trading port was located on this inland-facing side of the island, protected from the Atlantic waves

produced evidence of a Phoenician factory dating from the seventh century associated with pottery from Cyprus, Attica, and Ionia, as well as artefacts related to fishing. The island would have provided a convenient staging post for those wishing to explore the coastal regions to the south.

Some flavour of these trading expeditions into the wild is given by Herodotus, quoting stories he has heard from Carthaginians. The traders would land on the alien shore and lay out all the trade goods they had brought, and would then return to the ship and light a smoky fire. 'The natives, when they see the smoke, come down to the shore and, laying out to view so much gold as they think that the wares are worth, withdraw to a distance.' The traders would then come ashore again and 'if they think the gold enough they take it and leave but if it does not seem to them sufficient they go aboard the ship once more and wait patiently. Then the others approach and add to the gold until the traders are satisfied' (*Histories* 4.196). In this silent trade no one cheats since the exchange is mutually beneficial and it is in the interests of both partners that it should be repeated.

There is little that can yet be said of the intensity of this early Phoenician trade or of its vicissitudes, nor is it possible to give a proper analysis of the changing relations between the trading enclaves and the native populations, but the archaeological potential is there and will in time be realized. What is clear is that the sixth century was a time of rapid change—some refer to it as a period of crisis—when the old systems broke down and new imperatives began to drive a fresh wave of Atlantic exploration. But to understand this it is necessary first to explore the seismic changes under way in the Mediterranean.

In Mare Nostrum

The foundation of Carthage by settlers from Tyre in the late ninth century was motivated by the desire to develop a new commercial hub in the central Mediterranean. This was no mere way station on the route to the west—a convenient place to stop off for provisions and a little desultory trade—but a place very carefully chosen for its potential to grow rich on the unusually fertile hinterland that is now Tunisia. The great plains, well watered by the river Medjerda, provided grain in abundance, while coastal lands enjoyed the best of the Mediterranean climate, yielding all kinds of fruit and vegetables. Writing later of the lushness of the region Diodorus Siculus records:

8.4 (*Opposite*) The city of Carthage lay on the Bay of Tunis on a broad promontory. It may have been preceded by Utica, located on a bay to the north, close to the estuary of the Medjerda, but the silting of the bay eventually rendered the port unusable. Carthage, scoured by the sea, escaped these problems and thrived

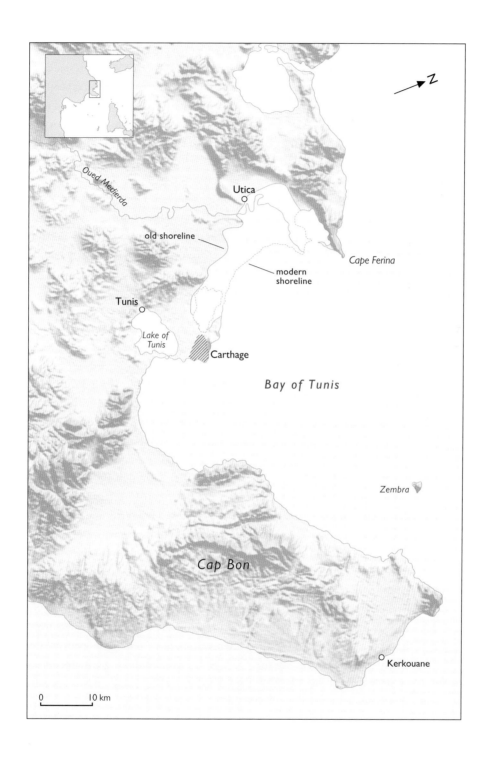

Oued Medjerda

Utica

old shoreline

modern
shoreline

Cape Ferina

Tunis

Lake of
Tunis

Carthage

Bay of Tunis

Zembra

Cap Bon

Kerkouane

0   10 km

It was divided into market gardens with orchards of all sorts of fruit trees ... The barns were filled with all that was needed to maintain a luxurious standard of living. Part of the land was planted with vines, part with olives and other productive trees. Beyond these cattle and sheep were pastured on the plains, and there were meadows filled with grazing horses. Such were the signs of prosperity in these regions, where leading Carthaginians had their estates.

(Diodorus Siculus 20.8.1–4)

The Carthaginians were known in the ancient world for their expertise in agriculture and wrote textbooks on the subject. It was fear of the country's abundance that encouraged the older Cato, in the mid-second century, to fling down lush North African figs as evidence of this before the Roman senate, demanding, as he so often did, 'Carthago delenda est' ('Carthage must be destroyed'). Carthage was founded to prosper by those who had a good eye for location. And prosper it did.

At the time when Carthage was founded, another power block was emerging in Etruria, where, between the ninth and seventh centuries, Villanovan villages coalesced into towns which soon grew to become the largest and most opulent in the central Mediterranean. The economic base for this spectacular growth lay in the rich metal deposits of the Colline Metallifere (Metal-Bearing Hills) behind the coastal towns of Populonia and Vetulonia and from the island of Elba close by. Iron from Elba was famous, while the hills of the mainland, in addition, produced ample supplies of copper, silver, and lead. Demand for metals drew Etruria into the sphere of the eastern Mediterranean networks, and soon quantities of exotic luxury goods were pouring in—raw materials like gold and ivory, together with high-value manufactured goods from Cyprus, Egypt, and the Levant, and fine figured pottery from the Greek workshops—influencing local craftsmen and creating a rapid cultural change characterized by archaeologists as the 'orientalizing period'. Soon craftsmen from around the eastern Mediterranean were moving to the thriving Etruscan cities to set up workshops to serve the demands of the elite. In many ways the Etruscans were experiencing the same astonishing transformation as were their contemporaries in Tartessos. But one difference was that, whereas Tartessos benefited from its relative isolation, the Etruscan cities had to share the Tyrrhenian Sea with other powerful entrepreneurs: the Greeks. It was to safeguard their trading interests that they soon developed an effective maritime force. The Greeks, for their part, were busy establishing settlements on the coasts of Sicily and southern Italy and around the Bay of Naples. These were self-sustaining citizen colonies usually set within fertile hinterlands able to produce agriculture surpluses to trade with the cities of the Greek homeland, where supplies of foodstuffs were always in demand. The colonization of the Tyrrhenian region had begun in the early eighth century, and already, by the middle of the seventh century, Magna Graecia had expanded to include much of the coastal region of southern Italy and Sicily.

For most of the eighth and seventh centuries Phoenicians, Greeks, and Etruscans lived in comparative harmony, but it was an unstable equilibrium that could easily be upset. The potential flash-points were at the western end of Sicily, where Phoenician cities were tightly juxtaposed with Greek, and in Campania, where the Etruscans had established control over a considerable territory using the Gulf of Salerno as their point of entry. The effect of this was to isolate the Greek cities around the Bay of Naples from the rest of Magna Graecia, an isolation further exacerbated when the Etruscans extended their control over the Tyrrhenian coast between Campania and Etruria.

The delicate balance was finally upset by events in the eastern Mediterranean. It began when, towards the end of the seventh century, eastern Greeks from the coasts and islands of Asia Minor began to take an active interest in the central and western Mediterranean. The first recorded contact was the visit of the Samian seafarer Kolaios to Tartessos about 630 BC, and it was probably about this time that, if Herodotus is to be believed, the Phokaians were exploring the Adriatic, the Tyrrhenian Sea, and southern Iberia in their penteconters. As a result of the reconnaissance the Phokaians decided to establish a colony at Massalia on the Golfe du Lion, an area in which the Etruscans had been actively trading for decades. According to Thucydides, the Carthaginians, allies of the Etruscans, tried to prevent this incursion but were defeated in a naval battle. The Phokaian confrontation with the Etruscans was further intensified when they established a colony at Alalia (now Aléria) on the east coast of Corsica and probably another at Olbia on the east coast of Sardinia. The Phokaian settlements were a direct threat to Etruscan commercial activity in what they had hitherto regarded as their own domain: it could not go unchallenged. A further blow to Etruscan naval supremacy came with the foundation of a colony on the island of Lipari by settlers from Rhodes and Knidos. The islands were strategically important, not only to the Etruscans but also to the Phoenicians.

Matters came to a head in 544 BC when the Persians, advancing westwards, annexed the Greek cities of Asia Minor, causing the entire population of Phokaia to take to their boats and flee. Some probably settled in the colony of Massalia, where the archaeological evidence shows an upsurge of activity around this time. Others settled at Alalia, causing fury among the Etruscans, who now, with the Carthaginians as allies, decided to oppose the settlement. Herodotus tells how a squadron of sixty Carthaginian ships were sent to join the Etruscan fleet of the same size and were met by sixty Phokaian ships. In the engagement that took place on the Sardinian Sea, possibly in the strait between Sardinia and Corsica, the Phokaians won the battle but lost forty of their ships, and of the remainder 'their beaks were so bent and blunted as to be no longer serviceable' (*Histories* 1.166). As a result the Phokaians decided to abandon Corsica and eventually settled at Velia on the Italian coast, safe within Magna Graecia. The exact date of the battle of the Sardinian Sea is unrecorded but it probably took place about 537 BC. In the aftermath the Etruscans founded a colony of their own on Corsica, perhaps taking over the site of the abortive Greek settlement.

The Carthaginians, meanwhile, were consolidating their hold on the western Mediterranean. Already, in 654–653 BC, they had founded a colony on Ibiza, the better to be able to reach the south coast of Iberia. Ibiza is on the same parallel as the Phoenician ports of southern Sardinia and could therefore be reached across the open sea by latitude sailing. From there it was only a short hop—less than a day's sailing—to Cabo de la Nao, welcoming the traveller to the friendly Iberian coast. The creation of a permanent base on Ibiza was a strategic move in the Carthaginian plan to strengthen her hold over the western Mediterranean. The old Phoenician colonies along the coast of southern Iberia now came increasingly under Carthaginian control, while, nearer home, Carthage drew the colonies on Sardinia and Sicily firmly into her sphere. The central position of Carthage was further enhanced when, in 573 BC, the Babylonians overran the Phoenician cities of the Levant, cutting the umbilical cord with the Levantine motherland and leaving Carthage as leader of the Phoenician west.

After the battle of the Sardinian Sea the maritime reach of the Etruscan cities became more and more restricted, not least as Carthaginian power grew. This, and their inability to dislodge the Greeks from the strategically vital Aeolian islands, meant that their sphere of influence was now restricted to the northern Tyrrhenian Sea. Attempts to take over the Bay of Naples by attacking the Greek city of Cumae in 525 BC failed. Hostilities continued, but the routing of an Etruscan fleet off Cumae in 474 BC marked the end of Etruscan aspirations in the region. Adding to their troubles was the rise of Rome, which had freed itself from Etruscan control about 510 BC.

Rome's new-found power was acknowledged the following year when a treaty was agreed between Carthage and Rome laying down, in some considerable detail, spheres of influence and rules of engagement. The text, recorded by Polybius, states:

> There is to be friendship between the Romans and their allies and the Carthaginians and their allies on these terms. The Romans and their allies are not to sail with longships beyond the Fair Promontory unless forced by storm or by enemies. It is forbidden for anyone carried beyond it by force to buy or carry away anything beyond what is required for the repair of his ship or for sacrifice and he must depart within five days ... The Carthaginians shall do no wrong to the peoples of Ardea, Antium, Laurentium, Circeii, Terracina or any other city of the Latins who are subject to Rome ... They shall build no fort in Latin territory ...

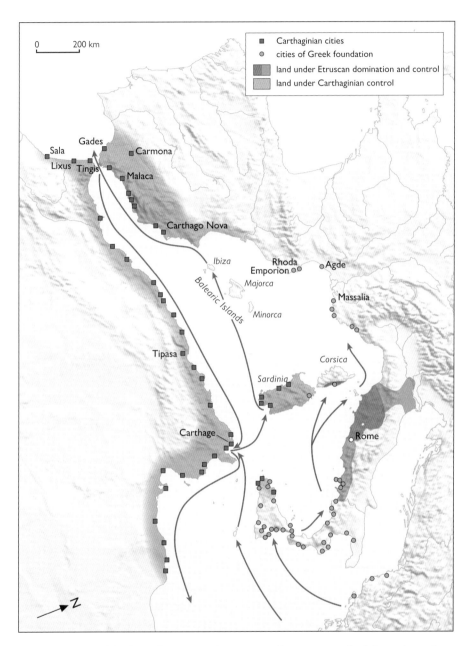

8.5 By the middle of the first millennium BC the western Mediterranean was divided into three spheres of influence: Greek, Punic (Carthaginian), and Etruscan. Etruscan interests were curtailed by Greek expansionism, which also threatened the Carthaginian sphere of influence. Later, when Etruscan power waned, Rome entered the competition on the side of the Greeks

That the treaty had to be reviewed on several occasions reflects the continuing tenseness of the situation.

Within what the Carthaginians regarded as their sphere of influence they were not always successful. In 490 BC off Cape Artemisium on the Iberian coast a Carthaginian fleet was destroyed by a Greek contingent, and ten years later on the north coast of Sicily at Himera a Carthaginian army was driven off by the Greeks. If Diodorus is to be believed, the Persians sent a delegate to Carthage to plan concerted attacks on the Greeks in their homeland and on Sicily (Diodorus Siculus 11.1). Both failed, the Carthaginians at Himera and the Persians at Salamis: 480 BC was a notable year for the Greeks. But the tensions continued to build, and from this time onwards the western Mediterranean south of a line from Sardinia to the Balearic islands, including the approach to the Strait of Gibraltar, became a no-go area for Greek shipping.

The growth of Roman power and their championing of the Greeks made it increasingly difficult for Carthage and Rome to coexist in the Mediterranean. That the uncomfortable equilibrium lasted for so long is surprising, but eventually, in 264 BC, the two powers found themselves at war over a territorial dispute on Sicily. The First Punic War, as it is now known, lasted until 241 BC. Rome emerged the victor, claiming Sicily as its first overseas territory, and a few years later Sardinia and Corsica were added to its nascent empire. Carthage, realizing that she had lost the Tyrrhenian, now turned her attention to Iberia as a potential centre of power well away from Roman influence. In 237 BC an expedition was sent to found a new city, Carthago Nova (now Cartagena), on a fine, well-protected harbour on the coast of Murcia. An added advantage of the site was that to reach it from Carthage one could sail north-west to the Galite islands off the north coast of Tunisia, and then along the latitude directly to Carthago Nova. The move initiated a new forward policy in southern Iberia, bringing the approaches of the strait even more firmly into the Carthaginian sphere.

The rest of the story may be briefly told. Conflict soon arose on the east coast of Iberia between Carthaginian interests and the Greeks settled around the Golfe du Lion, who were intent on expanding their trading operations down the coast of Iberia. Rome entered the dispute on the side of the Greeks and all-out war ensued (the Second Punic War, 218–201 BC), spreading to Italy and North Africa. In the end Rome triumphed and in doing so acquired all the Carthaginian territories in Iberia, leaving the Carthaginian empire reduced to its African homeland. Even so, Carthage was still seen as a threat to Roman interests in the central Mediterranean—a power to be annihilated at all costs. So it was that in 149 BC Roman armies landed in Africa, initiating the Third Punic War, which ended with the destruction of Carthage in 146 BC. It is a nice coincidence that in the same year Corinth also fell to the Roman army:

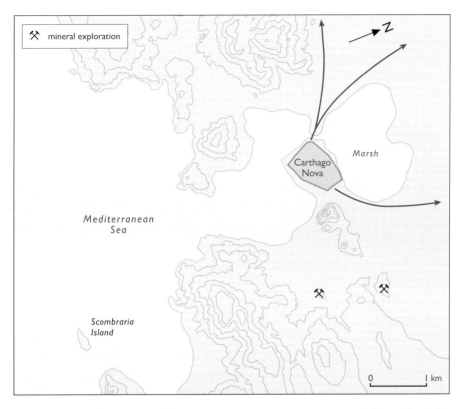

8.6 Carthago Nova (now Cartagena), founded by the Carthaginians in 228–227 BC following their defeat in the First Punic War, was intended to be the centre of their expansionist policies in Spain. The site was carefully chosen for its defensive qualities and its fine, well-protected harbour. It was also conveniently close to rich sources of silver

two of Rome's greatest maritime competitors had been brought to their knees within a few months of each other.

What stands out from these momentous events is the strength of the commercial imperatives that drove them. At first Carthage remained largely aloof as the Etruscans and Greeks contested their spheres of influence. It was the western Mediterranean that they saw as their own. But the influx of new waves of eastern Greeks at the end of the seventh century changed the dynamic, forcing the Carthaginians into alliances with the Etruscans against the Greeks. From their newly established forward base on Ibiza the Carthaginians could begin to restrict Greek access to Iberian waters south of Cabo de la Nao. As tensions grew during the sixth century, Greek shipping was excluded altogether, and the long, narrow Alboran Sea leading to the strait became a

Carthaginian preserve, while the Greeks were left to consolidate their holding around the Golfe du Lion.

It was during the gathering crises of the sixth century that the Carthaginians began to consider seriously the economic potential of the Atlantic, driven perhaps by the realization that the Mediterranean was fast filling with competitors.

The Atlantic-Facing Shore

The south-western extremity of Iberia, northwards from Gadir (Cádiz), offered a friendly coastline for sailors, its distinctive headlands like Cabo de São Vicente, Cabo Espichel, and Cabo da Roca aiding navigation, while the many protected inlets—the Odiel, the Sado, and the Tagus—provided safe and welcoming anchorages. It is around this coast that the early Phoenician traders had set up their enclaves. But north of the Tagus estuary, beyond the headland of Cabo Carvoeiro, the coastline changes. Distinctive features are few, while the low-lying land is fringed with endless moving sandy bars formed and reformed by longshore drift. Only Cabo Mondego stands out, signalling the approach of the river of the same name, on which the Phoenician traders founded their northernmost enclave. It is not until the river Miño is passed that the coastline becomes one of the distinctive formations—promontories, islands, and wide, sinuous inlets—so characteristic of the region now known as the Rías Baixas. It is here that a scatter of Phoenician goods signals the activity of traders intent on acquiring tin. Anyone thinking of venturing much beyond Cape Finisterre would be faced with two options: either to follow the north coast of Iberia backed by its formidable mountains, or to set out northwards across the Bay of Biscay into the unknown. There is no convincing evidence that the Phoenicians or the Carthaginians took either of these routes: Galicia appears to have been the northern extremity of their world.

The journey south from the Strait of Gibraltar along the coast of Morocco was comparatively easy once Cap Spartel had been rounded, particularly in late spring, when the power of the south-flowing current was augmented by the trade winds, allowing distances of 150 kilometres or more to be covered with ease within a twenty-four-hour period. The shoreline was signposted by recognizable headlands, while rivers flowing from the Atlas Mountains broke through the coastal reefs and sand-bars to provide safe havens for ships needing to heave to. It was along this coast that the Phoenicians established their trading enclaves. By the time Mogador was reached, the snow-capped peaks of the Atlas Mountains would have been a familiar sight, the range eventually meeting the sea between Cap Rhir and Agadir. Beyond, the wide and fertile flood-plain of the river Sous extends far inland between the High Atlas and the Anti-Atlas ranges. A further 150 kilometres along the coast, still in sight of the fading oceanwards end of the Anti-Atlas, Cap Drâa stands out. Immediately beyond is another fertile river valley, that of the river Drâa, which marks the southern limit of the hospitable Moroccan landscape and the beginning of the dreary, low-lying, arid coast where the Sahara meets the ocean—a monotonous, sparsely populated landscape stretching southwards for sixteen hundred kilometres. The stark contrast of the environmental divide marked by the river Drâa cannot fail to have impressed itself on the mind of a sailor intent on travelling south. It was a place to gather strength and courage before venturing onwards. After a journey of a day or so along the desert coast a sailor would have reached Cap Juby, from where, under clear conditions, the nearer of the Canary islands could be seen barely a hundred kilometres offshore. The challenge of ocean islands would surely have justified a detour.

But back on track again there was more interminable desert coast to follow until at last the river Senegal was reached, lush with vegetation and teeming with animal life including crocodiles and hippopotamuses. Thereafter the coast becomes more varied and interesting, with great river estuaries, like the Gambia and the Sierra Leone, interspersed with forest-clad hills tumbling down to the sea as the bulge of Africa is rounded and the coast begins to run due east, now well within the tropical zone. For the enterprising traveller the possibilities were endless. The temptation to carry on was encouraged by the Guinea Current, which in summer would have greatly facilitated the eastwards coastwise movement, drawing ships towards Cameroon.

The return journey, if begun in winter, would at first have been helped by the Guinea Current, now flowing in reverse to the west, but once around the bulge of Africa the predominant currents and winds were against a passage to the north in whatever season one travelled. Only by making careful use of local inshore currents, tacking where wind conditions allowed, and rowing when necessary could a painful progress be made back to the Strait of Gibraltar and to civilization. That attempts were made to explore the African coast is clear from the classical sources, but how far the adventurers went and what landfalls they made is the subject of lively debate.

The First Greeks to Reach the Atlantic

The first known Greek to reach the Atlantic was Kolaios of Samos, whose extraordinary voyage from the eastern Mediterranean to Tartessos (probably the port of Huelva) was made about 630 BC (pp. 250–1 above). That this pioneering voyage opened up the Tartessian market to Greek entrepreneurs, as Kolaios claimed, is supported by the discovery of Greek luxury goods dating from the late seventh to the early sixth century all along the coastal regions of southern Iberia. Goods of this kind were probably brought by the Phokaians, who, by the middle of the sixth century, had befriended the Tartessian king Arganthonios. The king, Herodotus reports, tried to get them to 'quit Ionia and settle in whatever part of his country they liked'. The offer was turned down, but they did accept funds to finance the rebuilding of the wall of their home town in the face of the growing Persian threat (*Histories* 1.163).

It was probably around this time that another Greek, Midakritos, himself quite possibly a Phokaian, was active along the Atlantic coast of Iberia. He is known only from a single mention in Pliny's *Natural History* (7.197) as the first person to import *plumbum* (in this case meaning tin) from the Cassiterides. If we are correct in locating these islands along the ria coastline of Galicia, then he will simply have been following the long-established routes used by the Phoenician traders. One intriguing possibility is that, since the route taken by Midakritos was essentially the same as that recorded in the periplus embedded in *Ora Maritima*, it might have been he who wrote the periplus. It is equally possible, however, that it was composed by a later Greek traveller who followed in the pioneer's wake.

Another Greek to visit the Atlantic, probably in the latter part of the sixth century, was Euthymenes of Massalia. No first-hand report of his voyage survives, but brief references to it are made by a number of later writers quoting from sources no longer extant which may themselves have been derivative. Unlike the other Greeks who ventured through the Strait of Gibraltar, Euthymenes turned south along the African coast. Details of what he saw are limited, but he observed the phenomenon of tides and he described a great river which contained crocodiles and hippopotamuses and was so large that fresh water flowed far out into the sea. He went on to speculate that strong winds blowing from the ocean drove the water inland so far that it eventually flowed into the Nile. The crocodiles and hippopotamuses he believed were proof of this since they were otherwise known only in the Nile. His muddled views on the flow of the water could have been coloured by observing the estuary when a combination of rising tide and onshore wind drove the surface water far upstream.

The great interest of the story lies not only in its initiation of the long-running debate on the source of the Nile, but in identifying which river it was that he saw. The most plausible suggestion is that it was the Senegal, in which case his journey must have taken him south of the Sahara. Another possibility, that it was the Drâa, on the northern edge of the desert, is less likely unless the river estuary and the wildlife have changed radically. Whichever was Euthymenes' river, his achievement in travelling far down the African coast was impressive.

That such a momentous voyage received so little attention in the Greek world may well be due to the secrecy with which the Massaliots guarded their maritime intelligence.

In this age of adventure many other Greeks may have sailed through the strait to explore the wonders of the ocean, but no record of their journeys was ever made public.

The Carthaginian Explorations of West Africa

By the end of the sixth century Carthaginian attention had become focused firmly on the potential of the Atlantic. The Greek adventurers who had begun to explore the ocean fringes, infiltrating themselves into the existing Phoenician trading networks, might reasonably have been seen as a threat to Carthaginian interests. After all, the way in which the Phokaians had appropriated large parts of the Etruscan sphere in the north-western Mediterranean and had set up colonies along the Gaulish coast must still have been fresh in the memory. So it was that in the last decade or two of the sixth century the Carthaginian elite began to sponsor their own expeditions into the Atlantic.

The two expeditions that we know most about from the classical sources are those of Hanno and Himilco, both members of the aristocratic Magonid family and perhaps even brothers. It is possible that they set out from Carthage at about the same time, passing together through the Strait of Gibraltar, Himilco going north and Hanno taking the southern route. Himilco's journey is hazy and ill-defined, while Hanno's is rich with topographical detail. Both men must have written accounts of their journeys for the Carthaginian state archives, but neither text survives. For Himilco's exploits we have to rely largely on the confusing *Ora Maritima*. Hanno, however, is better served since an abbreviated description of his journey was carved in stone and set up in the temple of Baal in Carthage. It was later translated into Greek and no doubt copied on many occasions. Only one version, known as Codex Heidelbergensis 398, transcribed in the tenth century AD, now survives. Copying is likely to have introduced many errors through misunderstanding and misreading, but, even so, the short text, eighteen paragraphs composed of only six hundred Greek words, is a precious survival.

Hanno, we are told, set out in sixty penteconters carrying thirty thousand men and women, together with grain and other supplies, to found colonies along the African coast. The figures can hardly be correct. Even if sixty ships were involved, a vessel about 35 metres long could hardly have carried five hundred passengers in addition to its fifty-man crew. It is an early reminder that numbers are very prone to scribal error and cannot be relied upon. This is particularly true when trying to assess distances based on number of days' sailing, though the aggregate of sailing days compiled from the Greek text is not very different from the thirty-five days' sailing recorded by the Greek historian Arrian, writing in the second century AD. If we accept the total of thirty-five days as the time taken for the outward journey and allow that Hanno could have averaged 150 kilometres each day, then he could possibly have travelled over five thousand kilometres, which would have taken him along the Gulf of Guinea to arrive not far from the mouth of the river Niger. Such calculations are, of course, subject to many reservations but at least offer a rough order of magnitude of what might have been. Much effort and ingenuity have been expended by commentators trying to match Hanno's description with the topography of the West African coastline, but such are the limitations of the original text that certainty will never be achieved, and at best all that can be offered is plausible guesses.

The first part of his Atlantic journey took Hanno along the coast of Morocco to a major river, the Lixus, probably to be identified with the Drâa, which flows along the southern side of the Anti-Atlas range. During this initial stage he built a temple to Poseidon on a wooded headland called Soloeis, possibly Cape Cantin north of modern Safi, and set up six cities for the colonizers he had brought with him from Carthage.

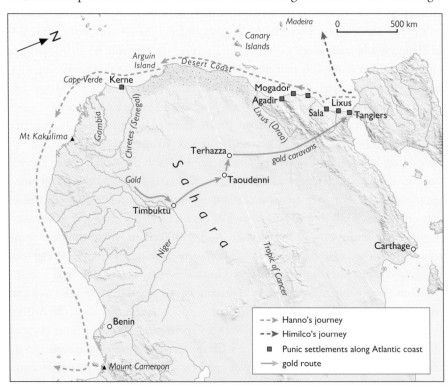

8.7 Carthaginian trading interests extended well down the Moroccan coasts, with trading posts established as far south as modern Agadir. Beyond this point only the more adventurous made their way, some, like the explorer Hanno, possibly getting as far as Cameroon. One of the attractions of Africa was gold found in the upper reaches of the river Senegal

8.8 The mouth of the river Senegal was an important focus for trade. It was probably here that the island settlement of Kerne, mentioned by classical authors, lay. Kerne was protected by a sand-bar from the Atlantic. The site has never been positively identified but the nucleus of the modern city of Saint-Louis corresponds well with the description of Kerne given by Hanno

Not all these settlements need have been new since his brief may have been to rein-vigorate old enclaves now in decline. Having dispensed with his passengers, he stayed for a while in the valley of the Lixus, making friends with the local nomadic Berber pastoralists, the Lixitai, who provided him with interpreters. We also learn that the inland regions were populated by Ethiopians (a general term used for black Africans), some of whom were unfriendly and lived in mountains infested with wild animals. The pause here would have allowed him to repair and restock the ships chosen for the exploratory part of the mission.

The next leg of the journey took Hanno along the desert coast where the Sahara meets the ocean. The text talks of a two-day journey, but, given the distance covered, this is likely to be a scribal error for nine days. Once past the desert he entered a more fertile region and came upon a great river called the Chretes. The text here is confused, but the simplest interpretation is that the party explored various branches of this river, in one of which they found crocodiles and hippopotamuses. In the estuary of the river were several islands, on one of which, called Kerne, they established a settlement, the

303

southernmost of the Carthaginian enclaves. Kerne survived the period of exploration and featured in later accounts. There has been much debate about the location of the great river, but the consensus is that it was the Senegal. Since the estuary has been much modified over the last two and a half millennia, Kerne may have disappeared under silt or been eroded away, though the suggestion that it may underlie the modern city of Saint-Louis is a reasonable possibility.

After Kerne the party continued southwards and then south-eastwards along the coast for twenty-six days, observing many wonders as they progressed. The land was populated by Ethiopians, who ran away when they saw the ships. They passed wooded promontories and came upon a great bay with a large island in it, where they heard 'the sound of flutes, cymbals and beating drums'. Sailing on, they passed a land 'full of burning incense from which fiery streams flowed down to the sea'. Further on 'the land was full of fire' and they saw 'an exceedingly high mountain called the Chariot of the Gods'. It took three days to pass the 'streams of fire' before reaching a bay called the Horn of the South. The account provides plenty of vivid detail, encouraging much speculation. Some commentators take the minimalist view, arguing that Hanno got as far as the coast of Sierra Leone. Others, impressed by the fiery mountain, believe that he sailed beyond the Niger delta to within sight of the volcano of Mount Cameroon.

One of the last things Hanno records is landing on an island 'filled with wild people. Most of them were women with hairy bodies which the interpreters called gorillas.' They chased them, capturing three, who 'bit and scratched ... We killed and skinned them and brought their hides to Carthage.' When, in 1847, a band of hitherto unknown hairy hominids was discovered in Gabon, they were given the name of gorillas, using Hanno's word. Hanno's hairy creatures may have been gorillas as we know them today, but equally they may have been chimpanzees, baboons, or humans. It is at this point that the narrative ends rather abruptly with a terse 'but we did not sail any further because we had run out of supplies'.

Hanno's periplus is a tantalizing partial record of one of the world's epic journeys. Behind its bland, matter-of-fact wording one can glimpse something of the emotions which the explorer must have felt: excitement, wonder, fear, and awe at the vastness of it all. What had been his intention? Had he planned to circumnavigate Africa and decided to turn back once he realized that the coast was turning south, or was it simply the realization that the distances were much greater than he had estimated that made him suddenly give up and make for home?

There is a later periplus which throws further light on trade along the African coast. It was ascribed in error to the late sixth-century explorer Scylax, but dates to the middle of the fourth century BC and is now referred to as Pseudo-Scylax. It describes the west coast of Africa down to the island of Kerne, where Phoenician traders were found to be in residence. In small boats they took their wares across to the mainland to trade with the Ethiopians, offering them aromatics, Egyptian glass, and Attic pottery in exchange for skins of both domestic and wild animals, elephants' tusks, and wine (presumably a local alcoholic brew). The natives were tall and good-looking, and the men were bearded. They rode horses and used bows and arrows and spears, and had a large settlement up-river, to which the Phoenicians sailed. Although the periplus could have relied, in part at least, on the earlier work of Hanno, the details it offers of the Kerne trading system are new and strongly suggestive of an eyewitness account. That the exotic goods available to the traders were drawn from Egypt and Greece shows that the Carthaginians were pragmatic in their commercial activities, motivated solely by what readily available goods turned the best profits. One surprise is that there is no mention of gold as a native resource. This was a gold-rich area, but there may have been local constraints on the movement of the metal which made it unavailable.

There is one further, rather curious reference to West African travel at this time, recorded by Herodotus (*Histories* 4.43). It concerns a Persian, Sataspes, who had been sentenced to death by impaling for 'violence towards a young woman'. The king, Xerxes, decided, however, that, instead of the sentence being carried out, Sataspes should be sent away to circumnavigate Africa in an anti-clockwise direction. No doubt relieved, Sataspes took ship in Egypt and sailed west through the Strait of Gibraltar and past Cape Soloeis, turning southwards down the coast. He followed this course for many months before growing tired of the adventure and turning back. On giving account of himself at the court of Xerxes, he described seeing pygmies wearing palm leaves who lived in large settlements and herded cattle, and explained that he had returned because his ships simply would not move any further. The king was unimpressed by the excuse and Sataspes was duly impaled. It is an odd story that might in some obscure way reflect the agreements that were being orchestrated at this time (about 480 BC) between the Persians and Carthaginians against the Greeks. A Persian-sponsored expedition into the Atlantic might have been a diplomatic move to warn off Greek explorers. Whether the unfortunate Sataspes had made a serious attempt at circumnavigation, or simply lurked about in the ports of the Moroccan coast picking up odd bits of information before returning, we shall never know.

For all their limitations, the periploi and other anecdotes about West Africa speak of a lively interest in the economic exploitation of the coastal region in the sixth and fifth centuries. It was commercially valuable knowledge, and the Carthaginians did such a good job of keeping it to themselves that the full extent of the Carthaginian enterprise will for ever remain shadowy.

Himilco's Adventures

When Himilco returned from his Atlantic voyage towards the end of the sixth century, he wrote a report which was kept 'in the secret annals of the Carthaginians'. Centuries later Pliny heard of it, but all he could report was that Himilco was sent to explore 'the parts beyond Europe', a phrase which might be taken to suggest that he sailed out into the Atlantic. The only other source to offer hints of Himilco's activities is *Ora Maritima*, the late Roman compilation which has already been described (pp. 282–4 above). In three separate places observations ascribed to Himilco are included. All refer to the wild, unfriendly ocean which 'can scarcely be crossed in four months', an assertion which might suggest that he attempted to sail directly across it. He talks of 'the sluggish liquid of lazy sea' with 'thickets of seaweed' which held the vessel back. There were monsters of the deep, 'and beasts swim around the slow and sluggishly crawling ships' (lines 117–29). To the west of the Pillars of Herakles 'the swell is boundless and the sea extends widely, the salt water stretches forth. No one has approached these waters, no one has brought his keel into that sea because there are no propelling breezes ... mist cloaks the air with a kind of garment, a cloud always holds the swell' (lines 380–9). In the final piece (lines 406–15), we return to the seaweed-clogged sea, and the great fear of monsters that skulked in the deep.

The absence of topographical detail may be the result of Carthaginian censorship of commercially valuable information, but taken at face value what survives of Himilco's report in *Ora Maritima* is redolent of an open-ocean voyage 'west of the Pillars of Herakles'. Some commentators have likened the 'sluggish ... lazy sea' to the doldrums and the 'thickets of seaweed' to the Sargasso Sea. This may indeed be so, but there remains a persistent belief in some of the more recent literature that Himilco journeyed north to Britain and Ireland and opened the way for Carthaginian traders to visit these islands. This belief is based solely on a misinterpretation of a few muddled lines in *Ora Maritima* referring to Holy Island (Ireland) and the island of the Albiones (Britain), juxtaposed with one of the extracts from Himilco. Since the two pieces may not be related at all, and anyway the islands may not be Britain and Ireland, the 'Albiones' referring to the tribe of that name in northern Iberia, the reasons for supposing that Himilco visited Britain are tenuous in the extreme. Moreover, there is no positive archaeological evidence for Phoenician or Carthaginian contact with Brittany, Ireland, or Britain in spite of centuries of archaeological activity in these regions.

What the archaeological data does show, however, is that imported Carthaginian material was reaching native hill-forts in north-western Iberia in some quantity, entering the country through coastal ports like La Lanzada on the Ría de Pontevedra and

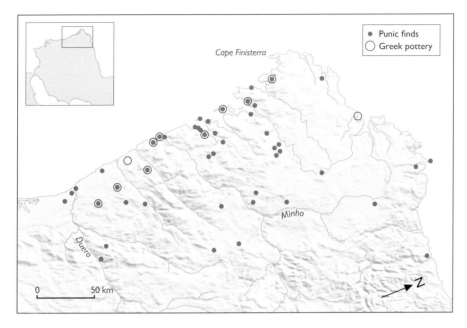

8.9 Between the fourth and second century Carthaginian interest in the metal-producing regions of north-western Iberia intensified, as is shown by the increasing quantity of Mediterranean material found in indigenous hill-forts. There seems, however, to have been little desire to explore the northern coasts or beyond

Museu do Mar on the Ría de Vigo. Eight sites are known to have recorded Carthaginian finds dating between the late sixth and fourth centuries, with the number rising to fifty between the fourth and second centuries, the imported material now including Punic and Greek pottery, Punic coins, and Mediterranean glass beads. The Carthaginian imports in Galicia are not only more numerous after about 400 BC, but also extend further round the coast as far as Cabo de Estaca de Bares, which effectively marks the divide between the Atlantic and the Cantabrian Sea. The virtual absence of imports beyond that along the north coast of Iberia is a clear indication that Galicia remained the northern extremity of Carthaginian enterprise.

The Isles of the Blest and Beyond

The four groups of Atlantic islands—the Canaries, Madeira, the Azores, and the Cape Verde islands—were all potentially within reach of the Carthaginian explorers. The nearest to the African mainland were the Canary islands, with the closest, Fuerteventura, being only a hundred kilometres from Cap Juby. The near islands, and

307

even Gran Canaria with its volcanic peak at nearly two thousand metres, would have been visible to coastal traffic. At the time when the Greeks and Carthaginians were venturing along the coast, a number of the islands were already occupied by people of Berber origin who had made the sea-crossing by about 1000 BC. Few explorers could have resisted making the slight detour to see what these mysterious places had to offer, not least because they would have been well aware of the myths about the Hesperides, the Isles of the Blest 'by deep eddying ocean'. When, at the end of the first millennium BC, King Juba II of Mauretania sent an expeditionary force to the islands, he probably did so in the knowledge of centuries of reported landings. Yet the sparse settlement evidence, apart from a few scattered finds and a carving of a hippos, suggests the islands had been only of passing interest, the Mediterranean traders being more intent on the richer pickings of the mainland coasts.

The island of Madeira and the smaller islands nearby—Porto Santa and Ilhas Desertas—lie much further out in the ocean, 640 kilometres from the African mainland and well out of sight of coastal traffic, but a ship blown off course or one making a determined reconnaissance of the open ocean could well have chanced upon them. There is one intriguing story told by Diodorus (5.19–20), who probably took it from the late fourth-century BC writer Timaeus, of a Carthaginian ship sailing along the African coast being blown out to sea and, after several days, coming upon a large fertile island with well-wooded mountains, navigable rivers, and a pleasant, temperate climate. The Etruscans, who heard of the discovery, expressed a wish to establish a colony there, but the Carthaginians were opposed and did their best to deflect the enterprise and nothing came of it. Apart from the mention of navigable rivers the description fits well with Madeira. The interest expressed by the Etruscans in the Atlantic may be seen in the context of the pressures created by the encroachment of Phokaian Greeks on the Etruscan sphere in the Mediterranean in the latter part of the sixth century BC. Who the Carthaginian was who made the discovery is unrecorded, but it is worth recalling that it was about this time that Himilco was exploring the ocean. Could it have been him?

The archipelago of the Azores, comprising ten major islands in all, lies thirteen hundred kilometres west of Cabo da Roca on the coast of Portugal, about halfway across the Atlantic. The chance of their having been visited in Carthaginian times is remote, but there is one discovery that deserves consideration. In 1749, after a violent storm, a hoard of coins contained in a pottery vessel was exposed on the beach of the most westerly of the islands, Corvo. The coins are no longer extant, but they were sent to Portugal and later Madrid, where they were identified, and eventually a paper was published claiming that two were Cyrenian and seven Carthaginian. The contemporary illustrations support this identification and allow the latest coins to be identified as belonging to the late third century BC. There has been much scepticism about the reported find,

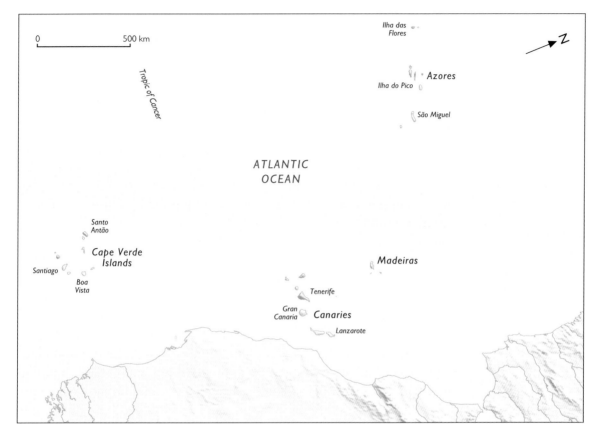

8.10 The near Atlantic islands and the sea around them have been called the Atlantic Mediterranean by French geographers to emphasize the similarities of the two seas and the fact that the islands were readily accessible to explorers coming from the Mediterranean

some commentators regarding it as imaginary or fake, others arguing that the coins found their way to the island sometime after the Portuguese settlement in the fifteenth century. A field survey of the island carried out in 1983 recovered sherds of what were then thought to be fourth- and third-century BC pottery, but the identification remains unverified. The response of those who dismiss the discoveries is understandable, but it must be stressed that there is no inherent reason why they should not be genuine—the result of a third-century voyage—perhaps a ship returning from the south and making a sweep out into the Atlantic to catch the prevailing westerlies to bring the vessel safely back to Iberia, much as the Portuguese learned to do a millennium later.

Of the Cape Verde islands there is little to be said. Lying 570 kilometres west of the African coast on roughly the latitude of the river Senegal, they would have been well out of sight of coast-hugging traffic, but the possibility of their discovery by Carthaginians as the result of accident or deliberate exploration cannot be ruled out. We must not underestimate the skills and curiosity of the Carthaginian navigators.

Pytheas of Massalia

The build-up of Carthaginian power at the western end of the Mediterranean and their growing hostility to the Greeks meant that from the fifth century access to the Atlantic would have become increasingly difficult for Greek, and even Etruscan, sailors. The ocean had become a Carthaginian preserve, and the rich metal resources of western Iberia were probably, by now, beyond the reach of the Greek world. As far as copper, gold, and silver were concerned, this posed no serious problem. Cyprus could supply all the copper that was required, gold could now be had from the northern Balkans, and huge supplies of silver had been discovered nearer to home in Attica. But tin was a rare commodity and the main source, in Galicia, was no longer available. Another commodity difficult to access was amber coming from Jutland and the Baltic. The main supply route had been across the Alps to the Po valley and the head of the Adriatic, but, with Etruscan influence increasing in the area after the beginning of the fifth century, the flow of amber was now under the control of Etruscan middlemen. The growing difficulty of getting hold of these two desirable commodities may have caused Herodotus, writing in the late fifth century, to take a particular interest in them, admitting that he could find out little about their origins and concluding somewhat weakly that 'nevertheless, tin and amber do certainly come to us from the ends of the earth' (*Histories* 3.115).

It may have been Herodotus' comments that inspired Pytheas of Massalia to set out on a remarkable journey of discovery, sometime about 320 BC, that would take him to the Atlantic and all round the coast of Britain, eventually returning home to write an account of his travels in a manuscript called *On the Ocean*. The text of *On the Ocean* no longer survives, but the book was read and quoted by other Greeks whose works are extant, and it is from these scraps that the outline of the journey and the phenomena encountered by Pytheas can be pieced together. Outstanding among his descriptions are details of the procurement of tin in Cornwall and of amber from the coast of Jutland.

Since Pytheas' journey was undertaken at a time when the Carthaginians controlled the Strait of Gibraltar, it is unlikely that he sailed into the Atlantic from the Mediterranean. The alternative would have been to go overland to the Garonne valley and then to follow the river to its estuary, the Gironde, where he would have caught his

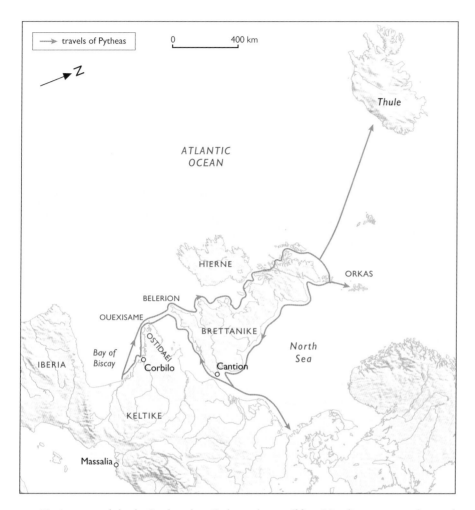

8.11 The journey made by the Greek explorer Pytheas, who set off from Massalia *c.*320 BC, can be traced in outline from extant classical sources. The reconstruction offered here is the simplest interpretation of the route using only the factual evidence. It is based on the assumption that Pytheas set out overland to explore the route by which tin was reaching Massalia, and for the rest of the journey used local shipping

first sight of the Atlantic. This is the route along which tin from Cornwall, and perhaps Brittany, was already reaching Massalia, and if he was interested in finding the source, it would have been logical for him to follow the supply route in reverse. From talking to local sailors in the Gironde estuary Pytheas could have learned about the great inward sweep of the Atlantic coast and picked up the specific information attributed to him that the northern shores of Iberia 'offer easier passage to Keltike than if you sail [there] by the Ocean'. In other words, he was implying that to reach the Atlantic coast

311

of France (Keltike) by sailing out into the ocean via the strait you would have to sail along the long and rugged north coast of Iberia: his trans-peninsular route to the coast of Keltike was much shorter.

Once on the Atlantic coast, possibly at the native port of Burdigala (Bordeaux), Pytheas could have joined a local ship bound for the Armorican peninsula (Brittany), observing as he went that it was a westerly projection from the European mainland (the word he uses is *kyrtoma*, meaning 'hump') 'not less than 3,000 stades long'. At the western extremity were a number of promontories, 'especially that of the Ostimioi which is called Kabaion, as well as the islands off it … the farthest of these Ou[e]xisame lies three days' voyage away'. Ouexisame is most likely to be Ushant, twenty kilometres off the west coast of Cape Finistère in Brittany, while Kabaion may be Pointe du Raz, beyond which lies Île de Sein.

Pytheas recorded a sun height on a latitude that coincides with the north coast of the Armorican peninsula before setting out, presumably on another local ship, for south-western Britain—one of the major sources of tin in the ancient world. Two classical sources, Pliny and Diodorus, refer to British tin production, both probably gleaning their information from the work of a Greek historian, Timaeus of Tauromenium (*c*.356–270 BC), who relied on Pytheas for his information on the Atlantic. The account reported by Diodorus is detailed:

> The inhabitants of Britain who live on the promontory called Belerion are especially friendly to strangers and have adopted a civilized way of life because of their interaction with traders and other people. It is they who work the tin, treating the layer which contains it in an ingenious way. This layer, being like rock, contains earthy seams and in them the workers quarry the ore, which they then melt down to clean of its impurities. Then they work the tin into pieces the size of knuckle-bones and convey it to an island which lies off Britain, called Ictis; for at the ebb-tide the space between this island and the mainland becomes dry and they can take the tin in large quantities over to the island on their wagons. (And a peculiar thing happens in the case of the neighbouring islands which lie between Europe and Britain, for at flood-tide the passage between them and the mainland runs full and they have the appearance of islands, but at ebb-tide the sea recedes and leaves dry a large space and at that time they look like peninsulas.) On the island of Ictis the merchants buy the tin from the natives and carry it from there across the Strait of Galatia [the Channel] and finally, making their way on foot through Gaul for some thirty days, they bring the goods on horseback to the mouth of the Rhône.
>
> (Diodorus Siculus 5.1–4)

Pliny's contribution is shorter and somewhat confused, but he adds the detail that the Britons used boats of wicker (*Natural History* 4.104).

There can be little doubt that the primary source relayed by Diodorus was a first-hand account written by someone who had visited the promontory and observed both the extraction and the trading of tin. It was just the sort of information that the Massaliots would have been anxious to have, offering a sense of control over the supply of this vital commodity. That the news was quickly picked up and reported by Timaeus reflects growing Greek interest in the distant Atlantic—a region that had been such a mystery to Herodotus.

The place name Belerion is generally thought to be the Penwith peninsula, the most south-westerly region of Cornwall, with Ictis identified as St Michael's Mount. But the possibility remains that other islands or promontories were also used as trading marts at this time. One such is Mount Batten in Plymouth Sound, where excavations have shown that a port-of-trade flourished in the first millennium BC. Mount Batten had access, via the river Tamar, to the rich tin sources found around the southern edge of Dartmoor. Within a kilometre of the site, at Plympton, two Greek coins have been found, one of Philip II of Macedon (reigned 359–336 BC), the other probably of Alexander III of Macedon (reigned 336–323 BC). That they were minted a little before the supposed date of Pytheas' voyage is tantalizing but may nothing more than a coincidence.

Only twenty-five kilometres from Plymouth Sound, where the river Erme reaches Bigbury Bay, the remains of a shipwreck have been discovered. The timbers of the vessel have long since rotted, but what remains is the cargo of tin ingots, some bun-shaped, others of a size and shape that resembled the astragalus (knuckle-bone) of a bovine. Although the Erme wreck is undated, it is ingots of this kind that Pytheas was describing. Clearly archaeology still has much to reveal about tin extraction in the south-west of Britain, but it is Pytheas' vivid first-hand description of what it was like to be there during the trading season that brings everything to life.

From Cornwall, Pytheas circumnavigated Britain, noting that it was roughly triangular and giving an accurate estimate of its size; it was probably from his account that Pliny learned of the many offshore islands and was able to name them. From Belerion the most likely onward route would have been northwards via St George's Channel and the Irish Sea and along the west coast of Scotland. Three sun heights were measured during his northern progress, one on the latitude of the Isle of Man, one on the latitude of the Isle of Lewis and the Outer Hebrides, and the third corresponding to the latitude of the Shetlands.

8.12 St Michael's Mount, off the south coast of Cornwall, has long been assumed to be the site of Ictis, the offshore market where tin was traded, though there is no conclusive archaeological evidence for this. Ictis was probably first described by Pytheas

Whether or not he ventured even further north is a matter of speculation, but Pytheas is quoted by the first-century AD writer Geminus as saying: 'The barbarians pointed out to us on several occasions the place where the sun lies down. For it happens around these places that the night is extremely short: two hours in some, three in others, so that after the setting, although only a short time has elapsed, the sun straight away arises again.' Such an observation could have been made anywhere on the south

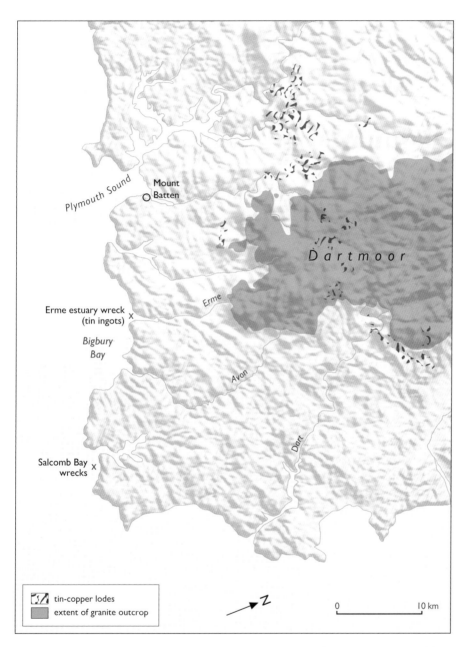

8.13 The south coast of Devon was visited by ships involved in the trade of tin and copper produced from the metal-rich ores around the Dartmoor massif. Mount Batten was a significant port-of-trade in the Iron Age—and is one of the possible candidates for Ictis. Wrecks carrying metal ingots and artefacts have been found in the Erme estuary and Salcombe Bay

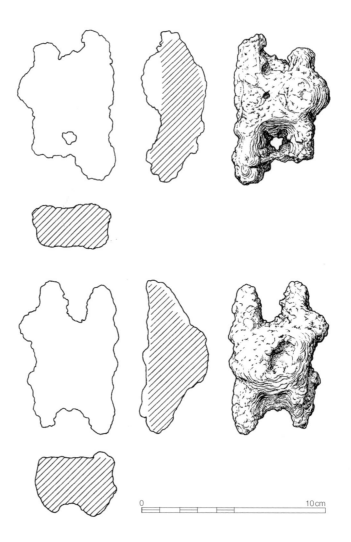

8.14 Tin ingots from a vessel that may have foundered on West Mary's rock in the estuary of the river Erme. The find is undated, but the ingots are of knuckle-bone shape of the kind first noted by Pytheas

coast of Iceland and implies that Pytheas, or at least his informants, had visited Iceland. Strabo reports Pytheas as saying that an island called Thule lies six days by sea north of Britain near the 'congealed sea'. This would fit with Iceland, which could indeed be reached in six days' sailing at speeds of between three and four knots. Descriptions of conditions in these far northern latitudes, ascribed to Pytheas by later writers familiar with his work, raise many questions. How far north did Pytheas actually travel? Did he glean a few observations from people who had made the trip to Iceland? Or was he simply making clever guesses about what lay north of Shetland? Assessing what is reported in the surviving scraps of *On the Ocean* transmitted by later writers, the simplest conclusion would be that he probably did make this epic journey into the unknown, most likely in the company of Britons already familiar with the northern reaches of the ocean.

Pytheas' return journey down the eastern side of Britain brought him into contact with indigenous people who had first-hand knowledge of the amber-producing region of Jutland. Given the fascination that amber held for Mediterraneans, it is tempting to think that he may have taken a detour across the North Sea to see for himself.

To complete the reconnaissance of Britain and to be able to finalize his measurements of circumference Pytheas must have sailed along the south coast from Kantion (Kent) back to Belerion, from where he could retrace his steps along the tin route to his home port of Massalia, there to write of his adventures in *On the Ocean*. For those who read it, people like his near-contemporary Timaeus of Tauromenium, the book would have been a revelation. A hundred and thirty years earlier, Herodotus had admitted to complete ignorance about the Atlantic coast of Europe, and the Carthaginian hold over the Strait of Gibraltar had prevented serious exploration. Now in a single work the nature of the ocean, with its great tidal ranges and fierce storms, its islands and people, and its icy northern extremities, had been brought into vivid focus and the world knew all about the extraction and distribution of the essential tin and magical amber. The far limits of the world were at last beginning to take on a reality.

The Impact of Pytheas' Journey

Inspiring though Pytheas' adventures would have been to his readers, there is no documentary evidence to suggest that others followed up his discoveries, nor is there any conclusive archaeological evidence of his, or other, Greek visits to Armorica or Britain. That said, there are finds from both regions that may hint at continued, if sporadic, contact with the Mediterranean world.

In Armorica a few coins of Mediterranean origin have been found, the most evocative of which was a gold stater minted in the Greek city of Kyrene between 322 and 315 BC. It was discovered attached to the root of a piece of seaweed washed up on the north coast of Finistère and would have been in circulation at the time of Pytheas' journey. Another tantalizing discovery is of a group of decorated standing stones (stelae) found concentrated on the Penmarc'h peninsula in the south-western corner of Brittany. Stelae were part of a long-established Armorican tradition, but most of the many hundreds known are undecorated, though some are carefully shaped and

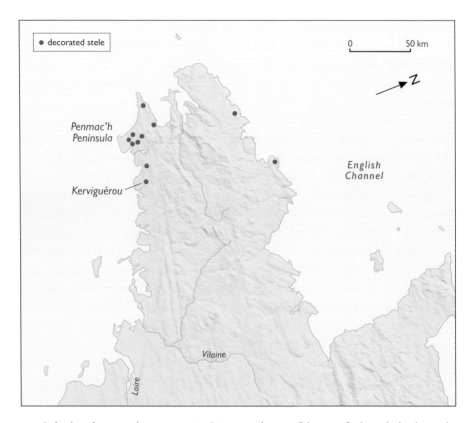

8.15 Stelae (standing stones) are common in Brittany, and many of the more finely worked stelae can be shown to be of Iron Age date. There is one group that is carefully decorated, often with fluting resembling Greek columns. They are predominantly coastal

occasionally fluted. Among the Penmarc'h group, however, are some ornamented with bands carved around the top and bottom composed of running spirals, chevrons, diamond latticework, and Greek-key motifs. It may be that the inhabitants of the region were simply an inventive lot delighting in developing decorative ideas, but the resemblance of at least one of the tall decorated pillars to the columns of Greek temples is striking and inevitably raises the question of whether we are seeing here a native copy of a Greek temple, perhaps one built in wood, erected somewhere on a Penmarc'h promontory by travelling Greeks to honour their patron deity—a not impossible hypothesis but one difficult to test.

8.16 (*Opposite*) The decorated stela from Kerviguérou, Melgven, Brittany, is one of the more elaborate. It is shown here as it appears from one side and with the full decoration drawn out. The similarity of the design to the Ionic column from Temple D at Metapontium in Italy is striking and raises the possibility that the Breton stela may have been inspired by a wooden temple put up by Greeks in Brittany

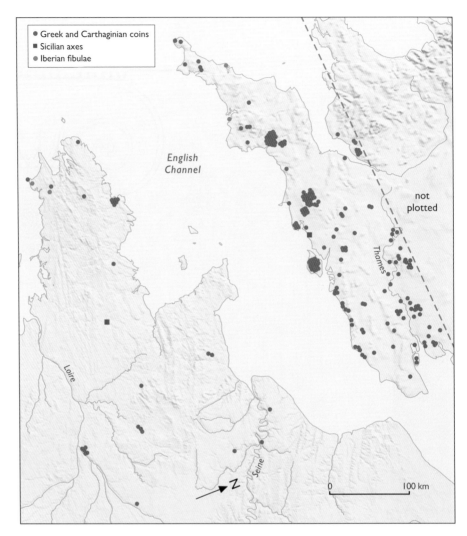

- Greek and Carthaginian coins
- Sicilian axes
- Iberian fibulae

English
Channel

not
plotted

Thames

Loire

Seine

N

0   100 km

8.17 Large numbers of Greek and Carthaginian coins have been found in Britain. Some certainly arrived in the prehistoric period and reflected trade with the adjacent continent, but many of them are likely to have been imports in the Roman period or were brought in much later by coin collectors. A few other items, like the Iberian-style fibulae (brooches) and the Sicilian axes, reflect Atlantic trade

In Britain, too, such evidence as there is of Greek contact is ambiguous. It consists of a number of Mediterranean coins of the fourth to second centuries scattered across the south-east of the island, together with isolated finds of Greek bronze vessels and Greek pots. The natural tendency of cautious archaeologists has been to explain these finds as late imports brought in by collectors in the Roman period or, much later, by antiquarians returning from the Grand Tour. But this won't quite do. That at least four of the Greek pots were recovered from the Thames, a favourite river for depositing votive offerings of metalwork in the Iron Age, hints that they may have been rare items of value dedicated to the gods as part of the same rituals as the native metalwork. How they arrived in Britain is unknown. Of the coin finds, a few have been found stratified in Iron Age contexts, and there are distinct concentrations in coastal regions, especially in Dorset, where an unusual number have been found in the area of Poole harbour, with other concentrations occurring around Exeter and on the Isle of Wight. It is quite possible that some of these finds were introduced during the fifth to second centuries by traders with access to Mediterranean goods, though whether directly by Mediterranean entrepreneurs or indirectly through Gaulish middlemen is a matter of debate. All that can safely be said is that expeditions to Armorica and Britain organized by Massaliots in the years following Pytheas' journey remain a distinct, but unproven, possibility.

Africa after the Fall of Gadir

The culminating act of the Second Punic War was the surrender of Gadir (Cádiz) to the Romans following the decisive battle of Ilipa (Alcalá del Río), fought on the banks of the Guadalquivir in 206 BC, in which the Carthaginian forces led by Hasdrubal Gisco were soundly beaten. With Gadir now in their hands the Romans had suddenly become an Atlantic power, though it was to take nearly two centuries before Atlantic Iberia came fully under Roman control. The long Lusitanian War, played out in Portugal, and the campaigns of the provincial governor Decimus Brutus in the north-west lasted from 155 to 136 BC: the Cantabri of the northern coastal region were only finally subdued in the hard-fought campaign of 26–16 BC.

The capture of Gadir (called Gades by the Romans) kindled Roman curiosity about the Atlantic, but it was not until about 150 BC that we hear of any serious attempt at exploration. Even then, the details are vague and are restricted to the statement by the historian Polybius that he had travelled on the ocean outside Spain and Gaul. Polybius had access to the account of Pytheas' voyage and may well have tried to follow the same route, travelling from Massalia to Narbo Martius (Narbonne) and then up the river Aude and via the Carcassonne gap to the headwaters of the Garonne. From here, using the long-established tin route, he could reach the Gironde estuary and then choose whether to travel north towards Armorica or south to explore the north coast of Spain. His account of this journey no longer survives, though his devastating critique of Pytheas, reported by Strabo, might suggest that he was damning the achievements of his predecessor the better to enhance his own more limited explorations. One interesting detail survives that may be relevant. Strabo records that Scipio Aemilianus, who was the patron of Polybius, questioned the Massaliots and people from Narbo and Korbilo about Britain but no one could (or would) tell anything worth recording. Perhaps it was Polybius who did the interrogating for his patron. To talk to the traders of Massalia and Narbo would have been a simple task, but Korbilo was somewhere on the estuary of the Loire, perhaps Nantes. This might imply that he got that far, unless, of course, traders from Korbilo could be found in the Mediterranean ports.

In 146 BC Polybius was present when Scipio dealt the death blow to Carthage. As historian-in-residence he was probably given privileged access to the archive of Carthaginian books and reports that would have become available, learning from them of the Carthaginian expeditions of discovery along the West African coast. It would have been a time of great excitement. Polybius' explorer instincts were stirred, and his patron, Scipio, agreed to make a fleet available to him: it was, after all, of strategic interest to Rome to assess the strength of the Carthaginian cities along the Atlantic coast. No doubt Polybius carried with him a copy of Hanno's periplus. Little is known of the journey beyond scraps recorded by Pliny. Polybius evidently knew of the island of Kerne and reported the unsurprising fact that 'beyond the mountain towards the west are forests full of the wild animals that Africa produces'. Mention of the river Banbotum, full of crocodiles and hippopotamuses, suggests that he may have reached the Senegal, or at least been aware of it. His original report does not survive, and it is impossible, from the garbled account of Pliny, to judge how much he was recording his own observations and how much he was simply copying sections of Hanno's periplus. At any event, his journey added little that was new.

Towards the end of the second century BC a very experienced traveller, Eudoxus of Kyzikos, decided to circumnavigate Africa in an anti-clockwise direction. He had already made two journeys to India via the Red Sea about 120 BC and, angered by having his cargoes confiscated by the court of Ptolemy, he decided to open up the route to India by way of the Atlantic, believing the contemporary wisdom that Africa did not extend south of the equator. He was further encouraged by believing that he had earlier found the wreck of a ship from Gades on the east coast of Africa. If sailors from Gades could make it to the Indian Ocean, so could he.

So it was that Eudoxus set out from his home at Kyzikos, on the south-western shore of the Sea of Marmara, with all his possessions and, trading as he went, eventually arrived at Gades. There he built a large ship, which towed two barges loaded with provisions. The expedition, which included craftsmen and physicians, set out southwards along the African coast and seems to have reached the tropics, where the ships ran aground. Undeterred, Eudoxus built a new vessel, a penteconter, from the timbers of the wrecks and proceeded with the journey, observing various tribes speaking Ethiopian (non-Berber) languages. The sequence of events now becomes confused, possibly because two separate journeys are conflated, but he eventually decided to turn back, discovering on the way home an uninhabited island with plentiful water which he thought would make a good winter base for a future expedition. Which island it was is impossible to say, but in all likelihood it was Madeira. The expedition finally landed on the Moroccan coast and Eudoxus travelled inland to the court of the Mauretanian king Bocchus I (c.120–80 BC), hoping that he would sponsor a new expedition. The king's negative response and the rumour that he was thinking of exiling him to an island persuaded Eudoxus to steal away, eventually returning to Spain.

Undaunted by his failure, Eudoxus began to prepare another expedition, this time comprising a large merchant ship and a penteconter, 'one for the open sea, the other for exploring the coast'. Equipping them with agricultural tools and seeds, he was clearly intending to overwinter on his newly discovered island, 'there to sow the seed and reap the harvest and complete the expedition as planned'. How he fared is unrecorded. Having built up the story, Strabo could only end, rather lamely: 'perhaps those who live in Gades or in Spain may be able to tell what happened to him after all [this]' (*Geography* 2.3.4). If they did know, nobody reported it. Eudoxus simply vanishes from history.

About 100 BC

By the end of the second century BC Rome had acquired a Mediterranean empire. To the original Tyrrhenian core of Italy, Sicily, Sardinia, and Corsica, she had added Greece and Macedonia, much of western Asia, the most fertile region of North Africa (roughly Tunisia), a large part of the Iberian peninsula, and the Mediterranean region of Gaul. In another century or so the Roman empire would encircle the Mediterranean, apart from Mauretania along the north-west African coast, and would face the Atlantic from the Strait of Gibraltar to the mouth of the Rhine.

In its early confrontation with Carthage, Rome had been forced suddenly to become a maritime power, in 261 or 260 BC building a fleet of a hundred quinqueremes and twenty triremes in, so it was claimed, sixty days, at the same time training thirty-three thousand rowers. Here was the determination that underlay Rome's spectacular rise to dominance. Naval fighting supremacy and tactical support were to prove crucial in many later engagements.

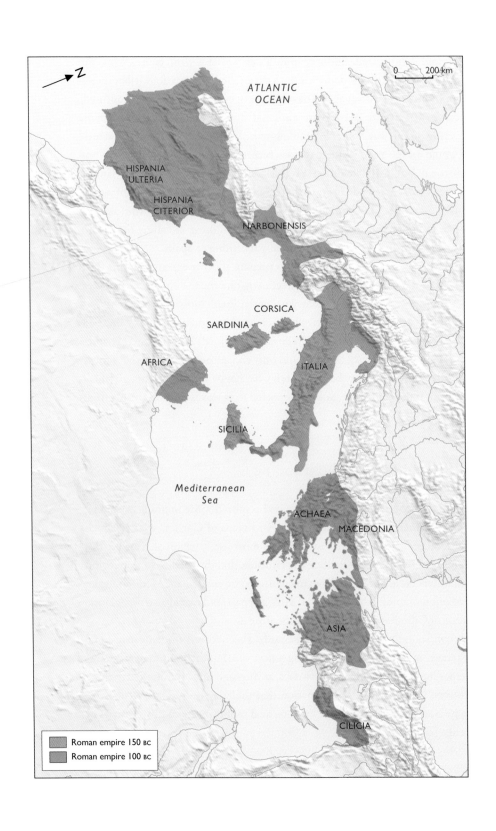

ATLANTIC
OCEAN

HISPANIA
ULTERIA

HISPANIA
CITERIOR

NARBONENSIS

CORSICA

SARDINIA

AFRICA

ITALIA

SICILIA

*Mediterranean
Sea*

ACHAEA

MACEDONIA

ASIA

CILICIA

0   200 km

Roman empire 150 BC
Roman empire 100 BC

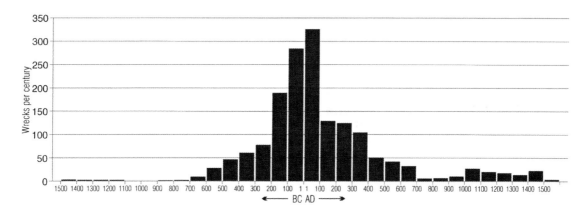

8.18 (*Opposite*) By 100 BC Roman expansion was still largely restricted to the Mediterranean region, although parts of Atlantic Iberia had begun to be incorporated into the nascent empire

8.19 (*Above*) If the number of shipwrecks so far discovered in the Mediterranean is a fair reflection of the annual volume of shipping, then the period from 100 BC to AD 100 saw maritime activity at its most intensive. This histogram of Mediterranean shipwrecks includes 1,646 recorded wrecks which are plotted assuming equal probability of sinking in any year during the date range of each wreck

8.20 (*Right*) Using ceramic data from the Vaunage in southern France, it is possible to show how wine from Italy replaced locally produced wine during the second century BC. A comparison of the quantities of wine amphorae to other types of pottery suggests that wine consumption rose considerably after 125 BC, when the Romans annexed the region

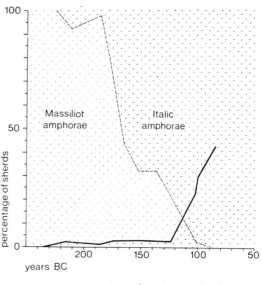

The success of the growing empire depended on the ability to move food, raw materials, and other commodities efficiently over long distances to provide for the burgeoning urban populations by addressing the imbalances caused by the uneven distribution of resources. Thus it was that grain had to be transported from the wheat-fields of Numidia (now western Tunisia and eastern Algeria) and from Egypt to satisfy the hungry proletariat of Rome. When overproduction through too heavy reliance on monoculture threatened, new markets had to be found for the suppliers. The estate owners of northern Italy, for example, soon discovered that the Gauls living beyond the boundaries of the province of Narbonensis were eager for wine, which they consumed undiluted in great quantity. Their passion was so great that they would give a slave for an amphora of wine, a deal greatly beneficial to the Roman estate owners, but then a Gaul with a surfeit of captives acquired through local warfare would think himself fortunate indeed to get so acceptable a quantity of wine in return.

So it was that, in moving surpluses around the Mediterranean, great merchant fleets came into being. Statistics based on counting the number of shipwrecks found around the coasts show an exponential rise in numbers after the end of the third century BC, peaking in the first century AD, and then declining rapidly again. Although the statistics may be affected by a number of variables, overall they must represent a boom in the volume of maritime traffic after the end of the Second Punic War. Another demonstration of the same phenomenon is given by the relative proportions of local wine amphorae compared to imported Italian amphorae found at settlement sites in southern Gaul. Early in the second century BC the ratio of imported amphorae sharply increases, ousting the local product altogether by about 100 BC. Concurrent with this is a very rapid increase in wine-drinking overall as the Roman lifestyle was adopted by the native elites. The wine produced in the northern Italian estates all had to be shipped from ports like Cosa (in modern Tuscany) to Massalia, from where it was transported by river and by road to Romanized consumers within Narbonensis and to the natives in the barbarian hinterland beyond. For the Roman shippers even the short sea journey was not without its risks, as the surprising number of shipwrecks found off the coast of Gaul bears witness.

The ships' masters who sailed the Mediterranean were the inheritors of a tradition going back into deep time. Their ancestors had learned how to navigate the Inner Sea and how to respond to its predictable moods. Over the many generations they had improved their vessels the better to suit them to the sea's vicissitudes. Sailors and ships alike had evolved to fit comfortably within this familiar maritime environment. Now the fast-growing empire was facing a new ocean altogether different from Mare Nostrum—one with a reputation for fearsome, unpredictable energies, an endless expanse fraught with danger.

9

The Atlantic Community,
100 BC–AD 500

The Roman military were not natural sailors. When forced to develop a naval force in the Mediterranean to counter the Carthaginians during the First Punic War (264–241 BC), they did so with efficiency and with conspicuous success, but then the Mediterranean was a familiar environment, its moods easily learned. In 206 BC, with the capitulation of Gadir (Cádiz), the Roman army faced an altogether different sea—the unpredictable Atlantic, an ocean without end. From time to time armies took to the sea, but always with foreboding: they were encroaching on the realms of Oceanus, and not infrequently the expeditions ended in disaster. Yet in the new lands they were to conquer, Atlantic Iberia, Gaul, and the islands of Britannia, they came upon indigenous populations living in symbiosis with the sea practising a tradition of seafaring thousands of years old. These were people who knew instinctively about the massive tidal ranges, the swells, and the sudden storms, and had braved them to settle some of the remotest Atlantic islands: the Orkneys and the Shetlands beyond the northern extremity of Scotland, and the Aran islands off the west coast of Ireland.

During the centuries of Roman occupation the indigenous seafaring tradition flourished, adopting technological improvements where these were advantageous, invigorated by the increased trading opportunities that the empire offered. Meanwhile, in areas beyond the frontiers, along the North Sea coast of Germany and Scandinavia, quite different maritime traditions were developing. Towards the end of the Roman occupation these northern seafarers began to extend their activities into the southern North Sea and the English Channel, bringing them into direct conflict with the waning powers of the empire.

Remoteness and Connectivity

The long Atlantic face of Europe from the Strait of Gibraltar to the Shetlands was a place of ambivalence. For the most part it was a confusion of rugged peninsulas of hard rock thrusting into the ocean, isolated slabs of land remote from each other but sharing the sea which bound them together in networks of connectivity. Remoteness and connectivity characterized the Atlantic façade. Remote places often accentuate human behaviour and the physical expressions of culture to create a distinct identity different from the 'other'. So it was along Atlantic-facing Europe. At about the time when the Romans were arriving, in the first century BC to the first century AD, distant cultural entities had emerged in Galicia, Armorica, south-western Britain and south-western Wales, north Wales, western Ireland, western Scotland, and the Hebrides and Northern Isles. Different identities were expressed in many ways, in the style of houses and settlements, artistic preferences in decorating pottery and metalwork, and in belief systems manifest in structures such as sauna baths and warrior statuary in Galicia, decorated menhirs and souterrains in Armorica, and the brochs and wheel-houses of the Western and Northern Isles.

Each region was distinctive, and yet there was much shared between them. Most widespread were the cliff castles, narrow promontories jutting out into the sea with a fortified barrier on the landward side. Often the barrier was a single wall and ditch, but sometimes it was multiple, and there was usually a single gate giving access. The defended area within was typically quite limited in size and often steeply sloping, providing comparatively little accommodation, but that people lived within is clear from the presence of hut sites and layers of occupation debris. Sites of this kind have been found along the Atlantic seaboard from Galicia to Shetland, the conventional explanation being that they were used in times of stress to provide protection for the community. This may have been so, but these 'forts' are so inhospitable and restricted that it seems likely that their prime purpose was other than for communal defence. One plausible explanation is that they were set aside as liminal places between land and sea, places where, perhaps, communication could be made with the ocean deities. Standing on these narrow

9.1 (*Opposite*) Castel Meur in Finistère is a dramatic example of the cliff castles found around the Atlantic coast of Galicia, Brittany, Britain, and Ireland in the Iron Age. The promontory is cut off from the land by earthwork defences. Since it is almost completely surrounded by the sea, it would be difficult for anyone on the promontory not to be aware that they were within the realms of the ocean

promontories today, the overriding impression is of being surrounded by the battering sea: the land seems very distant. The existence of sacred promontories around the south-west coast of Iberia is well attested in the periplus incorporated in *Ora Maritima*, and the astronomer Ptolemy lists many sacred promontories in his *Geography*.

Islands, too, could be liminal places sacred to the gods. Strabo, quoting Posidonius, writes of an island near the estuary of the Loire inhabited only by 'women of the Samnitae ... they are possessed by Dionysus and make this god propitious by appeasing him with mystic initiations as well as other sacred performances'. Once a year they took the roof off the temple and replaced it in a single day. Each woman brought a load of straw and one of their number was jostled so that she dropped the load, whereupon she was torn to pieces by the others, who carried the body parts in procession around the temple calling out joyfully to the god (*Geography* 4.4.6). Posidonius also describes a less extreme sacred island near Britain where sacrifices were performed like those 'in Samothrace that have to do with Demeter and Core'. Exactly what this means is unclear, but it was probably something to do with the fertility of the grain harvest. Another writer, Pomponius Mela, mentions the sacred island of Sena 'in the British sea facing the shore of the Ossimians' (an Armorican tribe), where an oracle presided. The tradition of sacred islands in the ocean remained strong during the later Christian period, some becoming places of repose for monks where there was nothing to distract them from communing with God; others were mythical places embedded in allegory. For the Atlantic communities, for whom the sea was an ever-present reality needing propitiation, islands and sea-girt promontories were the obvious locations where communication with the Other World could take place.

Another feature of the Atlantic-facing regions was the propensity for houses to be built to a circular plan, in contrast to much of continental Europe, where the usual house plan was rectangular. Circularity was clearly significant in these parts, but why this should be is obscure. It could be little more than a deeply rooted tradition, but the suggestion that it may have had something to do with solar symbolism is at least worthy of consideration. The solar disc sinking into the sea would have been in the daily consciousness of the ocean fringe communities, and it is a fact that many houses were aligned so that the rising sun would shine through the door, hinting at a deliberate link between siting and the movement of the sun.

Atlantic culture is also characterized by the skin boat, a vessel made of hides stitched together and stretched over a light wooden framework. Such vessels are mentioned in *Ora Maritima* in the context of the Oestrymnides, the tin-rich islands of the north-west Galician coast, and Strabo notes that 'boats of tanned leather' were in use along this coast up to the time of Brutus' campaigns in 138 BC (*Geography* 3.3.7). Skin boats are mentioned by Pliny, probably quoting Pytheas, when writing about the tin

9.2 The Castro de Baroña on the west coast of Galicia is a defended settlement of closely packed circular stone-built houses. Circular houses are characteristic of the Atlantic zone in the Iron Age

trade in south-western Britain in the late fourth century BC. Julius Caesar also saw skin boats in the south-east of Britain in the mid-first century BC and was sufficiently impressed by them to order similar vessels to be built to assist his troops in Spain during the civil war. The only direct representation we have of the form of one of these vessels is a gold model found in a first-century BC hoard at Broighter, County Derry, in Ireland. It depicts a large boat with sufficient accommodation for seven or eight rowers and with a central square-rigged mast and a steering oar. It was comparable in size to the 'Portable vessell of Wicker ordinarily used by the Wild Irish' illustrated in a late seventeenth-century drawing by Captain Thomas Phillips. Similar vessels, covered in tarred canvas not skins, are still in use off the west coast of Ireland today. Such boats are well suited to the Atlantic waves, a point made by J. M. Synge in his book *The Aran Islands* (1907):

9.3 The famous Broighter boat, found with other gold items in a hoard in County Derry, Ireland, provides a unique insight into Atlantic ships of the first century BC. The model, probably representing a hide vessel, has seven pairs of rowing oars, a steering oar, and central mast to take a square-rigged sail

a small sail was set up in the bow, and we set off across the sound with a leaping oscillation that has no resemblance to the heavy movement of a boat ... the men continued to row after it had gone up and as they occupied the four cross seats I lay on the canvas at the stern and the frame of slender laths which bent and quivered as the waves passed under them. When we set off it was a brilliant morning in April and the green glittering waves seemed to toss the canoe among themselves.

The speed and ease with which the skin boat rides the waves is also implicit in the description given in *Ora Maritima*: 'they ... marvellously fit out boats with jointed skins and often run through the vast salt water on leather' (line 106).

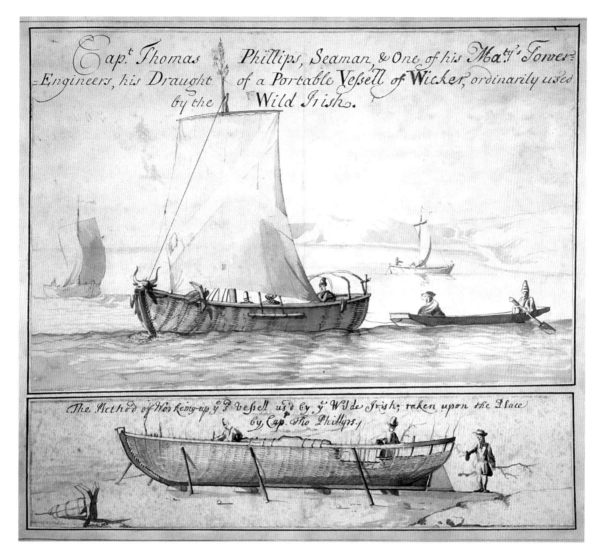

9.4 In the late seventeenth century Captain Thomas Phillips drew a rendering of a hide-covered currach which he described as 'a Portable Vessell of Wicker ordinarily used by the Wild Irish'. Currachs of this kind, covered with tarred canvas, are still used in western Ireland

There is no direct evidence of skin boats in Atlantic waters before the fourth century BC, but in all probability they were in use at least as early as the Mesolithic period. That their successors, the Irish currachs, still operate is a remarkable tribute to the simple versatility of the design. But the Atlantic maritime tradition was varied. Strabo mentions log boats on the Galician coast, and log boats continued on inland waters in

Britain and Ireland throughout the Iron Age and the Roman periods. There was also a tradition of sturdy plank-built vessels, as we shall see later.

The Narrowing Seas and Beyond

The narrowing English Channel and the North Sea opening out beyond offered very different sailing conditions from the Atlantic façade, and different patterns of seamanship developed to suit them. Strabo, writing half a century or so after Caesar's campaigns in Britain, says that four sea-passages between the Continent and Britain were regularly in use, with ships setting out from the estuaries of the Rhine, the Seine, the Loire, and the Garonne. By this time the whole of Gaul was in Roman hands, and much of the shipping using these routes would have been motivated by Roman commercial imperatives. According to Strabo the principal exports from Britain were grain, cattle, gold, silver, iron, hides, slaves, and hunting dogs. In return the Britons received 'ivory chains and necklaces, and amber gems and glass vessels and other trivial wares of that kind' (*Geography* 4.53). That the Britons were prepared to exchange valuable raw materials for knick-knacks Strabo considers laughable: Britons would have viewed the trade otherwise.

Caesar's campaigns had opened up diplomatic relations between the tribes of south-eastern Britain and Roman Gaul. Before that, different systems had prevailed. Caesar himself mentions that the tribes of Armorica were in direct trading contact with Britain, and this is well demonstrated by the archaeological evidence, which shows there to have been a major trading link between the north coast of Armorica in the vicinity of the Bay of Saint-Brieuc and the British port of Hengistbury Head on the Dorset coast, using Guernsey as a port-of-call on the way. One of the commodities carried by the Armorican middlemen between 120 and 50 BC was northern Italian wine transported in distinctive amphorae (Dressel type 1A). Another, shorter route between Nacqueville near Cherbourg and Hengistbury was used to export Kimmeridge shale from Dorset to Normandy. Further west there is some evidence of trade between northern Armorican ports like Le Yaudet and south-western Britain, where Plymouth Sound would have been a major point of entry. Eastwards of the Solent, as the Channel narrows, many much shorter Channel crossings offered themselves.

Once through the Strait of Dover the sea widens. Strabo describes how maritime traffic from the Rhine mouth coasted southwards towards the Channel's narrowest point before making the crossing to Britain. More direct routes probably led from the

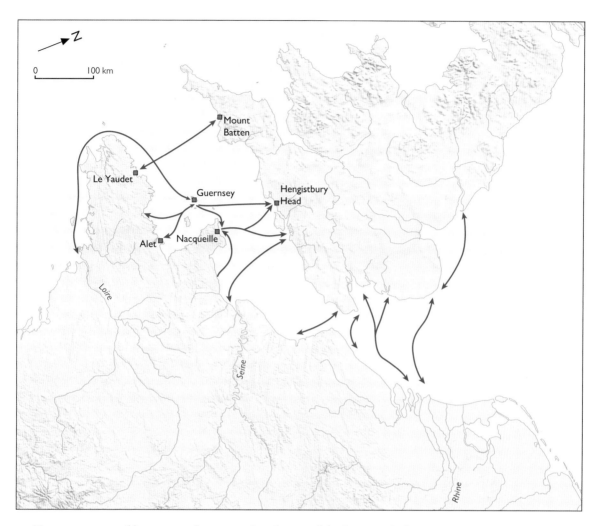

9.5 There were many possible sea passages between southern Britain and the Continent. Strabo, writing at the end of the first century BC, mentions that the Rhine, the Seine, and the Loire were favourite setting-off points. The ports named on the map have all produced archaeological evidence of cross-Channel trade in the first century BC

Rhine to the Thames, while, by sailing the latitude from the Rhine to the East Anglian coast and then following the coast northwards, the Yar estuary could be reached and, further on, the Humber estuary. These complex networks would have been in use for millennia before the Romans arrived on the continental coast. The indigenous sailors were skilled in making the crossings, their vessels honed to suit the sea in its many moods.

9.6 One of the valuable commodities widely traded in the Roman world was slaves. Strabo lists slaves as a principal export from Britain. This chain, for chaining six slaves together by their necks, was found in the Iron Age fort of Bigbury, near Canterbury, Kent

Perceptions of the Ocean

The knowledge of the Atlantic face of Europe was limited in the Graeco-Roman world to the few scraps that could be gleaned from the secretive Carthaginians, whose activities probably extended no further north than Galicia, and more detailed information on Armorica, Britain, and the North Sea provided by Pytheas. His near-contemporaries Dicaearchus of Messana and Timaeus of Tauromenium, and later writers like Eratosthenes of Kyrene, quoted Pytheas extensively and with approval, and so it was that some knowledge of the western fringes of the barbarian world entered into the awareness of Mediterranean scholars. But for the next 170 years nothing new was added: Pytheas remained the sole source.

By the middle of the second century BC the world was changing fast: Carthage was about to be wiped out and Rome was in expansionist mode. This was the context in which the Achaean aristocrat Polybius began to write his history of Rome in forty books. The first thirty-three covered the period from 220 to 153 BC. Book 34 was a geography, and the remaining books took the story up to the destruction of Carthage in 146 BC, an event which Polybius himself witnessed. The project took fifty years to complete, with the last corrections being made in 118 BC, and during this time Polybius undertook fieldwork of his own. He accompanied his patron, Scipio, in Spain and North Africa and he explored the route taken by Hannibal across the Alps, and following the fall of Carthage he was sent with a fleet to explore the west coast of Africa (p. 322 above). His claim that he made 'journeys through Africa, Spain, and Gaul and voyages on the seas that lie on the further side of these countries' implies that he visited the Atlantic coast of France, either by sailing northwards from Gades (Cádiz) or by taking the trans-peninsular Garonne–Gironde route to the Bay of Biscay. How far north his journeys took him is a matter of speculation. As we have seen, it may be that he reached Korbilo at the mouth of the Loire, but there is no evidence to suggest that he ventured beyond the south coast of Armorica.

It was in book 34, the 'Geography', that Polybius wrote about the ocean. Little now survives apart from a few quotations in later sources, but he used the opportunity to denigrate the work of Pytheas, dismissing much of it as lies and exaggeration. The violence of his attack suggests an intense jealousy. He conceived of himself as a pioneer explorer of the ocean and it may have been only on his visit to the library of Alexandria between 145 and 135 BC that he first came upon a copy of *On the Ocean*, learning that Pytheas had made a far more thorough exploration of the region nearly two centuries earlier. His disappointment would have been profound and he was not a man to give credit to others.

Whether or not there were systematic attempts to explore the Atlantic coasts is unclear. Strabo tells the story of a Roman who followed a Phoenician trader from Gades hoping to discover the way to the tin source in the Cassiterides and was lured onto shoals when the Phoenician deliberately beached his vessel to protect the secret. He goes on to say that later Publius Crassus managed to discover the route and made the information widely available. Since Strabo is writing here in the context of Spain, he is presumably referring to journeys up the west coast of Iberia to Galicia. The initial abortive attempt to find the route to the tin source may have come soon after Rome's acquisition of Gades in 206 BC. The Crassus who succeeded was probably P. Licinius Crassus, who was proconsul of Hispania Ulterior between 96 and 93 BC.

Roman military campaigns in Spain, Gaul, and Britain in the first century BC brought the Roman empire to the Atlantic coast of the European continent and for many made the ocean a reality. Yet Strabo, whose books on geography were largely completed by the end of the first century BC, had a curiously distorted view of the Atlantic region. *Geography* is a compilation stitched together largely from the work of others by an author who had never travelled further west than Italy and who held firmly fixed ideas about the order of the world which he did not allow to be upset by mere evidence. In his muddled view the Pyrenees and the Rhine were aligned north to south, and between the two the coast of Keltike (France) ran in a more or less straight line from south-west to north-east. Britain fronted the coast, the most easterly point, Kantion (Kent), being opposite the Rhine mouth, while the most westerly end lay opposite the Aquitanian Pyrenees. With this concept firmly fixed in his mind he was forced to reject Pytheas' nuanced description of the great westerly projection of the Armorican peninsula. Strabo also believed that Ireland lay north of Britain but was so close to the latitude at which he considered it too cold for humans to exist that it could only have been sparsely populated. For him the inhabited world ended between 55° and 58° north and since Pytheas wrote about people living beyond this limit he must be lying. It is also curious how little Strabo was influenced by new evidence that was being made available by contemporary Roman sources like the *Commentaries* of Julius Caesar. He was content instead to rely on his own cognitive geography and on very out-of-date sources.

The first century AD saw little improvement in geographical awareness. Pomponius Mela, a native of Spain, added a few scraps in three short, sketchy books written by AD 43, and the elder Pliny (d. AD 79) gathered together a vast scrapbook of miscellaneous information in his *Natural History*, calling on a range of sources and probably relying on Pytheas for much of his descriptions of Britain and its islands and of the amber-producing coast of Jutland. It was left to the Alexandrian astronomer Claudius Ptolemaeus (Ptolemy) to produce a tolerably accurate map of the known world about AD 150. Whether or not he actually drew maps is unclear, but he published lists of place names with latitudes and longitudes using the Canaries as the westernmost longitude, from which the others were calculated. It was from these that maps could be drawn. He had access to a very wide range of sources, including records compiled by sailors who knew the coasts of Ireland, which still lay beyond the boundaries of the empire. Allowing for minor distortions, which are probably the result of scribal errors, Ptolemy's map gives a remarkably accurate representation of the whole Atlantic coast from Kerne to Thule.

9.7 (*Opposite*) Two cognitive geographies of western Europe: (*a*) Strabo's view in the late first century BC; (*b*) Ptolemy's more accurate view in the second century AD

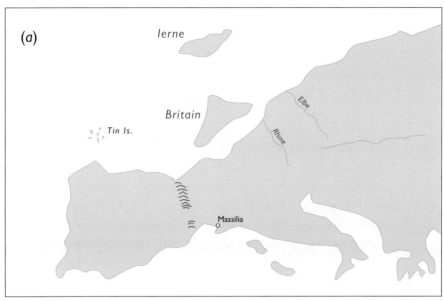

(a)

Ierne

Britain

Tin Is.

Elbe

Rhine

Massilia

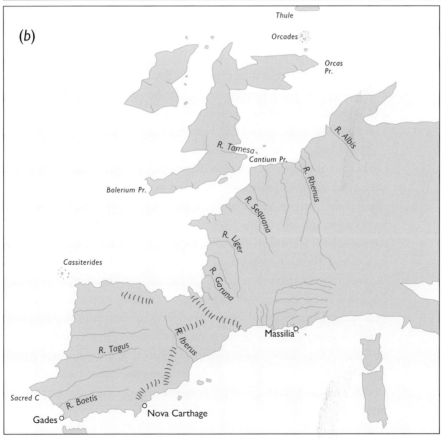

(b)

Thule

Orcades

Orcas
Pr.

R. Albis

R. Tamesa

Cantium Pr.

R. Rhenus

Bolerium Pr.

R. Sequana

R. Liger

Cassiterides

R. Garuna

Massilia

R. Tagus

R. Iberus

Sacred C

R. Baetis

Gades

Nova Carthage

Meanwhile in Africa

Following the destruction of Carthage in 146 BC the core of Carthaginian North Africa became a Roman province. Immediately to the west lay the kingdom of Numidia, and beyond that, stretching along the Mediterranean coast and down the west coast of Africa, roughly coincident with modern Algeria and Morocco, was the more diffuse kingdom of Mauretania. One of the Mauretanian kings, Bocchus I, had shown his suspicion of foreign adventurers by trying to restrict the activities of Eudoxus of Kyzikos about 100 BC, but for the most part friendly relations were maintained with the Roman world. A later ruler, Bogudes II, showed some interest in exploration, having sent an expedition to the tropics, but in 33 BC he decided to abdicate in favour of a more adventurous life in the entourage of Marcus Antonius, then fighting his Roman rivals in the east. When, out of this mêlée, Octavian (Augustus) emerged triumphant, he found that north-west Africa was without effective leadership, and to establish a degree of control he installed the heir of the Numidian kingdom, Juba II, as king of Mauretania in 25 BC. It was a sensible move. The Numidian kingdom had been absorbed into the Roman empire by Julius Caesar in 46 BC and the young Juba II taken to Rome to be brought up as a Roman citizen as part of a policy of educating the heirs to foreign thrones in Roman values and manners—a good investment should they be returned to take their thrones. In Rome, Juba met and married another royal exile, Cleopatra Selene, daughter of Marcus Antonius and Cleopatra. By sending Juba and his bride to rule Mauretania, Augustus was ensuring that the kingdom was likely to remain loyal to Rome and thus would need no military investment.

Juba II had an academic interest in Africa. In Rome he had been given access to books from the captured library of Carthage, among them a full account of Hanno's voyage, which in all probability included some mention of the offshore islands we know as the Canaries. As an educated man he will have been well aware of the Greek myths about the Isles of the Blest and the garden of the Hesperides and his curiosity was stirred. Sometime soon after his arrival in 25 BC he sent out an expedition to explore and himself took part. All seven of the major islands were given names based on their distinctive characteristics. One of them, because of its large population of dogs, was called Canaria, which now gives its name to the archipelago. The islands were said to be uninhabited, but traces of previous occupation were noted. On Junonia was what were thought to be the remains of a temple, and ruined buildings were seen on Canaria. In addition, the feral dogs and goats reflected earlier human habitation. In spite of the fertility of the islands and the congenial climate, no attempt was made to establish new settlements. Perhaps Juba was enough of a romantic to believe that the Isles of the Blest should remain unpolluted by mortals.

Juba's academic interest in Africa and his access to Carthaginian and Ptolemaic texts led him to write two books, *Libyka* on West Africa, and *On Arabia*, which included East Africa. His vision, like that of others before him, was that Africa was a squat continent lying wholly above the equator. For him, between where knowledge of West Africa ended and East Africa began there was only a comparatively short length of unexplored coast still to be navigated. Africa was now conceptually contained.

There is one further island footnote to add. During the civil wars of the late republican period, one of the contenders, Quintus Sertorius, fled to Mauretania about 80 BC and set himself up as a ruler of Tingis (Tangier). There he met and befriended a group of Iberian pirates who knew of two remote fertile islands in the Atlantic, probably Madeira, where they suggested he might settle. Though tempted by the idea of a quiet island retirement, Sertorius declined the offer and went on to fight a succession of engagements in southern Spain before being assassinated by one of his officers in 72 BC. The story is a reminder that there must have been many seafarers in Atlantic waters whose knowledge of distant islands never found its way into recorded history.

Roman Armies and the Ocean

The capitulation of Gades in 206 BC brought the Roman armies to the Atlantic. Standing on the city quay and looking west, a soldier would have confronted endless ocean on the edge of the world. The experience must have been profound. To a military strategist the ocean provided a natural frontier for the empire, and yet it was to take more than two hundred years to secure. Many obstacles stood in the way—civil war, recalcitrant tribes, the daunting overland distances that had to be covered—but behind it all there was an unspoken reluctance to tangle with the ocean. After a naval disaster in the North Sea in AD 16 one observer captured the ever-present fear by asking, 'why do we disturb the peaceful home of the gods?' (Seneca, *Suasoriae* 1.15).

Following Scipio's success at the battle of Ilipa in 206 BC, Rome became master of all the Carthaginian territories in Iberia, and by 194 BC had consolidated them into two provinces, Hispania Ulterior and Hispania Citerior, together occupying a strip between a hundred and two hundred kilometres wide along the Mediterranean coast from the Pyrenees to the Odiel–Tinto estuary. This created an inland frontier of some nine hundred kilometres facing hostile tribes, the confederation of the Celtiberi in the centre and the Lusitani in the west. Over the next forty years almost constant fighting along this frontier saw limited advances inland, with minor gains in the west extending Roman-held territory to the river Guadiana. In 155 BC the Lusitani intensified their raids on the Roman province, which culminated in the defeat of the governor

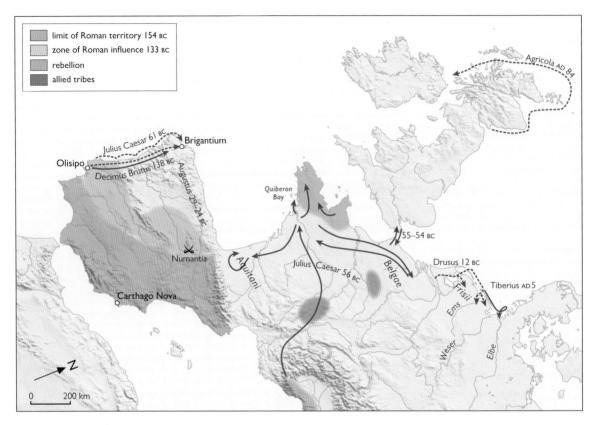

Legend:
- limit of Roman territory 154 BC
- zone of Roman influence 133 BC
- rebellion
- allied tribes

Labels on map: Agricola AD 84, Julius Caesar 61 BC, Brigantium, Olisipo, Decimus Brutus 138 BC, Augustus 29–24 BC, Quiberon Bay, 55–54 BC, Numantia, Aquitani, Julius Caesar 56 BC, Belgae, Drusus 12 BC, Frisii, Tiberius AD 5, Carthago Nova, Ems, Weser, Elbe, N, 0 200 km

9.8 Rome first made contact with the Atlantic when Gadir (Cádiz) was conquered in 206 BC. By 154 BC much of the south-west of Iberia has been incorporated into the new province of Hispania. Thereafter Rome's engagement with the Atlantic grew, culminating in the exploration of the coasts of Scotland and the Orkney islands under the direction of Agricola in AD 84

in 151 BC. Hostilities continued, with the Roman army thrusting north supported by sea-borne flotillas sailing along the Algarve coast—the first time the Atlantic had been put to military use by Rome. The aim of the Roman strategy was to drive a wedge between the Celtiberi and the Lusitani, isolating the latter against the ocean and forcing them to negotiate. The assassination of the Lusitanian war leader Viriathus in 138 BC brought resistance to an end, allowing Rome to extend the frontier as far north as the valley of the Tagus. Beyond that, between the Tagus and the Douro, the tribes were more lightly controlled.

In 138 BC Decimus Brutus, the provincial governor, began a campaign against the tribes of the north-west, having first established a supply base at Olisipo (Lisbon) on the Tagus estuary. His prime target was the Callaici, one of the principal tribes of metal-rich Galicia. This was presented as a retaliatory attack to punish the Callaici for their support of the Lusitani but in reality is more likely to have been a reconnaissance to find out about the tin and gold resources of the region and to assess the prospect of conquest. In the event, he returned with a considerable amount of booty, but, by the end of the campaign in 133 BC, the border of the Roman province had moved north only as far as the river Mondego, leaving the tribes of Galicia to themselves. While pressing events elsewhere in the Roman world deflected attention away from this remote mountainous region, the more entrepreneurial-minded remained curious about the metal resources, and it may well be that it was in this context that P. Licinius Crassus explored the sea-routes to the tin-bearing region sometime between 96 and 93 BC, opening up the trade route to those who wished to exploit it.

In 61 BC Julius Caesar was appointed governor of Hispania Ulterior, having already served as quaestor in the province eight years before. Aware of the opportunities offered by Galicia, both for quick military glory and for booty, he immediately raised a legion and marched north against the Lusitani and Callaici, his land-forces, supported by a fleet, converging on the native port of Brigantium (La Coruña). This was his first experience of the Atlantic and of its military uses—experience he was to make good use of a few years later in Armorica and Britain. The military gains were not followed up, largely because of events developing elsewhere, and the region remained unstable, with sporadic revolts breaking out among the Lusitani. It was not until the civil wars were over and Augustus had emerged as *princeps* (first citizen) that the new emperor could finally establish Roman control over the whole of northern Iberia by bringing to heel the mountain peoples—the Cantabri, the Austores, and the Galician tribes—in a series of campaigns between 29 and 24 BC. Even then, revolts were to continue for another eight years.

Caesar's lightning strike along the Atlantic coast in 61 BC amply demonstrated the advantage of sea-power as an effective way of supplying and reinforcing land-forces, but it is not clear whether special vessels were built on this occasion or local ships were commandeered. When he had found it necessary to dislodge dissidents from the Berlengas archipelago off the Portuguese coast, he had used local ships brought up from Gades, which suggests that suitable vessels were in short supply.

Four years after his first contact with the Atlantic in Iberia, Caesar found himself contending with the ocean again, this time on the coast of Armorica. In 58 BC, intent on a campaign of conquest, he had managed to get himself appointed to a command in Gaul. Given the size of the endeavour it is interesting that his second campaigning season (57 BC) was devoted to bringing the 'maritime regions' of Belgica and Armorica—that is, the entire Atlantic front from the Rhine to the Garonne—under control. He soon realized that the ocean would make an ideal western frontier and, by securing it first, the rest of Gaul could be brought more easily under Roman rule. To achieve this he led his forces among the Belgic tribes between the Seine and the Rhine, leaving Armorica to his general Publius Crassus. At first the Armorican tribes submitted, but during the winter a revolt broke out, led by the Veneti, whose territory lay on the southern side of the peninsula. Caesar responded quickly, sending one general to keep a watch on the Belgae and another to the Aquitani, between the Loire and the Garonne, thus containing the trouble to Armorica. Realizing that he was dealing with rebels in command of a strong naval force, he ordered a fleet of galleys to be built on the Loire and oarsmen to be recruited from the Province together with crews and pilots. Other vessels were requested from the Pictones and Santones, two of the coastal tribes between the Loire and the Garonne. This newly assembled naval force put to sea under the command of Decimus Brutus and made for the Gulf of Morbihan, where the Venetic fleet was known to be, while Caesar himself led land-forces into Venetic territory, attempting, unsuccessfully, to bring them to battle. Every time he attacked one of the fortified places, they simply stole away, so he decided to wait for the Roman fleet to appear, to defeat them at sea.

The naval battle fought out in the Bay of Quiberon is vividly described by Caesar. It was the Venetic ships that impressed him most:

> They were built and rigged in a different way from ours. Their keels were somewhat flatter, so they could cope more easily with the shoals and shallow water when the tide was ebbing. Their prows were unusually high and so were their sterns, designed to stand up to great waves and violent storms. The hulls were made entirely of oak to endure any violent shock or impact; the cross-beams, of timbers a foot thick, were fastened with iron bolts as thick as a man's thumb; and the anchors were held firm with iron chains instead of ropes. They used sails made of hides or soft leather, either because flax was scarce and they did not know how to use it, or, more probably, because they thought that with cloth sails they would not be able to withstand the force of the violent Atlantic gales or steer such heavy ships. ... They were so solidly built that our ships could not damage them with their rams, and their height made it hard to use missiles against them or seize them with grappling irons. Not only that: when a gale blew up and they ran before it they could weather the storm more easily and heave to more safely in the shallow water, and if left aground by the tide, they had nothing to fear from rocks and reefs.
>
> (*De Bello Gallico* 3.13)

9.9 An iron anchor together with an attached length of anchor chain dating to the first century BC was found in a hoard of ironwork in the Iron Age fort of Bulbury in Dorset. Caesar specifically mentions that iron anchor chains were used by the Venetic sailors of Brittany

From elsewhere in his description of the ensuing battle we learn that they were square-rigged and relied entirely on their sails, having no oars. The Veneti were able to muster 220 of these great ships, 'perfectly equipped with every kind of weapon'.

The Roman galleys were too low in the water to deal effectively with such high-sided vessels. The Romans were aware of this disadvantage and had armed themselves with sharp sickles mounted on long poles, with which they proceeded to cut the ropes holding the yards of the Venetic vessels, bringing down their sails. The disabled ships were then surrounded and boarded. When the wind suddenly dropped, those that had tried to make off were becalmed and captured. For the Roman soldiers watching from the cliffs the day-long battle must have been memorable. The detail in which Caesar describes the Venetic ships leaves little doubt about his fascination with these alien craft or his admiration for the way in which they had been so carefully adapted to local conditions. There was much for him to learn when next he had to face the Atlantic.

Towards the end of the campaigning season of 55 BC, Caesar turned his attention to Britain, justifying his interest by claiming that the Britons had been sending reinforcements to support Gaulish resistance, and adding, 'I thought it would be very useful merely to have visited the island to have seen what sort of people lived there and to get some idea of the terrain and the harbours and landing places' (*De Bello Gallico* 4.20). As a preliminary he interrogated

9.10 Depictions of Iron Age Atlantic vessels are rare. This coin of the British king Cunobelinus, minted in the early first century AD, shows a deep-hulled square-rigged vessel of the type described by Caesar in his confrontation with the Veneti

347

Gauls who traded with Britain and sent one of his warships to make a reconnaissance. The next stage was to amass the army at the point of shortest crossing and to assemble an invasion fleet comprised of the galleys built the previous year for his Venetic campaign, afforced with vessels requisitioned from the neighbouring Gaulish ports. In all, eighty transport ships were available in addition to the warships. The flotilla set off about midnight, with the leading ships reaching the British coast by early morning. The landing was not without its difficulties because the transports were too heavy to run ashore, but Caesar ordered his lighter galleys to be run up onto the beaches: 'The manoeuvre was very effective. The natives were greatly disturbed by the shape of the ships, the movement of the oars and the strange devices of our artillery.' The diversion allowed the troops the opportunity to disembark and establish a bridge-head.

Four days later the Romans paid the price of their inexperience. The eighteen vessels that were bringing the cavalry from Gaul were scattered and compelled to return by a sudden storm in the Channel. This coincided with a full moon, which Caesar admits he did not realize created exceptionally high tides. The combination of the high tides and the storms swamped the beached galleys, while several of the transports riding at anchor were battered and smashed, and 'the rest were unusable having lost cables, anchors and the rest of their gear'. It was a dangerous situation brought about largely by the Roman lack of understanding of the fast-changing moods of the Atlantic in autumn. After desultory skirmishes on land and negotiation with natives, and with weather conditions deteriorating, Caesar decided to withdraw to the relative safety of Gaul, using the damaged transports as best he could. The retreat was largely uneventful.

Caesar had learned a lot from the near-disaster of his foray into Britain in 55 BC, and in preparation for his next expedition in 54 BC he ordered specially modified ships to be constructed that could be loaded quickly and easily beached. They were lower and wider than Mediterranean vessels: 'I order that all these vessels should be suitable for both rowing and sailing, an arrangement made all the easier because of this low freeboard.' More than eight hundred vessels took part in the expedition, setting sail about sunset and arriving at midday after misjudging the tidal currents and being forced to row furiously to make the British coast.

The landing was unopposed and the troops marched off inland to engage with the Britons, leaving the fleet partly beached and partly at anchor. Once more there was a violent storm, which 'damaged almost all of our ships and cast them up on the shore. The anchors and cables had not held firm and the sailors and pilots could not cope with the force of the gale. As a result a great deal of damage had been done by ships colliding with each other' (*De Bello Gallico* 5.10). Fortunately for Caesar the ships were repaired before it was time to return to Gaul. Reading Caesar's detailed description of his confrontation with the sea it is clear that, while he was able to learn fast and show great flexibility, he was unnerved by the caprice of the ocean—the unaccountable suddenness with which everything could change. His calm concluding sentences to his British adventure, 'so we set sail in the evening and reached land at dawn. I had brought all the ships across in safety and we beached them', belie the dread and anguish he must have felt.

Caesar's conquest of Gaul brought the North Sea coast from the Channel to the Rhine into the Roman world. Beyond that lay a difficult coast of sand and shingle barriers backed first by marshland but further north fragmenting into elongated islands. It was this coastline that Augustus was referring to in his boast 'My fleet sailed on the Ocean from the mouth of the Rhine eastwards as far as the land of the Cimbri [Denmark?], to which, before that time, no Roman had gone into, either by land or by sea' (*Res Gestae* 26). How extensive was the exploration it is difficult to say, but two specific encounters are recorded. In 12 BC the military commander Drusus sailed down the Rhine after campaigning up-river and, having crossed a lake (perhaps a more extended version of the Zuider Zee), let his ships be grounded by a following tide. He was received by the local Frisians, who knew the waters well. Later, in AD 5, a Roman fleet sailed to the mouth of the Elbe to provide support for a land campaign being undertaken by Tiberius. These two rather ill-recorded events were only isolated incidents in the Roman probings northwards along the coast. In AD 16 Germanicus, campaigning in Germania, sailed his troops down the Ems to the North Sea to claim control of the Frisian islands, but somewhere on the ocean his fleet was caught in a violent storm and was scattered, some ships being driven across the North Sea to Britain. Germanicus made it back to the mainland, but the event was a reminder to all that the Ocean was not to be trifled with: it was an alien, hostile world where, as one eyewitness to the event wrote, there were immense monsters beneath the waves and men and ships could be torn apart by wild sea creatures. The stuff of overblown poetry perhaps, but a reminder of the Mediterranean world's deep-seated fear of the Ocean.

The final stages of Rome's exploration of the Atlantic came later in the first century AD with the conquest of Britain, an island which, even after Caesar's expeditions ninety years earlier, was still regarded with awe. When the emperor Gaius (Caligula) assembled an army to invade the island in AD 40, the troops rebelled at the prospect of crossing the ocean and the best the emperor could do was to make them collect seashells, perhaps to symbolize his control of the sea, but the embarkation was abandoned. Three years later, when the emperor Claudius was preparing a new invasion attempt, the troops again mutinied, saying that the ocean defined the edge of the world beyond which they were not prepared to go. Eventually they were persuaded to change their mind and the invasion proceeded without further problems, but it was to take thirty years for the island to be finally overrun.

The last stages of the conquest were in the hands of Julius Agricola, who arrived as governor in the summer of AD 78. Relying heavily on naval support, the armies marched northwards through Scotland, fighting a final decisive battle against the Caledonian resistance at Mons Graupius on the southern side of the Firth of Tay in the summer of AD 84. Agricola then instructed the navy to sail round the northern extremity of the island, as the historian Tacitus records:

> This coast of that remotest sea was first rounded at this time by a Roman fleet, which thus established the fact that Britain was an island. At the same time it discovered and subdued the Orkney Islands hitherto unknown. Thule, too, was sighted by our men, but no more—their orders took them no further and winter was close at hand.
>
> (*Agricola* 10)

Demonstrating that Britain really was an island, as Pytheas had already shown four hundred years earlier, would have satisfied the Roman mind. The island glimpsed in the distance was probably Shetland, but calling it Thule pays a nice homage to Pytheas. Thule lay beyond the inhabitable world and therefore was of no concern to Rome.

Commerce and Supply

Caesar learned quickly that the natives of the Atlantic coastal areas which he had encountered in Iberia, Armorica, and Britain had a long tradition of shipbuilding, creating craft well suited to the ocean conditions. They also engaged in lively trade, one maritime region with another. The piecemeal imposition of Roman rule over these countries changed comparatively little, other than adding an increased incentive to trade and providing peaceful conditions in which entrepreneurial activities could flourish. The need to supply the frontier troops, however, introduced a totally new imperative. By the end of the first century AD very large numbers of men were stationed along the Rhine and in northern Britain. Ease of troop movement, speed of supply, and the facility for rapid communications were developed, linking the frontier zones to the Mediterranean. The main artery ran northwards from the Golfe du Lion along the Rhône valley, branching at Chalon-sur-Saône, with one route leading to the Seine and thence to the Channel and another going via the Moselle to the Rhine frontier. Two important subsidiary routes strengthened the system. From Lugdunum (Lyon), by way of the Swiss lakes, the upper Rhine could be reached at Augusta Raurica (near Augst), while the roads through Langres led directly to the Channel port of Gesoriacum (Boulogne). These were the principal military supply routes to the north, but the long-established commercial routes across Gaul to the Atlantic, the one via the Rhône and Loire and the other from Narbo Martius (Narbonne) using the Garonne to the Gironde estuary, were still in active use. Thus, the estuaries of the great rivers—the Garonne, Loire, Seine, and Rhine—continued to provide the interfaces of the Mediterranean system with the Atlantic, strengthened by the new port facilities at Gesoriacum specifically developed to give quick and easy access to Britain. Between all these coastal outlets the flow of shipping would have been considerable.

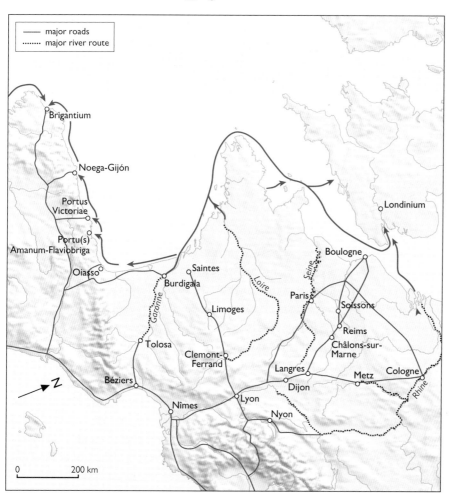

9.11 Trade between the Mediterranean and the Atlantic used the river routes of Gaul augmented by new roads built by the Romans. With the final conquest of the wilder parts of northern Iberia by Augustus in the late first century BC, a series of ports began to develop along the coast to serve the increasing volume of shipping

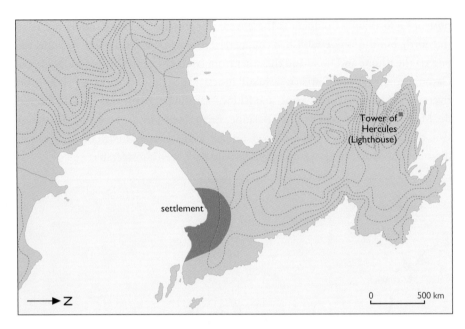

9.12 The focal port city in north-western Iberia was Brigantium (La Coruña), situated on a well-protected harbour. Here trade along the western and northern coasts of Iberia was articulated. Brigantium was also a convenient port for setting off across the Bay of Biscay. The great lighthouse on a high promontory overlooking the sea would have been a comfort to all navigating the waters

But what of Iberia? As we have seen, the archaeological evidence shows that Carthaginian traders were working the Atlantic coasts as far as the Ría de Viveiro on the north coast of Galicia from the fourth to the second century, but the rugged and treacherous coastline of Cantabria lay beyond their sphere of interest. The whole of the north coast of Iberia was an uncongenial environment for seafarers with few natural harbours. Beyond that lay the west coast of Aquitania, an almost continuous sand-bar backed by marshland stretching as far as the estuary of the Gironde. There was little in this eight-hundred-kilometre stretch of coast to attract maritime commerce.

One of the main terminal ports on the route from Gades and the Mediterranean was Brigantium (La Coruña), a rocky island which had become joined to the mainland by a sand-bar, creating a well-protected harbour sheltered from westerly and northerly winds. It had been the object of Caesar's thrust into Galicia in 61 BC. Finds of Graeco-Roman amphorae of the second or first century BC indicate something of its trading connections, and the harbour was dominated by two native castros, reflecting its importance. In the first century AD, under the Flavian emperors, the east harbour began to develop as a Roman port and the town was granted municipal status. It was sometime in the late first or early second century that the famous lighthouse

9.13 The famous Roman lighthouse at La Coruña, the Tower of Hercules, has been in almost constant use since the first century. It was refaced and heightened in the eighteenth century and modified again in the nineteenth century, but it is still largely of Roman workmanship

known as the Tower of Hercules was built to guide ships around the promontory. Roman investment in the port of Brigantium coincided with the development of other ports along the northern coastline of Cantabria and beyond: the unknown port at Noega-Gijon, Portus Victoriae (Santander), Flaviobriga (Castro Urdiales), Oiasso (Irún), and Lampurdum (Bayonne), which for the first time provided a system of safe havens enabling ships to journey in comparative safety from Brigantium to Burdigala (Bordeaux). Thus, in the first century AD the coastal route from the Mediterranean to the English Channel and North Sea became feasible for maritime traffic. It was, however, many times longer than the direct overland route through Gaul and it is unlikely that entrepreneurs or military suppliers ever considered it to be a serious competitor. At best the Atlantic offered a series of linked cabotage routes, with nodal ports like Brigantium and Burdigala serving as major hubs for transhipment between the different legs of the maritime system. That some ships' masters may have chosen to sail from Brigantium northwards across the Bay of Biscay to the Armorican peninsula is possible, but a journey taking a minimum of six days to cross one of the most unpredictable of seas is hardly likely to have become a favoured route.

The reality of coastal trade along the Atlantic route is demonstrated in the archaeological record by the distribution of products carried by the ships and by the occasional shipwrecks that have been found. Inscriptions also add some useful detail. The distribution of Dressel 1 amphorae is instructive. The amphorae were used to transport wine in the period from the mid-second century to the end of the first century BC from the estates where the wine was produced in northern Italy to the end users as far afield as Britain. The distribution map (Figure 9.14) gives a good indication of the dominant routes, from Massalia northwards along the Rhône to northern Gaul and from Narbo along the Aude–Garonne–Gironde route to the Atlantic. It was most likely from the Gironde estuary that ships transported the wine to the Armorican peninsula. The two separate distributions in Britain represent two chronologically different patterns of contact. The amphorae in the south central region are mainly of the 1A type common in the period 140–50 BC. These would have come from Armorica along with distinctive Armorican pots arriving at southern British ports like Hengistbury Head. The amphorae found in the Thames region were mostly of the 1B type, which were being widely traded between 60 and 10 BC and presumably arrived from the ports of northern Gaul. The Iberian distribution is quite separate, concentrating along the Atlantic coast, the ships coming directly from the Mediterranean via the Strait of Gibraltar. While it is possible that some of the cargoes reaching Armorica came by way of Atlantic Iberia, the more convenient route to the north-west was through the Gironde along the Gaulish coast.

Much the same story is told by the distribution of a different amphora type, Haltern 70, which dates from the late first century BC to the late first century AD. The amphorae were made in the Guadalquivir valley to transport wine, olives, and defrutum (a sweet liquid derived by boiling must—fermented grape juice). One route led through the Strait of Gibraltar to the ports of southern Gaul and then by the river routes through Gaul to the German frontier and to Britain. Another route led along the west coast of Iberia and is reflected in concentrations of amphorae in Galicia. Two shipwreck sites are known producing numbers of Haltern 70 amphorae, one in the Ría de Arousa near Pontevedra, the other off Cabo de Mar close to Praia do Areal. The amphorae that reached Britain in all probability came through Gaul using the short sea-route across the English Channel.

Direct trade between the Gironde estuary and Britain is well attested, at least by the third century AD, by two inscriptions found in Bordeaux. The first is the tombstone of L. Solimarius Secundinus, by origin a Treveran from the Moselle region. He is recorded as having been 'a merchant dealing with Britain'. The second is an altar erected in AD 237 to the goddess Tutela Boudig(a) by Marcus Aurelius Lunaris, who was an official working in the coloniae at York and Lincoln. The inscription records that he made a vow when he set out from York to Bordeaux to set up an altar to the

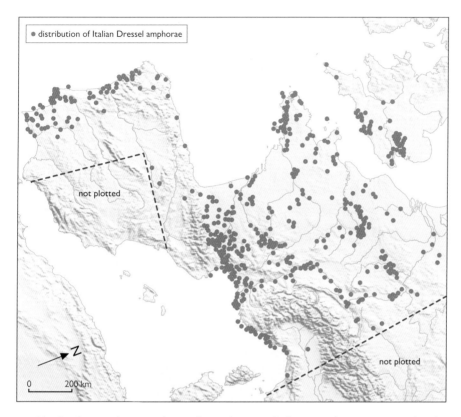

9.14 The distribution of wine amphorae of Dressel 1 type, which were used to transport north Italian wine during the first century BC, shows that the rivers of Gaul featured large among the routes in use. The two centres of distribution in Britain are of slightly different dates. Amphorae of the earlier type (Dressel 1A) were found in the Solent region and probably came from Brittany. After Caesar's conquest of Gaul, wine was imported into the Thames region from northern Gaul. The distribution in Atlantic Iberia suggests transport direct from the Mediterranean by sea

deity when he arrived. His touching faith in the goddess's protection is shown by the fact that he had the altar carved in York from the local millstone grit before he left and carried it with him on his long sea journey. The attraction of Bordeaux to both men may have been its ample supplies of good-quality wine.

A wreck site excavated in the harbour of St Peter Port on Guernsey adds further support to the vitality of the Bordeaux–Britain route in the late third century. The ship caught fire in the harbour with its cargo, comprising a commodity carried in barrels and large blocks of pitch, still on board. Analysis of the pitch suggests that it probably came from the pine forests of the Landes to the south of the Gironde estuary. Nothing can be said of the contents of the barrels, but it is tempting to suggest that it may have been wine loaded at Bordeaux alongside the pitch. Since much of the pottery on board

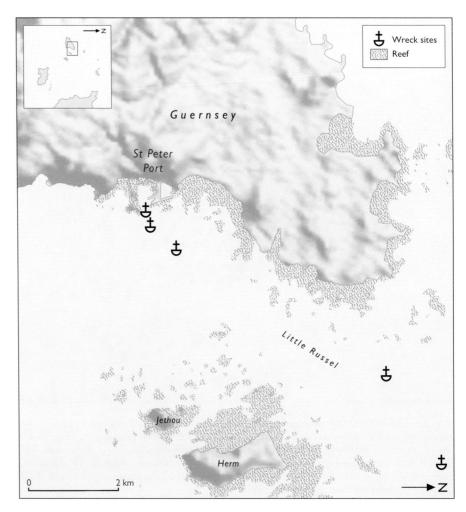

9.15 One of the principal sea-routes from Brittany to Britain led via Guernsey, allowing ships to call at St Peter Port to take on water. Five Roman wreck sites have been identified in the Little Russel channel—a reminder of the dangers of this stretch of water. The only wreck fully excavated is the St Peter Port wreck found within the modern harbour

used by the crew was acquired in London or other British east coast ports, the ship was probably on its homeward journey to Britain when disaster struck.

The journey from York or London to Bordeaux to bring back wine and pitch was a long haul. We have no idea what the outward-bound cargoes might have been, nor if there were trading stops en route, but something of the variety of commodities on the move is illustrated by four other shipwrecks: two off the north coast of Armorica, one on the approach to the Thames estuary, and one in London. The islands and reefs off Armorica were treacherous and must have claimed many ships. One, which came to grief on Les Sept-Îles near Ploumanac'h, was carrying a cargo of lead ingots, of which 271 were recovered, weighing a total of twenty-two tonnes. Some bore inscriptions mentioning the Brigantes and Iceni, two British tribes, suggesting that the cargo may have been of Pennine lead loaded at a British east coast port. It was presumably a British vessel, either outward-bound for Bordeaux and driven onto the islands in a storm, or making its way between the islands for an Armorican port like Le Yaudet to offload its cargo. The second Armorican wreck, dating to between the second and fourth centuries AD, foundered off Île de Batz near Roscoff. It was carrying a cargo of tin ingots, either Armorican tin on an outward journey, or Cornish tin on its way south. Of the Thames wrecks, one found on Pudding Pan Rock off the Kent coast was loaded with pottery tableware (*terra sigillata*) from northern Gaul. The other, found at Blackfriars in London, had brought a cargo of Kentish ragstone to the city. Together, the few

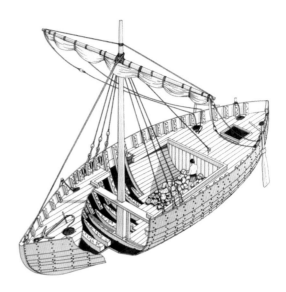

9.16 Reconstruction of the Roman ship found in the Thames close to Blackfriars Bridge in London. It was carrying a cargo of building stone from Kent when it sank

9.17 The excavation of the mast-step of the Blackfriars wreck. Some of the long nails used to attach the planking to the frames can be seen, their ends hooked over and driven back into the wood

wrecks that survive with their cargoes hint at the complexity and intensity of Atlantic maritime trade, everything from local cabotage of a few kilometres to long-distance voyages of fourteen hundred kilometres. The ports of the Atlantic seaboard must have been lively cosmopolitan places.

A microcosm of this maritime activity is illustrated by inscriptions found at two temple sites in the Scheldt–Rhine estuary where skippers about to sail across the southern North Sea solicited the protection of their favourite deities, the most popular of which was Nehalennia. One such skipper, Placidus son of Viductus, whose home had been in the Seine valley in the vicinity of Rouen, is also attested in York, where he sponsored public building works. Several others are recorded as *negotiatores Britanniciani* (traders with Britain). One man exported pottery to Britain; another was engaged in trade in wine and salt. These traders articulated the movement of goods and raw materials to and from the Rhine frontier zone. For some, their ships were engaged in the comparatively safe crossing to London and other eastern British ports; others had to look forward to much longer and more dangerous sea journeys. And then there was the waiting for the ships to return. The building of tension as the end of the sailing season was nearing and the ships had not returned would have been palpable. Little wonder that so much care was lavished on soliciting the protection of the deities.

Romano-Celtic Ships

Ships and boats of the types in use in north-western Europe during the period of the Roman occupation are well known from about thirty or so wrecks recovered from harbours and rivers. The vessels are sufficiently similar in constructional details to be regarded as belonging to a single shipbuilding tradition which has been called Romano-Celtic to reflect the possibility that some aspects of Mediterranean ship-building technology may have been adopted by the indigenous shipwrights. Of the vessels so far recovered three were sea-going: the ship dating to the mid-second century AD found in the Thames at Blackfriars, the late third-century ship found in St Peter Port harbour on Guernsey, and a smaller boat from Barlands Farm on the Severn estuary dating to about AD 300. Other more fragmentary remains from New Guy's House, London, and from Bruges may also belong to this group.

All share certain constructional techniques. They have flat keels composed of two or three planks with stem- and stern-posts attached. The planking is butted and caulked (with no sewing or mortising) and the planks are attached to the frames with long iron nails driven from outboard, sometimes through treenails, with the ends hooked and then bent over so that the hook bites into the frame. The method of framing is quite distinct. Heavy floor frames hold the keel and floor planks together, with lighter side frames to support the side-planking. The novelty lies in the sequence of construction. After the laying down of the keel and stern- and stem-posts, selected floor frames were attached, to which the lower hull planks were nailed before the rest of the floor frames were added. With the lower hull complete, side frames were attached, thus defining the shape of the upper hull, and the upper hull planks were then positioned and nailed to the framing. This type of composite construction is quite different from methods used in the Mediterranean, where the planked hull was formed first, before the frames were added, nor is it like the later method of setting up the frames before the planking is attached. It is intermediate between the two and seems to be an innovation of the North Atlantic shipbuilders.

These Romano-Celtic ships were solidly built vessels with planking between fifty and sixty millimetres thick attached by long iron nails to substantial frames. These features, together with the wide, flat bottoms and high sides, are the very characteristics that Caesar emphasized in his description of the Venetic ships he encountered in 56 BC. Like the Venetic ships, these were sailing vessels with their masts set about a third of the way from the bow at waterline. The only anchor known, from Bulbury in Dorset and dating to the first century BC (see Figure 9.9), was made of iron and was attached by a long iron chain of the kind adopted by the Venetic ships. All the principal characteristics, then, of the Romano-Celtic ships of the second and third centuries AD were already present in the north-eastern Atlantic in the first century BC, before the presence of Rome had made any significant impact. Hull construction, with its multiple-plank keel, could have evolved from the sewn-plank vessels of the earlier first millennium, and the use of a sail could equally well have developed in the Atlantic zone. The use of nails to attach the planking, however, was first adopted in the Mediterranean in the sixth century BC, and since it is quite an advanced piece of technology, the most parsimonious hypothesis would be that nailed planking and the square-rigged sail were first introduced into Atlantic waters by Phoenician and Carthaginian ships plying the west coast of Iberia. The advantage of these techniques would soon have been appreciated by the native sailors and adopted into their repertoire.

By the time the Roman armies were annexing Gaul and Britain, the local traders using the southern North Sea, the English Channel, and the seas around Armorica had evolved vessels that were well suited to the conditions in which they regularly sailed. Since it was these people and their successors who continued as traders, there was little imperative to adopt Mediterranean shipbuilding methods. Robust sailing vessels were more effective for managing the tides and winds than galleys with their low freeboard and limited cargo capacity.

9.18 The wreck found at Barland's Farm, Magor, Gwent, in the estuary of the Severn, seen here during excavation. The vessel dates to *c.* AD 300

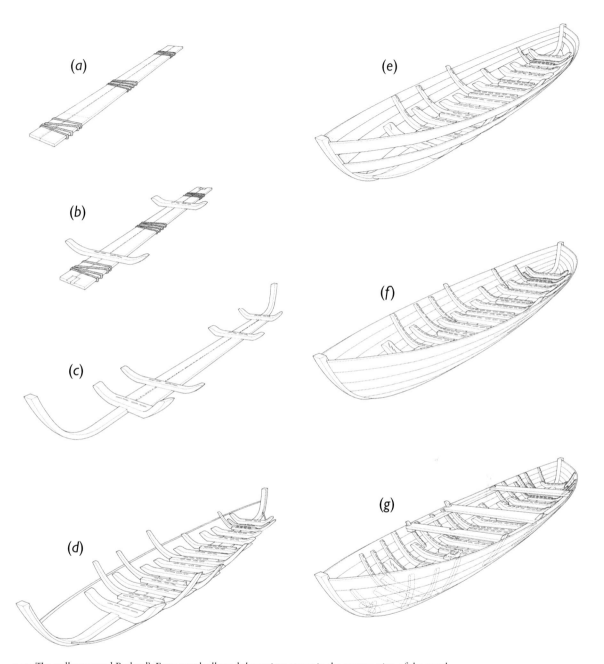

9.19 The well-preserved Barland's Farm wreck allowed the various stages in the construction of the vessel to be worked out

The Classis Britannica

In preparation for his abortive invasion of Britain in AD 40, Gaius (Caligula) had improved the port of Gesoriacum (Boulogne) on the Channel coast of Gaul, building a lighthouse to guide ships safely into the wide estuary of the Laine, where a permanent garrison had been stationed. He also ordered that an invasion fleet be assembled. In the event his aspirations came to nothing and it was left to his successor, Claudius, to complete the invasion three years later. After the landings had been made and the troops had begun to sweep across Britain, the invasion fleet would have become an essential support arm to the military, helping to move troops quickly when necessary and bringing up supplies as the army advanced. Eventually, when, by the end of the first century AD, the energy of the advance was spent and a frontier zone was being established in northern Britain, the fleet consolidated its Channel bases and settled into its peacetime support role. By this time it had formally been constituted as the Classis Britannica (British Fleet) under the command of a succession of prefects, one of whom, Lucius Aufidius Pantera (the only one known by name), appropriately set up an altar to Neptune at the port of Lympne in Kent.

The headquarters of the Classis Britannica was at Gesoriacum. On the British side of the Channel at Richborough, sited on the Wantsum Channel in east Kent, was the main bridge-head used at the time of the invasion and immediately after, but later, about AD 130, a rather more accessible base was established at Dover on the estuary of the Dour, guarded by a fort, with two lighthouses placed on the hills on either side to guide ships safely in. Subsidiary bases were probably maintained at Richborough, Reculver, and Lympne.

The activities of the fleet were varied. In the Weald of Kent they were involved in producing iron, presumably to supply military needs, while an inscription from the fort of Benwell on Hadrian's Wall records that a detachment from the fleet was taking part in construction work, a reminder that when not engaged in fighting the military were expected to install and maintain essential infrastructure.

One of the principal functions of the fleet would have been to patrol the sea-lanes to keep them safe for Roman shipping. Boulogne and Dover were well suited to control

9.20 (*Opposite top*) The Strait of Dover was of outstanding strategic and economic importance during the Roman period. By the second century it was protected by marines of the Classis Britannica (British Fleet) stationed in forts at Boulogne and Dover. Both ports could be identified from the sea by their prominent lighthouses, one at Boulogne and two at Dover

9.21 (*Opposite bottom*) Lucius Aufidius Pantera, prefect of the Classis Britannica, set up this altar in the second century, appropriately to the god Neptune. It was found at Lympne, Kent, on a site later to be reused as a Saxon Shore fort, and may have come from an earlier fort on the site

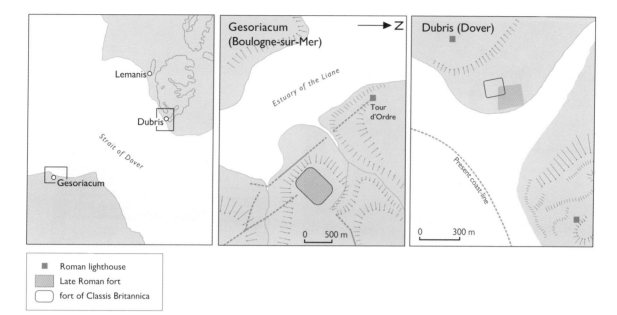

Lemanis

Dubris

Strait of Dover

Gesoriacum

Gesoriacum
(Boulogne-sur-Mer)

N

Estuary of the Liane

Tour
d'Ordre

0   500 m

Dubris (Dover)

Present coast-line

0   300 m

■ Roman lighthouse
▨ Late Roman fort
▢ fort of Classis Britannica

363

9.22 The Roman lighthouse surviving within the medieval castle of Dover is remarkably well preserved, but the present top storey is a medieval addition. It is one of two lighthouses sited to guide ships into the narrow harbour between towering chalk cliffs. This diagrammatic reconstruction shows how the Dover lighthouse would have looked in the late Roman period

the Channel at its narrowest point, but towards the end of the second century or early in the third, two new forts were established, one at Reculver at the northern end of the Wantsum Channel, where it could keep an eye on shipping in the Thames estuary, the other on the Norfolk coast at Brancaster, from where ships taking the east coast route to the north could be kept under surveillance. Reculver was garrisoned by a cohort of Baetasi from the Rhine mouth region, while Brancaster received a cohort of Aquitani from the south-west coast of Gaul: both forces would have had extensive experience of the sea. There is no record of why these new coastal forts were built but it may be that sea-borne attacks by Frisian and Frankish tribes from north of the Rhine mouth were becoming a significant threat.

Rival Emperors and Pirates

From the middle of the third century the western Roman empire entered a period of turmoil caused by Germanic tribes breaking through the Rhine frontier and exacerbated by contenders for power emerging in the west and challenging the central authorities in Rome. The troubles began in AD 253 with the incursion of Franks and Alemanni, who pillaged their way through much of Gaul as far south as Arles, creating conditions for usurping emperors to emerge, and unrest of various kinds continued until AD 296. It was a fraught half-century of political intrigue and civil warfare, and as the strength of maritime freebooters from the coastal region north and south of the Rhine mouth began to grow, so mastery of the sea became increasingly important. The first signs of trouble at sea came during the reign of Postumus (AD 259–68). Two of his coins bear the legends 'Neptuno Comiti' and 'Neptuno Reduci', referring to naval victories, presumably against pirate attackers somewhere in the southern North Sea or English Channel. After that the situation seems to have worsened. Finally, in AD 285 an experienced commander, Carausius, was appointed specifically 'to rid the seas of Belgica and Armorica' of Frankish and Saxon pirates. Carausius was a Menapian from the coastal region of northern Gaul (now Belgium) and had served at sea. His new command gave him control of the Classis Britannica, and he based himself at the fleet headquarters at Gesoriacum. Rumours soon circulated that he was allowing the pirates to raid and then intercepting them, confiscating the spoils for himself. Whether this was true or not, he was sentenced to death *in absentia* and took the only option open to him, which was to flee to Britain, where he set himself up as emperor.

That the coastal regions of Britain and Armorica were indeed being raided is implied by the large number of coin hoards being buried and the fact that several villas along the south coast of Britain were destroyed by fire at this time. Towns like Canterbury and Chichester were now being fortified by strong walls for the first time, and on the north and west coasts of Armorica promontories guarding estuarine ports at Alet, Le Yaudet, and Brest were also being strengthened with walls. It was about this time that a new series of coastal fortifications was erected along the south and east coasts of Britain from the Solent to the Wash, at Portchester, Pevensey, Lympne, Dover, Richborough, Bradwell, Walton Castle, and Burgh Castle, while the earlier forts at Reculver and Brancaster continued to operate. The new forts were massively built, with walls up to metres thick and with forward-projecting bastions to take ballistae. The dating of their

9.23 The Roman site at Richborough, Kent, was associated with the sea for four centuries. In AD 43 it served as a military supply base for the army. Later, as a gateway port to Britain, it was dominated by a monumental gate (*quadrifrons*) represented now by the massive rectangular foundation. In the third century the gate became a watchtower defended by a triple ditch system. Finally, in the late third century a stone-built fortification was erected with two ditches in front

366

construction is not very precise, but what evidence there is suggests that most, if not all, were constructed in the late third century. Taken together the evidence points to serious unrest in the coastal regions.

It may, of course, be that the new shore forts around the south and east coasts of Britain were a response by Carausius or his successor, Allectus, to possible attack by Rome to win back the rebel province. The threat was real and in the winter of AD 288–9 the emperor Maximian gave instructions for a new fleet to be built on the Rhine and the Moselle. What then happened is unclear. The official view was that bad weather prevented any action, but it is equally possible that Carausius was able to halt the planned attack at sea. A few years later, in AD 293, the central Roman authorities mounted a successful land attack on the Carausian base at Gesoriacum, as the result of which the Gaulish coast was lost to the rebels, who were confined thereafter to Britain. Not long afterwards Carausius was assassinated and Allectus became the new rebel leader. The end came in AD 296, when a new Roman invasion fleet, built in the estuaries along the Gaulish coast, set sail for Britain, one flotilla landing on the south coast in the Solent region, the other sailing down the Thames to take London. The invasion was successful. With the rebels beaten, Britain was restored to the empire and the pirate threat seems to have abated, at least for a while.

The beginning of the end came in AD 367 when tribes from Ireland and northern Britain joined with Saxons and Franks to make a concerted attack on the province of Britannia, during which the commander of the sea coast region (*comes maritime tractus*) was killed and unrest spread as far south as the Thames. It took several years to restore order, but the outcome was far-reaching. Three new coastal commands were instituted. Along the coast of Gaul the stretch from the Rhine to the Somme was put under the command of the *dux Belgicae secundae* while the rest of the coast from the Somme to the Gironde was made the responsibility of the *dux tractus Armoricani et Nervicani*. Between them the commanders had control of forts and fortified towns along the entire Atlantic coast of Gaul, where garrisons of frontier troops and naval flotillas were stationed. A similar arrangement was made for the south and east coasts of Britain, which were now put under the command of the *comes litoris Saxonici per Britanniam* (Count of the Saxon Shore), who also had two bases on the Gaulish coast enabling him to patrol the Channel to keep the sea-lanes open for traffic. Such a massive emphasis on coastal protection leaves little doubt that the North Sea and the English Channel were now under serious threat from sea-borne raids coming from the coastal regions beyond the Rhine frontier. One of the last images we have of these troubled times is of the Roman scout ships described by Vegetius. They were called *pictae*. Their small size and sea-green camouflage and their forty oars meant that they

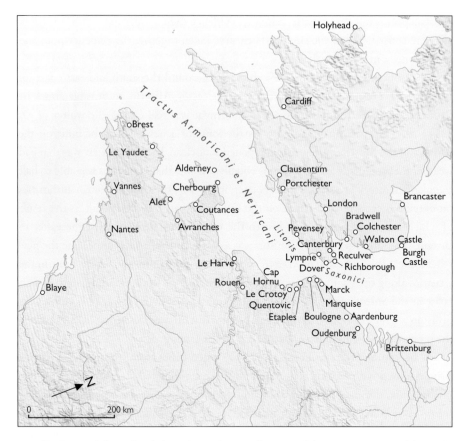

9.24 The Roman defences found along the north coast of France and the Low Countries and the south-east coast of Britain developed over several centuries. In the late fourth century they were divided into different commands

could move quickly across the seas unseen by raiders and report back on enemy movements. The sea raiders were now in the ascendancy.

The Nordic and North Sea Traditions

The rapid increase in raiding in the seas around Britain was the result of population growth north of the Rhine–Danube frontier, which put pressure on low-lying coastal areas already suffering from inundations caused by sea-level rise. The populations of these areas, now the Netherlands, coastal Germany, and Denmark, had little recourse but to take to the sea in search of new opportunities, first attacking Roman merchant shipping and raiding the coasts of Britain and Gaul, and later, as we shall see (pp. 397–9 below), seeking new land to settle in Britain and Gaul.

The eastern shores and seaways of the North Sea enjoyed a long tradition of seafaring, as displayed in the Bronze Age rock engravings of Sweden and in a series of ship remains that together enable us to trace the development in shipbuilding technology from the end of the Bronze Age to the fourth century AD. The sequence begins with the slender war canoe dating to about 350 BC found in a bog at Hjortspring on the Danish island of Als. The vessel had been dragged to an inland lake and left there, together with a quantity of weapons, as an offering to the deities, quite possibly in acknowledgement of a successful victory. It was about 18 metres long and 2 metres wide and could accommodate twenty rowers, probably using paddles. In outline it is very similar to vessels depicted on the later Scandinavian rock engravings. It was constructed from a hollowed-out bottom plank extending upwards with two side strakes on either side. The complex stem and stern were both extended to form a lower and an upper beak. What is of particular interest is the way in which the planks were attached using bevelled overlaps held by stitching. The inner frames were made of thin hazel ribs bent into shape and lashed to cleats integral with each plank, and were strengthened with cross-beams, the upper arms forming seats for the rowers. Every effort had been made to keep the vessel as light as possible by thinning the planks and using slender ribs so that the boat could move quickly through the water. A full-scale replica in sea trials reached a sustainable cruising speed of 4.7 knots with maximum sprint speed of 7.6 knots. The Hjortspring boat was the culmination of war canoe technology based on over a thousand years of boatbuilding experience, but inherent in its structure were techniques that were to develop into the distinctive Nordic tradition of the first millennium AD.

Overlapping planking was widely adopted in Scandinavia by the fourth century AD and is evident in western Norwegian boats from Valderøy and Halsnøy, where both have their planking sewn together outside the lap, as with the Hjortspring boat, but now the planks are fully overlapping. The next advance can be seen in the Swedish boat from Bjorke, dating to about AD 320, in which the overlapping strakes were fastened through the lap with iron nails clenched inboard by beating out the end of the nail over an iron washer. This is the earliest example of a clinker wash-strake, a technique that was to characterize Atlantic shipbuilding thereafter. Yet, in spite of this technically advanced innovation, the planks were still attached to the ribs using the traditional method of lashing through cleats.

It was a bog at Nydam in southern Jutland that was to produce the classic example of a Nordic ship of the early fourth century AD. Three vessels were found, of which Nydam 2 is the best preserved, measuring nearly 24 metres in length and nearly 4

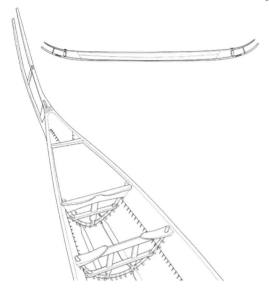

metres broad. It was clinker-built with overlapping strakes held by iron rivets and with the frames lashed to the planks through integral cleats, but novel features now included a thickened keel plank with regular fore and aft stems attached and a change of propulsion from paddling to rowing. It is quite possible that these innovations were learned from Romano-Celtic shipping encountered in the Rhine region. The Nydam boatbuilders used the best of indigenous traditional methods while adopting innovations from neighbours. It was vessels of this kind that raided the coasts of Britain and Gaul in the fourth century and caused such problems for the Roman defenders. They were to dominate events in the North Sea and beyond for centuries to come.

9.25 (*Opposite top*) The Hjortspring boat, dating to the late fourth century BC, was found deposited in a bog on the Danish island of Als. It was a development from the long canoes depicted on rock engravings in the Bronze Age. The deposition of the vessel and the weapons it contained suggest that it may have been a dedication to a deity made to celebrate a successful military engagement and in thanks for divine assistance

9.26 (*Opposite middle*) Full-scale reconstruction of the Hjortspring boat in action. It reached a cruising speed of 4.7 knots with a sprint speed of 7.6 knots

9.27 (*Opposite bottom*) Rock engraving from Hammer in south-eastern Norway, probably dating to the third or second century BC. The vessel depicted is very similar to the near-contemporary Hjortspring boat

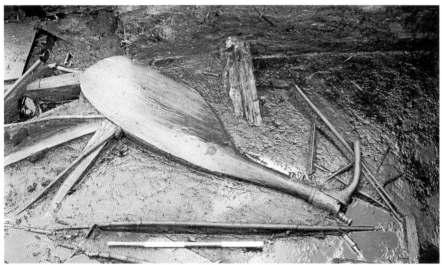

9.28 The Nydam boat, Nydam 2, found in southern Jutland in the nineteenth century, dating to AD 310–20. Two complete ships and parts of a third were discovered during the excavation of 1863–4. The planks of the hull were attached to each other with iron fastenings driven through overlapping planks

9.29 More recent excavations on the site of Nydam in 1989–97 brought to light many other details, including a complete steering oar

Far Horizons: Beyond Britain

When Agricola's expeditionary force rounded the northern edges of Britain in AD 84, receiving the submission of the Orkney islands on the way, it must have seemed that the north-western extremity of the world had been reached. But not quite. During his fifth season of campaigning, in AD 82, Agricola had been on the west coast of Scotland, overseeing the garrisoning of the region, from where, barely twenty kilometres away across the North Channel, he could see Ireland. The historian Tacitus takes up the story:

> In size it surpasses the islands of our sea but it is narrower than Britain. As for soil, climate and the character and lifestyle of its people, it differs little from Britain. The approaches and harbours are known due to trade and merchants. ... I have often heard him [Agricola] say that Hibernia could be conquered and occupied by one legion and a moderate number of auxiliaries.
>
> (*Agricola* 24)

In the event nothing came of the musings and Ireland was left to itself, beyond the empire yet locked to it by traders whose activities are reflected in a scattering of Roman trade goods found mainly in the eastern regions of the island. The distribution of artefacts, however, does scant justice to the knowledge which traders had of the island and which Ptolemy made use of in his *Geography*, compiled in the mid-second century AD. Not only was the coastline well known from maritime ventures, but the names of many tribes and settlements in the interior were recorded. Ptolemy comments that one merchant's tale he had gathered recounted that it took twenty days to cross the island from east to west. This implies that expeditions were being undertaken into the heart of the island. Whether these reports came from entrepreneurs from the Roman province or Irish traders is impossible to say. By the mid-second century, then, although Agricola's aspiration of conquest had not been realized, Ireland was by no means *terra incognita*.

It is understandable that merchants should seek to exploit the commercial opportunities of Ireland, but that more inquisitive spirits went further afield into the surrounding ocean is not impossible. Two observations may be relevant: the finding of a second-century AD Roman pot dredged by a trawler from the Porcupine Bank way out in the Atlantic, two hundred kilometres from the west coast of Ireland, and the discovery of three late Roman coins in south-eastern Iceland. How to explain these isolated discoveries? The coins could represent the chance visit of a Roman explorer or someone blown off course, but they could equally well have been taken to the island by visitors much later. The pot, on the other hand, is likely to have been lost or thrown

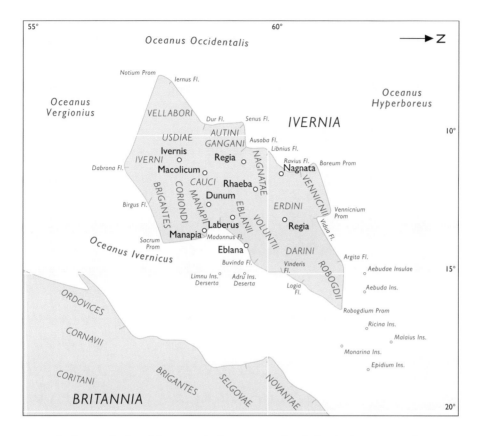

9.30 Ireland was evidently well known to the Romans, even though the island was never under Roman occupation. Ptolemy was able to record many places and tribes in the second century AD from information gathered from traders

overboard from a Roman ship, though whether the vessel was in the open ocean by choice or because of freak weather, we shall never know. These are tantalizing glimpses of expeditions that might have been.

A final speculation. Plutarch mentions that one Demetrius of Tarsus was commissioned to explore the islands around Britain. Could this be the Demetrius who made a dedication to Ocean and Tethys recorded in Greek on a bronze plaque found in York? The dedication is appropriate from someone just returned from an ocean voyage. But since Demetrius of Tarsus would have been active in British waters during the governorship of Agricola, his task may simply have been focused on the Western and Northern Isles. With so much to explore it seems unlikely that he had the time to probe the open Atlantic. This does not mean, however, that others were not drawn by their own natural curiosity to venture further afield.

373

κ.. ΕΝΤΑ ΚΥΜΑΤΑ
ΑΥΤΗС ΚΕ ΠΑΝΤΟ
ΙΕΡΑΤω ΟΝΟΜΑ

СΟΦΙΑ СΟΛΟΜωΝΤΟС

ΤΗΜΠΕΝΟΛΙΚΛΔΟΡΕ
ΞΕΠΟΡΙΕСΜΟΝ ΕΠΕ
ΝΟΗСΑΝ ΑΝΟΙ ΤΕΧΝΗ
ΤΗΝ ΔΕ СΟΦΙΑ СΑΤΕ
СΙ СΕΥΑСΕΝ ΠΑ ΘΕΝ
ΠΕΡΑ ΙΑΛ ΚΥΒΕΡΝΑ ΠΡΟ
ΝΟΙΑ ΟΤΙ ΚΑΙ ΕΝΟ Α
ΛΑССΗ ΙΑ ΟΙ ΚΑ ΟΔΑΝ
ΚΑΙΕΝ ΚΥΜΑΤΙ ΤΡΙ
ΚΟΝ ΑСΦΑΛΗ ΔΕΙΚΝΥ
ΟΤΙ ΔΥΝΑСΑΙ ΕΚ ΠΑΝ
ΤΟС СωΖΕΙΝ ΚΑΙ ΑΝΕΥ
ΤΕΧΝΗ ΠΕΤΙС ΕΠΙΒω
ΘΕΛΕΙС ΔΕ ΜΗ ΑΡΓΑ ΕΙ
ΝΑΙ ΤΑ ΤΗС СΟΦΙΑС ΕΡ
ΓΑ ΔΙΑ ΤΟΥΤΟ ΙΑΙ Ε
ΛΑΧΙСΤω ΞΥΛω ΠΙС
ΤΕΥΟΥСΙΝ ΑΝΟΙ ΦΥ
ΧΑС ΚΑΙ ΔΙΕΛΘΟΝΤΕС
ΚΛΥΔωΝΑ СΧΕΔΙΑ ΔΙΕ
СωΘΗСΑΝ

СΙΡΑΧ

ΙΠΛΕΟΝΤΕС ΤΗΝ ΘΑ
ΛΑССΑΝ ΔΙΗΓΗСΑΝ ΤΟ
ΤΙΝ ΚΙΝΔΥΝΟΝ ΑΥ
ΤΗС ΙΑΙ ΑΚΟΗΝ ωС
ΤΙωΝ ΗΜωΝ ΦΑΥ
ΜΑΖΟΜΕΝ ΚΑΙ ΕΚΕΙ
ΤΑ ΦΑΥΜΑСΤΑ ΚΑΙ ΠΛ

ΔΙ.. ΝΟΜΕΝ
ΚΙ С ΕΞΑΝΕ
ΛΑССΑ ΙΑΙ
ΜΕΓΕωС Θ
ΜΕΝΗ ΤΟΙ
ΕΙΝΕ ΕΠΕΙ
ΝΟΝ ΤωΝ
ΑΠ ΤΑ ΕΙ
ΔΙΑΛΑССΑ
ΜΗΝ ΕΠΑ
ΛΕΜΕ ΟΥ Φ
СΟΦΙΑ ΛΕΓΕΙ
ΤΙ ΘΕΝ ΤΑ
ΟΡΙ ΟΝ ΤΗ
ΕΙ ΠωС Θ
ΠΑΝΤωΝ
Κω ΤΑ
ΦΟΡΗ ΤΟС
ΤΑ Ο ΑΛΑ

Τ Θ СΟΛ ΕΚΤΙ

Θ ΑΛΑССΗС Ε
ΛΙ ΕΓω
ΧΟΝ ΦΑΥ
ΛΑССΑΝ ΤΟ
ΙΑΙ ΠωС Ε
ΑΥ ΜΕΝΗ
ΜΠΟΡωΝ
ΔΕ ΠΡΤΟ
ΠΑΝΤΟС
ΕΠΕΙ ΔΑ
ΤΗΝ ΕΝΑ
ΔΥΝΑΜΙ

10

An End and a Beginning, 300–800

At the beginning of the fourth century AD the future of the Roman empire looked secure. The late third century had been a difficult time. Various Germanic tribes had broken through the Rhine–Danube frontier and had raided deep into Gaul, a succession of contenders for power had set themselves up as emperors, and the economy had shown signs of serious failure. But in 284 the praetorian guard took charge and appointed a tough Illyrian soldier, Diocletian, to rule the empire. Immediately he set about putting things right. He had an acute understanding of the problems and a tenacity to get the job done, and his reforms were far-reaching. Border weaknesses were dealt with by creating special units, *limitanei*, who were permanently stationed along the frontier, and a field army, *comitatenses*, a rapid response force that could quickly be deployed to any danger zone. Galloping inflation was brought under control by currency reform and by strict price controls, while the problem of population decline and labour mobility was addressed by requiring sons to follow in their fathers' professions. Finally, to give stability to government he divided the vast and unruly empire into two parts, one centred in Rome, the other soon to be controlled from Byzantium (soon to become Constantinople), each ruled by an Augustus supported by a Caesar. The plan was that at the end of a twenty-year reign the Augusti would resign and the Caesars take over, appointing a new pair of Caesars. In 305 both Diocletian and his fellow ruler, Maximian, retired as agreed, and, although the system of succession soon broke down, it had created a period of stability long enough to allow the other sweeping reforms to take effect.

The centre of gravity of the empire had now moved east, and in 330 Constantine, who had fought his way to sole power six years before, inaugurated Byzantium to be the empire's capital: New Rome, soon to be renamed Constantinople. Yet, with all the changes, for the Romans, the Mediterranean was still 'Mare Nostrum'.

Two hundred years later everything had changed. The western empire was gone, subsumed by Germanic populations sweeping in from the north. Much of Iberia and south-western France was now ruled by Visigoths; Ostrogoths occupied Italy, the Balkans, and south-eastern France; central and northern France were in the hands of the Franks; the east of Britain had been settled by Saxons and tribes from Denmark; while most of North Africa had been overrun by the Vandals. The Mediterranean had ceased to be a Roman sea.

The Last Years of Mare Nostrum

The decisive naval battle of Actium, fought off the coast of Epirus in 31 BC between Octavian and the combined forces of Marcus Antonius and Cleopatra, brought the long period of civil war to an end. A few years later, in 27 BC, Octavian, now Augustus, could proclaim himself *princeps* (first citizen) and set about restoring the republic, which, in effect, meant inaugurating the empire. Although there were a few coastal regions still to be formally taken under Rome's wing, the Mediterranean was now, in reality, a Roman preserve: it was 'the great sea', the 'internal sea', 'our sea'.

With the civil war at an end and no other fleets to challenge Rome's authority on the 'internal sea', heavy battle units soon became an irrelevance. The navy's function was now reduced to keeping down the threat of pirate raids and providing transport for troops and officials when required. The time of the super-galleys was over. Augustus immediately set about reforming the navy, disbanding the massive combat units and instead setting up two squadrons, the larger based on Naples, the smaller on Ravenna. Both had some large vessels, but mostly the flotillas were made up of triremes with a few liburnians—light two-level galleys that could move fast and engage if necessary. Other much smaller squadrons, mainly of liburnians, were stationed elsewhere around the Mediterranean. The design of the ships changed too. No longer was there any need for the heavy and very expensive bronze-sheathed battering-ram. The ram was still retained, now with a blunt point, more symbolic than functional but quite sufficient to deal with pirates.

As the empire settled down to a long period of peace, so the volume of commercial traffic grew. Each year huge quantities of foodstuff had to be transported by sea from areas of production to regions where growing populations had outstripped their capacity to produce their own food. Grain, wine, olive oil, salted fish, and fish sauce (*garum*) were moved in ever-increasing quantities along the sea-lanes. Carthage and Alexandria were the main suppliers of grain to the consuming centres of Rome and Constantinople, while Iberia provided much of the oil, fish, and fish sauce. At Monte Testaccio, on the outskirts of Rome, where wine and oil were transhipped and the amphorae smashed up and discarded after their contents had been transferred to other containers, it is possible to estimate, by quantifying the distinctive globular amphorae (Dressel 20), that about 22,500 tonnes of Spanish oil reached Rome every year. Alongside bulk products the ships also carried other cargoes packed into spaces in between; it was in this way that pottery was transported. There were also vessels designed to carry special cargoes like the solidly built stone transporters and the bulk wine carriers fitted with *dolia* (very large ceramic containers). The annual tonnage of commodities carried between Mediterranean ports was enormous.

Roman cargo ships are frequently illustrated on mosaics and reliefs and show something of the variety of vessels in operation. There were two main types, one with a rounded prow, the other in which the prow is concave with a projecting cut-water at the waterline and a carved figurehead above. All had a square-rigged mainsail set forward of midships, sometimes of considerable width, and most vessels were also fitted with a smaller foresail set on a foremast fixed in position at a forward rake. In some cases a separate topsail was hoisted on the main mast, and the biggest freighters also carried a mizzen-mast. The additional canvas was designed to increase speeds. The emperor Gaius (Caligula) told a friend that the captain of ships bound for Alexandria drove them like racehorses. The fastest journey to be recorded from the Strait of Messina to Alexandria was six days, an average speed of six knots. The faster the cargo could be turned round, the more profitable the ship.

The troubled times beginning in the late third century focused anew upon the importance of having military command of the sea—a fear made real by the temporary secession of the province of Britannia (pp. 365–7 above). Some years later, in 324, when Constantine was making his bid for the throne, he was drawn into a sea-battle with his rival Licinius at the entrance to the Dardanelles. With no standing navies at his command Licinius was forced to gather some 350 triremes from Egypt, the Levant, and Asia Minor, while Constantine managed to put together a fleet of two hundred small thirty-oared and fifty-oared galleys. His victory against the much bigger vessels signalled the end of the age of the trireme. The future lay with smarter, faster ships.

The Germanic Threat to the Mediterranean

Many different tribes and tribal confederations occupied the great swath of forested land that lay north of the Rhine–Danube frontier stretching from the Pontic steppe to the North Sea. The region was beyond the reach of recorded history and the archaeological evidence is too ill-focused to allow the development and interaction of the tribes to be worked out in any detail, but what is clear is that a turbulence born of population pressures dominated the lives of the people. The presence of the Roman frontier made things worse since it prevented the natural flow of people from the north to the south. Instead, those close up against the frontier came under intolerable pressure from population build-ups behind them: their only recourse was to break through the barrier, and this they began to do in the late third century. Other factors exacerbated the situation. Nomadic tribes were moving from the Pontic steppe: first Sarmatians, then Alans, quickly followed by Huns, driving indigenous tribes westwards, adding to the scrabble for land along the North Sea coasts. Sea-level rises were causing extensive inundations, forcing people to move out. The Roman authorities tried to contain the problem by reorganizing the military dispositions along the frontiers in a way that encouraged the troops to settle and raise families, thus breeding new home-grown recruits. Germanic communities were also let in and settled on vacant land on the Roman side of the frontier in the expectation that they would want to protect their holdings from raiders coming from their former homelands.

For a while these measures served, but in 376 hordes of Visigoths crossed the lower Danube. Two years later the eastern Roman emperor, Valens, was killed in battle and the Visigoths went on to rampage through Greece, eventually moving westwards into Dalmatia in 401–8, and then into Italy, reaching the toe of the peninsula in 410. Meanwhile, in 401, Alans and Vandals had crossed the upper Danube, presaging a far more extensive incursion in 406–9 when Alans, Vandals, and Suevi surged through Gaul and into Iberia, the Alans settling in south-western Iberia, the Suevi taking the rest of the Atlantic region north of the Tagus. The Vandals settled in southern Iberia between 409 and 429. While these resettlements were in progress, the Visigoths began to push westwards from Italy in 412, eventually creating a vast Visigothic domain incorporating most of Iberia and the south-western quarter of France by about 480. In the east the Ostrogoths had settled much of the middle Danube region by about 450, and by about 500 they had established their hold over the Alps, most of Italy and Sicily, and large areas of south-eastern France. It had been a century of ceaseless upheaval, totally changing the face of Europe.

It would be wrong to think of the invading Germans as wild barbarians intent only on pillage and destruction. While this may have characterized the initial thrusts, the

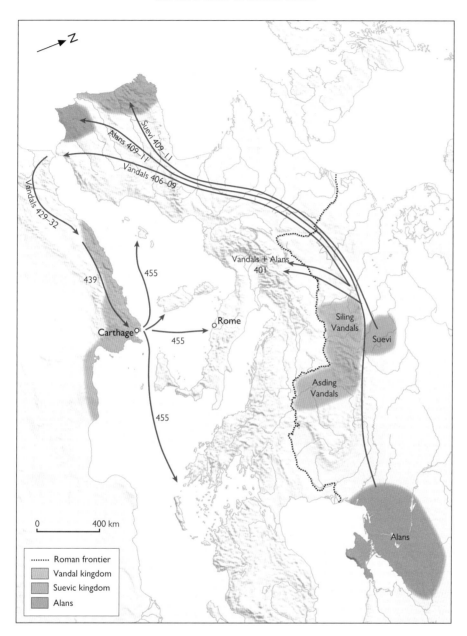

10.1 Pressure from tribes migrating from the east, together with an increase in population and deteriorating climatic conditions, forced people from north of the Roman frontier to break through to raid and to settle within the Roman provinces. One of the Germanic tribes caught up in these events was the Vandals, who moved south through Spain and into Roman North Africa in the early fifth century

379

newcomers were content to leave the regional Roman infrastructure largely intact, particularly the urban and rural systems that sustained the economy, and for the incoming elites to appropriate the controlling power. Thus it was that the towns and estates continued to thrive and Christianity flourished, the one noticeable difference being that alien elements were introduced into the decorative arts, generating a new visual energy.

The Germanic takeover of the western Roman empire in Europe had been largely land-based with little recourse to the sea. The Vandal conquest of North Africa was quite different. The Vandals' move into Iberia in 406–9, and the subsequent settlement of the south and east coasts, gave them ready access to the Mediterranean harbour towns with their long tradition of shipbuilding and seafaring. Harnessing these new-found facilities, they launched raids on the Balearic islands and the North African coast in 426, and three years later mounted a full-scale invasion of North Africa. The invasion force of Vandals together with Alans and Goths, divided into eighty units each of a thousand troops, was transported across the Strait of Gibraltar in May 429. Having landed with little opposition, they began their long march along the North African coast towards Carthage, taking one Roman city after another until Carthage itself finally succumbed in October 439. By maintaining a large fleet in the western Mediterranean the Vandals were able to prevent Rome from sending supplies and reinforcements to the provinces, and by capturing the port cities of North Africa, and in particular Carthage, they were able to cut off the supply of grain to Rome and the rest of Italy, thus adding to the empire's troubles. So strong had they become that in 442 Ravenna (which had replaced Rome as the centre of the western empire forty years before) gave official recognition to the Vandal kingdom in Africa. In 455, with their fleet now superior in the western Mediterranean, the Vandals launched a series of far-flung raids on the Balearics, Corsica, Rome, and the eastern Mediterranean. Rome succumbed, and the raiders carried away plunder and hostages selected from the Roman elite, among them the widowed empresses. Thereafter, with bases on the Balearics, Corsica, Sardinia, and Sicily, and their fleet ever active, the Vandals had control of the western Mediterranean.

Little is known of the Vandal fleet or the ships of which it was composed. Before their migration, as an inland people the Vandals can have had no tradition of seafaring, but after their arrival on the coast of southern Spain in 409 they soon appreciated the advantage of being able to command the sea. By commandeering ships and sailors from the Roman ports that came under their sway they were soon able to build an effective naval force. In the same way, on land the local provincial officials and estate managers provided them with the means to maintain the infrastructure of government and a thriving economy. The contribution of the invaders was to re-energize the tired provincial system.

The Empire Fights Back

By the middle of the fifth century the western Roman empire had largely succumbed to the barbarian incursions, a process which, symbolically at least, culminated in 476 when the child emperor of Rome, Romulus Augustulus, was deposed. Thereafter it was the eastern Roman empire, ruled from Constantinople, that remained to champion Roman culture—a Christian, Greek-speaking empire.

The accession of the emperor Justinian in 527 initiated a period of far-ranging reform within the empire and a new forward policy along its frontiers. Instability in the Vandal kingdom in North Africa, the Ostrogothic kingdom in Italy, and the Visigothic regime in southern Spain encouraged Justinian to turn his attention to the west, his vision being to restore the empire to something of its former boundaries. It was an audacious aspiration but it succeeded to a remarkable degree.

In 533 an invasion force of some fifteen thousand men under the Byzantine general Belisarius landed on the African coast and in a brief campaign defeated the Vandal armies. The Balearic islands, Sardinia, and Corsica were quickly brought under control, and thereafter North Africa provided a springboard for the attacks on the Ostrogoths in Italy, the first launched in 535. The campaigns against the Ostrogoths were hard-fought. Ravenna was taken five years later, but it was not until 561 that the peninsula was finally secured. Meanwhile, in 554 the outbreak of civil war in the Visigothic kingdom had provided the opportunity for Justinian to seize back much of southern Spain. The reconquest of the west had been a very costly enterprise, but the empire now controlled the entire Mediterranean coastline apart from Provence–Languedoc, which was held by the Franks, and a stretch of eastern Spain still in the hands of the Visigoths. Since neither state was much interested in maritime matters, the eastern Roman empire once again controlled the sea: Mare Nostrum had been restored.

Naval supremacy over the Germanic states was a major factor in the success of the Byzantine reconquest, but the fleets were probably never very large. In 508 the emperor Anastasius I was able to muster only a hundred galleys to attack the Adriatic coast of Italy. At this time the Ostrogoths had no ships with which to retaliate, and even when the war began in 535 with amphibious assaults on Italy, such ships as the Ostrogoths could bring to their defence were few. As the war progressed, the navies played an increasingly important part, both for transporting troops and for blockading cities. Belisarius used his fleet to good effect. The navy was instrumental in starving Ravenna into submission in 540, and later bringing in the grain needed to relieve the plight of the population. By this time the Ostrogoths had learned their lesson and were building ships similar to the Byzantine vessels. A few year later they were using them to blockade Byzantine-held cities, Naples in 543 and Rome from 545 to 552.

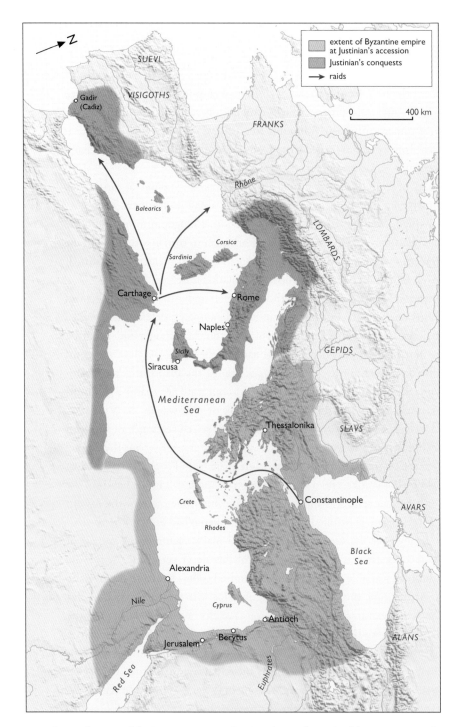

SUEVI

VISIGOTHS

Gadir
(Cadiz)

FRANKS

extent of Byzantine empire
at Justinian's accession

Justinian's conquests

raids

0   400 km

Rhône

LOMBARDS

Balearics

Corsica

Sardinia

Carthage

Rome

Naples

Sicily

GEPIDS

Siracusa

*Mediterranean
Sea*

Thessalonika

SLAVS

Crete

Constantinople

AVARS

Rhodes

*Black
Sea*

Alexandria

Nile

Cyprus

Antioch

ALANS

Jerusalem

Berytus

Red Sea

Euphrates

10.2   During the reign of the Byzantine emperor Justinian (527–65) a successful attempt was made, under the leadership of Count Belisarius, to reconquer one-time Roman territory around the western Mediterranean. The effort was costly and much of what was gained was soon lost

10.3 Theodoric, king of the Ostrogoths, established his capital at Ravenna in 493. One of the mosaics adorning the palace church (now Sant'Apollinare Nuovo) depicts merchant ships in the safety of the city's strongly defended harbour

The Byzantine Navy

The warships used during the reign of Justinian were similar to those operated by Constantine two centuries earlier, light galleys with only one level of rowers. That speed was their overriding characteristic is reflected in their name, dromon ('racer'). Byzantine control of the Mediterranean was short-lived. Around the European shores the Germanic states soon re-established themselves and a new Germanic people, the Lombards, moved into Italy, while in the late seventh century the Arabs began their spectacular conquest of the Levant and North Africa, reaching, then

383

10.4 A Byzantine dromon with two levels of rowers. From a twelfth-century manuscript

overrunning, much of Iberia by the early eighth century. In the face of these changes the Mediterranean became an increasingly hostile environment and the Byzantine navy had to evolve to meet the new challenges. No longer was the imperative simply to move troops and to blockade ports: now the vital commercial shipping lanes had to be protected, and ships threatening Byzantine territory had to be engaged at sea and deflected or destroyed. To meet this growing threat the composition of the Byzantine fleet began to change, the ships becoming larger and more heavily armed.

By one of the fortunate chances of history there survives a naval handbook, *Naumachia*, produced under the authority of the emperor Leo VI (reigned 886–912). It offers an incomparable description of the Byzantine navy as it was at the beginning of the tenth century: its ships and battle tactics, and much ancillary detail besides. The ships were still called dromons but were now larger, with two levels of oars, each level on each side having twenty-five rowers, making a ship's complement of a hundred. The size of the vessels varied, depending on how many marines were carried and how many of the rowers were to double up as marines. All the ships were partially decked with

fore and aft decks joined by side gangways and a central
catwalk, and some had additional fighting platforms forward and amidships. Most vessels were provided with a
mainmast and a foremast, while some of the larger vessels
also had a mizzen. In addition to the large fighting ships,
light vessels with one level of oars called *galeae* (hence
'galley') were still being built for tasks where speed was
of the essence.

In naval engagements the dromons often worked in
pairs, using their rams to disable the enemy. The handbook lays out the detail of how to go about it:

> One dromon comes alongside and grapples it; the
> enemy, as is their way, will run together to the side
> where the hand-to-hand fighting is taking place,
> with the aim of resting their own ship against the
> dromon. At this point another dromon will drive
> against the side of the enemy vessel near the stern
> and, in the collision, give that side a hard push.
> The first dromon, loosing itself from its lashings,
> can back off a bit so that the enemy vessel will not
> be leaning on it, and the other will then hit the
> enemy with full force, totally destroying the vessel
> with every man aboard.
>
> (Leo, *Naumachia* 69)

The other technique which the Byzantines perfected was
the use of Greek fire, a chemical concoction of crude oil
mixed with sulphur and quicklime which could be fired
or would burst spontaneously into flames if saltpetre
was added. Heated up and extruded from a bronze tube
(*siphon*) attached to the ship's bows, perhaps with the
aid of a pump, the long reach of the flames would have a
devastating effect on the enemy, as successive Arab navies
were to discover.

10.5 The life of Solomon illustrated with shipbuilding Byzantine
style. From a ninth-century manuscript

10.6 A Byzantine ship of the early ninth century with a lateen sail 'pouring fire on the fleet of the enemy', as the caption reads. This is the famous Greek fire in action. The manuscript dates to the fourteenth century

Shipbuilding techniques, whether for warships or for cargo ships, were also changing. By the seventh century new methods involving building the frame first and adding the planks later were beginning to be introduced. Three wrecks showing this innovation are known from as far afield as France, Sicily, and Israel. The most informative is the Yassi Ada 1 wreck, found off the south-west coast of Turkey, dating to about 625. It was a 21-metre-long cargo ship capable of carrying about sixty tonnes. The lower part of the hull was built shell first, the planks being kept in position in relation to each other with widely spaced mortises, not locked in position with dowels. Floor frames were then added. But above the waterline the construction method changed. Side frames were attached to the lower hull, and the planking of the upper hull was nailed to these in the frame-first manner. Vessels of this sort can therefore be regarded as transitional, paving the way for the fully frame-first style that was later to become the norm in the Mediterranean. As we have already seen (pp. 369–70 above), a similar transitional phase was also evident in shipbuilding in North Sea waters as early as the third century AD. While it remains a possibility that the Mediterranean was in some way being influenced by Atlantic developments, it is more likely that the shipwrights on the two seas arrived at the advantages of the frame-first method independently. The new technique enabled bigger ships to be built, but, of even more importance, it gave greater flexibility in designing a hull shape that allowed more seaworthy vessels to be constructed that were capable of long ocean passages.

Our knowledge of Byzantine shipbuilding has recently been greatly enhanced by the discovery and partial excavation of the Theodosian harbour of Constantinople during the construction of a railway line in the Yenikapı district of Istanbul. The harbour originally opened to the Sea of Marmara and was protected from the sea by two long moles. Built in the late fourth century, it functioned as a busy port until the late tenth or early eleventh century, when a series of violent storms drove in massive quantities of sand, greatly diminishing the harbour facilities, although it continued to be used for smaller vessels until the fifteenth century. Archaeological work which began in 2004 has identified the remains of at least thirty-seven wrecks sunk between the fifth and the eleventh century. Thirty-one of them were round sailing ships built for transporting cargoes; the remaining six were oared longships or galleys belonging to the Byzantine navy. It is one of the great discoveries of nautical archaeology, and when fully published will allow a detailed history of Byzantine shipbuilding to be written.

10.7 Excavations at Yenikapı, Istanbul, in 2006 exposed a number of wrecks dating from the fourth to the eleventh century lying in the Theodosian harbour. This vessel, number 13, dates to the eighth or ninth century

Trade in the Mediterranean and Beyond

When it sank off the south-west coast of Asia Minor, the Yassi Ada ship was carrying a cargo of 850–900 amphorae containing wine or oil taken on board somewhere in the Aegean, quite probably on the Asia Minor coast, together with a consignment of tableware known as Phokaian Red Slipware made in the same area. It may have been engaged in cabotage going from port to port, doing deals wherever there was a market, but it could have been bound for Alexandria, perhaps intending to take on a cargo of grain for the return journey. Grain exported from Alexandria and Carthage would have featured large in the cargoes of the time, but it seldom survives on wreck sites and it is therefore greatly under-represented in the archaeological record. Of the seventy or more wrecks dating from the fourth to the seventh century found in the

Mediterranean, by far the greatest number have produced amphorae for carrying wine and oil. Other cargoes included bronze artworks and other bronze goods, metal ingots, roof tiles, and grindstones. One, discovered at Marzamemi in Sicily, had on board the marble architectural fittings of an entire church. Cargoes were evidently varied, but by far the greatest volume of the goods transported would have been the staples, grain, wine, and oil.

While the goods carried by wrecks offer some indication of the routes in operation, a fuller picture comes from the distribution of distinctive types of pottery transported by ship which ended up being used and discarded on settlement sites. The most informative are specific types of amphora which are known to have been made in the Aegean region and in North Africa, and fine tableware, especially Phokaian Red Slipware and African Red Slipware from the Carthage region. The distribution and quantification of these types reflect both the extent and the intensity of maritime connections, but they cannot reveal the subtleties of the individual transactions.

The distribution of Phokaian Red Slipware illustrates the point. It was probably transported, along with amphorae of oil or wine, packed between the larger containers and is therefore often found on the same sites as the amphorae. It is known from many locations around the western Mediterranean, from the Golfe du Lion to the Levant

10.8 A reconstruction of the Yassi Ada wreck found off the south-west coast of Turkey dating to the seventh century. Structural details suggest that the vessel was lateen-rigged, as it is shown here

coast of Spain, but it was also shipped out into the Atlantic, turning up on sites along the estuaries of the Tagus, Mondego, Douro, and Gironde. More remarkably it is found in significant concentrations in south-western Britain and south Wales. These distributions reflect a sudden interest in the Atlantic seaways by Byzantine merchants, who were also carrying cargoes of African Red Slipware and wine and oil from the Aegean and North Africa. The Phokaian Red Slipware found in Britain dates to within the period 475–550, but mostly to the first quarter of the sixth century, before Justinian had re-established Byzantine authority in the western Mediterranean. This implies that the Byzantine shippers were dealing directly with the Visigoths in Iberia and southern France. In the late sixth century a passing reference in one of the *Lives of the Saints* mentions Greek merchants coming by ship from the eastern Mediterranean and sailing up the Guadiana to the inland town of Mérida. Similar merchant enclaves may well have been established at estuaries along the Atlantic coast of Iberia, echoing the situation fifteen hundred years earlier when the Phoenician merchants first explored the ocean.

In Britain it is conventional to class the North African and Phokaian Red Slipware plates together as A Ware and the amphorae as B Ware. They are frequently found in the same contexts, implying contemporaneous importation and use. The distribution extends along the Atlantic seaways from the Isles of Scilly to the west coast of Scotland, but by far the largest number of finds comes from Cornwall with a spread extending along the south coast into Devon and along the Severn estuary to Somerset and south Wales. The greatest concentration of imported pottery comes from the Cornish settlement of Tintagel, located high on a promontory jutting into the sea, quite possibly at this time the residence of a local king. There has been much debate about how many Byzantine ships braved the Atlantic to get to Britain and why. The minimalists point out that all the known pottery tableware and amphorae alike could have come in a single ship, but variation within the assemblages implies that several cargoes at the very least were involved. But why make so long a journey? Surely it was to acquire tin, for which Cornwall and Devon were famous. Indeed, in the seventh century Stephanus of Alexandria referred to tin as the 'British metal'. There is also a story told in the Life of St John the Almsgiver of a ship's captain (*naukleros*) being blown by a storm to Britain, where he was able to take on board a cargo of tin, which was miraculously turned into silver. The story may be a construct of a lively imagination, but it reflects the knowledge that Britain was a major tin producer. That said, the date range of the imported pottery found in Britain suggests that the Byzantine trading venture was short-lived, extending over perhaps little more than a generation.

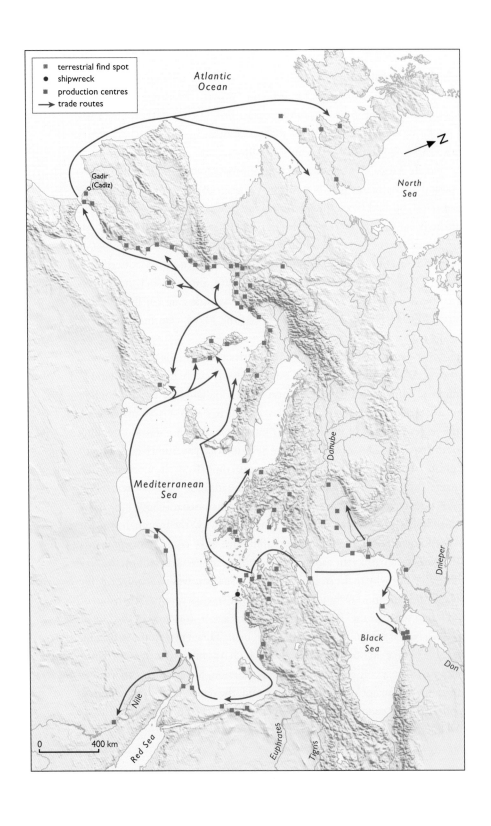

■	terrestrial find spot
●	shipwreck
■	production centres
→	trade routes

Atlantic
Ocean

North
Sea

Gadir
(Cadiz)

Mediterranean
Sea

Danube

Black
Sea

Dnieper

Don

Nile

Red Sea

Euphrates

Tigris

0   400 km

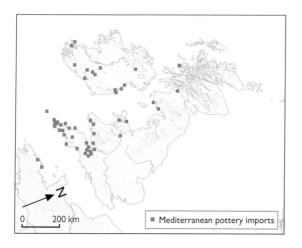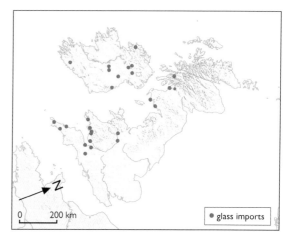

10.9 (*Opposite*) The distribution of distinctive amphorae made in western Turkey (a type known as LR 3B) reflects the shipping routes in operation in the fourth to the seventh century. Some ships left the comparative security of the Mediterranean to take their goods to Britain, probably in exchange for tin

10.10 (*Above*) The distribution of Mediterranean pottery and continental glass dating to the fifth to the seventh century illustrates the engagement of Mediterranean merchants with the western seaways of Britain in the immediate post-Roman period

The Arabs in the Mediterranean

In 627 the Byzantine emperor Heraclius led his army eastwards against the Sasanians, winning a decisive victory near Nineveh and bringing to an end a conflict that had sapped the energies of the empire for centuries. It marked, the Byzantines hoped, the beginning of a new era of peace and prosperity, but it was not to be. Five years earlier, in 622, the prophet Muhammad had led his followers to Medina in an epic journey, the *hijra* (flight), an event taken as the first year of the Islamic calendar and the beginning of an era that was to see Islam spread across the world from the Atlantic to Central Asia.

The expansion of the Arabs from their desert homeland was spectacular. By 632 they had gained control over the eastern shore of the Red Sea and a swath of the desert hinterland, and two years later the whole of the Arabian peninsula up to the river Euphrates was in Arab hands. Up to this point the Arabs had remained within their familiar ecological niche, the sparsely populated desert zone, but they now confronted two sedentary and long-established empires: the Sasanian empire in the east and the Byzantine empire in the west. Undeterred they advanced with astonishing speed,

391

by 656 conquering much of the Sasanian empire up to the Amu Darya (Oxus) and overrunning the Byzantine territories of Syria, Palestine, Egypt, and much of North Africa. So it was that only a generation after their triumph against the Sasanians, when they could reasonably have looked forward to a more stable and prosperous future, the Byzantine dream had been shattered.

The loss of the Levant, Egypt, and Cyrenaica was devastating. The Byzantines still had mastery of the sea and were able to regain control of Egypt in 645, but it was a brief advantage soon lost. All that could be done was to put energy into maintaining a strong land frontier along the Taurus Mountains of Asia Minor to prevent any further Arab advance there: the Levant and Africa had to be abandoned to their fate.

In Africa the Arab army advanced along the coastal route, taking the Egyptian frontier town of Barqa in Cyrenaica in 643 and Tripoli in Tripolitania four years later. There the advance rested for a while. In 665 a force penetrated the old Roman province of Africa (now Ifriqiya to the Arabs), where it met and defeated a contingent of Byzantine marines. Five years later, in 670, the Arabs took hold of what is now southern Tunisia, marking their successes with the foundation of the fortress town of Kairouan. It was from here in 682 that a lightning expedition to the west was mounted, led by Uqba ibn Nafi. Moving with great speed through the Maghrib, he reached Tangier, catching his first sight of the Atlantic before looping south through the Atlas Mountains to face the ocean again at Agadir. Here, so the story goes, he rode into the sea proclaiming, 'My God I call you to witness that if my advance were not halted by the Ocean I would go still further.' On his return journey he was ambushed and killed by Berbers working in coalition with Byzantine marines in eastern Algeria, a warning to all of the dangers of overextending lines of communication. The coalition then went on to capture Kairouan, driving the Arabs back to Barqa. It was a brief respite. The Arab army was back again in 695, re-establishing the base at Kairouan before moving on to capture Carthage in 698. Attempts by the Byzantines and the Berbers to win the city back failed, and with its loss the Byzantine grip on Africa finally came to an end.

As long as the local Berber tribes were prepared to join forces with the Byzantines, whose navy controlled the sea-routes, the Arab hold on Africa and the Maghrib would be under threat. The policy of converting the Berbers to Islam greatly lessened the problem, but the Arabs could not afford to neglect the sea. One of the first moves of the Arab leadership on capturing Carthage was to abandon the old city, whose harbours they considered to be too vulnerable, and to establish a new capital and fortress

10.11 (*Opposite*) The Arab advance into the Near East and North Africa in the eighth century was rapid and also extended well into western Europe in the early decades of the century. At the other end of the Mediterranean, Arab attacks on Constantinople were successfully repelled by the Byzantine state

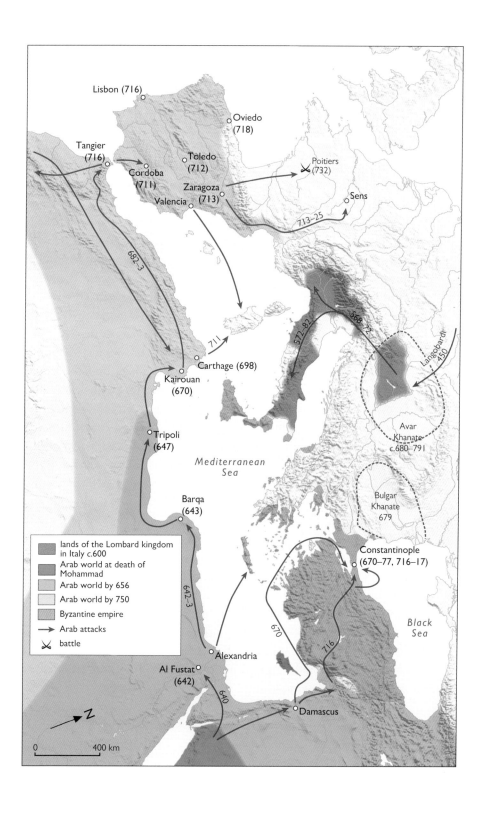

Lisbon (716)

Oviedo (718)

Tangier (716)

Toledo (712)

Cordoba (711)

Zaragoza (713)

Valencia

Poitiers (732)

Sens

713-25

682-3

711

Carthage (698)

Kairouan (670)

568-72

571-82

Langobardi 450

Avar Khanate c.680–791

Tripoli (647)

Mediterranean Sea

Barqa (643)

Bulgar Khanate 679

642-3

Constantinople (670–77, 716–17)

670

716

Black Sea

Alexandria

Al Fustat (642)

640

Damascus

N

	lands of the Lombard kingdom in Italy c.600
	Arab world at death of Mohammad
	Arab world by 656
	Arab world by 750
	Byzantine empire
→	Arab attacks
✄	battle

0   400 km

nearby at Tunis, on the shore of a well-protected inland lake, which they now connected to the sea by a navigable channel. At the same time the governor of Egypt sent a thousand Coptic shipwrights to construct a hundred warships. The foundation of Tunis and the construction of the fleet opened the way for the Arabs to begin to pick off the remaining Byzantine enclaves along the coast of the Maghrib and to turn their attention to the neighbouring sea and its attractive islands.

Meanwhile, the Arabs were not inactive in the eastern Mediterranean. By conquering Syria, Palestine, and Egypt they had acquired control over a long maritime interface inhabited by people whose ancestors had been building ships and sailing the Mediterranean for thousands of years. The governors of Egypt and Syria soon brought together the local shipwrights with craftsmen from Persia and Iraq to build a naval force, and to provide manpower Christian rowers were recruited locally. Their first maritime adventure brought Cyprus to its knees in 649, and a few years later Crete, Kos, and Rhodes were raided. In 655 the Arab and Byzantine navies met in their first full-scale battle. The engagement, which became known as the Battle of the Masts, took place off the coast of Lycia (south-western Asia Minor). Some five hundred Byzantine ships confronted an Arab fleet of two hundred. The battle lasted more than a day and ended in a devastating defeat for the Byzantines, whose emperor, Constans II, only narrowly managed to escape capture. How a relatively inexperienced Arab force could have managed to defeat a highly experienced Byzantine navy more than twice its size is difficult to say since the accounts are brief, but it may simply have been over-confidence on the part of Constans, who is said to have failed to array his fleet in battle formation before the attack. The battle had shown that the Byzantines could no longer rely on supremacy at sea: it was a grim realization, for without it Constantinople was now at risk.

The fear became reality in 670 when the Arab forces were shipped to Constantinople, establishing themselves at the nearby port of Cyzicus (formerly Kyzikos) for the winter of 670–1. The next year they moved off, but returned four years later, intending to stay. From Cyzicus they raided widely, keeping the Byzantine army occupied while other naval detachments captured Rhodes. Eventually, in 677, the Byzantine navy confronted the Arab fleet in force, making effective use of their new weapon, Greek fire. Many of the Arab ships were burned, and those that managed to get away were caught in a storm and destroyed. In the aftermath Rhodes was recovered and a treaty concluded with the Arabs.

The treaty was to hold for nearly forty years, but for the Byzantines it was a time of much internal dissent, which greatly weakened the state. Encouraged by this, the Arabs turned their attention once more to Constantinople, amassing a huge force of a hundred and twenty thousand men and a fleet of eighteen hundred ships. The army arrived in 717 and proceeded to blockade the city by land and by sea, but it was immediately confronted on land by Bulgars, who, in alliance with the Byzantines, attacked the Arab camp. At sea the Byzantine fleet, using Greek fire, drove the Arab ships to seek the safety of their port, Cyzicus, leaving the sea-lanes open so that the empire's ships could continue to supply the city. After a bitterly cold winter, during which large numbers of the besiegers died, the caliph sent reinforcements by land and by sea, but to little avail. The relief troops were dispersed by the Byzantine army before they could reach Constantinople, and many of the sailors, who were Christians recruited in North Africa and Egypt, deserted on arrival. Those besiegers who were left, now disease-ridden and starving, finally gave up after more than a year of suffering and made for home. Attacked by the Byzantine ships and devastated by storms, few of the Arab ships survived.

In the western Mediterranean the Arab forces were far more successful. Many sea-borne attacks were mounted on Sicily, Sardinia, and the Balearics, and in 710 the governor of Tangier sent an expeditionary force of four ships across the Strait of Gibraltar to explore the maritime approaches to Spain. The following year, armed with this new intelligence, he led an all-out invasion, and by 719 almost the entire peninsula, together with the coast of Languedoc, had succumbed to the Muslim armies. Thrusts northwards into the Frankish kingdom along the Rhône valley between 713 and 725, and through western France to Poitiers in 732, led to no new territorial gains for the invaders. However, by the early decades of the eighth century the political geography of the Mediterranean had changed out of all recognition. The Arab caliphate now controlled the entire Levantine, North African, and Iberian coastlines, and its ships sailed freely on the sea. All this was achieved in less than a hundred years.

The contribution of the Arabs to Mediterranean seafaring has been much discussed, but hard facts are few. Much of the debate has hinged on the origin and development of the lateen rig, that is, setting a triangular sail on a long yard attached at an angle to the mast, the sail running fore and aft rather than being set athwartships. The great advantage of this kind of rig over the square-rigged sail is that it enables the ship to tack against the wind. After the seventh century the lateen rig became increasingly popular in the Mediterranean and later was universally used in the Indian Ocean. One widely held view was that the technique developed in the Indian Ocean and was introduced into the Mediterranean by Arab shipbuilders. Such evidence as there is, however, suggests the reverse. Already during the early Roman empire square-rigged ships were being modified so that the yard could be swung to a fore and aft position when conditions demanded, and by the early second century lateen sails were in use on smaller boats. The Yassi Ada 2 wreck, dating to about 400, seems to have had a lateen rig, and it has been argued that the later Yassi Ada 1 ship of about 625 had two lateen sails. The evidence, then, suggests that by the sixth century the lateen rig had largely replaced the square rig in the Mediterranean and was probably the standard rig for the Byzantine dromon. When they arrived on the Mediterranean coast, the Arab commanders ordered fleets to be built by North African, Coptic, and Levantine shipbuilders, who would naturally have worked to the designs they were used to. Although we know that shipbuilders from the Persian Gulf and the Indian Ocean were also brought in, and may have introduced some technical innovations, the lateen rig was already a well-established Mediterranean convention. Indeed, it may be that it was the incomers who transmitted the idea back to the Indian Ocean.

As a desert people the Arabs had little experience of, or liking for, the sea. The great general Amr ibn al-As, who led the conquest of Palestine and Egypt, had strong views: 'If a ship lies still it rends the heart: if it moves it terrifies the imagination. Upon it a man's power ever diminishes and calamity increases. Those within it are like worms in a log, and if it rolls over they are drowned.' But prejudice was soon overcome and the Arab navies became a force to be reckoned with.

The Arab View of the Atlantic Ocean

Uqba ibn Nafi's grandiose gesture of galloping into the sea when he reached the Atlantic at Agadir in 682 is famous because of its symbolism: the Arab army had reached the edge of the world. Nothing and no one lay beyond, so one could rest on the land content in the knowledge that there were no more infidels to convert.

The Arabs had several names for the Atlantic. The tenth-century geographer al-Mas'udi called it the Green Sea or the Circumambient Ocean (al-Bahr al-Muhit), the latter echoing the early Greek concept of the ocean that surrounds the known world. But it was also 'Bahr al-Zulamat', the Sea of Perpetual Gloom, a place to be avoided at all costs. Al-Mas'udi was explicit: 'no ship can enter the ocean. It contains no inhabited land and no rational animals dwell there. Where it begins and where it ends are both unknown.' Calling the ocean 'al-Zulamat' was a specific reference to the use of the word in Koranic verse, which likens the state of the unbeliever to being 'in the depth of darkness, in a vast deep ocean, overwhelmed by billows, topped by billows, topped by dark clouds—depths of darkness, one above the other'. The Arabs had no love for the Atlantic.

And yet there were always the curious who would want to challenge the unknown. Al-Mas'udi tells of one such adventurer, a man named Khashkhash from Córdoba, who with a group of other young men 'set sail on the ocean in ships they had fitted out' and eventually returned with rich booty, though whether acquired by trade or by raiding is unrecorded; nor do we know the direction of their journey. This was not an isolated venture since al-Mas'udi refers to another of his writings, since lost, in which he had described the marvels of the ocean: 'what was seen there by men who have entered it at the risk of their own lives and from which some have returned safe and sound'. The Sea of Perpetual Gloom may not have been for the faint-hearted, but for some its challenge was irresistible.

The Beat of Hostile Oars

The story of the north-eastern Atlantic in the period 350–800 involves two inter-weaving narratives, a west side story about the Atlantic-facing lands—north-western France, western Britain, Ireland, and eventually the Faroe islands and Iceland—and an east side story, which focuses on the English Channel, eastern Britain, and the North Sea coasts of continental Europe. Both involve the movement of people, sometimes in large numbers, by sea.

The collapse of Roman centralized rule in Britain and north-western France in the early decades of the fifth century was, in part at least, the result of a new restlessness among the peoples living beyond the frontiers. Already, in the late third century, the seas around Britain were becoming dangerous because of pirates who attacked ships and raided the coast. We have already seen (pp. 367–8) that Saxons from north of the Rhine were becoming a serious threat in the southern North Sea and English Channel. At much the same time the west coast of Britain was coming under attack from Ireland, requiring that Roman forts be strengthened and new forts built. At about this time the officer in charge of a naval supply base somewhere in the Severn estuary, one Titus Flavius Senilis, dedicated a mosaic pavement in the temple of Nodens at Lydney; whether he was seeking the god's help for professional or personal reasons is not recorded. Then, in 360, Picts from north of Hadrian's Wall and Scotti from Ireland began to cause trouble in the north. Seven years later they were joined by Attacotti, probably from Ireland, and Saxons and Franks from continental Europe, in a concerted attack on the province, causing chaos as far south as the Thames. Raids from Ireland now increased in intensity, and by the end of the fourth century migrants were on the move: Scotti from the north of Ireland had begun to settle in north Wales, while the Déisi from southern Ireland were moving into south-west Wales. One contemporary Roman source, writing about the end of the fourth and beginning of the fifth century, says that the Irish rose up against the British and 'the sea foamed to the beat of hostile oars'. Stilicho, the general in charge of the defence of the Roman west, responded with force. Thereafter 'ice-bound Hibernia [Ireland] wept for the mounds of slain Scotti'.

But still the raids continued. This was the time when Niall of the Nine Hostages, high king of Ireland, led seven successful raids against Britain—at least according to Irish tradition. In all probability the flow of migrants into Wales continued into the fifth century, and in the early sixth century the Scotti from north-eastern Antrim crossed to Argyll to found the kingdom of Dál Riata. They were soon to give their name to the whole of northern Britain.

Meanwhile, in the east of Britain defensive measures had been taken against sea-borne attacks. The coastal forts from the Wash to the Solent and along the continental coast from the Rhine to Armorica had been strengthened and the command structure reorganized to counter Saxon raids. In addition, a series of watch-towers was built along the Yorkshire coast to provide early warning of hostile movements of Picts coming by sea from north of Hadrian's Wall. But all to little avail. Sometime soon after 407 there was a major incursion of Saxons into eastern Britain, and by the 420s and 430s the pace of immigration had intensified, with Saxons, Angles, and Jutes arriving in some numbers from the long continental coastline stretching from the Rhine mouth to the north of Denmark.

North-western France fared no better. In Armorica the barbarian inroads of 406–7 caused a complete breakdown in Roman authority and rebellion broke out. Attempts were made to re-establish centralized rule, but the unstable situation slipped into anarchy. There are some hints that soldiers were sent from Britain to try to maintain order, but, as Franks from across the Rhine moved into northern France and Saxons settled on the coasts of Lower Normandy, the last remnants of Roman authority collapsed. One final act remained. In the late fifth or early sixth century migrants from the south-west of Britain began to arrive in Armorica to settle, particularly in the northern coastal zone. According to the British monk Gildas, writing not long after, about 540, they were being driven out by the advance of the Saxons moving across Britain. There was no doubt an element of truth in this, but other factors, such as overpopulation or simply the desire to seek a new life as old systems collapsed, may have contributed. In any event, the migration saw a significant influx of Britons into Armorica, which henceforth became known as Brittany.

It seems that a shipload or two of the Britons were more adventurous than their contemporaries and sometime in the fifth century braved the Bay of Biscay to settle in Galicia. On arrival the community founded an abbey near Mondoñedo dedicated to Santa Maria de Bretoña. Judging by his Celtic name, Bishop Mailoc, who attended a council in Braga in 572, may have been a descendant of the pioneering community.

The period 350–550 was, then, a time of extensive folk wanderings, when thousands of people were on the move. It began with raids and ended with mass migration and resettlement. In all of this the sea was the facilitator.

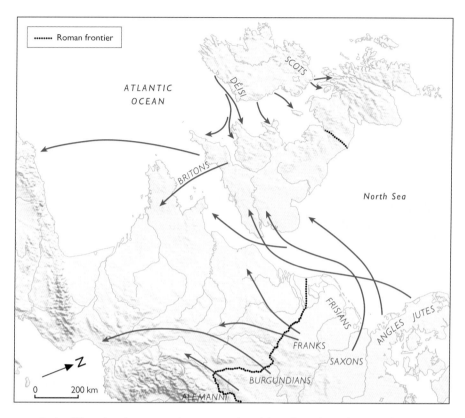

10.12 In the fifth and sixth centuries there was much mobility of population between the Continent, Britain, and Ireland using many of the long-established sea-routes. These centuries are often referred to as the migration period

The West Side Story

The episode of contact between the Byzantine world and south-western Britain in the late fifth or early sixth century was probably short-lived—a brief trading venture that had little significant effect on the British communities apart from providing the local elites with a few exotic goods with which to demonstrate their status. But the sixth century saw the beginning of a separate and more persistent network of maritime contacts, this time linking western France with south-western Britain and with communities all around the Irish Sea as far as the west coast of Scotland. The extent of the network is manifest in the distribution of glass and pottery vessels exported from western France. Two different types of pottery have been identified, known in English terminology as D and E Wares. D Wares were manufactured in western France in the region of Bordeaux or in the Loire valley in the sixth century and are known to French archaeologists as *Dérivées sigillées Paléochrétiennes*. Outside France they have been found at only seven sites along the Atlantic seaways between the Scilly Isles and Argyll. The E Wares are much more prolifically distributed and have been found at more than seventy different sites in western Britain and Ireland. The category includes a range of vessel types, mostly jars and beakers, with smaller numbers of bowls and jugs. They were manufactured in western France from the late sixth to late seventh century somewhere in the Loire valley, the Vendée, or Charente. The glass vessels, usually found on the same sites as the D and E Wares, were mostly conical drinking beakers, though a few bowls are known. They match types being made in Bordeaux. Taken together, then, the archaeological evidence clearly demonstrates extensive maritime links between western France and western Britain and Ireland spanning the sixth and seventh centuries.

What kinds of commodity were being carried in these glass and pottery vessels it is difficult to say with certainty. Most likely the cargoes were varied. Wine from the Bordeaux region probably featured large, but since it would have been carried in barrels it has left no archaeological trace. There are, however, documentary references to wine being used in western Britain and Ireland. Abbot Adomnán of Iona uses the metaphor of wine oozing from the crack in a large container, and commentaries on a lost

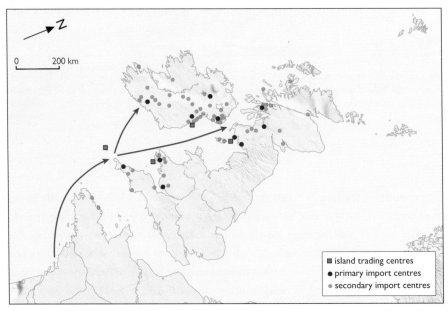

10.13 Maritime contacts were maintained between the west coast of France and western Britain and Ireland in the seventh century, during which time notions of Gaulish Christianity reached the Irish Sea region. Tangible evidence of this contact is to be found in the distribution in Britain and Ireland of pottery from western France (E Ware)

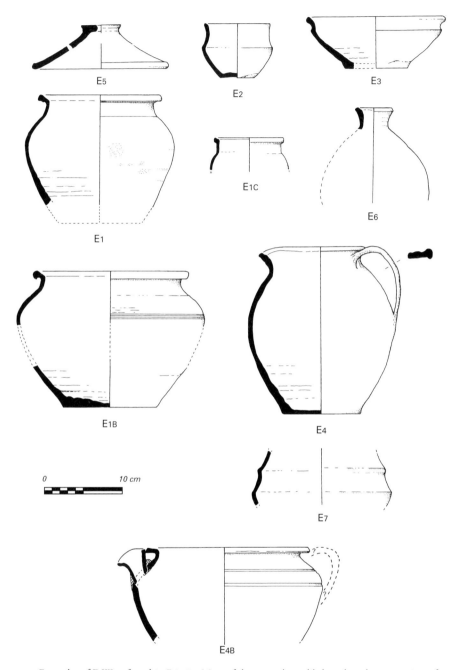

10.14 Examples of E Ware found in Britain. Most of these vessels are likely to have been containers for desirable commodities

Irish text, *Muirbretha* (Sea Judgements), mention wine as one of the many goods that could be encountered in a wrecked ship. The E Ware vessels themselves, though hardly distinguished examples of the potter's art, will have had a value as tableware in a largely aceramic area like western Britain and Ireland. The jars could also have been containers for imported commodities. Some have been shown to have been used to transport the reddish-purple dye madder. Others may have carried honey, spices, exotic nuts, and sweetmeats, all mentioned in Irish texts as coming from abroad. The glass vessels, too, would have been valuable trade goods, and contemporary Welsh sources refer to royal feasts where wine was drunk from glass beakers. The *Muirbretha* adds that among the goods found in shipwrecks were hides, iron, salt, gold, silver, furs, and horses. Some of these may have come from western France, not least salt, which was a commodity produced in abundance in the region.

That some of the trading ventures were organized on a regular basis is implied by a reference in the Life of Columba in which the saint anticipates the visit of a ship from Gaul, which duly arrives. The word used to describe the craft is *barca*, which denotes a trading vessel. It is tempting to see the remote monastic community on Iona counting the days until the Gaulish ship made its annual call bringing news of the outside world and the few luxuries that would make life bearable for another year. We learn from another source, the Life of St Philibert, of the monks on the island of Noirmoutier, just south of the Loire estuary, receiving traders: 'Irish ships with a diversity of goods on board put in at the island to provide the brethren with an abundance of shoes and clothing.' The text is a reminder that woollen fabrics and leather were among the more valuable of the exports from Ireland.

Saints and Seaways

The maritime networks that linked western France to the Irish Sea and beyond in the sixth and seventh centuries were motivated by commerce, but the ships also carried travellers, and with the travellers information could flow, bringing the culture of the two regions more closely together. It was probably in this way that Celtic Christianity—the type of Christianity that developed in western Britain and Ireland—received values and practices that distinguish it from the Roman type of Christianity which had taken root in the towns of eastern Britain. Ireland, beyond the boundaries of the empire, had remained largely pagan throughout the Roman occupation of Britain, but the fact that there was a small Christian community in the south-west of the island is implied by the dispatch of a Gaulish churchman, Palladius, by Pope Celestine to minister to the Christian Irish. Palladius arrived in 431, but little more is heard of him. A year later a

Briton called Patrick, who had spent some time in Ireland as a slave and had escaped on a merchant ship, decided to return to the island as a missionary. He, and Palladius before him, would have tried to impose a Roman urban-based model of Christianity by creating large territorial units, *parochia*, each served by a centrally placed church presided over by a bishop. The model was unsuited to the dispersed settlement pattern of Ireland, with its lack of centralized government, and by the end of the fifth century it had given way to a new system, monasticism.

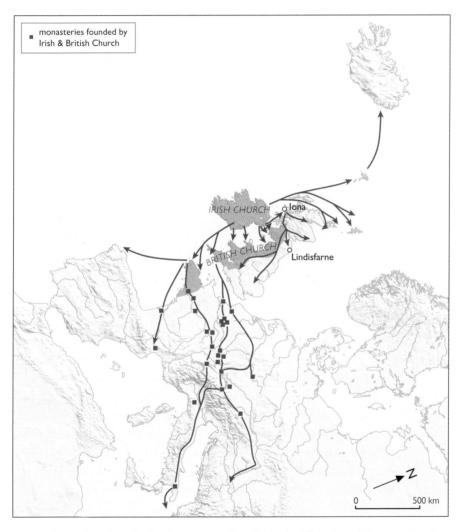

10.15 Holy men from the Irish Church were especially mobile in the fifth to the eighth century, founding religious establishments throughout Europe, though the majority concentrated their efforts in Brittany and in the North Atlantic, eventually reaching the Faroes and Iceland

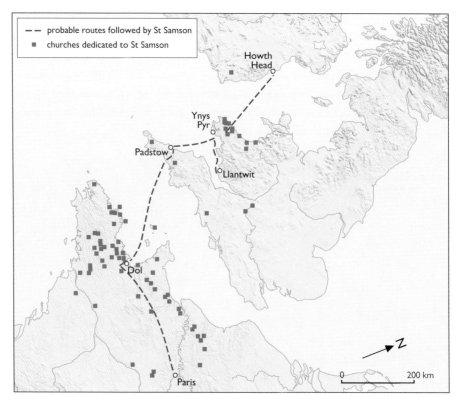

10.16 One energetic missionary was St Samson, who finally established himself in Dol in northern Brittany. The influence of his teaching is shown by the number of churches dedicated to him

Monasticism developed in the east, in Egypt and Cyrenaica. It combined mysticism with asceticism, its followers seeking to cut themselves off from the world the better to commune with God. Many sought a 'desert' place in which to found a monastic community; others of more extreme persuasion went off by themselves to become hermits and had, as one contemporary writer put it, 'no other occupation in their caves and caverns than to praise God day and night'. The values of monasticism had spread through Italy into southern Gaul before the end of the fourth century and, under church leaders like St Martin (316?–397), who became bishop of Tours, they flourished in western France. Growing hostility from the Episcopal Church, combined with the influx of Germanic settlers, drove many of those favouring the more ascetic form of Christianity to flee across the seas to western Britain and Ireland. A later document may be referring to this fifth-century exodus when it says, 'all the wise people (*sapientes*) on this side of the sea took flight to lands overseas, that is in Ireland, and wherever they went greatly increased the learning of those regions'. Those taking flight would have

404

used the Atlantic sea-routes already in operation. Once the traumas of the migration period had settled down, links between the diaspora and those who remained in France could be strengthened or re-established. Indeed, the intensity of the trading networks in the sixth and seventh centuries may, in no small part, be due to the social bonds dating back to that time.

The ideals of monasticism became firmly established in western Britain and Ireland during the fifth century. Superimposed on a tribal system, and with influences brought in by refugees from the Romanized zone of Britain, the Celtic Church emerged, distinguished not only by its scholarship and its practices but by the highly skilled craft schools for which it provided patronage.

Within the Celtic Church there were three classes of holy men: the bishops, who were peripatetic preachers moving around within their allotted territory; the holy men in charge of monasteries; and the *peregrini*, roaming monks in search of solitude. The third order was the most numerous and it was they who spread the message of the Celtic Church far and wide. Their journeys can often be traced from the distribution of the churches

10.17 This detail from a thirteenth-century stained-glass window in the cathedral of Dol in Brittany shows St Samson and his companions sailing from Cornwall to Brittany

dedicated to them. One, for whom a reliable Life survives, written in the early seventh century, is St Samson of Dol. He is first encountered in a monastery on Caldey Island, off the south coast of Pembrokeshire, meeting some Irish monks who were returning home after a visit to Rome. They encouraged him to go with them to Ireland, where he stayed for a while before returning to Caldey Island with a cart, which thereafter accompanied him on his travels. From Caldey Island he sailed to the north coast of Cornwall, staying at a monastery near Padstow for a short time before crossing the peninsula, probably to the Fowey estuary, where he embarked for Brittany on a boat that took him to the estuary of the Rance. Here he may have stayed at Alet, a small urban site fortified in the late Roman period. He then journeyed east to Dol, where he founded a monastic bishopric soon to become renowned throughout the land. His later travels took him on a political mission to Paris.

Many *peregrini* made similar journeys from the monastic centres of Ireland and Wales, but the Lives which describe their travels were written much later and contain much that is fanciful invention. Some monks took their ministry deep into Europe, reaching the Golfe du Lion, southern Italy, and the middle Danube, but many were

405

content to join in the wake of the Britons who had migrated to Brittany. For them the general pattern seems to have been to settle first on some offshore island, where they set up chapels and became hermits, and only later to move onto the mainland to minister to their brethren already settled there. The pause enabled them to establish their credentials and to negotiate with the community leaders to ensure a welcome. St Guénolé set himself up on the Île de Tibidy before moving to the mainland to found the abbey of Landévennec, while St Maudez stayed first on the Île de Bréhat before busying himself on the mainland.

Many of the holy men who made for the Continent became involved in the wider community, but other *peregrini* were more austere, preferring to find a place of solitude away from the temptations of the secular world. The monks who made their home on the stark pyramidal crag of Skellig Michael, thirteen kilometres out in the Atlantic off the coast of County Kerry, were making an extreme statement about their determination to give up the comforts and vanities of normal life. Here was a desert indeed, with little to sustain them other than the eggs of sea-birds and the few vegetables that could be persuaded to grow on their gale-torn garden patches. For much of the time they lived in or above the clouds, their world isolated by the unremitting rumble of the sea. Here the mind had little more to do than to focus on God and survival.

Other *peregrini* chose to explore the North Atlantic in search of their desert. The islands and peninsulas of the Atlantic face of Scotland offered ample opportunity, and several of the monasteries founded at the time became famous centres of Christian learning, among them Whithorn in south-western Scotland, founded by St Ninian, and Iona, established by St Columba in 563. Others were even more adventurous. The abbot of Iona, Adomnán, records three journeys made in the mid-sixth century by the monk Cormac ua Liatháin in search of a remote and deserted place far out in the ocean. On the second journey Cormac sailed north from Erris in County Mayo to visit Orkney, returning to land, this time at Iona, some months later. His third adventure was more enterprising. From somewhere in Scotland he sailed due north for fourteen days. His voyage 'extended beyond the limit of human wanderings and return seemed to be impossible'. Where exactly he went and what islands he may have visited are not recorded, but Cormac had been given some advice by the king of Inverness, who no doubt had a detailed knowledge of these northern waters and may have passed on information about distant islands, like the Faroes and even Iceland, the existence of which may have been common knowledge among northern sailors.

The Irish monk Dicuil, writing in the Carolingian court about 825, is another valuable source on the far north. He mentions many islands in the ocean north of Britain: 'on those islands hermits who sailed from [Ireland] have lived for roughly a hundred years'. That the islands were described as 'full of innumerable sheep and a great many different kinds of sea fowl' suggests that they were probably the Faroes, still notable for their sheep at the time of the later Norse settlement. His statement implies that the monks, the first inhabitants, had arrived in the early decades of the eighth century, bringing their sheep with them. He also knew that later, about 795, Irish clerics landed on Iceland:

> It is now thirty years since clerics, who have lived on that island from the first
> day of February to the first day of August, told me that not only at the summer
> solstice, but in the days on either side of it, the setting sun hides itself at evening
> hour as if behind a little hill, so that no darkness occurs during that very brief
> period of time but whatever task a man wishes to perform, even to picking the
> lice out of his shirt, he can manage as precisely as in broad daylight. … They deal
> in fallacies who have written that the sea around the island is frozen … But after
> one day's sailing from there to the north they found the frozen sea.

Dicuil's description, with its entertaining detail, is convincing evidence that there were already monks on Iceland in the last decade of the eighth century, though when they first arrived is unknown. The winter voyage he described is unlikely to have been the first. Indeed, the pioneers may date back to Cormac's time. The monks stayed until the arrival of the Norse settlers about 860. Their books, bells, and croziers were found by the incomers, and a few place names in the south-east of the island containing the word 'papa', indicating a religious origin, probably mark their early monastic sites.

What encouraged the monks who discovered Iceland to make their northern journey we shall never know for certain, but there may have been traditions going back to the time of Pytheas, or even before, that spoke of distant islands. Sailors blown off course who managed to return may have brought back sightings, and the flight of whooper swans, every year making their northward migration, would have alerted sailors to the existence of lands in the north. Knowledge of northern islands would have become part of local sea lore, and it was tales of this kind that would have encouraged Cormac to sail north in the mid-sixth century. His experiences will have added to local knowledge, inspiring further journeys until eventually landfall was made and the monks consolidated their precursors' first foothold.

The holy men spread the teachings of the Celtic Church far and wide along the Atlantic seaways from Galicia to Iceland in the period from the fifth to the eighth century. That they could achieve such a reach was born of two things: their faith with its adherence to the monastic way of life, and the long tradition of Atlantic seafaring of which they were the heirs. The stories of their ventures, embedded in the Lives and other texts, and the distribution of churches bearing the names of the founders, give the impression of sudden activity, but in reality we are glimpsing the impact of probably only a few hundred *peregrini* whose activities spanned two or three centuries. Since many of these would have chosen to travel in ships engaged in commercial exchanges, their travels demonstrate, for the most part, not unusual, God-driven maritime activity but the normal pattern of shipping movements along the seaways. That said, there were exceptions. The men who took ship and sailed to the Faroes and Iceland, and those whose fantastic stories are recorded in the *immrama* (the tales of voyages of the *peregrini*), were men apart who put their trust in God to take them where He willed across entirely unknown seas.

Of the boats in use at the time no material remains are known, but no doubt skin boats and plank boats continued to be built and used alongside each other. Indeed, both types are mentioned in the *Navigatio* describing the voyage of St Brendan. In chapter 4 Brendan and his fellow monks pitch their tent on a narrow creek and set about building their vessel. It was wooden-framed and covered with oxhides tanned with oak bark and stitched together, the joints smeared with animal fat to seal them. They then fixed the mast with a sail and steering gear, and loaded supplies for forty days, including spare hides for repair and fat for dressing the leather. The vessel was large enough to carry eighteen people. Later, after abandoning his skin boat on the coast of Ireland, Brendan built a wooden vessel. Adomnán also gives some details of the sailing currach used by Cormac on his voyage north. It had a keel with a prow- and stern-post and was covered with leather hides. The mast, sail, and rigging are also mentioned. The surviving texts, then, leave little doubt that skin vessels were widely used in the western and northern seas. They were flexible and resilient and would have suited the buffeting waves. But the probability is that plank boats continued to be made and used in these waters. Long winter journeys like those to Iceland would have demanded sturdy vessels of this kind.

The East Side Story

The presence of a relatively stable urban-based consumer society to the south of the Rhine–Danube frontier during the four hundred years or so of the Roman empire created the demand for a wide range of raw materials, many of which would have been supplied from what is now Germany, Poland, and Scandinavia. In return for grain, hides, furs, walrus ivory, honey, resin, and other forest products, the barbarian tribes received Roman consumer goods, most notably items of bronze and glassware. These imports are found across the North European Plain, and some were transported by sea to Scandinavia. One of the principal routes to the north lay by way of the Danish island of Fyn, thence via the Kattegat and Skagerrak to the Oslo fjord and westwards to the Atlantic coast of Norway. Another route led to the island of Bornholm and to the Baltic coast of Sweden. Trade with the Roman world initiated changes among the Scandinavian communities. Agricultural production intensified, and certain centres, by virtue of their command of the route nodes, became powerful, the power residing in the local elites. One such centre was Gudme in eastern Fyn. Begun in the first century BC, it became prosperous in the third and fourth centuries as Roman trade intensified. Gudme was an inland settlement, but a few kilometres away on the coast at Lundeborg lay its port, where each season trading took place and ships were repaired. Another trading centre of this period has been identified at Dankirke on the east side of the Jutland peninsula, a location that would have attracted trading vessels making their way northwards from the Rhine estuary along the North Sea coast of Germany.

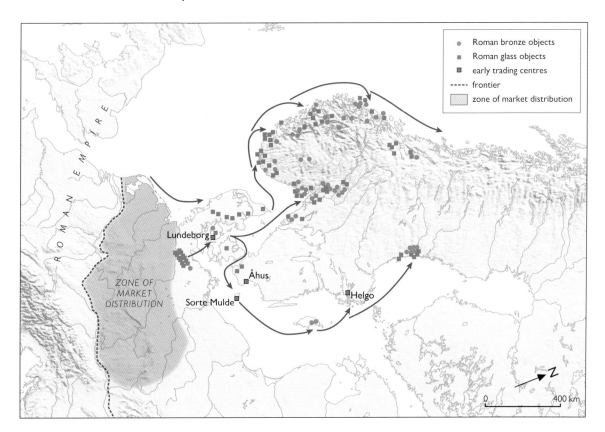

10.18 Roman consumer goods flowed through the northern frontier to the barbarian lands of Germany and Scandinavia. Across a broad zone adjacent to the frontier, goods were probably distributed directly through an embedded market system, but beyond they would have been transported by sea to trading centres in Scandinavia and then onwards along the existing maritime networks to distant ports

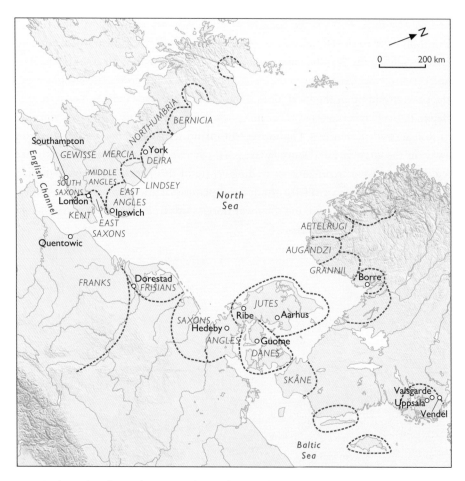

10.19 In the sixth and seventh centuries the North Sea and the Baltic were ringed by small kingdoms heavily dependent on the sea. Contact between them, sometimes over long distances, allowed ideas, beliefs, and materials to be exchanged

The collapse of the Roman west and the fury of the migrations that followed in the fifth and sixth centuries caused widespread disruptions around the shores of the southern North Sea but had little significant effect on Scandinavia except for the departure of groups of people from Jutland, who settled in eastern Britain. Farming communities continued to thrive and, as the turbulence of the migrations subsided, trade began to develop with the eastern Roman empire, now ruled from Constantinople. Old trading and production centres like Gudme continued and new ones emerged: places like Sorte Muld, on the island of Bornholm, and Helgö, an island on Lake Mälaren in central Sweden, both of which settlements began in the fourth century and became focal points in the development of the trading networks in the Baltic. At Helgö the discovery of a hoard of forty-seven Roman gold coins of the fifth and sixth centuries reflects links with the Byzantine world, and it was probably along these routes from the east that the bronze statuette of a Buddha, made in India in the sixth or seventh century, was brought.

It was in the Lake Mälaren region of central Sweden that a royal dynasty emerged, burying their elite in cemeteries beneath massive barrow mounds. These were the kings of the Svear, a tribe mentioned by the Roman historian Tacitus in the first century AD which was to give its name to Sweden. The earliest of the royal burials, dating to the sixth century, were interred with their gold and garnet-inlaid jewellery in a cemetery at Gamla Uppsala beneath burial mounds up to twenty metres high. The colossal input of labour needed for their construction testifies to the coercive power of the deceased nobility. Gamla Uppsala lies close to the river Fyris, where it flows into Lake Mälaren. Further up the river are two slightly later royal cemeteries, Valsgärde and Vendel, beginning in the seventh century, the latter giving its name to the period. Both contained the graves of the elite buried in their boats and richly furnished with grave goods. At Valsgärde, sited on the crest of a ridge overlooking the Fyris, fifteen boat burials were excavated: further up-river at Vendel there were fourteen, spanning the period from the seventh to the tenth centuries. Typically the dead aristocrat was

10.20 One of the most powerful of the sixth- and seventh-century polities was the Vandal kingdom of central Sweden. The individual chiefly centres can be identified by cemeteries of elite burials like Valsgärde, shown here. The hillock in the centre of the photograph, overlooking the river, was chosen as the location of the cemetery, represented now by a number of barrows

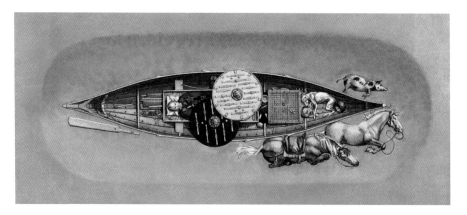

10.21 One of the characteristics of the elite Vandal burials was the use of a boat to contain the deceased and his or her grave goods. The reconstruction drawing is of a grave from Ultuna, Sweden

buried in the stern of his boat accompanied by his personal war gear: a sword, shield, spear, and sometimes a finely decorated helmet. In the bow of the boat the other grave goods were assembled: tools, drinking vessels, horse-gear, and domesticated animals including horses, dogs, cattle, sheep, and pigs. In one of the more elaborate graves at Valsgärde the dead man was provided with two horses complete with their gear and saddles, as well as a dog and a deer. To ensure his comfort he was laid on feather pillows.

The power of the Vendel period elite lay in their control of a range of commodities and their seafaring prowess. The clayey land of the Lake Mälaren region was well suited to intensive cattle production, providing not only an assured food source but also a plentiful supply of leather for export, while from the forest and mountain regions to the north and west came high-quality iron ore and furs. The lakes, home to abundant wildfowl, were a source of eiderdown. All these commodities would have been attractive to the Byzantine world. The sea played a dominant part in the lives of the Svear. The lake, stretching far inland and fringed with islands, was connected by a narrow strait to the Baltic with its deeply indented coastline and scattering of islands. Such an environment bred seamen whose entrepreneurial activities brought great wealth to their communities. It is little wonder that ships featured large in their burial rituals.

Around the North Sea a series of maritime kingdoms were developing at the same time as the kingdom of the Svear. The most spectacular was the kingdom of the East Angles in Britain, occupying much of the area of modern Suffolk and Norfolk, best known for its royal burial-ground at Sutton Hoo. The cemetery lies on a ridge overlooking the Deben estuary only thirteen kilometres from the sea—a situation similar to that chosen for the Vendel cemeteries, and, like them, the elite burials were marked by large barrow mounds. Two of the mounds covered ship burials. In the best preserved (mound 1) the dead man, whose body no longer survives in the acid soil, was placed in a chamber in the centre of the ship together with his weapons, including a finely decorated helmet, and a range of other valuable items, among them an ornate gold buckle and shoulder clasps, a purse containing thirty-seven Frankish gold coins, a number of bronze bowls and cauldrons, including one from Egypt, a harp, and a range of fabrics representing cloaks, blankets, and hangings. Together the finds suggest a date of about 630 for the burial. Who the dead king was is a matter of debate, but Rædwald is a strong possibility. The similarities to the Vendel period graves of Sweden are particularly striking, not only in the form of the burial but in the style of the weapons, especially the helmet. How to explain these similarities is more difficult. At the very least the two kingdoms must have been in close contact by sea, and it may be that intermarriage or the fostering of children helped to strengthen links between the two royal households.

10.22 The best known of the British North Sea kingdoms had its principal cemetery at Sutton Hoo, Suffolk. Excavations in 1939 brought to light evidence of an elaborate ship burial dating to the early years of the seventh century. Details of the hull structure were preserved in the sand, and the nails that clinched the hull planks remained in position, heavily oxidized

The form of ship used in the Sutton Hoo burial, though the timbers had completely rotted away, was preserved as a shadow in the sand with its rusted rivets still in position. Its careful excavation in 1939 is one of the great achievements of British archaeology. The ship was clinker-built, originally about 27 metres long. Its narrow planks were radially split and were without cleats on the inside to aid the attachment of the frames, which

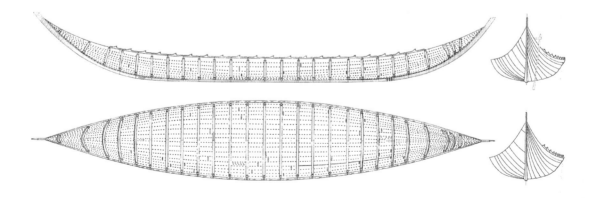

10.23 Reconstruction drawing of the Sutton Hoo ship

413

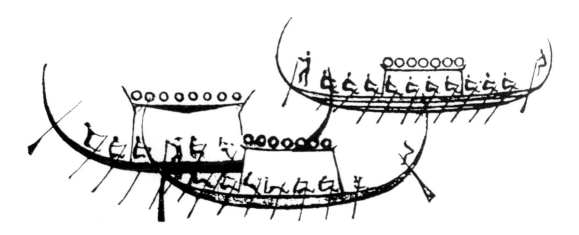

10.24 Vessels of the same type as the Vandal and Sutton Hoo ships are depicted as carvings on stones found on the island of Gotland in the Baltic Sea. The elegant vessels were powered by up to ten rowers. The carvings date to the fifth and sixth centuries

instead were fixed with treenails. Its keel swept high at bow and stern, giving the vessel a considerable rocker (curvature of the keel), while the cross-section at midships was near-circular. These characteristics would have given minimal resistance to the sea, suggesting that the ship was designed for rowing rather than sailing, an observation further supported by the absence of any evidence for a deep keel or fittings suitable for taking a mast. Another factor arguing against a sail is that with such a hull shape there would not have been sufficient lateral resistance to prevent leeway under sail.

Rowing vessels of the Sutton Hoo type were probably common in the North Sea and the Baltic, where there was a need for speed, persistence of travel, and a large crew that could exchange their oars for swords when necessary: they were ideal for raids and they clearly belonged to the same tradition as the Nydam vessel of the fourth century. But alongside them it is likely that sailing ships, cross-rigged with masts set near midships, of the kind in use on the southern North Sea during the Roman period, continued to be built. Engravings depicting such vessels are known in Denmark in the seventh century and on the memorial stones in Gotland from the eighth century. Such ships would have been better suited to carrying cargo, and as the volume of trade in the North Sea and the Baltic began to increase in the seventh century, so they would have become a more familiar aspect of the maritime scene.

The sea-borne migrations of the fifth century, with Saxons moving into Britain and Normandy, Angles into eastern Britain, and Jutes into Kent and the Solent region, had disrupted the long-established trade routes. But once the flurry of movement had subsided and the Franks, who had settled in the Rhineland and northern Gaul, had

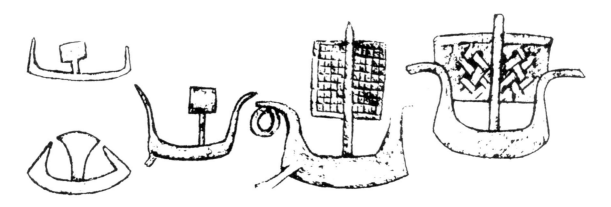

10.25 The Gotland stones also depicted sailing vessels, but these date to the sixth and seventh centuries

united under the leadership of Clovis (reigned 481–511), cross-Channel trade resumed and luxury goods, including glassware from the Frankish workshops, began to flood into south-eastern Britain through ports in Kent like Sarre on the island of Thanet and Fordwich on the Stour, downstream from Canterbury. Ports along the Sussex coast also began to receive Frankish traders. By the late seventh and early eighth centuries, as the Franks in the west and the Byzantines in the east created increasingly stable states, trade began to expand, encouraging the growth of a series of permanent markets along the continental interface with the North Sea and the Baltic. The new trading centres were usually on major river routes: Rouen and Saint-Denis on the Seine, Amiens on the Somme, Quentovic on the Canche, Dorestad on the Rhine, Wolin on the Oder, and Truso on the Vistula. Ports like Birka in Sweden, Kaupang in Norway, and Ribe and Hedeby in Denmark served the Scandinavian kingdoms, while around the south and east coasts of Britain major trading centres developed at Hamwic (the Saxon town of Southampton), London, Ipswich, and York. By the end of the eighth century the North Sea and the Baltic were criss-crossed by trading routes, creating a greater connectivity than had ever before been known. That two kings, Offa of Mercia and Charlemagne of the Franks, had to intervene in disputes to agree exact exchange rates is a reflection of the volume and complexity of the trade now under way.

There is little to be said of the cargo ships of the northern seas in the fifth to the eighth centuries, but to sail efficiently the longitudinal profile of the vessel needed to be straighter, with the ends more sharply upturned and with a higher freeboard, than the Sutton Hoo ship. The sailing vessels depicted on the Gotland memorial stones show that developments of just these kinds were under way in the eighth and ninth centuries. One response to these needs was to set the prow- and stern-posts at a sharp angle to the keel. It was this technique that was later to characterize the cog, the type of vessel that was to become the favoured work-a-day vessel of the Atlantic seaways. Demands for cargo ships in the seventh and eighth centuries were met with ingenuity by the shipwrights of the North Sea and the Baltic: it was a time of experimentation, and what emerged was to set the direction of shipbuilding for the next five hundred years.

The 450 years from the last decades of the Roman empire to the rise of the Vikings spanned the transition from the end of the ancient world and the beginning of the modern. It was a time of large-scale folk movement which disrupted and, in many cases, destroyed existing systems of connectivity. Although there was massive change, there was also a strong conservatism. The Byzantine empire laboured to maintain itself little changed, the Frankish empire which emerged in the west tried hard to re-create the values of the western Roman empire, while the Arabs, spreading far beyond their homeland, held fast to traditional values. In consequence the Mediterranean became an inward-looking sea, a place of little innovation. In the North Sea and the Baltic, trading intensified, calling for some experimentation with shipbuilding methods, though few felt any need to venture outside familiar waters. But on the Atlantic seaways a different spirit prevailed. While many, probably most, of those who took to the seas were traders plying long-established routes, some—the extremists of the Celtic Church—rose to the challenge of the ocean, seeing it as a place where God was intent to test them. The challenge led to the discovery of the Faroes and Iceland. Others, like the young men who set out from Córdoba, could not resist the lure of the unknown ocean, but for reasons that may have been more mercenary. The outer ocean was there to explore, and many, whether for religious or for commercial reasons, would soon be tempted to probe its limits.

11

The Age of the Northmen, 780–1100

In the later decades of the eighth century communities living in the maritime regions of Scandinavia began to move out of their traditional homeland, initiating what was to become a period of astonishing mobility—a mobility driven by three desires: to raid, to find new lands to settle, and to trade. This is the period conventionally known as the Viking Age. The first recorded warning of what was to come happened in, or soon after, 786 when three Norse ships landed on the coast of Dorset and a local official was killed. It was followed in 793 by a surprise attack on the Northumbrian monastery of Lindisfarne, and for the next sixty years the raids continued, devastating monasteries, churches, and towns in Britain, Ireland, and France, with a few of the more adventurous raiders targeting cities in Iberia and the western Mediterranean. There followed a period of fifty years during which time settlement became the principal objective, with Norse and Danish communities appropriating land in Scotland, England, Wales, and north-western France. In Ireland smaller trading enclaves were established on the more important estuaries. The desire for new land also drew settlers to the remote Atlantic islands of the Faroes, Iceland, and later Greenland, from where, about the year 1000, a few hardy souls completed the Atlantic crossing to land on the coasts of North America and become the first Europeans to engage with Native American peoples. In these two boisterous centuries the men—and the women who followed them—had driven themselves to extremes, always in competition with the unremitting Atlantic. That they achieved so much was due to the skill of the shipbuilders and navigators and to the human passion to seek out what lies beyond.

While these events were unfolding in the Atlantic involving Danes and Norwegians, Swedes were looking south-eastwards to continental Europe to develop their trading networks. Using the great rivers of central and eastern Europe, and making short overland portages where necessary, they were able to take their ships to the Black Sea and the Caspian, opening up unlimited opportunities to trade with the Byzantine empire and the Abbasid caliphate occupying much of the Near East. Suddenly Scandinavia had become a vibrant centre, with its networks extending from North America to Central Asia and from the Arctic to the Mediterranean. That this could have happened, and so quickly, was in large part due to social and economic changes under way in the Scandinavian homeland.

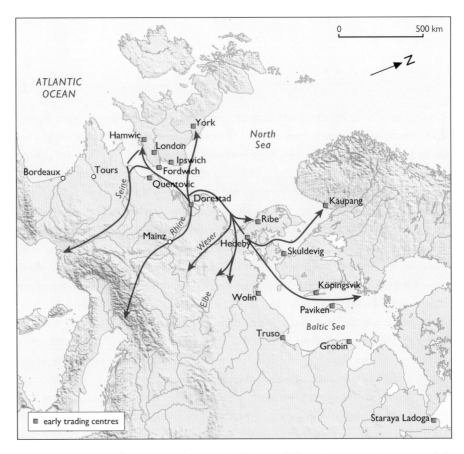

11.1 The trading networks developing between the Baltic and North Sea communities in the sixth and seventh centuries became increasingly active in the eighth century with new and flourishing ports becoming firmly established

Scandinavian Society

From the middle of the first millennium AD improvements in climate allowed many of the farming areas of southern Scandinavia to become more productive, while hitherto marginal land was being brought into cultivation. As the holding capacity of the environment increased, so the population began to grow, leading to far-reaching social changes. Social hierarchies developed, with chieftains holding power over many communities, and the residences of the more successful chieftains grew to become religious and economic centres.

By the late sixth and early seventh centuries many such centres existed in Scandinavia. In the territory of the Svear, around and to the north of Lake Mälaren, the chiefdoms were defined by the rich cemeteries of the Vendel period. This region was the nucleus of the later kingdom of Sweden. In the scattered lands and islands commanding routes between the North Sea and the Baltic, later to become Denmark, many chiefly settlements are known, at Dankirke on Jutland, Gudme on Fyn, Sorte Muld on Bornholm, and at Borre in Vestfold on the Oslo fjord. On the long Atlantic coast of Norway high-status sites have been identified at Klepp, Mære, and, further north, at Borg on Vestvågøy in the Lofoten islands on the Arctic Circle. All were in favourable areas where communities could develop self-sufficient economies and generate surpluses for trade. Already, by this early date, specialist trading centres had begun to emerge: Helgö on Lake Mälaren, Sorte Muld on Bornholm, and Lindeborg on Fyn.

In the eighth century, with the stabilization of the Frankish kingdom immediately to the south and the British kingdoms just across the North Sea, the volume of trade between the Scandinavians and their neighbours began to increase dramatically, leading to the growth of new specialized trading centres. At Ribe, on the west coast of Jutland, craftsmen and traders began to congregate about 705. A few years later land was apportioned into building plots served by a main street, and by the middle of the century it had become a fully fledged urban centre, replacing its neighbour Dankirke. Ribe was ideally sited to benefit from the fast-expanding North Sea trade. Meanwhile, in the first half of the eighth century, on the other side of the Jutland peninsula, a new port town began to develop at Hedeby on the Schlei fjord, and by the tenth century it had grown to be a major centre defended by a massive rampart. From its position it could command the Baltic Sea routes and facilitate trans-peninsular traffic between the Baltic and the North Sea. In Sweden the earlier trading centre of Helgö was eclipsed by the new trading port of Birka on the island of Björkö, which began to capture international trade around the middle of the eighth century. A little later, at the beginning of the ninth century, a new trading port began to develop at Kaupang in southern Vestfold at the head of the Oslo fjord.

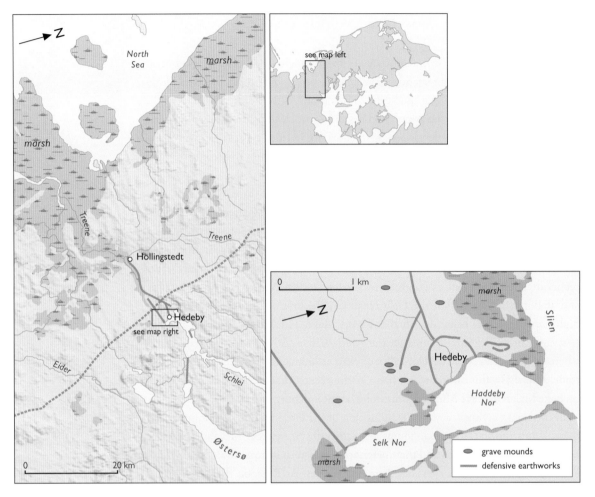

11.2 The port town of Hedeby was situated at the head of the Schlei inlet, providing direct access to the Baltic. Overland routes, protected by a series of defensive earthworks, linked via the river systems to the North Sea. The town therefore commanded the short trans-peninsular route between the two seas and grew rich on its control of trade

The quickening pace of trade was driven in no small part by the increasing demand by the Frankish, Byzantine, and British states for raw materials available only in northern latitudes in lands occupied by the Sami, the Finns, and the Balts, whose livelihood was based on hunting and gathering. The Scandinavians began to profit as middlemen. A rare insight into the nature of the procurement and trading processes involved is given by the activities of a Norwegian nobleman, Ottar, who visited the court of the English king Alfred in the late ninth century. His story was so fascinating to his Anglo-Saxon hosts that it was carefully written down. Ottar's home lay within the Arctic

11.3 Hedeby was founded by King Godfred in 808 as a merchant colony. The settlement soon became a centre for international trade and was defended with earthworks in the tenth century, but by 1100 it had been abandoned, its position usurped by the deep-water port of Schleswig. This reconstruction shows the town as it might have looked in the tenth century

Circle, probably near Tromsø. It is even possible that he lived at the elite settlement discovered at Borg in the Lofoten islands. He was a hunter and explorer in his own right, making long expeditions by ship, sailing north around the North Cape into the White Sea, there hunting whales and walrus—important sources of oil and ivory. He also received tribute from the neighbouring Sami:

> The skins of beasts, the feathers of birds, whale-bone and ship's ropes made from
> walrus hide and sealskin. Each pays according to his rank. The highest in rank
> has to pay fifteen marten skins, five reindeer skins, one bearskin and ten measures
> of feathers, and a jacket of bearskin or other skin, and two ship's ropes. Each must
> be sixty ells long, one made from walrus hide, the other from seal.

Having collected his annual tribute, Ottar sailed south to trade it for southern luxury goods in the markets of Kaupang and Hedeby. His visit to the court of Alfred, bringing gifts of walrus ivory, was probably intended to open up new markets with the English.

Increasing trade, allowing elites to accumulate wealth, encouraged the development of an even more hierarchical society, which eventually led to the emergence of larger kingdoms. The productive and fertile lands of Denmark were the first to be unified in the early eighth century, coinciding with the founding of Ribe as a royal centre. The

11.4 Coins issued by the town of Hedeby depict two types of ship, the proto cog (*upper row*) and the Viking type of vessel (*lower row*)

first king, Angantyr, was encountered by a visiting bishop from Utrecht, and thereafter a succession of kings is recorded. In Norway the widely dispersed nature of the settlements made unification difficult, but the process was begun by Harald Finehair in the 880s with the bringing together of Vestfold and the communities of south-western Norway. The more northern parts that remained outside the union were ruled by individual earls, and it was not until the end of the eleventh century that the country was finally united. Kings are first mentioned in the 820s among the Svear, but only in the late tenth century do we hear of a Swedish king whose authority extended from the east to the west coast. Thus, while Denmark was unified early, it took two to three centuries for Norway and Sweden to emerge as kingdoms. These were centuries of stress and disruption, with competing lineages fighting among themselves for power while rivalries within dynasties over questions of succession exacerbated the level of social tension.

Bringing these various threads together, we can see that the growing trade in exotic goods provided opportunities for elites to build power bases, leading to a more hierarchical and competitive society. This, combined with a steady increase in population, created

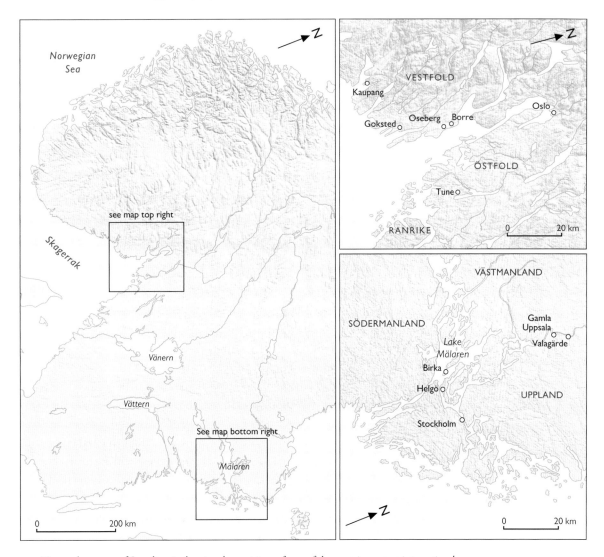

11.5 The southern part of Scandinavia showing the positions of two of the most important international ports of the tenth century, Birka on Lake Mälaren, Sweden, and Kaupang in Vestfold, Norway. Gokstad, Oseberg and Tune around the Oslo fjord were the locations of elaborate ship burials

heightened levels of stress and episodes of widespread conflict. As the social pressures intensified, there was an increasing incentive for entrepreneurial young men to leave home to seek their fortune by raiding and to return with booty and an enhanced reputation to support their claims for status and power. Others chose to go on trading expeditions, setting up trading posts in places like Ireland, where many opportunities for lucrative commercial activity were to be found. As knowledge of the outside world grew, so the attractions of

425

settlement abroad drew those seeking their own land away from the many constraints and uncertainties of home. Some joined the armies marauding in England and France, hoping to find estates to appropriate; others chose the more peaceful option of leading their families to uninhabited islands like the Faroes, Iceland, and Greenland, where land could be had for the taking without the need to fight. Whether raider, trader, or settler, all shared a common heritage: a homeland that was too constrained to hold them, a deeply rooted familiarity with the sea, and an insatiable curiosity which led them on.

People of the Sea

The first settlers who colonized Scandinavia after the last Ice Age were heavily dependent on the sea for their livelihood, and so it has always been. The three kingdoms which emerged during the Viking Age, all reliant on the sea, responded to it in different ways, depending on their geography. Denmark occupied a central position, the low-lying peninsula of Jutland and the dense scatter of islands to the east of it all but blocking the sea-lanes between the North Sea and the Baltic. The control of this route was crucial. There were three channels through: the Øresund between Sjælland and what is now the Swedish mainland, and the Storebælt and Lillebælt on either side of the island of Fyn. The Øresund is a difficult stretch of water with very strong currents, to be avoided if possible, but the other two channels were much safer to use. The northern approach to the channels was controlled by a flotilla based on the small island of Samsø, and in 726 a canal was cut across the island to facilitate the rapid deployment of guard ships. The Danes also controlled the broader approach to the Skagerrak and Kattegat by establishing their authority over the northern shores including the Oslo fjord. From their central position the Danes could engage with Baltic trade through the port of Hedeby and with the North Sea trade through Ribe. They were also ideally sited to act as middlemen between the Arctic hunters and the consumers of the increasingly urbanized Frankish empire. While their land was agriculturally productive and sufficient to provide subsistence for the resident population, they were entirely dependent on their control of the maritime trade routes to support the level of consumption to which the Danish elites had become accustomed.

The situation for those living along the Atlantic coast of Norway was very different. The deeply indented fjords and the inland mountain barrier made travel by land very difficult, but along the coast sheltered channels (*skergardr*), protected by islands and skerries, provided a comparatively safe passage from north to south; this was the 'north road'

11.6 Satellite photograph of the Norwegian coast, deeply incised by fjords and scattered with many islands. The sea naturally featured large in people's lives

which gave Norway its name. The steeply sided fjords, where the settlements clustered, offered only restricted land for cultivation and pasture, so the subsistence economy had to depend on hunting and fishing. Off the south-east coast, south of Cape Stad, and around the Lofoten and Vesterålen islands much further to the north, the fishing banks lay fairly close inland and offered ample catches. These fisheries were the training ground for mariners, who were drawn to the sea in increasing numbers to meet the needs of the growing population. The North Atlantic became their natural home and they learned to cope with its vicissitudes. The stands of fine timber growing on the lower mountain slopes and the copious supplies of iron from further inland provided the essential raw materials for generations of shipbuilders. The Norwegians were born to be sailors.

The communities of southern Sweden faced a different sea: the enclosed Baltic, where land was seldom out of sight. There was little reason for the Swedes to leave their sea. Productive land does not seem to have been in short supply, and they were ideally placed to gather raw materials from the hunters of the north simply by sailing along the low-lying shores of the Gulf of Bothnia and then to tranship their cargoes across the Baltic following the river routes to the markets of the Byzantine and Arab worlds. It was an enclosed, self-sustaining system.

The three emerging Scandinavian states, then, had different imperatives. The Swedes were content to develop their lucrative trading networks with the east; the Danes, while controlling the routes between the Baltic and the North Sea, were beginning to regard the North Sea and the lands beyond—England, Frisia, and France—as their legitimate sphere of interest; while the Norwegians, restricted by the harsh geography of their country, were forced to look outwards to the North Atlantic and its islands for their salvation.

Viking Ships

The spectacular maritime adventures of the Scandinavians could not have been achieved without significant improvements in shipbuilding technology. While it has been argued that the development of sailing ships in the seventh century was the catalyst for the Viking maritime endeavour, it is more likely that it was population pressures and social stresses at home that really drove the improvement in shipbuilding technology. Advances in shipbuilding at this time are well illustrated by a wreck discovered at Kvalsund on Nerlandsøy, Norway, dating to about 700. The vessel was quite small, only 18 metres long with space for ten pairs of oars, but the keel was now substantial enough to enable it to take the weight and stress of a mast. Another significant development was that the strakes (planks) which formed the hull were made of shorter lengths of timber nailed together, instead of single timbers stretching from stem to

11.7 The Oseberg ship, from Vestfold, Norway, was buried in an elite grave c.834. The vessel had been built about fourteen years earlier. The picture shows the ship during excavation in 1904

11.8 (*Right*) The Oseberg ship was restored and reconstructed in 1906–7. The finely carved decoration, seen here at the prow, suggests that the vessel belonged to a member of the elite. As reconstructed the ship is rather wide in the beam. Recent work has suggested that the vessel may have been distorted by the weight of the earth heaped above it and that originally it would have been narrower, with the sides correspondingly higher, making the ship far more seaworthy

stern, showing a new confidence in carpentry and enabling much larger ships to be built. For greater control the steering oar was now attached to the starboard side rather than being freely manipulated. These refinements are found in all the later ships of the Viking Age.

The variety apparent among Viking ships, and the advances in shipbuilding over time, are very clearly represented in a number of ship finds recovered from burials in Norway around the Oslo fjord, and from burials and as wrecks found in Denmark, most notably on Roskilde fjord and at the port of Hedeby. The Norwegian finds span the period 820–910, while the Danish finds tend to

11.9 The Gokstad ship was discovered in a burial mound in Vestfold, Norway. The ship, built of oak, was powered by sixteen pairs of oars with the oar holes placed in the third strake from the top. The vessel was built in the 890s and was buried *c.*910

11.10   In the Gokstad ship the mast was supported by a mast partner attached to the keelson

be later, dating from 850–1050. Thus, the differences that can be observed between the two groups may be due either to regional variation or to development over time.

The three Norwegian ships, from Gokstad and Oseberg in Vestfold, and Tune on the opposite side of the Oslo fjord in Østfold, were well preserved because they were used in burials and were covered by clay mounds, which prevented oxygen from getting to the wood. The earliest, from Oseberg, was built of oak about 820 and was buried as part of a funeral ceremony about fourteen years later. It was 21.5 metres long with a capacity for thirty rowers, fifteen a side, and was built with high curving stem and stern, elaborately carved. As reconstructed it has little freeboard amidships, but this may be due to distortions after burial caused by the weight of clay piled over it.

431

The vessel was designed to be rowed or sailed, but the fittings for the attachment of the mast—the keelson and the mast partner—were comparatively slight, implying that the vessel was not intended to sail in high winds; indeed, some have suggested that it was little more than a royal barge for ceremonial use in safe inshore waters.

The later Gokstad ship, built about 895 and buried fifteen years later, was a little larger than the Oseberg ship, with thirty-two oars. It had a more rounded profile with a much higher freeboard, and its keelson and mast partner were far more substantial, capable of supporting a mast of a size suitable for rough-sea sailing. Its greater depth gave space for cargo or ballast, which would have given added stability. The less well-preserved Tune vessel was also a sturdy ship, but rather smaller, with only twenty-four oars.

The three Norwegian vessels can best be regarded as general-purpose ships: vessels that could be used as warships in raids or for transporting cargo. With a length-to-breadth ratio of about 4:1 they were quite different from the warships found in Denmark, whose ratios of between 7:1 and 11:1 were designed to carry up to eighty oars with little room for cargo. The Danish ship finds, especially the Skuldelev ships deliberately sunk in Roskilde fjord to block the approach to the town in the eleventh century, and ships found during excavations around the Roskilde Viking Ship Museum, show something of the variety of vessels being built in the late Viking Age. There are sturdy cargo ships like Skuldelev 1 and sleek warships like Skuldelev 2/5 and Roskilde 6, which vary in length from 17 to 37 metres.

The earliest ship so far identified that can reasonably be regarded as a true longship was found in a burial at Hedeby and was probably built between 830 and 850: it was no more than 20 metres in length. Another burial find, from Ladby in Denmark, dating to about 900, was a metre or so longer. Both vessels were narrower than the Norwegian ships, with length-to-breadth ratios of about 7:1, but both were comparatively small, taking no more than thirty oars. A more substantial vessel, Hedeby 1, dating to about 985, was found partially burned in Hedeby harbour. It was extremely sleek, 31 metres long, with a length-to-breadth ratio of 11:1 and a capacity for sixty oars. But the most impressive of the longships is Roskilde 6. At 37 metres in length and with about eighty oars it is the largest longship so far known. It was built of Norwegian oak between 1018 and 1032 and was repaired with Baltic timber sometime after 1039. Its massive keelson not only supported a substantial mast and sail but also added strength to the centre of the long keel. With its forty rowing benches, this highly impressive vessel was clearly built under the authority of someone with considerable resources, perhaps even the king himself.

Alongside the longships there was a wide range of cargo ships—tubby vessels seldom more than 22 metres in length. Some, like Skuldelev 6, built in pine from western Norway about 1030, were only half that length. They were designed for a variety of

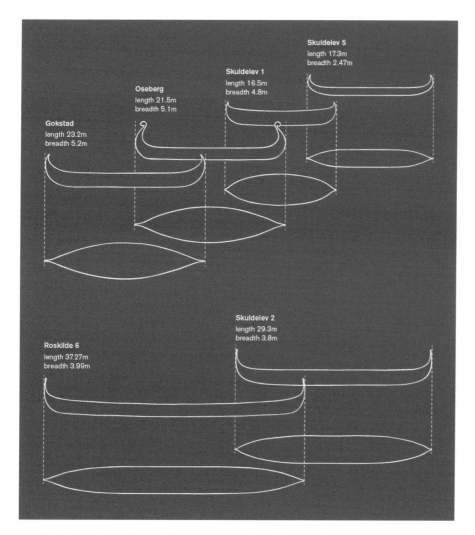

11.11 The relative shapes of some of the Norwegian and Danish ships reflect the purposes for which each was designed. The long, sleek vessels Skuldelev 2 and 5 and Roskilde 6 were warships built for speed and to carry a sizeable force of fighting men; the wide-bodied Skuldelev 1 was a cargo ship. Gokstad and Oseberg, of intermediate proportions, could have served a variety of purposes, including ceremonial

purposes from local journeys carrying farm produce from the fields to the market, to regular trading missions between Scandinavia and Ireland or Iceland, the form and capacity of the vessel being modified to suit its specific purpose and the waters in which it was intended to sail. Reviewing the remains of the vessels from Skuldelev and Roskilde on display in the Viking Ship Museum, Roskilde, and the replicas made of them, is to experience Viking Age shipbuilding at its most responsive—vessels built to

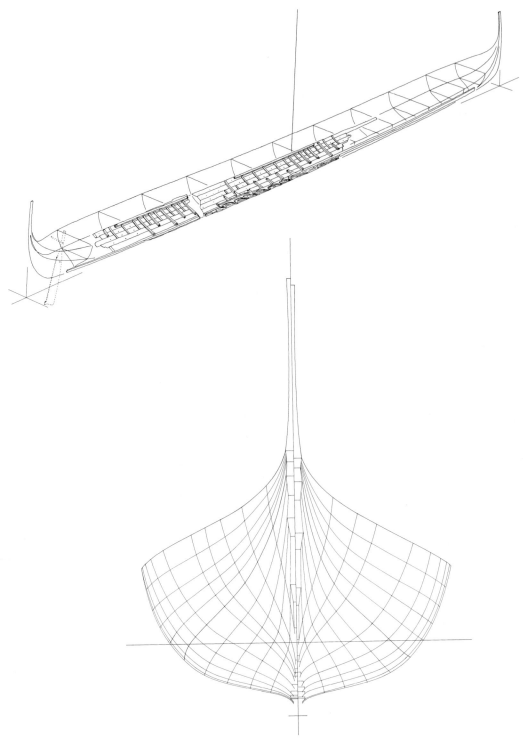

434

11.12 (*Opposite*) The Roskilde 6 vessel, found when the museum was being extended at Roskilde, Denmark, is the largest Viking ship so far discovered (37.27 metres from stem to stern) and could have accommodated eighty rowers. It was built *c.*1025. The reconstruction drawings are preliminary sketches

11.13 (*Above*) Part of the lower hull of Roskilde 6 during excavation in 1997

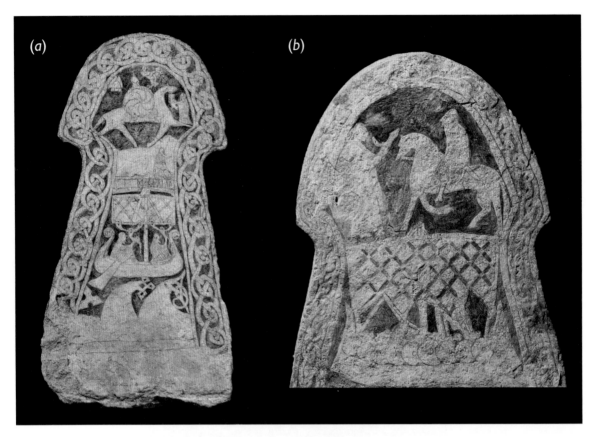

11.14 Images of ships were frequently depicted on the carved memorial stones found on the island of Gotland. (*a*) The Lillbjärs, Stenkyrka, stone, eighth to ninth century. The vessel is in the Viking style. (*b*) The Halla Broa stone, eighth to ninth century. In this example the ship has a vertical prow and stern. On memorial stones of this kind there may have been some artistic licence in the depiction of ships

satisfy all the varying needs of an enterprising seafaring community by craftsmen sure of their skills and with a deep understanding of what the sea demanded.

Facing the Ocean

However well built the ships, survival at sea depended on seamanship. Until the beginning of the eighth century Danish and Norwegian shipping for the most part kept to coastal waters, the Danes working the approaches to the Baltic and the coasts of Frisia down to the Rhine mouth while the Norwegians focused on the long, protected coastal passage between the mainland and the offshore islands and skerries. It was indeed a long passage.

436

11.15 The cemetery of Lindholm Høje, Sweden. The cemetery began in the seventh century and continued into the Viking period. Many of the graves were marked by settings of stones arranged in the form of a ship (*skibsætninger*). The prominence of graves of this kind reflects the close ties people had to the sea in the maritime region of Sweden

From the extreme south of Norway to Cape Stad was four degrees of latitude, and from Cape Stad to the North Cape was a further nine degrees. Sailors making this south-to-north journey would have quickly learned that the height of the sun measured at midday and the height of the Pole Star viewed at night increased or decreased as one progressed along the route. By constant observation and good memory it would have been possible to estimate the relative position of the vessel between departure and arrival. It is clear from the sagas that this technique of position-finding was widely used during the Viking Age. How far back in time the knowledge went is a matter of speculation, but there is no reason why foragers plying the same coasts in the Mesolithic period should not have been aware of these matters and used the information to position themselves during their seasonal hunting expeditions. By the early eleventh century astronomical knowledge was well established. One practitioner, Oddi Helgason, or Stjörnu-Oddi (Star Oddi) as he was known, had worked out details of the sun's azimuth measured in terms of half the sun's diameter, from which he was able to describe the sun's declination between the solstices.

All the time that coasting was the principal maritime activity, astronomical observations would have been used as an aid to positioning, but when ships began to sail into the open ocean, initially in search of fish on the more distant banks, being able to estimate latitude became of increasing importance: staying on a latitude gave the ship's master greater reassurance of returning safely to a familiar coast. By the eighth century, when journeys to the Faroes and the Shetlands were being made, requiring at least two days and nights at sea, a sailor wanting to journey to Shetland would sail up or down the Norwegian coast to a fixed point on the coast of Hordaland at around 60° north and then would sail out to sea, staying as close to the latitude as possible to reach Shetland. By maintaining the latitude on his return he could be sure of coming in sight of a coast that was familiar.

Measuring latitude afloat was more difficult than on land, but it could be done. The complexity of the sea lore that had to be committed to memory is nicely displayed in a mid-thirteenth-century text which describes how a party of men hunting off the Greenland coast were able to take measurements of the sun even at night.

> It was then freezing there at night, but the sun shone both night and day, and, when it was in the south, was only so high that if a man lay athwartships in a six-oared boat, the shadow of the gunwale meant the sun fell upon his face; but at midnight it was as high as it is at home in the settlement when it is in the north-west.

By the thirteenth century, after several centuries of open-ocean sailing, instructions for sailors showed that latitude sailing was by now so well established that ships' masters were prepared to keep the vessels on the open ocean, often out of sight of land, for long periods of time. In one of the recensions of the Icelandic *Landnámabók* (Book of Settlements), instructions for sailing from Norway to Greenland are given:

> From Hernar in Norway sail due west for Hvarf [now Cape Farewell] in Greenland, and then will you sail north of Shetland so that you can just sight it in clear weather, but south of the Faroe Islands so that the sea appears halfway up the mountain slopes; but steer south of Iceland so that you may have birds and whales therefrom.

The intention here is to stay on latitude but to give the ship's master reassuring sea-marks while keeping him well clear of dangerous coasts. By taking this course and sailing for sixteen hundred kilometres across the open sea, the vessel would eventually approach Greenland, a comfortable hundred kilometres or so north of its southern-most extremity, Hvarf. To make such a journey keeping to latitude was no mean feat of navigation given the need to counter currents and adverse winds.

The mention of sighting birds and whales south of Iceland is a reminder that there were many indications of position that a skilled sailor would have known. In all this, birds feature large. Certain sea-birds had distinct habits of feeding which kept them within a known radius of land, while the migrating flights of others indicated the direction of the feeding grounds where they were heading. The position of banks could be judged from the changing pattern of the swell or a proliferation of fish, while the approach to the east coast of Greenland was often signalled by the presence of floating ice. Such signs would have been both helpful and reassuring to a ship's company who had been at sea for many days on end.

If latitude could be established with reasonable accuracy by celestial phenomena, longitude could not. The only way to estimate distances travelled from east to west was by dead reckoning based on assessment of distance travelled in a day. The term *dægr-sigling* (day's sailing) is used in various texts, some implying that there were two *dægr* in every twenty-four hours, others that a day's sailing meant a full day, but to complicate matters further one source used the term to mean an actual distance of 144 nautical miles. These confusions apart, a sailor will have known what he understood by the term and would have applied it accordingly.

Navigation in the open sea in the days before the advent of the compass relied on the ability to observe the sun and the night sky. For short journeys taking only a few days a skilled mariner would have been able to forecast weather conditions and to hold back if the winds were unfavourable or the skies overcast, but for the longer journeys no such assurances could be given and the risk of adverse winds springing up or long periods of fog setting in had to be faced. Changes of wind direction driving the vessel off course could be countered so long as the sun or the Pole Star could be seen, but with the onset of fog it was easy to lose all sense of direction—to lose one's reckoning. Such a state, known as *hafvilla*, is mentioned on a number of occasions in the sagas. It was often preceded by a drop in the wind and the development of fog. The *Laxdæla Saga* (one of the Icelandic sagas) describes just such an event: 'They met with bad weather that summer. There was much fog and the winds were light and unfavourable, what there were of them. They drifted far and wide on the high sea. Most of those on board completely lost their reckoning.'

There is a record of one ship remaining in this state for two weeks. Crews would have dreaded the *hafvilla* more for its fearsome disorientation than for any danger. So long as they remained on the open sea away from land, they could wait for the skies to clear to give them the direction and allow them to regain their correct latitude. In one famous example in the later tenth century a Norwegian sailor, Bjarni Herjolfsson, set out from Iceland to join his father in Greenland, but 'the fair wind died away and northerly winds and fogs succeeded and they did not know which way they were going and this went on for many days'. Eventually the sun broke through and they were able to get their bearings, but when land was sighted, Herjolfsson realized they were past the longitude of Greenland. By resetting their course he eventually arrived safely at his father's settlement. The land they had glimpsed was the eastern seaboard of North America.

The many stories told in the sagas leave little doubt that the Norwegians of the Viking Age were remarkable sailors, willing to face the dangers of the open North Atlantic in their small craft armed only with the accumulated experience of generations passed on in oral traditions, and their grim determination. Their exploits in the northern ocean, before the advent of the compass, are little short of astonishing.

The Earliest Overseas Adventures: Britain and Ireland, 783–850

The *Anglo-Saxon Chronicle* provides a convenient date for the beginning of the Viking adventures overseas, for under the year 793 it tells us that, on 8 June, 'the ravages of heathen men miserably destroyed God's church on Lindisfarne with plunder and slaughter'. The sea-borne attack on the Northumbrian monastery was a shocking event, but it may not have been the first recorded confrontation between Norse seamen and the British Isles. Sometime between 786 and 802 three shiploads of Northmen had landed on Portland off the Dorset coast and had killed a royal official who went to meet them, assuming them to be traders. They were a long way from home and were evidently spying out the potential of southern Britain, but whether they were intent on raiding or trading remains unknown.

These early recorded encounters raise the question of the date and progress of the first Norse incursions into the British Isles and Ireland. The logic of geography would suggest that the earliest landfalls, made by ships sailing westwards from southern Norway, would most likely have been on the Shetlands, the Orkneys, and Caithness. Shetland was only two days' and two nights' sail from Hordaland and could well have been discovered by boats venturing westward into the open ocean in pursuit of shoals of fish. Sightings of distant islands would have attracted the curious-minded, encouraging them to explore still further, and once the Northern Isles and adjacent coasts were known, more adventurous souls would have been drawn on to the Western Isles, soon to discover Ireland and the Irish Sea. Indeed, it may have been by continuing on this route that the three ships recorded in the *Anglo-Saxon Chronicle* eventually found themselves off the Dorset coast. Raiders soon followed. The monastery on Iona, prominent in the western seaways, suffered three attacks, in 795, 802, and 806, and the Irish annals record twenty-six Viking attacks on monasteries in the period 795–820. For the most part these early encounters would have been small-scale ventures involving only a few vessels at a time.

Raiding was evidently a significant part of the process of interaction between Norway and the countries described as *vestan um haf* (west over the sea), but so, too, were trade and settlement. Which took precedence is not always easy to say. Traditionally there seems to have been the assumption that raiding was the spearhead, but the situation may have been more complicated. Given the pressure on land at home, the imperative to find new lands to settle may have taken priority. Initial contacts by fishermen, under way by the eighth century, opened the way for people to establish new homes in the Northern Isles and Caithness by peaceful means, or by force. Place names and genetic evidence show there to have been a considerable Norse incursion into these areas, and there is ample archaeological evidence from both settlements and burial sites to support this, though it is difficult to say how early in the eighth century the influx began. It may have been from these newly settled areas that many of the raiding parties set out to pillage the Western Isles and Ireland. The *Orkneyinga Saga* gives an intriguing account of what purports to be the lifestyle of the Viking Svein Asleifarson in the mid-twelfth century. It is clearly anachronistic since raiding was long since over by this time, but the story may well embody a memory of life as it had been on Orkney two centuries before:

> In spring he had more than enough to occupy him, with a great deal of seed to sow, which he saw to carefully himself. Then, when the job was done, he would go off plundering in the Hebrides and in Ireland on what he called his 'spring trip', then back home just after midsummer, where he stayed until the cornfields had been reaped and the grain was safely taken in. After that he would go off raiding again and never come back until the first month of winter was ended. This he called his 'autumn trip'.

The settlement of the Hebrides and of the adjacent western coasts of Scotland probably followed not long after the initial settlement of the Northern Isles, providing a new springboard for further attacks on Ireland and the lands around the Irish Sea.

The raids on Ireland began in 795 with the plundering of the monastery on Rathlin Island off the north-west coast. Three years later it was the turn of St Patrick's Island near the town of Skerries in County Dublin. By 807 the raiders were exploring the west coast, attacking Inishmurray off Sligo and Roscam in Galway Bay. In 821 there were raids on Howth and Wexford Harbour. The next year it was the turn of Cork, and in 824 the remote monastery perched on Skellig Michael was attacked and its father superior taken hostage. For the next four years the raiders concentrated on the east coast. In all probability the Welsh monasteries also came under attack at this time, but records are sparse. These early raids were small-scale hit-and-run affairs, picking off monasteries that were within easy reach of the sea, enabling the raiders to be off before local resistance could be organized. On those occasions when local forces were gathered in time to confront the raiders, the Vikings fared badly, presumably because their numbers were small.

Throughout the 830s pressure intensified. This is best explained by supposing that Norse settlers from the Western Isles were now joining those coming from the Northern Isles and from Norway, the more distant bands leapfrogging over the recently settled islands. Raids came thick and fast. In 831 north Louth was attacked, and the wealth of the religious establishments in Armagh became a particular attraction the following year, when multiple raids were mounted. Now emboldened by success, and coming in larger forces, the raiders began to venture further inland, making forays thirty to forty kilometres from the sea. Every year there were many attacks involving increasing numbers of raiders. The fact that they were now taking place late in the year suggests that the Vikings were overwintering on small islands. The year 837 saw a massive force of sixty ships sail up the Boyne and the Liffey, while another fleet used the Shannon to reach Lough Derg, where they pillaged and burned the monastery on Holy Island. Two years later a Viking fleet sailed up the river Bann to Lough Neagh, using it as a base to plunder the north. That they were still there in 841 implies that they were now regularly overwintering. It was for this year that the first *longphorts* were recorded, one at Linn Dúachaill, County Louth, the other at Dublin. These were permanent fortresses built to protect both the men and their ships. The appearance of *longphorts* marks a new phase in the Viking enterprise. The *Annals of St Bertin* sum up the situation, recording that by 847, 'after they had been under attack from the Vikings for many years, the Irish were made tributaries to them; the Vikings have possessed themselves without opposition of all the islands round about and have settled on them'. That said, attempts by the Vikings to take over inland areas were successfully resisted by the Irish kings, who won a series of land-battles fought between 845 and 848, killing many hundreds of invaders.

Throughout the first half of the ninth century the aim of the Vikings had been to gather loot, mainly from ecclesiastical establishments within easy reach of the sea. They also took captives: churchmen and other members of the elite who could be ransomed for a good price and, increasingly, ordinary men and women who could be sold on to become slaves working on farms in the Western and Northern Isles and in Norway. As trading networks developed, slaves became an increasingly valuable commodity in the markets of the Arab world. Little wonder that the threat of the Northmen was a fearsome prospect for a monk cowering in the remote solitude of his monastery. On one stormy night a monk recorded his appreciation of the weather, scribbling in the margins of a manuscript:

> The wind is fierce tonight
> It tosses the sea's white hair
> I fear no wild Vikings
> Sailing the quiet main.

In the North Sea and Beyond, 750–850

Until the middle of the ninth century the Norwegians concentrated their overseas activity on northern and western Britain, while the Danes restricted their activities to the North Sea, the English Channel, and beyond. It was probably threats from Denmark that prompted King Offa of Mercia to order the defence of the Kentish coast in 792, and it is worth considering whether it was the Danes rather than Norwegians who raided Lindisfarne in 793 and Jarrow or Monkwearmouth on the Tyne the next year. At this early stage the Danish activity, such as it was, focused on England rather than the North Sea coast of mainland Europe, which was part of the strong centralized Frankish kingdom controlled by Charlemagne. The Frisian coastal zone had passed to the Franks in the 770s and Saxony was finally conquered in 804, bringing the Carolingian empire to the very borders of Denmark. Tensions between the two states grew, and in 810 the Danish king Godfred tried to pre-empt an attack planned by Charlemagne by sending a fleet of two hundred ships to ravage the coast and islands of Frisia, which they did with some success. The tense situation ended when Godfred was assassinated, and an uneasy peace was concluded.

The death of Charlemagne in 814 heralded a period of uncertainty, providing the Danes with the opportunity to attack. In 819, while a large Danish fleet was still at sea threatening the coast of Saxony, a flotilla of thirteen Danish ships set out to raid the Carolingian coast. They attacked Flanders, the Seine estuary, and western Poitou, and took the island of Noirmoutier south of the Loire estuary. Here they overwintered, making several forays along the coast of Aquitania before returning home with much booty later in 820. Without an adequate navy the Franks were able to do little to counter sea-borne attacks. Particularly vulnerable was the coast of Frisia and Flanders, where the major trading ports offered attractive prizes for raiders. The important port of Dorestad was attacked and destroyed in 834 with much slaughter, those who survived being carried off as slaves. It was attacked again in 835 and 836, and raids on Frisia continued the following year, when the island of Walcheren in the estuary of the Scheldt was plundered and used as a base for further raids. Eventually, in 850, Dorestad was ceded to the Danes, who, in return, were expected to protect the Frisian coasts from further attack.

With the death of the Carolingian king Louis the Pious in 840, internal strife caused by the succession dispute greatly weakened the empire, triggering a new bout of sea-borne raids. In 841 the *Annals of St Bertin* record that 'Danish pirates sailed down the Channel and attacked Rouen, [and] plundered the town with pillage, fire and sword …'. They also raided the rich churches along the Seine, including Jumièges and Saint-Wandrille. The Seine remained a popular destination with Viking warlords and in 845 they had penetrated as far as Paris, which was only saved when the king paid a

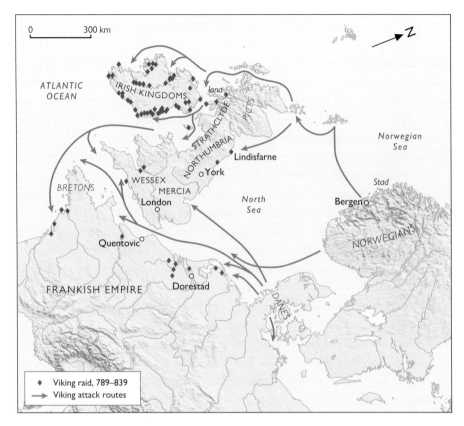

11.16 The first recorded Viking raid on Britain dates to 789. For the next fifty years Norse and Danish seafarers raided the coast of Britain, Ireland, and France. To counter attacks fortifications were erected along the coasts of the Netherlands and Belgium

massive tribute in gold and silver. The trading post of Quentovic, on the coast north of the Somme estuary, was attacked in 842 and much of the settlement destroyed 'except for those buildings which [the attackers] were paid to spare'. The following year it was the turn of Nantes on the Loire to suffer. Here, besides the loot and protection money, there were wealthy businessmen to take hostage. The Viking war bands who made their bases on the Seine and the Loire were probably largely Danish in origin, but the *Annals* also mention Norwegians from Vestfold settling on an island and raiding the coasts of Aquitania. It is possible that they arrived via the Irish Sea.

From the base on the Loire further expeditions went south. In 844 a force entered the Gironde estuary and sailed up the Garonne to Toulouse, and four years later Saintes and Périgueux were attacked. The Vikings who had explored the Garonne continued south in 844 to probe the coasts of Galicia and Andalucía. The first port reached, La

Coruña, put up an effective resistance, but at Lisbon, Cádiz, and Seville the raiders were more successful, even holding Seville for a time before being ousted by superior Muslim forces. It was a serious engagement. The bodies of slain Vikings were strung up on the palm trees in the city for all to see, and two hundred Viking heads were sent to allies in Tangier as a display of the city's prowess and resilience. The *madjus* ('heathen wizards'), as the attackers were called, had seen the wealth and opportunities of Andalucía, but it was to be fifteen years before they returned.

For the first thirty years or so of the ninth century, England lay outside the Danish sphere of interest, their activities being focused on the opportunities offered by the European coastline of the Carolingian empire, but after a series of successes in Frisia they turned their attention to Britain, in 835 landing a large contingent on the Isle of Sheppey in the Thames estuary, from where further raids could be mounted. Thereafter attacks intensified. In 838, somewhere in Cornwall, the West Saxons defeated a Viking force which had landed on the north coast of Somerset. In 842 Vikings who had recently raided the Frankish port of Quentovic crossed the Channel to attack its English counterpart, Hamwic, in Southampton Water. Nor did the east coast escape. Raids were mounted on Lindsey and, in 844, on the coast of Northumbria: England was now firmly in the sights of the Danes, and in 850 a large Danish force together with its fleet overwintered on the Isle of Thanet, east Kent. It was the beginning of a new chapter.

Atlantic Adventurers, 850–900

The Viking enclaves now established on the Seine and the Loire continued their raiding expeditions late into the second half of the ninth century using the sea and rivers to get them to within striking distance of lucrative objectives, particularly the main towns that could be forced to pay protection money or, if they defaulted, could be pillaged. The situation is vividly summed up by Ermentarius of Noirmoutier, who in the 860s, looking back over the previous decades, wrote:

> The number of ships increases, the endless flood of Vikings never ceases to grow bigger. Everywhere Christ's people are the victims of massacre, burning, and plunder. The Vikings overrun all that lies before them, and none can withstand them. They seize Bordeaux, Périgueux, Limoges, Angoulême, Toulouse; Angers, Tours, and Orléans are made deserts. Ships past counting voyage up the Seine, and throughout the entire region evil grows strong. Rouen is laid waste, looted and burned: Paris, Beauvais, Meaux are taken. Melun's stronghold is razed to the ground, Chartres occupied, Évreux and Bayeux looted, and every town invested.

Allowing for a degree of exaggeration there can be little doubt that Viking enthusiasm for well-rewarded adventures was taking its toll on France. Plunder was a prime motive, but bound up with this was a desire for fame. To have led a successful expedition and to return home with loot and stories of wild daring was a sure way to gather followers and to enhance one's status within the broader community. The more exotic the lands visited, the greater the reputation gained.

These mixed motives lay behind an audacious expedition led by two Danes, Bjorn and Hastein, which set out with sixty-two ships, probably from the Loire, in 859. Their voyage to the south, following the one made fifteen years earlier, was to last for four years. The early stages were not auspicious. After some desultory raids in northern Iberia, two of the ships, laden with gold and silver, were captured by Muslims somewhere off the coast of Portugal. Further disappointment followed when, having sailed up the Guadalquivir, they found Seville was well able to defend itself. Moving on, they sailed through the Strait of Gibraltar, plundering Algeciras on the way, before crossing to the coast of North Africa, where they rounded up a large haul of captives. Some were exchanged for ransom; others were sold as slaves. Among those captured were native Africans—'blue men' and 'black men'—who were eventually traded on to Ireland. The Danes continued along the coast of Murcia to the Balearics, thence to the French coast, raiding as they went. Narbonne was one of the towns to suffer. It was now late in the year and time to find a safe place to overwinter. The Rhône delta had its attractions and they were able to find a convenient island in the Camargue where the ships and men would be safe. From here they launched raiding expeditions up-river, attacking Arles, Nîmes, and Valence, but the Franks responded vigorously. In spring the force journeyed eastwards along the coast and round the Gulf of Genoa. One of their aims seems to have been to raid Rome—a worthy goal for a Viking intent on enhancing a reputation. In the event they found a city which they understood to be Rome and spent some time gaining entry, but when they found that it was in fact Luna they set it on fire and slaughtered the male inhabitants. From there they sailed up the Arno, sacking Pisa and Fiesole before continuing their journey south. The sources are unclear about what happened then but hint that the Vikings may have reached Alexandria before beginning the return to Gibraltar. Once through the strait they were attacked by a Muslim fleet but continued undaunted. When they eventually reached Navarre, they took the opportunity to strike inland and captured Pamplona, gaining huge returns by ransoming wealthy captives. In 862 the force arrived back on the Loire, having lost two-thirds of their ships.

By the standards of the time this would have been an honourable venture, a feat of skill and daring displaying leadership of a high order. The remnants of the force had returned with shiploads of plunder and exotic foreign captives, but even more

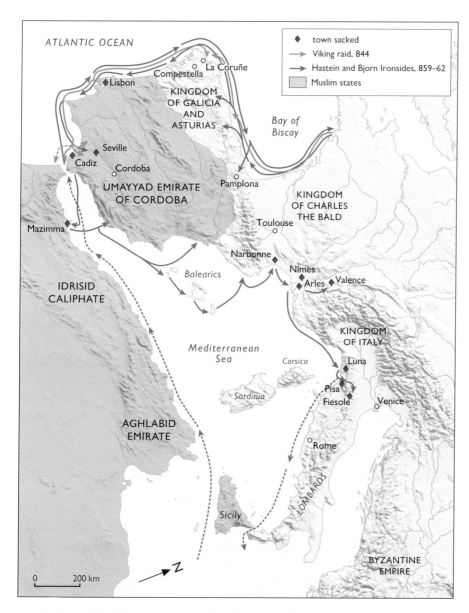

11.17 In the middle of the ninth century the Viking raiders became more ambitious. In 844 one expedition raided along the Atlantic coast of Iberia, reaching the Strait of Gibraltar. Fifteen years later another group set off for the Mediterranean on an expedition that was to last four years. After sacking Pisa they probably sailed into the eastern Mediterranean, but no details of this part of the adventure are recorded. Eventually the remnant of the expedition returned home

importantly, they had stories to tell of foreign places no Viking had ever been before. This was adventure at its most flamboyant.

The Danes in England, 850–900

The growing confidence of the Danish armies encamped in the estuaries of the Somme and the Seine posed a new threat to the English kingdoms. The island was rich, its rulers divided, and it was only a day's journey away. The overwintering of a Danish army on Thanet in 850 and on Sheppey the following year marked the beginning of a new phase in the confrontation. Kent and the Thames estuary was a favoured point of entry, and in 851 a massive force said to have involved 350 ships approached, attacking Canterbury and London, but was defeated by the English. Nine years later, in 860, a navy sailed from the Somme along the English Channel to Southampton Water intent on taking Winchester but was repelled. In these two failed attempts the Danes had learned something of the strength of the kingdom of Wessex, and it may have been this knowledge that encouraged them to turn to easier targets in the east of England.

A new determined effort came in 865, when what was described as 'a great heathen army' crossed to East Anglia and took up winter quarters. How many men were involved is unknown but estimates tend to favour anything between a thousand and three thousand. This was far more than a raid: it was an attempt to establish control of a territory. For the next four years the Danish army was on the move through East Anglia, Mercia, and Northumbria, fighting when necessary and taking protection money and supplies when agreements could be reached. It was an ordered progression through the midlands and the north designed to demonstrate strength and to gather political and strategic information. The land grab began when, in 869, the king of East Anglia was killed and his kingdom was appropriated. The submission of Mercia and Northumberland followed, with land in both kingdoms being taken for settlement. The colonization of Mercia began in 874 and of Northumberland two years later: the conquerors 'shared out the land of the Northumbrians, and they proceeded to plough and support themselves'.

Meanwhile, Wessex stood firm. In 871 a Danish force had marched on Reading, where they were joined by 'a great summer army' presumably newly arrived via the Thames. Wessex was persuaded to make peace, and an unstable equilibrium ensued. A second attempted invasion of Wessex was mounted in 875 with little success. In 877–8 the Danish army took up winter quarters at Gloucester in preparation for a third attempt. After some initial gains the Danes, led by King Guthrum, were finally beaten by the West Saxons at Edington in Wiltshire. A new Danish army had arrived

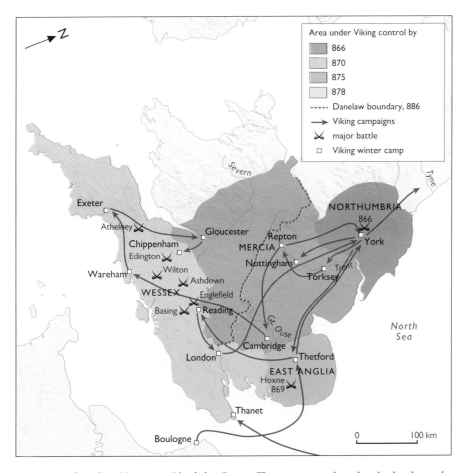

11.18 In 865 the Viking 'Great Army' landed in Britain. They overwintered on the island and over the next thirteen years rampaged widely, as far west as Exeter and as far north as the river Tyne

at Fulham on the Thames to join the attack on Wessex but, hearing of the defeat, they fled the country and turned their attentions instead to France and the Low Countries. After eight years of fighting, Wessex, under its king, Alfred, remained intact and was greatly strengthened by the experience. When two more Danish armies arrived in Kent and the Thames estuary in 892, one of 250 ships, the other of eighty, they could make little headway and eventually dispersed, some to East Anglia, some to Northumberland, and the rest back to the Seine estuary.

The number of Danish fighting men arriving in England between 865 and 892 was considerable. Though many will have died in battle and some returned to the Continent, a high percentage settled down in the east, the midlands, and the north—a

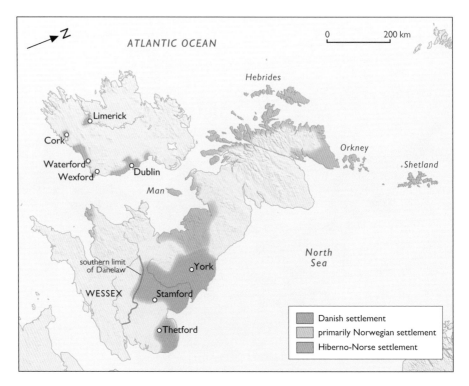

11.19 By the end of the ninth century large parts of Britain had been settled by Danes and Norwegians. In Ireland, in spite of extensive raiding, only small enclaves of Vikings had managed to settle to found trading colonies

fact well attested by the dense distribution of Scandinavian place names which respect the boundary formally agreed by Alfred and Guthrum defining the southern limit of Danish interests, the Danelaw. The leading Danes took over existing estates from English owners, opening up the country for migrants from Denmark seeking new opportunities. A lively trade developed across the North Sea with Jorvik (York) serving as the main port of entry. The archaeological evidence shows that contacts between eastern England and Denmark were maintained throughout the tenth century, during which time people moved freely to and fro across the North Sea.

The escalation of the Danish onslaught after 850 alerted the English to the growing importance of ships in the defence of the realm. King Alfred had personal experience of this. In 875 we learn from the *Anglo-Saxon Chronicle* that the king 'went out to sea with an armed fleet and fought with seven ship-rovers, one of whom he took and dispersed the others'. Later, in 882, the king was again at sea confronting four Danish ships. He 'took two wherein all the men were slain and the other two surrendered'. The

11.20 The Orkney and Shetland islands were heavily settled by Norwegians. Here at the Brough of Birsay, Orkney, a settlement of Viking longhouses can be seen. Settlement began *c*.800, and in the early twelfth century a church was built (in the square enclosure). Birsay has the attraction of being a fertile island. It can be reached only at low tide, giving the residents a degree of protection

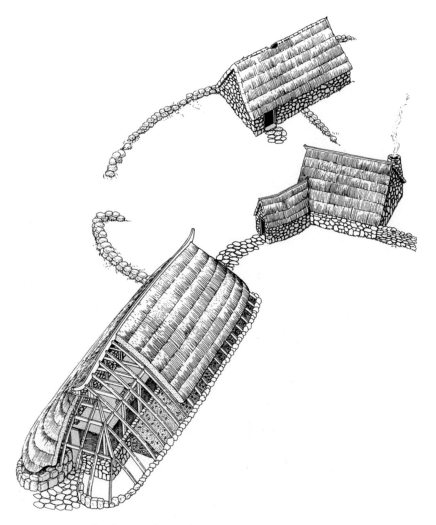

11.21 Reconstruction of a Viking Age farmstead excavated at Ribblehead, North Yorkshire. The longhouse was accompanied by ancillary buildings serving as a kitchen and a workshop

engagements were small-scale, but the first-hand experience was put to good use when in 896 the king set about organizing an English navy, issuing instructions for

> building longships against the esks [Danish warships], which were full-nigh twice as long as the others. Some had sixty oars, some more; and they were both swifter and steadier, and also higher than the others. They were not shaped either after the Frisian or the Danish model, but so as he himself thought that they might be most serviceable.

452

11.22 The Viking cemetery excavated at Westness on Rousay, Orkney, contained a range of burials, of which the richest was of a female. Two boat burials of males were also found. In the one shown here the prow and stern of the boat were packed with stones defining a central burial chamber

No actual English warships of this period have yet been found, but if they were indeed as revolutionary as they sound, it raises the intriguing question of the relationship of Alfred's longships to the longships of the Danes, the earliest of which so far known are Hedeby 1, dating to 985, which had about sixty oars, and Roskilde 6, dating to about 1025, which had about eighty oars. Could it be that Alfred's innovations inspired Danish shipbuilders?

453

11.23 Danish tombstone found in St Paul's churchyard in London. It is decorated in the energetic Ringerike style dating to the eleventh century. Originally the stone would have been elaborately painted

The only English vessel of this period so far discovered is a cargo boat found in the marshes of Kent at Graveney. She was built in the 890s and abandoned about 950. The hull was built plank first of cleft oak, iron-fastened in clinker style, and sits broadly in the Nordic tradition, being double-ended with a side steering oar and a mast taking a square sail stepped amidships. But there are differences. She was fuller in section with massive close-spaced floor timbers and her planks were fastened with nails driven through treenails—characteristics which hark back to methods used in much earlier Romano-Celtic vessels. Given the complex cultural history of the southern North Sea region, this combination of traditions is not surprising.

Alfred's creation of an English navy, and the system of fortified settlements (burghs) which he initiated to provide local militias at strategic points throughout the kingdom, greatly increased the military strength of Wessex, while the long conflict with the Danes generated a new sense of English identity. Under his successors, Edward

11.24 The Graveney boat, excavated on the Kentish marshes east of Faversham in 1970, was built *c*.895 and abandoned fifty years or so later. Although the vessel shares constructional features with contemporary Nordic boats, there are significant differences which suggest that the British shipwrights were largely following their own traditions

the Elder and Athelstan, the English territories held by the Danes were systematically reconquered, and towards the end of his reign (924–39) Athelstan could claim to be 'king of the Anglo-Saxons and Danes' and 'king of the whole of Britain'.

Settlers and Traders around the Irish Sea

Events in Ireland in the 840s showed that the local kings were strong enough to rein in the excesses of Viking aggression, forcing those already settled to realize that there were no easy pickings to be had. But by now Dublin was established as a defended Viking enclave, and soon others were to spring up at estuaries around the coast, at Wexford, Waterford, Cork, and Limerick. They could, of course, be used as bases from which to mount raids along the rivers or by sea, but they were above all centres for commerce, increasingly serving as ports-of-trade. Such facilities were of value to the indigenous population since they provided markets for their produce and access to goods from overseas. They were also centres where craftsmen could congregate, creating a wide range of products to meet local needs. Since the Viking ports were advantageous to the Irish, they could be tolerated, allowing an uneasy symbiosis to develop, but increasingly the Irish kings looked on them with envy.

Constrained by the aggressive attitude of the Irish war leaders and by competition among themselves, the Vikings began to look to other lands around the Irish Sea. In 866 the Dublin-based Vikings turned their attention to Pictland (present-day Scotland north of the Forth), overrunning the country and extracting tribute. Four years later they captured Dumbarton, bringing the Britons of Strathclyde (Cumbria and Lowland Scotland) under their control and returning triumphant in two hundred ships laden with loot and large numbers of captives: it had been a lucrative venture. But in Ireland pressures were building as squabbles between the different Viking enclaves and increasingly aggressive attitudes towards them from the Irish began to take their toll. The permanent trading enclaves in which the Vikings had settled in Ireland had greatly reduced their mobility and made them easy prey. In 866 they were driven out of northern Ireland, and over the next few decades the settlements at Wexford, Waterford, and Limerick were attacked and defeated. Finally, in 902 the joint Irish forces of Brega and Leinster descended on the prize, Dublin. 'The pagans were driven from the fortress of Dublin and they abandoned a good number of their ships, and escaped half dead after they had been wounded and broken.' Many of those driven out of Ireland settled on the Isle of Man and in the coastal regions of Cheshire. Some went to Cumbria; others chose to join in with the settlement of Iceland.

The Tenth Century and Later

For the next two centuries Norwegians and Danes were active in western France, Britain, and Ireland, sometimes working separately, sometimes together, and sometimes in opposition to each other. The picture is complex but may be briefly summarized.

In France the Carolingian kings came to accept the inevitable, that the main river estuaries, especially the Seine and the Loire, were a Viking domain. By building bridges and fortifications they could hinder attacks on cities further up-river, but in the lower estuaries the Vikings were here to stay, and by formally recognizing the fact in treaties and land agreements the French hoped that those already in possession of land would prevent other raiders from approaching from the sea. Thus it was that the Northman Rollo was recognized as the count of the Rouen district in 911. Over time Rollo's successors extended their hold over north-western France as far west as the Cotentin peninsula, allowing other Northmen to settle, including some arriving from Ireland, creating the duchy of Nor(d)mannia: Normandy. In the lower Loire valley a similar policy was adopted in 921 by granting the Northmen large tracts of land around Nantes. Between the two areas of settlement lay the peninsula of Brittany, which, throughout the ninth century, had been subject to sporadic Viking raids. Now it became a focus for renewed Viking interest. In the early years of the tenth century the remnants of the roving Norwegian army, aided by Rollo, began a series of increasingly powerful attacks which, in 914, led to the overrunning of the entire peninsula, forcing some Bretons to flee to England. The fight-back began in 936 when the exiles, aided by the English, captured Nantes and began to flush out the pillaging bands. Although the Northmen from the Seine region mounted further raids in the 940s and 960s, Brittany managed to maintain its independence.

Meanwhile, in Ireland, Viking raiding began again with the arrival of a great fleet at Waterford in 914. It had come from Brittany, having spent time en route raiding in the Severn estuary. More arrived the following year. In 917 leaders of the Norse dynasty exiled from Dublin to northern England returned to join in the assault, eventually retaking the city. Then followed a long period of conflict during which the Viking enclaves sometimes served as allies of the Irish kings in their incessant strivings for supremacy. There was now frequent movement across the Irish Sea as the aspirations of the Viking rulers of Dublin and York began to intermesh. It was a confused period of endemic warfare which was still rumbling on when the Anglo-Norman armies arrived in Ireland in 1170. During this time there were raids on Wales. Anglesey and the Lleyn peninsula were subject to attack in 961 from Dublin and in 980 and 987 from the Western Isles, while place name evidence suggests that Vikings had settled in south-west Wales and were regularly sailing along the Welsh south coast.

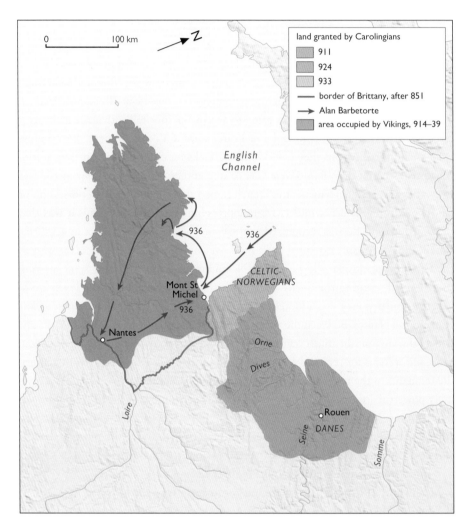

11.25 In the early tenth century Danes were allowed to settle in the lower Seine valley, the settlement rapidly expanding westwards to the Cotentin, where Norwegians from Ireland arrived to make their homes. The territory was known as the land of the Northmen, Nor(d)mannia (Normandy). Other groups of Vikings attempted to take over Brittany but were eventually repelled

Nor was England to escape. Raids resumed in 980, and in 991 ninety ships carrying two or three thousand men arrived at Folkestone. It was a joint expedition led by a Norwegian, Olaf Tryggvason, and a Dane, Sven Forkbeard, both of whom saw campaigning in England as a way of boosting their reputations at home. For the next twenty-five years Scandinavian armies rampaged through England until finally, in 1017, England was brought under the control of the Danish king Cnut, who by the time of

458

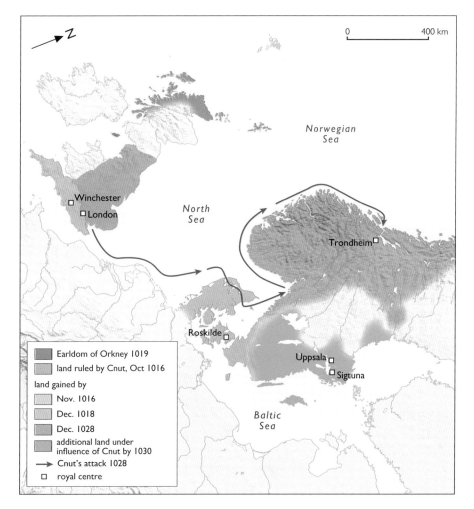

11.26 The story of the North Sea kingdom of the Scandinavians culminated in the reign of King Cnut, who was ceded most of central and northern England in 1016 and went on to create a kingdom embracing England, Denmark, and much of Norway and Sweden

his death in 1035 had extended his domain to include England, Denmark, and Norway. The dispute that followed his death led to the Norman invasion of 1066. But this was not quite the end of Scandinavian claims on England. Three years later a Danish fleet of 240 ships was sent to the east coast to support those opposed to the Norman takeover, while at the same time a Norse fleet from Ireland arrived in the Severn estuary, but the interventions had no lasting effect. A final attempt to challenge Norman supremacy came in 1075 when a large Danish and Norwegian fleet landed on the east coast and managed to sack York, but by now the Norman overlords were firmly in

459

control. It was the last Scandinavian attack on England—nearly three hundred years after three shiploads of men had landed on the Dorset coast and killed a local official.

The tenth and eleventh centuries saw the seas around Britain and Ireland alive with shipping involved in raiding, trading, and territorial conquest. By now the divide between Danish and Norwegian spheres of interest had broken down and the two countries often worked together. The settlements, too, were no longer exclusive. Those living in the enclaves in Ireland were of mixed Norse and Irish ancestry, and settlers from Ireland were allowed to take up land in the Cotentin peninsula as the Norman successors of the original Danes who had settled around Rouen extended their domain to the west. While the available texts focus on the main raids and advances, there was a great deal of mobility going on behind them. In this the sea played a crucial role. The cultural mix is nicely shown by the ships found in and around Roskilde fjord in Denmark, dating to the eleventh century. By carefully studying the tree rings of their timbers it is possible to show that various of the vessels were built of locally grown Danish oak, but two were constructed of Norwegian timber, probably in Norway. These were the cargo boat Skuldelev 1, built of pine from western Norway, and the warship Roskilde 6, the oak for which came from south-eastern Norway: it was later repaired with Baltic oak. Even more interesting was the small warship Skuldelev 2, which was built of oak grown in the region of Dublin in 1042 and repaired twenty years later with British oak. These tiny glimpses remind us of the interconnectivity of the Viking world and the huge importance of the sea in allowing the Scandinavians to maintain their highly distinctive mobile lifestyle.

To New Lands across the Ocean

The discovery of the Faroe islands by the Norwegians probably took place in the early decades of the ninth century, and settlement followed quickly. The islands had been occupied by a few Christian monks for a century or so. They had introduced sheep, the numbers of which so impressed the Norse newcomers that they named the islands Færeyjar (Sheep Islands). If any monks still remained, they would have quickly departed when their solitude was invaded by the incoming pagan settlers. Where the settlers came from is a matter of debate. One possibility is that they arrived directly from Norway only a few days' sail away, their discovery the result either of deliberate exploration of the open sea or of a fishing vessel being blown west by an adverse wind. The other possibility is that they were reached by Norse settlers coming from the Northern or Western Isles who had learned of these northern outposts from local people familiar with stories of the wandering monks. Some support for this view comes from a report in the sagas that the first settler was Grim Kamban, a name which suggests that he may have come from Ireland or the Hebrides. Once the islands had been rediscovered, knowledge of them spread fast and families from the overpopulated coasts of Norway braved the sea-crossing in search of land to settle. What they found was a cluster of windswept islands, the largest only thirty kilometres long, but a landscape very similar to the lands from which they had come. The feral sheep and the seals provided a basic food source to be augmented by the cattle and seed-grain they brought with them. Other essential imports were wood for boatbuilding and repairs, and, for home building, metal tools, whetstones, and soapstone vessels. The main product of the islands was wool and woollen fabric used to make sails. The ethos of the islanders was very different from that of their compatriots in the Hebrides: their very remoteness removed the temptation to raid and focused all their energies on extracting a livelihood from their harsh environment.

Iceland was even more remote, thirteen hundred kilometres from the Norwegian coast. In good weather with a fair wind the crossing could be made in a week, but adverse conditions could extend the journey to a month or more. To reach Iceland required considerable feats of seamanship and vessels strong enough to endure the battering of the ocean. Since Iceland had already been settled by Irish monks, its existence would have been known to the inhabitants of the Western and Northern Isles and, when the Norse settlers arrived, would soon have passed into the sea lore of the North Atlantic communities. According to two Latin texts of the twelfth century, Iceland was discovered by a Swede, Gardar Svavarsson, and two Norwegians, Floki Vilgerdarson and Naddodd. These explorers, and probably others, may well have been inspired by rumours circulating in the middle of the ninth century of the huge ice-covered island far out in the ocean. Once a sure sea-route had been established, migrants, displaced by the political upheavals that gripped south-eastern Norway, began to make their way to the new land. Some came in large groups led by their chieftain. Others were families of younger sons forced to move as populations outgrew the holding capacity of their home. The progress of the settlement was recorded by Ari Thorgilsson in the early twelfth century in the *Landnámabók*, in which the first 430 settlers and their holdings are listed. In the period between 870 and 930 some twenty thousand people arrived in Iceland. Most of the early settlements took place around the west and north coasts, where the best land was to be had in sheltered valleys. The south coast was at first avoided. It was inhospitable and dangerous, 'nothing but sands and vast deserts and a harbourless coast, and, outside the skerries, a heavy surf'. Even so, the latecomers managed to find a few niches to settle.

Most of the early settlers seem to have reached Iceland from Norway, either by way of the Faroes or by sailing the open sea along the latitude, but some came from the

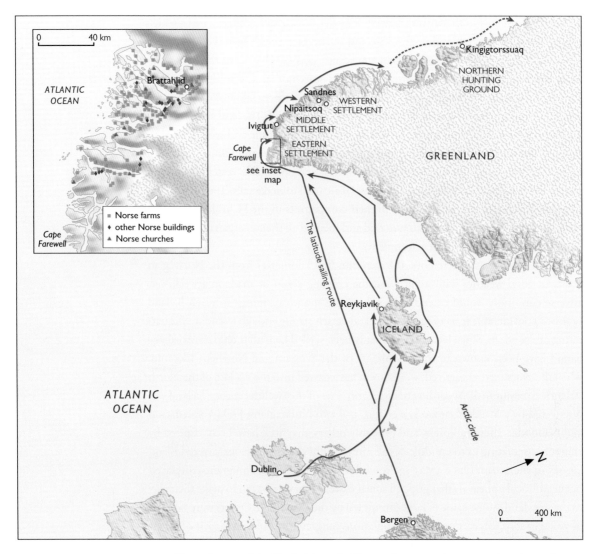

11.27 The exploration of the North Atlantic by Norse sailors was an heroic episode in human history. Driven by economic pressures at home and by an innate desire to explore, they colonized Iceland and went on to establish enclaves along the west coast of Greenland. Their feats of seamanship, sailing for long periods out of sight of land across a difficult ocean, were remarkable

Western Isles. Later in the middle of the tenth century, as the Irish kings made life increasingly difficult for the Viking enclaves, Norse settlers from Ireland, together with their Irish slaves and wives, made the journey to Iceland. That the inflow of new immigrants was not inconsiderable is clear from the high percentage of Celtic DNA in the present Icelandic population. By the early eleventh century the total population of the island had probably reached sixty thousand. Movement of people on this scale across a sea as hostile as the North Atlantic was unprecedented. Everything—people, animals, timber, and household and farming equipment—had to be carried by ship. The *Landnámabók* gives some indication of what this meant. Some immigrants, like Geirmund the Swarthy, sailed with four ships. Others might have two ships or one, or a single ship might be shared: each according to the wealth of his or her household. The vessels used were ocean-going cargo ships variously known as the *hafskip*, *kaup-skip*, and *knörr*, with a capacity to carry thirty to fifty people together with animals, food supplies, and equipment. Queen Aud, a Norwegian who made the journey from Caithness to Breidafjordur in western Iceland via Orkney and the Faeroes, took with her, in addition to essential equipment and livestock, her family, friends, and servants, together with twenty freedmen. It would have been an uncomfortable existence cooped up on a heavily loaded *knörr* for several weeks on end.

11.28 One of the better-known Viking settlements on Iceland was excavated at Stöng in 1939. It consisted of an extended longhouse with an attached dairy and latrine accessed from within the hall. It has been reconstructed using squares of turf laid on dry-stone foundations in the manner of the original building

11.29 Miniature from a late thirteenth century Icelandic manuscript of the law of seamen (*Farmannalög*) showing shipbuilding in progress. Much of the timber for the Icelandic ships had to be imported from Scandinavia

Iceland had birch-woods in the most protected valleys, which provided some usable timber, but for housebuilding and shipbuilding heavier timbers had to be imported from Norway. The early settlers brought their own with them. Later it became one of the principal imports, together with meat. In return Iceland produced bales of woollen cloth, hides, skins, and furs, and the much-valued white falcon, favoured as diplomatic gifts. To sustain the island population a regular pattern of trade developed, managed by merchants, some of whom lived partly in Norway and partly in Iceland. The volume of shipping was never very great but remained at a level sufficient to support the life of the islanders, at least until the early fourteenth century, when the Black Death disrupted the established systems, but by that time new trading networks were beginning to develop with England and the Continent.

Among those who arrived to make a new life for themselves on the island were people who had been exiled from their homeland in Norway or who had thought it wise to distance themselves from criticism or threats of violence. One of these was Thorvald Asvaldsson, who had been involved in a feud in which someone had been killed. He and his family, including his 16-year-old son Eric (Eric the Red), arrived on Iceland about 965, long after all the good land had been taken. The best they could do was to set themselves up on the inhospitable coast of Hornstrandir. Later, when Eric married, he moved to a better farm but became involved in a succession of feuds, which ended by him killing two of his enemy's sons, for which he was tried and banished overseas for three years. As a boy he had heard the story of the sighting of a land far to the west, some sixty years before, by a sailor who had been blown off course. Forced to leave Iceland, and with the blood feud still raging in Norway, Eric persuaded his friends to help him fit out a ship to search for the fabled land, and about 985 he set sail west across the ocean. Eventually a landing was made on the barren and inhospitable east coast of Greenland. The explorers then sailed south down the coast to Hvarf, the southernmost extremity of Greenland, rounded the headland, and made their way northwards along the west coast, where they found a far more congenial landscape of deep anchorages and long fjords flanked by rich grasslands. After spending the winter on an island, the next spring Eric found a fjord to his liking (which he named named Eiriksfjörd, now Tunulliarfik fjord) and there built a house at Brattahlid, which thereafter served as the political centre of what became known as the Eastern Settlement. He later sailed some 650 kilometres up the west coast, finding another suitable location for what was to become the Western Settlement.

His period of exile now over, Eric returned to Iceland, but since the blood feud was far from forgotten, he decided to make his home in Greenland—the name which he gave the new land to encourage others to follow him. The next summer he left Iceland for good, accompanied by friends, with others to follow. In all, fourteen ships made the journey, bringing about five hundred settlers, together with all their animals and their belongings. A further eleven ships set out but failed to arrive, either having turned back or having perished during the journey. The Eastern Settlement was said to have consisted of 190 farms, the Western Settlement of about ninety, with a smaller cluster of twenty farms, known as the Middle Settlement, in between. Archaeological surveys suggest that this is likely to be a considerable underestimate.

The climate of Greenland can be shown to have been significantly warmer from the ninth to the thirteenth century than it is today, which explains how it was that the farms could flourish. The rich pastures around the fjords allowed sheep, goats, and cattle to be reared, while seals could be hunted. Regular hunting expeditions were also made to hunting grounds in the far north between 70° and 75°. Climatic deterioration, the encroachment of Inuit hunters, and piracy eventually brought the Greenland settlements to an end in the fifteenth century.

The settlement of Greenland in the last decades of the millennium was an astonishing achievement. It shows how the circumstances of a single charismatic person's life can lead to exploration and colonization. Eric the Red's situation was probably similar to that of many young men who found themselves on the edge of society, disenchanted or disfranchised by the vagaries of a volatile world, their circumstances and natures tipping them into adventure. It was symptomatic of the Viking Age.

To the Edge of the Ocean

One of the settlers who followed Eric the Red to Greenland was Bjarni Herjolfsson. He was an experienced sailor who owned a merchant vessel and made regular trips between his family home in Iceland and Norway. His story, as recorded in the *Grænlendinga Saga*, tells how, on returning to Iceland from a trading voyage, he discovered that his father had sold his farm and left for Greenland. Without unloading his ship he decided to sail on to join his family, admitting to his crew, 'our voyage will appear rash, seeing that none of us has experience of the Greenland sea'. No doubt he took advice from those who had, and set out on a course that would bring him to the east coast of Greenland so that he could then turn south to round Hvarf to reach the Eastern Settlement. But after three days the wind dropped and fog descended and they totally lost their bearings, sailing far south of the cape into the unknown sea. When the fog eventually lifted, Herjolfsson was able to adjust his course but was now so far west that he was in sight of the coast of North America. First the explorers saw a thickly wooded, hilly country, then, two days later, a low-lying wooded land, and finally, after a further three days, a mountainous icy land. On each occasion Herjolfsson refused to land, knowing from the unfamiliar territory that he was far to the south-west of Greenland.

After four more days at sea, they made the west coast of Greenland and Herjolfsson was able to join his family. He had done with seafaring and settled down to a farmer's life.

Herjolfsson's sighting of North America took place about 986. Fourteen years later Leif, son of Eric the Red, bought Herjolfsson's ship and set out to retrace his journey in reverse. Having sailed up the west coast of Greenland, he crossed the Davis Strait to discover a flat, barren, icy land which he called Helluland (Flatstone Land), where they made landfall. The exact location of Helluland is debatable but it was probably Baffin Island. He then turned south along the Labrador coast, anchoring and going ashore to explore the thickly wooded low-lying countryside which he named Markland (Woodland). A further two days' sailing out of sight of land took them past a cape to

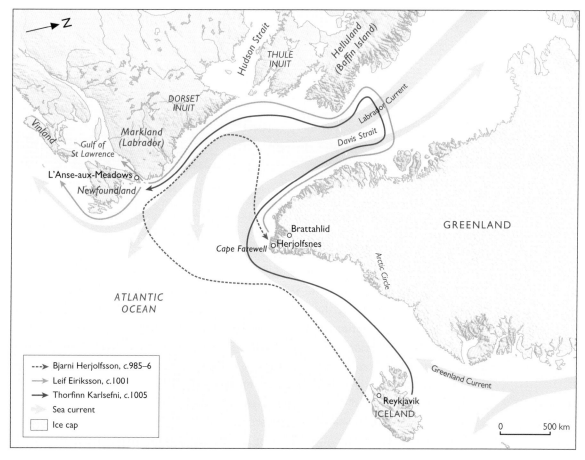

11.30 The ultimate thrust of the Nordic seamen sailing from Iceland and from Greenland was to explore the coast of North America from Baffin Island to Newfoundland or beyond. The first landing of a European on the American continent took place *c.*1000

467

11.31 Only at L'Anse-aux-Meadows on the northern extremity of Newfoundland has a convincing Viking Age settlement been found. The reconstruction is based on excavated evidence but the windows are a modern requirement. One of the essential activities carried out here was ship repairing

a river, where they landed and made camp for the winter, enjoying the plentiful wild salmon and noting the lush pasture. This he called Vinland (probably Newfoundland) after the wild vines or berries that abounded. During the winter they felled timber and loaded their ship, and the following spring set out on an uneventful return voyage to Greenland, benefiting from a constant fair wind.

In the following years, Greenlanders returned to North America. Leif's brother Thorvald led one expedition but was killed in an encounter with hostile native Americans. A year or two later an attempt was made to set up a colony in Vinland. The expedition was led by a Norwegian, Thorfinn Karlsefni, who had married Thorvald's widow. Sixty men and five women set out with their livestock and equipment. After making a safe landing and establishing homesteads, they began to stockpile timber, fur, and hides to send back to Greenland. Trading also began with the native Americans, but the relationship soon deteriorated and when spring came Karlsefni decided that it was unsafe to stay and the would-be colonists all returned home. The final voyage was

468

led by, among others, an illegitimate daughter of Eric the Red, but a falling-out between the leaders, resulting in many deaths, quickly brought the expedition to an end.

The detailed stories of the voyages to North America are recorded in the *Grænlendinga Saga*, but Vinland is mentioned in a number of other sources over the next two or three centuries and there can be little doubt that about AD 1000 Greenlanders were making journeys to the coasts of North America. Dramatic archaeological evidence of Norse settlement was discovered on the northernmost tip of Newfoundland at L'Anse aux Meadows, located where a small stream flows into Épaves Bay. The settlement, dating to the late tenth to early eleventh century, was short-lived but is likely to have been occupied by a Norse community seeking to establish a base for further explorations. That they had a forge and were extracting bog iron shows a high degree of self-sufficiency. Among the items which the smith made were iron rivets necessary for repairing boats. Here, in all its simplicity, was life on the edge of the world.

The Viking Achievement

Norse and Danish sailors had begun to sail out of their coastal waters probably by the mid-eighth century: 250 years later they were making the first attempts to settle in North America. Population expansion and the resulting unrest no doubt played a part in driving young men to explore the potential of the north-western Atlantic. Where suitable farming lands were available for settlement, families could follow even if it meant taking over other people's land by force. Similar situations had happened on other occasions in Europe's long early history, but what stands out about the Scandinavian achievement is the audacious scale of it all and the fact that it meant confronting some of the fiercest sailing conditions in the world. It is almost as if human imagination, once presented with the challenge, found it irresistible.

But we are now entering a historic period in which texts are available to offer explanations for motives, albeit texts written a century or more after the events and therefore relying on folk memory with all the opportunities that offers for embellishment. Yet what the sagas report has a ring of truth. They tell of a society on edge, where tempers can get out of hand, bursting into violence, and where blood feuds can go on for years. Difficult families are forced into exile, leaving young men like Eric the Red with little option but to find new homes overseas. Then, on that remote Greenland shore, perhaps it was sibling rivalry that spurred Leif Eiriksson and his brothers and sisters and in-laws to push themselves still further to make that final thrust across the sea to America. In stories like these we can begin to glimpse something of the reality of the timeless contest between humans and the sea.

12

The New European Order,
1100–1400

After the frantic and brutal energy of the Viking era Europe settled down to a protracted period of endemic warfare as states vied with each other for territory and dominance, driven on by the ambitions of their aspiring elites. All this created the grey noise of history. But something more fundamental was beginning to emerge: a new commercial imperative which began to transcend the shifting boundaries of the nascent nation states. Suitably motivated, people in different countries could work together for what they, from their own perspectives, perceived to be a common good. But noble motives and commercial self-interest were inextricably bound up. The Crusaders are an example of this. From the year 1095, when Pope Urban II called on the Christian world to amass forces to drive the Muslims out of the Holy Land, until 1270, when Louis IX led the Eighth Crusade against Tunis, tens of thousands of young men from western Europe made their way to the east under the flag of Christianity. But this was far more than a Holy War: it was a scramble for loot, land, and trading opportunities. The Christian sack of Constantinople in 1204 during the Fourth Crusade and the dismemberment of the Byzantine empire, to the commercial advantage of Venice and other Latin interests, was symptomatic of the whole episode: market forces and the rapidly growing power of trading cities were beginning to override political boundaries and the squabbling of kings.

Of all the boundary disputes being fought out in Europe, of greatest consequence was the prolonged fight between the Christian kingdoms and the Muslim states in Iberia. The Christian advance began with the spectacular victory of the kings of Castile, Aragón, and Navarre, reinforced by a detachment of French knights, against the Muslim Berber Almohads at Las Navas de Tolosa in 1212. Thereafter the push to the south was rapid, with the towns of Córdoba, Jaén, and Seville falling in quick succession. By 1262 the entire Guadalquivir valley had been wrested from the Muslims, and advances into the Sierra Nevada soon reduced Muslim-held territory to a small enclave: the Nasrid kingdom of Granada in the extreme south of the peninsula. The importance of this sequence of events was that the Strait of Gibraltar was no longer under Muslim domination, allowing shipping to flow freely between the Atlantic and the Mediterranean for the first time in five hundred years. Whereas trade between the Mediterranean and north-western Europe had been conducted overland, the sea-route through the strait along the Atlantic coast now came into its own, making it very much easier to move bulk consignments of goods. One of the consequences of this was a growing confidence among Portuguese and Spanish seafarers, leading to their spectacular achievements in the fifteenth and sixteenth centuries. Another result of the opening up of the strait was that Mediterranean seafarers could now begin to venture into the Atlantic to explore its many commercial possibilities.

The Atlantic soon became a busy sea-route, the haunt of professional sailors who came to know its many ports. One was the sea-captain from Dartmouth described in Chaucer's *Prologue*, who decided to make the pilgrimage to Canterbury in the fourteenth century, riding 'as best he could' a farmer's horse. This 'excellent fellow', tanned brown by the sun, had frequently pilfered draughts of vintage wine behind the vintner's back in Bordeaux: 'few were the rules his tender conscience kept'. If he captured a ship, he would make his prisoners walk the plank. But he was a talented navigator. In reckoning tides, currents, and moons, 'no one from Hull to Carthage was his match … he knew all the havens as they were from Gotland to the Cape of Finisterre, and every creek in Brittany and Spain'. He was one of a growing body of sailors finding lucrative employment along the Atlantic seaways as maritime trade began to thrive in the thirteenth and fourteenth centuries. Such men had little concern for transient political boundaries.

A History—in Brief

Between 1100 and 1400 the borders of the European states were in constant flux, and yet the main blocks remained surprisingly consistent. In the centre lay the German empire emerging from the eastern part of the Carolingian empire and stretching from the North Sea and the Baltic to the Mediterranean to include northern Italy. At best it was a loose confederation of separate states acknowledging varying degrees of allegiance to the king and emperor.

Bordering Germany to the south-east was what remained of the Byzantine empire, which, by the beginning of the twelfth century, had been reduced to the Balkans and western Asia Minor but still included the Aegean islands together with Crete and Cyprus. Pressure from recently arrived nomads settling north of the Danube was largely contained, but the Seljuk Turks on the eastern border were a constant threat and it was to help check this that the emperor looked to the Christian west to assist—a plea that led to the First Crusades in 1096. This was the beginning of the end for the empire. By opening the way for the envious Latins from the west the Byzantines had sealed their fate. In 1204 the armies of the Fourth Crusade, led by the doge of Venice, Enrico Dandolo, stormed and sacked Constantinople. In the aftermath the ripe old empire was torn apart. The core of the land empire was divided up among the Frankish barons, while only the periphery—the empire of Nicaea in Asia Minor—remained in Byzantine hands. For Dandolo it was the opportunity he had been anticipating. He saw to it that the Venetians were established in the most favoured part of Constantinople and took possession of a string of islands, including Crete, Rhodes, and Euboea, vital to the development of their maritime empire. The Cyclades were offered to Venetian nobles and became the duchy of Archipelago. It was a land grab carefully calculated to give Venice a dominant position in the eastern Mediterranean over their rival Genoa. It provided them with secure bases commanding the major sea-lanes without the inconvenience of having to administer large territories. The antagonism between Genoa and Venice is a theme to which we shall return (p. 482).

The southern part of Italy, together with Sicily, played a significant part in Mediterranean commerce, serving as a convenient bridge between Europe and the Muslim states in North Africa. Its crucial position is shown by the desire of the larger polities to have control over its ports and harbours. From 1091, when it was taken over by Norman warlords, it changed hands four times before finally becoming independent in 1295, belonging successively to Henry IV, the Angevins, and the Aragonese.

In Iberia the unremitting contest between the Christian north and the Muslim south provided the driving narrative throughout the medieval period. In the eighth and ninth centuries the northern kingdoms of Asturias (later León), Aragón, and Navarre stood out alone against the Muslim advance, but over time resistance was strengthened by tribes encouraged down from the mountains of Cantabria in the north to settle in the frontier regions between the upper reaches of the Douro and the Ebro. Here they established an impressive array of fortifications, becoming known as Castilians. As their power grew, they absorbed the kingdom of León. Thereafter Castile and Aragón became the two principal powers in northern Iberia, often competing, but united in their desire to drive out the Muslims. In 1085 Alfonso VI of León and Castile thrust south to the Tagus valley, capturing the important city of Toledo. In the Muslim south it was a time of change. More warlike communities moved in from the Atlas Mountains across the strait, first the Almoravids in 1086, and later the Almohads in 1147, heralding a more aggressive stance against the Christian north. This in turn encouraged the northern kingdoms of Castile, Aragón, and Navarre to work together more closely to face the threat. Their early success at the battle of Las Navas de Tolosa in 1212 marked a turning point, and by the middle of the century the Muslim foothold in Spain had been reduced to the kingdom of Granada, which held on for another two centuries. In the rest of the peninsula the triumphant states of Castile, Aragón, Navarre, and Portugal jostled for power and territory, and it was during this period that Aragón began to expand its interests in the Mediterranean, taking control of the Balearics, Sardinia, and Sicily, and ports in southern Italy, including Naples.

By the late thirteenth century the political divisions of Iberia were beginning to crystallize. With the treaty of Alcañices, signed in 1297, the boundaries of Portugal were recognized, bringing much of the Atlantic face of the peninsula under a single authority. With its sheltered estuaries and copious supplies of good timber, Portugal soon began to develop as a maritime state, playing an increasing part in the burgeoning sea-borne trade between northern Europe and the Mediterranean. Castile, too, had its outlets to the Atlantic, the most significant of which was the estuary of the Guadalquivir, guarded by Cádiz. Its thriving port city of Seville, sufficiently far up-river to ensure safety from sea raiders, had the great advantage of direct access to the highly productive countryside of Andalucía. Castile, like Portugal, could begin to develop its maritime commerce. However, internal division in Iberia would not be healed until 1469, when Ferdinand of Aragón and Isabella of Castile were married. Now the last thrust south could begin, and in 1492 the Muslim kingdom of Granada was finally conquered.

The conquest of England by William duke of Normandy in 1066 set in train a series of events which, by 1180, saw the entire Atlantic zone of France, together with most of Britain and Ireland, under the control of a single monarch, Henry of Anjou, who had succeeded to the throne of England in 1154 as Henry II. The Angevin empire over which Henry ruled had been assembled through inheritance and marriage, augmented by force of arms. Henry, as duke of Normandy, was also king of England. Additional French territories accrued through further inheritances, and his marriage to Eleanor of Aquitaine added Aquitaine and Gascony. He could also claim authority over the princes of Wales and the king of Scotland, and to complete his Atlantic portfolio, Brittany and Ireland were beaten into submission by military force.

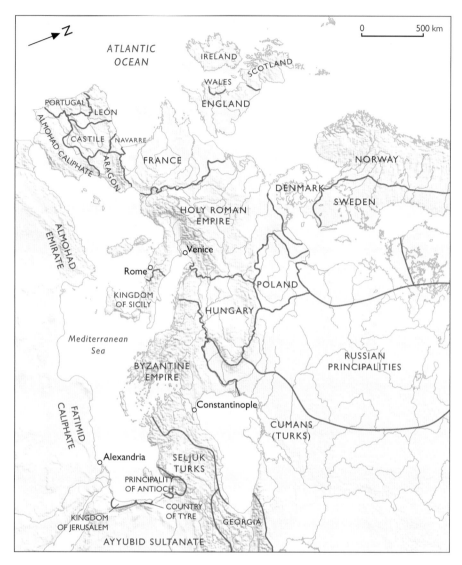

12.1 Europe *c.*1200 had begun to take on a familiar form with the emergence of nation states, but the whole of the southern Mediterranean coast was still under the control of Islamic polities

Spectacular though the creation of the Angevin empire was, it lacked political coherence: it had been stitched together too quickly out of disparate parts over which there were many claims. It soon began to disintegrate, and by the early decades of the thirteenth century the French kings had reclaimed substantial territories, leaving only Gascony in English hands. A hundred years later, in 1337, the French seized Gascony,

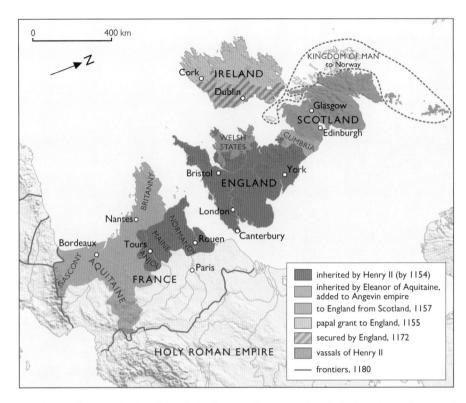

12.2 By 1180 Britain, Ireland, and the whole of western France constituted the Angevin empire, created during the reign of Henry II by marriage, inheritance, and conquest. It was short-lived

precipitating a lasting struggle between England and France which became known as the Hundred Years War. Gradually English possessions in France were stripped away until, by 1543, only Calais remained. Although war was intermittent, England suffered many raids from the sea, while large areas of France were ravaged as competing armies tramped backwards and forwards across the countryside.

The sea-borne trade between England and Atlantic France, which flourished in the period from the mid-twelfth century until the outbreak of the Hundred Years War, declined during the fourteenth and fifteenth centuries, but the major ports of Nantes, La Rochelle, Bordeaux, and Bayonne continued in operation, serving the many ships making the long haul between the North Sea and the Mediterranean. During the thirteenth century, when the Gascon wine trade with Britain was flourishing, Bordeaux doubled in size, and even during the long war following the loss of Gascony economic imperatives meant that British trade with France continued, though on a reduced scale. When there was a profit to be made, a way could always be found.

476

In the North Sea region the fury of the Norwegian and Danish attacks from the sea was all but over by the early eleventh century, and the failure of the Danish expeditions to regain England after the Norman Conquest of 1066 brought raiding to an end. Norway retained its overseas possessions of the Faroes, and took control of the settlements on Greenland in 1261 and Iceland in 1263. But in Scotland Norse possessions were lost one after the other: Ross, Caithness, and Sutherland at the beginning of the thirteenth century and the Hebrides and Man in 1266. Only the earldom of Orkney, comprising Orkney and Shetland, remained, until it was finally ceded to Scotland in 1468–9 and formally annexed a few years later. Meanwhile, Denmark had been turning its attention to the Baltic, organizing crusades against the pagan peoples living around the southern and eastern coasts as far north as the Gulf of Finland. For a brief period, in the first half of the thirteenth century, the Danes held extensive territories, but their nascent empire was soon lost to German expansion. Once established on the Baltic, the German cities began to assume control of trade, creating a confederation of merchant guilds which became known as the Hanseatic League, or the German Hansa. By the fourteenth century the Hansa extended from the Rhine mouth to the Gulf of Finland, embracing Sweden and with agencies in Norway and England. Its very existence, spanning political divides, showed that commerce was fast becoming the significant force, transcending political boundaries.

The Mediterranean Economy

At the beginning of the eleventh century there were two big players in the Mediterranean world, the Byzantine empire and the Muslim states; the Christian west was of little significance. At this stage the Byzantine emperors still ruled the Balkans and Asia Minor, together with Crete and Cyprus and a part of southern Italy. From this enviable position they were able to command trade routes from Scandinavia and from the east and to dominate maritime movements throughout much of the eastern Mediterranean. The Muslim world, stretching along the whole of the North African coast and incorporating the Levant and much of Iberia, had control over the southern Mediterranean, while from bases in the Balearics and Sicily they were able to maintain a significant presence in the western Mediterranean. They were, however, politically fragmented, and this lack of a centralizing authority weakened their power at sea. The Latin states had shown comparatively little interest in the Mediterranean, but coastal cities like Venice, Genoa, Pisa, Naples, and Amalfi were already developing trading links with the Byzantine empire and with Syria and Egypt. The initiative lay with a growing class of merchant venturers who were prepared to invest in ships and cargoes in the expectation of making good cash returns. To facilitate their ventures, some set up trading stations abroad: both Venice and Amalfi early on had merchants resident in Constantinople.

In spite of the political turmoil of the eleventh century, Mediterranean maritime trade developed its own systems and momentum, little concerned with the conflicts going on around. Christian merchants freely traded with anyone willing to engage with them, but Muslim traders were more restricted since the teachings of Islam frowned upon commerce with the infidel. Nevertheless, trade flourished, facilitated by Jewish merchants, who were to be found throughout the Mediterranean and were particularly active in Iberia and in Egypt. Documents found in a synagogue in Old Cairo show that not only did their trading networks extend the length of the Mediterranean, but they also helped to articulate the Indian Ocean trade with their agents permanently based in India. Cairo was now a major gateway for eastern products reaching the Mediterranean, avoiding territories controlled by Turks.

Each of the trading ports of the Latin west had its own favoured routes. The little port of Amalfi on the west coast of Italy developed a network linking Italy, Tunisia, Egypt, and Constantinople. Venice focused on the Adriatic and the routes to the Byzantine empire, while Genoa and Pisa began by extending their influence in the Tyrrhenian Sea, first clearing Corsica and Sardinia of Muslim pirates. Trade was still on a fairly limited scale, based largely on the shipping of raw materials like metals, timber, linen, leather, oil, and slaves from areas where they were produced in surplus to wherever there were consumer markets. Alongside this, luxuries from the east—silk, spices, perfumes, and pearls—were introduced into the Mediterranean system through Cairo or Constantinople.

The system, which had been developing throughout the tenth and eleventh centuries, began to change quite dramatically towards the end of the eleventh century as a result of a series of far-reaching political upheavals. In the east the power of the Byzantine empire was increasingly weakened by pressure from the Seljuk Turks, while in the west, in Iberia, the Christian advance against the Muslim states was well under way, culminating in the reconquest of the Mediterranean coast of Valencia by the Castilian leader El Cid in 1094. But it was the Crusades that were to have the greatest effect by unleashing the might of the Latin west on the Mediterranean. Under the banner of Christ many thousands of young men marched and sailed to the Holy Land with the avowed intent of freeing the holy sites from Muslim control, but whatever the rhetoric, the effect was a land grab leading to the establishment of four Crusader states along the length of the Levant. It was a short-lived enterprise, difficult to sustain at such a distance in so hostile an environment, and under Mamluk attack in 1291 the entire edifice collapsed.

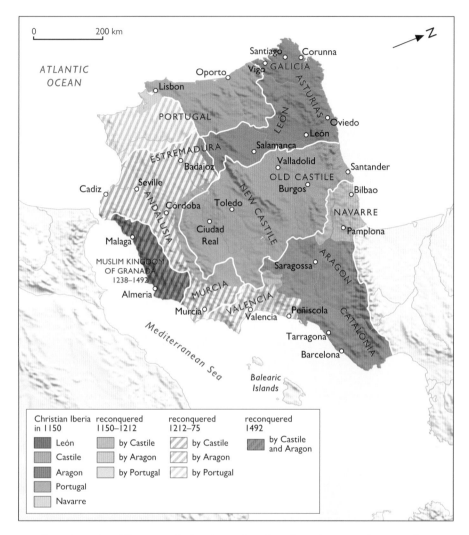

12.3 From the mid-twelfth century the kingdoms of northern Iberia began to advance south against the Muslim caliphates. The Reconquista was not completed until the kingdom of Granada was finally conquered in 1492

The real significance of the Crusades was that they introduced the Latin west to the commercial potential of the Mediterranean. The sack of Constantinople by the Fourth Crusade in 1204 provided the west, most particularly Venice, with unrestricted access to the markets of the Byzantine world. With Constantinople under a tight rein and the Muslim world in disarray, the Mediterranean was now wide open. This much was recognized by the French monarchy, who, in the early decades of the thirteenth

479

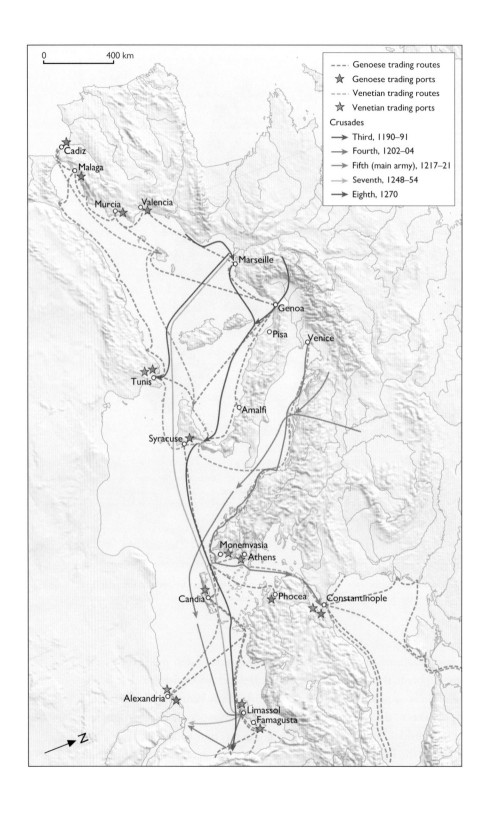

0   400 km

Genoese trading routes
★ Genoese trading ports
Venetian trading routes
★ Venetian trading ports
Crusades
→ Third, 1190–91
→ Fourth, 1202–04
→ Fifth (main army), 1217–21
→ Seventh, 1248–54
→ Eighth, 1270

Cadiz
Malaga
Murcia   Valencia
Marseille
Genoa
Pisa
Venice
Tunis
Amalfi
Syracuse
Monemvasia
Athens
Candia   Phocea   Constantinople
Alexandria
Limassol
Famagusta
N

12.4 (*Opposite*) The rise of the Italian trading cities of Venice, Genoa, Pisa, and Amalfi established competing trading networks throughout the Mediterranean and the Black Sea and extending into the Atlantic. Genoa and Venice soon became the dominant forces and set up trading enclaves in many of the major ports. The Crusades added to mobility by sea

12.5 (*Above*) After the Fourth Crusade in 1204 Venice established a trading enclave in Constantinople, but in 1261 their Genoese competitors set up a rival colony on the opposite side of the Golden Horn at Pera (Galata)

century, extended the royal domain down to Languedoc and built a new port at Aigues-Mortes on the coast of the Camargue to provide both a staging point for future Crusades and a commercial outlet to the Mediterranean. While the Crusader states existed, ports like Antioch, Tripoli, Beirut, Tyre, and Acre were much frequented by Italian and Provençal merchants, who were encouraged by trading concessions and were allowed to establish residential quarters for the merchants. Thus it was that the entrepreneurs of the west were drawn into ever more intensive trade relations with the east, sailing the length of the Mediterranean.

The beneficiaries of all the maritime activity, be it trade or the transportation of Crusader armies, were the cities of the European coast of the western Mediterranean and the Adriatic: Barcelona, Aigues-Mortes, Marseille, Genoa, Pisa, Naples, Amalfi, and Venice. Great rivalry existed between them, the more successful eventually squeezing out their smaller competitors until, by the end of the thirteenth century, Barcelona, Genoa, and Venice had emerged as the dominant forces. Each commanded routes leading deep into the European hinterland, each had ample supplies of good timber for shipbuilding, and each had a defined stretch of sea that they could regard as their home waters. Of these benefits, the first was the most important because Europe offered unlimited markets for Mediterranean commodities and in return could supply raw materials in short supply in the Mediterranean, particularly wool, cloth, and tin. By dominating the entry points to Europe the merchants resident in these ports-of-trade were able to facilitate the two-way passage of goods and to grow rich on the proceeds.

While the merchants of Aragón based in Barcelona had comparatively easy access to the rich valley of the Ebro, the plains of central Spain, and the southern flanks of the Pyrenees, merchants from Genoa and Venice had to cross the Alps to reach the markets of central and northern Europe. In the tenth century the favoured route from Venice was along the Adige, passing through Verona, to cross the mountains by the Brenner Pass. From Genoa the way lay via the pass at Mont Cenis to Chambéry and thence to the Rhône, but with the opening of the Schöllenen bridge in the 1230s the more direct route via the Italian lakes and the St Gotthard Pass gained in popularity. These alpine crossings were far from easy. Brigandage, wild animals, avalanches, and sudden changes of weather conditions were ever-present dangers.

The merchants who made the journey were aiming for the fairs held in the towns of northern Europe. Most towns held weekly markets and annual fairs, but as population, productivity, and trade increased, some regions developed cycles of fairs, with the fair passing from town to town over a trading season, which could last almost the entire year. The earliest of the major cycles came into being in Flanders, with the fair moving between Bruges, Torhout, Mesen, Lille, and Ypres between February and November,

12.6 For a long time France paid little attention to the Mediterranean, but in 1240 Louis IX began to develop the new port town of Aigues-Mortes in the Camargue to serve as an outlet to the Mediterranean and a place of embarkation for Crusaders. That the appearance of the town remains little changed is the fortunate result of the rapid silting up of its harbour

but the most important was the cycle of Champagne fairs shared between six towns lying between Saint-Denis (Paris) and Chalon-sur-Saône. The cycle began at Lagny in January and ended at Troyes in December. It was to these fairs that Flemish cloth and English wool, so much in demand, was brought to exchange for Mediterranean commodities, saving the Italian merchants from having to make the additional onward journey to Flanders. The pattern began to change at the beginning of the fourteenth century with the opening of the central Alpine passes, which offered a more direct route to the North Sea ports of Bergen op Zoom and Antwerp and the major German trading centres at Frankfurt am Main and Leipzig with their onward links to the Baltic.

483

12.7 Before the opening up of the Strait of Gibraltar to Christian shipping in the thirteenth century, trade between the Mediterranean and the North Sea was overland, using the passes through the Alps. To facilitate trade, cycles of fairs were held in the towns of Champagne and Flanders. In the early fourteenth century, with increased use of the Brenner Pass, new market centres developed on routes leading to the Baltic

Another factor affecting the volume of transalpine trade was the opening up of the sea-route between the Mediterranean and the North Sea at the end of the thirteenth century, following the advances of the Christian armies against the Muslim states in Iberia. With the Strait of Gibraltar now a comparatively safe passage, maritime trade could begin to develop. The earliest record of this is of two Genoese vessels setting out for north-western Europe in 1277. By the end of the century Genoese and Venetian galleys were making the journey to the markets of Flanders and England on a regular basis. Sea travel had advantages over the transalpine routes. It was safer, and ships could carry greater volumes of cargo. The breaking of Muslim domination over the Strait of

Gibraltar in the middle of the thirteenth century was a turning point in maritime history. Not only did it allow the trading system of Europe to be reordered, but it paved the way for the Genoese, the Castilians, and the Portuguese to create partnerships which led to the exploration of the Atlantic, and eventually the Iberian-led discovery of America and the development of a sea-route to the Indian Ocean.

Mediterranean Ships, 1100–1400

In the Middle Ages, as in times past, two types of vessel were in use in the Mediterranean: longships driven by oars but also provided with lateen sails carried on one or more masts, and round ships relying solely on the wind. The longships, or galleys, developed from a long-established Mediterranean tradition rooted in the early first millennium BC. By the eleventh century AD, they were powered by oarsmen working in two levels, one above the other, with the lower oarsmen being below deck. But by the beginning of the thirteenth century all the oarsmen were above deck, working now two to a bench and four to a bank. A little later a third oarsman was introduced to each bench, creating a vessel known as a trireme *alla sensile* ('in the simple fashion'). From about 1290 this became the approved arrangement and was considered to be the most efficient means of propulsion. The number of banks of oars varied, usually between eighteen and twenty-five. The galleys were also provided with between one and three masts carrying lateen sails. These were used for long voyages, but in combat situations the sails could be reefed and the masts lowered. A raised prow served as a fighting platform. It was brought to a sharp point tipped with iron, which could lodge in the enemies' timbers to facilitate boarding. At the stern a raised poop deck giving greater visibility provided the station for the captain and helmsman. The galleys were very effective in Mediterranean waters. The oars gave them manoeuvrability when entering and leaving crowded harbours, while the lateen-rigged sails enabled them to sail fast even close to the wind. When the wind dropped, the oars could be brought into use. The Italian galley was the culmination of two thousand years of shipbuilding tradition.

By the fifteenth century a heavier class of galley known as the *galea grossa* was being built. These could serve as merchant galleys or could be converted to become fighting ships. They were slower than the ordinary galleys, with higher freeboards, which gave them an advantage in fighting since they would tower above smaller vessels. When used as merchant vessels their larger size gave them a greater cargo-carrying capacity. There were also smaller galleys with two oarsmen to each seat, galliots, which usually had eighteen to twenty banks of oars, and fustas with ten to fifteen banks. Smaller still

12.8 The maritime interests of Venice are reflected in this fourteenth-century relief on the façade of the basilica of St Mark illustrating the story of Noah building the Ark

were bergantines, with one oar to each seat and ten to fifteen banks. These little vessels performed a number of functions. In battle they could be used to pass messages or transport reinforcements: they were also effective in hit-and-run raids.

Alongside the slender galleys were a variety of round merchant ships usually known as nefs, characterized by their large carrying capacity. They were driven only by lateen-rigged sails. The larger nefs could carry five hundred tonnes of cargo but required a crew of more than a hundred men to manage the sails. At both fore and aft there were raised towers supporting state rooms which provided comfortable accommodation for passengers able to afford them.

Such provision is a reminder that there were many travellers in the Mediterranean looking for passages on merchant ships. Besides diplomats and merchants there was an unceasing stream of Christian pilgrims travelling to the Holy Land. Even Muslim pilgrims making their way to Mecca on the haj were prepared to use Christian ships. And from time to time there were Crusaders to transport. Venice provided two hundred ships to take the army of the Fourth Crusade to Constantinople, and half a century later the Genoese shipyards were busy fulfilling an order from Louis IX to supply him with ships for his Crusades against the Egyptians and Tunisians. And then there were the cargoes to transport. All around the Mediterranean, commodities from Europe, Asia, and Africa poured into the port cities, ready to be transhipped. Slaves from the Slavonic regions brought to the Aegean, gold from across the Sahara taken to the North African ports, cloth and tin from north-western Europe, olive oil, soap, and leather from Iberia, and a wealth of luxuries from the east, including the much-desired silks, spices, and gemstones—all

12.9 (*Opposite*) (*a*) A Venetian *galea grossa* (heavy galley) of the mid-fifteenth century, lateen-rigged but also powered by 170 or more rowers. The need to provide for such a large crew meant that the cargo capacity was limited to low-volume, high-value goods. (*b*) A Venetian galley *alla sensile*. The smaller, sleeker build of the vessel, crewed by about 140 rowers, meant that these galleys were much faster and more manoeuvrable, ideal for naval engagements

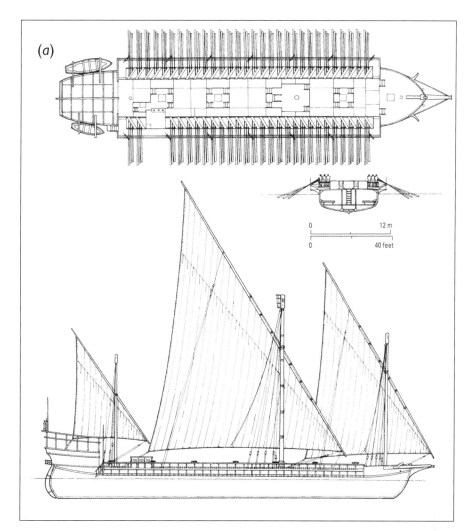

(a)

0   12 m

0   40 feet

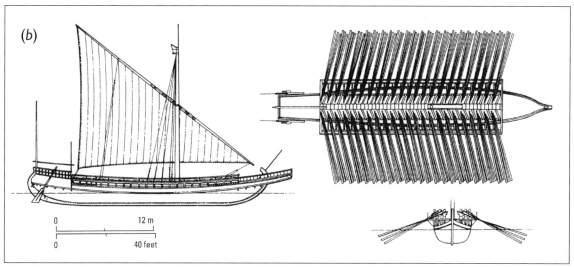

(b)

0   12 m

0   40 feet

12.10 Drawing by Raphael of a Venetian galley in sailing mode with oars at rest. This small vessel is a galliot or a fusta

were carried across the Mediterranean on the palimpsest of criss-crossing routes in unending cycles of exchange and on a scale never before witnessed.

The Atlantic Economy

The cessation of Viking raids in the eleventh century allowed trade along the Atlantic seaways to begin to pick up, and by the fourteenth century it was flourishing. Standing back from the complex network of trade routes that grew up over time, we can resolve the systems into three: the southern system linking Britain and Ireland to western France and western Iberia, the North Sea and Baltic system dominated by the Hanseatic League, and the North Atlantic system involving Scandinavia, Iceland, and Greenland and eventually Britain. All three were interlinked and changed over time as political events had their effect. The Reconquista in Iberia saw the Castilians and the Portuguese begin to play an increasing role from the early thirteenth century, while the rise of the Angevin empire in the twelfth century and subsequent wars between England and France affected the volume and direction of trade. In the north the decline of Norway as a sea-power opened the way for England to begin to exploit Iceland and its fishing grounds. Underlying these superficial political shifts was the prime mover of demography. The steady and quite rapid growth of population in Europe in the early Middle Ages generated increasing demands for goods and created tensions. The pressures were partially relieved by the Crusades, which, in turn, enhanced the volume of trade by opening up the eastern markets to west Europeans. Then came the ravages of the Black Death, which broke out in the Crimea in 1346 and spread rapidly across the whole of Europe, killing perhaps a third of the population and disrupting economic systems. Gradually things stabilized, and by the beginning of the fifteenth century Europe had recovered, to be gripped by a new energy.

Before we look at the movement of goods along the Atlantic routes something must be said about pilgrimage. The 'finding', in 812, of the bones of St James, son of Zebedee, at Santiago de Compostela in the extreme north-west of Iberia provided a rallying point for the Christian opposition to the Muslim occupation of Iberia, which had begun a hundred years before. It was not long before the town began to attract pilgrims from the western states of Christian Europe journeying by land from various centres in France, by way of Aragón, Navarre, and León, to pay homage to the saint's remains. It is no exaggeration to say that these pilgrim routes through northern Iberia helped to bind the Christian kingdoms together, strengthening their common purpose and encouraging cooperation against the Muslim states in the south. The desire to visit the shrine of St James also caught the imagination of the British and the Irish, many of

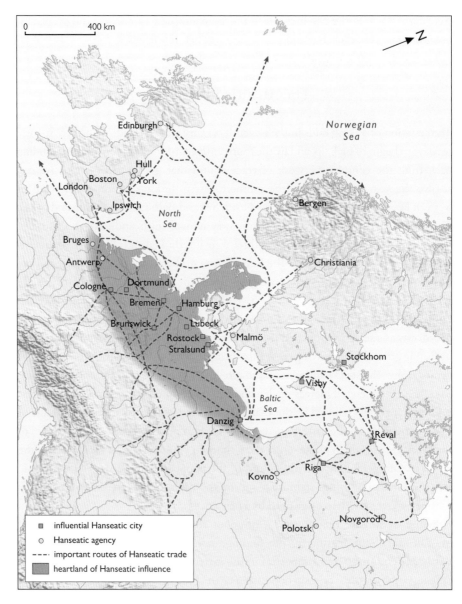

0   400 km

Norwegian Sea

Edinburgh

Hull
Boston   York
London
Ipswich

Bruges
Antwerp
Cologne   Dortmund
Bremen   Hamburg
Brunswick   Lübeck
Rostock
Stralsund

North Sea

Bergen

Christiania

Malmö

Stockholm

Visby

Baltic Sea

Danzig

Reval

Kovno   Riga

Polotsk   Novgorod

◼ influential Hanseatic city
○ Hanseatic agency
--- important routes of Hanseatic trade
▨ heartland of Hanseatic influence

12.11 By the fifteenth century the Hanseatic League controlled much of the maritime trade in the Baltic and North Sea. Besides the main trading cities of the Hansa, agencies were established in other trading ports

490

whom chose to make the pilgrimage by sea. Bristol and Dublin became the principal assembly points. Ships from Bristol carrying hundreds of pilgrims at a time might stop at Plymouth to pick up more, while in Dublin the numbers were so great that hostels were set up to house them while they waited for a sailing. Many of the other ports of southern Britain and Ireland also provided ships to meet pilgrim demand. Some of those who set out disembarked at Bordeaux and made the rest of the journey by road; others chose to sail directly across the Bay of Biscay to Galicia in cramped conditions that must have been far from comfortable, constantly shouted at by seamen trying to manage the ship, frustrated by a crush of seasick landsmen cluttering up the decks.

The numbers making the pilgrimage by sea could be very considerable. In 1189 between ten and twelve thousand pilgrims landed at La Coruña over a short period of time. Fearing the consequences of such an invasion, the authorities drove the pilgrims back and forbade them from proceeding to the shrine. The pilgrim traffic established a regular sea-route to Galicia, while the surpluses of timber and tin on offer for export attracted commercial shipping. With the gradual opening up of Portugal and the Castilian-held region of Andalucía, ships were drawn even further to the south, and by the early thirteenth century Castile, through ports like Seville, was trading regularly with Bristol, Southampton, London, and Bruges.

Each region of Atlantic Europe produced commodities that were in demand in other regions, and so maritime trade grew in volume, moving surpluses from one port to another. Seville was famous for its olive oil and dried fruits—raisins, dates, and figs—so much in demand in northern Europe to provide sweetness to the diet before sugar became widely available. Andalucía also produced wine and high-quality leatherwork. Portugal, through its principal ports of Lisbon and Oporto, exported wine and cork grown in its cork oak forests. Santander and Bilbao offered Cantabrian iron and forest products like resin, fur, and dye-wood. Gascony was primarily a producer of good-quality wine exported in vast quantities through Bordeaux and Bayonne. In the middle of the fifteenth century, 3 million gallons were transported to England alone in a single year. Gascon wine all but replaced the wine from Rouen and allowed the English taste for wine to continue to be satisfied in the face of declining English wine production during the climatic downturn of the fourteenth century. Other products exported via Bordeaux were alum and potash, used in dressing cloth, and the all-important dye-wood. Brittany's contribution to the flow of exports was restricted to salt, produced by evaporation in the salt-pans of Guérande in the Loire estuary, and dried fish. The principal exports from England were wool and grain, with lesser quantities of tin and lead. Up to the mid-fourteenth century England exported mainly raw wool, but from then cloth exports increased until, by the early decades of the sixteenth century, cloth amounted to more than 90 per cent of England's total wool export. The other great cloth producer in the early Middle Ages was Flanders, which benefited from copious supplies of fuller's earth, needed for processing fabrics, found in the Scheldt valley. Bruges became the market centre for Flemish cloth, which was exported through its port of Sluys. Finally, there was Ireland, whose main products were sea-fish—herring, hake, pollock, and cod—together with salmon caught in its fast-flowing rivers. Hides and other skins added to the list of exports, and by the fifteenth century linen for clothes and sail-making was becoming available in increasing quantity. The variety of bulk commodities being transported along the Atlantic sea-routes was considerable, but we should not forget the minor cargoes—honey, wax, tallow, metalware, pottery, and a host of other consumer goods—that could be packed in the spaces between the bulkier items. It was into this well-established network that Mediterranean galleys were to introduce an array of eastern exotics when they began to venture into the Atlantic (pp. 502–6 below).

But who carried all these goods? The procedures were complex. Sometimes, of course, it was the ship belonging to the port where the goods were collected for export. On other occasions it was visiting ships from the ports where the commodities were to be consumed or distributed. But there were also middlemen. Bristol, for example, received tin and fish from Cornwall, and a wide range of fish, together with hides and linen, from Ireland, which its merchants repackaged for transmission to overseas ports. Bordeaux, on the other hand, relied largely on foreign ships to distribute its wine. In one year in the early fourteenth century local records show that two hundred ships left the harbour. Of these, only five belonged to local ship-owners. The others were ships from England, Flanders, Brittany, and the town of Bayonne. Records of English ships leaving Bordeaux in 1409–10 show that they came from the ports of Dartmouth, London, Hull, Bristol, Fowey, and Plymouth. Bristol sent only nine of the seventy-eight ships in that year. In another year only half the ships offloading Gascon wine at Bristol were locally registered. Some came from Bayonne and La Rochelle, while others came from other British ports. Some regions gained a reputation for being reliable carriers. The sailors of Bayonne, together with their Basque neighbours, were available for hire. They occupied the region between the Atlantic coasts of Iberia and western France and could serve to link the two. Similarly, the Bretons, fearless sailors with little to offer but their fish and salt, were prepared to act as middlemen between the north and the south. Transhipment was a complex process, made more so by the multitude of different strategies adopted by the merchant venturers.

The axis between London and Bruges marks a convenient divide between the Atlantic system and the North Sea–Baltic systems. There was, of course, a considerable degree of overlap between them, with shipping passing along the English Channel from one to the other, but from the twelfth century the North Sea and the Baltic came under the domination of the Hanseatic League. This confederation had its unofficial capital at Lübeck, a town founded in 1143 in Slavonic lands recently colonized by the Germans. Two hundred towns joined the league, stretching from the Rhine mouth, across northern Germany, and northwards along the Baltic coast to the Gulf of Finland. Agencies (*kontors*) were set up more widely to look after the league's interests in important trading centres like London, Bruges, Bergen, Visby (on the island of Gotland), and Novgorod. In the thirteenth and fourteenth centuries the league dominated commercial activities in the Baltic and was effective in supporting its members' interests in the North Sea, but its power began to wane in the fifteenth century in the face of British and Dutch interventions.

Spread in an arc from the Rhine to Finland, the Hanseatic towns had complete control of the flow of commodities between inland Europe and the Baltic and North Sea. The Hansa was a contained, self-sustaining system, but for some goods it had still to deal with the outside world. One of these was salt, which came under great demand as the need for salted herring to feed the fast-growing population increased. Since good-quality salt was produced in quantity in Guérande, on the south coast of Brittany, and in the Bay of Bourgneuf, just to the south of the Loire estuary, the Hansa organized fleets of up to fifty vessels each year to bring back what was required. By the early fifteenth century the salt convoys had extended their reach as far south as the Sado estuary at Setúbal in southern Portugal, where the salt produced was of particularly high quality. On the outward journeys the ships carried mainly grain. In addition to salt, their return cargoes included dried fruit, olive oil, and wine. The freedom with which the Hansa were able to trade in western France and Portugal is in sharp contrast to the restrictions they placed on merchants working the North Sea.

In the North Atlantic the communities settled in Iceland and Greenland maintained their sailing traditions, but the energy shown by the pioneers was soon spent. The toll taken by having to eke out an existence in such a harsh environment was one factor; another was the lack of good timber for shipbuilding. When a vessel reached the end of its life, some timbers could be reused, but to build a new ship the islanders were dependent on supplies of fresh timber reaching them from Norway, and the flow could be unreliable. Even so, sufficient ships were kept in good order to sustain the local economies and to create the surpluses needed to exchange the essential supplies from Europe. Not only had the Greenlanders to provide themselves with fish, but they had, each year, to sail far north to the hunting grounds of Nordseter for walrus to build up stocks of ivory, walrus-hide ropes, and oil essential for trading. The Icelanders could rely on a demand for their rough woollen cloth, but they too had to keep fishing fleets to supply their own needs. The rapidly increasing demand for stockfish (dried unsalted whitefish) by the European states in the fourteenth century gave a new impetus to Icelandic seafaring and encouraged sailors to move away from local waters, venturing south to the Faroes and Shetland in pursuit of migrating shoals. Some ships owned by island traders also made the three-week journey to Norway, but, even so, the islands came increasingly to rely on the arrival of Norwegian ships to keep the trade routes open. From the middle of the thirteenth century, traffic to Greenland and Iceland, the Faroes, and Shetland was almost entirely dominated by Norway.

In 1262, after a difficult period caused by internal dissent, the Icelanders, who had hitherto been proudly independent, decided to put themselves under the authority of the Norwegian Crown. In return for the Icelanders paying annual taxes to Norway, the latter agreed to send six trading ships each year to Iceland. This particular provision, which was reinforced in subsequent agreements, hints at a certain desperation—the fear that the lifeline to Europe might fail if left only to market forces. By the mid-fourteenth century, when trade with Iceland was at its peak, between ten and twenty ships were sent each year. This flourishing ocean trade came at a time when Norwegian foreign trade was otherwise in rapid decline, a decline caused in no small part by the growing dominance of the German Hansa. Iceland provided the Norwegians with trading opportunities beyond the interference of the Hansa at just the time when the market for stockfish was growing—a demand that Iceland was well placed to meet. It looked as though things were set fair for both partners. But it was at just this time that the Black Death struck, bringing trade virtually to a standstill. In 1347 twenty ships sailed to Iceland, but in 1349 the number was reduced to one, and for two years, 1350 and 1355, no ships sailed at all. It was a desperate time for the islanders. Towards the end of the century numbers picked up again, but it was not to last. Heavy taxes were now being imposed on Icelandic imports, and, with the shift of political power in Norway away from the west coast to Oslo, trade between Bergen and Iceland declined to virtually nothing—a decline exacerbated by the sacking of Bergen by German pirates in 1393 and 1394. It was only the appearance of English ships, first recorded in Iceland in 1412, that saved the situation. It is a story to which we shall return (pp. 543–6 below).

Greenland fared worse. Communication with the settlements was becoming very irregular by the fourteenth century. Seldom did more than one ship a year make the journey, and there was one period in the middle of the century when no ship appeared for nine successive years. Climatic deterioration, leading to worsening ice conditions and the advance of hostile Inuit, added to the troubles of the settlers. The last that is heard of them was news brought back to Norway in 1410 by a group of Icelanders who had been driven off course and had been marooned on Greenland for several years.

Thereafter the settlers continued their existence in isolation from the rest of the world, the last ones dying out by the end of the fifteenth century.

Atlantic Ships

By the eleventh century there were three main types of ship being built in Atlantic Europe: Nordic-style ships, vessels called cogs, and hulcs. All three traditions had their origins in the North Sea region going back to the early centuries of the first millennium AD.

We have already considered the Nordic tradition in the early stages of its development in Scandinavia, represented by the famous Gokstad and Oseberg ships and the vessels found in and around Roskilde. Typically the vessels were built plank first of cleft oak, iron fastened in clinker style. There was much variety within the general tradition, and the boat found at Graveney in the marshes of Kent, dating to the ninth century, seems to represent an English variant retaining Romano-Celtic characteristics (p. 454 above).

One of the best-known boatbuilding events of the earlier Middle Ages was William of Normandy's preparation for transporting his foot soldiers and cavalry across the English Channel in 1066. The Bayeux Tapestry shows in charming detail the felling of the trees, the preparation of the planks, and the crafting of the characteristic double-ended vessels. The shipwrights at work here were only a few generations on from the Viking raiders who had settled in the lower Seine valley with their leader, Rollo.

From the eleventh century onwards evidence for the development of Nordic-style ships comes from wrecks, notably those found at Hedeby, Skuldelev, and Bergen, and from depictions incorporated into the seal-stamps made for coastal towns for use in sealing commercial and legal transactions. As wrecks become rarer from the thirteenth and fourteenth century, so seals take their place as a primary source of evidence. The ships are now bigger. Some had decks fore and aft, but larger vessels were decked throughout, providing shelter for the crew and the cargo. The deck timbers offered the added advantage of bracing the hull, giving it greater strength. It was usual for castles to be built on the prow and stern, and fighting tops were often fitted to the mastheads. The castles could be used as fighting platforms when needed, but they also provided good lookout positions and shelter. These vessels retained their traditional means of propulsion and steerage, with the mast set amidships and the rudder side-mounted. Nordic-style ships would continue in use into the fourteenth century, but by the early 1200s they had already begun to give way to the cog.

12.12 The Bayeux Tapestry, which depicts Duke William's invasion of Britain in 1066, includes scenes of shipbuilding on the Normandy coast in preparation for the sea-crossing to Pevensey. The ships under construction are in the Nordic tradition

Cogs were first mentioned in a document referring to Frisian ships in the ninth century. Thereafter the type grew in regard throughout the medieval period, becoming the vessel of choice among the merchants of the German Hansa. Their popularity spread along the Atlantic seaways, and at the beginning of the fourteenth century the first cogs are recorded in the Mediterranean. Characteristically, cogs were flat-bottomed vessels with flush-laid bottom planking and clinker-built sides with a sharp transition between the bottom and the sides. Their distinctive longitudinal profile is created by straight stem- and stern-posts set at a sharp angle to the keel. The sides were high, creating a larger cargo space, the sheer-line rising gently at the stern and rather higher at

12.13 (*Opposite top*) The official seals of the English coastal towns often depict ships in recognition of the town's maritime heritage. This thirteenth-century seal of Winchelsea in East Sussex illustrates a vessel built in the Nordic tradition with castles fore and aft

12.14 (*Opposite bottom*) An English manuscript of 1271 showing two Nordic-style ships engaged in battle with mariners fighting from the fore and aft castles

the bow. Rudders were often mounted on the stern-post, and invariably there was a single square-rigged mast set amidships.

The origin of the cog lay in the Romano-Celtic tradition of boatbuilding which flourished in the Rhine mouth area in the first few centuries of the first millennium AD. These vessels were designed specifically for use on rivers and in estuaries as bulk carriers, and it was among the Frisians of the Low Countries that they continued to develop. Cogs are well represented by wrecks (some eighteen are known from the Netherlands to Sweden) and the type is often depicted on seal-stamps. The earliest wrecks, all from Denmark, date to the late twelfth century, while the latest, from the Netherlands, belong to the early decades of the fifteenth century.

12.15 Coin issued by the town of Hedeby showing a vessel with near-vertical stem- and stern-posts in the style of a cog

The best preserved by far is the cog found in the Weser, down-river from Bremen. Dendrochronological evidence shows that she was built about 1380 and is one of the largest known, at around 23 metres in length, with high sides (4.3 metres), giving a cargo-carrying capacity in the order of a hundred tonnes. Judging by the frequency with which cogs were depicted on seals and mentioned in contemporary texts, they were becoming particularly favoured in the thirteenth century, their popularity lasting throughout the fourteenth century and into the fifteenth, when new styles of ship design began to replace them. With its robust stability and large hold capacity, the cog was everywhere to be seen in the North Sea and the Baltic carrying bulky cargoes in comparative safety with a minimum input of costly manpower. The cog was the merchant's way to fortune.

498

12.16 Two cogs engaged in combat from a fourteenth-century English manuscript

The third type of Atlantic ship was the hulc, a name first mentioned in an English charter of about the year 1000. The word is Anglo-Saxon and means a husk of corn or a pea pod, presumably reflecting the shape of the vessel. A ship which might be thought to look like a pod is engraved on the town seal of Shoreham, Sussex, dating to 1295, which also carries an inscription helpfully identifying the vessel as a hulc. No wreck has yet been identified, though timbers claimed to be from hulcs have been found reused on waterfronts on the Thames. To describe the vessel, we have therefore to rely on contemporary depictions in manuscripts, paintings, engravings, and carvings. The hulcs were double-ended ships without stem- or stern-posts, strongly curved longitudinally, and built of planks of even width swept up at the ends. The planking ends on a sheer-line well clear of the water. Illustrations clearly show the ships to have been clinker-built, but some appear to indicate reverse-clinker planking, with each plank overlapping inboard the upper edge of the plank below. Both bow and stern were fitted with castles, and the single mast was stepped amidships; rudders were

12.17 The well-preserved remains of a fourteenth-century cog were excavated in the river Weser not far from Bremen. This scale model is closely based on the excavated remains

12.18 Besides ships of Nordic tradition and the distinctive cogs there was a third type of vessel, known as a hulc, in use in the early Middle Ages. It is characterized by the way in which its planks sweep up to end on horizontal timbers. A typical hulc is depicted on the twelfth-century font now in Winchester Cathedral. The font was made in northern France of Tournay marble

stern- or side-mounted. Where the hulc originated is difficult to say, but the earliest known image is on a coin minted at the port of Quentovic, near Étaples on the Channel coast of France, in the ninth century. Its popularity in England suggests that it developed somewhere along the coast of the English Channel or of eastern England.

In the thirteenth century the hulc began to rival the cog. Its great advantage was that it could be built with straight runs of sawn timber, making it cheaper and quicker to build than the cog or Nordic-style vessels, for which each plank had to be individually shaped. The form of the hull, with its wide ends, provided capacious cargo space exceeding that of a cog of equivalent length. The ratio of building costs to tonnage would have given the hulc a significant advantage over the cog.

From the eleventh to the fourteenth century the preferred type of warship in England was the galley (*galea*) powered by rowers. In the ninth century King Alfred had ordered the construction of specifically designed warships with sixty oars to defend England against the Danes. Galleys propelled by oars and sail continued to feature in the island's defence, coming to prominence again in the early thirteenth century, when war between England and France began. In 1204 King John ordered forty-five galleys to be stationed at various English ports and another five in Ireland. Between 1209 and

12.19 A hulc seen here in an English manuscript of 1118–40. Like the hulc on the Winchester font, it was built in reverse clinker style with the lower edge of each plank placed behind the upper side of the plank below it

1212 a further twenty were ordered, together with thirty-four other vessels, and later in the century, in 1294, a royal command went out for twenty galleys, each of 120 oars. Even bigger vessels of 132 and 152 oars were constructed for the English at Bayonne in the mid-1320s. But by the mid-fourteenth century, although galleys continued to be built, cogs fitted out for fighting began to take over, their advantage being their greater height. Towering above the galleys, their fighting men, ranged on the deck and on the fore- and sterncastles, could easily pick off their opponents. The ubiquitous cog had once again come into its own.

What is surprising about shipping in the Atlantic zone in the early Middle Ages is that, though there were small improvements in shipbuilding technology, there was little real innovation in design. Shipwrights worked largely within traditions established half a millennium earlier. Symptomatic of this conservatism was a reliance on the single square-rigged mast with all the limitations it placed on sailing. It was not until the late fourteenth century that new ideas in ship design and navigation began to be introduced. By then the Atlantic horizons were broadening.

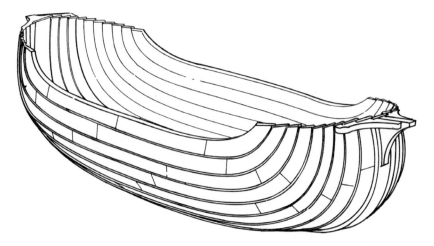

12.20 Reconstruction drawing of a hulc. The hull is built of short lengths of plank joined with scarfs spaced to minimize weakness. All the planks end on a horizontal well above water-level to reduce the risk of rotting

Between the Seas

Until the early thirteenth century, the Strait of Gibraltar was controlled by the successive Muslim polities which ruled Iberia, in later centuries by the Almoravids, who arrived from the Atlas Mountains in 1086, and the Almohads, who advanced from much the same area in 1147. It was a dangerous stretch of water for Christian ships and few attempted to sail between the two seas. Nor did the Muslims have much interest in exploiting the Atlantic any further than their own shores. For them, Seville and Almería marked the western extremity of a trading network extending along the North African coast to Egypt and the Levant, and to the Red Sea and the Indian Ocean beyond. They had little need for regular contact with the Christian north, though vessels bringing cargoes of slaves were always welcome in North African ports.

Until the beginning of the twelfth century the Iberian ports seem to have been largely the preserve of Muslim traders, but the Italian merchant cities were alive to the opportunities they offered. In the late eleventh century a Genoese vessel is recorded to have visited Málaga and another put in to Almería in 1120. From these early beginnings the Genoese were able to build up a profitable traffic with the ports of Andalucía, and by the end of the twelfth century they had negotiated treaties giving their ships safe passage and their merchants favourable tariffs. Gradually colonies of Genoese merchants grew up in the ports of Almería, Málaga, Cádiz, Seville, and Lisbon, the merchant families showing themselves to be adept at maintaining their

12.21 The city of Genoa, seen here in the late fifteenth or early sixteenth century, is situated on the narrow coastal plain backed by the Ligurian Alps. It was therefore outward-looking and more dependent on the sea than its rivals. The absence of a productive hinterland meant that its inhabitants concentrated on seamanship and trade

own identity while living in harmony with their hosts. It was a symbiotic relationship. The Genoese could transport English and Flemish wool and fabrics bought in the Champagne fairs to the ports of Andalucía and there take on board the much-desired produce of Granada: sugar, dried or preserved fruits, and saffron. They could also acquire Saharan gold, to which Málaga had privileged access. With their monopoly of the Iberian ports firmly established, the Genoese found themselves in a particularly favoured position when the Reconquista began to wrest the south from Muslim control.

12.22 Seville, seen here in a sixteenth-century painting by Alonso Sánchez Coello, was a river port owing its prosperity to the agriculturally productive valley of the Guadalquivir and to its easy access to the Atlantic, a day's sailing down-river. Even when still under Muslim domination, Genoese traders had established a lively enclave here. The painting shows the departure of Spanish ships bound for America in 1498

The forward thrust of the Christian armies—a coalition of Castile, Aragón, and Navarre, strengthened by cohorts of French knights—in the middle of the thirteenth century made spectacular gains. Córdoba fell in 1236, Seville in 1248, and Cádiz in 1262. Now the whole of the Guadalquivir valley was under Castilian control, and by 1275 the Muslims had been reduced to the kingdom of Granada. With concessions in the Granadian ports of Almería and Málaga and in the newly won Castilian ports of Seville and Cádiz, Genoa had the best of both worlds. Málaga, now the principal outlet for the kingdom of Granada, was of vital importance to shipping wishing to make the passage from the Mediterranean to the Atlantic since it was here that ships could wait in safety until the wind conditions were favourable, but it was Seville, with its direct access to the Atlantic, that became the pivot between the two seas. In the late thirteenth century a contemporary writer listed the merchandise passing through the city. It came from Alexandria, North Africa, Pisa, Genoa, and Sicily, from Portugal, western France, and England, and from Catalonia, Aragón, and inland France: 'ships come up the river every day from the sea, including *naves*, galleys, and many other sea-going vessels'.

With the Strait of Gibraltar now open, shipping began to flow more freely, but it was slow progress at first. In 1277 Nicolozzo Spinola sent the first Genoese galley out into the Atlantic en route for the Flemish port of Sluys to acquire cloth, and the next year two Genoese galleys set sail, stopping at Southampton, Sandwich, and London on the way to the Flemish markets. It was not long before the Venetians joined in, and by 1298 flotillas of galleys were sailing annually from the Italian merchant cities to Flanders.

Nor were the Atlantic seamen slow off the mark. A Florentine chronicler, Giovanni Villani, wrote in 1304:

> At this time people came from Bayonne and Gascony in their ships which in Bayonne they call cogs, through the Strait of Gibraltar, on buccaneering expeditions in the Mediterranean, where they inflicted much damage. After that time people from Genoa, Venice, and Catalonia began to employ cogs for their seafaring and abandon the use of their own large ships owing to the seaworthiness and lower cost of cogs. Thus, great changes were wrought in the ship form of our fleet.

Villani's comment is revealing. Quite simply the great Mediterranean galleys were ill-suited to the long Atlantic journey. They needed large crews of rowers, which were expensive and had to be fed and watered. Since space on board was at a premium and was largely devoted to cargo, the galleys had to make frequent stops to take on new supplies. This extended the journey time, adding further to the cost. The most popular ports of call along the route were Lisbon, La Coruña, La Rochelle, and Nantes, where there were Italian agents in residence who facilitated the stopovers. Rivalries between the Genoese and Venetians led them to try to avoid each other as much as possible. Thus, while the Genoese favoured the Galician port of La Coruña, the Venetians made for El Ferról. The Genoese also tended to use the smaller Breton ports in preference to Nantes.

In spite of the inefficiencies of the great galleys, the Venetians maintained their annual convoys well into the fifteenth century. The outlook of their owners remained stolidly Mediterranean. The Genoese, meanwhile, showed their adaptability. Immediately after the Reconquista they quickly increased their presence in Seville and Cádiz, building up very substantial merchant enclaves and in doing so creating for themselves a new Atlantic identity. Already in the early thirteenth century the Genoese had begun to adopt large round ships of Atlantic type. By the end of the century round sailing ships were accompanying their galleys on the Atlantic run, and by about 1340 the commercial galleys had been dispensed with altogether. Round ships suited the Genoese style of trading since they were used to carry relatively low-value, high-bulk cargoes between the Strait of Gibraltar and the English Channel at speed with fewer stops en route, and thus more cheaply, allowing the financial return on the journeys to be quickly recouped. Although the Genoese were careful to maintain their distinctiveness, through intermarriage and by being prepared to serve in the government of the towns or in the interests of the Crown they made themselves a valued part of the Castilian community. Thus it was that, in the fifteenth century, their reputation for trustworthiness and their skills at sea put them at the forefront of Atlantic exploration.

The arrival of the Venetian and Genoese galleys in English and Flemish ports was an event eagerly awaited. They brought with them a treasure of high-value goods from the Mediterranean and the east, spices and dried fruits, silks, and damasks, and a wide range of exquisitely crafted wares, including armour, gold-work, and fine leather. Some brought less exciting, though no less important, cargoes like alum from Phocaea (formerly Phokaia) on the coast of Asia Minor, so useful in the processing of cloth. Putting in at ports like Southampton and London, the Italian merchants could offload some of their spectacular goods in exchange for English cloth and wool, lead and tin, and hides from Ireland brought in through Bristol, and in the ports of Flanders they could take on board the Flemish cloth for which the region was famous. On their return, if cargo space allowed, they could pick up sea-salt from the salt-pans of Guérande, the Bay of Bourgneuf, and Setúbal.

With the opening up of the Atlantic route in the fourteenth century the trans-peninsular trade through the Alps to the Champagne and Flemish towns fell into decline. Italian merchants whose predecessors had had to make the dangerous journey through the Alps could now stay comfortably at home waiting for their ships to return.

The Best of Both Worlds

For six hundred years Muslim control of the Strait of Gibraltar had meant that there was little free mixing of Atlantic and Mediterranean shipping, but suddenly, with the Reconquista, the constriction fell away and by about the year 1300 ships of both seas could come and go as they pleased. In south-western Iberian ports like Lisbon, Cádiz, and Seville sailors from both the Atlantic and the Mediterranean would have marvelled at the alien craft among which they found themselves. And with the flotillas of Mediterranean galleys making their annual journeys to the north, shipbuilders in

England and Flanders were soon introduced to quite different styles of construction and rigging. There was much for everyone to learn.

The fourteenth century was a time of experiment. Until 1300 most northern ships had been square-rigged and built shell first with frames added later, the planks of the hull being overlapped and nailed together in clinker style. The Mediterranean vessels were lateen-rigged, their hulls built frame first with planks laid flush in carvel style. It was the French who were the first to introduce Mediterranean methods of ship-building to the north. The French Crown was well aware of the quality of the galleys that were being built along the south coast in ports like Narbonne, Aigues-Mortes,

12.23 Highly glazed basins (*bacini*) were fixed on the outside walls of several churches in Pisa. Made by Muslim craftsmen and depicting Muslim ships, they were meant to proclaim the success of Pisan merchants in penetrating Muslim markets

and Marseille. Indeed, in the thirteenth century Louis IX had commissioned galleys from Genoa and Venice to transport troops engaged in the Crusades. So it was that in 1294 the French brought shipbuilders from the Mediterranean ports to Rouen on the river Seine, where, in a part of the royal dockyard known as Le Clos des Galées, they were put to work constructing galleys in Mediterranean style for the French navy. Thereafter, until 1416, Mediterranean craftsmen kept the galleys in repair, building new ones when required. The French were so impressed by the fighting potential of galleys that they employed squadrons of Genoese galleys to augment the French navy in the prolonged conflict with the English.

The benefits of the northern cog were quickly appreciated by the Genoese, as we have seen, and by the early fourteenth century the three-masted lateen-rigged galley with side rudder was soon being replaced by the cocha, a version of the cog, with a single square-rigged sail and a stern rudder but built frame first in Mediterranean style. These sailing vessels were cheaper to build and man and were much easier to handle in a following wind than the more cumbersome galleys with their lateen rig. However, since the lateen rig had some advantages, not least that it enabled the vessel to sail closer to the wind, it was not long before cochas were being fitted with a second mizzen-mast towards the stern to take a lateen sail, thus combining the best of both rigs. The earliest reference to this style of two-master is in a Catalan contract of 1353; the vessel also had a small sail on a bowsprit. Thereafter the two-mast cocha (or nan, as it was sometimes called) became common in the Mediterranean. In the Atlantic these vessels were known as carracks. A further improvement was the addition of a square-rigged foremast, giving greater sail power. The earliest illustration of a three-master appears in a Catalan manuscript of 1406. The Genoese and the Catalans were clearly at the forefront of this rapid advance in shipbuilding design in the late fourteenth and early fifteenth century, and it was the Genoese who were responsible for introducing these innovations to the Atlantic.

12.24 Bench end, originally in the Chapel of St Nicholas, King's Lynn, dating to *c.*1415. It shows a typical carrack rigged with a square mainsail and a lateen mizzen

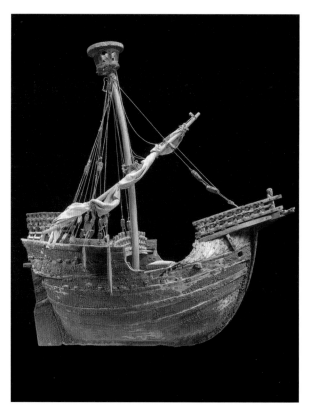

12.25 (*Left*) Model of a carrack dating to *c*.1450, with a single square-rigged mainsail. The model was an ex-voto from a church in Catalonia

12.26 (*Right*) An Italian engraving of *c*.1470–80 showing a three-masted carrack. The small triangular topsail was a Mediterranean development

The English were slow to adopt these new styles of rigging. The first two-masters were not built until the early fifteenth century (in Southampton), the *Anne* in 1416 and the *Grace Dieu* between 1416 and 1418, and the square foresail does not appear until the 1430s. The frame-first carvel style of build was not adopted until the late fifteenth century. The first recorded vessel to be built in this style was a three-master constructed at Dunwich between 1463 and 1466. Frame-first construction required skills which the north European shipbuilders were slow to learn. When they wanted ships of this kind they, like the French, had to import specialist craftsmen from the Mediterranean. Similarly, when the English acquired frame-built ships, in warfare or by piracy, they had to hire experienced foreigners to repair them. Northern Europe did not fully adopt frame-first construction until the sixteenth century.

The three-master built frame first with carvel planking at Dunwich in 1463–6 belonged to a class of small, fast ships known as caravels, a type which originated in Portugal in the thirteenth century as two-mast, lateen-rigged fishing vessels. In 1448 'a certain ship or barge called *Le Carvell* of Oporto in Portugal' was given leave to trade to England. It is the first written reference to such a ship from Iberia in English waters, but already, in 1439, the duke of Burgundy was having 'une caravelle' built by Portuguese shipwrights somewhere near Brussels, and others were being built about this time at Sluys in Flanders. The caravel was a big, broad vessel which had developed out of Mediterranean and Atlantic traditions on the Atlantic coast of south-western Iberia. It was fast and manoeuvrable, well suited to the open Atlantic. These vessels, and the men who grew up with them, were soon to spearhead the exploration of the ocean.

The Atlantic Mediterranean

The Atlantic Mediterranean is the term used by French historians to refer to that part of the Atlantic lying immediately outside the Strait of Gibraltar bounded by the island groups of the Canaries, Madeira, and the Azores. To that extent it can claim to be a 'middle sea', and in the fourteenth century it became the preserve of Mediterranean sailors. Sailors knew these waters before 1300. Muslim traders, hugging the shore, made regular journeys between the ports along the coast of Morocco, and fishermen, Muslim, Portuguese, and Galician, exploited the nearby sea, attracted by the sardines and tuna that abounded. How adventurous they were is unrecorded, but they would have had a keen understanding of the winds and currents, and would have been able to offer a store of invaluable wisdom to those who now emerged from the Mediterranean.

The opening up of the Atlantic to the Mediterranean Christian polities in the second half of the thirteenth century offered enticing opportunities for maritime entrepreneurs, among whom the Genoese were the first to take up the challenge. Some, as we have seen, were content to send flotillas of trading vessels northwards to England and Flanders. Others, showing more spirit of adventure, once beyond Gibraltar turned south to see what they could find. For the Genoese, whose access to eastern trade goods was becoming ever more restricted through competition with the Venetians, the Atlantic was the sea of opportunity. So it was that in 1291 two Genoese, the Vivaldi brothers, set off in a galley 'for regions of India by way of the Ocean', their route presumably taking them down the coast of Africa, in the wake of the Carthaginians and Greeks more than a millennium and a half before, in the expectation of being able to

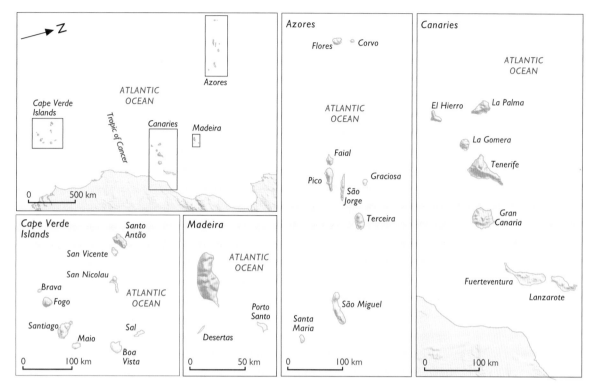

12.27 From the twelfth century the islands of the Atlantic Mediterranean became increasingly attractive to sailors and traders from the Mediterranean. The development of the carrack with its flexible rigging greatly facilitated exploration

open up the highly profitable route to the Indian Ocean. Nothing more was heard of them. Others no doubt followed. Some, with less ambition, were encouraged by knowing that explorers of the classical period had discovered the Fortunate islands just off the African coast. In the first century AD, Pliny had given a full description of the island group, naming several of them. One, Canaria, was soon to give its name to the archipelago. In the 1340s Petrarch records that the Genoese had sent armed ships to the Canary islands within the memory of his parents, presumably in the early decades of the century.

The first visit for which there is any detailed record was that of the Genoese trader Lanzarotto Malocello, who set himself up on the island named after him sometime before 1339. Thereafter the voyages of exploration came thick and fast. In 1341 a major expedition set sail. It was under Italian command, with Genoese and Florentines playing a leading role, but it seems to have been a cooperative venture inspired by the Portuguese and with Castilian involvement. They explored at least thirteen of the 'isles called Newfound', of which six were inhabited. News of the discovery eventually reached the Florentine poet Boccaccio, through whose writing the record survives. In the following year, 1342, at least four voyages were licensed to sail from Majorca. That the ships were to be cogs suggests that by now it was becoming general knowledge that galleys were not well suited to Atlantic conditions.

The appearance of Majorcans in Atlantic exploration is interesting. Majorca had been finally freed from Muslim rule by the kingdom of Aragón in 1229, and for a while, in the late thirteenth and early fourteenth century, it had become an island kingdom living off the sea. During this time it was used as a staging post for Genoese expeditions to the west. Benefiting from the many sailors and traders who used its ports, Majorca soon became a centre for map-making, producing, alongside prestigious maps for wealthy clients, the more practical portolans—sailing instructions illustrated by sea-charts for use by sailors. In 1343 the island was absorbed into the kingdom of Aragón, under whose authority subsequent expeditions were sent. With the Canary islands becoming better known, and stories of the pagan island tribes beginning to circulate, missionary zeal now became the driving force. The first recorded mission, in 1351, established the diocese of Fortuna on Gran Canaria. Five missionary expeditions are recorded over the next thirty or so years.

Growing knowledge of the islands is reflected in the maps of the period. The beginnings of their accurate recording can be seen on the Dulcert Map of 1339, which shows three of them in roughly their correct positions. By the time the Catalan Atlas (Figure 2.16) was compiled about 1380, eleven islands were mapped, and on Guillem Soler's map of 1385 the islands are shown correctly spaced in relation to the African coast and at approximately their right scale.

While Mediterranean traders and missionaries were making visits to the Canaries, the Portuguese and Castilians were beginning to contemplate outright colonization. In 1345 the king of Portugal 'turned the eyes of our mind' to the task of subjugating the islands and sent out a reconnaissance expedition. In the same year the Castilians asserted their claim, but little came of it and there the matter rested for a while, until 1370, when Portugal claimed rights over two islands. To counter this, expeditions were sent from Seville, and so the dispute escalated. In the early years of the fifteenth century, two other contenders joined the race: Jean de Béthencourt and Gadifer de La Salle, both members of the Norman aristocracy. The original intention seems to have been to claim the islands for France, but in the event the leaders came to rely heavily on Castilian support and had to acknowledge homage to the king. The Norman colonization, which began in 1408, was only a partial success. Lanzarote, Fuerteventura, and El Hierro were occupied, the larger, more fertile islands escaping their grasp. But it was a beginning, and since the Norman mercenaries admitted subservience to the Castilian Crown, Spain's claim was established. This did not prevent Béthencourt's successor from selling the lordship of Lanzarote to the Portuguese in 1448, an act which led to a long dispute that was not resolved until the Canaries were assigned to Spain in 1479.

Reaching the Canary islands required no great feat of seamanship since the winds and currents carried ships southwards along the African coast. Returning was more difficult, especially in cogs, which could not sail close to the wind. The return journey along the coast could be made in a brief period in midwinter, but for the rest of the year it was necessary to sail out into the ocean in a north-westerly direction to reach the band of westerlies which would drive the ships back to the Iberian coast. It was in this way that the uninhabited islands of Madeira and the Azores were discovered. Although there are no fourteenth-century textual references to them, Madeira is clearly marked on maps from the mid-fourteenth century, and groups of islands are shown roughly in the position of the Azores, though rather strung out and oversized. The latitude is more or less accurate but the longitudes are out, which is to be expected given that the only way of assessing longitude at the time was by dead reckoning. Maps of the later fourteenth century show eight islands in the Azores archipelago, suggesting that all except the most westerly, Corvo, had been visited. No attempt seems to have been made to settle them until the Portuguese colonization of the early fifteenth century.

That the island rim of the Atlantic Mediterranean was discovered, explored, and partly colonized within a few decades in the fourteenth century was a notable feat of seamanship. It was driven by men with a deep curiosity and sense of adventure, spurred on, no doubt, by a desire for fame, missionary zeal, and simple avarice. Their task was made easier by the technological advances of the age. Sturdy oceanworthy vessels were now being built, the compass was widely used, and this, together with improvements in dead reckoning, made it possible for skilled cartographers to produce increasingly accurate portolan charts criss-crossed with rhumb lines enabling mariners to navigate to specific islands with ease. With the technology in place, and the Atlantic Mediterranean now a familiar sea, it was time to explore other horizons.

13

The Ocean Conquered,
1400–1510

It is not easy to gauge the mood in the western Mediterranean during the fourteenth century. It was a time of huge change driven by the devastations of the Black Death. The European population had been cut by a third, its Christian beliefs had been shaken to the core, and the old certainties of the feudal system had been fatally undermined. What emerged by the end of the century was a new world bursting with new opportunities but one still constrained by the husk of old value systems. Throughout the twelfth and much of the thirteenth century, Europe had been united in its Crusades against the Muslim world in the Holy Land, but the fall of the Crusader states to the Mamluks in 1291 had brought the dream and the unity of purpose it inspired crashing to the ground. There were, however, other religious objectives to motivate the young. In 1270 Louis IX had already deflected the Eighth Crusade to Tunis, no doubt with a watchful eye on the economic advantages to be gained by involvement in the Maghrib, a place where the African gold caravans ended and only a short sea journey from his new base at Aigues-Mortes in the Rhône delta. Meanwhile, in Iberia the Christian polities were united in their desire to drive out the Moors, an aspiration finally achieved with the reconquest of the kingdom of Granada in 1492.

The protracted Reconquista did much to sustain chivalric ideals in Christian Iberia. The Moor provided a vision of the 'other' against which the disparate Christian states could unite, giving their young males a well-focused target to pit themselves against in pursuit of glory. But throughout the fourteenth century the search for new horizons began. Africa was an obvious attraction. Not only was the Maghrib still in the hands of the Moors, but the country was a source of many desirables, including gold, and in the more distant recesses of the continent there were pagan peoples in desperate need of being introduced to the benefits of Christianity. Here, then, was an objective worthy of both the European Christian elite and their financial backers.

Dom Henrique

Since the treaty of Alcañices, signed by Portugal and Spain in 1297, the relationship between the two countries had been uneasy. The marriage of Princess Beatrice of Portugal to Juan I of Castile meant that Portugal would eventually pass to Castile by succession. This was far from acceptable to the merchants of Lisbon. With the accession of João I as king of Portugal in 1385, hostilities quickly intensified, leading to the decisive battle of Aljubarrota late in the year, from which Portugal emerged triumphant.

The English had supported the Portuguese cause, and the alliance was strengthened still further when King João married Philippa, daughter of John of Gaunt. The third child of the union was the Infante Dom Henrique, born in 1394. Like his brothers, Henrique took part in the capture of Ceuta, a Muslim port on the African coast opposite Gibraltar, in 1415. He acquitted himself well and four years later, at the age of 25, he was appointed governor of the Algarve. The Ceuta expedition, which founded the first Portuguese enclave on the African mainland, was an audacious act designed in part to utilize the surplus energies of the army, which had had little to occupy it since the end of hostilities with Castile, and partly to gain control of the port through which much of the gold coming by caravan across the Sahara was channelled. It could also be justified as another step in the triumphant advance of Christianity against the Moors. Henrique, then, grew up at a time when the young state of Portugal was beginning to flex its muscles, searching for a direction in the fast-changing world. On taking up his new appointment in 1419, Henrique set up his new home at Sagres, close to Cape St Vincent in the extreme

13.1 Miniature of Dom Henrique (1394–1460), more popularly known, from the nineteenth century, as Henry the Navigator. Dom Henrique was the third surviving son of João I of Portugal and Philippa of Lancaster, daughter of John of Gaunt

13.2 The fifteenth-century Catalan Atlas shows the world as it was believed to be at the time of Dom Henrique. The map shows the Sinus Aethiopicus, the east–west gulf that was believed to extend around the south side of Africa. This belief reflects the concepts of Ptolemy in the second century

south-west of Portugal. His entire horizon to the west and the south was bounded by the ocean, and it was on this chosen geography that he focused much of his creative energies.

The aims, aspirations, and achievements of the Infante Dom Henrique, or Henry the Navigator as he has been popularly known since the nineteenth century, have been caught up in a veil of nautical romanticism originating with his admirer and biographer Gomes Eanes de Zurara and embroidered by others since. More rigorous historians have encouraged us to leave aside notions that he set up a school for navigators on the windswept heights of Sagres, where he studied and taught cosmology and stellar navigation, and to see him as a man of his time, a younger son driven by filial duty, with an abiding faith in his own horoscope; a member of the knightly Order of Christ and, as one modern historian has said, a man brought up in the 'shabby swagger' of a chivalric world lacking in ancient riches. He still had a crusading fervour, but he was driven by a desire to see his country prosper and by a deep-seated natural curiosity.

From Sagres, Henrique's cognitive geography was outward-looking, to the islands of the Atlantic Mediterranean and to the west coast of Africa. The islands had potential for colonization, while the African coast provided the prospect of being able to tap into the flow of Saharan gold nearer to its source. In the four decades from his arrival in the Algarve until his death in 1460, he provided the inspiration and the patronage that encouraged a succession of ships' captains to push the boundaries of knowledge southwards down the African coast to Sierra Leone and westwards to the Azores.

Throughout this time his principal concern was to take control of the Canary islands, which the Castilians considered to be their preserve. The latter had already established their presence on Lanzarote, Fuerteventura, and El Hierro, but the larger populated islands of Tenerife, Gran Canaria, La Palma, and La Gomera had resisted colonization and were potentially there for the taking. Expeditions to Gran Canaria and La Gomera in 1434 achieved little apart from slaves, and the pope's intervention two years later in favour of the claims of Castile brought further expeditions to a temporary halt. There were subsequent Portuguese ventures between 1440 and 1454 but without success. Expeditions continued after Henrique's death in 1460 but ceased altogether when, in 1479, the treaty of Alcáçovas-Toledo finally agreed the rights of Castile to all the island group. The reason why Henrique and the Castilians were so intent on acquiring the Canaries was that they were seen to be a convenient base from which the Saharan gold route on the African mainland could be accessed. While the islands were not of themselves particularly productive, they were a source of orchil, derived from moss, and a resin, dragon's blood, both used in dyeing, and they offered a ready supply of slaves. But then slaves could be acquired at many other points on the African mainland, as the Portuguese pioneers soon found out.

While the unsuccessful attempts were being made on the Canaries, the Portuguese were intent on colonizing the unoccupied islands of Madeira and the Azores. Soon after his arrival in the Algarve, Henrique had sent an expedition to Madeira and its neighbour, Porto Santo, but little seems to have come of it, and as late as 1436 Madeira was described as suitable only for hermits. Yet three years later, in June and July 1439, ships were being dispatched to Madeira and the Azores carrying settlers, together with the sheep and seed-grain necessary to support them. Over the next decade or so Madeira was apportioned out to enterprising feudal lords whose task it was to bring out settlers and encourage them to stay, a task made easier by the fact that many of

13.3 The Sagres peninsula near Lagos on the Algarve, jutting out into the Atlantic, is traditionally the place where Dom Henrique established a school of navigation. Standing on the peninsula and looking south, there is nothing to see but ocean extending without limit down the west coast of Africa. It is easy to appreciate the challenge presented to would-be explorers

those who arrived were criminals or people sent into exile. Madeira's climate was well suited for the production of sugar, which was much in demand, but the cultivation of sugar-cane and the extraction of sugar was a capital-intensive enterprise. It was, however, an enterprise in which Genoese financiers were very willing to invest, and Dom Henrique was himself a partner in a Madeiran sugar mill built in 1452. The industry prospered to the satisfaction of the capitalists, and by 1480 sixty to seventy shiploads of sugar were being exported annually.

The Azores were not suited climatically for sugar production, but were prolific in producing wheat, sheep, and cattle, and became a major grain supplier to Portugal.

Settlement was on a feudal basis, with a peasantry brought in from the mainland serving under 'captains' who had the right to grant leases of five years or more while retaining control of the flour mills and bread ovens, and the extraction of salt. The success of the island colonies owed much to the organizing enterprise of Dom Henrique and to the financial backers he encouraged to invest in his vision. The islands benefited particularly from the enterprise of Italians who traded and settled there, but they also gained much from incomers from the southern Netherlands encouraged by the special trading privileges negotiated with Bruges. These entrepreneurs also extended their interests to Madeira, and by the end of the fifteenth century one-third of Madeira's sugar production was being shipped to the Low Countries.

Early in the sixteenth century, when transatlantic trade with America began to develop, the Azores became a port of call for ships using the prevailing westerly winds, on the return journey, to drive them on to Europe. Similarly, for those coming from the Far East around the southern tip of Africa and striking out across the ocean on the south-easterly trades to reach the westerlies, the appearance of the archipelago signalled a welcome haven and the beginning of the last haul before the comforts of home.

Gold, Slaves, and India

Dom Henrique's determined efforts to develop the islands gave a boost to the Portuguese economy, but his main objective remained African gold, and to gain access to it he needed his captains to explore the coastline for suitable places to tap into the indigenous trade routes. A major thrust south past the latitude of the Canaries got under way about 1421. Cape Non—the point beyond which it was believed lay the impassable torrid zone—was soon passed, and in 1434 an able ship's captain, Gil Eanes, rounded Cape Bojador, a dangerous passage because of the reefs and shallows which extended far out into the ocean. His physical achievement was much praised, but its real significance lay in breaking the psychological barrier presented by these landmarks, which had loomed threateningly in the minds of sailors. Thereafter the advance was rapid. Nuno Tristão passed Cabo Blanco in 1442 and later landed on the island of Arguin (modern Mauritania), sheltered by the curve of the cape, where a trading colony was set up. From here, over the next thirty years, merchants travelled inland to meet up with the caravans transporting gold northwards through the desert. Arguin also gained the dubious reputation of being Europe's first slaving station in Africa. In 1444 Tristão reached the mouth of the river Senegal, and in the same year Dinis Dias rounded Cape Verde. Two years later, Tristão was exploring the mouth of the Gambia when it seems he was killed. The discovery of the two rivers provided a major incentive for exploration, attracting adventurers like the Genoese trader Antoniotto Usodimare, who sailed far up the rivers to Mali in the 1450s, and the Venetian navigator Alvide da Ca' da Mosto, whose interest in the natural history and anthropology of the region is manifest in his vivid writings.

Henrique and his brother Pedro had encouraged and sponsored the exploration, and as news of the discoveries spread it became essential for Portugal to claim its monopoly. In 1455, in a masterstroke of diplomacy, Henrique persuaded the pope to issue a bull recognizing Portugal's right to the entire coastline, 'extending from Cape Bojador and Cape Non through all Guinea and passing beyond to the southern parts'. Anyone who interfered in the Portuguese domain would be excommunicated.

By the time of Henrique's death in 1460, the coast had been explored as far as Sierra Leone and there was a reluctance to go much further. At this latitude the familiar

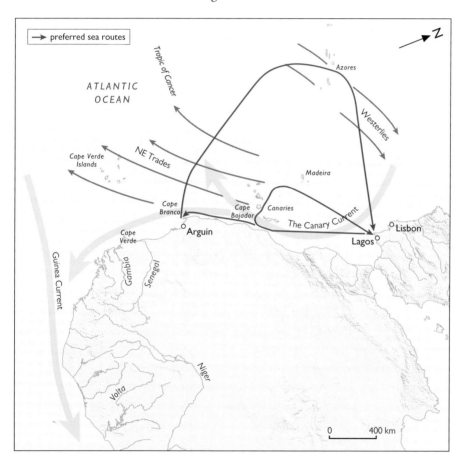

13.4 The currents and winds of the Atlantic facilitated sea travel down the west coast of Africa, but the return journey was more difficult, requiring wide sweeps to be made out into the ocean to pick up the westerlies needed to drive the vessel back to Europe. In this way Madeira and the Azores became familiar to sailors

North Star could hardly be seen above the horizon, making navigation uncertain, and anyway, the Senegal and Gambia rivers offered sufficiently rich pickings to satisfy the traders. Perhaps more to the point, the Portuguese king, Afonso V, was now involved in crusading in Morocco with the intention of capturing Tangier and Arzila, thus gaining control of the Strait of Gibraltar; Guinea was a long way away from his immediate concerns. But in 1469 interest in the African coastline picked up again when the king leased the whole African enterprise, except for the port of Arguin and the Cape Verde islands, to a Lisbon merchant, Fernão Gomes, in return for an annual rent and an agreement to explore a hundred leagues of coast annually. Gomes was a man of energy who picked his captains well, and over the five years in which the lease was to run, his men explored 3,200 kilometres of coastline, across the Bight of Benin and past the Niger delta. The island of Fernando Pó (Bioko), in sight of Mount Cameroon, was glimpsed, at which point the coast turned south. The last of his captains crossed the equator and rounded Cape Lopez, reaching latitude 2° south. In 1475, when the lease was up, Gomes made no effort to renew it. The outbreak of war between Portugal and Castile, which saw the Castilians sending privateering fleets to the Guinea coast, made continued trade and exploration both dangerous and expensive. Although the Portuguese lost the war on land, they were more successful at sea, and in the treaty of Alcáçovas-Toledo, which brought the war to an end, Castile accepted the Portuguese monopoly of fishing, trade, and navigation along the whole of the West African coast. The same treaty also affirmed Portugal's rights to Madeira and the Azores.

The revival of interest in trade and exploration which followed was actively encouraged by the new king, João II, who came to the throne in 1481. The Portuguese hold on the Guinea coast was strengthened and a forward policy instigated, the king funding a series of expeditions, led by experienced mariners, designed to chart the passage around the southern tip of Africa to the Indian Ocean. The new objective inspired fresh energy and enthusiasm. The ships carried stone columns, *padrões*, to erect on prominent headlands to mark the progress of the advance. The first was set up in 1483 at the mouth of the Congo by Diogo Cão, who sailed for some distance up the great river, where the second *padrão* was erected. He returned to Portugal in 1484, but the following year he was back again, continuing his journey southwards as far as Cape Cross at 21° south. Here he set up another *padrão* before turning north to spend more time reconnoitring the river Congo en route back to Portugal. In his two expeditions he had explored 2,500 kilometres of coast.

One of the problems that Cão had encountered was finding food along the tropical coastline. So it was that when his successor Bartolomeu Dias left Lisbon in 1487 he took, in addition to his two caravels, a store-ship, which he left anchored at Angra Pequena before proceeding along the unknown coast. The winds and currents were

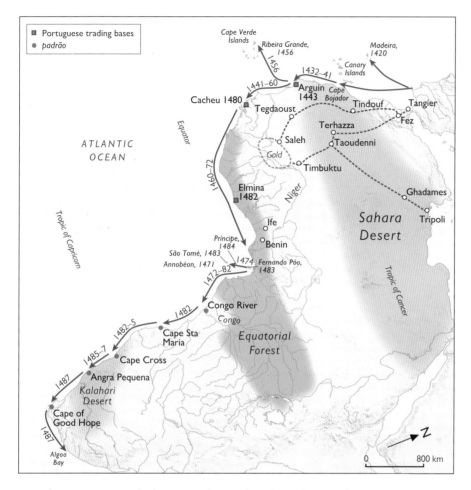

13.5 After Dom Henrique's death in 1460 enthusiasm for exploring the coast of Africa continued, spurred on by the desire to find a way around the continent to get to the Indian Ocean and the wealth it offered. As the Portuguese explorers pushed south, entrepreneurs followed behind, setting up trading bases at Arguin (now Mauritania), Cacheu (Guinea-Bissau), and Elmina (Ghana) to exploit gold, slaves, and ivory obtainable from the indigenous peoples of the coastal regions eager to engage in trade

now very much against his southern progress, so at Cape Volta he struck out south-south-west to catch the prevailing westerlies, which carried him around the southern cape of Africa without seeing it, to Algoa Bay, where he realized that they had reached the edge of the Indian Ocean. Having decided that they had come far enough, Dias began the return journey, only then sighting the cape, which he named the Cape of Storms. Back at the store-ship at Angra Pequena, he erected a *padrão* on Point Dinas before setting off for Lisbon, where the ships finally berthed in December 1488.

For the next ten years the records are silent, but the strong probability is that many exploratory voyages were made during this time to test the winds and currents by sweeping further and further out into the western Atlantic to find the optimal conditions for the southern journey, rather than face the slog against contrary winds encountered when hugging the coast as Cão and Dias had done. Thus, when an expedition led by the nobleman Vasco da Gama set out from Lisbon in July 1497 intent on reaching India, they would have had access to the knowledge gained over the decade of reconnaissance, which they used to good effect. From the Canaries the ships sailed directly to the Cape Verde islands and then began a massive sweep westwards out into the open Atlantic before picking up the westerlies, which drove them to the African coast at St Helena Bay, a few degrees north of the Cape of Storms. There they 'saluted the captain-major by firing our bombards, and dressed the ship with flags and standards'. They had been four months at sea. From there they coast-hopped up the east coast of Africa, sailing as far north as Malindi

13.6 (*Above left*) In the later years of the fifteenth century it was customary for the Portuguese explorers to set up marker stones (*padrões*) to record the progress of their thrust south. The *padrão* at Cape Cross, Namibia, bearing the arms of Portugal, was erected by the explorer Diogo Cão. A replica marks its original location

13.7 (*Above*) The inscribed *padrão* at Ielala near Matadi at the mouth of the river Congo

13.8 During the period of Portuguese expansion, Lisbon, the base from which the fleets usually set out, flourished and expanded over the surrounding hills. The lively waterfront is seen here in a painting of the sixteenth century

before setting course across the Indian Ocean to Calicut. Da Gama had set out with four ships—two caravels and two square-rigged nãos—each carrying twenty guns. The inclusion of square-rigged vessels is a further indication that the ships' masters were confident of finding favourable following winds in the Atlantic, since they perform poorly close to the wind. The heavy armament reflected the mood of the expedition. It was an aggressive thrust into a new world which the Portuguese intended to dominate, and da Gama's violent behaviour in the Indian Ocean set the scene for the conflict that was to follow. On the way home the ships sailed straight from the Cape of Storms to the Cape Verde islands and then looped westwards to pick up the westerlies, which

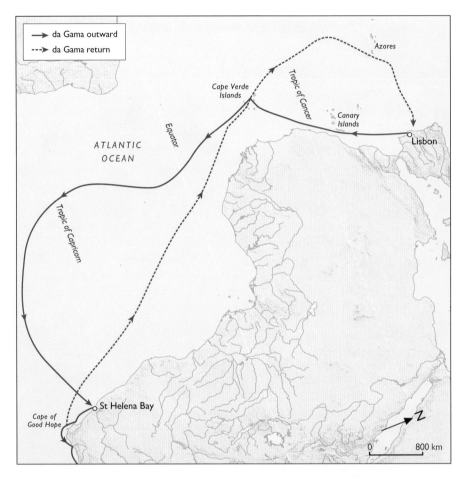

13.9 Vasco da Gama had learned much about Atlantic navigation from those who had gone before him. Instead of trying to make the difficult passage down the coast of Africa, he took a wide loop out into the Atlantic, eventually making land at St Helena Bay in south-west Africa before following the coast into the Indian Ocean. His return journey took him from the Cape of Good Hope (which he called the Cape of Storms) out across the open ocean

brought them to the Azores and to Lisbon, arriving in July 1499. The outward and homeward courses which da Gama had set were to be followed by East India ships for centuries to come.

While the Portuguese captains were pioneering the route to India, other entrepreneurs were developing the Guinea coast and islands. As well as the trading colony at Arguin, two fort factories were built on the African mainland of Cacheu (now in Guinea-Bissau) in 1480 and at São Jorge da Mina, or Elmina (now in Ghana), in 1482. The site for Elmina was agreed by negotiation with local chiefs, and the fort was built

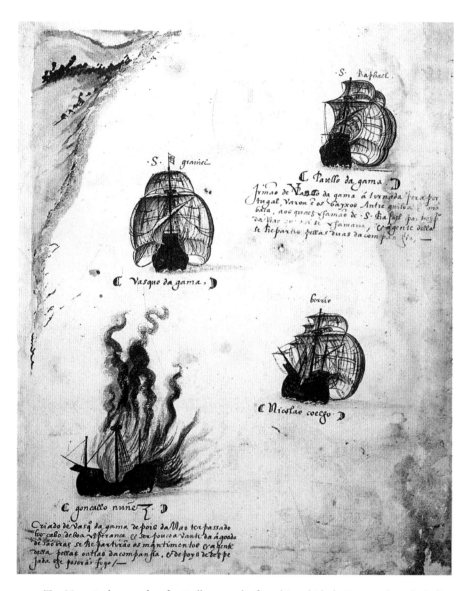

13.10 The *Memoria das armadas* of 1568 illustrates the four ships which da Gama took to the Indian Ocean in 1497

of dressed stone shipped out from Portugal. When complete it was garrisoned by sixty soldiers and soon became the centre around which a native settlement grew. Another factory was set up at Gató on the river Benin to deal specifically with the trade in slaves. The principal exports from the Guinea coast were gold, slaves, and the coarse, pungent malagueta pepper, but other local products included ivory, copper, gum, wax,

13.11 St George's Castle, guarding the trading centre established by the Portuguese at Elmina in 1482. This Dutch print dates to the sixteenth century

palm oil, and ostrich eggs. In return, the indigenous population received cloth and a wide range of hardware. At first, in the last decades of the fifteenth century, the volume of trade was not great, amounting to between twelve and fifteen Portuguese ships a year carrying a total of about five hundred slaves, but over the next century it was to increase dramatically.

The various islands off the west coast of Africa, the Cape Verde islands off the coast of Senegal and the islands of the Bight of Bonny off Cameroon, proved difficult to colonize because of their tropical climate, which was inhospitable to Europeans. Attempts to settle the Cape Verde islands in 1462 met with little enthusiasm, largely because they were too remote from Portugal, but the energetic Genoese trader Antoniotto Usodimare, who followed in the wake of the explorers, established a viable community on the largest island, Santiago, based on slave-run sugar plantations in the 1480s, and the island served as a port of call for ships going to and from

13.12 St George's Castle, Elmina, still dominates the port today

the Indian Ocean. In the Bight of Bonny sustaining island colonies was even more difficult, but on São Tomé, by the 1490s, there was a small settlement of some fifty Europeans, all exiled criminals, who ran sugar plantations with slave labour and traded with the nearby coast for slaves, copper, and pepper. Another colony was founded in Príncipe in 1500, but for all the settlers in this remote corner of the sea it was a precarious existence.

The Portuguese achievement in this century of discovery had been considerable. The entire Atlantic coast of Africa had been explored, the Azores, Madeira, and the Cape Verde islands had been colonized, and sufficient had been learned of the winds and currents of the Atlantic to allow ships to make sweeping ocean journeys out of sight of land for months on end to cover the huge distances between Portugal and the Cape of Storms, soon renamed the Cape of Good Hope by a king well satisfied with the achievements of his ships' captains.

Securing the Canary Islands

The Canary islands had been in contention between the Castilians and the Portuguese since 1345, when both royal households had laid claim to them. As we have seen (pp. 510–13), Castilian colonization of Lanzarote, Fuerteventura, and El Hierro, led by Norman lords, began in 1402, but the contested sale of the lordship of Lanzarote to Dom Henrique in 1448 renewed Portugal's interest in the Canaries and attempts were made over the next six years to seize the island from its settlers and to conquer Gran Canaria. Success in exploring the African coast, however, distracted Dom Henrique and interest lapsed. The war that broke out in 1474, when Afonso V of Portugal challenged Ferdinand and Isabella for the crown of Castile, brought the issue of control of the Canaries once more to prominence. In 1478 seven Portuguese caravels were dispatched to the islands, and in response Castile sent its own naval force to resume conquest. One of the reasons for Castilian concern was that the Crown wished to reassert its rights over the Spanish conquistadors who were active in the islands. These private enterprises were too small-scale to be effective: what was needed to ensure firm and permanent control was a new state-sponsored expedition properly financed. The treaty of Alcáçovas-Toledo of 1479, which brought the war between Portugal and Castile to an end and affirmed Castilian rights to the islands, provided a new incentive.

The central figure in the Castilian enterprise was Alonso de Quintanilla, a senior official in the treasury. His achievement was to bring together a group of financial backers, mostly Genoese merchants from Seville, who saw the prospects of colonizing the Canaries as a worthwhile investment. The islands offered access to the gold routes along the African coasts and were a ready source of slaves and dye-stuffs. They were also fertile and could be brought into cultivation for sugar-cane to supply the ever-increasing European demand. The conquest of the three large and populous islands, Gran Canaria, La Palma, and Tenerife, and the quelling of rebellions on La Gomera, which had already been partially conquered, was presented as a crusade against unbelievers—essentially a continuation of the Reconquista now in its final stages on the Spanish mainland. The native population, tribes who used no metal, put up a spirited resistance, but by exploiting native rivalries and by employing conversion to Christianity as a divisive tool to confuse the locals, the Castilian conquest proceeded apace, though not without its setbacks. Gran Canaria was subdued by 1483, La Palma in 1492, and Tenerife in 1496. On La Gomera, the only island on which the Castilians had installed feudal lords, rebellions rumbled on for over a decade but were finally crushed in 1489.

The settlement of the Canaries marked the crucial first stage in the creation of the Castilian empire. It was important for two reasons. The first is that the financial arrangements masterminded by de Quintanilla, involving Genoese merchant bankers, were to serve well in providing support for the later expeditions to America. The second is that La Gomera, one of the westerly islands in the Canaries, with its excellent deep-water harbour, was perfectly sited for ships planning to make the westward passage across the Atlantic using the north-easterly trade winds. This would have been well understood by seafarers used to sailing in these waters. It was no surprise, then, that in 1492, only three years after La Gomera was finally subdued, Columbus chose the port as the setting-off point for his journey to the Caribbean.

The Cognitive World of Columbus

The extent of the Atlantic, or the Ocean Sea as it was generally known, was a great source of academic debate in the fifteenth century. By the 1430s Majorcan maps were placing the Azores in approximately their correct positions and beyond were a plethora of islands well known in legend—places like Hy-Brasil, Antillia, and the islands visited by Brendan—to inspire those thinking of further exploration. Between 1462 and 1487 at least eight expeditions were commissioned by the Portuguese to look for Antillia and other new islands in the west, mostly setting out from the Azores, and in the 1480s British sailors sailed from Bristol in an attempt to find Hy-Brasil and other islands in the North Atlantic.

Alongside this flurry of practical excitement others were speculating on the size of the Ocean Sea. Classical texts were becoming widely available. Ptolemy's writings were known in the early fifteenth century, and knowledge of Strabo's *Geography* was circulating in Italy as early as 1423, though it was not fully available in print until 1469. A careful reader of the text would have been struck by Strabo's quotation from Eratosthenes suggesting that it was possible to sail from Iberia to India along the same parallel. That the world was a globe was widely recognized, and so, too, was the concept of a single land-mass, Eurasia, stretching around it. The debate focused on two issues: Was there another land-mass, the Antipodes, somewhere to be found? And what was the circumference of the earth and the width of the Ocean

13.13 Christopher Columbus, in a portrait painted some years after his death

Sea between the two extremities of Eurasia? The Antipodean debate was largely theoretical, though much favoured by Italian humanists; of more practical interest was the width of the Ocean.

One writer influential on all these matters was Pierre d'Ailly, cardinal of Lorraine, who hypothesized that the Antipodes might not be a separate continent but a continuation of a known land-mass. He was also firmly of the belief that the Atlantic was narrow. Another supporter of this latter view was Paolo Toscanelli, a Florentine cosmographer who, in 1474, wrote a letter to Fernão Martins, canon of Lisbon, who was gathering data for the Portuguese king. In the letter Toscanelli gave his opinion that the distance westwards between the Canaries and Cipangu (Japan) was about 7,200 kilometres and from Cipangu to Cathay (China) was a further 3,200 kilometres. These calculations depended on Marco Polo's considerably inflated estimate of the length of Asia from east to west. Toscanelli had also worked out that a degree of latitude at the equator represented 72 kilometres, when the actual figure is 96 kilometres. Thus, his estimate of 7,200 kilometres between the Canaries and Cipangu fell significantly short, the actual distance being nearly 17,000 kilometres. Belief in the narrow Atlantic was very attractive to those who were contemplating sailing westwards to China, but it was a delusion.

It was in this atmosphere of excited debate and speculation that Christopher Columbus (Cristóbal Colón, or Cristoforo Colombo) spent his formative years. Born in Genoa in 1451, the son of a weaver, Columbus was soon drawn to the sea. Stories of his early years speak of him voyaging to the Levant as an employee of a Genoese bank and later, after being shipwrecked off Cape St Vincent, making his way to Lisbon, where he seems to have continued to work for the same bank before moving to Madeira. There he met and married a Portuguese noblewoman whose brother was the governor of Porto Santo, a small island not far from Madeira. Later journeys took him to the Portuguese factory of Elmina on the Guinea coast, and possibly also to Iceland. By the age of 30 he had acquired an extensive knowledge of the Atlantic, and although he was not a professional seaman he had a good grounding in navigation and had gathered some knowledge of hydrography. More to the point, he developed a fascination for the geography of the Ocean Sea, reading and annotating books like Pierre d'Ailly's *Imago Mundi*, and corresponding with other theorists. In 1481 he wrote to Toscanelli and was sent in reply a copy of the data on the Atlantic which Toscanelli had prepared for the king of Portugal. Columbus was now contemplating an ocean crossing. He wanted to believe, as d'Ailly did, 'that the sea is navigable in a very few days if the wind is fair', but Toscanelli's estimate of 7,200 kilometres between the Canaries and Cipangu suggested that the journey would be too great. Perhaps it was youthful enthusiasm emboldened by a degree of self-deception that encouraged him

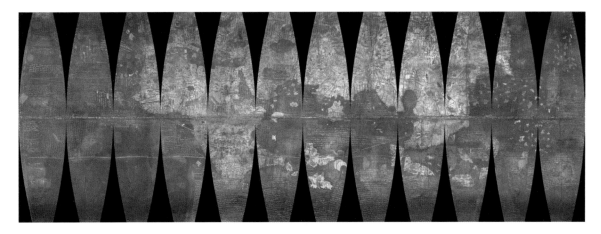

13.14 The earliest terrestrial globe was created by Martin Behaim in 1492 (see Fig. 1.15). He followed the belief of Columbus and others that Eurasia was of considerable expanse and that therefore the distance between Europe and China across the Atlantic was correspondingly quite short

to rework the figures in the margins of his copy of *Imago Mundi* using estimates for the circumference of the world calculated by a ninth-century Arab geographer. This and other adjustments allowed him to arrive at a figure of 4,800 kilometres for the distance between the Canaries and Japan, far more manageable in the boats of the time. Confident that the crossing was feasible, he drew up a scheme, which he presented to Toscanelli, receiving in reply a second letter praising his 'magnificent and grand desire to navigate from the parts of the east to the west'. His ideas now formed, it was simply a matter of finding a financial sponsor.

In 1484 Columbus took the obvious step of presenting his grand scheme to King João II of Portugal. The prospects were carefully considered by a panel of experts and rejected. At the time all the Portuguese maritime effort was focused on exploring the route along the African coast to the Indian Ocean. Cão had just returned from his first successful exploration and it would have been clear to the Portuguese that it was only a matter of time before a route to the east would be found. Columbus next turned his attention to gaining the support of the Castilians, putting his case before Ferdinand and Isabella, but they were unconvinced. He also sent his younger brother Bartholomew to England and France to try to solicit royal patronage, but neither country showed any serious interest. There was nothing for it but to continue to work away at the Spanish, which he did with great persistence, eventually, in 1492, persuading Ferdinand to back the venture. Why the king changed his mind is a matter of speculation, but that the Portuguese were gearing up to make a final burst into the Indian Ocean following Dias's successful rounding of the Cape of Storms

(Good Hope) in 1488 must have been a significant incentive: this was Spain's last chance to get to the Indies by the western route before Portugal laid claim to the Indian Ocean. Another factor was that the financial package which had been created to support the colonization of the Canaries had proved successful, and profitable to the Genoese bankers, who were now more than willing to provide the king with loans for the new venture, not least because it was to be led by one of their own countrymen. So it was that a contract was drawn up between Ferdinand and Isabella and Columbus known as the *Capitulations of Santa Fe*, later expanded into a more detailed document: 'For as much as you, Cristóbal Colón, are going by our command, with some of our ships and with our subjects, to discover and acquire certain islands and mainland in the ocean …'. The document goes on to specify Columbus' status as admiral of the Indies and viceroy and high admiral of Castile, and to agree that he could claim one-tenth of all the profits of trade. It was a deal with which Columbus could be well satisfied.

13.15 The marriage of Ferdinand and Isabella, shown here on a gold double excelente of Ferdinand II minted in Seville in 1475, united the kingdoms of Aragón and Castile into one powerful country. Both monarchs were consistent supporters of Christopher Columbus in his desire to explore the lands on the other side of the Atlantic

Preparations and the First Voyage

In May 1492 Columbus travelled to the small Andalucían port of Palos de la Frontera, which had been ordered to provide the expedition with two caravels for twelve months. The ships chosen were the *Niña* and the *Pinta*. Columbus needed a third ship and eventually settled on the *Santa Maria*, a não, a larger, more round-bodied vessel: it was far from ideal because it was slower than the caravels, but it was all that was available. This he charted as his flagship, appointing the owner, Juan de la Cosa, an experienced sailor, as its master. To command the two caravels he engaged three brothers of the Pinzón family. Martín, a seaman of considerable experience, was appointed captain of the *Pinta* with his younger brother Francisco as master, while the youngest, Vincente, captained the *Niña*. The *Santa Maria* had a crew of forty men; the two caravels each had about twenty-five.

Precise details of the three vessels are not recorded, but the two caravels were probably about 21 metres long and 7 metres broad, single-decked but with a raised quarterdeck providing limited sleeping accommodation for the captain and master.

13.16 This book, owned by Columbus, contained a hand-coloured compass and a table of winds and hours of daylight at different latitudes

They were probably three-masted: the *Pinta* was square-rigged, but the *Niña* started out as a lateen rig and was refitted as a square rig in the Canaries before the Atlantic crossing began. The *Santa Maria*, a typical não, perhaps as much as 25 metres in length and 8.5 metres broad, was square-rigged on its fore- and mainmast with a lateen-rigged mizzen. All three ships were lightly armed.

The fleet set sail on 3 August bound for the Canary islands, where the vessels were repaired and got ready for their ocean journey. This involved rerigging the *Niña* and recaulking the *Pinta*, which was also fitted with a new rudder. After taking on board fresh supplies, the vessels set sail on 6 September. From his own experience of Atlantic sailing and by consulting other seamen, Columbus would have built up a good under-standing of the Atlantic wind systems. He would have known that the Canaries lay on the northern edge of the north-easterly trade winds, while the Azores lay on the latitude of the prevailing westerlies. Thus, the simplest way to cross the ocean was to sail south-west from the Canaries to pick up the trade winds to provide the following wind for the journey west. Another reason for starting from the Canaries was that, like Toscanelli, Columbus believed that the Canaries lay on the same latitude as Cipangu at about 28° north. By starting at this point and sailing down the latitude, he would be sure to reach his destination. In planning his return journey he would have understood that the surest way to reach Iberia was to set off in a north-easterly direction in the hope of picking up the westerlies to drive him safely eastwards towards Europe. All of this would have been within the scope of his cognitive geography, much of it gained from personal experience, and would have provided the basis of his planning. In the event the first voyage, outward and homeward, went almost exactly according to plan.

On 12 October, after a largely uneventful ocean voyage of thirty-three days, land was sighted. The expedition had crossed the Sargasso Sea. There had been unrest among the crew as the time on the open ocean lengthened, but progress had been good: just before the sighting, they had travelled a record sixty leagues (330 kilometres) in a single day. In all, it had been a remarkably successful journey. The land they had come upon was the island of San Salvador in the Bahamas, and on their landing next day they were greeted by friendly natives. Columbus believed they had found one of the islands off Japan, and for the next three months they continued their exploration, landing next on Cuba and then on Hispaniola, where on 24 December the *Santa Maria* ran aground and had to be abandoned. Just before this event the *Pinta* had sailed off on her own, so Columbus had no option but to set up a small fort, La Navidad, and leave most of his crew there, the remainder, including himself, sailing off in the *Niña*. The two caravels met up off the coast of Hispaniola and on 16 January 1493 began their homeward journey, sailing northwards to pick up the westerlies. Storms encountered on the way separated the two vessels and Columbus had to put in to the Azores before landing on the banks of the Tagus and proceeding to Lisbon, to be politely received by King João. On 3 March the *Niña* took Columbus back to Palos, coincidentally arriving just as Martín Pinzón was steering the storm-battered *Pinta* into port. The expedition had taken six months.

The discoveries of new islands in the west delighted Ferdinand and Isabella but raised urgent questions of the spheres of influence claimed by Spain and Portugal. The situation was now far more complicated, not least because there was the real prospect that Spain would reach Asia by sailing west before Portugal got there by sailing eastwards around Africa. Under existing agreements Portugal had rights to all lands south of an east–west line drawn through the Canaries, but this no longer suited Spain, who

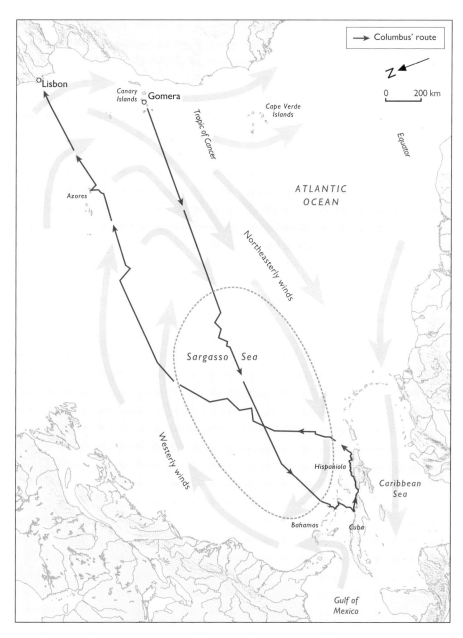

13.17 Columbus' first voyage in 1492 set off from the Canary islands and his plan was to sail down the latitude to reach Japan. His first sight of land was the island of San Salvador. His return journey, picking up the westerlies, took him back to Lisbon via the Azores

13.18 This fifteenth-century woodcut celebrates Columbus landing on San Salvador in 1492, his progress watched by an intent King Ferdinand

called on the assistance of a pliant pope prepared to issue a succession of bulls favourable to Spain. The Portuguese objected, threatening to send a massive fleet to defend her interests in the Atlantic. In the event, a degree of sense prevailed when, in 1494, the two countries managed to negotiate an agreement, which became known as the treaty of Tordesillas, by which a longitude was agreed through the middle of the Atlantic. To the east of the line, newly discovered territories would belong to Portugal; to the west, to Spain. What no one knew at the time was that the eastern part of South America lay in the Portuguese sphere and, when discovered six years later, Brazil, as it became known, was incorporated into the growing Portuguese empire.

Later Voyages and Discoveries, 1493–1503

Columbus was to make three more voyages, sailing from Spain in 1493, 1498, and 1502. The first of these, which set out in September 1493, was a massive expedition comprising seventeen ships carrying a colonizing force of more than fifteen hundred men to settle Hispaniola. When it was discovered that the original settlement of forty men who had been left at La Navidad had been wiped out by disease, a new city, called La Isabela, was founded on the north side of the island. Columbus, who seems to have had

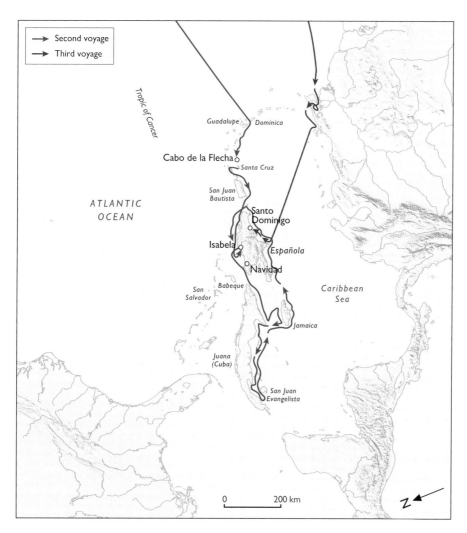

13.19 Columbus made a further three voyages. During the second and third voyages he explored certain of the Caribbean islands and made brief contact with the mainland of South America

539

little interest in becoming a colonial administrator, was content to leave this aspect of his mission to his brother Bartholomew. The initial foundation failed and the main settlement was moved to the south side of the island and re-established as Santo Domingo.

For Columbus the prime aim was exploration. The expedition had set off from the Canaries as usual but had taken a more southerly course to make better use of the north-easterly trade winds. This brought them to the Dominica Passage, between the islands of Dominica and Guadeloupe in the Lesser Antilles, from where they were able to follow the curve of the Leeward islands, skirting Puerto Rico, to Hispaniola. Having established the base at La Isabela, Columbus set off again to explore the southern shore of Cuba (Juana), encountering Jamaica en route, before returning to La Isabela. Two compulsions drove him: the desire to find a profitable source of gold and the hope of identifying a route through the maze of islands to China. In both he was disappointed, and on 10 March 1496 he sailed for Spain, reaching Cádiz fifty-three days later.

Meanwhile, Ferdinand and Isabella remained intent on colonizing the newly found land to provide a sustained source of income. Another 350 colonists had been sent out with additional supplies in January 1498, and in May Columbus left on his third expedition with a fleet of six vessels. From the Canaries three vessels were sent on to Santo Domingo, while Columbus took the remaining three south to the Cape Verde islands before setting a course west across the ocean, sailing on the latitude. He was hoping to use the trade winds to take him to explore more southerly regions than he had hitherto seen. In reality the latitude he steered was rather too far south and brought him into the doldrums, where they were becalmed and drifted for eight days, but eventually the winds picked up and the ships saw the three peaks of an island which they named Trinidad. Entering the Serpent's Mouth between Trinidad and the mainland of South America (at what is now Venezuela), Columbus was impressed to see huge volumes of fresh water pouring out into the sea and, realizing that this implied the presence of a great river (actually the Orinoco), he knew that he must be viewing the edge of a continent. He was very unwell at this stage, and his thoughts may have rambled, but he was thinking on a grand scale: 'I have come to believe that this is a vast continent, hitherto unknown,' he wrote, speculating that it might be the Garden of Eden, the Earthly Paradise which 'all men say is at the end of the Orient'. In other words, was this the great projection of land stretching from China that some classical writers like Ptolemy believed to exist? His preconceptions forced him to reject the more obvious possibility that he had found an entirely new continent quite separate from Eurasia.

But Columbus' time was running out and it was necessary to deliver what remained of the supplies he was carrying to Santo Domingo, so he set a north-westerly course across the open Caribbean to Hispaniola, reaching the island at the end of August

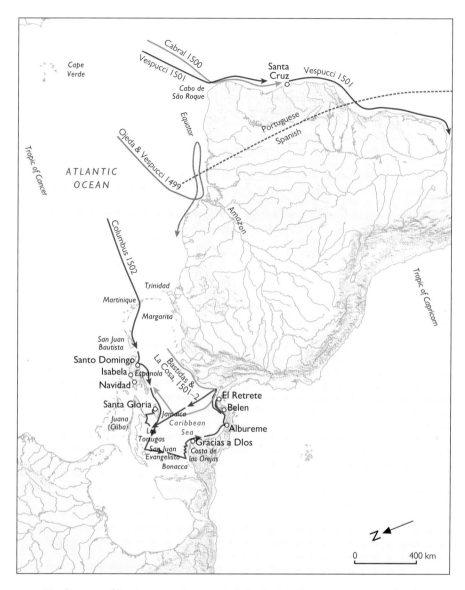

13.20 The discovery of South America began with Columbus' third voyage in 1498. His fourth voyage explored part of the coast of Central America between 1502 and 1504. Meanwhile, between 1499 and 1502 other expeditions had discovered much of the Atlantic coast of South America as far south as the Rio de la Plata

1498. The situation among the settlers had deteriorated drastically and there was open rebellion, which Columbus and his brothers failed to contain. News reached Spain, and in 1500 a new governor was sent by Ferdinand and Isabella to restore some semblance of order. Having assessed the situation, the governor immediately arrested Columbus and his family and sent them back to Spain in chains. It was clear to all that Columbus was an incompetent administrator and could not be allowed to continue, but he was also a national hero and on his arrival the monarchs thought it prudent to restore some of his privileges, including the title Our Admiral of the Ocean Sea.

Columbus was to make one last voyage in search of the way through to China and the Orient, sailing in May 1502 with four caravels and making the crossing from the Canaries to Martinique in the Windward islands in just twenty-one days. After putting into Santo Domingo, he sailed westwards to the island of San Juan Evangelista, off the south coast of Cuba, south of modern Havana. Then, picking up a new wind, he set a course south-west to the Islas de la Bahia (which he named Bonacia), just off the coast of Honduras. A few days later he landed on the Honduran coast (La Costa de las Orejas), claiming it for Spain. The next months were spent exploring the coasts of Nicaragua, Costa Rica, and Panama as far as the Gulf of Darien. Promising sources of gold were identified, but hostile natives made it difficult even to begin to exploit them. Nor was there any sign of a way through to China. It is one of the ironies of history that, when Columbus anchored at El Retrete on the north coast of Panama, he did not realize that he was merely sixty kilometres from the Pacific.

The rest of the expedition was a near-disaster. With only two serviceable ships, both leaking and crammed with 130 men, he set out for Santo Domingo, but storms and adverse winds drove them off course and they ended up landing on Jamaica, beaching the now useless ships and turning them into a stronghold. Marooned on the island with few supplies, their only hope was to get help from Santo Domingo. A canoe was fitted out and two men volunteered to make the 400-kilometre journey. Miraculously they managed it, and eight months later a caravel arrived to announce that help was being sent. By this time, morale had collapsed and many of the men were in outright mutiny, but eventually, in June 1504, a relief ship arrived to carry Columbus and those loyal to him back to Hispaniola. They had been marooned for nearly a year and a half. Another stormy crossing of the Atlantic passage saw Columbus safe on Spanish soil in November 1504. Now suffering severely from arthritis, he died two years later at the age of 55.

Columbus' abysmal failure as a colonial administrator and his arrogance and delusions of grandeur should not be allowed to obscure his remarkable achievements. Although not the most skilled of navigators, he had a keen understanding of wind patterns and was good at dead reckoning. He also had an acute sense of geographical space. This is most vividly demonstrated by the course he set across the Caribbean from the coast of Venezuela to Santo Domingo during his third voyage. Sailing blind across 1,200 kilometres of ocean, he was able to reach land little more than 130 kilometres off target. It was a spectacular feat of navigation. But perhaps his greatest legacy sprang from his belief in himself, which drove him to sail where few of his contemporaries were prepared to venture. His achievement in reaching land and returning to tell the tale was an immediate spur to others and unleashed new energies.

Two of the men who had taken part in the adventure in 1492, Alonso de Ojeda and Vincente Pinzón, inspired by Columbus' discoveries during his second voyage, set out separately in 1499 to explore the coast of South America. While Ojeda sailed westwards along the coast of Venezuela, Pinzón seems to have travelled eastwards, perhaps reaching as far as the Amazon estuary. It may be no coincidence that the following year, 1500, the Portuguese sailor Pedro Álvares Cabral, en route to the Indian Ocean, made a great sweep westwards and landed on the coast of Brazil. Although often presented as a happy accident, it may well have been a deliberate attempt by the Portuguese to see if the continent of South America, which was just coming into focus, extended east of the Tordesillas line into the Portuguese sphere. Such a discovery would, and indeed did, have significant political and economic repercussions.

Another entrepreneur who was taking an interest in the South American coast at this time was the Florentine businessman Amerigo Vespucci, a resident of Seville. Although some doubt attaches to the stories circulating about his explorations, he does seem to have made two voyages. The first, in 1499 along the coasts of Venezuela and Guyana, was made in Spanish ships. The second, made under Portuguese authority in 1501, began around Cabo de São Roque at about 6° south and continued down the coast, reaching beyond the estuary of the Rio de la Plata to Patagonia, a distance of some 3,200 kilometres from his initial landfall. For his achievement in reconnoitring so much of the coastline of the new continent it was popularly named after him: America. No longer could there be any doubt that a vast land-mass lay between the Atlantic and the Orient.

Meanwhile in the North Atlantic

In the North Atlantic patterns of maritime trade were changing. The isolated communities of Iceland and Greenland relied heavily on ships arriving from Norway to bring the necessities of life that the islanders could not themselves produce in return for their stockfish, wadmal (coarse woollen cloth), and oil. But by the end of the fourteenth century the system had begun to break down, with the incoming ships failing to arrive on a regular basis. So it was that, when the English began to explore the Icelandic market in the early fifteenth century, the islanders were, at least at first, welcoming. The first recorded English ship arrived in 1412, and thereafter the numbers rapidly increased. The first English ports to send ships were the east coast ports led by Hull and Lynn, but from 1424 Bristol became the major player, and by the 1440s other west coast ports in Devon, Cornwall, and Wales were sending vessels.

The large English merchant ships brought back considerable cargoes, particularly of stockfish and herring. In return the English merchants offered woollen broadcloth, linen, beer, wine, and wheat flour. The demand by the English merchants created tensions, particularly with Denmark and Norway, who saw their lucrative trading monopoly at risk. Agreements were negotiated requiring the English to trade under licence, but more often than not the restrictions were flouted, and they led, in the second half of the century, to outright hostility between the English ports and the Danish state and the Hansa. Although English merchant ships and fishing doggers (sturdy two-masted vessels) were still operating in the 1470s and 1480s, by the end of the century the volume of merchant shipping had dramatically declined, leaving only the doggers to make their annual runs to the Icelandic fishing grounds.

The century or so of open-ocean sailing had brought many changes to English ship construction. Sails and rigging were much improved, with the introduction of topsails and spritsails greatly increasing manoeuvrability. Hull construction, too, was modified, with the introduction of higher bows designed to cope better with the fierce North Atlantic. Navigational aids had also improved, with the compass now in widespread use on the Iceland run. The ship's master would have carried a lodestone, so essential for remagnifying the needle, as well as sounding leads and an hourglass to time the length of the tacks, enabling his dead reckoning to be improved. So it was, in the last decades of the fifteenth century, that England now had merchant and fishing fleets well used to the rigours of North Atlantic sailing, and when, about 1480, political difficulties with the Danes and the Hansa made Icelandic trade an increasingly uncertain prospect, it was inevitable that ship-owners would begin to look elsewhere for their profits.

Since early medieval times there had been stories of an island called Hy-Brasil way out in the ocean somewhere to the west of Ireland. While it could have been yet another island myth born of imagination, it is not impossible that ships had occasionally reached the shores of North America and returned to tell the tale. To such stories would have been added much firmer information passed on by the Icelanders about Helluland, Markland, and Vinland, visited by their Greenland cousins. An English sailor on the Iceland run would have been well aware of the existence of land in the west: the time was now right to begin to explore the new opportunities which this offered.

It was the men of Bristol who took the initiative. The earliest record of a ship sailing in search of Hy-Brasil is in 1480. The next year another ship sailed carrying a large quantity of salt. The early records are scanty and incomplete, but the salt-laden ship sailing in 1481 implies that the Bristol captains had already discovered rich fishing grounds, most probably the Newfoundland Banks. By 1490 two or three ships a year were leaving Bristol for the western Atlantic, suggesting that the new fishing grounds were being exploited on a regular basis, and it is more than likely that landings were being made on the North American coast. That this was so is supported by a letter sent by an English merchant, John Day, then resident in southern Spain, to the 'Grand Admiral', most likely Columbus. The letter, written in the winter of 1497 just after John Cabot had returned from landing on Newfoundland, said that Day was certain that the land Cabot had explored 'was found and discovered in the past by men from Bristol who found "Brasil" as your Lordship well knows. It was called the Island of Brasil and it is assumed and believed to be the mainland that the men of Bristol found.' (This is to some extent supported by a letter sent by the Spanish envoy in London to Ferdinand and Isabella in 1498 saying that 'the people of Bristol have for the last seven years sent out every year two, three, or four caravels in search of the island of Brasil and the Seven Cities'.) Although the Bristol merchants managed to keep their activities reasonably quiet, the evidence supports the view that from the 1480s they were fishing on the Newfoundland Banks and visiting the neighbouring North American coasts. How they viewed the land they had discovered is unrecorded, but they would most likely have considered it to be an easterly projection of Asia.

Such a view would have been consistent with the beliefs of the Venetian entrepreneur John Cabot. Cabot was of the opinion that the region then being explored by Columbus was much too far east to be the approaches to Japan or China and that the quickest way from Europe to the Orient would be found at high northern latitudes. Having failed to interest the Spanish and the Portuguese in his proposals—both of whom were energetically pursuing their own preferred routes to the east—he turned to England and in 1495 went to London to present his ideas to King Henry VII and to raise money from the Italian merchant community to finance an expedition. The king, no doubt mindful of his misjudgement in failing to invest in Columbus a few years earlier, agreed to issue Cabot with a patent to explore.

Cabot may already have known of the discoveries of the Bristol sailors a decade or so earlier. At any event Bristol was a logical place to start from, given the experience of its seamen with the North Atlantic. So it was there that he went to plan for his first voyage in 1496. All that is known of what happened is contained in John Day's letter to Columbus: 'Since your Lordship wants information relating to the first voyage, here

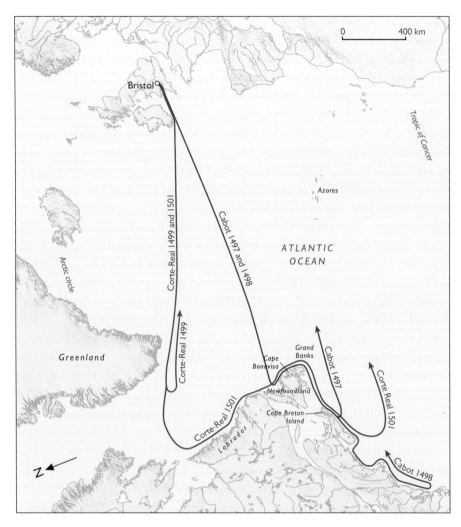

13.21 While the Spaniards were busy plotting the coasts of South America, a number of expeditions set out from Bristol between 1496 and 1501 to explore the coast of North America, which had probably been visited a few years before by ships from Bristol searching for new fishing grounds

is what happened: he went with one ship, he fell out with his crew, he was short of supplies and ran into bad weather, and he decided to turn back.'

Lack of success did not deter Cabot or his sponsors. In 1497 a new expedition was prepared. The patent under which he was sailing was explicit. It gave him leave to explore the eastern, western, and northern seas together with 'whatsoever islands, continents, regions or provinces of heathens or infidels, in whatever part of the world placed, which before this time were unknown to Christians'. The scope is clear.

546

Everything outside the Spanish interests in the southern part of the Atlantic was fair game except for the already Christianized regions of Iceland and Greenland. Cabot sailed from Bristol on 2 May 1497 in a small ship, the *Matthew*, with about twenty men, at least two of whom were Bristol merchants. Most of what is known of the voyage comes from John Day's letter. Having rounded Ireland, he set a course westwards on the latitude, making landfall on the coast of North America on 24 June. There is no certainty where the landing was made, but most commentators favour Newfoundland, some preferring Cape Dégrat at the extreme north end, others Cape Bonavista, partway down the east coast. After this first and only landing 'they spent about one month discovering the coast … and returned to the coast of Europe in fifteen days'. The month would have allowed him to explore the coast of Newfoundland and possibly Cape Breton Island and part of Nova Scotia. During his travels he was impressed by the abundance of fish like those found in Iceland and sold as stockfish in England, and by the forests of tall timbers suitable for making masts. The expedition saw traces of human activity but encountered none of the indigenous population. The exploration over, with a fair wind they made good progress across the Atlantic and reached Brittany 'because the sailors confused him, saying that he was heading too far north' before sailing on to Bristol. It had been a successful and straightforward journey, helped by the fact that many of his small crew were probably already quite familiar with this part of the North Atlantic. The king was pleased and Cabot became something of a celebrity.

Cabot's final voyage departed from Bristol in May 1498. Five ships started out, four fitted out by Bristol merchants, the fifth by the king. That some carried trade goods implies that the intention was to make contact with the indigenous tribes. One of the ships was caught in a storm and had to put in to Ireland, but the rest continued. The progress of the expedition is obscure and much debated, but it seems to have involved setting up a Christian mission before embarking on a long voyage of exploration down the east coast of America, perhaps as far as the areas being explored by the Spaniards. This would explain why, on Juan de la Cosa's map of about 1500, the coastline of America is shown with tolerable accuracy marked with English flags. There is some evidence to suggest that Cabot was back in London by May 1500. If some part of the expedition had penetrated so far south as to impinge on the legitimate Spanish sphere, it would have been politically embarrassing for the English, which may be one reason why it was kept quiet.

Nothing is known of John Cabot after his return in 1500, but Henry VII continued to encourage voyages to Newfoundland and the adjacent areas, perhaps intent on finding a north-west passage to the Orient. One of Cabot's collaborators, William Watson of Bristol, was sent with royal support to explore the 'new found land' in 1499 and 1500, and other Bristol-based initiatives set off in 1502 and 1503. While seeking a north-west passage will have been a tempting aim, settlement and fishing were now important considerations. One expedition, led by John Cabot's son Sebastian in 1504, seems primarily to have been concerned with fishing, but his second expedition in 1508–9 was one of exploration, taking him north past Labrador and possibly Baffin Island, and south as far as Florida, thus consolidating England's claim to the North American coastline.

John Cabot's discoveries alerted the Portuguese king to the possibility that some of the newly found land might lie on the Portuguese side of the Tordesillas line, and in 1499 he issued a patent to João Fernandez, a farmer from Terceira, one of the islands of the Azores, to explore in the north-western Atlantic. For the next few years Fernandez together with Gaspar and Miguel Corte-Real and João Martins—all residents of Terceira—were actively involved in expeditions. Fernandez was a landholder under the patronage of the Corte-Real family. He was present in Bristol, probably as a trader, from as early as 1486 and must have been aware of the stories of new lands across the ocean now circulating in the port. Nothing is known of the voyage of 1499, but the next year he was accompanied by Gaspar Corte-Real on a northward journey, when the southern tip of Greenland, probably Cape Farewell, was spotted; they were prevented from landing, either by adverse weather conditions or by ice floes. They firmly believed that what they were seeing was the eastern extremity of Asia. Fernandez remained in Bristol and in 1501 became chief of an Anglo-Portuguese syndicate which received letters patent from Henry VII. His brief from the Portuguese king was to 'discover and find anew' heathen lands, confining him to somewhere between Newfoundland and Greenland.

In the same year, 1501, Gaspar Corte-Real set out with three caravels on a separate voyage in an attempt to find the land seen the previous year. After finding the sea frozen they changed course, probably crossing the Davis Strait to the coast of Labrador, noting many large rivers flowing into the sea. The geography is obscure, but it is possible that they reached Cape Chidley on the south side of the Hudson Strait as well as exploring the east coast of Newfoundland. Two of the original ships returned to Lisbon in October 1501 but the third, carrying Gaspar, was lost. The next year Miguel Corte-Real set out to find his brother, but his ship, too, failed to return. The flurry of reconnaissance in the early years of the sixteenth century quickly established the importance of the Newfoundland fishing grounds. By 1506 the quantity of fish being brought back to Portugal was so great that the king thought it worthwhile to levy a tithe at ports where the fish was unloaded.

Sebastian Cabot's return to England in 1509 is a convenient point to bring this story to a close. The northern fishing grounds were now being regularly exploited by the

English and the Portuguese. The Normans had already joined in, and it was not long before the Bretons and Basques arrived. The fishing fleets crossing the ocean from Europe to the Newfoundland Banks set an annual rhythm which was to last until today. And what of the northern route to the Orient? The Corte-Real brothers had failed to find it and had died in the attempt. Others were to follow.

By now most of the Atlantic coast of the Americas was known, if somewhat sketchily, from Baffin Island to Patagonia. The task was finally completed in 1520, when Ferdinand Magellan, a minor Portuguese noble, discovered the strait to be named after him, between the Patagonian mainland and the island of Tierra del Fuego, opening the way to the Pacific. In a mere thirty years of extraordinary human endeavour, the endless Ocean Sea had at last been contained.

14

Reflections on the Ocean

Anyone thinking or writing about history has to begin by trying to understand the environment in which the action takes place. There are really two environments to bear in mind: the actual physical ecozone as it was at the time of the event, and the world as it was conceived to be by those who inhabited it. The first may have been different from the present day but can be reconstructed by archaeologists and other scientists. The second, the cognitive world of the past, is very much more difficult for us to comprehend. A Greek sailor like Kolaios, looking out on the Atlantic around 630 BC, will have had a very different view of the great ocean from that of Dom Henrique two thousand years later. For the Greek the ocean extended to the liminal edge of the world, where lay some kind of paradise peopled by the shrill-voiced Hesperides and where the sun mysteriously disappeared at the end of every day. It was a place of total wonder, generating a frisson of danger and excitement. For Dom Henrique it was an ocean of opportunity, offering him the chance to fulfil his chivalric duties to his lineage and his god: to make his country and his religion prosper. Unlike the Greek, he knew much of the ocean tides and currents and had information about the islands scattered off the African coast. He was also aware that the world was spherical and that somewhere across the ocean lay land.

The cognitive geographies of Kolaios and Dom Henrique were very different, but as humans they shared a genetic make-up that programmed them to respond in similar ways to stimuli and situations. Besides the normal animal behaviour of feeding, reproduction, and care of young, humans are genetically hardwired to have the ability for

551

abstract, imaginative thought enabling them to create myths and gods, but they also share an acquisitive nature manifest in their desire to gather exotic goods and to be in command of knowledge. It is through the ownership of these rare attributes, both tangible and intangible, that some are able to exercise power. Our genetic structure, therefore, determines the way in which society configures its belief systems and its systems of social hierarchy.

Scientists have recently isolated a gene, DRD4-7R, which, it is claimed, predisposes those who possess it to want to travel: the popular press have named it the wanderlust gene, and it is said to be present in about 20 per cent of the human population. No doubt, on more careful analysis, the matter will prove to be far more complex, but that a significant percentage of humans are genetically predisposed to travel, to satisfy an innate curiosity, is amply demonstrated in the narrative we have examined throughout this book. The unknown engages the human imagination and draws the curious out of the familiar *place* they inhabit into the threatening, but ever exciting, *space* beyond. So it has been ever since the first hominids began to move out of Africa.

The Sea Challenges; the Sea Transforms

The sea, in its formless state of perpetual motion, is starkly different from the land. Conceptually it is anti-land, the antithesis. What the land is, the sea is not. To venture onto it is a deliberate act of defiance: it is to challenge wild disorder. In doing so, the sailor knowingly enters into a competition that can end only with his return to land or his death. The sense of competition may for some have been an attraction in itself, as it is for lone ocean sailors today, but for most there would have been the lure of material gain either by acquiring actual commodities or by gaining esoteric knowledge which itself offered social reward.

The movement of commodities from areas of production to areas of consumption—trade in its various guises—pervades the narrative. The acquisition of obsidian from Melos by the Mesolithic and Neolithic communities of the Greek mainland, the boatload of Tartessian silver brought home to Samos by Kolaios, the Gascon wine transported in great quantity to England, all have the appearance of being examples of the simple movement of materials from producer to consumer where the carrier would have made a profit in the transaction. But trade is seldom simple. The obsidian from Melos may have changed hands many times in socially directed cycles of redistribution before reaching the Franchthi Cave, while the ships carrying Gascon wine to England came from many different ports and would have been available for hire, their masters willing to carry any cargo for anyone. And all the time there would have been owner-captains, men like Kolaios, prepared to go from port to port selling off one cargo and taking on board new goods whenever there was a quick profit to be made.

All those involved, the ship-owners, the captains and the crew, and those who owned the cargoes, were taking risks. They were in constant competition with the sea, and, acutely aware of this, they felt the need to placate the gods. This is vividly demonstrated by the altars set up at the temples on the Rhine mouth to the local Roman deity Nehalennia in anticipation of, or in thanks for, a successful voyage, and by the ex-voto boat models hung up in Catalan churches in the Middle Ages by ships' masters grateful to be safely back home.

By allowing safe passage the sea was giving. It gave in other ways, by offering food to supplement the land-based diet—fish that had to be caught, sea mammals hunted on ice floes, and the occasional whale washed up on the strand. For some communities such resources were of vital importance. The Norse settlers on the east coast of Greenland depended on regular fishing expeditions to augment their daily diet and on their annual trips to the hunting grounds in the north to obtain seal oil and the walrus ivory used to trade for the essential goods their restricted ecozone was unable to supply. As the population of western Europe grew, so fishing became increasingly important to feed the people. By the beginning of the sixteenth century, fleets of ships were leaving ports in Portugal, the Basque country, Brittany, and Britain for the fishing grounds of Newfoundland, bringing home their salted catch at the end of the season. It was the intensification of these fishing expeditions in the North Atlantic, driven by demographic need, that helped to build the maritime capability of the west European states—a capacity that was to become a dominant factor in later world history.

The sea also facilitated raiding and migration, which were often closely linked. The episode of the 'sea peoples' in the twelfth century BC, the resettlement of Britain and Brittany in the fifth century AD, and the remarkable Viking phenomenon beginning in the eighth century AD, all began with a restless mobility in which sea raiding played an important part before the flow of people on the move grew to become a migration. The sea facilitated the speed and the spatial extent of these events: it is almost as though it enhanced the intensity of the demographic swell—a force first initiated by the failure of the homeland to provide sufficient resources to support the population and then driven on by that inherent human need for acquisition.

While the drivers for raiding, migration, and resettlement were environmental and genetic, societies were often able to call upon their belief systems—the result of the human ability to think imaginatively and to construct myths—to provide the justification for their acts. Discontented Greeks wanting to set up colonies would consult the gods through the oracle and would gain assurance from the belief that it was the gods' will that they faced the sea to reach the foreign shore. They were travelling under divine guidance and with a purpose. Similarly, the thousands of young men who set off on Crusades, often braving the sea to reach the Holy Land, did so under the comforting mantle of their Christian faith, their aim being to protect the holy sites from the infidel. That this involved pillaging, killing, and the appropriation of other people's land was of no consequence: they were secure in their beliefs. Much the same is true of the European onslaught on America, which had such a devastating effect on the native American populations. Here the frantic scrabble for gold, and the land grab that ensued, could be presented as the acceptable consequence of taking the comforts of Christianity to the benighted savage.

What emotional part did the sea play in all this? For a Viking setting out to raid the monasteries of Ireland or a Spaniard to lay waste the central American civilizations, could it be that by placing themselves at the mercy of the ocean they were seeking reassurance through the rite of passage? By travelling beyond the threshold of their world they were also separating themselves from the certainties and controls of their previous life. Some such tissue of beliefs seems to have lain behind the way in which the Irish Christian *peregrini* viewed the sea. By taking to the sea, and trusting in God's guidance, they would pass from their old life to the new. For many this meant being led to a desert place, usually a remote island, there to indulge a life of solitary contemplation. But for a few who returned home, like St Brendan, it was the revelation of the journey that gave them new life. Spending time at sea, in a transitional world of wild disorder, was a transformative experience.

The Closed Sea, the Open Ocean

In the names people in the past gave to their seas we can glimpse something of how they viewed them. By Roman times the Mediterranean was 'Mare Nostrum', 'Our Sea', something familiar. Rome lay at the centre of the contained sea and by the end of the first century BC controlled its entire perimeter. When it was that the Mediterranean communities first began to be conscious of the nature of their closed sea it is difficult to say. Some sense of its real limits may have begun to form in the last centuries of the second millennium BC, when there are hints of Mycenaean activity in the western Mediterranean, but the moment of truth probably came in the tenth century BC with the first Phoenician journeys from the Levant westwards across the sea and through the Strait of Gibraltar to Huelva. This was probably the first time that individual ships made the journey from one end of the Mediterranean to the other. From that moment the new cognitive geography for 'Our Sea', as a circumscribed space, came into being. This cannot fail to have had an effect on the way in which Mediterranean people subsequently viewed the world. The Ionian vision which developed in the sixth century BC of the Mediterranean lying in the middle of a roughly circular land-mass surrounded by 'the circumambient ocean' persisted for a very long time. It was a comforting view—a world contained and knowable—and it helped to generate a closed, Mediterranean-centred mindset. While the Phoenicians were prepared to sail beyond to explore the nearby fringes of the Ocean, the Greeks showed very little interest in it, the poet Pindar warning against venturing beyond the Pillars. For the Romans the only advantage of the Ocean was that it formed a convenient boundary for the empire: expeditions to Britain were looked upon as acts of recklessness, challenging the gods. Even latecomers like the Arabs, having learned to become a Mediterranean people, viewed the Atlantic—the Sea of Perpetual Gloom—with distaste if not trepidation. Later still, with the growth of commercially driven maritime city states like Venice and Genoa, it is surprising how little interest was taken in the world beyond the Mediterranean, even though the Genoese indulged in a cursory exploration of the nearby Atlantic islands. For the Mediterraneans, their sea remained their world.

Those communities who lived along the Atlantic coastline shared an entirely different world-view. Imagine looking out daily on an ocean that had no bounds. There was the western horizon, but what, if anything, lay beyond? Was it the edge of the world? For tens of thousands of years only imagination could offer answers, inspired by the daily setting of the sun and the intricate rhythms of the sea.

Perceptions would have changed when the Greek vision of a spherical world gradually came to be accepted after the middle of the first millennium BC, but how long these ideas took to become embedded in the consensus of the Atlantic community it is difficult to say. Some may have become familiar with such beliefs in the first centuries of the first millennium AD, but it would not have been until the early Middle Ages that these notions became more widely known outside the Mediterranean. For those who were prepared to accept that the earth was a globe, cognitive geography changed. As Eratosthenes had said in the late third century BC, by travelling due west from Europe one would eventually reach the eastern extremities of Asia. The Ocean was no longer endless: it could be crossed. Whereas, before, the only incentive to sail out into the open Ocean had been to hunt for mythical islands, now there was a real prospect of status-enhancing achievements and access to profitable commodities. The new enticements dramatically changed attitudes to the Ocean, luring ships further and further west to see what lay beyond.

On the Sea

In the millennia of prehistory humans wishing to take to the sea had various options available to them. They could make rafts of logs, build simple craft by sewing together tightly bound bundles of reeds, or inflate skins to provide a swimmer with added buoyancy. All these constructions were well within the technical ability of early hunter-gatherers using simple stone tools. Later, as toolkits became increasingly sophisticated, more deliberately engineered craft could be built. One of the most basic was the log boat hollowed out with stone axes aided by hardwood wedges. With added outriggers and with two or more log boats joined together, a craft capable of taking to the open seas could be concocted. A totally different kind of vessel, requiring only a basic toolkit of stone blades and points, could be made from skins stretched over a light wooden framework. Such vessels could face open-ocean conditions and be built large enough to carry a sizeable crew or bulky cargo.

The widespread introduction of copper alloy tools in the fourth to the third millennium BC opened up entirely new possibilities facilitated by more sophisticated carpentry. Planks could be made, cleats cut, and complex mortise and tenon joints made. This was the beginning of plank-built vessels. Later improvement included the introduction of the sail and the use of nails to attach planks to the frames—copper nails at first and then iron as the metal became more widely available. Later still, in the North Sea zone, planks were overlapped and nailed together along the edges, clinker-style. These technological improvements went hand in hand with the development of increasingly sophisticated toolkits. By the end of the first millennium BC the technology was in place to allow more complex plank-built vessels to be constructed. Thereafter it was simply a matter of improvements to design until the late nineteenth century, when the mass production of sheet steel initiated entirely new methods of shipbuilding. In the twentieth century the ability to extract aluminium from bauxite and the development of resin-based compounds opened up further possibilities.

Methods of propulsion also changed over time, beginning with paddling and developing to rowing, which, in the big Venetian galleys of the fifteenth century, reached heights of technical efficiency. When the sail was first used is a difficult matter to decide, but that the wind could be caught and manipulated to propel a craft is not a particularly sophisticated idea, nor is the construction of a serviceable sail difficult. As we have seen, there are reasons for suggesting that some kind of sail might have been used to speed up journeys from Asia Minor to Cyprus as early as the eighth millennium BC. The advantage of a sail would have been evident to Egyptians wanting to sail upstream on the Nile, and it was probably in the Nile valley, in the fourth millennium BC, that the regular use of the sail began, soon spreading to the eastern Mediterranean.

The vector for the spread of the sail the length of the Mediterranean and out into the Atlantic was most likely the Phoenician expansion that began in the tenth century BC, though it remains a possibility that simple sails may already have been used in both the Mediterranean and the Atlantic. The sail was generally employed as an adjunct to rowing to provide extra power when the wind was right. Sail-only propulsion started to become the norm throughout the Atlantic from the twelfth century, but not until much later in the Mediterranean.

For most of the second millennium little changed, apart from the development of increasingly complex rigs, until the introduction of steam-power in the nineteenth century, first as an adjunct to wind-power and then replacing it altogether. Thereafter oil, and later nuclear power, brought changes of their own.

Knowing the Sea

However skilled was the shipbuilder, success at sea depended on the knowledge of the crew and their ability to use it. A sailor had to learn the currents and the winds, and in the Atlantic had to understand the complexity of the tides. He had to be conversant with the movement of the stars to establish true north, and to be able to use the heights of the sun and selected constellations to sail along the latitude when that was advantageous. Perhaps most importantly of all, he had to carry in his mind a cognitive map in which to position himself at all times.

When and where these skills were first developed is a matter of speculation. Navigation, in the sense of position-finding and the ability to return to the point of origin, are the skills of the hunter-gatherer and are likely to have become innate at a very early stage in human development. Many bands of migrating hominids moving out of Africa and into Asia and eventually Australia will have used the coastal zone as an easy passage, learning as they went the huge potential of the sea as the provider of a varied array of food. Similarly, the early hunter-gatherers who peopled the Mediterranean zone and western Europe will have found the littoral environment a congenial place to be and will have begun to adapt their food-gathering regimes to benefit from the seasonal variety on offer. It was in this context that the first tentative moves would have been made away from the comforting solidity of the land, enticed by the ready sources of food and driven on by that embedded human curiosity we have so often emphasized.

Around the shores of the Mediterranean and along the Atlantic coast there is ample evidence of coastal-zone gathering strategies in the Middle and Upper Palaeolithic period, and there can be little doubt that, during this long period, hunter-gatherers were sea-going, though to what extent they can be regarded as seafaring—willing and able to travel out of sight of land—is debatable. The hunting bands who reached Crete by boat in the Middle Palaeolithic, making long open-sea voyages, can be regarded as properly seafaring, but this is likely to have been exceptional. For the most part, this long formative period of inshore journeys in pursuit of fish, sea-birds, and sea mammals is best regarded as sea-going. It was a nursery in which the skills of the sailor were refined. It was the climatic challenges of the Younger Dryas (10,800–9600 BC) that drove coastal hunter-gatherers more fully to embrace the sea.

Maritime hunter-gatherers and land-based farmers for a long time occupied different worlds, but in the eastern Mediterranean in the ninth millennium BC a symbiosis began which saw farmers taking to the sea to colonize new ecological niches, first on Cyprus, then on Crete, and a little later crossing the Aegean to the Greek mainland. Not long afterwards, in the middle of the sixth millennium, farming communities, most likely aided by coastal hunter-gatherers with maritime skills, began their remarkable advance the length of the Mediterranean and out into the Atlantic. It was this period of intense mobility between 9000 and 5000 BC that saw the beginning of seafaring in Europe. The knowledge gathered during this time, and the maritime skills so finely honed, established the seafaring tradition that continues to this day. While naval architecture has seen various technical developments, there have been comparatively few major advances in the skills base of the mariner. The widespread introduction of the magnetic compass and of charts and portolans in the thirteen century AD was a major step forward. So, too, was accurate time measurement used to establish longitude in the eighteenth century. But it could well be argued that it was not until the last hundred years, with the development of radar, echo sounding, and satellite navigation, that there has been a fundamental change in navigation.

The Challenge of the Sea of Perpetual Gloom

The familiar Mediterranean offered little challenge to seafarers after the tenth century BC, by which time the Phoenicians had established their regular pattern of voyages embracing the whole sea from one end to the other. Thereafter the Mediterranean remained a largely inward-looking world, content with itself. It is surprising how rarely the Phoenician maritime achievement has been given credit by recent historians. From their narrow coastal strip in the Levant the Phoenicians were forced by geographical circumstance to look outwards to the sea, and, by virtue of their position on the interface between Egypt and Mesopotamia, they were the inheritors of the technical advances of both worlds. Already by the tenth century they had become the most accomplished sailors of the ancient world and were later widely recognized as such by the Greeks and the Egyptians. There is nothing too far-fetched in the story told by Herodotus that, about 600 BC, Phoenician sailors were commissioned by the Egyptians to circumnavigate Africa, and succeeded in doing so. A century or so later they were exploring the Atlantic coasts. Why their achievement should have been so played down is probably due to the prejudice of recent centuries, the worship of every-thing Greek during the eighteenth-century Enlightenment, and the admiration for Roman imperialism during the colonial surge in the nineteenth century. Just as both Greeks and Romans, for different reasons, despised their Phoenician rivals, so it was that school pupils were taught to be uncritically dismissive of them. Archaeological evidence is doing much to correct the imbalance and to present the reality of the Phoenician achievement.

By making regular journeys through the Strait of Gibraltar from the tenth century BC, the Phoenicians came into contact with the deeply rooted maritime traditions of the Atlantic communities of Europe and Africa and would no doubt have learned quickly from them as they established trading enclaves along the coasts of Portugal and Morocco. The Atlantic posed an entirely new challenge. That they relished it we may be sure, but we know little of their engagement apart from the journeys of Hanno down the coast of Africa and of Himilco, who seems to have sailed out into the open ocean. Yet they must have been but two of the many sailors drawn into the unknown. The Canaries, probably Madeira, and possibly the Azores were visited during this time. How many set sail and how many returned we shall never know.

A few Greeks were also attracted to the Atlantic, passing through the Strait of Gibraltar to explore the ocean coasts, but details are lacking. The one journey of which we have some information, that of Pytheas about 320 BC, was rather different in that it was a journey of discovery probably using local boats. Nonetheless, its scope was impressive. Pytheas explored the seas around Britain, possibly reaching as far north as Iceland. He gathered information by observation, but he would have learned much from the local sailors.

The only hint we have that a few may have been drawn to the open ocean lies in a comment by Strabo. Referring to Eratosthenes' belief that by setting off from Iberia and sailing along the latitude one could reach the eastern extremities of Asia, Strabo remarks that those who had tried, and returned to tell the tale, turned back because of the emptiness of the ocean. The implication of Strabo's words is that some, possibly many, had tried to sail across the Atlantic. Nor should we regard this as surprising: it would have been stranger if no one had risen to the challenge.

The possibility remains, therefore, that someone—Phoenician or Greek—may have crossed the ocean. From time to time a claim is made that an artefact found on the mainland of America must have been carried there by a European traveller before Columbus, but nothing convincing has yet been presented. Some are fakes, most are dubious, and the few that seem genuine may have been transported much later. The very considerable literature that has grown up around these claims is not without interest, but it reflects more on human credulity than on ancient exploration. That said, the balance of probability is that the occasional ship with a live Phoenician or Greek crew did reach the American coast, carried there by the north-westerly trades and currents. Computer simulations of natural drift show that for most of the year vessels starting at the Canaries would probably make landfall somewhere in the Americas, particularly if setting out between September and June, within a two-hundred-day period, which is considered to be the maximum for a human to survive in an open boat. The cultural or genetic impact of such landings would, however, have been negligible and very difficult to recognize.

For the Phoenicians and the Greeks, open Atlantic exploration would have been a minority activity, there being little real incentive except to satisfy the desire for travel and adventure. But by the early medieval period the commercial impetus to reach the Orient and its riches had become a compulsion, encouraged by a better understanding of geography. So it was that the Portuguese and the Spanish, encouraged by Genoese expertise and finance, began their Atlantic adventures: the Portuguese sea-captains under royal patronage forging the route laboriously around Africa to the Indian Ocean, the Spanish sponsoring Columbus in his plan to use the north-easterly trades to cross the ocean in the expectation of reaching Japan and eventually China.

The Atlantic must always have exercised a fascination over those who daily looked out upon it, but through the opacity of time their responses are difficult for us to glimpse. Chance finds, like a group of Roman coins from the south coast of Iceland and a pot found in the Atlantic far to the west of Ireland, hint at patterns of otherwise unknown voyages, echoes of which come down to us in the rich vein of voyage stories (*immrama*) preserved in the Irish vernacular literature. The *immrama* record a tradition of seafaring that was continued by Irish monks who braved the North Atlantic to settle on the Faroe islands and on Iceland. Perhaps in these anecdotal fragments we are glimpsing something of the rich pattern of exploratory seafaring that endured through the first millennium BC and the first millennium AD in these northern Atlantic waters—a continuum that linked the mariners who told Pytheas stories of Iceland across time to the Norse fishermen who first set out to settle there and went on to explore still farther, eventually reaching America. They were all part of the ever-present underswell of maritime engagement demanded by the Ocean.

GLOSSARY OF NAUTICAL TERMS

A brief glossary of nautical terms used in this book is offered here. Readers wishing to explore this fascinating world further are recommended to the fuller glossary in S. McGrail, *Boats of the World* (Oxford, 2001), and to I. C. B. Dear and P. Kemp (eds.), *The Oxford Companion to Ships and the Sea* (2nd edn, Oxford, 2005). The following glossary benefits from both sources.

athwartships   From one side to the other of the ship.

batten   A light strip of wood fastened over a *seam*, or light flexible strip of wood used to lay out curved lines or establish hull contours.

bergantine   Two-masted vessel, square-rigged on the foremast and fore and aft rigged on the mainmast.

bilge   A region between the sides and the bottom of the boat.

bireme   An oared vessel with two levels of oarsmen, one above the other.

bow-post   *See* stem.

bowsprit   A large *spar* or boom running out from the *stem* of a vessel, to which the foremast *stays* and sometimes a *spritsail* are attached.

brace   A rope attached to the ends of the *yards* of a vessel for the purpose of trimming the sail to suit the wind.

caravel   Originally used to describe a Portuguese fishing boat with *lateen* rigging but later used to include larger merchantmen with lateen sails on two masts. This type of vessel was *carvel-built*.

carvel-built   Sometimes used to describe a *frame-first* build with flush-laid *strakes*.

caulk   To insert material between two *strakes* or other timbers to form a watertight junction.

cleat   A projection usually integral to a *plank* to which other fittings may be fastened or a line made fast.

clench   To bend, hook, or otherwise turn the end of a metal fastening so that it will not draw out under stress.

clinker-built   A form of boatbuilding in which the *strakes* are placed so that they partly overlap one another, usually upper strake outboard of lower strake, but occasionally the reverse arrangement is found.

cocha   A type of *cog* with a single square-rigged sail and a stern rudder but built *frame first*.

cog   A type of vessel, broadly built, without a *keel* or with a simple keel-*plank* to which the *stem-* and *stern-posts* were attached, and with high *freeboard* to provide capacity for cargo. Primarily a coastal merchant vessel, but also used as a ship of war.

cross-beam   A timber extending across the vessel.

currach   A small boat made from a light timber framework covered with hides, used in recent times in Scotland and Ireland but of great antiquity, probably going back to the Mesolithic period.

cut-water   The forward edge of the *stem* or prow around the waterline.

dogger   A sturdy two-masted fishing vessel originally of Dutch origin. Formerly used for deep-sea fishing in the North Sea.

draft   The vertical distance between the waterline and the lowest point of the hull.

floor timber   A transverse timber extending across the bottom of a vessel from the *keelson* to the *bilges* creating a nearly horizontal platform to the point to which the vessel's side begins to turn towards the vertical.

frame   A transverse member made up of more than one piece of timber, usually *floor timbers* and pairs of futtocks (which support the side-*planking*), and set against the planking.

frame first   A vessel is said to be built *frame* first when the hull shape is determined by the framing, which is the prime element in design and strength.

freeboard   The height of sides above the waterline, measured at the centre of a vessel.

galley   An oared fighting ship of Mediterranean origin with one or more levels of oars. They had one or two masts, taking *lateen* sails, which could be lowered and stowed before action.

gunwale   The upper edge of a ship's side.

halyard   A rope or tackle used for raising or lowering a sail, *yard*, *spar*, or flag.

helm   The handle or tiller by which the rudder is managed. The term may be used to include the whole steering gear.

hippos (*pl.* hippoi)   Small boat rowed by three to five rowers, so named by the Greeks because of its horse-head prow (Greek *hippos*). Usually applied to Phoenician vessels.

hulc   An early medieval vessel simply constructed with rounded bow and *stern* and without a *keel*. The *planks* are upturned fore and aft so that the cut ends are out of the water.

keel   The lowest longitudinal strength member, extending the length of the vessel, to which the *stems* are joined forward and aft.

keelson   Centre-line timber on top of the floors but fixed to the *keel*, adding to the longitudinal strength and stiffness of the vessel. May have a *mast-step* incorporated.

lateen rig   A triangular sail set on a long *yard* at an angle of about 45 degrees to the mast. The forward end is attached low down; the rear end peaks high.

lath   A light longitudinal *batten* laid over *caulking* to protect it, and held in place by fastenings.

lee shore   The shore towards which the (prevailing) wind blows.

lodestone   Magnetic oxide of iron. An iron bar stroked with a lodestone, if freely suspended, would align itself north–south.

longship   A long, narrow, double-ended ship with a shallow draught, propelled by oars and usually having a single mast with a square-rigged sail.

mast partner   A structure, often a *cross-beam*, at deck level, locating and supporting a mast.

mast-step   A fitting used to locate the heel of a mast.

mizzen   The principal sail on the mizzen-mast of a ship (the mast aft of the main-mast), set in *lateen* rig.

mortise and tenon   A method of fastening flush-laid *planking* in which free tenons are fitted into mortises cut in the meeting edges of adjacent planks. After the planking is assembled the tenons may be pierced by *treenails*, one through each plank.

não   Spanish term used during the late Middle Ages for a ship; not a specific type of vessel.

nef   A type of French merchant ship of the late Middle Ages. Three-masted with a single square sail on the fore- and *mizzen*-mast and a square mainsail and topsail on the mainmast.

outrigger   A float or pontoon fixed with struts to a small boat, parallel to and at some distance from it, for the purpose of increasing stability.

penteconter   Ancient Greek ship with fifty oars.

plank   A length of wood which, together with others attached end to end, makes up a *strake*.

poop deck   The aftermost and highest deck, often forming the roof of a cabin in the *stern*.

portolan A collection of sailing directions describing harbours, coasts, estuaries, etc., illustrated with charts.

quarterdeck The upper deck of a ship to the *stern* of the mainmast, from which the captain or master commands the vessel.

quinquereme A *galley* rowed by oarsmen arranged in groups of five, perhaps with three levels of oars, one above the other, the top two each pulled by a pair of men, the bottom by one.

reef To shorten sail by tying up the lower portion using reef points—short lengths of rope attached to the sail.

rhumb line A line on a chart which intersects meridians at the same oblique angle along which a ship might sail in a constant direction.

rib A simple form of *frame*. This term may be more appropriate than 'frame' when applied to small open boats.

rocker The fore and after curvature of a *keel* or bottom of vessel.

run To sail with the wind from the *stern* sector.

scarf A tapered or wedge-shaped joint between timbers of similar section at the join.

seam A juncture of two timbers required to be watertight.

sheer-line The upward curve of the deck towards the bows and the *stern*.

sheet A single line used to trim the foot of a sail to the wind.

side timber A framing timber supporting the side-*planking* between the *floor timbers*. It may be adjacent to a floor but is not fastened to it.

spar A general term for a wooden pole used in a ship's rigging.

spritsail Small square sail suspended from a bowsprit, a mast projecting in advance of the bow.

stays Ropes leading from the masthead fore and aft to support the mast.

stem or stem-post Foremost timber forming the bow of a vessel. The bottom is joined to the *keel*. It forms the timber to which the front ends of the *strakes* are attached.

step The block in which is fixed the heel of a mast or capstan.

stern The after end of the ship where the steering gear is usually situated.

stern-post A vertical or near-vertical timber attached to the *keel* at the aft end of a vessel. In later vessels the rudders were hung from them.

strake A single *plank* or combination of planks stretching from one end of a boat to the other.

T and O map From *orbis terrarum*, or 'orb of the lands', representing the physical world as an 'O' with a 'T' inside, as described by Isidore of Seville (*c.*560–636).

topsail   Sail set above the working sails in a fore-and-aft rigged vessel. It may be split in two, each with its own *yard*. On the mainmast it is called the main topsail and on the foremast, the fore topsail.

transom   A beam set across the vessel, usually at the *stern* or bow. At the stern it may be bolted to the *stern-post* to provide the framing for a flat rear.

treenail   A wooden peg or dowel, usually of oak, used to join two timbers. It may be secured at each or either end by the insertion of a wedge.

triaconter   Ancient Greek galley with fifteen rowers to each side.

trireme   An oared vessel with three levels of oarsmen, one above the other.

umiak   A large Inuit boat consisting of a light wooden frame with skins drawn over it and propelled by paddles.

wash-strake   An additional board fitted to the side of a boat to prevent the sea from washing over.

yard   A wooden *spar*, comparatively long and slender, suspended at its centre from, and forward of, a mast to support a square sail which is bent to it.

A GUIDE TO FURTHER READING

In the pages to follow some suggestions for further reading are offered for those who feel inclined to learn more about the subjects discussed in this book. In making the suggestions I have been very selective, choosing books and papers which I have found to be reliable and useful. Where possible, works in English have been given preference, but for some subjects it is necessary to venture into other European languages. Most of the works cited have extensive bibliographies which will allow the reader to delve deep into any subject and quickly to discover the primary sources. It is there that the fascination really begins.

Human interaction with the sea over tens of thousands of years is a 'grand narrative', and to appreciate its flow it is necessary to view it from above so that the rhythms can be properly understood, but there are so many intriguing sub-narratives that the temptation to focus in and explore is irresistible. In each chapter I have given in to the temptation so as to relish some of the detail that underpins the big history. The reader who wants to know more will find references there and will be able to burrow down to whatever level of detail he or she wishes.

There is a great difference between the kind of literature available to support the prehistoric and the historic parts of this long story. One of the reasons for this is that, while historians have been researching and analysing their documents for centuries, producing increasingly mature and nuanced studies, prehistory is a young discipline experiencing an exponential growth in the quantity of data being daily published as the result of new excavations and new analytical techniques. During the time taken to write this book, discoveries on Crete have revolutionized our understanding of early seafaring, and current work on ancient DNA, when fully published, will allow us to look at human mobility in entirely new ways. The disparity in the data means that, for the early chapters, I have usually had to turn to papers published in conference proceedings and journals, while for the later period there are many good books of synthesis from which to choose.

One of the joys in embarking on a story such as the one we are exploring here is that new discoveries and fresh scholarship are constantly adding to it, refocusing our perspective and refining our understanding. The narrative offered here is an introductory overview; this Guide to Further Reading is the first step on a journey of exploration that can last a lifetime.

CHAPTER 1. THOSE IN PERIL ON THE SEA

There is no better way to understand the eternal conflict between humans and the ocean—the Sea of Perpetual Gloom—than to read two novels, Victor Hugo's *The Toilers of the Sea* (1866) and Pierre Loti's *Pêcheur d'Islande* (The Icelandic Fisherman, 1886). Both are dramatic works presenting the sea as an irresistible force, constantly demanding, and treating mere humans as pawns to be mocked. A more rational, but no less fascinating, work is *The Sea: A Cultural History* (London, 2011), beautifully written by the anthropologist John Mack. It is the best introduction to the human–sea interaction at present available.

The legends and folk-tales about the sea can be found in the many popular works on folklore. Émile Souvestre's work *Le Foyer Breton: contes et récits populaires* (1844) presents the famous Breton legend of the inundated city of Ker-Is, a topic also given full modern treatment in C. Guyot, *The Legend of the City of Ys*, trans. D. Cavanagh (Amherst, Mass., 1979). The lost land of Lyonnesse is discussed in A. D. H. Bivar, 'Lyonnesse: The Evolution of a Fable', *Modern Philology*, 50 (1953), 162–70. A general collection of belief systems pertinent to the Atlantic and Baltic are conveniently presented in P. Lysaght, S. Ó Catháin, and D. Ó hÓgáin, *Islanders and Water-Dwellers* (Dublin, 1999); this is fairly solid stuff written for an academic audience. A much easier read is a delightful collection of sea stories collected before the Second World War along the coast of Galway by Heinrich Becker and published as *Seaweed Memories: In the Jaws of the Sea* (Dublin, 2000). *The Colloquy of the Two Sages* (Paris, 1905), mentioned for its treatment of the liminal intertidal zone, is edited and translated by Whitley Stokes.

The compulsion to travel and the power of esoteric knowledge is brilliantly presented by Mary Helms's *Ulysses' Sail* (Princeton, 1988), its subtitle, *An Ethnographic Odyssey of Power, Knowledge, and Geographical Distance*, giving some flavour of its wide scope. Some of the aspects explored by Helms are given further treatment in Robin Lane Fox's *Travelling Heroes: Greeks and their Myths in the Epic Age of Homer* (London, 2008). The more specific theme of pilgrimage is explored in J. McCorriston, *Pilgrimage and Household in the Ancient Near East* (Cambridge, 2011). The voyage in Irish mythology is discussed in A. and B. Rees, *Celtic Heritage: Ancient Tradition in*

Ireland and Wales (London, 1961), ch. 16, while the *peregrini*, the wandering monks, are given full treatment in E. G. Bowen, *Saints, Seaways and Settlements in the Celtic Lands* (Cardiff, 1977).

For understanding the early Greek view of the universe, Hesiod's *Theogony* and *Works and Days* are essential reading, both brought together with useful notes in M. L. West's translation (Oxford, 1988). Homer's *Iliad* and *Odyssey* are also vital sources available in many editions. Similarly, Herodotus' *Histories*, also available in many editions, should be consulted both for the insights it provides and for the sheer pleasure of reading the prose. From the huge array of works on Greek myths I would recommend the lively but scholarly book by S. P. Kershaw, *A Brief Guide to the Greek Myths* (London, 2007). The way in which an understanding of the universe developed in the classical world is presented with great scholarship in J. O. Thomson, *The History of Ancient Geography* (Cambridge, 1948), which, though a vintage text, is still invaluable. K. Clarke, *Between Geography and History* (Oxford, 1999), is a scholarly analysis of the geographical and historiographical tradition in the second and first centuries BC. The various classical writers who record ocean voyages, Hanno, Avienus, and Pytheas, will be introduced in the further reading for the appropriate chapters.

The *immrama* (voyages) have a considerable literature. I have already mentioned the useful introduction in Rees, *Celtic Heritage*. Another helpful overview, with special reference to *The Voyage of Máel Dúin*, will be found in M. Dillon, *Early Irish Literature* (Chicago, 1948), ch. 6. The voyage is also analysed in E. Johnston, 'A Sailor on the Seas of Faith: The Individual and the Church in the Voyage of Máel Dúin', in J. Devlin and H. B. Clarke (eds.), *European Encounters: Essays in Memory of Albert Lovett* (Dublin, 2003), 239–52. Brendan's exploits are conveniently discussed in G. Burgess, *The Voyage of St Brendan* (Exeter, 2002). The myth of Atlantis is the subject of a vast literature varying widely in its value. Since the story is considered here to be an allegory that Plato invented for the purposes of debate, two citations are sufficient: P. Vidal-Naquet, *The Atlantis Story: A Short History of Plato's Myth* (Exeter, 2007), and W. Warman, *Character, Plot and Thought in Plato's Timaeus–Critias* (Leiden, 1977), the latter giving a detailed consideration of the context of Plato's invention. The world in which Isidore of Seville was writing is well described in R. Collins, *Early Medieval Spain: Unity in Diversity, 400–1000* (London, 1983).

The whole subject of mythical islands in the Atlantic is attractively summed up and put into context in D. S. Johnson's lively little book *Phantom Islands of the Atlantic: The Legends of Seven Lands that Never Were* (New York, 1994). The influence of the legendary islands on later explorers is considered in T. J. Westropp, 'Brasil and the Legendary Islands of the North Atlantic', *Proceedings of the Royal Irish Academy*, 30 (1912), 223–60.

Finally, the Arab travellers: although not impinging too much on the subject matter of the book, the horizons and motivation of medieval Arab travellers are interesting to explore. Two books are recommended: A. M. H. Shboul, *Al-Mas'udi and his World* (London, 1979), and D. Waites, *The Odyssey of Ibn Battuta* (London, 2010).

CHAPTER 2. THE COMBAT THAT IS CALLED NAVIGATION

We begin at the beginning, with plate tectonics. Good discussions can be found in general works on physical geography like P. L. Hancock and B. J. Skinner (eds.), *The Oxford Companion to the Earth* (Oxford, 2000), but for a reader interested in the development of the debate, a collection of papers published in *Scientific American* between 1950 and 1970 brought together in J. T. Wilson (ed.), *Continents Adrift* (San Francisco, 1971), make fascinating reading. The Messinian Salinity Crisis is usefully summarized in A. Mather, 'Tectonic Setting and Landscape Development', in J. Woodward (ed.), *The Physical Geography of the Mediterranean* (Oxford, 2009), 5–32, and in more detail in K. J. Hsü, *The Mediterranean Was a Desert: A Voyage of the Glomar Challenger* (Princeton, 1987). The debate on the Zanclean flood event is laid out in P.-L. Blanc, 'The Opening of the Plio-Quaternary Gibraltar Strait: Assessing the Site of the Cataclysm', *Geodinamica Acta*, 15 (2002), 303–17, and D. Garcia-Castellanos et al., 'Catastrophic Flood of the Mediterranean after the Messinian Salinity Crisis', *Nature*, 462 (2009), 78–81. On the flooding of the Black Sea, there has been much excited debate. Useful papers are to be found in V. Yanko-Hombach et al. (eds.), *The Black Sea Flood Question: Changes in Coastline, Climate and Human Settlement* (New York, 2006), to which L. Giosan, F. Florin, and S. Constantinescu, 'Was the Black Sea Catastrophically Flooded in the Early Holocene?', *Quaternary Science Reviews*, 28 (2009), 1–6, can be usefully added.

For the geography of the Mediterranean, the most convenient source is J. C. Woodward (ed.), *The Physical Geography of the Mediterranean* (Oxford, 2009). Details of the wind systems in the Mediterranean are given in the Meteorological Office publication *Weather in the Mediterranean* (London, 1962). Other useful works on aspects of the Mediterranean include I. N. Vogiatzakis, G. Pungetti, and A. M. Mannion (eds.), *Mediterranean Island Landscapes: Natural and Cultural Approaches* (New York, 2008), and J. Blondel et al., *The Mediterranean Region: Biological Diversity in Time and Space* (Oxford, 2010).

The Atlantic is considered throughout its complex history in P. Butel, *The Atlantic* (London, 1999), and M. W. Sandler, *Atlantic Ocean: The Illustrated History of the Ocean that Changed the World* (New York, 2008). One of the most convenient ways of understanding the coastal geography of the Atlantic is by selectively using the Geographical

Handbook Series prepared by Britain's Naval Intelligence Division in the 1940s to provide basic information for those planning military and naval operations. Understandably there is an emphasis on coastal geography. Volumes were prepared as follows: *Belgium* (Cambridge, 1944), *France* (Cambridge, 1942), *Morocco* (Oxford, 1941–2), *Portugal* (Oxford, 1942), and *Spain* (Oxford, 1944). Other basic sources are the Admiralty Pilots and the Tidal Stream Atlas (Hydrographic Department). The currents in the Atlantic and the biomass they generated in the ocean are topics well explained in J. R. Coull, *The Fisheries of Europe: An Economic Geography* (London, 1972).

In approaching the question of early Greek knowledge of cosmology and sailing, two useful sources are D. R. Dicks, *Early Greek Astronomy to Aristotle* (London, 1970), and S. McGrail, 'Navigational Techniques in Homer's *Odyssey*', *Tropis*, 4 (1996), 311–20. Pytheas' use of sun heights is described in B. Cunliffe, *The Extraordinary Voyage of Pytheas the Greek* (London, 2001), while the late Roman poem *Ora Maritima* by Rufus Festus Avienus is available in translation with helpful notes in J. P. Murphy's edition (Chicago, 1977). Strabo's understanding of the Atlantic is given in his *Geography* 1.1 and 4. Rutters and portolans are comprehensively treated in T. Campbell, 'Portolan Charts from the Late Thirteenth Century to 1500', in J. B. Harley and D. Woodward (eds.), *The History of Cartography*, 3 vols. (London, 1987–2007), i. 371–463, and in J. T. Lanman, *On the Origin of Portolan Charts* (Chicago, 1987). The different schools of map-makers, in particular the Majorcan school, are discussed in the context of the exploration of the Atlantic from the Mediterranean in F. Fernández-Armesto, *Before Columbus: Exploration and Colonization from the Mediterranean to the Atlantic, 1229–1492* (Philadelphia, 1987). The subject of sea-charts is considered more widely in P. Whitfeld, *The Charting of the Oceans: Ten Centuries of Maritime Maps* (London, 1996), and M. Mollat du Jourdin and M. de La Roncière, *Sea Charts of the Early Explorers, 13th to 17th Century*, trans. L. Le R. Dethan (London, 1984). The subject of navigation is covered in a classic text, E. G. R. Taylor, *The Haven-Finding Art: A History of Navigation from Odysseus to Captain Cook* (London, 1956), and in A. D. Aczel, *The Riddle of the Compass: The Invention that Changed the World* (New York, 2001).

Finally, two general books that offer good contextual introductions to the themes explored in this book are Butel, *The Atlantic*, and M. Mollat du Jourdin, *Europe and the Sea*, trans. T. L. Fagan (Oxford, 1993).

CHAPTER 3. TAKING TO THE SEA

The ability of our distant ancestors to take to the sea—the Mediterranean and the Atlantic—during the Palaeolithic period raises a number of difficult questions that are currently engaging archaeologists. To begin to understand the European evidence it is helpful to look at the rest of the world. Some of the more useful papers include R. G. Bednarik, 'Seafaring in the Pleistocene', *Cambridge Archaeological Journal*, 13 (2003), 41–66; J. F. O'Connell, J. Allen, and K. Hawkes, 'Pleistocene Sahul and the Origins of Seafaring', in A. Anderson, J. H. Barrett, and K. V. Boyle (eds.), *The Global Origins and Development of Seafaring* (Cambridge, 2010), 57–68; J. B. Bulbeck, 'A Parsimonious Model for *Homo Sapiens* Colonization of the Indian Ocean Rim and Sahul', *Current Anthropology*, 48 (2007), 315–21; J. M. Erlandson, 'Anatomically Modern Humans, Maritime Voyaging, and the Pleistocene Colonization of the Americas', in N. G. Jablonski (ed.), *The First Americans: The Pleistocene Colonization of the New World* (San Francisco, 2001), 59–62.

Of crucial importance to the debate on the origins of seafaring in the Mediterranean was a Wenner-Gren Workshop held in 2012 generating twenty-one significant papers edited by A. J. Ammerman and T. Davis in *Island Archaeology and the Origins of Seafaring in the Eastern Mediterranean* and published in two parts in *Eurasian Prehistory*, 10–11 (2013–14). Together these papers make essential reading for anyone interested in the rapidly evolving field. Particular excitement focuses on recent Palaeolithic discoveries on Crete which are presented in one of the papers, C. Runnels et al., 'Lower Palaeolithic Artifacts from Plakias, Crete: Implications for Hominid Dispersals', *Eurasian Prehistory*, 11 (2014), 129–51. The debate continues in C. Runnels, 'Early Palaeolithic on the Greek Islands?', *Journal of Mediterranean Archaeology*, 27 (2014), 211–30, and T. P. Leppard, 'Modeling the Impacts of Mediterranean Island Colonization by Archaic Hominins: The Likelihood of an Insular Lower Palaeolithic', *Journal of Mediterranean Archaeology*, 27 (2014), 231–53. The early occupation in the caves on Gibraltar and its maritime implications are discussed in C. B. Stringer et al., 'Neanderthal Exploitation of Marine Mammals in Gibraltar', *Proceedings of the National Academy of Sciences*, 105/38 (2008), 14319–24, and R. N. E. Barton, C. B. Stringer, and J. C. Finlayson (eds.), *Neanderthals in Context: A Report on the 1995–1998 Excavations at Gorham's and Vanguard Caves, Gibraltar* (Oxford, 2012), esp. K. Douka and T. F. G. Higham, 'Marine Resource Exploitation and the Seasonal Factor of Neanderthal Occupation: Evidence from Gibraltar'.

To approach the vast literature on the Late Glacial Maximum and its impacts on human society in Europe, C. Gamble, *The Palaeolithic Societies of Europe* (Cambridge, 2009), offers a very thorough introduction with ample references to the literature. On the Cosquer Cave near Marseille, see J. Clottes, J. Courtin, and L. Vanrell, *Cosquer redécouvert* (Paris, 2005); for the Nerja Caves and other southern Spanish sites, A. Morales-Muñiz and I. Rosello-Izquierdo, 'Twenty Thousand Years of Fishing in the Strait: Archaeological Fish and Shellfish Assemblages in Southern Iberia', in T. C. Rick and M. Erlandson (eds.), *Human Impacts on Ancient Marine Ecosystems: A Global*

Perspective (Berkeley, 2008), 243–78. Evidence for maritime exploitation in France is briefly summarized in J.-J. Cleyet-Merle and S. Madeleine, 'Inland Evidence of Human Sea Coast Exploitation in Palaeolithic France', in A. Fischer (ed.), *Man and Sea in the Mesolithic: Coastal Settlement Above and Below Present Sea Level* (Oxford, 1995), 303–8. Disparate evidence for the earliest seafaring in the central Mediterranean is critically brought together in M. A. Mannino, 'The Question of Voyaging by Foragers Who Lived in the Central Mediterranean', *Eurasian Prehistory*, 11 (2014), 165–84.

The warming climate following the Last Glacial Maximum and the later Younger Dryas and its effect on human settlement are explored in S. Mithen, *After the Ice: A Global Human History, 20,000–5000 BC* (Cambridge, 2003). A very useful overview of the causes of the Younger Dryas is given in D. J. Meltzer and V. T. Holliday, 'Would North American Paleoindians Have Noticed the Younger Dryas Age Climatic Changes?', *Journal of World Prehistory*, 23 (2010), 1–41. A meteor strike as the possible cause of the climatic downturn is considered in A. M. T. Moore and D. J. Kennett, 'Cosmic Impact, the Younger Dryas, Abu Hureyra and the Inception of Agriculture in Western Asia', *Eurasian Prehistory*, 10 (2013), 57–66.

The cave site at Franchthi on the Gulf of Argos features large in discussions of the Mesolithic and Neolithic exploitation of the sea. The standard presentation of the lithic evidence is C. Perlès, *Les Industries lithiques taillées de Franchthi (Argolide, Grèce), i: Présentation général et industries paléolithiques* (Bloomington, 1987). Other important papers on the subject by the same author include 'Long Term Perspectives on the Occupation of Franchthi Cave: Continuity and Discontinuity', in G. N. Bailey et al. (eds.), *The Palaeolithic Archaeology of Greece and Adjacent Areas* (London, 1999), 311–18, and 'The Mesolithic of Franchthi: An Overview of the Data and Problems', in N. Galanidou and C. Perlès (eds.), *The Greek Mesolithic: Problems and Perspectives* (London, 2003), 79–88. To these should be added M. C. Stiner and N. D. Munro, 'On the Evolution of Diet and Landscape during the Upper Palaeolithic through Mesolithic at Franchthi Cave (Peloponnese, Greece)', *Journal of Human Evolution*, 60 (2011), 618–36.

The cave site of Akrotiri Aetokremnos on Cyprus is central to the discussions of early seafaring and has been the subject of lively debate, particularly on the interpretation of the faunal remains. The literature has proliferated since the first substantive discussion of the find by the excavator A. H. Simmons: 'Humans, Island Colonization and Pleistocene Extinctions in the Mediterranean: The View from Akrotiri Aetokremnos, Cyprus', *Antiquity*, 65 (1991), 857–69. The same author reviewed the subsequent debate in a useful summary, 'Akrotiri-Aetokremnos (Cyprus) Twenty Years Later: An Assessment of its Significance', *Eurasian Prehistory*, 10 (2013), 139–56, and also in his more wide-ranging book *Stone Age Sailors: Palaeolithic Seafaring in the Mediterranean*

(Walnut Creek, Calif., 2014). Other early Cypriot sites relevant to the first peoples of the island are Aspros and Nissi Beach, for which see A. J. Ammerman, 'Tracing the Steps in the Fieldwork at the Sites of Aspros and Nissi Beach on Cyprus', *Eurasian Prehistory*, 10 (2013), 117–38.

The spread of hunter-gatherer communities from the North European Plain to Sweden and Norway following the retreat of the ice sheet is explored by Lou Schmitt in a series of papers, 'The West Swedish Hensbacka: A Maritime Adaptation and a Seasonal Expression of the North-Central European Ahrensburgian', in Fischer (ed.), *Man and Sea in the Mesolithic*, 161–70; L. Schmitt et al., '"Why They Came": The Colonization of the Coast of Western Sweden and its Environmental Context at the End of the Last Glaciation', *Oxford Journal of Archaeology*, 25 (2006), 1–28; L. Schmitt, 'A Note concerning Flake Axes and Umiaks', *Oxford Journal of Archaeology*, 32 (2013), 119–22. The spread of hunter-gatherers up to the coast of Norway is discussed in S. Bang-Andersen, 'Colonizing Contrasting Landscapes: The Pioneer Coast Settlement and Inland Utilization in Southern Norway 10,000–9,500 Years before Present', *Oxford Journal of Archaeology*, 31 (2012), 103–20.

An interesting paper that reflects on the question of developing appropriate methodologies for discovering elusive coastal Mesolithic sites is C. Runnels, 'Mesolithic Sites and Surveys in Greece: A Case Study from the Southern Argolid', *Journal of Mediterranean Archaeology*, 22 (2009), 57–73. The application of that methodology to Crete yielded remarkable results presented in T. F. Strasser et al., 'Stone Age Seafaring in the Mediterranean: Evidence from the Plakias Region for Lower Palaeolithic and Mesolithic Habitation of Crete', *Hesperia*, 79 (2010), 145–90.

The cave site of Grotta dell'Uzzo in Sicily, with a long sequence of use, is introduced in R. Leighton, *Sicily before History: An Archaeological Survey from the Palaeolithic to the Iron Age* (London, 1999). The important faunal sequence is fully discussed in A. Tagliacozzo, *Archeozoologia della Grotta dell'Uzzo, Sicilia* (Rome, 1993), with the maritime implications being specifically considered in M. A. Mannino et al., 'Marine Resources in the Mesolithic and Neolithic at the Grotta dell'Uzzo (Sicily): Evidence from Isotope Analysis of Marine Shells', *Archaeometry*, 49 (2007), 117–33.

A perceptive overview of our present knowledge of early seafaring in the Mediterranean, assessing the strengths and weaknesses of the evidence and the need for further study, is given in two papers by A. J. Ammerman beginning and ending the Wenner-Gren Workshop held in 2012: 'Introduction', *Eurasian Prehistory*, 10 (2013), 1–30, and 'Setting our Sights on the Distant Horizon', *Eurasian Prehistory*, 11 (2014), 203–36. Both are essential reading.

The situation along the Atlantic coast in the Mesolithic period is summarized in B. Cunliffe, *Facing the Ocean: The Atlantic and its Peoples, 8000 BC–AD 1500* (Oxford, 2001), ch. 4. A number of relevant papers will be found in three monographs: A. Fischer (ed.), *Man and the Sea in the Mesolithic* (Oxford, 1995); R. Young (ed.), *Mesolithic Lifeways: Current Research from Britain and Ireland* (Leicester, 2000); M. González Morales and G. A. Clark (eds.), *The Mesolithic of the Atlantic Façade* (Tempe, Ariz., 2004). The Portuguese evidence is well introduced in two papers: J. Roche, 'Spatial Organization in the Mesolithic Sites of Muge, Portugal', and J. E. Morais Arnaud, 'The Mesolithic Communities of the Sado Valley, Portugal, in their Ecological Setting', both in C. Bonsall (ed.), *The Mesolithic in Europe* (Edinburgh, 1989), 607–13, 614–31. For the Mesolithic of the north coast of Iberia, see M. González Morales and M. A. Fano Martínez, 'The Mesolithic of Cantabrian Spain: A Critical Review', in N. Milner and P. C. Woodman (eds.), *Mesolithic Studies at the Beginning of the 21st Century* (Oxford, 2005), 14–29.

A useful overview of the Mesolithic in Scotland is given in N. Finlay, G. Warren, and C. Wickham-Jones, 'The Mesolithic in Scotland: East Meets West', *Scottish Archaeological Journal*, 24 (2002), 101–20; and a number of interesting issues, including the exchange of different stone types in the west of Scotland, are discussed in D. Telford, 'The Mesolithic Inheritance: Contrasting Neolithic Monumentality in Eastern and Western Scotland', *Proceedings of the Prehistoric Society*, 68 (2002), 289–315. One of the classic excavations of a maritime community took place on Oronsay. The results and analyses are published in P. Mellars, *Excavations on Oronsay: Prehistoric Human Ecology on a Small Island* (Edinburgh, 1987). The significance of the site is further considered in S. Mithen (ed.), *Hunter-Gatherer Landscape Archaeology: The Southern Hebrides Mesolithic Project, 1988–1998* (Cambridge, 2000).

For Scandinavia, an excellent survey of the Mesolithic and Ertebølle cultures is given in T. D. Price, *Ancient Scandinavia: An Archaeological History from the First Hunters to the Vikings* (Oxford, 2015), with full bibliographies. Log boats of the Ertebølle period are briefly discussed in C. Christensen, 'Mesolithic Boats from around the Great Belt, Denmark', in B. Coles, J. Coles, and M. S. Jorgensen (eds.), *Bog Bodies, Sacred Sites and Wetland Archaeology* (Exeter, 1999), 47–50. For the important site of Tybrind Vig, where paddles and a log boat have been found, see S. H. Andersen, 'Tybrind Vig', *Journal of Danish Archaeology*, 4 (1985), 52–69.

A very brief introduction to the spread of early farming to Europe is given in B. Cunliffe, *Europe between the Oceans, 9000 BC–AD 1000* (London, 2011), chs. 4 and 5. Cyprus features large in the debates about the development of shipping in this period. A broad overview of the problem is provided in A. B. Knapp, 'Cyprus's Earliest Prehistory: Seafarers, Foragers and Settlers', *Journal of World Prehistory*, 23 (2010), 79–120. Questions of the dating of the earliest Neolithic on Cyprus are discussed in S. W. Manning, 'Temporal Placement and Context of Cyro-PPNA Activity on Cyprus', *Eurasian Prehistory*, 11 (2014), 9–28. The question of the types of boat used and the periodicity of voyaging is intriguingly explored in J.-D. Vigne et al., 'The Transportation of Mammals to Cyprus Sheds Light on Early Voyaging and Boats in the Mediterranean Sea', *Eurasian Prehistory*, 10 (2013), 157–76.

The spread of Neolithic lifestyles by enclave colonization throughout the Mediterranean and into the Atlantic was introduced in a seminal paper by J. Zilhão, 'The Spread of Agro-Pastoral Economies across Mediterranean Europe: A View from the Far West', *Journal of Mediterranean Archaeology*, 6 (1993), 5–63. There has been much new work and new radiocarbon data since then, which Zilhão has reviewed in a book chapter (with an updated bibliography) focusing carefully on the process of the spread: 'Early Food Production in Southwestern Europe', in C. Renfrew and P. Bahn (eds.), *Cambridge World Prehistory*, 3 vols. (Cambridge, 2014), iii. 1818–34. The implications for seamanship are considered by Zilhão in 'Early Prehistoric Navigation in the Western Mediterranean: Implications for the Neolithic Transition in Iberia and the Maghreb', *Eurasian Prehistory*, 11 (2014), 185–200.

For maritime mobility in the central Mediterranean the most relevant paper is R. H. Tykot, 'Obsidian Procurement and Distribution in the Central and Western Mediterranean', *Journal of Mediterranean Archaeology*, 9 (1996), 39–82. The La Marmotta log boat is considered in M. A. Fugazzola Delpino and M. Mineo, 'La piroga neolitica del lago di Bracciano, La Marmotta', *Bullettino di Paletnologia Italiano*, 86 (1995), 197–266.

CHAPTER 4. TWO SEAS, MANY RESPONSES, 5300–1200 BC

There are several books that provide general background reading for this chapter. The broader cultural background is well covered in three books: C. Broodbank, *The Making of the Middle Sea* (London, 2013); B. Cunliffe, *Facing the Ocean* (Oxford, 2001); T. D. Price, *Ancient Scandinavia* (Oxford, 2015), all with useful references. The physical evidence of boats is conveniently brought together in S. McGrail, *Boats of the World: From the Stone Age to Medieval Times* (Oxford, 2001), while copper extraction, which is an important thread in this chapter, is considered in its European context in W. O'Brien, *Prehistoric Copper Mining in Europe, 5500–500 BC* (Oxford, 2015).

The spread of farming to the Atlantic zone of Europe begins with the appearance of Cardial Ware enclaves referred to in the last chapter. The spread of Danubian influences to the west is helpfully summed up in G. Verron, *Préhistoire de la Normandie* (Rennes, 2000), while the complex situation in Brittany, where different cultural influences intertwine, is carefully presented and analysed in C. Scarre, *Landscapes of Neolithic Brittany* (Oxford, 2011). For the spread of the Neolithic to Britain, about which a very great deal has been written, the best authoritative summary (with a copious bibliography) is A. Sheridan, 'The Neolithisation of Britain and Ireland: The "Big Picture"', in B. Finlayson and G. Warren (eds.), *Landscapes in Transition* (Oxford, 2010), 89–105. The possible causative effect of climate change is outlined in R. Tipping, 'The Case for Climate Stress Forcing Choice in the Adoption of Agriculture in the British Isles', in the same volume, 66–76. The extremely interesting question of the transport of domesticated animals by boat to Mesolithic Ireland is considered in A. Tresset, 'French Connection II: Of Cows and Men', in I. Armit et al. (eds.), *Neolithic Settlement in Ireland and Western Britain* (Oxford, 2003), 18–30, and P. C. Woodman and M. McCarthy, 'Contemplating Some Awful(ly Interesting) Vistas: Importing Cattle and Red Deer into Prehistoric Ireland', in the same volume, 31–9.

Very little of a general nature has been written about megalithic monuments in Atlantic Europe in recent years, though the subject has developed apace. Some idea of the debates now under way can be gained from the fifty or so specialist papers given to an international symposium held in Santiago de Compostela in April 1996: A. A. Rodríguez Casal (ed.), *O Neolitico atlántico e as orixes do megalitismo* (Santiago de Compostela, 1997). The 860 pages in various languages are not for the faint-hearted. Among the more recent (and more accessible) regional reviews are L. Oosterbeek, 'Megaliths in Portugal: The Western Network Revisited', in G. Burenhult and S. Westergaard (eds.), *Stones and Bones: Formal Disposal of the Dead in Atlantic Europe during the Mesolithic– Neolithic Interface, 6000–3000 BC* (Oxford, 2003), 27–37; C. Scarre, *The Landscapes of Neolithic Brittany* (Oxford, 2011); A. Sheridan, 'French Connections I: Spreading the *Marmites* Thinly', in Armit et al. (eds.), *Neolithic Settlement in Ireland and Western Britain*, 3–17, and the same author's 'Ireland's Earliest "Passage" Tombs: A French Connection?', in Burenhult and Westergaard (eds.), *Stones and Bones*, 9–26. Megalithic art along the Atlantic seaways has been thoroughly discussed in E. Shee Twohig, *The Megalithic Art of Western Europe* (Oxford, 1981). More recently an international conference held in Rennes generated a useful series of papers: J. L'Helgouac'h, C.-T. Le Roux, and J. Lecornec (eds.), *Art et symboles du mégalithisme européen* (Rennes, 1997). The fascinating subject of the Neolithic cosmologies is explored in C. Ruggles, *Astronomy in Prehistoric Britain and Ireland* (London, 1999). The symbols thought to represent boats carved on a rock at Borna in the Bay of Vigo and on the megalithic tombs of Mané Lud in Brittany are discussed by F. Alonso, 'Prehistoric Boats in the Rock-Paintings of Cádiz and in the Rock Carvings of Northwestern Spain', in C. Westerdahl (ed.), *Crossroads in Ancient Shipbuilding* (Oxford, 1994), 11–19.

Debates about Copper Age developments in southern Iberia are dominated by considerations of the fortified sites which have been the focus of excavation for many decades. The context for these has been explored in two books by Robert Chapman: *Emerging Complexity: The Later Prehistory of South-East Spain, Iberia, and the West*

Mediterranean (Cambridge, 1990) and *Archaeologies of Complexity* (London, 2003). Useful references which introduce some of the main sites are A. Arribas Palau and F. Molina, 'Los millares: nuevas perspectivas', in W. H. Waldren, J. A. Ensenyat, and R. C. Kennard (eds.), *IInd Deya International Conference of Prehistory: Archaeological Techniques, Technology and Theory. Recent Developments in Western Mediterranean Prehistory* (Oxford, 1991), 409–19; E. Sangmeister and H. Schubart, *Zambujal: die Grabungen 1964 bis 1973* (Mainz, 1981); N. H. Savory, 'The Cultural Sequence at Vila Nova de S. Pedro', *Madrider Mitteilungen*, 13 (1972), 23–37. Aspects of the large nucleated settlement in the Guadalquivir valley are discussed in M. E. M. Costa Caramé et al., 'The Copper Age Settlement of Valencina de la Concepción (Seville, Spain): Demography, Metallurgy and Spatial Organization', *Trabajos de Prehistoria*, 67 (2010), 85–177, and F. Nocete, 'The Smelting Quarter of Valencina de la Concepción (Seville, Spain): The Specialized Copper Industry in a Political Centre of the Guadalquivir Valley during the Third Millennium BC (2750–2500 BC)', *Journal of Archaeological Science*, 35 (2008), 717–32. For the debate about the earliest copper metallurgy in Spain, see A. Ruiz Taboada and I. Ruiz Montero, 'The Oldest Metallurgy in Western Europe', *Antiquity*, 73 (1999), 897–903, and F. Nocete, 'The First Specialized Copper Industry in the Iberian Peninsula, Cabezo Juré, 2900–2200 BC', *Antiquity*, 80 (2006), 646–54. The copper mines in Mediterranean France are discussed in P. Ambert et al., 'The Copper Mines of Cabrières (Hérault) in Southern France and the Chalcolithic Metallurgy', in T. L. Kienlin and B. W. Roberts (eds.), *Metals and Societies* (Bonn, 2009), 285–95.

The Bell Beaker phenomenon has generated a vast literature. One useful recent compilation of papers, generated by a symposium, is F. Nicholas, *Bell Beakers Today: Pottery, People, Culture, Symbols in Prehistoric Europe* (Trento, 2001). The classic study of the Iberian region in which the Maritime Bell Beaker originated is R. J. Harrison, *The Bell Beaker Cultures of Spain and Portugal* (Cambridge, Mass., 1977), which presents a lot of the material evidence. Among the recent studies of Maritime Bell Beakers in Atlantic contexts, the monograph by L. Salanova *La question du campaniforme en France et dans les îsles anglo-normandes* (Paris, 2000) is the most comprehensive. The spread of Bell Beakers to southern France has been reviewed in M. Vander Linden, 'For Whom the Bell Tolls: Social Hierarchy vs. Social Integration in the Bell Beaker Culture of Southern France (Third Millennium BC)', *Cambridge Archaeological Journal*, 16 (2006), 317–32. The evidence for Beaker involvement in the earliest copper production in Ireland is presented in W. O'Brien, *Ross Island: Mining, Metal and Society in Early Ireland* (Galway, 2004). For the arrival of Beaker influences in southern and eastern Britain, see S. Needham, 'Transforming Beaker Culture in North-West Europe: Processes of Fusion and Fission', *Proceedings of the Prehistoric Society*, 71 (2005), 171–218. Early gold-work is extensively discussed in G. Eogan, *The*

Accomplished Art: Gold and Gold-Working in Britain and Ireland during the Bronze Age (Oxford, 1994). Evidence to suggest that non-Irish gold sources were significant is presented in C. D. Standish et al., 'A Non-Local Source of Irish Chalcolithic and Early Bronze Age Gold', *Proceedings of the Prehistoric Society*, 81 (2015), 149–77.

The question of trade between Africa and Iberia in the Chalcolithic and Early Bronze Age was surveyed in R. J. Harrison and A. Gilman, 'Trade in the Second and Third Millennia BC between the Maghreb and Iberia', in V. Markotic (ed.), *Ancient Europe and the Mediterranean* (Warminster, 1977), 91–104, with extensive references to earlier literature, and in C. Poyato Holgado and A. Hernando Grande, 'Relaciones entre la península Ibérica y el Norte de Africa: "marfil y campaniforme"', in E. Ripoll Perelló (ed.), *Actas del Congreso Internacional 'El Estrecho de Gibraltar', Ceuta, 1987*, 2 vols. (Madrid, 1988), i. 317–29. The supply of ivory is explored in T. X. Schuhmacher, J. L. Cardoso, and A. Banerjee, 'Sourcing African Ivory in Chalcolithic Portugal', *Antiquity*, 83 (2009), 983–97. A useful summary of the Chalcolithic and Early Bronze Age in Morocco is given in G. Souville, 'Témoignages sur l'Âge du Bronze au Maghreb occidental', *Comptes Rendus des Séances de l'Académie des Inscriptions et Belles-Lettres*, 130 (1986), 97–114. Evidence of early copper working in Portugal is detailed in two papers: R. Muller and J. L. Cardoso, 'The Origin and Use of Copper at the Chalcolithic Fortification of Leceia (Oeiras, Portugal)', and R. Muller and A. Monge Saores, 'Traces of Early Copper Production at the Chalcolithic Fortification of Vila Nova de Sao Pedro (Azambuja, Portugal)', both in *Madrider Mitteilungen*, 49 (2008), 64–93, 94–114. For the Argaric culture in south-eastern Iberia, see P. V. Castro et al., 'Agricultural Production and Social Change in the Bronze Age of Southeast Spain: The Gatas Project', *Antiquity*, 73 (1999), 846–56; V. Lull, 'Argaric Society: Death at Home', *Antiquity*, 74 (2000), 581–90; V. Lull et al., 'Las relaciones políticas y económicas de El Argar', *Menga: Revista de Prehistoria de Andalucia*, 1 (2010), 11–36.

For the central Mediterranean, the distribution of obsidian continues to provide insights into connectivity: see R. H. Tykot, 'Obsidian Procurement and Distribution in the Central and Western Mediterranean', *Journal of Mediterranean Archaeology*, 9 (1996), 39–82. There are also useful papers in R. H. Tykot, J. Morter, and J. E. Robb (eds.), *Social Dynamics in the Prehistoric Central Mediterranean* (London, 1999). For the impact of Bell Beakers on the central Mediterranean, see Y. Bokbot, 'La civilizacion del vaso campaniforme en marruecos y la cuestion del sustrato calcolítico precampaniforme', in M. Rojo Guerra, R. Garrido Pena, and I. García Martínez de Lagrán (eds.), *El campaniforme en la península Ibérica y su contexto europeo* (Valladolid, 2005), 137–59.

Prehistoric log boats from Ireland, some of which may have been sea-going, are briefly discussed in M. Fry, 'A Creature of the Deep: The Dugout Boat in Sea-Going Mode: Evidence from the Shores of the North of Ireland', in M. Meek (ed.), *The*

Modern Traveller to our Past (Dublin, 2006), and K. Brady, 'The Logboats in the Lake', *Current Archaeology*, 292 (July 2014), 10–15.

Bronze Age plank-built boats from Britain are comprehensively reviewed in McGrail, *Boats of the World*, 184–91, and R. van de Noort, 'Argonauts of the North Sea: A Social Maritime Archaeology for the 2nd Millennium', *Proceedings of the Prehistoric Society*, 72 (2006), 267–87. The best-preserved of the plank-built boats from Dover is fully described in P. Clark (ed.), *The Dover Bronze Age Boat* (London, 2004). The reconstruction of the Dover boat is further discussed in O. Crumlin-Pedersen, 'The Dover Boat: A Reconstruction Case-Study', *International Journal of Nautical Archaeology*, 35 (2006), 58–71. The vexed question of whether these plank-built vessels could sail on the open sea is fully debated in two papers by J. Coates: 'Early Seafaring in Northwest Europe: Could Planked Vessels Have Played a Significant Part?', *Mariner's Mirror*, 91 (2005), 517–30, and 'The Bronze Age Ferriby Boats: Seagoing Ships or Estuary Ferry Boats?', *International Journal of Nautical Archaeology*, 34 (2005), 38–40. The British plank-built boats are considered in their broader context in R. van de Noort, 'Exploring the Ritual of Travel in Prehistoric Europe: The Bronze Age Sewn-Plank Boats in Context', in P. Clark (ed.), *Bronze Age Connections: Cultural Contact in Prehistoric Europe* (Oxford, 2009), 159–75.

The rich iconography of boats in rock carvings and on bronzes in Scandinavia is a major source of information about sea-going. A lively introduction to Scandinavian rock engravings is J. Coles, *Shadows of a Northern Past: Rock Engravings of Bohuslän and Østfold* (Oxford, 2005). Scandinavian ship iconography is exhaustively dealt with in F. Kaul, *Ships on Bronzes: A Study of Bronze Age Religion and Iconography* (Copenhagen, 1998). Further shorter studies include the same author's 'Social and Religious Perceptions of the Ship in Bronze Age Northern Europe', in P. Clark (ed.), *The Dover Bronze Age Boat in Context: Society and Water Transport in Prehistoric Europe* (Oxford, 2004), 112–37, and K. Kristiansen, 'Seafaring Voyages and Rock Art Ships', in the same volume, 111–21. The importance of sea travel to trade along the coast of Norway is presented in B. Solberg, 'Exchange and the Role of Imports to Western Norway in the Late Neolithic and Early Bronze Age', *Norwegian Archaeological Review*, 27 (1994), 111–26.

CHAPTER 5. THE EASTERN MEDITERRANEAN CAULDRON,
5300–1200 BC

The eastern end of the Mediterranean and the lands surrounding it—Egypt, the Near East, Asia Minor, and the lands and islands of the Aegean—constitute one of the most intensively studied regions in the world, and unsurprisingly the literature is vast.

That said, the following books provide the essential background: C. Broodbank, *The Making of the Middle Sea* (London, 2013), offers a comprehensive overview; M. van de Mieroop, *A History of the Ancient Near East, ca.3000–323 BC*, 2nd edn (Oxford, 2011), is a succinct introduction to part of the period; I. Shaw (ed.), *The Oxford History of Ancient Egypt* (Oxford, 2000), presents a series of essays offering overviews of each period (the first ten of which are relevant to this chapter). These three volumes provide an easily accessible background reading for this chapter. The following additional sources may be helpful in following up details.

For the rise of the early urban states in Mesopotamia, D. Wengrow, *What Makes Civilization?* (Oxford, 2010), is a short but interesting overview, while P. Charvát, *Mesopotamia before History* (London, 2002), and J. N. Postgate, *Early Mesopotamia: Society and Economy at the Dawn of History* (Cambridge, 2004), provide the archaeological background in more detail. The Uruk expansion is widely covered, most conveniently in G. Algaze, *The Uruk World System* (Chicago, 2005). The Levantine coastal zone is introduced in J. N. Tubb, *Canaanites* (London, 1998). For a detailed consideration of the evidence from Syria, see P. M. M. G. Akkermans and G. M. Schwartz, *The Archaeology of Syria: From Complex Hunter-Gatherers to Early Urban Societies, c.1600–300 BC* (Cambridge, 2003). This includes discussions of important sites like Ugarit (in modern Ras Shamra) and Ebla (south-west of Aleppo) and the routes from the Mediterranean coast to Mesopotamia. The port of Byblos in Lebanon and its network are described in M. Saghieh, *Byblos in the Third Millennium BC: A Reconstruction of the Stratigraphy and a Study of the Cultural Connections* (Warminster, 1983), and in H. Frost, 'Byblos and the Sea', in C. Doumet-Serhal (ed.), *Decade: A Decade of Archaeology and History in the Lebanon* (Beirut, 2004), 316–47. The developing relationship between Egypt and the Levant are considered in T. E. Levy and E. C. M. van den Brink, 'Interaction Models Egypt and the Levantine Periphery', in E. C. M. van den Brink and T. E. Levy (eds.), *Egypt and the Levant: Interrelations from the 4th through the Early 3rd Millennium BCE* (Leicester, 2002), 3–38.

The development of boats on the Nile is laid out in some detail in S. McGrail, *Boats of the World: From the Stone Age to Medieval Times* (Oxford, 2001), 14–54, with extensive references to the published sources. The well-preserved Cheops boat is fully discussed in P. Lipke, *Royal Ship of Cheops* (Oxford, 1984). Other useful works include R. L. Bowen, 'Egypt's Earliest Sailing Ships', *Antiquity*, 34 (1960), 117–31, and S. Wachsmann, *Seagoing Ships and Seamanship in the Bronze Age Levant* (College Station, Tex., 1998).

Turning now to the Aegean, C. Broodbank, *An Island Archaeology of the Early Cyclades* (Cambridge, 2000), presents not only the cultural narrative but an in-depth discussion for the developing importance of the sea. Details of the Aegean boat models and engravings are given in McGrail, *Boats of the World*, 105–11, to which should be added the engravings at Strophylas on Andros, described in C. A. Televentou, 'Strophylas: A Neolithic Settlement on Andros', in N. Brodie et al. (eds.), *Horizon: A Colloquium on the Prehistory of the Cyclades* (Cambridge, 2008), 43–53. For the significance of the Kastri group of pottery, see P. Sotirakopoulou, 'The Chronology of the "Kastri Group" Reconsidered', *Annual of the British School at Athens*, 88 (1993), 113–36. The evidence of contact with Miletos is outlined in A. M. Greaves, *Miletos: A History* (London, 2002). For the port of Mochlos on Crete, see J. S. Soles, 'From Ugarit to Mochlos: Remnants of an Ancient Voyage', in R. Laffineur and E. Greco (eds.), *Emporia: Mycenaeans and Minoans in the Central and Eastern Mediterranean* (Austin, Tex., 2005), 429–39, and J. S. Soles, 'Mochlos Boats', in E. Mantzourani and P. P. Betancourt (eds.), *Pilistor: Studies in Honor of Costis Davaras* (Philadelphia, 2012), 187–200.

The internationalism, which many writers have recognized as a significant development in the Early Bronze Age Aegean, is analysed in detail in D. Catapoti, 'Further Thought on the International Spirit: Maritime Politics and Consuming Bodies in the Early Cyclades', in G. Vavouranakis (ed.), *The Seascape in Aegean Prehistory* (Aarhus, 2011), 71–89.

A very readable introduction to the Minoan world is presented in J. L. Fitton, *Minoans* (London, 2002). More detailed papers on a range of relevant subjects will be found in E. G. Clive (ed.), *The Oxford Handbook of the Bronze Age Aegean* (Oxford, 2010), including important chapters on chronology. The disputed date of the eruption of Thera is discussed in S. W. Manning, *A Test of Time: The Volcano of Thera and the Chronology and History of the Aegean and East Mediterranean in the Mid Second Millennium BC* (Oxford, 1999), and in C. W. Shelmerdine (ed.), *The Cambridge Companion to the Aegean Bronze Age* (Cambridge, 2008), 105–18. The specific theme of Minoan command of the sea is discussed in R. Hägg and N. Marinatos (eds.), *The Minoan Thalassocracy: Myth and Reality* (Stockholm, 1984), and M. H. Wiener, 'The Isles of Crete? The Minoan Thalassocracy Revisited', in D. A. Hardy (ed.), *Thera and the Aegean World III*, 3 vols. (London, 1990), i. 128–60. The justly famous Thera wall paintings are introduced in N. Marinatos, *Art and Religion in Thera* (Athens, 1984), and L. Morgan, *Miniature Wall Paintings of Thera: Study in Aegean Culture and Iconography* (Cambridge, 1988). The maritime paintings have been considered in many papers, often arriving at conflicting conclusions, including S. Wachsmann, 'Thera Waterborne Procession Reconsidered', *International Journal of Nautical Archaeology*, 9 (1980), 287–95; the same author's *Seagoing Ships and Seamanship in the Bronze Age Levant* (Texas, 1998); J. G. Younger, 'A View from the Sea', in G. Vavouranakis (ed.), *The Seascape in Aegean Prehistory* (Aarhus, 2011), 161–83.

The Mycenaean world is attractively introduced in L. Schofield, *The Mycenaeans* (London, 2007), with a useful guide to further reading. Possible trading sites on the North African coast west of the Nile delta, at Marsa Matruh and Bates's Island, are discussed in D. and A. P. White, 'Coastal Sites of Northeast Africa: The Case against Bronze Age Ports', *Journal of the American Research Centre in Egypt*, 33 (1996), 11–30, and D. White (ed.), *Marsa Matruh* (Philadelphia, 2002). The Late Bronze Age shipwrecks in the eastern Mediterranean are described from a structural point of view in S. McGrail, *Boats of the World: From the Stone Age to Medieval Times* (Oxford, 2001), 122–5. More detail on the Uluburun vessel and its cargo is given in three papers by Cemal Pulak, 'Uluburun Shipwreck: An Overview', *International Journal of Nautical Archaeology*, 27 (1998), 188–224; 'Who Were the Mycenaeans Aboard the Uluburun Ship?', in R. Laffineur and E. Greco (eds.), *Emporia: Mycenaeans and Minoans in the Central and Eastern Mediterranean* (Austin, Tex., 2005), 295–310; 'The Uluburun Shipwreck and Late Bronze Age Trade', in J. Aruz, K. Benzel, and J. Evans (eds.), *Beyond Babylon: Art, Trade, and Diplomacy in the Second Millennium BC* (New Haven, 2008), 289–310. For the Cape Gelidonya wreck, see G. F. Bass, 'Cape Gelidonya: A Bronze Age Shipwreck', *Transactions of the American Philosophical Society*, 57/8 (1967).

Trade, mobility, and connectivity in the eastern and central Mediterranean are subjects discussed in a collection of papers in N. H. Gale (ed.), *Bronze Age Trade in the Mediterranean* (Jonsered, 1991). The same broad themes are brought together in a stimulating paper by S. Sherratt, 'Circulation of Metals at the End of the Bronze Age in the Eastern Mediterranean', in C. F. E. Pare (ed.), *Metals Make the World Go Round: The Supply and Circulation of Metals in Bronze Age Europe* (Oxford, 2000), 82–97. For a broad overview of the impact of the Mycenaeans, A. F. Harding, *The Mycenaeans and Europe* (London, 1984), sets the scene. The gradual build-up of Mycenaean influence in the central Mediterranean is carefully assessed in A. Cazzella and G. Recchia, 'The "Mycenaeans" in the Central Mediterranean: A Comparison between the Adriatic and Tyrrhenian Seaways', *Pasiphae*, 3 (2009), 27–40. Evidence of the later Cypriot contact with the central Mediterranean is presented in detail in F. Lo Schiavo, E. Macnamara, and L. Vagnetti, 'Late Cypriot Imports to Italy and their Influence on Local Bronze Work', *Papers of the British School of Rome*, 53 (1985), 1–71, and L. Vagnetti and F. Lo Schiavo, 'Late Bronze Age Long Distance Trade in the Mediterranean: The Role of the Cypriots', in E. Peltenburg (ed.), *Early Society in Cyprus* (Edinburgh, 1989), 217–43.

Sardinia features large in these accounts. A useful collection of background papers is presented in R. H. Tykot and T. K. Andrews (eds.), *Sardinia in the Mediterranean: A Footprint in the Sea* (Sheffield, 1992). The Bronze Age is given extended treatment in G. S. Webster, *A Prehistory of Sardinia, 2300–500 BC* (Sheffield, 1996). For a more detailed consideration of the impact of external influences on indigenous developments, see A.

Russell, 'Foreign Materials, Islander Mobility and Elite Identity in Late Bronze Age Sardinia', in P. van Dommelen and A. B. Knapp (eds.), *Material Connections in the Ancient Mediterranean* (London, 2010), 106–26.

The possible impact of Mycenaeans on southern Iberia is discussed in M. Almagro Gorbea and F. Fontes, 'The Introduction of Wheel-Made Pottery in the Iberian Peninsula: Mycenaean and Pre-Orientalizing Contacts?', *Oxford Journal of Archaeology*, 16 (1997), 345–61, and J. C. Martín de la Cruz, 'El valle medio del Guadalquivir', in S. Celestino, N. Rafel, and X.-L. Armada (eds.), *Contacto cultural entre el Mediterráneo y el Atlántico, siglos XII–VIII a.C.: la precolonización a debate* (Madrid, 2008), 289–99. The Mycenaean pottery found at Montoro in the Guadalquivir valley is fully presented in J. C. Martín de la Cruz, 'Mykenische Keramik aus bronzezeitlichen Siedlungsschichten von Montoro am Guadalquivir', *Madrider Mitteilungen*, 29 (1988), 77–92. A convenient catalogue and discussion of the various ship carvings and paintings which may represent eastern Mediterranean vessels, including the Pontevedra carving, are provided in A. Rey da Silva, *Iconografía náutica de la península Ibérica en la protohistoria* (Oxford, 2009).

CHAPTER 6. EXPLORING THE ENDS OF THE WORLD, 1200–600 BC

The best introduction to the Mediterranean in this period is C. Broodbank, *The Making of the Middle Sea* (London, 2013), ch. 9. For the Atlantic, see B. Cunliffe, *Facing the Ocean* (Oxford, 2001), chs. 7 and 8, and my *Britain Begins* (Oxford, 2013), ch. 8. Another useful overview is M. Ruiz-Gálvez Priego, *La Europa atlántica en la edad del Bronce: un viaje a las raíces de la Europa occidental* (Barcelona, 1998).

Of crucial importance to the fast-developing story of the opening up of the Atlantic to Mediterranean merchants are the discoveries being made at Huelva in southern Spain. The Huelva hoard has been discussed in detail in M. Ruiz-Gálvez Priego, *Ritos de paso y puntos de paso: la ría de Huelva en el mundo del Bronce Final europeo* (Madrid, 1995). Recent ideas on the development of the carp's-tongue swords are presented in D. Brandherm and C. Burgess, 'Carp's-Tongue Problems', in F. Verse et al. (eds.), *Durch die Zeiten: Festschrift für Albrecht Jockenhövel zum 65. Geburstag* (Rahden, 2008), 133–60. The exchange of elite artefacts between the eastern Mediterranean and Iberia is explored in R. J. Harrison, *Symbols and Warriors: Images of the European Bronze Age* (Bristol, 2004), chs. 7 and 8; A. Mederos Martín and R. J. Harrison, '"Placer de dioses": incensarios en soportes con ruedas del Bronce Final de la península Ibérica', *Complutum Extra*, 6 (1996), 237–53; A. Mederos Martín, 'La conexión levantino-chipriota: indicios de comercio atlántico con el Mediterráneo oriental durante el Bronce Final, 1150–950 AC', *Trabajos de Prehistoria*, 53 (1996),

95–115. The excavations at Huelva that have produced evidence of tenth-century or earlier Phoenician contact are discussed in F. González de Canales Cerisola, L. S. Pichardo, and J. L. Gómez, *El emporio feniso precolonial da Huelva, c.900–770 BC* (Madrid, 2004); the same author's 'The Precolonial Phoenician Emporium of Huelva, ca.900–770 BC', *Bulletin Anticke Beschaving*, 81 (2006), 13–29; A. J. Nijboer and J. van der Plicht, 'An Interpretation of the Radiocarbon Determinations of the Oldest Indigenous–Phoenician Stratum Thus Far, Excavated at Huelva, Tartessos (South-West Spain)', *Bulletin Anticke Beschaving*, 81 (2006), 31–6. Some aspects of the finds from the excavation are considered in a broader Mediterranean context in A. Mederos Martín, 'Fenicios en Huelva, en el siglo X AC, durante el reinado de Hîrām I de Tiro', *Spal*, 15 (2006), 167–88. The question of equating Tartessos in Spain with Tarshish in the Bible is thoroughly discussed in C. López-Ruiz, 'Tarshish and Tartessos Revisited: Textual Problems and Historical Implications', in M. Dietler and C. López-Ruiz (eds.), *Colonial Encounters in Ancient Iberia: Phoenician, Greek and Indigenous Relations* (Chicago, 2009), 255–80.

Various papers relevant to the Cypriot contact with the central Mediterranean were given in the further reading for Chapter 5. The contacts between Egypt and the Near East are summarized in I. Shaw, 'Egypt and the "Outside World"', in I. Shaw (ed.), *The Oxford History of Ancient Egypt* (Oxford, 2000), 314–29; W. V. Davis (ed.), *Egypt, the Aegean and the Levant* (London, 1995); R. Redford, *Egypt, Canaan and Israel in Ancient Times* (Princeton, 1992). For the sea peoples, see N. Sandars, *The Sea Peoples: Warriors of the Ancient Mediterranean, 1250–1150 BC* (London, 1978), and T. and M. Dothan, *Peoples of the Sea: The Search for the Philistines* (New York, 1992). For the Hittites, T. Bryce, *The Kingdom of the Hittites* (Oxford, 2005).

The rise of the Phoenicians is considered in many works. One of the classic accounts is D. Harden, *The Phoenicians* (Harmondsworth, 1980). The Phoenician world is also well covered in the many essays brought together in a lavishly illustrated exhibition catalogue, S. Moscati (ed.), *The Phoenicians* (Milan, 1988). The Phoenician homeland in the Levant is fully considered in M. E. Aubet, *The Phoenicians and the West: Polities, Colonies and Trade*, 2nd edn (Cambridge, 2001), in which the cities of Tyre and Sidon are described, with references to more detailed publications. The same volume gives a full consideration of the Phoenician thrust into the western Mediterranean together with an account of Gadir (Cádiz). It also provides a summary of the Phoenician enclaves along the coast of Andalusia, to which should be added the same author's 'Mainake: The Legend and the New Archaeological Evidence', in R. Osborne and B. Cunliffe (eds.), *Mediterranean Urbanizations, 800–600 BC* (Oxford, 2005), 187–202. Another useful source, assessing a wide range of evidence, is A. Neville, *Mountains of Silver and Rivers of Gold: The Phoenicians in Iberia* (Oxford, 2007). A detailed account of the Phoenician enclaves established along the Portuguese coast is given in A. M. Arruda, *Los Fenicios en Portugal: Fenicios y mundo indígena en el centro y sur de Portugal, siglos VIII–VI AC* (Barcelona, 2000). For a shorter, updated account, see the same author's 'Phoenician Colonization on the Atlantic Coast of the Iberian Peninsula', in Dietler and López-Ruiz (eds.), *Colonial Encounters in Ancient Iberia*, 113–30. The effect of colonial contact on indigenous communities in the lower Tagus valley is discussed in A. M. Arruda, 'Alto de Castello's Iron Age Occupation (Alpiarça, Portugal)', *Zephyrus*, 74 (2014), 143–55. There have been few detailed publications of the Phoenician colonies along the Moroccan coast, but a good overview of the current state of scholarship is given in chapter 1 of F. López Pardo and A. Mederos Martín, *La factoría fenicia de la isla de Mogador y los pueblos del Atlas* (Tenerife, 2008), with much of the rest of the book being devoted to the Phoenician settlement on Mogador. A full report on the excavation on Mogador is given in A. Jodin, *Mogador: comptoir phénicien du Maroc atlantique* (Rabat, 1966). The most recent work is briefly noted in *Archaeology Worldwide*, 1 (2014), 52–4.

The earliest archaeological evidence for Carthage is discussed in R. F. Docter et al., 'New Radiocarbon Dates from Carthage: Bridging the Gap between History and Archaeology?', in C. Sagona (ed.), *Beyond the Homeland: Markers in Phoenician Chronology* (Leuven, 2008), 379–422, and R. Docter et al., 'Punic Carthage: Two Decades of Archaeological Investigation', in J. L. López Castro (ed.), *Las ciudades fenicio-púnicas en el Mediterráneo occidental* (Almería, 2008), 85–103.

The south-west of Iberia is a focal area for the interaction of the Mediterranean and the Atlantic in the early first millennium. The principal issues are outlined in B. Cunliffe, 'Core–Periphery Relationships: Iberia and the Mediterranean', in P. Bilde et al. (eds.), *Centre and Periphery in the Hellenistic World* (Aarhus, 1993), 53–85. An up-to-date discussion of the Late Bronze Age warrior stele is offered in R. J. Harrison, *Symbols and Warriors: Images of the European Bronze Age* (Bristol, 2004). The later stele with inscriptions in Celtic are presented in J. T. Koch, *Tartessian: Celtic in the South West at the Dawn of History* (Aberystwyth, 2009). One of the classic papers exploring the broader context for the Phoenician interest in south-western Iberia is S. Frankenstein, 'The Phoenicians in the Far West: A Function of Neo-Assyrian Imperialism', in M. T. Larsen (ed.), *Power and Propaganda (Mesopotamia 7)* (Copenhagen, 1979), 263–94. It was, however, written long before the discovery of tenth- and ninth-century Phoenician enclaves. The famous cemetery of La Joya, Huelva, is published in J. P. Garrido Roiz and E. Orta García, *Excavaciones en la necrópolis de 'La Joya', Huelva II* (Madrid, 1979). A summary of the orientalizing period in south-western Iberia is given in R. J. Harrison, *Spain at the Dawn of History: Iberians, Phoenicians and Greeks* (London, 1988).

The early development of Euboea as an active trading community is explored in M. Popham, 'Precolonisation: Early Greek Contacts with the East', in G. R. Tsetskhladze and F. De Angelis (eds.), *The Archaeology of Greek Colonisation* (Oxford, 1994), 11–34, and M. Popham and I. C. Lemos, 'A Euboean Warrior Trader', *Oxford Journal of Archaeology*, 14 (1995), 151–8. Evidence that Euboeans and Phoenicians cooperated in early trading operations is considered in J. Boardman, 'Early Euboean Settlements in the Carthage Area', *Oxford Journal of Archaeology*, 25 (2006), 195–200. The early Greek presence at the port of Al Mina on the coast of Syria has been frequently debated in, for example, J. Boardman, 'Al Mina and History', *Oxford Journal of Archaeology*, 9 (1990), 169–90, and J. Waldbaum, 'Greeks *in* the East or Greeks *and* the East? Problems in the Definition and Recognition of Presence', *Bulletin of the American Schools of Oriental Research*, 305 (1997), 1–18. The subject of early Greek colonists in the Tyrrhenian Sea is reviewed in M. Pallottino, *A History of Earliest Italy*, trans. M. Ryle and K. Soper (London, 1991), ch. 3. Two perceptive papers present the early colonial settlement at Pithekoussai: D. Ridgway, 'Phoenicians and Greeks in the West: A View from Pithekoussai', and J. N. Coldstream, 'Prospectors and Pioneers: Pithekoussai, Kyme and Central Italy', both in Tsetskhladze and De Angelis (eds.), *Archaeology of Greek Colonisation*, 35–46, 47–60.

The standard work on Greeks in Iberia is A. J. Domínguez Monedero, *Los griegos en la península Ibérica* (Madrid, 1996). The subject is discussed in the context of developing trading networks in Cunliffe, 'Core–Periphery Relationships: Iberia and the Mediterranean'. Two classic studies of Greek material found in Iberia are B. Shefton, 'Greeks and Greek Imports in the South of the Iberian Peninsula: The Archaeological Evidence', in H. G. Niemeyer (ed.), *Phönizier im Westen* (Mainz, 1982), 337–70. For a thought-provoking discussion of the social impact of the Greek contact, see P. Rouillard, 'Greeks and the Iberian Peninsula: Forms of Exchange and Settlement', in Dietler and López-Ruiz (eds.), *Colonial Encounters in Ancient Iberia*, 131–51. For Massalia (Marseille), see A. T. Hodge, *Ancient Greek France* (London, 1998).

The Atlantic Bronze Age is a popular subject with an extensive literature. The standard study of the material evidence is A. Coffyn, *Le Bronze final atlantique dans la péninsule ibérique* (Paris, 1985). Two useful collections of edited papers making major contributions to the debate are C. Chevillot and A. Coffyn (eds.), *L'Âge du Bronze atlantique* (Beynac, 1991), and S. Oliveira Jorge (ed.), *Existe uma idade do Bronze atlântico?* (Lisbon, 1998), with some papers in English. The changing intensity of maritime contacts along the Atlantic seaways is carefully considered in C. Burgess and B. O'Connor, 'Iberia: The Atlantic Bronze Age and the Mediterranean', in S. Celestino, N. Rafel, and X.-L. Armada (eds.), *Contacto cultural entre el Mediterráneo y el Atlántico, siglos XII–VIII a.C.: la precolonización a debate* (Madrid, 2008), 41–58.

Among the elite artefacts reflecting connectivity along the Atlantic façade, caul-drons are discussed in S. Gerloff, *Atlantic Cauldrons and Buckets of the Late Bronze and Early Iron Ages in Western Europe* (Stuttgart, 2010). The spits for roasting meat are considered in C. Burgess and B. O'Connor, 'Bronze Age Rotary Spits: Finds Old and New, Some False, Some True', in H. Roche et al. (eds.), *From Megaliths to Metals: Essays in Honour of George Eogan* (Oxford, 2004), 184–99. Flesh-hooks for lifting the meat from the boiling cauldrons are treated in S. Needham and S. Bowman, 'The Dunaverney and Little Thetford Flesh-Hooks: History, Technology and their Position within the later Bronze Age Atlantic Zone Feasting Complex', *Antiquaries Journal*, 87 (2007), 53–108. An interesting anthropological model for understanding the Final Atlantic Bronze Age in Iberia is presented in R. Harrison and A. Mederos Martín, 'Patronage and Clientship: A Model for the Atlantic Final Bronze Age in the Iberian Peninsula', in C. F. E. Pare (ed.), *Metals Make the World Go Round: The Supply and Circulation of Metals in Bronze Age Europe* (Oxford, 2000), 133–50. The intriguing question of Celtic being the lingua franca of the Atlantic zone is introduced in Cunliffe, *Britain Begins*, ch. 7 (with a bibliography), 508–9, and my 'Celtic from the West: The Contribution of Archaeology', in B. Cunliffe and J. T. Koch (eds.), *Celtic from the West: Alternative Perspectives from Archaeology, Genetics, Language and Literature* (Oxford, 2010), 13–38. The Bronze Age shipwrecks found in British waters are described in K. Muckleroy, 'Middle Bronze Age Trade between Britain and Europe: A Maritime Perspective', *Proceedings of the Prehistoric Society*, 47 (1981), 257–97, and D. Parham, S. Needham, and M. Palmer, 'Questioning the Wrecks of Time', *British Archaeology* (Nov.–Dec. 2006), 43–6. Mediterranean bronzes imported to Britain are summarized in S. Needham and C. Giardino, 'From Sicily to Salcombe: A Mediterranean Bronze Age Object from British Coastal Waters', *Antiquity*, 82 (2008), 60–72. Finally, evidence from Phoenicians trading along the coast of Atlantic Iberia beyond the Phoenician enclaves is summarized in A. González-Ruibal, 'Facing Two Seas: Mediterranean and Atlantic Contacts in the North-West of Iberia in the First Millennium BC', *Oxford Journal of Archaeology*, 23 (2004), 287–317.

CHAPTER 7. OF SHIPS AND SAILS: A TECHNICAL INTERLUDE

The study of ancient shipping has generated an extensive general literature which makes the evidence widely available in serious but readable books: L. Casson, *Ships and Seamanship in the Ancient World*, 2nd edn (Princeton, 1986), and S. McGrail, *Boats of the World: From the Stone Age to Medieval Times* (Oxford, 2001), offer detailed studies fully referenced. Two other books, both by Lionel Casson, can also be recommended: *The Ancient Mariners*, 2nd edn. (Princeton, 1999), and *Ships and Seafaring in Ancient Times*

(London, 1994). An invaluable source of ancient representations of ships and boats presented in the context of a thorough overview is to be found in L. Basch, *Le Musée imaginaire de la marine antique* (Athens, 1987). For readers interested in the finer technology of boatbuilding across the world, B. Greenhill, *Archaeology of the Boat* (London, 1976), is a readable introduction. Two standard works dealing with specific types of vessel are J. Morrison and R. Williams, *Greek Oared Ships, 900–322 BC* (Cambridge, 1968), and J. Morrison and J. Coates, *The Athenian Trireme* (Cambridge, 1986).

Staying with the Mediterranean, a thoughtful overview for the earlier period is provided in C. Broodbank, '"Ships A-Sail from over the Rim of the Sea": Voyaging, Sailing and the Making of Mediterranean Societies, *c*.3500–800 BC', in A. Anderson, J. H. Barrett, and K. V. Boyle (eds.), *The Global Origins and Development of Seafaring* (Cambridge, 2010). Pre-classical Mediterranean ships are fully discussed in S. Wachsmann, *Seagoing Ships and Seamanship in the Bronze Age Levant* (College Station, Tex., 1998). A series of specialist papers on Phoenician shipping are presented in V. Peña, C. G. Wagner, and A. Mederos (eds.), *La navegación fenicia: tecnología naval y derroteros* (Madrid, 2004). Two collections of papers introducing a wide range of themes of direct relevance to Mediterranean shipping in the classical period will be found in R. L. Hohlfelder (ed.), *The Maritime World of Ancient Rome* (Ann Arbor, 2008), and D. Robinson and Andrew Wilson, *Maritime Archaeology and Ancient Trade in the Mediterranean* (Oxford, 2011).

An up-to-date listing of Mediterranean shipwrecks is provided in A. J. Parker, *Ancient Shipwrecks of the Mediterranean and Roman Provinces* (Oxford, 1992). For some of the specific wrecks mentioned in the chapter: P. Pomey, 'Les Épaves grecques et romaines de la place Jules-Verne à Marseille', *Comptes Rendus des Séances de l'Académie des Inscriptions et Belles-Lettres*, 139 (1995), 459–84; J. R. Steffy, 'Kyrenia Ship: An Interim Report on the Hull Construction', *American Journal of Archaeology*, 89 (1985), 71–101; M. L. Katzev, 'Kyrenia 2: Building a Replica of an Ancient Greek Merchantman', *Tropis*, 1 (1989), 163–75; A. Tchernia, P. Pomey, and A. Hesnard, *L'Épave romain de la Madrague de Giens*, *Gallia*, 34th suppl. (1978); P. Pomey, 'Le Navire romain de la Madrague de Giens', *Comptes Rendus des Séances de l'Académie des Inscriptions et Belles-Lettres*, 126 (1982), 133–54.

For early Greek navigational skills, see S. McGrail, 'Navigational Techniques in Homer's *Odyssey*', *Tropis*, 4 (1995), 311–20; S. Medas, 'L'orientamento astronomico: aspetti tecnici della navigazione fenicio-punica tra retorica e realtà', in Peña et al. (eds.), *La navegación fenicia*, 43–53. Pytheas' taking of sun heights, and the use that Hipparchos made of them to estimate latitudes, are discussed in D. R. Dicks, *The Geographical Fragments of Hipparchus* (London, 1960), 179–93, and B. Cunliffe, *The Extraordinary Voyage of Pytheas the Greek* (London, 2001).

Much less has been published on Atlantic shipping in this period. For a general survey of the Atlantic regions, see B. Cunliffe, *Facing the Ocean: The Atlantic and its Peoples* (Oxford, 2001). More specifically on seafaring, see my 'Seafaring on the Atlantic Seaboard', in Anderson et al. (eds.), *Global Origins and Development of Seafaring*. For the rock engravings and paintings of boats from around the coasts of Iberia, see L. and M. Dams, 'Ships and Boats Depicted in the Prehistoric Rock-Art of Southern Spain', in T. F. C. Blagg, R. F. J. Jones, and S. J. Keay (eds.), *Papers in Iberian Archaeology* (Oxford, 1984), 1–12; F. Alonso, 'Prehistoric Boats in the Rock-Paintings of Cádiz and the Rock-Carvings of Northwestern Spain', in C. Westerdahl (ed.), *Crossroads in Ancient Shipbuilding* (Oxford, 1994), 11–19; A. Rey da Silva, *Iconografía náutica de la península Ibérica en la protohistoria* (Oxford, 2009).

The poem *Ora Maritima* by Rufus Festus Avienus, which incorporates an early Massaliot periplus, has been the subject of much close scrutiny. The most convenient text, with brief commentary, is *Ora Maritima*, ed. J. P. Murphy (Chicago, 1987). The editor relies on geographical identifications made by A. Schulten, *Avieno: Ora Maritima (Fontes Hispaniae Antiquae I)* (Madrid, 1922). A more carefully argued commentary on the geography of the periplus is given in C. F. C. Hawkes, *Pytheas: Europe and the Greek Explorers* (Oxford, 1975), 17–26. A further attempt to disentangle the Atlantic geography of *Ora Maritima* is offered in Cunliffe, *Extraordinary Voyage of Pytheas the Greek*, 41–6.

CHAPTER 8. EXPLORING THE OUTER OCEAN, 600–100 BC

Although this chapter is concerned with the Mediterranean impact on the Atlantic coastal areas, it is necessary to know something of the political developments in the Mediterranean to understand the context for the interaction. Definitive historical accounts of the period can be found in the various volumes of *The Cambridge Ancient History*. An engaging narrative account of the period is given in chapters 5–9 of D. Abulafia, *The Great Sea: A History of the Mediterranean* (London, 2011); M. Torelli, 'The Battle for the Sea Routes, 1000–300 BC', and G. Rickman, 'The Creation of Mare Nostrum, 300 BC–500 AD', both in D. Abulafia (ed.), *The Mediterranean in History* (London, 2003), 99–121, 127–49. The disruptive impact of events in the Near East on the Phoenician homeland is carefully analysed in M. E. Aubet, *The Phoenicians and the West: Polities, Colonies and Trade*, 2nd edn (Cambridge, 2001). The vying powers in the Tyrrhenian Sea and the eventual emergence of Rome as pre-eminent are thoroughly treated in M. Pallottino, *A History of Earliest Italy*, trans. M. Ryle and K. Soper (London, 1991), and T. Cornell, *The Beginnings of Rome: Italy and Rome from the Bronze Age to the Punic Wars, c.1000–264 BC* (London, 1995). The conflicts between

Rome and Carthage are explored in B. Craven, *The Punic Wars* (London, 1980), and D. Hoyos, *Hannibal's Dynasty: Power and Politics in the Western Mediterranean* (London, 2003). For the archaeology and history of Carthage, see S. Lancel, *Carthage: A History* (Oxford, 1995).

The geography of the Atlantic coastline of Europe and Africa is best understood using a good atlas in combination with Google Earth. Helpful descriptions will be found in the relevant volumes of the Naval Intelligence Division's Geographical Handbooks, *Morocco* (1941–2), *Portugal* (1942), and *Spain* (1944). Another useful source is *Africa Pilot*, i: *Comprising Arquipélago dos Açores, Arquipélago da Madeira, Arquipélago de Cabo Verde, and Islas Canarias*, published by the Hydrographic Office (London, 1953). The evidence for the earliest Greek contact with southern Spain is presented and discussed in B. B. Shefton, 'Greeks and Greek Imports in the South of the Iberian Peninsula: The Archaeological Evidence', in H. G. Niemeyer (ed.), *Phönizier im Westen*, Madrider Beiträge 8 (Mainz, 1982), 337–70. For a more recent and wide-ranging treatment of the Greek impact, see A. J. Domínguez Monedero, *Los griegos en la península Ibérica* (Madrid, 1996). The two Greeks who are known from the classical sources to have explored the Atlantic, Midakritos and Euthymenes, are discussed in M. Cary, 'The Greeks and Ancient Trade with the Atlantic', *Journal of Hellenic Studies*, 44 (1924), 166–9; M. Carey and E. H. Warmington, *The Ancient Explorers* (London, 1929); R. Carpenter, *Beyond the Pillars of Hercules*, 2nd edn. (London, 1973). The most recent and most scholarly of the studies is D. W. Roller, *Through the Pillars of Hercules* (London, 2006), ch. 1.

The Carthaginian exploration of the Atlantic coast of Africa and Europe has generated a considerable literature and we must be selective. The journey of Hanno along the African coast has been outlined in R. Carpenter, *Beyond the Pillars of Hercules*, 2nd edn. (London, 1973), 81–100; J. Ramin, *Le Périple d'Hannon* (Oxford, 1976); A. Mederos Martín and G. Escribano Cobo, 'El periplo norteafricano de Hannón y la rivalidad gaditano-cartaginesa de los siglos IV–III a.C.', *Gerión*, 18 (2000), 77–107; Roller, *Through the Pillars of Herakles*, ch. 2, with a full text and translation, 129–32. The evidence for the journey made by Himilco is assessed in B. Cunliffe, *The Extraordinary Voyage of Pytheas the Greek* (London, 2001), 42–4, with the relevant texts in full. The archaeological evidence suggesting that Phoenicians and Carthaginians did not venture further north than north-western Iberia is presented in A. González-Ruibal, 'Facing Two Seas: Mediterranean and Atlantic Contacts in the Northwest of Iberia in the First Millennium BC', *Oxford Journal of Archaeology*, 23 (2004), 287–316. The archaeology of the Atlantic coast of Africa is less well known, but two detailed reports present evidence from the two best-known sites: F. López Pardo and A. Mederos Martín, *La factoría fenicia de la isla de Mogador y los pueblos del Atlas* (Tenerife, 2008), and C. Aranegui Gascó (ed.), *Lixus, colonia fenicia y ciudad púnico-mauritana: anotaciones sobre su ocupación medieval*, Saguntum Extra 4 (Valencia, 1995).

The Atlantic islands are considered in the context of their historical settlement in P. Mitchell, 'Towards a Comparative Archaeology of Africa's Islands', *Journal of African Archaeology*, 2 (2004), 229–50, and in their mythological context in P. T. Keyser, 'From Myth to Map: The Blessed Isles in the First Century BC', *Ancient World*, 24 (1993), 149–67. Evidence for the early settlement of the islands is outlined in Roller, *Through the Pillars of Herakles*, ch. 3. The archaeology and early history of the Canary islands is presented in detail in A. Mederos Martín and G. Escribano Cobo, *Fenicios, púnicos y romanos: descubrimiento y poblamiento de las Islas Canarias* (Las Palmas, 2002). The intriguing discovery of a hoard of Carthaginian coins on the island of Corvo in the Azores is described in T. Monod, 'Les Monnaies nord-africaines anciens de Corvo (Açores)', *Bulletin de l'Institut Fondamental d'Afrique Noire*, series B35 (1973), 231–4, 548–50. Fieldwork attempting to throw light on the site of the supposed discovery is reported in B. S. J. Isserlin, 'Did Carthaginian Mariners Reach the Island of Corvo (Azores)? Report on the Results of Joint Field Investigations Undertaken on Corvo in June, 1983', *Rivista di Studi Fenici*, 12 (1984), 31–46. The interest shown by the Moroccan king Juba II in the Canary islands is discussed in D. W. Roller, *The World of Juba II and Kleopatra Selene: Royal Scholarship on Rome's African Frontier* (London, 2003).

The Atlantic journeys made by the Massaliot explorer Pytheas have long excited interest, and many ingenious reconstructions of his route have been offered. For a minimalist view, setting the journey in its contemporary and archaeological context, see Cunliffe, *Extraordinary Voyage of Pytheas the Greek*. Most of the textual fragments on which the account is based are conveniently brought together in Pytheas of Massalia, *On the Ocean*, trans. C. Horst Roseman (Chicago, 1994). A selection of the potentially relevant archaeological evidence referred to includes, on the classically decorated stelae from southern Brittany, M.-Y. Daire and A. Villard, 'Les Stèles de l'Âge du Fer à décors géométriques et curvilignes: état de la question dans l'Ouest armoricain', *Revue Archéologique de l'Ouest*, 13 (1996), 123–56; on a shipwreck with tin ingots, A. Fox, 'Tin Ingots from Bigbury Bay, South Devon', *Proceedings of the Devon Archaeological Society*, 53 (1997), 11–23; on the port-of-trade of Mount Batten, B. Cunliffe, *Mount Batten Plymouth: A Prehistoric and Roman Port* (Oxford, 1988). For Greek coins found in Britain, J. G. Milne, *Finds of Greek Coins in the British Isles* (Oxford, 1948), since when there have been many more discoveries. For Greek pottery found in Britain, B. Cunliffe, *Iron Age Communities in Britain*, 4th edn. (London, 2005), 463–5, and R. Bradley and A. M. Smith, 'Questions of Context: A Greek Cup from the River Thames', in C. Gosden et al. (eds.), *Communities and Connections: Essays in*

Honour of Barry Cunliffe (Oxford, 2007), 30–42. Other commentaries on the journey of Pytheas include M. Cary and E. H. Warmington, *The Ancient Explorers* (London, 1929), 33–40; R. Carpenter, *Beyond the Pillars of Hercules* (London, 1973), 143–98; C. F. C. Hawkes, *Pytheas, Europe and the Greek Explorers* (Oxford, 1975); Roller, *Through the Pillars of Herakles*, ch. 4.

The later explorations of the African and European coasts in the second and first centuries are conveniently summarized in Roller, *Through the Pillars of Herakles*, ch. 6. The activities of Polybius are considered in scholarly detail in F. W. Walbank, *Polybius* (Berkeley, Calif., 1972), and the travels of Eudoxus in J. H. Thiel, *Eudoxus of Cyzicus*, Historische Studies 23 (Groningen, 1939).

We return finally to a brief assessment of the Roman world in the period after the Third Punic War when the Roman economy was rapidly expanding. Essential reading includes K. Hopkins, *Conquerors and Slaves* (Cambridge, 1978), and P. Garnsey, K. Hopkins, and C. R. Whittaker (eds.), *Trade in the Ancient Economy* (London, 1983). The evidence for maritime transport in the western Mediterranean is explored in A. J. Parker, 'Shipwrecks and Ancient Trade in the Mediterranean', *Cambridge Archaeological Review*, 3 (1984), 99–107, while the importance of the wine trade is demonstrated in A. Tchernia, 'Italian Wine in Gaul at the End of the Republic', in Garnsey et al. (eds.), *Trade in the Ancient Economy*, 87–104, and in A. Tchernia, *Le Vin de l'Italie romaine: essai d'histoire économique d'après les amphores* (Rome, 1986).

CHAPTER 9. THE ATLANTIC COMMUNITY, 100 BC–AD 500

The archaeological evidence for the disparate communities living along the Atlantic seaways at this time is summarized in B. Cunliffe, *Facing the Ocean* (Oxford, 2001), chs. 9 and 10, while my 'Seafaring on the Atlantic Seaboard', in A. Anderson, J. H. Barrett, and K. V. Boyle (eds.), *The Global Origins and Development of Seafaring* (Cambridge, 2010), 265–74, gives an account of the ships in use in the late prehistoric period, including a discussion of the texts referring to skin boats. For the Broighter model, see A. W. Farrell and S. Penny, 'The Broighter Boat: A Reassessment', *Irish Archaeological Research Forum*, 2 (1975), 15–28. The fascinating question of sacred islands has not yet received the attention it deserves, but Strabo's *Geography* contains several of the key descriptions.

The question of cross-Channel trade between Britain and Gaul has received much attention. An essential background paper is S. McGrail, 'Cross-Channel Seamanship and Navigation in the Late First Millennium BC', *Oxford Journal of Archaeology*, 2 (1983), 299–337. The archaeological and textual evidence is discussed in B. Cunliffe, 'Relations between Britain and Gaul in the First Century BC and Early First Century

AD', in S. Macready and F. H. Thompson (eds.), *Cross-Channel Trade between Gaul and Britain in the Pre-Roman Iron Age* (London 1984), 3–23. A more detailed assessment of the links with Brittany is presented in B. Cunliffe and P. de Jersey, *Armorica and Britain: Cross-Channel Relationships in the Late First Millennium BC* (Oxford, 1997). Three of the ports involved in this trade have been excavated: for Alet, see L. Langouet, *La Cité d'Alet: de l'agglomeration gauloise à l'île de Saint-Malo* (Saint-Malo, 1996); for Nacqueville, A. Lefort and C. Marcigny, 'Reprise des études sur le site Âge du Fer d'Urville-Nacqueville: bilan documentaire et perspectives de recherche', in C. Marcigny (ed.), *Archéologie, histoire et anthropologie de la presqu'île de La Hague (Manche)* (Beaumont-Hague, 2008), 62–121; for Hengistbury, B. Cunliffe, *Hengistbury Head, Dorset*, i: *The Prehistoric and Roman Settlement, 3500 BC–AD 500* (Oxford, 1987).

Roman perceptions of the ocean are reviewed in D. W. Roller, *Through the Pillars of Herakles* (London, 2006), ch. 7, and R. Chevallier, 'The Greco-Roman Conception of the North from Pytheas to Tacitus', *Arctic*, 37 (1984), 341–6, while their views of Britain are explored in P. C. N. Stewart, 'Inventing Britain: The Roman Creation and Adaptation of an Image', *Britannia*, 26 (1995), 1–10. A broader view of the way in which the classical geographers conceptualized the world beyond the Mediterranean is explored in O. J. Thomson, *The History of Ancient Geography* (Cambridge, 1948), which remains a classic. The place of Polybius, Posidonius, and Strabo in creating a cognitive geography is discussed in some detail in K. Clarke, *Between Geography and History: Hellenistic Constructions of the Roman World* (Oxford, 1999). The significance of the Moroccan king Juba II to the developing understanding of Africa is thoroughly analysed in D. W. Roller, *The World of Juba II and Kleopatra Selene: Royal Scholarship in Rome's African Frontier* (London, 2003).

The Roman conquest of Spain, Gaul, Britain, and Germany is a vast subject which is treated in the relevant volumes of *The Cambridge Ancient History*. Other helpful accounts which deal with individual provinces include S. J. Keay, *Roman Spain* (London, 1988); L. A. Curchin, *Roman Spain: Conquest and Assimilation* (London, 1991); J. F. Drinkwater, *Roman Gaul* (London, 1983); A. King, *Roman Gaul and Germany* (London, 1990); C. M. Wells, *The German Policy of Augustus* (Oxford, 1972); S. S. Frere, *Britannia*, 3rd edn (London, 1987); D. Mattingly, *An Imperial Possession: Britain in the Roman Empire* (London, 2006). On more specific aspects of early Roman military confrontation with the sea, Caesar's own accounts of his battle with the Veneti and his crossings to Britain are worth reading. A lively translation is provided in Julius Caesar, *The Battle for Gaul*, trans. A. and P. Wiseman (London, 1980). For North Sea engagements, see Wells, *German Policy of Augustus*. For Britain in the first century AD, Tacitus, *Agricola*, is the appropriate text. The edition edited by R. M. Ogilvie and I. Richmond (Oxford, 1967) provides a full commentary.

The subject of trade along the Atlantic seaways and across the North Sea in the Roman period has generated an extensive, if scattered, literature. Three very comprehensive reviews of the evidence of trade with Iberia are J. L. Naveiro López, *El comercio antiguo en el N. W. Peninsular: lectura histórica del registro arqueológico* (La Coruña, 1991); C. Carreras and R. Morais, 'The Atlantic Roman Trade during the Principate: New Evidence from the Western Façade', *Oxford Journal of Archaeology*, 31 (2012), 419–41, and Á. Morillo, J. S. Domínguez, and C. Fernández Ochoa, 'Hispania and the Atlantic Route in Roman Times: New Approaches to Ports and Trade', *Oxford Journal of Archaeology*, 35 (2016), 267–84. For Gaul, Britain, and the North Sea, see M. Fulford, 'Pottery and Britain's Trade in the Later Roman Period', in D. P. S. Peacock (ed.), *Pottery and Early Commerce: Characterisation and Trade in Roman and Later Ceramics* (London, 1977), 35–84, and M. Fulford, 'Coasting Britannia: Roman Trade and Traffic around the Shores of Britain', in C. Gosden et al. (eds.), *Communities and Connections: Essays in Honour of Barry Cunliffe* (Oxford, 2007), 54–74; F. M. Morris, *North Sea and Channel Connectivity during the Late Iron Age and Roman Period, 175/150 BC–AD 409* (Oxford, 2010).

Various shipwrecks are mentioned in the chapter. The Sept-Îles wreck found off the north coast of Brittany containing a cargo of British lead is published in M. L'Hour, 'Un Site sous-marin sur la côte de l'Armorique: l'épave antique de Ploumanac'h', *Revue Archéologique de l'Ouest*, 4 (1987), 113–32. The wreck carrying blocks of pitch found at St Peter Port is described in detail in M. Rule and J. Monaghan, *The Gallo-Roman Trading Vessel from Guernsey* (St Peter Port, 1993). The Pudding Pan wreck, carrying pottery from Gaul, sunk in the Thames estuary, is reported in M. Walsh, *Pudding Pan: A Roman Shipwreck and its Cargo in Context* (London, 2016). The vessel from Bruges is discussed in P. Marsden, 'Boat from the Roman Period Found at Bruges, Belgium, in 1899, and Related Types', *International Journal of Nautical Archaeology*, 5 (1976), 23–56. The same author examines the vessels from New Guy's House and Blackfriars, London, in *Ships of the Port of London: First to Eleventh Centuries AD* (London, 1994). The Barland's Farm boat from the Severn estuary is fully reported in N. Nayling and S. McGrail, *The Barland's Farm Romano-Celtic Boat* (York, 2004). An excellent (brief) summary of vessels built in the Romano-Celtic tradition will be found in S. McGrail, *Early Ships and Seafaring: European Water Transport* (Barnsley, 2014), 124–35.

Evidence for the Classis Britannica (British Fleet) is outlined in H. Cleere, 'The Classis Britannica', in V. A. Maxfield (ed.), *The Saxon Shore: A Handbook* (Exeter, 1989), 18–22, with references to ironworking in the Weald. The naval base at Boulogne is presented in the same volume in R. Brulet, 'The Continental Litus Saxonicum', 45–77, especially 62–72. The fort at Dover is fully reported in B. Philp, *The Excavation of the Roman Forts of the Classis Britannica at Dover, 1970–1977* (Dover, 1981). The Roman lighthouse at Dover Castle has most recently been reassessed in K. Booth, 'The Roman Pharos at Dover Castle', *English Heritage Historical Review*, 2 (2007), 8–21.

The late third- and fourth-century events in the North Sea and English Channel were closely tied to empire-wide convulsions. The part played by Carausius in all this is carefully discussed in P. J. Casey, *Carausius and Allectus: The British Usurpers* (London, 1994), and H. P. G. Williams, *Carausius: A Consideration of the Historical, Archaeological and Numismatic Aspects of his Reign* (Oxford, 2003). The coastal defences and the Saxon shore have been treated in a number of works: S. Johnson, *The Roman Forts of the Saxon Shore* (London, 1979), presents the facts in their broader historical context; V. A. Maxfield (ed.), *The Saxon Shore: A Handbook* (Exeter, 1989), gives details of all the major structures; while A. Pearson, *The Roman Shore Forts: Coastal Defences in Southern Britain* (Stroud, 2002), offers an up-to-date reassessment.

The Nordic tradition of shipbuilding is introduced in S. McGrail, *Boats of the World: From the Stone Age to Medieval Times* (Oxford, 2001), 207–10, and is covered in a series of wide-ranging essays published in O. Crumlin-Pedersen, *Archaeology and the Sea in Scandinavia and Britain: A Personal Account* (Roskilde, 2010), well illustrated and with copious references. The definitive publications of the Hjortspring boat are G. Rosenberg, *Hjortspring fundet* (Copenhagen, 1937), and O. Crumlin-Pedersen and A. Trakadas (eds.), *Hjortspring: A Pre-Roman Iron-Age Warship in Context* (Roskilde, 2003). The early discoveries of the Nydam boats are described in H. Shetelig, 'Das Nydamschiff', *Acta Archaeologica*, 1 (1930), 1–30. The result of the more recent excavations are summarized in F. Rieck, 'The Ships from Nydam Bog', in L. Jørgensen, B. Storgaard, and L. G. Thomsen (eds.), *The Spoils of Victory: The North in the Shadow of the Roman Empire*, trans. J. Manley and A. Daly (Copenhagen, 2003), 296–309.

Among the scraps of evidence for Roman exploration we might list the Roman pot found on Porcupine Bank, 250 kilometres west of Ireland, noted in S. P. Ó Ríordáin, 'Roman Material in Ireland', *Proceedings of the Royal Irish Academy*, 51C (1947), 35–82, especially 65–6. For a more recent updating of the lists of Roman material from Ireland, see I. Bateson, 'Roman Material from Ireland: A Re-Consideration', *Proceedings of the Royal Irish Academy*, 73C (1973), 21–97, and the same author's 'Further Finds of Roman Material from Ireland', *Proceedings of the Royal Irish Academy*, 76C (1976), 171–80. A full account of the Roman world's view of Ireland is given in P. Freeman, *Ireland and the Classical World* (Austin, Tex., 2001). The spread of Roman material along the North Sea coast into Germany and Scandinavia is brought together (with extensive references) in Morris, *North Sea and Channel Connectivity during the Late Iron Age and Roman Period*. Finally, the Roman coins found in Iceland were first reported in H. Shetelig, 'Roman Coins Found in Iceland', *Antiquity*, 23 (1949), 161–3, and have more recently been discussed again in J. M. Alonso-Núñez, 'A Note on Roman Coins Found in Iceland', *Oxford Journal of Archaeology*, 5 (1986), 121–2.

CHAPTER 10. AN END AND A BEGINNING, 300–800

The chapter begins with changes to the government of the Roman world introduced by Diocletian at the end of the third century which were to have a dramatic effect on European history. S. Williams, *Diocletian and the Roman Recovery* (London, 1985), provides an excellent account of the man and his times. The later Roman empire and what followed has been a popular subject for historians. Three fine recent studies can be recommended: B. Ward-Perkins, *The Fall of Rome and the End of Civilization* (Oxford, 2005); P. Heather, *The Fall of the Roman Empire: A New History* (London, 2005); C. Wickham, *The Inheritance of Rome: A History of Europe from 400 to 1000* (London, 2009). The relevant chapters of *The Cambridge Ancient History*, xiii (1998) and xiv (2000), provide well-balanced narratives of the period. For the development of the Byzantine world, two texts are recommended: a collection of essays, C. Mango (ed.), *The Oxford History of Byzantium* (Oxford, 2002), and, for a carefully considered overview, A. Cameron, *The Byzantines* (Oxford, 2006).

The subject of shipbuilding and seafaring in the Mediterranean in the period is best approached through L. Casson, *Ships and Seafaring in Ancient Times* (London, 1994), before turning to the more substantial and thoroughly referenced book by the same author, *Ships and Seamanship in the Ancient World*, 2nd edn. (Princeton, 1986). For the broader context, see A. Cameron, *The Mediterranean World in Late Antiquity* (London, 1993), and J. H. Pryor, *Geography, Technology and War: Studies on the Maritime History of the Mediterranean* (Cambridge, 1988), both of which are essential reading. A useful summary of first-millennium developments is given in A. Wilson, 'Developments in Mediterranean Shipping and Maritime Trade from the Hellenistic Period to AD 1000', in D. Robinson and A. Wilson (eds.), *Maritime Archaeology and Ancient Trade in the Mediterranean* (Oxford, 2011), 33–59. Rome's port area and the huge mound of broken amphorae are discussed in E. Rodríguez Almeida, *Il Monte Testaccio: ambiente, storia, materiali* (Rome, 1984), while the functioning of the port is analysed in D. J. Mattingly and G. S. Aldrete, 'The Feeding of Imperial Rome: The Mechanics of the Food Supply System', in J. Coulston and H. Dodge (eds.), *Ancient Rome: The Archaeology of the Eternal City* (Oxford, 2000), 142–65. The technological changes in Mediterranean shipbuilding in this period are considered, with examples from actual wrecks, in S. McGrail, *Ships of the World* (Oxford, 2001), 158–64. Other sources on Byzantine shipping include J. Pryor and E. Jeffreys, *The Age of Δρομοω: The Byzantine Navy ca.500–1204* (London, 2006), and V. Christides, 'Byzantine *Dromon* and Arab *Shini*: The Development of the Average Byzantine and Arab Warships and the Problem of the Number and Functions of the Oarsmen', *Tropis*, 3 (1995), 111–22. The spectacular collection of ships found in the Theodosian harbour of Constantinople is introduced in C. Pulak et al., 'The Shipwrecks at Yenikapı: Recent Research in Byzantine Shipbuilding', in D. N. Carlson, S. M. Kampbell, and J. Leidwanger (eds.), *Maritime Studies in the Wake of the Byzantine Shipwreck at Yassıada, Turkey* (College Station, Tex., 2014), 102–15. An older source, H. R. Lewis, *Naval Power and Trade in the Mediterranean, AD 500–1000* (Princeton, 1951), though out of date in places, is still very useful. On the ever-popular subject of Greek fire, see J. Haldon, 'Greek Fire: Recent and Current Research', in E. M. Jeffreys (ed.), *Byzantine Style, Religion and Civilization: In Honour of Sir Steven Runciman* (Cambridge, 2006), 290–325.

The migrations of Germanic and steppe people through Europe and into the Mediterranean region, where acculturation with the indigenous Romanized people took place, have been presented in a number of scholarly but readable accounts. A good place to begin is with an essay by M. Todd, 'Barbarian Europe, AD 300–700', in B. Cunliffe (ed.), *The Oxford Illustrated Prehistory of Europe* (Oxford, 1994), 447–82. Then, more specifically for the Goths, P. Heather, *The Goths* (Oxford, 1996); M. Rouche, *L'Aquitaine des Wisigoths aux Arabes, 418–781: naissance d'une région* (Paris, 1979); R. Collins, *Visigothic Spain* (Oxford, 2004). For the Vandals in the Mediterranean region, the standard text is C. Courtois, *Les Vandales et l'Afrique* (Paris, 1955). The broader North African context is provided by S. Raven, *Rome in Africa*, 2nd edn (Harlow, 1984), with more details in A. Schwarcz, 'The Settlement of the Vandals in North Africa', in A. Merrills (ed.), *Vandals, Romans and Berbers: New Perspectives on Late Antique North Africa* (Aldershot, 2004), 49–57. For Italy at this time, see N. Christie, *The Lombards* (Oxford, 1996), and J. Moorhead, *Theodoric in Italy* (Oxford, 1992). The achievements of Count Belisarius are discussed in R. Boss et al., *Justinian's War: Belisarius, Narses and the Reconquest of the West* (Hull, 1993).

The Byzantine trade in pottery and wine throughout the Mediterranean and from the Mediterranean to the Atlantic is carefully assessed in T. Papaioannou, 'A Reconstruction of Maritime Trade Patterns Originating from Western Asia Minor during Late Antiquity, on the Basis of Ceramic Evidence', in D. Robinson and A. Wilson (eds.), *Maritime Archaeology and Ancient Trade in the Mediterranean* (Oxford, 2011), 197–210. Other relevant accounts include P. S. Peacock and D. F. Williams, *Amphorae and the Roman Economy* (London, 1986), and D. Pieri, *Le Commerce du vin oriental à l'époque byzantine, V^e–VIIe siècles: le témoignage des amphores in Gaule* (Beyrouth, 2005). The evidence for Byzantine trade along the Atlantic coast of Iberia is presented in P. Reynolds, *Hispania and the Roman Mediterranean, AD 100–700* (London, 2010). For the extension of the trade to Britain and Ireland, see A. Harris, *Byzantium, Britain* *and the West: The Archaeology of Cultural Identity, AD 400–650* (Stroud, 2003). Byzantine and other imported pottery in the islands was listed and discussed first in C. Thomas, *A Provisional List of Imported Pottery in Post-Roman Western Britain and Ireland* (Redruth, 1981); more recently in E. Campbell, *Continental and Medieval Imports to Atlantic Britain and Ireland, AD 400–800* (York, 2007), and A. Kelly, 'The Discovery of Phocaean Red Slip Ware (P.R.S.W.) Form 3 and Bii Ware (LR1 Amphorae) on Sites in Ireland: An Analysis within a Broader Framework', *Proceedings of the Royal Irish Academy*, 110 (2010), 35–88.

The impact of the Arabs on the Mediterranean is discussed in J. Shahîd, *Byzantium and the Arabs in the Sixth Century*, 2 vols. in 4 (Washington, 1995), and, more briefly, by R. Hoyland, 'The Rise of Islam', in Mango (ed.), *Oxford History of Byzantium*, 121–8. The broader economic relationships between the Arabs and the Christian west are discussed in R. Hodges and D. Whitehouse, *Mohammed, Charlemagne and the Origins of Europe* (London, 1983). For a massively detailed account of trade in this period, full of fascinating detail, try M. McCormick, *Origins of the European Economy* (Cambridge, 2001). The life of the Arab traveller al-Mas'udi, who wrote about the Atlantic (among other things), is explored in A. M. H. Shboul, *Al-Mas'udi and his World* (London, 1979).

The North Sea region from the end of the Roman period is not well understood, but J. Hayward, *Dark Age Naval Power*, 2nd edn (Hockwold-cum-Wilton, 1999), provides an invaluable and balanced overview giving much detail. For the late Roman period, S. Johnson, *The Roman Forts of the Saxon Shore* (London, 1976), offers a broad survey of the coastal installations which can be augmented by the various essays in V. A. Maxfield (ed.), *The Saxon Shore: A Handbook* (Exeter, 1989). One of the contributions, S. C. Hawkes, 'The South-East after the Romans: The Saxon Settlement', 78–95, introduces some of the more important material evidence relevant to the arrival of Germanic settlers. Another collection of useful papers, this time dealing with aspects of the ships, is S. McGrail (ed.), *Maritime Celts, Frisians and Saxons* (London, 1990).

The movement of Christian *peregrini* along the Atlantic seaways is set out in the classic work by E. G. Bowen, *Saints, Seaways and Settlements in the Celtic Lands*, 2nd edn (Cardiff, 1977), which builds on his earlier work, *The Settlement of the Celtic Saints in Wales* (Cardiff, 1954). These journeys are put into a broader context in M. Dillon and N. Chadwick, *The Celtic Realms* (London, 1967). To these should be added a recent careful assessment of the archaeological and historical evidence clearly presented in J. Wooding, *Communication and Consensus along the Western Sea Lanes, AD 400–800* (Oxford, 1996). These four books provide the essential background to understanding the mobility of people along the Atlantic fringes in the centuries after the collapse of Rome. The archaeological reality of the networks is nicely illuminated in E. Campbell,

Continental and Mediterranean Imports to Atlantic Britain and Ireland, AD 400–800 (York, 2007). An excellent short introduction to the Irish vernacular literature of which the voyages of the *peregrini* form a part is M. Dillon, *Early Irish Literature* (Chicago, 1948), while Irish law is set out in all its fascinating detail in F. Kelly, *A Guide to Early Irish Law* (Dublin, 1988). A particularly attractive introduction to the myths surrounding Atlantic islands is D. S. Johnson's fascinating book *Phantom Islands of the Atlantic: The Legends of Seven Lands that Never Were* (New York, 1994). For a scholarly discussion of the skin boat in the Atlantic tradition, J. M. Wooding, 'St Brendan's Boat: Dead Hides and the Living Sea in Columban and Related Hagiography', in J. Carey, M. Herbert, and P. Ó Riain (eds.), *Studies in Irish Hagiography: Saints and Scholars* (Dublin, 2001), 77–92. For the works of the monk Dicuil, translated and edited by J. J. Tierney, see Dicuil, *Liber de mensura orbis terrae* (Dublin, 1967), which includes the earliest reference to Christian monks visiting Iceland. The subject of early Irish monks on Iceland is explored in K. Ahronson, *Into the Ocean: Vikings, Irish and Environmental Change in Iceland and the North* (Toronto, 2015), while the question of the *peregrini* in the North Atlantic is considered in detail in papers published in B. E. Crawford (ed.), *The Papar in the North Atlantic: Environment and History* (St Andrews, 2002). The movement of people between south-western Britain and Brittany was clearly articulated in a classic work by N. K. Chadwick, *Early Brittany* (Cardiff, 1969), while the archaeological evidence is laid out in P.-R. Giot, P. Guigon, and B. Merdrignac, *The British Settlement of Brittany: The First Bretons in Armorica* (Stroud, 2003). The issues have been looked at in a different perspective in C. Brett, 'Soldiers, Saints and States? The Breton Migrations Reunited', *Cambrian Medieval Celtic Studies*, 61 (2011), 1–56.

The events in the North Sea and Baltic region are complex and interwoven. A good place to begin is with T. D. Price, *Ancient Scandinavia: An Archaeological History from the First Hunters to the Vikings* (Oxford, 2015), chs. 7 and 8, with copious references. The Vendel period is widely explored in J. P. Lamm and H.-Å. Nordström, *Vendel Period Studies* (Stockholm, 1983). Early trading bases are described in P. O. Nielsen, K. Randsborg, and H. Thrane (eds.), *The Archaeology of Gudme and Lundeborg* (Copenhagen, 1994). Sutton Hoo is best appreciated through M. Carver, *Sutton Hoo: Burial Ground of Kings?* (London, 1998). The famous ship is presented in detail in R. Bruce-Mitford, *The Sutton Hoo Ship-Burial*, i (London, 1975). For a comprehensive study of the Gotland memorial stones, see E. Nylen and J. P. Lamm, *Stones, Ships and Symbols: The Picture Stones of Gotland from the Viking Age and Before* (Stockholm, 1988). The question of Carolingian naval power in the North Sea is given full consideration in J. Haywood, *Dark Age Naval Power*, 2nd edn (Hockwold-cum-Wilton, 1999), ch. 5. For technological aspects of sixth- and seventh-century vessels, see S. McGrail, *Boats of the World: From the Stone Age to Medieval Times* (Oxford, 2001), 210–12.

CHAPTER II. THE AGE OF THE NORTHMEN, 780–1100

There are many good books on the Viking Age introducing the themes explored in this chapter. The best place to begin is with J. Graham-Campbell (ed.), *The Cultural Atlas of the Viking World* (Abingdon, 1994), not only for the quality of the individual contributions but also for its maps and other illustrations. Also strongly to be recommended are the collection of specialist essays brought together in P. Sawyer (ed.), *The Oxford Illustrated History of the Vikings* (Oxford, 1997). Good overviews are provided in R. Hall, *Exploring the World of the Vikings* (London, 2007), and S. Brink with N. Price (eds.), *The Viking World* (London, 2008). Of the older works, a classic treatment is G. Jones, *A History of the Vikings* (Oxford, 1968), which is particularly good on the historical details. An essential companion for anyone reading about the Vikings is J. Haywood, *The Penguin Historical Atlas of the Vikings* (London, 1995), both for the quality of the maps and for the succinct texts that accompany them. There are several good regional studies which have much to offer: K. Randsborg, *The Viking Age in Denmark* (London 1980); A. Ritchie, *Viking Scotland* (London, 1995); M. Redknap, *Vikings in Wales* (Cardiff, 2000); D. Griffiths, *Vikings of the Irish Sea* (Stroud, 2010); N. S. Price, *The Vikings in Brittany* (London, 1989).

The economic changes under way in the North Sea which impacted on the development of Scandinavian society are well assessed in R. Hodges, *Dark Age Economies: The Origins of Towns and Trade, AD 600–1000* (London, 1982), and the same author's *Dark Age Economics: A New Audit* (Bristol, 2012). A differently focused view is offered in M. Carver, 'Commerce and Cult: Confronted Ideologies in 6th–9th-Century Europe', *Medieval Archaeology*, 59 (2015), 1–23. Of the major trading bases in Scandinavia: for Helgö, see A. Lundström (ed.), *Thirteen Studies on Helgö* (Stockholm, 1988); for Birka, B. Ambrosiani and B. G. Eriksson, *Birka-Vikingastaden* (Stockholm, 1996); for Kaupang, D. Skre and F. A. Stylegar, *Kaupang: Vikingbyen* (Oslo, 2004); for Hedeby, H. Jankuhn, *Haithabu: ein Handelsplatz der Wikingerzeit* (Neumünster, 1986).

Viking ships have been a favourite subject generating a considerable literature. An excellent up-to-date short introductory essay is G. Williams, *The Viking Ship* (London, 2014). Another useful summary is P. Pentz, 'Ships and the Vikings', in G. Williams, P. Pentz, and M. Wemhoff (eds.), *Vikings: Life and Legend* (London, 2014), 202–27. For more detailed studies, see A. W. Brøgger and H. Shetelig, *Viking Ships: Their Ancestry and Evolution*, rev. edn (Oslo, 1971); O. Crumlin-Pedersen (eds.), *The Skuldelev Ships I: Topography, Archaeology, History, Conservation and Display* (Roskilde, 2002); the same author's *Viking-Age Ships and Shipbuilding in Hedeby/Haithabu and Schleswig* (Roskilde, 1997); T. Sjøvold, *The Viking Ships in Oslo* (Oslo, 1985). A reader looking for a more discursive treatment of North Sea ships and seafaring cannot do better than to read O. Crumlin-Pedersen's *Archaeology and the Sea in Scandinavia and Britain: A Personal Account* (Roskilde, 2010). This is the published version of six talks given in 2008 as the Rhind Lectures in Edinburgh, which offer a broad view of ships and seamanship in its many aspects distilled by one of the great experts on the subject. Navigation and seamanship in the North Atlantic is brought vividly to life in G. J. Marcus, *The Conquest of the North Atlantic* (Woodbridge, 1980), ch. 15, which draws extensively on the Icelandic sagas.

The progress of the Viking raids is described in the various works listed at the beginning of this section, most fully in Jones, *A History of the Vikings*. Other studies on aspects of the raids are to be found in D. Bates, *Normandy before 1066* (London, 1982); A. Willemsen, *Vikings! Raids in the Rhine/Meuse Region, 800–1000* (Utrecht, 2004); D. Ó Corráin, *Ireland before the Normans* (Dublin, 1972); C. Etchingham, *Viking Raids on Irish Church Settlements in the Ninth Century* (Maynooth, 1996).

A useful collection of papers on the 'great heathen army' in Britain is brought together in J. Graham-Campbell et al. (eds.), *Vikings and the Danelaw* (Oxford, 2003). Another useful compilation is W. Davies (ed.), *From the Vikings to the Normans* (Oxford, 2003). The latest phase of Danish rule in Britain as part of Cnut's kingdom is described in M. K. Lawson, *Cnut: The Danes in England in the Early Eleventh Century* (London, 1993), and, in a broader Scandinavian context, in a series of papers in A. Rumble (ed.), *The Reign of Cnut* (London, 1994).

The Scandinavian exploration of the north-western Atlantic begins with the settlement of the Faroe islands, discussed in S. Dahl, 'The Norse Settlement of the Faroe Islands', *Medieval Archaeology*, 14 (1970), 60–73. For the discovery and settlement of Iceland and Greenland, G. J. Marcus, *The Conquest of the North Atlantic* (Woodbridge, 1980), offers a spirited discussion of the literary evidence. Other useful accounts include G. Jones, *The Norse Atlantic Saga*, 2nd edn (Oxford, 1986); J. H. Barrett (ed.), *Contact, Continuity and Collapse: The Norse Colonization of the North Atlantic* (Turnhout, 2003); A. Mortensen and S. V. Arge (eds.), *Viking and Norse in the North Atlantic* (Tórshavn, 2005). More specifically on the settlement of Iceland, a useful translation of the classic text is by H. Pálsson and P. Edwards, *The Book of Settlements: Landnámabók* (Manitoba, 1972). For accounts of the settlement, B. C. Einarsson, *The Settlement of Iceland: A Critical Approach* (Reykjavik, 1955), and J. Byock, *Viking Age Iceland* (London, 2001). The evidence of Norse settlement in Greenland is summed up in K. Krogh, *Viking Greenland* (Copenhagen, 1967), and more recently in J. Arneborg and H. C. Gulløv (eds.), *Man, Culture and Environment in Ancient Greenland* (Copenhagen, 1998). Finally, America. A useful introduction providing a translation of the sagas is M. Magnusson and H. Pálsson, *The Vinland Sagas: The Norse Discovery of America* (London, 1965). Other useful sources include A. S. Ingstad, *The Norse*

Discovery of America, 2 vols. (Oslo, 1985), and W. W. Fitzhugh and E. I. Ward, *Vikings: The North Atlantic Saga* (Washington, 2000). The famous Norse settlement at L'Anse aux Meadows in Newfoundland is described in the first volume of A. S. Ingstad's *Norse Discovery of America*. For a more recent description, H. and A. S. Ingstad, *The Viking Discovery of America: The Excavation of a Norse Settlement at L'Anse aux Meadows, Newfoundland* (St John's, 2000).

CHAPTER 12. THE NEW EUROPEAN ORDER, 1100–1400

To introduce the period covered by this chapter the reader is recommended to begin with the relevant chapters in David Abulafia's comprehensive overview *The Great Sea: A Human History of the Mediterranean* (London, 2011). The Atlantic is less well served, but a useful perspective is offered in P. Butel, *The Atlantic* (London, 1999). The complex history of Europe at this time is not easy to access in short, readable form, but the relevant maps and commentaries in J. Haywood, *Cassell's Atlas of World History* (Abingdon, 1997), offer a good visual introduction.

For more detail on the historical background, S. Runciman's three-volume *History of the Crusades* (Cambridge, 1951–4) is incomparable, providing an essential narrative thread throughout much of the period. The Genoese are thoroughly presented in S. A. Epstein, *Genoa and the Genoese, 958–1528* (Chapel Hill, NC, 1996). For Italy and Sicily, see D. Abulafia, *The Two Italies: Economic Relations between the Norman Kingdom of Sicily and the Northern Communes* (Cambridge, 1997). For Venice, see D. Nicol, *Byzantium and Venice: A Study in Diplomatic and Cultural Relations* (Cambridge, 1988), and F. C. Lane, *Venice: A Maritime Republic* (Baltimore, 1973). Interlocking events in the western Mediterranean are carefully analysed in D. Abulafia, *The Western Mediterranean Kingdom, 1200–1500: The Struggle for Dominion* (London, 1997), and are presented in relation to the opening up of the Atlantic in F. Fernández-Armesto, *Before Columbus: Exploration and Colonization from the Mediterranean to the Atlantic, 1229–1492* (Philadelphia, 1987). For Iberia, W. M. Wall and P. Cachia, *A History of Islamic Spain* (Edinburgh, 1965), offers a succinct summary, while O. R. Constable, *Trade and Traders in Muslim Spain: The Commercial Realignment of the Iberian Peninsula, 900–1500* (Cambridge, 1994), relates the economy to the broader Mediterranean. The Reconquista is treated in D. Lomax, *The Reconquest of Spain* (London, 1978). The maritime empire of Henry II is discussed in R. R. Davies, *The First English Empire: Power and Identities in the British Isles, 1093–1343* (Oxford, 2000). See also C. T. Allmand, *The Hundred Years War* (Cambridge, 1988), and M. Barber, *The Angevin Legacy and the Hundred Years War, 1250–1340* (Oxford, 1990).

Trade in medieval Europe is attractively introduced using stories of individual merchants in J. and F. Gies, *Merchants and Moneyman: The Commercial Revolutions, 1000–1500* (London, 1972), and in a classic collection of papers, E. M. Carus-Wilson, *Medieval Merchant Venturers* (London, 1954). For a broad overview, see N. J. G. Pounds, *An Economic History of Medieval Europe*, 2nd edn (Harlow, 1994), and for the all-important overland trade routes, J. E. Tyler, *The Alpine Passes* (Oxford, 1930). The various volumes of the *Cambridge Economic History of Europe* are an invaluable source for those seeking detailed treatments.

The development of Mediterranean shipping in the Middle Ages is best approached through the seminal work of J. H. Pryor, *Geography, Technology and War: Studies in the Maritime History of the Mediterranean, 649–1571*, 2nd edn (Cambridge, 1992). A series of relevant papers are brought together in J. Morrison (eds.), *The Age of the Galley: Mediterranean Oared Vessels since Pre-Classical Times* (London, 1995). The pilgrim traffic to Santiago de Compostela is discussed in R. Collins, *Early Medieval Spain* (Oxford, 1983), and J. Sumption, *Pilgrimage: An Image of Medieval Religion* (London, 1975). An important collection of papers dealing with Bristol trade, trade with Iceland, the export of English wool and cloth, and the Gascon wine trade by E. Carus-Wilson are brought together in *Medieval Merchant Venturers* (London, 1954). For more recent work on the Gascon wine trade, see M. James, *Studies in the Medieval Wine Trade* (Oxford, 1971), and J. Barnard, *Navires et gens de mer à Bordeaux ver 1400* (Paris, 1968). Maritime trade with Spain and Portugal is treated in W. Childs, *Anglo-Castilian Trade into the Middle Ages* (Manchester, 1978), and the same author's 'Anglo-Portuguese Relations in the Fourteenth Century', in J. L. Gillespie (ed.), *The Age of Richard II* (Stroud, 1997), 27–49. The position of Ireland in the trading networks is well covered in T. O'Neill, *Merchants and Mariners in Medieval Ireland* (Dublin, 1987). Icelandic trade both with Scandinavia and later with England is explored in G. J. Marcus, *The Conquest of the North Atlantic* (Woodbridge, 1980), to which should added W. Childs, 'England's Icelandic Trade in the Fifteenth Century: The Role of the Port of Hull', *Northern Seas Yearbook 1995* (Esbjerg, 1995), 11–31. For the position of Breton seamen, see H. Touchard, *Le Commerce maritime breton à la fin du moyen âge* (Paris, 1967). For the Hanseatic League, P. Dolliger's *The German Hansa* (London, 1970) sets the broad scene. More specific detailed studies of the Hansa include J. A. Gade, *The Hanseatic Control of Norwegian Commerce in the Later Middle Ages* (Leiden, 1951), and T. R. Lloyd, *England and the German Hansa, 1157–1611* (Cambridge, 1991).

Atlantic shipping in the Later Middle Ages is briefly introduced in O. Crumlin-Pedersen, *Archaeology and the Sea in Scandinavia and Britain: A Personal Account* (Roskilde, 2010), 113–24, and is explored in more detail in S. McGrail, *Ships of the World* (Oxford, 2001), 226–57. An older work, which still has much to offer, is B.

Greenhill, *Archaeology of the Boat* (London, 1976), chs. 16–19. For a more extended treatment, see I. Friel, *The Good Ship: Ships, Shipbuilding and Technology in England, 1200–1520* (London, 1995), and R. W Unger (ed.), *Cogs, Caravels and Galleons: The Sailing Ship, 1000–1650* (London, 1994). Other useful publications include A. F. Christensen, 'Hanseatic and Nordic Ships in Medieval Trade: Were the Cogs Better Vessels?', in C. Villain-Gandossi, S. Busuttil, and P. Adam (eds.), *Medieval Ships and the Birth of Technological Societies*, i: *Northern Europe* (Valletta, 1989), 17–23; O. Crumlin-Pedersen, 'To Be or Not To Be a Cog: The Bremen Cog in Perspective', *International Journal of Nautical Archaeology*, 29 (2000), 230–46; B. Greenhill, 'The Mysterious Hulc', *Mariner's Mirror*, 86 (2000), 3–18. The standard scholarly work for representations of medieval ships on seals is H. H. Brindley, *Impressions of Casts of Seals, Coins, Tokens, Medals and Other Objects of Art in the Seal Room of the National Maritime Museum* (London, 1938).

The flotillas of galleys sailing from Venice and Genoa to England and the Low Countries are discussed in E. Byrne, *Genoese Shipping in the Twelfth and Thirteenth Centuries* (Cambridge, Mass., 1930), and R. Lopez, 'Market Expansion: The Case of Genoa', *Journal of Economic History*, 24 (1964), 445–64.

The early exploration of the Atlantic following the opening up of the Strait of Gibraltar in the thirteenth century is elegantly presented in Fernández-Armesto, *Before Columbus*, outlining the activities of the early explorers, mainly Genoese, in the context of Mediterranean geopolitics. For the early maps so important in these enterprises, see P. Whitfield, *The Charting of the Ocean: Ten Centuries of Maritime Maps* (London, 1996), and M. Mollat du Jourdin and M. de La Roncière, *Sea Charts of the Early Explorers, 13th to 17th Century*, trans. L. Le R. Dethan (London, 1984). For the Catalan Atlas, see G. Grosjean (ed.), *Mapamundi: The Catalan Atlas of the Year 1375* (Zurich, 1978). The discovery of the Atlantic islands is outlined in C. Verlinden, 'La Découverte des archipels de la "Méditerranée atlantique" (Canaries, Madères, Açores) et la navigation astronomique primitive', *Revista Portuguesa de História*, 16 (1978), 105–31, and A. Tejera Gaspar and E. Aznar Vallejo, 'Lessons from the Canaries: The First Contact between Europeans and Canarians, c.1312–1477', *Antiquity*, 66 (1992), 120–9.

CHAPTER 13. THE OCEAN CONQUERED, 1400–1510

The century or so of contact between men and the Atlantic has long fascinated their successors, generating a massive literature, much of it derivative. Fortunately we are blessed with several recent books which present and analyse evidence from the original sources and assess past interpretations. Together they provide the essential reading for this chapter. The best place to begin is with J. H. Parry's splendid overview *The Age of Reconnaissance: Discovery, Exploration and Settlement, 1450–1650* (London, 1963). In part 1 of the book the questions of the ships, seamanship, and navigation are thoroughly discussed, with the second part providing a narrative of the discoveries. It should, however, be remembered that this is a venerable text. More recent work has challenged some of the detail and added much that is new. Parry's pioneer work should be augmented by five texts recommended as essential reading. F. Fernández-Armesto, *Before Columbus: Exploration and Colonization from the Mediterranean to the Atlantic, 1229–1492* (Philadelphia, 1987), which, as the subtitle explains, gives an account of the political context and early stages of Atlantic exploration, stressing the involvement of the Genoese. P. Russell, *Prince Henry 'the Navigator': A Life* (Yale, 2001), is a beautifully balanced assessment of Dom Henrique and his part in the Portuguese explorations and colonizations up to the time of his death in 1460. G. Ames, *Vasco da Gama* (Harlow, 2005), takes the story of the Portuguese endeavour up to their arrival in the Indian Ocean. Of the massive literature on Christopher Columbus, the most nuanced is F. Fernández-Armesto, *Columbus* (Oxford, 1991). Finally, D. Hunter's *The Race to the New World: Christopher Columbus, John Cabot and a Lost History of Discovery* (New York, 2011) provides a fascinating account of political context of the first Atlantic crossings using sources that have only recently become available. Other titles which give alternative treatments or fill in details include J. Cummins, *Christopher Columbus* (London, 1992); S. E. Morison, *Portuguese Voyages to America in the Fifteenth Century* (Cambridge, Mass., 1940); F. J. Pohl, *Amerigo Vespucci: Pilot Major* (New York, 1944).

Contemporary descriptions of the explorations and other related documents are published by the Hakluyt Society, London. These include G. E. de Azurara, *The Chronicle of the Discovery and Conquest of Guinea*, trans. C. R. Beazley and E. Prestage, 2 vols. (1896–9); *The Journal of Christopher Columbus during his First Voyage, 1492–3*, ed. C. R. Markham (1893); *A Journal of the First Voyage of Vasco da Gama, 1497–1499*, ed. E. G. Ravenstein (1898); *The Letters of Amerigo Vespucci*, ed. C. R. Markham (1894); *The Voyages of Cadamosto*, ed. G. R. Crone (1937); *Select Documents Illustrating the Four Voyages of Columbus*, ed. C. Jayne, 2 vols. (1930–3).

Among the huge literature that has accumulated around voyages of discovery, opening up fascinating avenues for further reading and research, a few leads may be given here: L. A. Vigneras, 'New Light on the 1497 Cabot Voyage to America', *Hispanic American Historical Review*, 36 (1956), 503–6, referring to a newly discovered letter written by John Day to Columbus describing the voyage; A. A. Rudock, 'Columbus and Iceland: New Light on an Old Problem', *Geographical Journal*, 136 (1970), 177–89, discussing a claim that, if true, has many fascinating implications; E. Jones, 'Alwyn Ruddock: John Cabot and the Discovery of America', *Historical Research*, 81 (2008),

224–54, outlining the claims made of the discovery of new documents relating to Cabot's journeys; S. McGrail, 'Columbus' Trans-Atlantic Voyages in 1492–3', *Medieval History*, 23 (1992), 76–91, giving an experienced mariner's view of Columbus' first voyage. Although the impact of the early colonists on indigenous cultures lies beyond the scope of this book, it is a subject of some fascination which the reader may well wish to explore. A good place to start is with a collection of essays edited by W. Bray, *Europe and the Americas, 1492–1650* (Oxford, 1993), which examines various aspects of the clash of cultures; especially relevant to our chapter is the essay by K. Deagan and J. M. Cruxent, 'From Contact to Criollos: The Archaeology of Spanish Colonization in Hispaniola', 67–104.

CHAPTER 14. REFLECTIONS ON THE OCEAN

This chapter reflects on what has gone before. One paper to end with is R. T. Callaghan's 'Drift Voyages across the Mid-Atlantic', *Antiquity*, 89 (2015), 724–31. It raises the timeless question of the extent to which human activity is conditioned by geography.

ILLUSTRATION SOURCES

The information for the maps in this volume was compiled by the author using a wide variety of sources. Unless otherwise stated, the maps were produced by Encompass Graphics Ltd.

The author and publishers wish to thank the following for their kind permission to reproduce the illustrations:

Chapter 1 opener: David Lyons/Alamy Stock Photo; **1.1** Wikimedia Commons; **1.2** © The Trustees of the British Museum; **1.3** Engraving from a map of 1598 by Olaus Magnus, akg-images; **1.4** John Eagle Photography; **1.5** Hemis/Alamy Stock Photo; **1.6** De Agostini Picture Library/J. E. Bulloz/Bridgeman Images; **1.7** Posta Faroe Islands; **1.8** J. O. Thomson, *History of Ancient Geography* (Cambridge University Press, 1948), fig. 11; **1.9a** Gerhard Milstreu and Flemming Kaul, The National Museum Copenhagen; **1.9b** Gerhard Milstreu, Tanum Rock Art Museum Underslös; **1.10** © iStock.com/inigofotografia; **1.11** Nick Hogan, University College Cork; **1.12** David Lyons/Alamy Stock Photo; **1.13** © The British Library Board, Harley 4751 f. 69; **1.14** Biblioteca Nazionale Centrale di Roma; **1.15** Germanisches Nationalmuseum, Nürnberg.

Chapter 2 opener: NASA/VRS/Science Photo Library; **2.1a and b** Redrawn from *Readings from Scientific American, Continents Adrift* (San Francisco, 1970), pp. 106, 1; **2.2** Illustration by Richard Bonson from D. Attenborough, *The First Eden: The Mediterranean World of Man* (Wm Collins and BBC, 1987); **2.3, 2.4** Author: various sources; **2.5** NASA/VRS/Science Photo Library; **2.6** Redrawn from M. Ponsich, 'La navigation antique dans le détroit de Gibraltar' in R. Chevalier (ed.), *Mélanges offerts à Roger Dion* (Paris, 1974); **2.7** Author; **2.8** Author: various sources; **2.9** Commission Air/Alamy Stock Photo; **2.10** Author: various sources including J. R. Coull, *The*

Fisheries of Europe: An Economic Geography (London, 1972); **2.11** Author: modified from B. Cunliffe, *Facing the Ocean* (Oxford, 2001), fig. 12.2; **2.12** B.A.E. Inc./Alamy Stock Photo; **2.13, 2.14** Author: various sources; **2.15** Heritage Image Partnership Ltd /Alamy Stock Photo; **2.16** Bibliothèque Nationale, Paris, France/Index/Bridgeman Images; **2.17a** Harry Ransom Center, University of Texas at Austin; **2.17b** The Bodleian Libraries, University of Oxford, MS. Pococke 375, fols. 3ᵛ–4ʳ.

Chapter 3 opener: age fotostock/Alamy Stock Photo; **3.1** Author: various sources; **3.2** Redrawn from J. C. Shackleton et al., 'Coastal Palaeogeography of the Central and Western Mediterranean During the Last 125,000 Years and its Archaeological Implications', *Journal of Field Archaeology* 11 (1984), 307–14; **3.3** Author: various sources; **3.4** Fanny Broadcast/Gamma-Rapho/Getty Images; **3.5** Redrawn after C. Scarre (ed.), *The Human Past* (London, 2005), p. 178; **3.6** Mary C. Stiner; **3.7** Redrawn with modifications after J. C. Shackleton and T. H. van Andel, 'Prehistoric Shell Assemblages from Franchthi Cave and the Evolution of the Adjacent Coastal Zone', *Nature* 288 (1980), fig. 1; **3.8** Harry Tzalas; **3.9** Redrawn after S. Manning and L. Hulin, 'Maritime Commerce and Geographies of Mobility in the Late Bronze Age of the Eastern Mediterranean: Problematizations' in E. Blake and A. B. Knapp (eds.), *The Archaeology of Mediterranean Prehistory* (Oxford, 2005), fig. 11.1; **3.10** Redrawn with modifications from S. Bang-Andersen, 'Colonizing Contrasting landscapes', *Oxford Journal of Archaeology* 31 (2012), fig. 1; **3.11** age fotostock/Alamy Stock Photo; **3.12** L. Schmitt et al., 'Chronological Insights, Cultural Change, and Resource Exploitation on the West Coast of Sweden during the Late Palaeolithic/Early Mesolithic Transition', *Oxford Journal of Archaeology* 28 (2009), fig. 7; **3.13** T. F. Strasser et al., 'Stone Age Seafaring in the Mediterranean: Evidence from the Plakias Region for Lower Palaeolithic and Mesolithic Habitation in Crete', *Hesperia* 79 (2010), fig. 3. Photo by Nicholas Thompson. Courtesy of the Trustees of the American School of Classical Studies at Athens; **3.14** Redrawn from T. E. Strasser et al., 'Stone Age Seafaring in the Mediterranean: Evidence from the Plakias Region for Lower Palaeolithic and Mesolithic Habitation in Crete', *Hesperia* 79 (2010), fig. 2a; **3.15** Redrawn from J. M. Arnaud, 'The Mesolithic Communities of the Sado Valley, Portugal, in their Ecological Setting' in C. Bonsall (ed.), *The Mesolithic in Europe* (Edinburgh, 1989), fig. 1; **3.16, 3.17** Lennart Larsen/National Museum of Denmark; **3.18** From a drawing by Eva Koch in C. Christensen, 'Mesolithic Boats from around the Great Belt, Denmark' in B. Coles et al. (eds), *Bog Bodies, Sacred Sites and Wetland Archaeology* (Exeter, 1999); **3.19** Based on N. J. Russel et al., 'The Exploitation of Marine Molluscs in the Mesolithic of Western Scotland: Evidence from the Ulva Cave, Inner Hebrides' in A. Fisher (ed.), *Man and Sea in the Mesolithic* (Oxford,

1995), fig. 1; **3.20** Redrawn from D. Talford, 'The Mesolithic Inheritance: Contrasting Mesolithic Monumentality in Eastern and Western Scotland', *Proceedings of the Prehistoric Society* 68 (2002), fig. 6, which is based on various sources; **3.21** Author: various sources; **3.22** Drawing by Emili Cortell. Museo Arqueológico Municipal de Alcoy, Alicante, Spain; **3.23** Redrawn from data in R. H. Tykot, 'Obsidian Procurement and Distribution in the Central and Western Mediterranean', *Journal of Mediterranean Archaeology* 9/1 (1996), fig. 10; **3.24** © Museo delle Civiltà – Museo Preistorico Etnografico L. Pigorini, su concessione del MiBACT; **3.25** Redrawn with modifications from J. Zilhão, 'From the Mesolithic to the Neolithic in the Iberian Peninsula' in T. D. Price (ed.), *Europe's First Farmers* (Cambridge, 2000), fig. 6.3.

Chapter 4 opener: Robert Harding/Alamy Stock Photo; **4.1, 4.2** Author; **4.3** Collection Musée de Préhistoire de Carnac/Photo: H. Neveu-Derotrie; **4.4** Miguel Medina/AFP/Getty Images; **4.5** From G. Bailloud et al., *Carnac. Les premières architectures de pierre* (Paris, 1995), p. 89; **4.6** Redrawn from C. Scarre, *Landscapes of Neolithic Brittany* (Oxford, 2011), fig. 2.7; **4.7** Hemis/Alamy Stock Photo; **4.8** Redrawn after P.-R. Giot, *Barnenez Cairn, Guennoc, Vol I* (Rennes, 1987), figs. B2 and B3; **4.9** Redrawn after A. Sheridan, 'The Neolithization of Britain and Ireland: the "Big Picture"' in B. Finlayson and G. Warren (eds.), *Landscapes in Transition* (Oxford, 2010), fig. 9.1; **4.10** Redrawn after multiple sources including M. J. O'Kelly, *Newgrange Archaeology, Art and Legend* (London, 1982), figs. 3 and 22; **4.11** Archaeo Images/Alamy Stock Photo; **4.12** Redrawn after G. Bailloud et al., *Carnac. Les premières architectures de pierre* (Paris, 1995), p. 65; **4.13** © Underwater Archaeology Unit, DAHRRGA. Photo by Karl Brady; **4.14** from an enhanced photograph published by M. and S. J. Pequart and Z. Le Rouzic, *Corpus des signes gravés des monuments mégalithiques du Morbihan* (Paris, 1927), pl. 44; **4.15** Redrawn after F. Alonso Romero, 'Hallazgo de un petroglifo con representaciones esquemáticas de la Edad del Bronce', *Zephyrus* 25 (1974), 295–308; **4.16, 4.17** Author: various sources; **4.18** Reconstruction realized by V. Salvatierra por M. Salvatierra – Universidad de Granada; **4.19, 4.20** Author: various sources; **4.21** © The Trustees of the British Museum; **4.22** Redrawn using data from T. X. Schumacher et al., 'Sourcing African Ivory in Chalcolithic Portugal', *Antiquity* 83 (2009), fig. 6; **4.23** Redrawn from data provided in G. Souville, 'Témoignages sur l'âge du bronze au Maghreb occidental', *Académie des Inscriptions et Belles-Lettres* (Paris, 1986), figs. 1 and 3; **4.24** From G. Souville (cited above), fig. 4; **4.25** Main picture, Hull and East Riding Museum: Hull Museums; inset, Institute of Archaeology, Oxford; **4.26, 4.27** © Canterbury Archaeological Trust Ltd; **4.28** Author; **4.29** Lennart Larsen/National Museum of Denmark; **4.30** Deutsches Schiffahrtsmuseum; **4.31** Knut Helskog; **4.32 top** National

Museum of Denmark; **4.32 bottom** Juraj Lipták/The National Museum Copenhagen; **4.33** Robert Harding/Alamy Stock Photo; **4.34** K. Kristiansen, 'Seafaring Voyages and Rock Art Ships' in P. Clark (ed.), *The Dover Boat in Context* (Oxford, 2004) fig. 13.3; **4.35** SHFA_id7191. Kville 151, Ödsmål. Rubbing. D. Evers 1970. <www.SHFA.sc>.

Chapter 5 opener: akg-images/Andrea Jemolo; **5.1, 5.2** Author: various sources; **5.3** Author; **5.4** Author: various sources; **5.5** Picade LLC/Alamy Stock Photo; **5.6** Based on various sources including J. Haywood (ed.), *The Cassell Atlas of World History* (London, 1997), map 1.17; **5.7** Shelley Wachsmann, *Seagoing Ships and Seamanship in the Bronze Age Levant* (Texas A & M University Press, 1998); **5.8** akg-images/Andrea Jemolo; **5.9** DeAgostini/Superstock; **5.10** Estate of Paul Johnstone; **5.11** Peter Schmid/Paul Lipke, Montague, MA; **5.12** From *History of Seafaring*, edited by George F. Bass (Thames & Hudson Ltd, London, 1972); **5.13** Republished with permission of Princeton University Press from *Ships and Seamanship in the Ancient World*, Lionel Casson, 1971; permission conveyed through Copyright Clearance Center, Inc.; **5.14** Various sources including data from C. Broadbank, *An Island Archaeology of the Early Cyclades* (Cambridge, 2000), fig. 103; **5.15** Universal Images Group North America LLC/Alamy Stock Photo; **5.16** Redrawn from various sources; **5.17** © Ashmolean Museum/Mary Evans; **5.18** The Art Archive/Alamy Stock Photo; **5.19** C. Broadbank, *An Island Archaeology of the Early Cyclades* (Cambridge University Press, 2000), fig. 23; **5.20** © The Egypt Exploration Society; **5.21** Author: various sources; **5.22** Duby Tal/Albatross/Alamy Stock Photo; **5.23** De Agostini Picture Library/G. Dagli Orti/Bridgeman Images; **5.24, 5.25** © Ashmolean Museum/Mary Evans; **5.26** akg-images/jh-Lightbox_Ltd./John Hios; **5.27** Author: various sources; **5.28** © The Trustees of the British Museum; **5.29** Redrawn using data from U. Yalçin et al., *Das Schiff von Uluburun: Welthandel vor 3000 Jahren* (Bochum, 2005), fig. 10; **5.30** Multiple sources including A. Harding, *The Mycenaeans and Europe* (London, 1984), figs. 16 and 55 and C. Broadbank, *The Making of the Middle Sea* (London, 2013), fig. 8.67; **5.31a** Redrawn from A. Gonzalez-Rubal, 'Facing two seas: Mediterranean and Atlantic contacts in the Northwest Iberian of the First Millennium B.C.' in *Oxford Journal of Archaeology* 23 (2004), fig. 2 and T. J. Maarleveld in P. Clark (ed.), *The Dover Boat in its Context* (London, 2004), fig. 15.1; **5.31b** Redrawn from F. Alonso, 'Prehistoric Boats in the Rock-Paintings of Cádiz and in the Rock-Carvings of Northwestern Spain' in C. Westerdahl (ed.), *Crossroads in Ancient Shipbuilding* (Oxford, 1994), fig. 3.

Chapter 6 opener: Paisajes Españoles S.A; **6.1** Redrawn from various sources including M. Ruiz-Gálvez Priego, *Ritos de Paso y Puntos de Paso* (Universidad

Complutense, Madrid, 1995), fig. 3; **6.2** From M. Ruiz-Gálvez Priego (cited above), lámina 2; **6.3** Redrawn using data from D. Branderm and C. Burgers, 'Carpe-tongue problems' in *Durch die Zeiten* (Rahden, 2008), figs. 3 and 5; **6.4** Author: various sources; **6.5i** © Griffith Institute, University of Oxford; **6.5ii** Courtesy of the Oriental Institute of the University of Chicago; **6.6** Author: various sources; **6.7a** Nina Jidejian, *Tyre through the Ages* (Dar El-Mashreq Publishers, Beirut, 1986); **6.7b** María Eugenia Aubet Semmler; **6.8** George Gerster/Panos Pictures; **6.9** © The Trustees of the British Museum; **6.10** Author; **6.11** Heritage Image Partnership Ltd/Alamy Stock Photo; **6.12** Author: various sources; **6.13** Multiple sources including R. Hanson, *Symbols and Warriors* (Bristol, 2004), fig. 2.2; **6.14** Author: multiple sources including B. Cunliffe, 'Core–Periphery Relationships: Iberia and the Mediterranean' in P. Bilde et al. (eds.), *Centre and Periphery in the Hellenic World* (Aarhus, 1993), fig. 4; **6.15** Paisajes Españoles S.A.; **6.16** Multiple sources including M.-E. Aubet, *The Phoenicians and the West* (Cambridge, 1993), figs. 46 and 48; **6.17** Based on S. Lancel, *Carthage. A History* (Oxford, 1995), fig. 22; **6.18** Redrawn after J. Koch, *Tartessian 2* (Aberystwyth, 2011), p. 4 with modifications and additions; **6.19** akg-images/Album/Oronoz; **6.20** From J. P. Garrido Roiz and E. Orta Garcia, *Excavaciones en la Necrópolis de 'La Joya*, Huelva II (Madrid, 1978); **6.21** Photo: Ángel Martínez Levas. Museo Arqueológico Nacional, Spain (N.I. 28562); **6.22** Redrawn from M. Popham, 'Precolonisation: early Greek contact with the East' in G. R. Tsetskhladze and F. De Angelis (eds.), *The Archaeology of Greek Colonisation* (Oxford, 1994), fig. 2.12; **6.23** Multiple sources; **6.24, 6.25** Author: multiple sources; **6.26** Philippe Foliot/Photothèque, Aix Marseille Univ, CNRS, Minist Culture & Com, Centre Camille Jullian, Aix-en-Provence, France; **6.27** Redrawn from R. J. Harrison, *Symbols and Warriors* (Bristol, 2004), figs. 8.2 and 8.3; **6.28** From J. Koch, *Tartessian 2* (Aberystwyth, 2011), p. 30.

Chapter 7 opener: G. Revéillac/Photothèque, Aix Marseille Univ, CNRS, Minist Culture & Com, Centre Camille Jullian, Aix-en-Provence, France; **7.1** drawing after P. Pomey, AMU-CNRS, Centre Camille Jullian, Aix-en-Provence, France; **7.2** Photothèque, Aix Marseille Univ, CNRS, Minist Culture & Com, Centre Camille Jullian, Aix-en-Provence, France; **7.3a** Ch. Durand & G. Revéillac/Photothèque, Aix Marseille Univ, CNRS, Minist Culture & Com, Centre Camille Jullian, Aix-en-Provence, France; **7.3b** Philippe Foliot/Photothèque, Aix Marseille Univ, CNRS, Minist Culture & Com, Centre Camille Jullian, Aix-en-Provence, France; **7.4** M. E. Aubet, *The Phoenicians and the West* (Cambridge University Press, 1993), fig 10, redrawn from an original drawing published by Layard; **7.5** Heritage Image Partnership Ltd/Alamy Stock Photo; **7.6** © The Trustees of the British Museum; **7.7** De Agostini Picture Library/G. Dagli Orti/Bridgeman Images; **7.8** Nic

Flemming; **7.9** Photo © RMN-Grand Palais (musée du Louvre)/Stéphane Maréchalle; **7.10** © The Trustees of the British Museum; **7.11** Antoine Chene/Photothèque, Aix Marseille Univ, CNRS, Minist Culture & Com, Centre Camille Jullian, Aix-en-Provence, France; **7.12** Ancient Art and Architecture Collection Ltd./Mike Andrews/Bridgeman Images; **7.13** J. F. Coates, 1992. © The Trireme Trust; **7.14** De Agostini Picture Library/Bridgeman Images; **7.15** redrawn from S. Mcgrail, *Ships of the World* (Oxford University Press, 2001), fig. 4.42; **7.16** G. Revéillac/Photothèque, Aix Marseille Univ, CNRS, Minist Culture & Com, Centre Camille Jullian, Aix-en-Provence, France; **7.17** drawing J.-M. Gassend, M. Rival, CNRS, Centre Camille Jullian, after P. Pomey, 1997 c: 99; **7.18a and b** Redrawn from S. Medas, 'L'orientamento astronomico: aspetti tecnici della navigazione fenicio-punica fra retorica et realtà' in V. Peña et al. (eds.), *La Navegación Fenicia* (Madrid, 2004), p. 45; **7.19a and b** Redrawn from A. Arruda, *Los Fenicios en Portugal* (Barcelona, 2000), fig. 6; and A. Mederos Martín et al., *Arte Rupestre de la Prehistoria de las Islas Canarias* (Gobierno de Canarias, 2003), p. 132; **7.20** Author: various sources; **7.21** Paisajes Españoles S.A.

Chapter 8 opener: Skyscan.co.uk/I. Hay; **8.1** Redrawn from A. Gonzàlez-Ruibal, 'Facing Two Seas: Mediterranean and Atlantic Contacts in the Northwest of Iberia in the First Millennium B.C.', *Oxford Journal of Archaeology* 23 (2004), fig. 5; **8.2** Redrawn after A. Jodin, *Mogador Comptoir phénicien du Maroc atlantique* (Tangier, 1966), figs. 2 and 3; **8.3** © Eddydegroot/Dreamstime; **8.4** Author; **8.5** Author: various sources; **8.6** Redrawn after S. F. Ramallo Asensio, *Carthago Nova. Puerto Mediterráneo de Hispania* (Fundación Cajamurcia, 2011), p. 32; **8.7** Author: various sources; **8.8** Syndicat d'Initiative Saint-Louis, Sénégal; **8.9** Redrawn after A. Gonzàlez- Ruibal, 'Facing Two Seas: Mediterranean and Atlantic Contacts in the Northwest of Iberia in the First millennium B.C.', *Oxford Journal of Archaeology* 23 (2004), fig. 8; **8.10, 8.11** Author; **8.12** Skyscan.co.uk/I. Hay; **8.13** Author: various sources; **8.14** A. Fox, 'Tin Ingots from Bigbury Bay', *Proceedings of the Devon Archaeological Society* 53 (1995), fig. 5; **8.15** Redrawn from M.-Y. Daire and A. Villard, 'Les stèles de l'age de fer à décors géométriques et curvilignes. Etat de la question dans l'ouest armoricain', *Revue Archaeologique de l'Ouest* 13 (1996), fig. 11; **8.16** From a drawing in M.-Y. Daire and A. Villard (above), figs. 2, 14, and 18; **8.17** Redrawn from B. Cunliffe, 'Britain, the Veneti and Beyond', *Oxford Journal of Archaeology* 1 (1982), fig. 5; **8.18** Author: various sources; **8.19** Fig. 2.3 from A. Wilson, 'Developments in Mediterranean Shipping and Maritime Trade from the Hellenistic Period to AD 1000' in D. Robinson and A. Wilson, *Maritime Archaeology and Ancient Trade in the Mediterranean* (Oxford University School of Archaeology, 2011), using data collected by Julia Strauss; **8.20** From B. Cunliffe, *Greeks, Romans and Barbarians: Spheres of Interaction* (London, 1988), fig. 32.

Chapter 9 opener: Arcaid Images/Alamy Stock Photo; **9.1** Maurice Gautier; **9.2** Photo: Barry Cunliffe; **9.3** Heritage Image Partnership Ltd/Alamy Stock Photo; **9.4** By permission of the Pepys Library, Magdalene College, Cambridge; **9.5** Author; **9.6** Courtesy of Manchester Museum, The University of Manchester; **9.7** Redrawn from various sources; **9.8** Author; **9.9** Institute of Archaeology, Oxford; **9.10** Jane Bottomley/Chris Rudd Ltd; **9.11**, **9.12** Author; **9.13** LOOK Die Bildagentur der Fotografen GmbH/Alamy Stock Photo; **9.14** Author: various sources; **9.15** Author using information provided by Richard Keene; **9.16** Caroline Caldwell © Museum of London; **9.17** Peter Marsden; **9.18** © GGAT HER Charitable Trust; **9.19** Original image © GGAT HER Charitable Trust, edits © Oxford University Press; **9.20** Author; **9.21** From C. R. Smith, *Report on the Excavations Made on the Site of the Castrum at Lymne in Kent in 1850* (London, 1852), pl. 7; **9.22 left** Shutterstock; **9.22 right** © Historic England Archive; **9.23** Arcaid Images/Alamy Stock Photo; **9.24** Author: various sources; **9.25** Jette Elkjær/Viking Ship Museum, Roskilde, Denmark; **9.26** The Viking Ship Museum, Roskilde, Denmark. Photo: Rikke Johansen; **9.27** Redrawn from O. Crumlin-Pedersen, *Archaeology and the Sea in Scandinavia and Britain* (Roskilde, 2010), fig. 1.34; **9.28** © Landesmuseen Schloss Gottorf, Schleswig; **9.29** Per Poulsen/National Museum of Denmark; **9.30** Various sources.

Chapter 10 opener: Bibliothèque nationale de France, Ms Grec 923 f. 206v; **10.1**, **10.2** Author: various sources; **10.3** The Art Archive/Alamy Stock Photo; **10.4** Burgerbibliothek Bern, Cod. 120.II, f. 119r; **10.5** Bibliothèque nationale de France, Ms Grec 923 f. 206v; **10.6** Granger Historical Picture Archive/Alamy Stock Photo; **10.7** Istanbul Archaeological Museums; **10.8** Ryan C. Lee; **10.9** Redrawn after T. Papaioannou, 'A Reconstruction of the Maritime Trade Patterns Originating from Western Asia Minor during Late Antiquity on the Basis of Ceramic Evidence' in D. Robinson and A. Wilson (eds.), *Maritime Archaeology and Ancient Trade in the Mediterranean* (Oxford, 2011), fig. 11.6; **10.10** Redrawn after E. Campbell, *Continental and Mediterranean Imports to Atlantic Britain and Ireland, A.D. 400–800* (York, 2007), figs. 45 and 83; **10.11** Author: various sources; **10.12** Author; **10.13** Special thanks to Ewan Campbell; **10.14** E. Campbell, *Continental and Mediterranean Imports to Atlantic Britain and Ireland, A.D. 400–800* (York, 2007), fig 21; **10.15** Author: various sources; **10.16** Redrawn after E. G. Bowen, *Britain and the Western Seaways* (London, 1972), fig. 35; **10.17** From E. G. Bowen (above), fig. 34; **10.18** Redrawn using data from U. L. Hansen, *Der romische Import im Norden* (Copenhagen, 1987), map 32 with additions; **10.19** Redrawn after O. Crumlin-Pedersen, *Archaeology and the Sea in Scandinavia and Britain* (Roskilde, 2010), fig. 4.1 and M. Carver, *Sutton Hoo: Burial Ground of Kings?* (London, 1998), fig. 27; **10.20** Swedish National Heritage Board, photo by Jan Norman, 1993; **10.21** painting by Þórhallur Þráinsson; collection of Lennart Hulth; photo by John Ljungkvist; **10.22** Granger Historical Picture Archive/ Alamy Stock Photo; **10.23** © The Trustees of the British Museum; **10.24, 10.25** Erik Nylén, 'Bildstenar'(1978).

Chapter 11 opener: © Museum of Cultural History, University of Oslo/Erik Irgens Johnsen; **11.1** Author: various sources; **11.2** Author using various sources including T. D. Price, *Ancient Scandinavia* (Oxford, 2015), fig. 8.15 and G. Jones, *A History of the Vikings* (Oxford, 1973), map 5; **11.3** Picture Press/Jochen Stuhrmann und Tim Wehrmann for GEO; **11.4** D. Ellmers, *Frühmittelalterliche Handelsschiffahrt in Mittel- und Nordeuropa* (Neumünster, 1972); **11.5** Author: various sources including G. Jones, *A History of the Vikings* (Oxford, 1973), maps 2 and 4; **11.6** NASA; **11.7** © Museum of Cultural History, University of Oslo/Olaf Vaering; **11.8, 11.9, 11.10** © Museum of Cultural History, University of Oslo/Eirik Irgens Johnsen; **11.11** Paul Goodhead © The Trustees of the British Museum; **11.12** The Viking Ship Museum, Roskilde, Denmark. Illustration by Morten Gøthche; **11.13** The Viking Ship Museum, Roskilde, Denmark. Photo by Werner Karrasch; **11.14a** Gabriel Hildebrand/ The Swedish History Museum; **11.14b** Gotlands Museum, photo by Raymond Hejdström; **11.15** VisitAalborg; **11.16** Author: various sources; **11.17** Author using data from J. Haywood, *The Penguin Historical Atlas of the Vikings* (London, 1995), pp. 58–9; **11.18** Author using data from J. Graham-Campbell (ed.), *Cultural Atlas of the Viking World* (London, 1994), p. 129; **11.19** Author: various sources; **11.20** © Historic Environment Scotland (John Dewar Collection); **11.21** Copyright of York Museums Trust (Yorkshire Museum); **11.22** Sigrid Kaland; **11.23** Heritage Image Partnership Ltd/Alamy Stock Photo; **11.24** © National Maritime Museum, Greenwich, London; **11.25, 11.26** Author: various sources; **11.27** Author: various sources including G. Jones, *A History of the Vikings* (Oxford, 1973), map 13; **11.28** Mats Wibe Lund; **11.29** Folio 61v of mid-14th-century Icelandic manuscript, *Skarðsbók Jónsbókar* (AM 350 fol.). Photographer: Jóhanna Ólafsdóttir. Photograph provided by the Árni Magnússon Institute for Icelandic Studies; **11.30** Author; **11.31** Russ Heinl/All Canada Photos /Superstock.

Chapter 12 opener: British Library, Arundel 93 fol. 155/© British Library Board. All Rights Reserved/Bridgeman Images; **12.1** Author; **12.2, 12.3** Author: various sources; **12.4** Author: various sources including J. Haywood, *The Cassell Atlas of World*

History (London, 1997), maps 3.11 and 3.17; **12.5** British Library Arundel 93 fol. 155 / © British Library Board. All Rights Reserved/Bridgeman Images; **12.6** Arco Images GmbH/Alamy Stock Photo; **12.7** Various sources; **12.8** O. Böhm; **12.9a and b** Roger Smith and Malcolm Swanston of Arcadia Editions Ltd; **12.10** Venice, Accademia, photo © 2016 Scala, Florence, courtesy of the Ministero Beni e Att. Culturali; **12.11** Author: various sources; **12.12** Musée de la Tapisserie, Bayeux, France, with special authorization of the city of Bayeux/Bridgeman Images; **12.13** © National Maritime Museum, Greenwich, London; **12.14** © The Fitzwilliam Museum, Cambridge; **12.15** Christer Åhlin/The Swedish History Museum; **12.16** ©The British Library Board, Royal 10 E.IV f. 19; **12.17** Deutsches Schiffahrtsmuseum; **12.18** John Crook; **12.19** By permission of the President and Fellows of Corpus Christi College, Oxford; CCC Ms 157 f. 383; **12.20** B. Greenhill, *Archaeology of Boats* (A. & C. Black, 1976); **12.21** The Art Archive/Alamy Stock Photo; **12.22** Museo de América, Madrid; **12.23** SBAAAS Pl dia 27468, courtesy of MiBAC/Soprintendenza Pisa, Prot 2338, 20 September 2016; **12.24** © Victoria and Albert Museum, London; **12.25** collection Maritiem Museum Rotterdam; **12.26** © National Maritime Museum, Greenwich, London; **12.27** Various sources.

Chapter 13 opener: Grobler du Preez/Alamy Stock Photo; **13.1** Bibliothèque nationale de France; **13.2** De Agostini Picture Library/Bridgeman Images; **13.3** Photolocation Ltd/Alamy Stock Photo; **13.4** Author; **13.5** Author: various sources including J. Haywood, *The Cassell Atlas of World History* (London, 1997), map 3.18; **13.6** Grobler du Preez/Alamy Stock Photo; **13.7** Museu de Marinha, Lisbon; **13.8** Câmara Municipal de Cascais/Condes de Castro Guimarães Museum (MCCG-BIB-14); **13.9** Various sources; **13.10** Granger Historical Picture Archive/ Alamy Stock Photo; **13.11** Wikimedia Commons; **13.12** Seth Lazar/Alamy Stock Photo; **13.13** Museo Naval, Madrid; **13.14** Germanisches Nationalmuseum, Nürnberg; **13.15** Fitzwilliam Museum, University of Cambridge, UK/Bridgeman Images; **13.16** Biblioteca Colombina. Sign. 10-3-4; **13.17** Various sources; **13.18** Granger Historical Picture Archive/Alamy Stock Photo; **13.19**, **13.20**, **13.21** Various sources.

Chapter 14 opener: © airn/Shutterstock

The publisher apologizes for any errors or omissions in the above list. If contacted, they will be pleased to rectify these at the earliest opportunity.

Picture Research by Sandra Assersohn

INDEX